The Persistence of Hollywood

Thomas Elsaesser

 Routledge
Taylor & Francis Group

NEW YORK AND LONDON

First published 2012
by Routledge
711 Third Avenue, New York, NY 10017

Simultaneously published in the UK
by Routledge
2 Park Square, Milton Park, Abingdon, Oxon OX14 4RN

Routledge is an imprint of the Taylor & Francis Group, an informa business

© 2012 Taylor & Francis

Library of Congress Cataloging-in-Publication Data

Elsaesser, Thomas.
The persistence of Hollywood / by Thomas Elsaesser.
p. cm.
Includes bibliographical references and index.
1. Motion pictures—United States.   2. Motion picture industry—United States.
I. Title.
PN1993.5.U6E44 2011
791.430973—dc23

2011024177

ISBN: 978–0–415–96813–3 (hbk)
ISBN: 978–0–415–96814–0 (pbk)
ISBN: 978–0–203–15250–8 (ebk)

Typeset in Minion
by RefineCatch Limited, Bungay, Suffolk

Printed and bound in the United States of America on acid-free paper by
Sheridan Books, Inc.

Table of Contents

Acknowledgments and Places of Previous Publication

This book has been in the making for quite some time, dating back to 2002, when the idea was first proposed to me by Bill Germano, then the New York Senior Vice President of Routledge and a friend from many previous years' encounters in New York, London and Amsterdam. To him goes my gratitude for having initiated the project; thanks also to his successors as commissioning editors at Routledge, first Matthew Byrnie and then Erica Wetter, for having shown both patience and persistence.

Along the way, many friends, students and colleagues have taken an interest, some, like Amy Kenyon, making a detailed inventory and offering helpful comments, others overcoming my scruples about re-publishing essays more than forty years old: special thanks in this respect must go to Drehli Robnik, who "discovered" for himself my essay on Sam Fuller, and to Joe McElhaney, who still liked my piece on "Vincente Minnelli" enough to include it in his essay collection on the director. Seunghoon Jeong has been a most attentive interlocutor in New York, his fertile mind fully attuned to the subject. I extend thanks also to Jon Lewis and JD Connor, for generously showing me part of their ongoing research at different stages, and to Michael Wedel, for his in-depth knowledge of contemporary Hollywood.

However, my very special appreciation goes to Warren Buckland, who agreed to shoulder the not inconsiderable task of reading the entire manuscript—including several essays that did not make it into the final selection. He then prepared a report that became the blueprint both for revising the order of the chapters and for highlighting the common themes and arguments. Insofar as the collection does have a measure of coherence, it owes it in no small degree to Warren's analytical understanding of American Cinema and his expertise as editor. He also took time out copy-editing, pruning, making some structural changes and completing footnotes. Besides the many hours of labor this saved me, having him on the project in the final stages had the invaluable effect of making sure that this time, I would see it through to the end. This book is dedicated to Peter Wollen, my first benefactor and taskmaster as editor of a film magazine, and to the memory of Richard Winkler (1942–2001), who first shared with me the pleasures of writing on the cinema.

The following places of previous publication should be mentioned:

"The Name for a Pleasure that has No Substitute: Vincente Minnelli" was first published as "Vincente Minnelli," in *The Brighton Film Review* 15 (December 1969): 11–13; and 18 (February

1970): 20–22. Published with "Preface 1979" in *The Musical*, ed. Rick Altman (London: Routledge Kegan Paul 1981), 8–27.

"All the Lonely Places: The Heroes of Nicholas Ray" was first published as "Nicholas Ray," in *The Brighton Film Review* 20 (May 1970): 12–16 and 21 (June 1970): 15–17.

"Sam Fuller's Productive Pathologies: The Hero as (His Own Best) Enemy" was first published as "*Shock Corridor*," in *Sam Fuller*, ed. P. Wollen and D. Will (Edinburgh: Edinburgh Festival, 1972), 79–85 and "*The Crimson Kimono*," *The Brighton Film Review* 8 (1969): 11–12.

"Cinephilia: Or the Uses of Disenchantment" was first published in *Cinephilia: Movies, Love, and Memory*, ed. Malte Hagener and Marijke de Valck (Amsterdam: Amsterdam University Press, 2005), 27–44.

"Why Hollywood?" was first published in *Monogram* 1 (April 1971): 4–10.

"Narrative Cinema and Audience Aesthetics: The *Mise-en-Scène* of the Spectator" was first published as "Narrative Cinema and Audience-Oriented Aesthetics," in *Popular Television and Film*, ed. Tony Bennett (London: BFI, 1981), 270–82.

"Transatlantic Triangulations: William Dieterle and the Warner Bros. Biopics" includes material first published as "Film History as Social History: William Dieterle and the Warner Bros Bio-Pic," in *Wide Angle* 8, 2 (1986): 15–31.

"The Dandy in Hitchcock" was first published in *The McGuffin* 14 (November 1994), 15–21, and subsequently republished in *Hitchcock Centenary Essays*, ed. Richard Allen and S. Ishii Gonzales (London: British Film Institute, 2000), 3–14.

"Too Big and Too Close: Alfred Hitchcock and Fritz Lang" was first published in *The Hitchcock Annual*, ed. Richard Allen and Sidney Gottlieb, 12 (2003), 1–41.

"Robert Altman's *Nashville*: Putting on the Show" includes material first published as "Putting on a Show: Robert Altman's Nashville," *Persistence of Vision* 1 (Summer 1984): 35–43.

"Stanley Kubrick's Prototypes: The Author as World-Maker" was first published as "Evolutionary Imagineer: Kubrick's Authorship," in *Stanley Kubrick*, ed. H.P. Reichmann (Frankfurt: Kinematograph no. 20, Deutsches Filmmuseum, 2004), 136–47.

"The Pathos of Failure: Notes on the Unmotivated Hero" was first published in *Monogram* 6 (1975): 13–19.

"*Auteur* Cinema and the New Economy Hollywood" was first published as "American Author Cinema: the Last or First Great Picture Show," in *The Last Great American Picture Show: New Hollywood Cinema in the 1970s*, ed. T. Elsaesser, A. Horwath and N. King (Amsterdam: Amsterdam University Press, 2004), 37–68.

"The Love that Never Dies: Francis Ford Coppola and *Bram Stoker's Dracula*" was first published as "Specularity and Engulfment: Francis Ford Coppola and Bram Stoker's *Dracula*," in *Contemporary Hollywood Cinema*, ed. Steve Neale and Murray Smith (London: Routledge, 1998), 191–208.

"The Blockbuster as Time Machine" was first published as "The Blockbuster: Everything Connects, But Not Anything Goes," in *The End of Cinema—As We Know It*, ed. Jon Lewis (New York: New York University Press, 2001), 11–22.

"Digital Hollywood: Between Truth, Belief and Trust"was first published as "The New-New Hollywood: Beyond Distance and Proximity," in *Moving Images, Culture & the Mind*, ed. Ib Bondebjerg (Luton: University of Luton Press, 2000), 187–204.

Permission for reprinting has kindly been granted by Amsterdam University Press, New York University Press, the editors of The Hitchcock Annual, The British Film Institute, Taylor & Francis (Routledge), Deutsche Filmmuseum Frankfurt and University of Luton Press.

Excerpt from "The Public Enemy" by Richard Maltby, *Senses of Cinema*, 29 (November–December 2003). Copyright 1999–2011 Senses of Cinema Inc. and the contributor. Reproduced by permission.

General Introduction

Film Criticism, Film Theory

The present collection spans almost forty years of writing about the cinema. At first, I was just filling notebooks in the dark and copying intellectual postures and critical stances from my peers. But returning to England from Paris in September 1968, where for the preceding twelve months I had more or less slept, dreamt and lived under the looming presence of Henri Langlois at his Cinémathèque inside the Palais de Chaillot, it was easy to believe that maybe a mission awaited me. In the heady days of French cinephilia and Parisian politics the idea that the cinema was worth devoting one's life to,[1] did not seem at all absurd, in spite of (or because of) not possessing either the arrogance or the confidence to think of making films oneself. For the subsequent twenty years, I dedicated myself to this mission of making the cinema the most important measure of (my) life. But all the while, I was acutely aware of a split in practice: that between being a film critic—proffering value judgments to an (imagined) audience of my peers—and being a teacher, formulating a project for "film studies" as a university discipline. It began innocently and polemically in 1964, when I started to write for a student newspaper and went on to found a university film magazine in 1968, followed by a short-lived, but surprisingly well-remembered successor, *Monogram*, begun in 1971.[2]

When *Monogram* ceased publication in 1975, I began to write for other journals and newspapers, for *Framework, Screen* and *Positif*, even *New Society* and once or twice for the *Guardian*. From the mid-1980s I continued reviewing irregularly, first for the *Monthly Film Bulletin* and then for *Sight & Sound*. To those familiar with the film culture in Great Britain at the time, this may seem an odd career move, since my natural home would have been *Movie*, rather than its sworn enemy, *Sight & Sound*. But already from 1972 onwards, I did not have to make a living from reviewing, which absolved me from certain existential worries and perhaps for that reason, gave me a different outlook on the house journal of the institution whose mission it was to serve film culture at the intersection of education and the general public: the British Film Institute. The BFI—in the shape of the Education Department—had supported us intellectually and financially in the days of *Monogram*, and when I chose to write for the *Monthly Film Bulletin*, at the invitation of Richard Combs, it was because I liked the idea of being published in a trade supplement whose main purpose was to furnish accurate credits and reliable plot synopses for current releases. The opinion pieces I did for the *MFB* on Hans Jürgen Syberberg or Peter Greenaway were low-key, which gave me a chance to develop my ideas or champion marginal directors like Ruy Guerra or Raoul Ruiz in the protective shadow of relative obscurity. When the *Monthly Film Bulletin* was merged with *Sight & Sound*, I began to write longer pieces, but these have, on the whole, been more selective—and often also more retrospective—in their choice of films, topics or filmmakers: for successive editors of *Sight & Sound*, from Penelope Houston and John Pym, to Philip Dodd and Nick Thomas I was mostly their man for German cinema and European art films.

As a teacher of film studies my role has been much more ambiguous: in Great Britain, courses in film for undergraduates and graduates only date back some thirty years, and I cannot avoid taking responsibility for having been one of those younger academics (in my case, with a PhD in English and Comparative literature) who came to a university position on the back of the second wave of Higher Education expansion in the early 1970s. In tune with the students, but a Trojan horse for the institution, I helped give a home in academia to something which several of my senior colleagues in the English department abominated, and many of my fellow critics considered a joke: the academic study of the cinema. Since 1975, then, I have been fighting various institutional battles and journalistic skirmishes that first disguised, then defined, and several times since redefined and reconstructed "film studies" as a field to be researched and a subject to be taught at university.

Being part of a university, one often has a very reified relation to one's subject, seeing it in the (un) holy trinity of a "methodology" (a set of rules, routines and procedures), a "body of knowledge" (a finite number of more or less secured empirical facts or data), and finally, a collection of canonical "works" or "texts" (of individual films to be classified into seminal and masterpieces, and more recently, into classics and cult-films). Since by definition, the task of a university teacher is to instruct the young by making a problem out of something that to them seems obvious, there is perhaps no need to dwell at length on the fact that this reified object known as a discipline, becomes, when taken outside the university, largely stripped of its legitimating purpose and to those outside, in the "real world," seems very nearly meaningless.

During roughly the same period, the function of film criticism underwent changes, as did the fortunes of film magazines and film journals. The major complaint was that reviewing had become indistinguishable from advertising.[3] What struck me, however, as a film historian as well as a critic, was how much film reviewing had always been a service industry. Being a service is its "first nature," so to speak: a fact which—after years as the editor and chief author of *Monogram* and contributor to the *Monthly Film Bulletin*—I came to accept not without a certain perverse satisfaction. As a film historian I also noticed, not without a certain surprise, that many of the main questions and key concepts of the evolving discipline were first posed and formulated by film *critics*. In the past, this had had much to do with the general hostility of universities (but also shared by the "serious" cultural establishment) towards sustained reflections on the cinema. Nonetheless, the impact made by working critics on the agenda of film studies in the 1960s and 1970s is, in retrospect, astonishing. As an example I could cite one of my fields of research, the German cinema: its history and interpretation has until recently been almost exclusively shaped by two working critics, Siegfried Kracauer and Lotte Eisner.[4] Neo-realism and *auteurism* are other examples: it was mainly thanks to the reviews and essays of André Bazin that Italian neo-realism advanced to one of the most enduring paradigms of the aesthetics not only of the European cinema, but of the cinema, cementing a hegemony of realism, against which Christian Metz entered into a polemical dialogue, the very dialogue between "realism" and "constructivism" to which film studies owes its first entry into the university, under the name of semiology of the cinema. Similarly, our understanding of Hollywood, its canonical directors and cinematic masterpieces, also comes from critics: François Truffaut, Claude Chabrol, Jean Douchet and those filmmaker-critics (Eric Rohmer, Jacques Rivette, Chris Marker) who wrote for *Cahiers du cinéma* in the 1950s and 1960s, as well as Andrew Sarris in New York, who popularized *la politique des auteurs* by turning it into *the auteur theory*, and Pauline Kael, who fought it. Finally, *film noir* and *melodrama*—standard topics of the theoretical discourse of film studies—are genres originally named by critics, often in the midst of more or less polemical trench warfare.

Cinephilia: Love, Nostalgia and Disenchantment

This book, then, is in its first part about the British version of the phenomenon of *cinephilia*, the love of cinema. But it is also about the history of what has happened to cinephilia, as it migrated from little film magazines into university film classes. For after starting as a French-inspired preference for Hollywood movies, this passion for and persistence of Hollywood began to split into the "paradigm wars" of film theory for us teachers, and into various forms of cultism and fandom for subsequent generations of students, before it became all but absorbed by some of the varieties of cultural studies, only to re-emerge, since the 1990s on the Internet in blogs, list-servers and social networks.

Love of cinema, as an emotion that blurs the boundaries between movies and life, blending critical partisanship with melancholy regret, has existed, in one form or another, since the 1920s. But at the limit, when it makes one believe that the latter—life—can only be endured by a sustained involvement with the former—movies—it can also be more precisely located in history and more circumscribed geographically. In the essays that follow, cinephilia is inseparable from *auteurism*, as promoted by the French *auteur*-critics around *Cahiers du cinéma* of the 1950s and early 1960s, becoming muted while Hollywood was under attack during the 1970s, before it mutated into a carefully balanced ambivalence during the battles around the different definitions of "classical (narrative) cinema."

The term classical cinema, although also borrowed from André Bazin, emerged in the critical vocabulary at first in Britain in the late 1960s and then in the US in the 1970s, at a moment in time, in other words, when both the existence of the *auteur* and the reality of classical Hollywood (almost by definition, if one accepts that "a theory is often the funeral of a practice") were rapidly becoming obsolete, part of the past, and poised for a nostalgic embrace: by then it had become a cinephilia not without a touch of necrophilia.[5]

Nonetheless, the discussions around classical cinema were often conducted with great passion and even animosity, signs of the affective investment essential to cinephilia. What made the affectivity even more ambivalent was that partisanship took place against the background of bidding (painful, triumphant?) farewell to the idea of the cinema as (traditional) art form, promoted after 1945 through neo-realism and the (mainly European) *auteur* directors from Jean Renoir, Luchino Visconti and Roberto Rossellini to Ingmar Bergman, Max Ophuls and Andrzej Wajda. What replaced it was the sense of the cinema as in some ways a synthetic, but at the same time symptomatic (that is to say, typically modern) mythology, an idea first suggested by Edgar Morin in France and Parker Tyler in New York, but made respectable through Claude Lévi-Strauss and, above all, Roland Barthes.

That the debate around cinephilia played itself out across a complex cultural matrix, at a particular historical conjunction, is evident also when one contextualizes topographically the fact that it was Paris where the terms of the vocabulary and the canonical works were established, as well as the stances and attitudes rehearsed. For many of the younger generation in Britain and the US, pilgrimages to Paris were *de rigueur*; it became a case of "playing at being French," while the French themselves, a decade earlier—through jazz in St Germain des Prés, the Gallimard *serie noire*, Gide, Sartre and Camus' admiration for William Faulkner, Dashiell Hammett and Ernest Hemingway—had been "playing at being American." This, at least, is part of the history that an early essay of mine, "Two Decades in Another Country" (1975), wanted to present about the migration of French love for Hollywood in the 1950s and 1960s.[6] The companion piece, thirty years on, is the essay on "Cinephilia," included in the present volume, which recapitulates some of the personal details of this story, but also tries to give a more theoretical turn to the developments in and beyond the 1970s. It tracks the persistence of cinephilia in the formations that (on the face of it) seem to be its opposite, the cinephobic strand of French film theory, inaugurated—in the pages of the very same *Cahiers du cinéma*, no less—with essays, such as the one on John Ford's YOUNG MR LINCOLN or those other brilliant "deconstructions" of Hollywood ideology,[7] which so profoundly marked "*Screen* theory" in Britain,[8] and continued to influence the way film studies was taught in the United States well into the 1990s.[9]

Why Hollywood?

If I return to my own involvement in these debates, the critical rather than meta-critical essays that I published between 1967 and 1975 reflect a double agenda. On the one hand, writing for a public rather than for myself began with a more or less mimetic adoption of the unalloyed *auteurism* of *Cahiers du cinéma* and *Movie*, in the articles I published in the *Brighton Film Review*, two samples of which are the essay on Nicholas Ray (written, flushed with excitement, from seeing his films and meeting Ray after his lecture at the National Film Theatre) and on Sam Fuller. The latter I had also met in London in 1968, whereupon I persuaded my collaborators on the *BFR* to do a special issue on Fuller (graciously acknowledged by the director in a letter sent to us from Los Angeles). The essay on SHOCK CORRIDOR reprinted here was commissioned by Peter Wollen for the Edinburgh Retrospective booklet of 1969.

By the time the Fuller and Ray essays were published, I had already tried to extend *auteurism* to include questions of genre and ideology. I was particularly interested in the complementary-compensatory function that genres have for Hollywood,[10] and how this related to an overall cultural-ideological project that appeared unique to the American cinema, namely to reshape the nation, after WWII, in the image of its mass media. It gave it a quasi-anthropological function neither captured by the extreme aesthetic value suddenly placed on Hollywood genre films by *auteurism* and cinephilia, nor acknowledged by an also quite extreme ideological critique and deconstruction of Hollywood. The result was a number of hybrid pieces, one of which I devoted to Vincente Minnelli (1970), whom I saw putting forth a complementary, but unified "vision" by alternating between making musical comedies and melodramas, much the same way Peter Wollen had shown the *auteur* "Howard Hawks" to be made up of binary pairs, in which comedies and Western, seemingly antithetical genres, conditioned and necessitated each other.[11] My own post-*auteurist* essays did not follow a strict structuralist agenda, as inaugurated by Wollen and subsequently laid out by *Screen*, but rather initiated a more general reflection about the American cinema (in the pages of *Monogram*), where we tried to understand how Hollywood worked as an integrated, but flexible system, which led to some first specifications (and more unsecured speculations) about what the term "classical cinema" could signify.

If I was therefore in the late 1960s/early 1970s—somewhat fortuitously, but as it turned out, also fortunately—involved in the formulation of one of the several versions of what is now generally referred to as "classical Hollywood" cinema, the underlying interest was as much ethnographic-anthropological as it was aesthetic and political. In the 1990s I was intrigued to find myself figure occasionally as witness for both the defense and the prosecution, as it were, in the so-called "paradigm wars" (Jane Gaines) or "form wars" (Bill Nichols).[12] Film studies had its most creative period in the 1980s, leading to a lively polemic between *Screen* theory (notably represented by Laura Mulvey, Stephen Heath, Colin MacCabe) and positions (headed by David Bordwell, Noël Carroll) that later were gathered together under the title of *Post-Theory*. Without directly entering into the debate, I did "respond" to an invitation to contribute to a special issue of *Film Criticism*, where I tried to re-assess my position about the cinema, in the face of a general paradigm shift, tilting the profession towards cultural studies, while also acknowledging the need to engage openly with the changes that had transformed Hollywood in the 1980s and 1990s.[13] For the present volume I expanded these thoughts into a partly autobiographical essay, paying a special tribute to Peter Wollen, and trying to put the London scene around *Screen* and the emergence of cultural studies in context ("Film Studies in Britain: Cinephilia, *Screen* Theory and Cultural Studies").

The shift of my cinephile horizon was also occasioned by a change of location from the University of Sussex in Brighton to bohemian West London, and the re-founding of the *Brighton Film Review* as *Monogram*, encouraged by my first contacts (besides Peter Wollen) with Laura Mulvey, Jon Halliday, Sam Rohdie and Geoffrey Nowell Smith, most of whom were my seniors by a few years, and especially in matters political, far more sophisticated and erudite. The first programmatic statement of this encounter, where I mapped a position both distinct from that of *Screen*, but—as I hoped— open to exchange and debate, was "Why Hollywood?" where I tried to spell out some of the principles behind our continued interest in studying the classical cinema systematically, and how we intended to do it in a historical-critical context. I highlighted the drive-oriented (male) hero, the linear narrative trajectory in the form of a journey or a quest, the strong character-centered motivation and the interlocking causal chain of actions. But what was also important to me was to identify a psycho-social element of affect, energy and emotion, which at first I attributed to the directors' world view: Sam Fuller's paranoid/violent heroes, Nicholas Ray's romantic protagonists with their Dionysian energies, but also destructiveness, Minnelli's more aestheticized psychic drive and emotional *joie de vivre*, but also often taken to the point of excess, delirium and even death—and therefore akin to the *jouissance* that Roland Barthes had identified in modernist texts. I saw in these directors and their work an *immanent* critique of American ideology, which finally seemed to me more interesting than merely to apply the standard (European) *ideological* critique from outside the films and from outside the culture that produced and sustained them.

Subsequently, I extended this immanent critique and my sense of these films as limit experiences which, I realized, I had projected onto my favorite Hollywood *auteurs*, partly no doubt in order to rescue the "good (Hollywood) object" from the withering critiques by my peers. Depersonalizing the good object somewhat, I turned the diagnostics around, looking towards the audience, trying to analyze the emotional-bodily force field—the psychic matrix of reception, as I called it—into which the spectator is immersed by the "cinema experience." It was the other side of cinephilia: a state of mind sensitive to the place, the space, the time, the big screen, the darkened auditorium. The result was "Narrative Cinema and Audience-Aesthetics," presented initially to one of the BFI Education Department's evening seminars in the early 1970s, where it fell somewhat flat, or rather, it fell between several reigning or emerging orthodoxies: an experience which strengthened my resolve to chart a path in dialogue with but nonetheless also distinct from that of *Screen*.

Film studies in Britain, from the mid-1970s onwards, and increasingly through the 1980s, began to develop along somewhat divergent trajectories. At the center was *Screen* magazine, which had turned to psycho-semiotics, with a series of remarkable and hugely influential articles, published in quick succession by Colin MacCabe on the "classic realist text,"[14] Stephen Heath's major articles on narrative,[15] and especially Laura Mulvey's article which practically founded feminist film theory,[16] all of them vigorously continuing the critical engagement with Hollywood. Although taking off from a different vantage point, one has to add here the analyses of entertainment forms, commissioned and researched by members of the Birmingham Centre for Contemporary Cultural Studies. While *Screen* theory relied heavily on Althusser's interpretation of Lacan, the Birmingham School extended and made productive the theoretical bases of Gramscian Marxism, impervious and generally hostile to psychoanalysis. The subjects broached by cultural studies tended to include the cinema, but also marginalized it, turning more towards other media, artifacts and objects of popular culture, such as television, soap opera, women's magazines, popular music, spectator sports or fashion.

However, throughout the 1970s (1972–79) there was at least a third strand of inquiry linking British writing to popular cinema, perhaps more an accidental conjuncture of three individual essays, each author pursuing more or less his own interests, rather than forming a school, but each continuing an engagement with Hollywood, notably around genre, which with hindsight seem to have features in common. Three authors produced widely quoted articles outside the *Screen* orbit, two appearing in *Movie* and one in *Monogram*. My own essay on melodrama "Tales of Sound and Fury," from 1972 was followed by Richard Dyer's *Movie* essay on the musical, "Entertainment and Utopia," from 1977[17] and Robin Wood published "An Introduction to the American Horror Film" in 1979.[18] All three essays looked at the deviant, non-conformist or excessive genres of Hollywood symptomatically, that is, in order to read from them a dynamic, critical engagement with big issues in US-American society, gender and the family. Each essay, while certainly affected by structuralist method, eschewed grand theory, concentrating instead on a close analysis of a particular corpus of films, and treating seriously, as the *auteurists* had done, films with stereotypical plots and often despised generic forms.

Film Analysis as System

During the 1980s, my essays and lectures tended to take up the tenets of *Screen* theory only to the extent that I adopted and tried to make my own the analyses of Raymond Bellour, inspired by a personal encounter, by his essays on The Big Sleep, on Gigi and The Lonedale Operator, but less so by his better-known work on Hitchcock. My brief section on the opening of The Big Sleep, and the longer analysis of The Public Enemy are an oblique tribute to Lévi-Strauss' influence on his work, especially in the way Bellour framed the question of classical cinema as one of (mythological) extension and (textual) volume. For me, he lucidly formulated an essential (formal, but also ideological) tension in Hollywood cinema between the linear, goal and drive-oriented surface structure, which sustains a conscious, motivational engagement with the protagonist, and a "depth" structure, following a quite different logic, with richer extensions in symbolic and emotional space. Bellour allowed me to retain from *auteurism* an immanently critical, reflexive and self-referential dimension, while also keeping in focus the question of genre, star and studio, which is to say, the "systemic" features of Hollywood's self-organization and self-regulation; and finally, even as he devoted more of his critical energies to video and installation art, Bellour proved a valuable reference in my efforts to define—formally, but especially anthropologically, in the way American cinema speaks to America and through America to the world—what retroactively became classical Hollywood, as the studio-era was re-assessed, during the (second) phase of "New Hollywood," starting around 1975, when the American film industry itself underwent its most momentous changes for thirty or forty years.

The differences between my early essays on Hollywood as a coherent set of rules, patterns and practices, written as these changes were taking place and the rules were broken, and "Film as System" reflect above all the division between critic and teacher. For the sake of my students and pedagogy, I needed to formalize my more intuitive insights, leading to an extended statement of how to read Hollywood films closely within the routines of academic study. In "Film as System" I concentrated on openings, in order to show how carefully crafted these foreshadowing and retrospective effects are that give the classical Hollywood film its "body," its memory of itself, as well as its many effects of "realism" as coherence, its dense semantic texture and reliably pleasurable self-consistency. The essay is expository and thus the one most directly indebted to structuralism (and to Thierry Kuntzel, himself a video-artist and a friend of Bellour's), but I took care to enlist and compare several different methodological entry points (including those provided by David Bordwell, Peter Wollen, Edward Branigan), pairing them off against each other, seeing them as complementary, and assessing the consequences of their methodological choices for the practice of close textual analysis. A more contextual approach is taken in the two-part chapter that gives the book its title, *The Persistence of Hollywood*, where I lay out the general frameworks within which I think one needs to understand the formal features as well as the historical dynamics that allow Hollywood to be in constant change and yet stay the same, to be the most adaptive *and* the most conservative, the most revolutionary *and* the most reactionary force in global culture: a perplexing and paradoxical anthropological phenomenon that will never have been studied enough.

Self-divided not only between critic and scholar, but also between formalism and historical analysis, I also continued with my other tradition of contextualization, derived from Siegfried Kracauer's socio-psychological model of "modernity and the mass-media," which I tried to combine with Edgar Morin's more explicitly socio-anthropological model of the cinema. The result was a series of articles, which returned to the question of genre and the studio-system, but now as a more complex set of historical determinants. These included censorship, national politics, the representative hero, while also paying attention to the formal constraints or stylistic pressures bearing upon the classical mode in the 1930s and 1940s. In this sense, several essays highlight the history of Warner Bros., focusing on its gangster films and the biopics as typical formations/deformations of a historical imaginary and its public sphere, and thus are attempts to both place and displace the terms of the debate around the classical. Placing classical cinema formally and displacing it historically, the notion of genre comes back as something that regulates norms and deviance (in matters of ethnic, class and gender identities) for a particular community at a particular point in time. While genre seems to loom large, almost as an anthropological category, the essays try to ground the definition of genre also in the narratological work that came out of structuralism, especially Propp and Greimas. These considerations around the gangster film and the William Dieterle biopics from the 1930s, with their male stars as focal points (James Cagney, Paul Muni) were originally preceded by a collaborative piece written with a colleague during the summer of 1975 in Berlin, featuring another Warner Bros. film, THE ROARING TWENTIES, starring both Cagney and Humphrey Bogart.[19] Also relevant in this context is the most "extra-territorial" director to have ever worked with and for Warner Bros., Stanley Kubrick. The prototypical role his films were to play in the transition from classical "in-house" studio films to post-classical "outsourcing" is evaluated at the end of the section on *auteurs maudits* and mavericks.

In the 1960s and 1970s, we used to think of the cinema as the last creative, individual art form, as an expressive medium, and we celebrated its heroes, the *auteurs*. In this respect, the gap between Hollywood, the European art cinema and the political and formal avant-garde cinemas was not as wide as it often seemed. But in the course of the final decades of the 20th century we realized more and more that the cinema—all of cinema—had been like an invisible film, a material immaterial substance, in which the century had been captured or had inscribed itself. Likeness, trace, imprint, cast, script or Turin shroud: we know it is legible, even if we don't always know how to decipher or translate it. The "image" the century has left: is it thanks to, or in spite of the work of the *auteurs*? The question poses itself, since so much of our collective and individual memory is made up of photographic and filmic images whose authorship is, for all intents and purposes "anonymous." If Andy Warhol was one of the first to recognize this,[20] it was Jean Luc Godard who was able to give this sense of the cinema as the "veritable history" of the 20th century its most definitive form and documentation, in his *Histoire(s) du cinema (1988–98)*.[21] His collision-compilation of a hundred years of cinema still relies on and endorses the *auteurs*, drawing on Hitchcock, Renoir, Dreyer, Rossellini, Lang, Murnau as well as George Stevens and Sidney Lumet, but the discourse is that history speaks through them, their "individual vision" more a vehicle for the historical unconscious—or the historical imaginary—of cinema. Perhaps this is what Godard finally meant when, twenty years earlier, he proposed a counter-cinema.[22]

Such conclusions suggest that the more impersonal theories of the cinema—say the sociological one of a Siegfried Kracauer, or the anthropological one of an Edgar Morin, and even the formalist case for classical cinema—have proven more prophetic. Will they be more productive for the 21st century than the *auteurist* studies we were conducting in the 1960s? Will they prove more relevant than even the anti-*auteurist* psycho-analytical and semiotic analyses of the classical American cinema? The verdict is not yet in, but the chances are that the director as *auteur*-entrepreneur will flourish in the digital era, even if *auteurism* as we have known and debated it will become a nostalgic memory before being revived as a "cult" interest.

What, then, do we make of these abandoned sites of film scholarship, or how to account for their revival and persistence? In other words: what was the function of authorship studies and what their status today? I can only answer in a personal manner: I started my life as a critic with essays on Nicholas Ray, Sam Fuller and Vincente Minnelli—two outsiders of the Hollywood system, and one an aesthete who for a long time was considered a mere *metteur en scène* rather than an *auteur*.[23] What interested me (but not only me) was how these filmmakers had been able to create a world, "their" world in this impersonal medium, and even more in this impersonal industry, which was the Hollywood studio system. The model was that of antagonism and "critique," the individual artist pitted against the system.

As a historian, I also felt obliged—and frankly, attracted—to study this Hollywood "system" in more detail, from within its own logic, rather than as merely the negative foil of the *auteur*'s struggle for autonomy. The socio-historical and anthropological approaches interested me more than the political-polemical ones, but I never abandoned the *auteurist* bias, except perhaps to extend it into a historical, as well as aesthetic inquiry, with a weakness for European directors working in Hollywood. Wanting to document the efforts required to maintain integrity and a personal vision among strangers, I transferred the old *Cahiers du cinéma* preference for the Hollywood outsider to mainly German-speaking directors at the margins, concentrating on refugees, self-exiles, displaced persons in one form or another—from Ernst Lubitsch, F.W. Murnau and Fritz Lang, to Joe May, E.A. Dupont and Robert Siodmak, then to William Dieterle, Walter Reisch and Douglas Sirk. But I was also fascinated by the English Hitchcock in the Californian sun, and Roman Polanski, the Pole with French connections, surrounded by tragedy and scandal in L.A., and I became intrigued by Americans displaced in Europe, notably Orson Welles, Joseph Losey and Stanley Kubrick.

The *auteurs* were thus only one polarity of the dialectic: the other was the effort to read the American cinema as symptomatic, taking the pulse of the *Zeitgeist*, registering the shifts in the cultural history, rendering palpable the mass-media unconscious already alluded to when I mentioned Kracauer and Morin. The more critical I became of Kracauer in relation to Weimar Germany and its cinema, the more Kracauerian I remained in my estimation of the Hollywood cinema. For years I could do little more than either ignore this contradiction, or at best register the tension between the two positions. I consoled myself by thinking of Raymond Bellour, whose symptomatic readings of Hollywood across especially the work of Hitchcock seemed to me to display a similar oscillation—between describing Hollywood as a "complete world," and making Hitchcock—surely the most eccentric and unrepresentative representative of what Hollywood stood for and still stands for—the embodiment and symbol of these closed worlds or mythologies.

Hollywood Defined Through Its Outsiders

In my teaching I kept alive the debate around the "classical," but increasingly I found myself looking at Hollywood classicism as also the product of its non-American, immigrant, self-exiled directors, so that the classical—after the exploration of genre—finds itself in each case folded back into a discussion of an *auteur*-director also trailing another national tradition and being part of an international history. Among several possible papers I have selected a study of one of the least recognized *auteurs* across the Europe-Hollywood-Europe axis: William Dieterle, both Warner Bros. studio hack and eminent European. I follow it with chapters on Orson Welles, Alfred Hitchcock and Fritz Lang.

Each essay is less concerned to establish their *auteurist* credentials, that is the thematic coherence of their work (which—in contrast to Minnelli, Fuller, Ray—has always been incontestable, even where it was challenged, as in Pauline Kael's book on CITIZEN KANE).[24] Rather, the chapters situate these figures in a multi-layered cultural history of Europe and Hollywood, exploring the personal as well as stylistic signifiers of the national character-(mask) they felt themselves called upon to put on and represent. This positioned their work within and at the margins of the classical, and opened it up to various kinds of non-classical styles or the historical deviations (Baroque, Expressionist or Edwardian). The section also raises issues of continuity and discontinuity in the critical-evaluative paradigm, further taken up in an essay that marks the beginning of the transitional phase starting in the 1970s and ending in the early 1990s. Devoted to Robert Altman's pioneering, multi-track and multi-strand narrative ensemble film NASHVILLE (1975), it tries to show how creatively aware but also divided this director was, regarding the different "crises": his work pointed in a direction that Hollywood did not take. The Kubrick essay has been placed here, because Kubrick is not only extra-territorial, but also "too late/too soon" in relation to the classical/post-classical shifts in 1960s/1970s Hollywood. It is around Altman and Kubrick that one can track once more a critique "from within" of the classical, and show how these directors each develop their version(s) of the post-classical by pathologizing the classical, by "prototyping" it, or by re-"turning" the classical against itself.

The Post-Classical as Classical-Plus

Section IV concentrates on post-classical Hollywood, in the gradual, but not always peaceful self-invention from "New" Hollywood to Global Hollywood, and from the on-location filmmaking by directors like Bob Rafelson and Monte Hellman, to the digital post-production work of George Lucas and Steven Spielberg. The tension is between the centrifugal forces of globalization, money and the different delivery systems for Hollywood "product" (as "the industry" or "the business" not only encompasses film and television production, but becomes interlaced with the music business, advertising and the military) and the centripetal forces of cultural and high-tech "clustering," which shows that place and location still matter, when it comes to having a skill-base, as well as requiring the flow of "information" that only circulates among "tribal" communities. Equally contradictory is the pull towards outsourcing, sub-contracting and specialization on the one hand, and the "winner-takes-all" logic, which finally keeps so much economic power and cultural capital in the hands of so few.

It was as a way of encouraging myself to once more participate directly in the debates around the after-life of the "classical cinema" (and what it might mean to speak of a post-classical cinema, now applied to Hollywood since the 1980s rather than to the New Hollywood of the early 1970s) that in 2002 I co-wrote a book on the distinction between classical and post-classical cinema when applied to typical special effects "action-films" like DIE HARD, on "time travel films" like BACK TO THE FUTURE.[25] Earlier I had published an essay on the relation of classical cinema to television series, to ride films and studio-tours, which aligns a certain textual-temporal logic (that of seriality, of the sequel and the prequel) with an economic and marketing logic, each becoming allegorized versions of the other.[26] Although not included, it should be seen as a companion piece to "New Economy Hollywood," which in turn is a "sequel" to "The Pathos of Failure," first published in 1975, in that it tries to analyze, thirty years after, what might have been the several kinds of industrial logics underlying the "New Hollywood" and its transformation into the blockbuster culture of the 1980s and beyond.

By invoking once more the Hollywood-Europe-Hollywood dialectic, but also by a more specific application to Hollywood of the idea of post-Fordist industrial production, I want to offer an explanatory model that is both specific enough and capacious or "flexible" enough to understand the personal *auteurist* element of the change from "New Wave" to "New Economy" Hollywood, while taking account of the industrial changes usually referred to as the package unit system and the corresponding shift in emphasis from production to post-production, and from post-production to marketing. A key figure in these transitions, and an *auteur* who himself is only too (self-)conscious of "embodying" several paradigms of American film history, including those of its mavericks, *auteurs maudits* and misfits is Francis Ford Coppola. It is with an analysis of his Bram Stoker's Dracula and its multi-layered references to both literature and cinema, to the national and the international, to Hollywood as intensely obsessed with "America" and increasingly multi-national and global that I try to make the transition to the entrepreneurial *auteur*—first to Steven Spielberg's transformation of the blockbuster into a kind of time-machine and memory-generator, and second, with an analysis of James Cameron (and his blockbuster hit Avatar), who rather than being opposed to the system, embodies and represents it, though in an intriguingly (self-) contradictory way.

The collection is brought to a close with two attempts to understand the "persistence of Hollywood" in the digital age. The first tries to account for the rapid adoption of the new digital production and post-production methods not through focusing on the new technology, but in relation to different regimes of knowledge, belief and trust, while the final chapter—my most synthesizing effort to date—extends this analysis into more encompassing historical frameworks of the "American century," economic models of "creative destruction" and anthropological schemata, affecting the body and the senses, but ultimately turning on self-regulation as self-reference, providing access for all and keeping the system "open," while tightly controlling both access and openness.

All five sections of this collection have a double focus, as it were: the way they engage with time and time-shifting, not in the sense of science fiction, but as they try to grapple with the seeming paradox of Hollywood's continuity and change, its ability to appear to remain the same "fantasy island," while constantly revolutionizing key areas of its engagement with the "real world" of finance, labor, management, technology and global trade. The fact that the essays span the period from the late 1960s to the present, with an emphasis on the 1970s and 1990s, makes them symptomatic of these periods of accelerated change.

I
Flashback: Of Objects of Love and Objects of Study

1
Film Studies in Britain: Cinephilia, Screen Theory and Cultural Studies

It All Started in the Sixties . . .

That the question of film studies as a distinct discipline and its relation to cultural studies *can be asked*, is a tribute to the success which in the 1980s and 1990s assured film (and television) studies in the universities something of a privileged place, as a young, innovative and provocatively hybrid discipline: one of the few so-called "growth areas" in the humanities. That the question *has to be asked* in the new century means that past success as well as present dis/reorientation have to be seen in context. One such context is the emergence of film studies in Britain in the 1970s and 1980s, the place and the period that have shaped my own contribution most directly. I begin on a personal note and will conclude with some speculations on the possible fate of film studies after its encounter with cultural studies. Probably sharing a professional profile with several film scholars of my generation, I began writing about film in the early 1960s as a student of literature. I arrived at the University of Sussex in 1963, involved myself in running a university film club and began by compiling program notes. After my BA I stayed on for a PhD, eventually also organizing festival-like retrospectives: among others, one in 1971 on German avant-garde films from the 1960s. I began teaching film and cinema courses in a department of English and American Studies around 1973 (at the University of East Anglia), initially as an addition to the Modern Language & Literature program, but always with the aim of developing an autonomous Film Studies Department. This finally came to pass in 1976, and I continued to develop the subject throughout the 1980s. By the time I left in 1991 we were teaching film studies at undergraduate level, we had an internationally recognized MA program, as well as supervising PhD students.[1] Before recapitulating the formation of the discipline from this personal vantage point in more detail, a flashback is in order, to—what else—the Sixties.

Following the call for a "white-hot technological transformation" by the then Labour Prime Minister Harold Wilson, Britain in the 1960s underwent major expansion in its higher education system (the foundation of the so-called "New Universities," which included both Sussex and East Anglia), where new disciplines and interdisciplinary work, especially in the humanities, was being actively encouraged. But London was also the center of much intellectual ferment in the field of politics and culture (around the journal *New Left Review*, for instance) and a magnet for anyone seriously interested in cinema (studies). Between the mid-1960s and mid-1970s, several internal "revolutions" at the British Film Institute were taking place, resulting in a specially set up Education Department, a new publications policy (the "Cinema One" book series, pamphlets, working papers, journals), and an active program of supporting schools and universities to teach film as an academic subject.[2] The fact is that during the 1970s and 1980s Britain emerged as the most vibrant country in Europe with respect to film studies, producing a very diverse film culture that acted as a conduit for ideas between Paris and the United States, while also sustaining a remarkably focused and yet internationally highly influential home-grown intellectual debate about the cinema, its theory and history. Why this should have been so deserves a broader study than I can give it here, but it can be traced to the combined, although by no means always convergent effects of institutional initiatives (notably at the BFI and at several of the "New" universities, at the Society for Education in Film and Television [SEFT], as well as through the retrospectives at the Edinburgh Film Festival and at the National Film Theatre in London). Add to that the different, if short-lived magazine publications and their editors and contributors, some of whom were nothing less than brilliant and occasionally charismatic individuals, as well as a thriving avant-garde filmmaking movement around the London Co-op, and you have an effervescent mix, but also a community committed for the long term. The diversity of this film culture can be measured by remembering that it ranged from Hollywood cinephilia to promoting the structuralist avant-garde, from *auteurism* to new approaches to genre, from archival research on "early cinema," to work in television and popular culture, from studies of "national cinema" to feminism and psychoanalysis, from conferences on realism and Bert Brecht to debates about ethnographic film and documentary, from "political" cinema and Eisenstein to the "New Hollywood" of Robert Altman, Arthur Penn, Martin Scorsese and Francis Coppola. Among the journals, it is *Screen* that is most often cited as the center of all this activity, but as I shall argue, it was by no means the only film magazine of note, the diversity being a vital aspect of the "ecology" of this film culture and its robustness. Finally, among the active individuals were Robin Wood, Victor Perkins, Sam Rohdie, Ben Brewster, Richard Dyer, Jonathan Rosenbaum, Stephen Heath and Colin MacCabe, but also a remarkable number of couples: Peter Wollen and Laura Mulvey, Geoffrey Nowell-Smith and Rosalind Delmar, Claire Johnston and Paul Willemen, Andi and Pam Engel, Richard Collins and Christine Gledhill, Pam Cook and Jim Cook, John Ellis and Rosalind Coward (which may go some way to explain the early and intense engagement with feminism and film theory).

Jean Luc Godard's LE MÉPRIS

My own involvement in this London film culture started, as mentioned, around a university film club in Brighton, which in one sense was a natural follow-up to my affiliation with a film club in my 'teens during the 1950s in Germany, one of those distinctly middle-class *Film-Gilde* institutions, devoted to "realism," whether Italian neo-realism, much valued by my parents, who loved de Sica's MIRACLE IN MILAN and Fellini's LA STRADA, or in the form of psychological realism of the Ingmar Bergman or Kurosawa variety, much prized by myself, at a time when going to the cinema meant stealing a glimpse at what adults did, when they thought the children were not watching.

The Brighton film club I joined in 1964 was quite different from the *Gilde*-Club: it defined itself in the mirror of French *auteurism* of the late 1950s and worshipped Hollywood, and so in another sense from Bergman movies, by joining it I put a symbolic end to my adolescence. For my new friends quickly attacked this German middle-class taste and eventually browbeat me into agreeing that Bergman's THE SILENCE, despite its sexual frankness and existential "angst," was not as important for the cinema as John Ford's THE MAN WHO SHOT LIBERTY VALANCE. I could see for myself that Jean-Luc Godard was an exciting director not just in and for the present, but because he opened up the past: he had made me curious about Vincente Minnelli, when Michel Piccoli in LE MÉPRIS insisted on wearing his hat at all times, because Dean Martin did so in SOME CAME RUNNING. But that a Western with John Wayne should be more serious than WILD STRAWBERRIES or THE SEVENTH SEAL seemed inconceivable to the aesthetic orthodoxy I grew up with.

Ever since I was sixteen, I had been drawing up lists of the films I *needed* to see and taking copious notes immediately after the screenings of those that I did manage to catch at a local movie theater or the film club. But what galvanized all of this, and made cinephilia so completely distinct from other juvenile obsessions, such as stamp collecting or drawing up the weekly top-ten hit parade, was the encounter with the films of Godard. Mesmerized by A BOUT DE SOUFFLE in 1960 and VIVRE SA VIE in 1962, baffled by LE PETIT SOLDAT in 1963, it took a screening of LE MÉPRIS in London in 1964 to make the idea of *studying film* an urgently felt necessity. If someone had asked me at that time André Bazin's famous question from 1958, "qu'est-ce que le cinema?" I would probably have answered: "cinema is whatever Jean-Luc Godard happens to be doing *right now*." Film studies, as far as I was concerned, was initially born from the wish to catch up with Godard, and from the realization that words (that is, our training in literature) were all we had to cope with the heady confusion of feelings, action and thought that was cinema.

LE MÉPRIS confounded most profoundly any ideas one might have entertained about the "essence" of cinema, either as ontology (cheating death, by preserving the imprint of life, according to Bazin), or as driven by an inherent teleology (mimetic realism, for instance). It confronted one with the fact that film was the most total art ever invented, but also the medium in which one could speak about anything that mattered in life. In LE MÉPRIS, the cinema was as much a black box of infinitely receding depths in time and space, as it was a white surface covering an ontological void. In Godard's film the screen could at any point revert to its flat and two-dimensional state, right in the middle of telling a fictional narrative, proving that neither deep focus nor greater and greater "realism" could possibly be the direction in which the cinema was heading. LE MÉPRIS brought back the "graphic" in the photographic, and gave a "scriptural" dimension even to Cinemascope. It showed that color was as much a matter of rendering surfaces opaque and impenetrable, as its palette conferred transparency to objects, or allowed light to emanate from the texture of a dress and the complexion of a face. Since anything could enter a Godard frame, be it a page from a book, a photo clipped from a newspaper, a street scene or a staged tableau vivant, his images had the iconic-semiological status of posters (of which quite a few were prominently featured in LE MÉPRIS). That is, they were as much topological-tropological maps as they were visual representations, they were as much a crowded canvas of picture emblems from the time of Giotto (with a nod to Elie Faure) as they were dispositions of objects in post-Euclidean space (with a salute to Picasso's *Demoiselles d'Avignon*).

Sound and language, too, deployed their own distinct ontology in Godard's cinema. He first of all returned words to their status as graphic signs and pictograms, which is what they were prior to becoming articulate sounds in the "talkies." And to the all-talking film, Godard restored the pause, the "mute" intermittence, as well as the eloquence of silence, while his soundtrack was voice *and* noise, even before it was music or speech. In LE MÉPRIS, Georges Delerue's music keeps spreading its chromatically lush wings into soaring heights of feeling, only to break off so abruptly each time, either shocked into silence or hushed by an invisible conductor. This music is a character in its own right: it moves among the protagonists, inserts itself between them, and like the voice of some Shakespearean Ariel conversant with Bert Brecht's epic theater, it provides its own comment on the action—ironic, ominous and incorrigibly optimistic in turn.

LE MÉPRIS made me realize—long before I saw, for instance, Anthony McCall's work or Dan Graham's installations—that the projection of an image might be nothing but a cone of light, cutting a slice of geometry out of space. At the very next moment, though—for instance, when the ancient statue of Neptune, eyelessly scanning a fallen world in a 360° circle, and yet fixing us with a piercing gaze—the image could conjure up a depth in both mythic time and philosophical thought that stretched into infinity. When in the opening scene, Raoul Coutard's camera, moving with stately grace along the tracks so inexorably laid out for it, began to swivel, at the end of the credits spoken by Brice Parain as if he was God(ard) himself, and finally turned towards us, spectators in the darkened room, I became conscious of my vulnerability inside my imagined invisibility, as the single, square face of a menacing alien was suddenly upon me. All but swallowing the screen and me with it, this camera-mouth made palpable how tight was the space, physical as well as metaphysical, in which any fiction sustains the illusion that what we see is taking place "out there," before it folds back upon itself, mirror-like doubling the apparatus in a *mise-en-abyme* of infinite regress that finally excludes the human subject altogether.

But what perturbed me most, and for the first time made me want to write about "the cinema" in 1964, was Michel Piccoli, demonstrating six different ways of stepping through a door (in which the central pane of glass is missing). It occurs early on in the film, when Camille (Brigitte Bardot) and Paul Javal (Piccoli) visit for the first time the flat Michel had bought for them from the money that Prokosh (Jack Palance) had advanced him for his work as script-doctor on Prokosh's Hollywood-in-Italy production of *The Odyssey*. The couple is already seriously at odds with each other, with Camille suspecting that Michel had "sold" her to Prokosh, in order to secure the deal. The scene starts with them entering the apartment, a desultory exchange ensues, while both, on their own, explore the different rooms and views, and it ends with Camille bending down to look at herself in a gilt-framed mirror, casually stacked against a wall. Quite possibly an homage to a Buster Keaton gag (from *The Haunted House*), Piccoli's movements back-and-forth—sometimes opening the supposedly glazed door and closing it behind him, sometimes just stepping through the empty pane, then again, opening the door and still stepping through the pane—outline a complex moral geometry. At the time, it struck me as a metaphor of the cinema, as much as it evidently was a comment on the passages, dead-ends and false openings of the couple's marriage. A metaphor for the "frame" as well as the "screen," for what separates and what connects, for the limits between what is inside and what is outside, the scene is also a metaphor for the difference between the literal and the metaphoric itself. Never before in a film had I felt so strongly the possibility that the (non-)drama of the solitude of two human beings in the company of each other—echoes of Bergman, or of Rossellini's VIAGGIO IN ITALIA—could become a theoretical treatise on "what is cinema" in miniature. Documenting the documentary dimension within any diegetic space, and demonstrating how the make-believe of fiction arises from within the materiality of a setting or a décor, Piccoli's *viaggio in camera* was for me one of Godard's most Bazinian moments, achieved by means that were quite un-Bazinian. It taught me that telling a story for Godard would always mean "painting the space between" his characters, rather than providing any firm ontological ground they might be able to share, even in moments of intimacy, tenderness or anticipated domesticity. A "door" would always be in the way: half-open, half-closed, half-solid, half-glazed, but in any case, forever half-finished.

Cinephilia in the Sixties and Film Writing as (Surrogate) Film Making

Godard propelled the wish to reflect on the cinema, but he did so in a dramatic/traumatic way. He lodged the desire for a theory of cinema through the cinema itself, but his films foreclosed that very possibility, because the standards he set were so far in advance of everything else that happened in the cinema up to that time. The experience was so traumatic, and Godard became so emblematic, I think, because his films fostered the illusion that writing about films was already halfway to making them, and that making films was the most authentic manner of being engaged in the world, or quite possibly in transforming the world: not only one's own, but that of one's culture and society. Hence the fatal ambition to become a film activist, which meant—in a gesture that both copied *Cahiers du cinéma* and harked back to the avant-garde movements of the 1920s—to write for and edit a film magazine, which I eventually did in 1968.

Among the books I read to prepare myself for the task in the years between 1964 and 1968 was neither André Bazin's four volumes *Qu'est-ce que le cinéma?* (1958–62) nor Siegfried Kracauer's *Theory of Film* (1960) but *Le cinéma ou l'homme imaginaire* by Edgar Morin, published in 1956, who took a distinctly anthropological view of the 7th Art. Besides Morin, it was Robert Warshow's *The Immediate Experience* (1962), and especially Parker Tyler whose essays I devoured, written mostly during the 1950s but collected in the 1960s as *The Hollywood Hallucination*, and as *Sex, Psyche, Etcetera in the Film*. What had prepared me for Tyler were the occasional pieces by the English critic Raymond Durgnat, whose iconoclasm was generously spiced with Adou Kyrou's and Robert Benayoun's brand of surrealism, which had survived in the pages of *Positif*, the Parisian antagonist of *Cahiers du cinéma*, and a magazine that hated Godard. Morin, Warshow, Tyler and Durgnat gave my understanding of cinema an ethnographic-anthropological slant and a broadly cultural-historical grounding, reinforced by my university studies in European Romanticism and Modernist literature, 19th century historiography and 20th century politics.

The reading prescribed by my friends, after they had converted me to Hollywood, was slightly different. What gave them such self-confidence was a subscription to *Movie* magazine, edited by Ian Cameron, which started appearing in 1961. Sometimes regarded as a clone (or rather, in those days a "carbon copy") of *Cahiers du cinéma*, it was admired by us for its intransigent militancy vis-à-vis other positions, notably that of *Sight & Sound*, the house journal of the British Film Institute. Realism, for instance, was attacked by *Movie* not because it privileged the cinema's mechanical reproduction of reality over its expressive-constructivist potential, nor did Ian Cameron and Victor Perkins object to British "kitchen sink" cinema because of its manifestly middle-class "angry young men" rather than authentic working-class heroes. *Movie* abhorred the realist credo because it was championed by *Sight & Sound*: the victory of good taste over cult and camp, of pragmatism over passion: a prescriptive, well-meaning, understated consensus of those who enjoyed the cinema, but in moderation, and who, when given the choice, would probably prefer a good novel, or an evening at the theater. *Movie* writers, on the other hand, argued openly among themselves over the merits of Richard Brooks' Elmer Gantry (1962) or the significance of John Frankenheimer's The Manchurian Candidate (1962) for the future of Hollywood. For *Movie*, Hollywood stood for *mise-en-scène*, and *mise-en-scène* stood for the manifestations of a soul, at once more violent and more vulgar, more ideologically ambiguous and more bracingly naive than seemed enshrined in either the *Cahiers du cinéma* cult of *auteurs* or Lindsay Anderson's *Free Cinema* movement. *Movie* loved Otto Preminger and Joseph Losey, when the reputation of the first had already entered into free fall, and the second had not yet been adopted by *Sight & Sound*, which did so only after Losey's successful collaboration with Harold Pinter on The Servant and Accident.[3]

A Paris Pilgrimage

Movie's Hollywood, then, was not exactly the Hollywood of *Cahiers* or of Bazin. Granted: Hitchcock, Hawks and Welles were mentioned, but they did not—at least not in the early years—provide the touchstones. Insofar as it looked to Paris, *Movie* was closer to the MacMahonists (of *Présence du cinéma*), and when it invited art critics to contribute, it was people like Lawrence Alloway, an influential voice of British pop art, who was sympathetic to Hollywood movies, to advertising and comics, and who, in a study of movie iconography (published in one of *Movie*'s first issues), had extolled the values of "mass popular art" and its cross-fertilizations with high art, rather than antagonism.[4] *Movie* embraced not only gangster pictures and *film noir*, but saw even in the Frank Tashlin movies with Jerry Lewis the energy and vitality of the new youth culture (which had not yet been given this name). From *Movie* I learnt to love (though these were also *Cahiers'* favorites) the MGM musicals of the Arthur Freed unit; above all, Vincente Minnelli's THE BANDWAGON but also Nicholas Ray's PARTY GIRL. The license *Movie* gave us to like these "trashy" films was exhilarating, since they were championed by this very English, very Oxford team of Young Turks. In retrospect, it seems that *Movie* was much more closely aligned in sensibility if not in personnel with the emergent British pop scene at the art colleges, with Mick Jagger's music and Mary Quant's boutiques, than was realized at the time. With hindsight it is possible to reconstruct how much *Movie* had correctly read the signs of the times in matters of fashion and style, and what a (small but significant) service it had rendered British youth in matters cinema and visual design.

Nonetheless, for anyone interested in the cinema in the 1960s, the pull of Paris was irresistible. No sooner had I finished my first university undergraduate degree and begun a doctorate, than I enrolled at the Sorbonne. I did not take any courses, but spent my daytime hours at the Rue Richelieu Bibliothèque Nationale, and the evenings—usually from 7 p.m. to midnight, at the Cinematheque. By then, armed with a copy of Andrew Sarris' *American Cinema: Directors and Directions* (which had become the cinephile's equivalent of the Ten Commandments, while also appealing to the "top-ten" collector in me, with its lists of must-see films and classifications of directors, from the "Pantheon directors" down to those that offered "less than meets the eye"), I shuttled every night between the Palais de Chaillot and the Rue d'Ulm. Henri Langlois was famous for his inspired programming, which would combine a rare Mizoguchi melodrama with an Allan Dwan Western, or show Jacques Tourneur's BUILD MY GALLOWS HIGH on the same evening as Marcel Carné's LE JOUR SE LÈVE. I must have seen six hundred films in the eight months I spent in Paris, and filled several spiral bound notebooks with comments scribbled in the dark. No sooner had I returned to England and re-established contact, I went ahead and started a university film magazine in late 1968, the *Brighton Film Review*. Its slightly better known, but also relatively short-lived successor was *Monogram*, begun in 1971. The name was chosen to advertise our allegiance to Hollywood (with a nod to Godard who had dedicated his first film A BOUT DE SOUFFLE, to Monogram, a B-movie studio). The fact that *Monogram* promoted Hollywood in the early 1970s, at the height of anti-Vietnam protests and in the wake of May '68 was an act of loyalty in the guise of provocation: instead of writing about Glauber Rocha or Michael Snow, we published articles on Michael Powell and Raoul Walsh, Sam Peckinpah and Robert Aldrich. Besides celebrating Douglas Sirk, Vincente Minnelli and Joseph Losey, we also attacked the British Cinema and David Lean, yet almost in spite of ourselves, we also kept faith with Ingmar Bergman, Federico Fellini and Luis Buñuel.

What was so special about French cinephilia, and why was it important for what became film studies in Britain? In a subsequent chapter, I shall try to give a more thorough answer, but the cinephilia I became initiated into around 1963/4 in Brighton and London did include dandified rituals strictly observed when "going to the movies," either alone or, less often, in groups. And as I shall argue, cinephilia was always a gesture towards cinema already framed by nostalgia and other retroactive temporalities, by pleasures tinged with regret, even as they register as pleasures. Without cinephilia, there would not have been film studies, certainly not for my generation in Great Britain, but with film studies—some would say—we also created the gravediggers of cinephilia.

Film Theory as Screen Theory—Mourning Work for Cinephilia?

One is always convinced that one's experience of life is unique, and that the choices one makes are self-directed and premeditated. Thus, I did not ask myself why it was that during the same years that I founded a film magazine in Brighton, there also appeared in London *Afterimage, Cinemantics, Cinema Rising, Enthusiasm, Cinema* (Cambridge University) and only a little later *Framework* (University of Warwick) and *Filmform* (Newcastle University). They all kept their distance from, but certainly felt the gravitational pull of *Screen*, refounded in 1971, and dramatically reversing the decline of the Society for Education in Film and Television (SEFT). Nor did I realize at the time that pilgrimages to Paris similar to mine (as well as to Rome) had been undertaken a few years earlier by Peter Wollen, Laura Mulvey, Geoffrey Nowell-Smith and Jon Halliday: all regular writers for *Screen* and major figures in the emergence of film studies in Britain.

The parallels and coincidences thus focus attention on the conjunctural dynamics that led from French-inspired cinephilia and *auteurism* to film studies in Britain, but also highlights once more some crucial institutional factors. For me, Peter Wollen was the key figure, not so much as a writer, but as the man at the Education Department of the British Film Institute in charge of publications. I first met him when I needed a print subsidy for *Monogram*, and although he must have raised an eyebrow or two at our editorial policy, he immediately promised financial support, and also encouraged us to attend and give papers at the regular fortnightly BFI/*Screen* workshops. There, we often enough got into a fight with Sam Rohdie, the abrasive but brilliant first editor of the new *Screen*, but we also met our peers from the other publications—Tony Rayns, Simon Field, Ian Christie, Silvia Harvey, Steve Crofts, as well as the other staff of the BFI Education Department: Ed Buscombe, Alan Lovell, Colin McArthur, Jim Kitses and Christopher Williams. Wollen, in an interview from 2001, traced his own development within this configuration:

> When I came back [from Tehran in 1963] I started writing for the *New Left Review*. This was a magazine, which had originally been founded by an older generation of people, the generation of people like Edward Thompson, Raymond Williams and Richard Hoggart. But then a new generation appeared and took over, most of them coming from Oxford, people I had known such as Perry Anderson, Robin Blackburn, Alexander Cockburn, and others. . . . The first things I wrote for the *NLR* were about contemporary politics. But I was interested in film and Perry Anderson, who was the editor, wanted the magazine to be modeled on something like *Les Temps Modernes*, and he wanted cultural coverage as well as political coverage. So the idea came of writing about film and that's when I did my first film pieces, under the name of Lee Russell.
>
> Then I got a job at the British Film Institute in the Education Department, which was run by somebody called Paddy Whannel, who wrote a very good book with Stuart Hall early in the 1960s. It was a pioneering book in the field that later became known as "Cultural Studies." It turned out that he had read what I had written in *New Left Review* and he asked me, quite unexpectedly, if I would like to come and work with him at the BFI. . . . We were supposedly an Education Department, we held seminars, we published things, first pamphlets, then a series of books, the *Cinema One* series, which I ended up editing. . . . The purpose of the Education Department in the BFI was to launch film education in English schools and universities as a serious subject, alongside the other arts. Painting, literature, music—it was taken for granted that they would be part of the curriculum. So one of the basic goals of the Education Department was to support anyone who wanted to teach film in schools or universities. And one way to support them was by publishing books, which they could use in class. So that was the context in which [my own] *Signs & Meaning in the Cinema* was written. There was also a French influence because already the journal *Communication* had been launched in France, where it introduced the ideas of semiology and structuralism. [. . .]
>
> Very soon after *Signs & Meaning* came out the first serious film courses in universities were developed. As a result of that I was invited to teach in a university for the first time, so in that sense, it changed things radically for me, at least. The immediate reaction to the book was one of polarization. You got people who supported it—"about time too, now we have a proper book of film theory in England"—and people who hated and loathed it— "what is all this garbage? We don't need all this to understand and appreciate film!" It certainly created some

controversy. [But] we went ahead and founded *Screen* magazine, which was a militantly theoretical journal. That also came out of the BFI Education Department.[5]

Considering that in the 1970s, the BFI headquarters were in Dean Street, parallel to Wardour Street, where the big Hollywood studios had their press screening rooms, and that SEFT's *Screen* office in Old Compton Street was only a few hundred yards from the BFI, while around the corner was Meard Street, where the *New Left Review* has its home, it becomes clear how powerfully a shaping force was exerted by this small topographical Soho "square" in Central London on the intellectual contours and personal networks of film studies not just for London but extending all over Britain in its formative decade.[6] *Monogram*'s writers came from Brighton, *Cinema* was edited in Cambridge, and *Framework* at the University of Warwick.

As Wollen points out, *Screen*'s intellectual lineage was also in Paris. Not *Cahiers du cinéma* and Langlois' Cinemathèque, but formed by the journal *Communications* and Christian Metz's and Roland Barthes' seminars, which were attended by Stephen Heath and Colin MacCabe, two of the intellectual engines behind the new *Screen* offensive. Their articles, together with those by Wollen, Mulvey, Ben Brewster and others, alongside translations from Metz, Jean-Louis Comolli and Raymond Bellour, are now generally identified under the name of "*Screen* theory," by which is meant a volatile blend of Saussurean linguistics, Lévi-Straussian structuralism, Althusserian Marxism and Lacanian psychoanalysis, which together elaborated a theoretically very sophisticated, but for their opponents hermetically sealed and tautological critique of bourgeois (psychological) realism, patriarchal modes of gender representations and the "realist effect" of the "cinematic apparatus."[7] Specific technical terms such as "suture," "interpellation," "subject-construction," "mirror-stage" and "the gaze" are identified with *Screen* theory, which developed the early insights of Lévi-Strauss, Barthes and Greimas (theirs was a general theory of culture as a language of verbal and visual signs, whose meaning is determined by their position within a structure of oppositions and equivalences) in the direction of a theory of gendered subjectivity and vision, which has had an enormous influence on film theory, feminism, visual culture studies and art history.

Were one to analyze *Screen* theory from within its own theoretical premises, one might be forgiven for detecting among the theorists themselves a dynamic of desire and its disavowal, as much caught in mis-cognition and the mirror-phase as that characterizing the "viewing subject" of Hollywood cinema: given the common "cinephile" origins of almost everyone in British film culture in the 1960s and 1970s, the subsequent ambivalences shown vis-à-vis Hollywood films[8] suggest a protracted self-exorcism and painful auto-analysis. In this sense, *Screen* theory's decade-long deconstruction of Hollywood can be seen as a kind of extended funeral service or mourning work for cinephilia, where the very loss of the once loved object intensifies the effort to master this loss by a theory of "subjectification" and "interpellation."

Similarly, though in a different register, a closer look at the London scene in the 1970s, under the aspect of personal friendships/rivalries, domestic partnerships, local proximity and the brief flowering of film magazines thanks to funds from the BFI, indicates the presence of several kinds of Oedipal ambivalences and of Melanie Klein's good/bad object relations. It may explain *Screen*'s "discovering" Douglas Sirk (as a "good" *auteur*, because of his associations with melodrama and the woman's film), the dissenting reassessments of neo-realism, or the rivalries over who "owned" Hitchcock: *Sight & Sound*, *Screen* or *Movie*. My own ambivalence towards *Screen*—contributing to the special Sirk-issue, but polemicizing in the pages of *Monogram* against *Cinéthique* (but also meaning *Screen*); gratefully accepting shelter in the *Screen* offices as *Monogram*'s post-room and business address, but keeping up a mock-antagonism with Sam Rohdie, its then editor—fits the same pattern of "productive paranoia." Sometimes a good enemy is better than a best friend, as Bert Brecht (or Carl Schmitt) might have put it.

The more general argument would be that it was a deferred but also disavowed cinephilia, which provided one part of the driving force behind *Screen* theory. The intellectual brilliance and theoretical difficulties of the theory both covered over and preserved the fact that ambivalence about the status of Hollywood as the good/bad object persisted, notwithstanding that the "love of cinema" was now called by different names: voyeurism, fetishism and scopophilia.[9] Such terms, beyond their technical meaning within Freudian discourse, make it evident that by 1975/76 the cinephilia to which this generation owed its knowledge of the cinema, had been dragged out of its closet, and revealed itself as a source of disappointment: the magic of the movies, in the cold light of day, had become a manipulation of regressive fantasies and the place for masculinity to protect itself from castration anxiety and sexual difference. Especially the feminist project which took its cue from Claire Johnston, Pam Cook and above all Laura Mulvey made this ambivalence towards "classical" Hollywood remarkably productive, and it is not altogether irrelevant to this moment in history that Mulvey's call, at the end of her famous essay, to forego visual pleasure and dedicate oneself to un-pleasure was not always heeded.

Pleasure, consumption and popular culture became a political issue par excellence in Britain,[10] but not for *Screen*, whose writers had maintained a very explicit commitment to the pared-down Marxist aesthetics of the historical avant-garde (notably Russian constructivism and Brecht) and to the (British, and to a lesser extent, American) anti-aesthetics of the political avant-garde. As filmmakers, Laura Mulvey and Peter Wollen were themselves part of this avant-garde, with films like PENTHESILIEA (1974) and RIDDLES OF THE SPHINX (1977) and as writers of a number of key articles redefining modernism and avant-garde practice for a contemporary and by the 1970s highly politicized generation. Godard's own turn away from citing and pastiching Hollywood films, towards a militant, ascetic and verbal cinema during the years of the "Dziga Vertov Group" served as an example also for Mulvey/Wollen,[11] occasionally leading to polemical exchanges with filmmakers from the London Co-op, such as Peter Gidal, Steve Dwoskin and Malcolm Le Grice, who had a more formalist understanding of film, more in tune both with the New York avant-garde and with filmmakers in Germany and Austria, for whom *Screen* showed little interest.[12] Journals like *Afterimage* and *Framework* had a wider coverage of international cinema—including European art- and avant-garde cinema, Asian and "Third" cinema, as well as the new film cultures that began to develop around the smaller film festivals in Italy, Canada and Latin America—but by the same token, these magazines exerted only a limited influence on the formation of film studies as an academic discipline, for which *Screen* and the BFI ultimately provided the necessary intellectual pedigree and institutional momentum.

In retrospect, one of the great achievements of *Screen* has been the bond it managed to forge between theory and practice, between intellectuals and avant-garde directors. In this it renewed a tradition from the 1920s. If, for instance, one traces back film theory to its "origins," we find that the most significant impulses have come from filmmakers (Sergei Eisenstein, Dziga Vertov, Jean Epstein, Louis Delluc, John Grierson) and film critics (Rudolf Arnheim, Béla Balázs, Siegfried Kracauer, Lotte Eisner), with the occasional art historian contributing an important essay (Elie Faure, André Malraux, Erwin Panofsky). The central thrust of this intervention was to defend (and define) film as an art form (and a "language"), and to free the cinema from the stigma of being a mere mechanical reproduction of reality. While it can be argued that the coming of sound put an end to their efforts, the manner in which *Screen* adopted the rather dry academic discourse of Metz's semiology and adapted it into the weapon for a new militancy was unique. By empowering a certain form of filmmaking as well as a redefinition across the cinema of what is art, *Screen*'s intellectual enterprise does indeed deserve the epithet "heroic," however brief this moment was to have been.

By the mid-1980s, a certain turning point was in evidence. *Screen*'s policy of (mainly French) high theory could be seen to have paid off: it had achieved the BFI Education Department's goal to provide the "texts" and set the intellectual agenda that enabled one part of this diverse film culture of the 1960s to enter into the university and establish the British version of film studies. But the insistence on this particular theory, which defined films as a language and the spectator as subject to mis-cognition and ideological interpellation also set the scene for a number of divisions. By then, many of the independent film magazines offering other perspectives (including *Movie, Monogram, Cinema, Cinema Rising, Filmform*) had either ceased publication or appeared only very sporadically, partly because the superior clout of *Screen*—intellectual and institutional—had overshadowed their attempts to evolve alternative approaches to cinema. *Screen* had also split the filmmaking communi-ties, some of whose members did not feel enabled by high theory, while others, among them a number of women's filmmaking collectives (notably the London Women's Film Co-op, the Sheffield Film Co-op and the Berwick Street Collective) clearly benefitted from the high profile that *Screen* had given to feminist issues and the politics of gender, while not necessarily following the theoretical line of *Screen*'s famous contributors.

Film Studies in the University: A Trojan Horse?

What Peter Wollen in the interview mentions only in passing is the background to his own appoint-ment at Essex University in 1976. This initiative began from within the BFI (led by Ed Buscombe), and was aimed at encouraging universities to formally establish film studies by offering them funding for a three-year appointment which the university was subsequently to take on and make permanent. I was myself directly involved in the scheme at the University of East Anglia, where I regarded it as an ideal opportunity to extend the teaching of film by adding another colleague. In the end, five posts were filled, all at "new universities": Robin Wood went to Warwick, Richard Dyer was hired at Keele, Ben Brewster at Kent, Peter Wollen at Essex and Charles Barr at East Anglia. Of the five, only Keele and Essex did not make their posts permanent, and to this day, the three others—Warwick, Kent, East Anglia—are recognized as the leading film studies departments in the country, having substantially expanded in size and produced, over the past three decades, a majority of the graduates and doctorates that currently teach film and media in Britain. While film studies is now successfully established at most universities in Britain, Oxford and Cambridge are still holding out, and even the Colleges that make up London University have found it difficult to catch up on the roughly ten-year lead that the three "provincial" university film departments were able to build up.[13]

Nevertheless, the difficulties that film studies initially faced in these universities were consider-able. Most academics in the humanities distrusted a subject so obviously popular and pleasurable, but without a list of recognized classic authors, canonical texts or a secured and proven method for studying them. Here, French cinephilia proved invaluable, because it permitted one to propose a curriculum set up in the mirror image of literature. *Cahiers du cinéma*'s and Andrew Sarris' pantheon *auteurs* (Orson Welles, John Ford, Alfred Hitchcock, Fritz Lang, Jean Renoir, Max Ophuls, Howard Hawks, Kenji Mizoguchi), and undisputed masterpieces (CITIZEN KANE, LA RÈGLE DU JEU, SUNRISE, MODERN TIMES, THE BIG SLEEP, VERTIGO, LETTER FROM AN UNKNOWN WOMAN) served us well in establishing introductory courses, while the French passion for *mise-en-scène* criticism allowed us to conduct the kind of close textual reading familiar to students of poetry and the modern novel. But as indicated, "out there" in the world of politicized film theory and the cut and thrust of intellectual debate, these very authors, canons and methods were shown to be deeply flawed ways of under-standing the cinema and its political-ideological role in perpetuating bourgeois individualism and gendered subjectivity. Had we not been reading Roland Barthes about the death of the author, or Michel Foucault on "what is an author"? Had we not learnt to deconstruct the textually smooth surface of John Ford's YOUNG MR. LINCOLN? Not in order to uncover layers of deeper meanings, or recover the personal vision of the director within the studio system, but rather, to practice an "active reading" which makes the films say "what they have to say *within* what they leave unsaid, to reveal their constituent lacks; these are neither faults in the work . . . nor a deception on the part of the author . . .; they are its *structuring absences*."[14] The very split discussed above, between cinephile *auteurism* and *Screen* theory's ideological assault on Hollywood, finally worked in favor of film studies inside the academy, because it answered to literary studies' own crisis in its methodological self-understanding as well as its own doubts about canon-formation. Film studies' ability to draw on Barthes' structuralism, Saussurean semiology, Lacanian psychoanalysis and Derrida's deconstruction not only made it a useful ally for a younger generation of literary theorists. It also raised the intellectual stakes generally, because the study of a "low" medium turned out to require "high theory" from its practitioners and thus gave film theorists a special advantage in the "identity wars" that began in the early 1980s.[15] It is in this sense that one can speak of film studies as having been the "Trojan horse" of these wars, introducing structuralism, psychoanalysis, feminism and post-structuralism in the humanities, thereby internally polarizing the existing subjects and areas of expertise, while providing powerful impulses for departmental renewal and cross-disciplinary cooperation.

Film Studies: A Victim of Its Success?

In some sense, then, this is a double success story. An emerging interest in the serious study of the cinema in the 1960s—sparked off by revitalized European filmmaking in the form of several *nouvelle vagues*, some outstanding directors, and a new appreciation of "classical" Hollywood—was able to bundle its energies for a decade around film magazines, around the BFI—at that time an enlightened, if often divided public institution—and a generation of politically committed, polemically gifted and intellectually hungry men and women, many of whom (and this is the second part of the success story) were able during the next decade—the mid-1970s to the mid-1980s—to find teaching positions in the "new universities" or at other institutions of higher education, where their theoretical sophistication, as indicated, often gave them a vanguard role also with respect to the older, more established disciplines.

But this success could not disguise a certain paradox or a-symmetry. As an academic discipline, film studies constructed its object according to the rules that obtain within the humanities, and these, as I tried to show, were largely set by literary studies and realist or modernist discourses (rather than, say, by communication studies, sociology, economics, history or art history). But the cinema also exists in the culture and the economy at large, as one of the great popular arts and entertainment forms of the 20th century. This existence as an industry and the films' presence in society as popular culture are shaped by a dynamic in which academic work plays next to no part. Our essays and books rarely reached the general reader, and working film critics had little time for film theory, which they found abstruse, elitist and patronizing. Furthermore, what is striking about the disciplinary conception of the cinema as a body of "texts" (the canonical masterpieces, a body of work by recognized directors or rare discoveries in archival vaults) is the degree to which it "privatizes" the film experience and aligns it with reading a book, not least in order to give the cinema the degree of (modernist) autonomy and (medium) specificity required by works that aspire to be recognized as "art" in the 20th century. By contrast, what is striking about the cinema as a public sphere and popular practice has been the *loss of autonomy and specificity* that individual films have undergone over the same thirty years, a process which also began in the mid-1970s, when Hollywood was able to revive its economic success with a new kind of film experience, namely the blockbuster, combining a different sound-space with spectacle values, such as special effects and thrilling action sequences. As movie theaters became showcases for new products of the ever-growing media entertainment industries, and these products (mainly event movies and blockbuster spectacles) came to be seen as "content" that could be packaged around different "platforms" and thus exploited by other media industries (above all, by television, the videogame market and the music business), the films themselves, while still the prime experience, had difficulty in retaining their status as either "texts" or individually "authored" artifacts: with DVD releases, directors' cuts and bonus packages they no longer command the space of singularity and closure we traditionally expect of a "work (of art)." Not only have the sequel, prequel or series become almost the norm of mainstream film production; the other aggregate states of the cinematic event just mentioned make up the major part of a film's economic potential, whose commodity status appears further confirmed by the DVD, with its slick packaging and ubiquitous marketing. This loss of autonomy and specificity, critics (and filmmakers) have lamented as the "decay" or even the "death" of cinema.[16] It is a debate that not only touches the transfer from photographically based images to digitally shot and edited film, or signifies the end of the referential bond that the celluloid-based moving image has with reality. It also alludes to the sheer ubiquity and total availability of film, depriving us of the sense of event and occasion that traditionally was associated with "going to the movies"—and with cinephilia.

For it is worth recalling here another aspect of cinephilia. If I am right in arguing that (British) film studies emerged out of the cinephilia of the early 1960s, it inherited the habit of valuing not only the singular work and the director as uniquely creative *auteur*, but also the unique experience of a film's performance as a projected event. This event, as I mentioned above, was tied to a place, a space and a time, usually that of its single showing at a cinémathèque, or it required the special effort of catching one's favorite film at a second-run cinema or (for the TV generation) on late-night television. Yet, however much we now may prize the fond memory of these moments, I also recall the difficulties of renting 16 mm copies for teaching: what would I have not given in those early days of film studies for a video copy or DVD of an Ozu, Renoir or Welles to be available at home or in the seminar-room! At the same time, I cannot help notice the paradox that the availability of films on video-tape or DVD has left us with: these very technologies of (digital) storage tend to favor the (contentious) "close textual analysis" as the dominant pedagogical *practice*, while the films' ubiquity in a vastly expanded media space tends to contradict such a concentration on the individual film from the point of *theory*. Structuralism and post-structuralism were in this sense "centrifugal" and dispersive theories of textual ensembles, not ways of conferring closure on a text upon itself. While in the early days of film studies, our experience was that of the film as (singular) *performance* and our theory was that of the film as *book/text/narrative*, the experience today is of the DVD as *book* (chapter divisions, pause-button, "leafing through" with fast-forward or rapid scanning), while theory tells us we require a different conceptual vocabulary: often enough one where the *performative*, the "embodied" and the "located" play a significant role, and the cultural context of reception forms the horizon of analysis.

Perhaps one needs to go beyond this paradox. In truth, several kinds of division of labor have taken place in the last thirty years, during which "the cinema" has found itself refigured many times over. First, a different division of film production and film culture has occurred. In the 1970s, one could talk about "classical Hollywood," "New Hollywood," "author's cinema," "avant-garde cinema" and "Third Cinema." Now, there is global Hollywood, the international art cinema and "world cinema." The avant-garde has migrated into the museum and the art world, the *auteur* has become a creative entrepreneur promoting him/herself as a "quality brand," and the film festival circuits decide what is a "new wave" (and thus part of the "international art cinema") and what is "world cinema" (and thus part of "themed" programming on topical issues).[17] Second, inside the academy and its institutions, there is "film studies," "media studies," "cultural studies," "visual theory," "gender studies," "new art history," "image anthropology," "post-colonial studies" and many more disciplines and sub-disciplines, all claiming to have something significant to say about film and the cinema, or using films to exemplify issues of critical concern. Finally, there is the ever-widening gulf between the film critic, working for a newspaper, writing in a journal or curating retrospectives for a film festival, and the film scholar, attending conferences, teaching film classes and writing textbooks or monographs—read almost exclusively by students and fellow scholars.

Cultural Studies in Opposition to *Screen* Theory?

One of these divisions of labor I want to highlight in particular: that between film studies and cultural studies. During the "identity-politics wars" of the 1980s, *Screen* theory was not the only intellectual resource. On the contrary, its emphasis on subjectivity and gender seemed to foreclose other important markers of difference, such as class, ethnicity and community- and peer group-identity. Wollen rightly points out that much of the background to the BFI Education Department's work originated not from France and French intellectual trends, but from two sources of British radical thought: the founding generation of the *New Left Review*, among them Raymond Williams and Edward Thompson and, second, from the initiators of what would become the Birmingham Centre for Contemporary Cultural Studies, founded by Richard Hoggart in 1964 and coming to international prominence above all through Stuart Hall, its director from 1968 to 1979.

The continuing vitality of British film studies into the 1980s and its extension into media studies in the 1990s, I would argue, depended on both: on the philosophically trained, often very abstract French system thinkers, translated and transmitted by *Screen*, and the more empirical, historically informed and politically more tough-minded scholars around what eventually came to be known as "cultural studies" or the Birmingham School. Its intellectual agenda—the study of popular culture on a broader front and the nuanced valorization of its pleasures—has often been interpreted as a reaction to *Screen* theory's reliance on psychoanalysis and "apparatus theory," which concentrated on the textually constructed spectator, defined as passive, subjectified and a-historical, leaving no trace of his/her presence, either in society or in the films. But it is important to recall also what *Screen* theory and the Birmingham School had in common, before identifying their differences. Both put the focus on reception and the spectator, rather than on the artist-creator-author. Both drew on Marxism, even if on different tendencies of Western Marxism: *Screen* famously relied on Louis Althusser's concept of "interpellation" while cultural studies preferred Antonio Gramsci and his idea of "hegemony." Both had a common heritage in Lévi-Strauss and Barthes, and considered films to be analyzable in terms of "text" and as a species of "language," but while *Screen* had followed Metz's route from Saussurean linguistics to Lacanian psycho-semiotics, Birmingham had adopted the more "empowering" approach of Roman Jakobson, summarized in Stuart Hall's famous formulation of the communication circuit as a process of "encoding/ decoding" in which a "popular text" (a term that goes beyond the cinema to encompass all the products of commercial mass culture) usually provides options—here following Michel de Certeau—for a preferred (or hegemonic) reading, an oppositional (or counter-hegemonic) and a negotiated reading, where the reader, while recognizing the text's dominant codes, is able to resist or reconstruct meaning in such a way as to reflect local experiences and promote personal or group interests. Hall's formulation proved immensely influential because it empowered spectators, users and consumers to become their own meaning-makers, in line with de Certeau's redefinition of resistance as the use of "bricolage" and "tactical knowledge." Hall's "negotiated readings" offered an alternative to several positions, which were felt to be excessively pessimistic or conceptually flawed: first, that of *Screen* and the textually "constructed," "positioned" and "divided" subject-spectator. But equally important with respect to contemporary cultural theory was the Birmingham School's challenge to the positivism of empirical communication studies, and to the negativity of the Frankfurt School's analyses of the "culture industry." Hall and his students also distanced themselves from the nostalgia of a British strain of cultural analysis (identified with Matthew Arnold, F.R. Leavis and also Richard Hoggart), which longed for an "authentic" popular or working-class culture, while condemning as sterile the mass-media culture coming from the United States after 1945 and taken up so enthusiastically by working-class youth in Britain in the 1950s. Hall was also right, insofar as popular music in Britain (the Rolling Stones, the Beatles, the Who, all the way to David Bowie and Brian Ferry) as well as British pop art (Richard Hamilton, Peter Blake, Eduardo Paolozzi) had turned out to be enormously creative and internationally successful, precisely by reworking American "imports" and by "negotiating" the preferred meanings of mass-produced culture into a uniquely local idiom. Punk's "counter-hegemonic readings" of negative stereotypes from mainstream society are also proof of Hall's insight, and his followers were able to do remarkable field-work among other "minority" groups, such as teenage girls, gays, lesbians and blacks to examine these communities or sub-cultures' creative use of mass-market commodities and their "negotiation" of prejudice and stereotyping.

Cultural studies, which thus emerged (methodologically) in parallel to film studies, and (politically) in opposition to mass-communication studies, devoted itself to a new definition of the popular arts and entertainment industries, trying to take aboard a certain "democratic" understanding of the motives, desires and pleasures among those who "use" the mass media for their own group-identification (youth-cultures), self-differentiation (sub-cultures) and self-definition (fans). In line with reception studies in literature and the focus on the (gendered) spectator of feminist film theory, but also determined to enable the "consumer" as "producer" (if not exactly in the way that Bert Brecht or H.M. Enzensberger had envisioned),[18] cultural studies can also be understood as a way of mapping the fields of film and media history in a new way, by speaking about specific "texts" in a manner that shows how these are embedded in the wider (social) histories of popular entertainment, life-styles and consumption, domestic leisure and the "public sphere." More specifically, cultural studies has also tried to define for the popular a specific form of aesthetic production (formula, the stereotype, pastiche, intertextuality, irony), exploring subcultures' relation to style, and returning, besides to Lévi-Straussian "bricolage," to Mikhail Bakhtin's notion of "carnival" and the "dialogical" with respect to popular culture: regardless of its commercial origins and commodity status.[19]

In this respect, cultural studies has been an invaluable ally for another counter-movement to "high theory" also within film studies, namely the turn to "cinema history" and "media archaeology," as it developed in the 1980s around the study of the "origins" of cinema, which saw a revival of interest in "early" and "silent" cinema at festivals and academic conferences. The history of cinema (as opposed to film history) became an academic paradigm in its own right in the 1990s under the heading of "cinema and modernity" or "cinema and visuality," drawing on the work of Walter Benjamin, Georg Simmel and Siegfried Kracauer. Now often also referred to as the "cinema of attractions," this paradigm around visual culture, spectacle and display offers itself as another version of reception studies, and an alternative to the traditional emphasis in film studies on narrative, narratology and paratexts, inspired by literary structuralism and Gérard Genette. Most of this work in early cinema takes a broadly "cultural" and "intermedial" rather than a "medium-specific" approach, which is to say, it is more interested in the (trans-media, multi-cultural and media-historical) category of *modernity* than in the (literary and art-historical) category of *modernism*.

One can thus, by the 1990s, speak of two generations of (academic) film studies in Britain, at once related to each other and subtly opposed to each other. In contrast to the (first phase of) film studies, derived from and ambivalent towards cinephilia, the (second phase of) film studies, inspired by cultural studies has broadened its scope both synchronically (by taking in other manifestations of visual and popular culture) and diachronically (by extending its historical reach to include "pre-cinema" and, I am tempted to add, "post-cinema"). It is thus able to make good also the demand to pay attention to the materiality and heterogeneity of media practices and media technologies, from a perspective that can also include the digital media, one of the distinguishing features of "media theory." But instead of the latter's tendency towards a post-McLuhan form of technological determinism, film studies as cultural studies aims to rescue the popular-as-progressive from radical theory's disenchantment with both high culture and mass entertainment. Thus it has, for instance, in the wake of Stuart Hall, amply documented the sophistication and discrimination (the traditional hallmarks of educated taste) of popular reading strategies, as well as their subversive, activist, interventionist and deconstructive potential.[20] It has also made axiomatic what in film studies remained contested territory: that cultural production is always "post-production," the appropriation and transformation of already existing texts, discourses and cultural ready-mades.

Abducted by Cultural Studies, Rescued by Philosophy?

The itinerary I have been trying to trace has an avowedly personal dimension, and thus cannot claim to be impartial or even representative. But it is one that is embedded in a number of institutional contexts, which in turn are part of the history of film and cultural studies in Britain, where "London" (here exemplified by the British Film Institute and *Screen* magazine) exerted a gravitational pull, but one that was balanced by various regional forces, especially the "new universities" that first established academic film studies (Warwick, East Anglia, Kent), by the Edinburgh Film Festival that became the home for a mixture of avant-garde filmmaking (with a strong feminist slant), cinephile retrospectives (of Sam Fuller, Douglas Sirk, Frank Tashlin, Raoul Walsh, Jacques Tourneur) and specific debates (such as the one on Foucault, France and "popular memory"), and last but not least, by the Birmingham Centre for Contemporary Cultural Studies, which provided the most significant intellectual counterweight to *Screen* theory in the 1980s, with a world-wide response. By the 1990s, the Birmingham brand had all but eclipsed what I called the first phase of British film studies. The "politics of representation" around race, class, gender and sexual orientation have become such prominent features of academic discourse in the humanities across the disciplines that it would be fair to say that British cultural studies (by now critiqued, modified, adapted and indeed "negotiated" by local practitioners in the United States, Australia, and also in Northern Europe) has not only "subsumed" and thereby thoroughly redefined film studies in many universities, but also become something of a "hegemonic" force in the way we approach the manifestations of all culture: be it high culture or popular culture, be it literary culture or media culture, be it the crass commercialism of television and tourism, or the slightly more subtle commerce of the art world and exhibition practice.

The question that poses itself at such a juncture is twofold. One: can film studies remain comfortable within such a broad brief, or does it need to extricate itself from this embrace and find its own re-definition? And two, can cultural studies, such as it is currently constituted, veritably assume the task that seems to have fallen to it, namely to provide instruments precise enough and sensors delicate enough to ensure the critical readability—for this what is at stake—of all that is now subsumed under culture? Does not the fact that "culture" can no longer be opposed to "nature" (no more than "nature" can be opposed to "technology") require also a redefinition of cultural studies? In answer to the first question, I note that ever since Gilles Deleuze's cinema books, published in the late 1980s and widely read and discussed in the 1990s, the cinema, or rather "film" has entered an entirely different space of reflexivity and conceptualization. More decisive in this "philosophical turn" of film studies than the possible exhaustion of the paradigms of "representation" and the questions of "identity" (both of which Deleuze pointedly avoids) may have been the crisis into which the cinema has been plunged by digitization. Seemingly depriving it of its material basis in photography, the digital image is said to alter the very ground of many of film's key characteristics, both as a technical medium and an art form, such as fiction versus documentary, realism versus illusionism, montage versus long take, movement versus stillness, irreversible linearity versus simultaneity. But when film studies aligns itself with philosophy and when philosophy (across a spectrum that ranges from "continental" philosophy to cognitivism, and also including Stanley Cavell and Anglo-American pragmatism) takes an interest in the cinema, many other issues of a non-technological nature are also at stake, affecting questions of evidence and epistemology, but also of ontology, "disclosure" and "being." One can thus be fairly optimistic that in the decade to come, film theory will re-invent itself, even if (or perhaps because) the cinema as we have known it for its first hundred years, has indeed passed away. Here, too, as in the case of *Screen* and cinephilia, a (new) theory may well turn out to be the funeral of a practice.

The second question: can cultural studies assume the role it has inherited from literary studies, and if so, on what disciplinary basis—anthropological, sociological, aesthetic, hermeneutic or historical?—I find much more difficult to speculate about. There are different claims, for instance from art history, reviving the ambitions of Aby Warburg and extending them in the direction of an image-anthropology, which would speak also in the name of moving images in film and installation art, and not only of the framed static image of painting and photography. From the side of media studies, a generalized concept of medium (along the lines of "the difference that makes the difference," Gregory Bateson's famous definition of "information") seems to compete with a more specific idea of a "technological ('cyber') culture," in which human beings and their symbolic (inter)actions (i.e. "culture") are understood as the products of their information media and technologies, rather than vice versa.

From my own perspective as (still) a film scholar, I am somewhat skeptical about many of these claims when they come with totalizing aspirations, since I see them above all as staking out potential or actual territory in university departments and research allocations. Cinema's comparative insignificance as a "serious" contender in major research funding exercises sometimes seems a blessing in disguise. Precisely because of its somewhat "performative" position in the academy, hovering over several disciplines, such as literary studies, art history, philosophy or communication studies like a butterfly or hummingbird, film studies when called upon to construct for itself a viable history and theory, knows better than other disciplines that such self-definitions are largely the function of a process that in many ways has only just begun, and is happening largely outside of its control: the transformation of the classic humanities based primarily on written texts, their history and hermeneutics into one where sounds and images play a much larger role. In this process, dependent as it is on the overall space allowed to the study of culture (texts, images, representation and symbolic actions), under pressure to legitimate itself vis-à-vis the hard and social sciences, and to prove itself "useful," film studies is better off neither to strive for autonomy, nor to have imperial ambitions. While its "place" in the curriculum seems largely secure—thanks to the double conjuncture of the moving image's popularity among students, and the perceived social and economic relevance of what is known as "the media"—the "space" (discursive, institutional, aesthetic) is, as I have tried to indicate, far from uncontested, which allows it (if it wants to) to periodically reinvent itself and remain experimental, curious, adventurous, bold and even promiscuous: in short, "opportunistic," meaning that it can seize opportunities when they present themselves. This is how I have known film studies, this is how I have practiced it, and this is how I would like to remember it.

2

The Name for a Pleasure that has No Substitute: Vincente Minnelli

Preface (1979)

When this article was published early in 1970 in the Brighton Film Review, *the house journal of the film society of the University of Sussex,* auteur *studies had already become quite unfashionable.*[1] *And among the genres, the reputation of the musical (after the mid-1960s box-office and critical failure of big-budget productions such as* HELLO, DOLLY!*) was probably at its lowest point ever. Knowing that I was addressing myself to students who bought and read the magazine mainly for its bi-weekly listings rather than for the lengthy articles we smuggled in at the back, I nevertheless felt sufficiently involved in the gathering momentum in Britain around questions of* auteur *versus genre, structural versus thematic criticism, ideological versus textual analysis, to want* The Brighton Film Review *to contribute to these debates. The convenient provincialism of a seaside university gave us the cover to argue, for instance, in favor of our cinephile obsessions, while nonetheless keeping a watchful eye on what* Screen *and other film magazines were doing. Though committed readers of* Movie *and the yellow issues of* Cahiers du cinéma, *we put less emphasis on* auteurist *themes and gave more attention to "style." We tried to be informative and broadminded enough not to scare off our readers, but we nonetheless hoped that our expository manner carried a polemical edge that London would take note of (it did).*

The essay on Minnelli, occasioned by a small retrospective we had been organizing, wanted to push auteur *studies a little further in the direction of genre (claiming that all of the director's films were musicals at heart, with the melodramas a form of musical turned inside out), while opening up the rigid boundaries drawn around genre in the studies on the Western or the gangster film, published by the British Film Institute.*[2] *I therefore related the concept of the musical itself to some more general notion of a "drive- or goal-oriented" structure that I claimed was underpinning all Hollywood filmmaking of the time. The individual genres and their historical mutations could then be understood as partial aspects of a totality whose overall constellation was centered elsewhere. Perhaps the argument ended up being somewhat circular: Minnelli is seen by me as an* auteur *because his practice of the musical/melodrama genre allowed one to study the dynamic structures to which much of ("classical") Hollywood style conforms. At the same time, his aesthetic exemplified these principles by the way his films transgressed or exceeded them. I am quite sure that at the time I failed to see just how close such a set of equations came to undermining the dominant opposition "auteur versus the system" on which a good deal of the polemics of the* auteur *theory depended.*

After positing this "drive-oriented" structure, the article does not pursue this point, except to explain its presence in terms of the exigencies of audience identification, rather than as a critique of American society of the time, or as a reflection of ideological conflict. In this (as in other articles written at that time) I wanted to explore the idea that Hollywood's global strategy had always been aimed at binding its audiences on a psychic-affective level: in other words, "realism" (the representation of a reality) was not the main issue, but the embodiment of affective intensities and emotional energies were. In Minnelli, the continuities and breaks, in short, the modulations of the drive and its obstacles, define both the narrative and the visual rhetoric (the mise-en-scène) *of a given film. They also create the illusion of unity that constitutes the "style" specific to not just this director's work (I also wrote about Douglas Sirk, Nicholas Ray and Sam Fuller in this vein). What seemed to make Minnelli exemplary, and for me put him on a par with Jean Renoir and Fritz Lang, was that in his films the act of seeing, the constraints and power relations it gave rise to, appeared so uncannily foregrounded that the action always tended to become a metaphor of the more fundamental relation between spectator and* mise-en-scène, *audience and (invisible, because ubiquitous) director. Fortuitously, but perhaps fittingly, my article ends with a brief analysis of* Two Weeks in Another Town, *which Paul Mayersberg in* Movie *had already called a "testament film."[3] There the director (visible, but split between two protagonists) loses control over his creation, evidently also a comment on the changes that were taking place in Hollywood filmmaking during the Sixties: the very same changes that made the* auteur *and* mise-en-scène *criticism (whose unspoken third term had always been the studio-system, its implied "other") historically obsolete as a determining force, and by the same token, available as a theoretical construct.*

What remains is to ask why critics should have invested, and still invest, so much energy in the auteur *theory, given that it had always been perverse, deliberately flying in the face of what we know about mass media, popular culture and their history. Auteurism's victories always had to be snatched from the jaws of common sense. In the history of the American cinema, apparently so completely dedicated to the impersonality and invisibility of the storyteller's hand, the fingerprints of the specialist and flourish of the stylist had always been intermittently visible. Whether the "trouble" in the system, or the icing on the cake: it was the fate or privilege of the* auteur *critic to attribute such "extra" touches or an "excess" of talent to the director. And this probably for good reason: film studies in the 1970s and 1980s appeared to have settled the vexing question of why films give us pleasure, by deciding that in the cinema the spectator enters into a dialogue not with an "other"—be they the characters or their creators—but with his or her own split self, whether Marxian or Lacanian. Insofar as* auteur *criticism perhaps never sufficiently acknowledged the narcissism of the cinephile, it stood exposed by its fanatical identification with the narcissism of the filmmaker. But for those who talk to themselves most intensely through the intermediary of an (imaginary) "other" or a (external) "supplement," there will remain the need, however rhetorically displaced or nostalgically recalled, to reinvent the author, if only, as Roland Barthes has remarked, because his disappearance would imply, finally, also that of the critic and reader. The* auteur *is the fiction, the necessary fiction one might add, become flesh and body in the director, for the name of a pleasure that has no substitute in the sobered-up deconstructions of the authorless voice of either ideology or the system.[4]*

Vincente Minnelli (1970)

Vincente Minnelli's critical reputation has known a certain amount of fluctuation. Admired (or dismissed) in America as a "pure stylist" who, in Andrew Sarris' phrase "believes more in beauty than in art," his work reached a zenith of critical devotion during the late 1950s and early 1960s in France, with extensive studies in *Cahiers du cinéma*, especially in the articles by Jean Douchet and Jean

Domarchi, who saw in him a cinematic visionary obsessed with beauty and harmony, and an artist who could give substance to the world of dreams.

In England *Movie* took up his defense, from the first number onwards. But strangely enough, the contributors concentrated almost exclusively on Minnelli's dramatic films of the early 1960s (a memorable article by Paul Mayersberg on Two Weeks in Another Town comes to mind), and gave rather cursory treatment to the musicals, while the later films, such as Goodbye Charlie (1964) and The Sandpiper (1965) were passed over. With this, Minnelli joined the legion of American directors whose work was supposed to have suffered decline, if not total eclipse in the Hollywood of the middle and late 1960s.

The following remarks are a first attempt to disentangle a few essential characteristics from a singularly rich and varied body of work, and to trace some of the dominating lines of force in his style. Above all, I am concerned with the fundamental *unity* of Minnelli's vision. At the risk of displeasing the genre critics and antagonizing those who share the view that thematic analysis generally exhausts itself in what has (rather summarily) been referred to as "schoolboy profundities," I would like to look at some of Minnelli's constant themes and furthermore, conduct some kind of special pleading for Minnelli as a *moralist*, even though this will mean flying in the face of the "stylist" school—both of the Sarris variety and *Movie*, who claim for Minnelli as for Cukor that he never writes his own scripts, and therefore never uses other people's material for the propagation of his own views, that he confines himself to the interpretation, the *mise-en-scène* of the ideas of others, and that, consequently, his work is best regarded as lacking in consistent themes, and rather excels on a supreme level of visual competence.

I think this is a fundamental misunderstanding. True, there are superficially two "Minnellis"— one the virtual father of the modern musical, and the other the director of dramatic comedies and domestic dramas. Other critics—even sympathetic ones—would probably claim a different Minnelli for almost every film—the loving "pointillist" of American period pieces or of "Gay Paree" (Meet Me in St. Louis, Gigi, An American in Paris), the catalyst for Gene Kelly and Fred Astaire musicals (Ziegfeld Follies, Yolanda and the Thief, The Pirate, The Band Wagon, Brigadoon), the ingenious vulgarizer of painters' lives (Lust for Life) and best-selling novels (The Four Horsemen of the Apocalypse), the handyman who puts together a star vehicle for an ambitious producer (The Reluctant Debutante), and lastly perhaps the "difficult" director of such problem pieces as Some Came Running, Home from the Hill, and of Hollywood self-portraits—The Bad and the Beautiful and Two Weeks in Another Town.

Altogether, Minnelli has directed some thirty-two films, not counting the episodes and sketches contributed to other people's films. It might seem difficult to find a personal vision in as vast an oeuvre as his, not to mention the fact that all films (except one) have been made in the MGM studios, under the supervision of a few, themselves very gifted and articulate, producers like John Houseman (four films) and Arthur Freed (twelve). But surely anyone who is reasonably familiar with his films will see in Minnelli more than the glorification of the *metteur-en-scène*, the stylish craftsman of the cinema, the dandy of sophistication. I for one am convinced that Minnelli is one of the purest "hedgehogs" working in the cinema—an artist who knows one big thing, and never tires to explore its implications. In Walter Pater's famous phrase, all romantic art aspires to the status of music. My contention is that all Minnelli's films aspire to the condition of the musical. In this resides their fundamental unity. However, in order to substantiate this point, I shall insert a few remarks to explain what I mean by "musical."

The classic Hollywood cinema is, as everybody knows, *the* commercial cinema par excellence— out merely to entertain. Usually this is taken to be a fundamental drawback, at worst utterly precluding its products from the realms of serious art, at best, presenting the film-maker with formidable odds against which he has to test his worth, as artist *and* entrepreneur. I shall try to show how deeply Minnelli's conception of his art, indeed his "philosophy" of life, are formed by the conflict between the necessity of circumstance and the vital need to assert—not so much one's self, but rather one's conception of meaning, one's vision of things. It furnishes his great theme: the artist's struggle to appropriate external reality as the elements of his own world, in a bid for absolute creative freedom. When I say artist, I hasten to add that this includes almost all of Minnelli's protagonists. (Insofar as they all feel within them a world, an idea, a dream that seeks articulation and material embodiment.)

Yet there is another side to the "commercial cinema" syndrome, which is rarely ever given its full due. (At least in England: in France, the *Positif* and *Midi-Minuit* critics have always paid tribute to the commercial cinema *qua* commercial cinema.) I am referring to the fact that perhaps the enormous appeal of the best Hollywood cinema, the fundamental reason why audience-identification and immediate emotional participation are at all possible, lies in Hollywood's rigorous application of the *pleasure principle*—understood almost in its Freudian sense, as the structure that governs the articulation of psychic and emotional energy. It seems to me that a vast number of films "work" *because* they are built around a psychic law and not an intellectual one, and thus achieve a measure of coherence which is very difficult to analyze (as it must be extremely difficult for a film-maker to control and adhere to), and yet constitutes nevertheless an absolutely essential part of the way the cinema functions—being indeed close to music in this respect.

For a superficial confirmation of this fact, namely that there is a central energy at the heart of the Hollywood film which seeks to live itself out as completely as possible, one could point to the way in which—superimposed on an infinite variety of subject matters—the prevalent plot-mechanisms of two major genres of the American cinema (the Western and the gangster film) invariably conform to the same basic pattern. There is always a central dynamic drive—the pursuit, the quest, the trek, the boundless desire to arrive, to get to the top, to get rich, to make it—always the same graph of maximum energetic investment.

For the spectator, this means maximum emotional involvement, which depends upon, and is enhanced by, his maximum aesthetic satisfaction—or rather, by the skilful manipulation of his desire for as total a sense of satisfaction as possible. Intellectual insight and emotional awareness are transmitted in the best American cinema exclusively as a drive for *gratification*, which the audience shares with the characters. The more a film director is aware of this interrelation of morality and aesthetics in the cinema, the more his *mise-en-scène* will be concerned with the purposeful ordering of *visual* elements, to achieve a kind of plenitude and density, which inevitably, and rightly, goes at the expense of ideas. In other words, there seems to exist, particularly in the American cinema, an intimate relationship between the *psychological* drives of the characters (i.e., the motives *beneath* the motives that make them act), the *moral* progression which they accomplish, and the *aesthetic* gratification afforded to the audience by the spectacle; and these are held together by some profound mechanism, identical in both audience and characters—be they criminals, detectives, gunfighters, shop-assistants, song-writers or millionaires.

Perhaps one of the most interesting consequences of this fact is that this, if true, would entail a thoroughly different concept of cinematic realism, which would have nothing to do with either literary realism or the realism of pictorial art. For what seems to me essential to all of Minnelli's films is the fact that his characters are only superficially concerned with a quest, a desire to get somewhere in life, that is, with any of the forms by which this dynamism rationalizes or sublimates itself. What we have instead, just beneath the surface of the plots, is the working of energy itself, as the ever-changing, fascinating movement of a basic impulse in its encounter with, or victory over, a given reality. The characters' existence is justified by the incessant struggle in which they engage for total fulfilment, for total gratification of their aesthetic needs, their desire for beauty and harmony, their demand for an identity of their lives with the reality of their dreams. Minnelli's films are structured so as to give the greatest possible scope to the expansive nature of a certain vitality (call it "will," or libido)—in short, to the confrontation of an inner, dynamic, reality and an outward, static one. Minnelli's typical protagonists are all, in a manner of speaking, highly sophisticated and cunning day-dreamers, and the *mise-en-scène* follows them, as they go through life, confusing—for good or ill—what is part of their imagination and what is real, and trying to obliterate the difference between what is freedom and what is necessity.

What, in this context, characterizes the Minnelli musical is the total and magic victory of the impulse, the vision, over any reality whatsoever. The characters in his musicals transform the world into a reflection of their selves, into a pure expression of their joys and sorrows, of their inner harmony or conflicting states of mind. When Gene Kelly begins to dance, or plays with the first words of a song, say in BRIGADOON, the world melts away and reality becomes a stage, on which he and Cyd Charisse live out their very dream. Or when Louis Jourdan, in utter confusion about his feelings, rushes to the Jardin du Luxembourg to sing the title number of GIGI, Minnelli leads him into a wholly mysterious, wholly subjective landscape of the imagination, pregnant with the symbols of his newly discovered love for the one-time schoolgirl. Such a confrontation with their innermost worlds always gives the characters a kind of spontaneous certainty from which, ultimately, they derive their energy.

The Minnelli musical thus transforms the movements of what one is tempted to call, for lack of a better word, the "soul" of the characters into shape, color, gesture and rhythm. It is precisely when joy or sorrow, bewilderment or enthusiasm, that is, when emotional intensity, becomes too strong to bear that a Gene Kelly or a Judy Garland has to dance and sing in order to give free play to the emotions that possess them. And it is hardly exaggerated to compare what Minnelli did for the musical with Mozart's transformation of the comic opera. One only needs to hold a Busby Berkeley musical—with its formally brilliant but dramatically empty song-and-dance routines and elaborate visual compositions—against even an early and comparatively minor Minnelli effort, say, the "Limehouse Blues" sequence from ZIEGFELD FOLLIES, to see how the musical with Minnelli has been given an authentic spiritual dimension, created by a combination of movement, lighting, color, decor, gesture and music which is unique to the cinema.

Thus defined, the world of the musical becomes a kind of ideal image of the medium itself, the infinitely variable material substance on which the very structure of desire and the imagination can imprint itself, freed from all physical necessity. The quickly changing decor, the transitions in the lighting and the colors of a scene, the freedom of composition, the shift from psychological realism to pure fantasy, from drama to surreal farce, the culmination of an action in a song, the change of movement into rhythmic dance—all this constitutes the very essence of the musical. In other words, it is the exaltation of the artifice as the vehicle of an authentic psychic and emotional reality. Minnelli's musicals introduce us into a liberated universe, where the total freedom of expression (of the character's creative impulse) serves to give body and meaning to the artist's vitality in the director, both being united by their roles as *metteurs-en-scène* of the self.

The paradox of the musical, namely that a highly artificial, technically and artistically controlled decor and machinery can be the manifestation of wholly spontaneous, intimate movements, or the visualization of submerged, hardly conscious aspirations, becomes not only Minnelli's metaphor for the cinema as a whole, but more specifically, it makes up his central moral concern: how does the individual come to realize himself, reach his identity, create his personal universe, fulfil his life in a world of chaos and confusion, riddled with social conventions, bogus with self-importance, claustro-phobic and constricting, trivial and above all artificial, full of treacherous appearance, and yet impenetrable in its false solidity, its obstacles, its sheer physical inertia and weight?—epitomized in the sticky, rubbery substance Spencer Tracy has to wade through, as he is trying to reach the altar, in the nightmare sequence of FATHER OF THE BRIDE. Minnelli's answer, surprisingly enough for this supposedly obedient servant of other people's ideas, is a plea for chaos, where his characters embrace flux and movement, because it is closest to the imagination itself. Minnelli's motto might well be that "better no order at all than a false order."

And here we have the crux of the matter: for the Minnelli musical celebrates the fulfilment of desire and identity, whose tragic absence so many of his dramatic films portray. Looked at like this, the dramas and dramatic comedies are *musicals turned inside out*, for the latter affirm all those values and urges, which the former visualize as being in conflict with a radically different order of reality. In his non-musical films—from THE CLOCK to HOME FROM THE HILL, from THE COBWEB to TWO WEEKS IN ANOTHER TOWN—tragedy is present as a particular kind of unfreedom, as the constraint of an emotional or artistic temperament in a world that becomes claustrophobic, where reality suddenly reveals itself as mere decor, unbearably false and oppressive. That is when the dream changes into nightmare, when desire becomes obsession, and the creative will turns into mad frenzy.

It is in this absence of that freedom which the musical realizes and expresses through dance and song, through rhythm and movement, by indicating that peculiar fluidity of reality and dream which alone seems to offer the possibility of human relationships and of a harmonious existence—it is in the absence of this that Kirk Douglas or Judy Garland, Robert Mitchum or Glenn Ford and Ronny Howard (THE COURTSHIP OF EDDIE'S FATHER) suffer anguish and despair, neurosis and isolation, spiritual and physical enclosure, if not death. And it is precisely the possibility, the promise of a return to chaos, to movement, which saves Judy Holliday (BELLS ARE RINGING), Gregory Peck and Lauren Bacall (DESIGNING WOMAN), Rex Harrison and Kay Kendall (THE RELUCTANT DEBUTANTE) in the dramatic comedies from becoming hopelessly trapped in their own worlds.

Minnelli's films invariably focus on the discrepancy between an inner vision, often confused and uncertain of itself, and an outer world that appears as hostile because it is presented as a physical space littered with obstacles. Life forces upon the characters a barely tolerable sense of rupture, and the Minnelli universe has its psychological *raison d'être* in a very definite and pervasive alienation. But instead of lamenting this modern condition, almost all his films concentrate on portraying the energies of the imagination released in the individual during this process of (social?) decomposition. Too often this has been seen merely as a total abandon to the faculty of make-believe, of the beautiful appearance through which Minnelli is supposed to celebrate Hollywood escapism.

This view, even if applied only to the musicals, is an untenable simplification. Minnelli's concern is always with the possibilities of a human creativeness asserting itself in and through a world which is so obviously imperfect. True, imperfections are taken for granted, they are global, because Minnelli is dealing not with a given reality, but with the psychological and emotional predicament it produces. Two types of heroes come to symbolize this situation: the artist and the neurotic, two ways of dealing with the actual which are obviously not unrelated. That he sees them as intimately connected states of being constitutes the coherence of his moral vision and the unity of his themes.

Whereas the "neurotic" dilemma is either treated comically (THE LONG, LONG TRAILER, the dream becoming a nightmare, or GOODBYE CHARLIE, in which the reincarnated hero involuntarily under-goes a sex-change) or tragically (HOME FROM THE HILL, THE FOUR HORSEMEN OF THE APOCALYPSE), art and neurosis form the explicit subject of THE BAD AND THE BEAUTIFUL, LUST FOR LIFE, TWO WEEKS IN ANOTHER TOWN. Even in the musicals, where the triumph of the creative temperament seems assured, it is not by a "naïve" assertion of will-power or happy-go-lucky bonhomie, but through a complex process of metamorphosis which transforms both the individual and his world. For the inner vision is essentially flawed, and so long as the protagonist cuts himself off from life, his dream is static, a passive nostalgia or worse, a self-limiting delusion. As a consequence, the external world seems to him nothing but oppressive, false and alien—an attitude which none of Minnelli's films vindicate as an adequate response, though they often make it their starting point.

Three of Minnelli's greatest musicals, THE PIRATE, BRIGADOON and THE BAND WAGON, open with such typical situations of the "self-in-exile." In THE PIRATE Judy Garland, about to be married to a fat, wealthy businessman, sighs over her fate and looks romantically into the distance while dreaming of Macoco, the legendary Caribbean pirate, coming to take her away. In BRIGADOON, a disenchanted Gene Kelly, playing an American tourist, stalks about in Scotland, having lost his way in the wilderness of the Highlands. And in THE BAND WAGON, Fred Astaire in the role of a once-famous star gets off the train in New York to discover that the big party at the station is cheering some other celebrity.

Though these may seem archetypal situations of the genre, they recur in all of Minnelli's films, whether musical or not. THE COURTSHIP OF EDDIE'S FATHER is a particularly striking example, with father and son feeling completely lost in their own home (a family situation common to at least a dozen Minnelli films). And the implications are finally made explicit in TWO WEEKS IN ANOTHER TOWN, where the hero is first seen in a mental hospital. In other words, Minnelli starts from a characteristic disorientation about the relation of self and world, from which originates the impulse towards action. Whatever his protagonists do becomes therefore automatically identified with a desire to realize themselves by transcending an indifferent or restrictive environment.

This makes the Minnelli character live in the tension of a necessary isolation and an inevitable drive towards domination. It is as such a central theme of the American cinema. But whereas one easily assumes this to be in Minnelli's earlier films an exclusively aesthetic concern—a need for beauty, for living out a romantic fantasy—the moral dimension is never obscured. And if the very early films do emphasize the final articulation of a harmony, the later ones turn to the ambiguous conditions of the creative will itself, whether in the form of a self-destructive obsession (LUST FOR LIFE), a manic manipulation of others (THE BAD AND THE BEAUTIFUL) or a tenacious determination (HOME FROM THE HILL).

In some of the earlier films, for example, Minnelli's attitude can be seen to alternate between optimism about the individual's potential to make the world conform to his dreams, and an equally acute sense of the tyranny over others implicit in its realization. But this is never blown up to the dimensions of ponderous moralizing; on the contrary, it is always contained in the insignificant story, the unprepossessing event. In MEET ME IN ST. LOUIS, for example, near-tragedy ensues when the father of the household decides to move his big family to New York, and thus to uproot them from their small self-contained world. It is the typical Minnelli dilemma of the will of the individual opposed to the always fragile fabric of human harmony. The father's announcement of his intention falls on the family like a bolt out of the blue, and their world is visibly coming to a halt. In tears, the family scatters to various parts of the home, leaving the mother and father alone. The mother begins to play a song on the piano as the father sings, and it is the sound of their harmonizing that gradually brings the rest of the family out of hiding. As they gather near the father and mother, Minnelli's editing conveys the precise feeling of a rhythm recommencing, and the characters "circulate" once more through the house as if their blood had begun to flow again, with gestures and movements that approximate a graceful dance. By contrast, in FATHER OF THE BRIDE, the same situation is inverted, and Spencer Tracy, as the father, is progressively more exiled from his own home because of the banal and conventional ideas and preconceptions which his wife and daughter are trying to foist upon him.

The clearest expression of a corresponding optimism is in THE CLOCK. It is the story of a GI on a twenty-four-hour leave and a girl from the country who happen to meet in a railway station. In this film, full of the most unpromising stereotype material, Minnelli magnificently communicates the elements of his vision. For example, the obligatory stroll through Central Park becomes the pivot where the real New York in all its oppressive strangeness transforms itself into an integral part of the couple's experience of themselves. As they listen to the bewildering noise of the city, the sounds merge into a kind of music, and through its rhythm, the couple find each other—the city literally brings them together. This is important, because the film is built on the tension between the fatality of the clock, the diffuse chaos of the city, and the will of the lovers. Against a world circumscribed by time and ruled by chance (their initial encounter, the various accidental separations, the careless indifference that surrounds them), Minnelli sets the determination of the couple to realize a common happiness. Insignificant though they are in the human sea, their naive trust in love-at-first-sight appears as heroic because it is supported by a belief in the human will and its power to transcend the given. Judy Garland and Robert Walker here exemplify the Minnelli "philosophy" par excellence: the freedom of the individual, his creative potential, consists in perceiving order and design in chaos, whose meaning is revealed when it becomes dance. The film opens with a crane shot into the crowd at Pennsylvania station, showing the aimless movement. It ends with the camera craning out from the station, and as Judy Garland is seen walking away, even the crowd has a regular flow and a definite rhythm.

Although the polarity between two worlds, or world-views, is Minnelli's central structural device, the meaning of the themes is defined by the nature of the energy which the characters bring to bear on the world as they find it. The spectrum is wide, with innumerable shades and variations. Whether it is the genteel "joie de vivre" of MEET ME IN ST. LOUIS, the instinctive stubbornness of Eddie in THE COURTSHIP OF EDDIE'S FATHER, the dream of a luxury caravan (THE LONG, LONG TRAILER) or the fantasy life of a switchboard girl (BELLS ARE RINGING)—common to all of them is the sense that without this energy the world would always disintegrate into mere chaos.

As with many Hollywood directors, the basic purpose of Minnelli's handling of visual elements is to encourage audience identification. But no other director has such a keen and differentiated eye for the mesmerizing qualities of a setting, a particular decor. Not inappropriately, Jean Domarchi once compared Minnelli to Hitchcock, saying their conception of the cinema is "alchemistic": the elements of Minnelli's *mise-en-scène* are indeed geared towards producing an overall impression of unreality, wholly engrossing the spectator by a sense of timing and a fluidity of movement which exaggerates the natural relativity of time and space in the cinema to a point where the visual spectacle becomes a kind of hallucination.

This means that the mechanism of identification (or projection) normally understood rather crudely as referring only to the audience's empathy with the protagonist, is amplified to include the setting, which no longer functions as an objective point of correlation, but becomes wholly absorbed into the action as the natural extension of the protagonist's being. The characterization of the Minnelli hero therefore reduces itself to the barest outlines of a specific individuality. His role is to indicate a sequence of psychological situations of general significance, and not to illustrate the ramifications of a unique case. What matters is not his character (i.e. his moral principles, his credibility as a rational and sentient human being) but his personality (i.e. the set of attitudes and physical responses he displays in given situations).

Where it is a question of substantiating or explaining a human relationship in terms of psychological motivation, Minnelli therefore invariably presents the conflict as a clash of settings, an imbalance of stylistic elements, such as a contrast of movements or a disharmony of colors or objects. The bright yellow caravan in the landscape of THE LONG, LONG TRAILER, for example, jars so painfully that in itself it suffices to undermine the couple's pretensions to a free and natural life. At other times the violence of a gesture is set off against an otherwise smooth or harmonious visual surface, and when Barry Sullivan in one of the opening scenes of THE BAD AND THE BEAUTIFUL slams down the telephone, an incongruous but highly dramatic contrast is created in opposition to the dream-like setting in which an actress is being filmed by the camera-crew. Minnelli constantly reduces his stories to their moments of visual intensity, where he can project the dramatic conflicts into the decor. Where other directors use the cinematic space to clarify the intellectual complexities of their plots (Otto Preminger, Lang), Minnelli relates distance (or lack of distance) to varying degrees of subjective intensity. Thus, an important function of the *mise-en-scène* is to interiorize the rapport that exists between spectator and action, by reproducing a similar tension of identification and projection within the film itself—achieved very often by a typical Minnelli camera movement which consists of an unobtrusive, but very fluid, traveling forward, interrupted by an almost imperceptible craning away usually held as a general shot until the fade-out. This makes the Minnelli hero emerge in many ways as the creator *and* spectator of his own life, realizing himself most fully in a world which he can transcend by using it as the decor of his own *mise-en-scène*. Conversely, the moment of rupture—doubt, despair, nightmare—is equally dramatized in the interrelation of hero and environment, and the world of objects becomes either solid and immobile, or bristles with a recalcitrant life of its own.

In these cases, it is the gesture, sometimes aggressive, more often hesitant, which is extended into the alien territory that defines the protagonist's sense of personal identity, and the most subtle changes in his state of mind are relayed through his position and behavior as his body responds to the setting. Barry Boys in an article on THE COURTSHIP OF EDDIE'S FATHER has given a fine analysis of the opening of the film, with Eddie precariously poised in the once familiar kitchen, which through the death of his mother has become a hostile world.

This means that there is an obvious analogy between the approach of his characters to their predicament and the cinematic medium. Thus the mechanism of projection and identification are reflected in Minnelli's films as the two phases of a character's development: projection of his vision upon an environment, identification (or breakdown of an identification) with a decor, a created world.

In the musicals, where the characteristics of Minnelli's cinema are most transparent, one can see a kind of recurrent pattern of situations, which forms the archetypal Minnelli structure (what differentiates his non-musical films is mainly that though these situations are present, they are not necessarily in this order): 1. The moment of isolation (the individual vision as imprisonment). 2. The tentative communication (the vision materializes as decor). 3. The rupture (the decor appears as mere appearance and delusion). 4. The world as chaos. 5. The world as spectacle/the spectacle as world.

In a sense, this pattern represents a kind of catharsis of vision, to which corresponds the clarification of emotions through the purging of their opposites: what emerges from the contradictory impulses of solitude and euphoria, frustration, despair and delirious monomania is a measure of self-fulfilment, often merely implicit—where all emotional extremes feed into the creation of "the show," and where the energy is finally disciplined in the movement of the dance. The classic example of this is THE PIRATE: Judy Garland (Manuela), dreaming of the pirate, sees Macoco materialize in Gene Kelly, only to discover that he is an impostor—a discovery that creates emotional chaos for her (she loves him all the same) and actual chaos on the island (there is a price on his head). Manuela, finally renouncing her romantic fantasies, joins Kelly's humble theatrical troupe, and the film ends with an ironic number, significantly entitled "Be a Clown."

Likewise, in BRIGADOON, Gene Kelly's desire for another world materializes in the legendary village of Brigadoon where he meets the girl of his life, only to discover that the whole village and its inhabitants will have to disappear again for another hundred years. He returns to New York, but the mad chaos in the fashionable bar makes him long so much for the enchanted world of Brigadoon that he returns to Scotland, and miraculously, Brigadoon appears once more, conjured up by his faith. But now Brigadoon is threatened by one of the inhabitants who wants to escape from the magic spell and live a "real" life. The villagers hunt him down and he is finally killed. Gene Kelly on the other hand, marrying Fiona, his dream girl, accepts the "unreality" of Brigadoon and is prepared to live for only a day every hundred years—a metaphor for the artist living only through his art, whatever the cost to "real life."

In THE BAND WAGON, too, the pattern is in evidence. Here it is particularly the different stages of Astaire's re-immersion into the world of show business, the different and often disastrous shows, that liberate the character from his wholly egocentric projection, and by a series of debunking maneuvers and parodies (e.g. the staging of *Oedipus Rex*), Minnelli establishes the idea of the spectacle as the measure of things. This is summed up in the theme song "That's Entertainment": "everything that happens in life/can happen in a show . . . anything, anything can go/The world is a stage/the stage is a world/of entertainment."

The notion of the artist as actor, however, not only relates the hero in a complex way to his environment, it also allows Minnelli to pursue the theme of artistic creativity into its most banal guises, where a common human denominator—the role-playing of all social life—serves to illuminate what is after all normally considered a privileged state of being. An essentially artistic temperament is revealed in all those who—from switchboard girl to Hollywood tycoon—want to act upon a given reality, change it, transform the material of their lives through the energy of an idea, an obsession, or merely the tentative groping to live up to the boldness of their imagination. But this theme of an energy in search of a material form hardly ever communicates itself in Minnelli as achievement. On the contrary, it is radically relativized as process—a permanent becoming—and rhythm, gesture and color are the properly cinematic signs of a spontaneous and contagious vitality, embodied in the musical as in no other genre.

Thus, despite the obvious difference between Judy Holliday's blunt vivaciousness in BELLS ARE RINGING and Leslie Caron's spiritual and graceful sensibility in GIGI, both films share the common drive for a liberation which inevitably leads to the spectacle, and both films are, in this sense, concerned with the ethics of the *mise-en-scène*—in one film understood as the (benevolent) influence on other people's lives, in the other as the assumption of a role in a formalized and stylized society. In BELLS ARE RINGING, Judy Holliday wants to play the good fairy to the clients of a telephone answering service, but at first she creates merely confusion, chaos and mischief. But although her role-playing makes her seem unreal to herself, her clients eventually bind together—to produce a theater-play. In an important aspect, however, her predicament highlights one of the inspirations of Minnelli's art. Through Judy Holliday's escapades we see a dichotomy between the richness of the American imagination and the restrictive force of a conventional morality. Significantly, the police handcuff her for her flight of fancy, ironic symbol of society's attitude to the creative artist.

If BELLS ARE RINGING concerns the responsibility of the *metteur-en-scène*, GIGI is an example of the apprenticeship of the *mise-en-scène*. Gigi has to learn how not to be natural, how to calculate her movement and judge the meaning of each gesture. She has to learn the conscious use of appearance, as a way of retaining a personal spontaneity and freedom through the language of social grace. In GIGI it is difficult to know how to take this aesthetic education—the color symbolism tells the story of a degradation, with Gigi's red and green becoming gradually a merely fashionable mauve and pink. On the other hand, the process seems inevitable, and Minnelli obviously prefers a conscious grace to a false innocence. In this sense, GIGI more than any other film is about the commercial cinema. And by subjecting his inspiration to the rigors of the system, Minnelli himself seems to praise the chains that tie the Hollywood artist so often to the banal story, the vulgar sentiment, the platitudinous cliché. However, unlike other aesthetic moralists such as Max Ophuls or Renoir with whom he has much in common, Minnelli has a wholly American reliance on an unbroken stream of vitality and energy. But as with them, what defines value for him is the *conception* of the world, not its material basis. In this sense, even the most "unreal" of his melodramas or musical comedies acknowledges a level of existence, a dimension of the actual that many a European director studiously ignores, and which Hollywood itself seems to have lost under the impact of TV-style instant realism. Who is then to say whether Minnelli's aestheticism is pernicious mystification or not rather the realism of the truly cinematic artist?

But Minnelli himself has dramatized the dilemma of film-making explicitly in his two films THE BAD AND THE BEAUTIFUL and TWO WEEKS IN ANOTHER TOWN. In both films seemingly fundamental moral distinctions between art and life are seen to become more and more ambiguous, as the laws and conditions of film-making impose themselves on an already inauthentic model of life. The film-to-be, the artifact, assumes the dimensions of an inexorable necessity, exposing the moral flaws and human weaknesses of those involved in its creation—a banal point perhaps, had not Minnelli balanced this indictment of Hollywood in THE BAD AND THE BEAUTIFUL by the dramatization of a grandiose, all-devouring obsession of an artist who spares neither himself nor others in order to remain true to his inspiration. Through the character of producer Jonathan Shields—cynical, cunning and demonic, who sacrifices everything in order to make films—Minnelli explores the nature of his own commitment to the cinema. Shields, by destroying their private lives, liberates the creative potential of his director, scriptwriter and leading lady, who had all been imprisoned by their petty worries and emotional fixations. THE BAD AND THE BEAUTIFUL shows the visionary as the most ruthless realist, dominating a world with an energy so radical that it can only come from the intimate knowledge of its degradation.

Art as the destruction of "ordinary" life—this is the central ambiguity which is at the heart of Minnelli's vision. And in LUST FOR LIFE, the film about Vincent Van Gogh, he pays homage to a greater artist, yet at the same time sharpens his own theme to its paroxysm. The Nietzschean intensity of Van Gogh's vision produces paintings of life as no human eye has ever seen them, but it is also a demonic urge that dissolves and severs all human bonds and finally destroys Van Gogh himself. In the film, the two sides are linked symbolically. As his isolation grows, the yellow colors of a superhuman light invade the canvas. But here Minnelli confronts a dilemma that transcends the framework of Hollywood, namely that of the morality of art itself. What are the values it creates, whom does it serve and to what ends?

If these questions receive an ambivalent answer in Minnelli's films, where the artist finally redeems and justifies his trespass on "life," it is partly because for Minnelli the artist is not privileged in either status or sensibility. All those who are capable of experiencing existence by its intensity ("Why must life be always measured by its duration?"—this complaint of Deborah Kerr in TEA AND SYMPATHY is symptomatic) and have the courage of their inspiration are artists in Minnelli's films, whether creative in an accepted sense or not.

It is when dealing with the "real" artist, as in LUST FOR LIFE, that the question of the value of ordinary life becomes problematic, and in TWO WEEKS IN ANOTHER TOWN the demonic element in the Shields-Van Gogh personality is portrayed as unambiguously neurotic and incapable of dealing with his life. Through Jack Andrus (all three characters, significantly, are played by the same actor—Kirk Douglas) Minnelli insists above all on the human price to be paid for the artist's venture. For in this film, the "art" is shown to be inept, and the society is simply decadent. The assertive energy which in the early films bridged or compensated for the rupture is explicitly and nostalgically evoked by Minnelli quoting his own THE BAD AND THE BEAUTIFUL. A feeling of guilt and failure, by contrast, always makes reality seem apocalyptic. In TWO WEEKS it is the spectacle in its corrupt form (one director taking over from another, everyone working behind one another's back) that comes to dominate, and the central protagonist, instead of being the force that precariously balances two mutually complementary orders of reality, is a schizophrenic, just released from a mental hospital. Although the film in the end appears to suggest the possibility of a new start, this is both a return and an escape, and the outcome is finally left open. What weighs, however, more heavily is the "death" of the director in the film—Minnelli's alter ego, but also his counter-self—whose once creative vision has turned into a morbid and self-destructive introspection, to which he finally succumbs.

3
All the Lonely Places: The Heroes of Nicholas Ray

To those familiar with Nicholas Ray's films,[1] his moral and existential preoccupations are well known: solitude of the individual in a depersonalized world (DANGEROUS GROUND, 1951), revolt and violence of the adolescent (REBEL WITHOUT A CAUSE, 1955), the problematic nature of adulthood and maturity in an atomized society, the double-binds and mis-communication intertwining the generations and the sexes (BIGGER THAN LIFE, 1956), and lastly, the frustrations of self-expression and the goals of self-fulfilment, which make even artistic creation a perversity (IN A LONELY PLACE, 1950).[2] With these themes of isolation, the outsider and social anomie, Ray's films fit more into a European tradition in style and sensibility, and yet they are also part of Hollywood 1950s mainstream, in the way their director was socially committed and "liberal" without being explicitly on the political left.

In interviews Ray was one of the most articulate and communicative of Hollywood directors. As he readily admitted, his films are very personal, with a network of constantly recurring obsessions, and his characters share a lot of his own traits, down to their gestural mannerisms, as was strikingly apparent during a personal appearance at the National Film Theatre in London, in 1969, as part of the retrospective that originally inspired this essay. These autobiographical traits along with his air of an intellectual no doubt helped in making Ray one of the most celebrated of auteurs *in the* Cahiers du cinéma *canon of the 1950s. To his admirers—reaching from Jean-Luc Godard, François Truffaut and Jacques Rivette[3] to critics as different as Fereydoun Hoveyda, Michel Mourlet and Bernard Eisenschitz[4] —his directorial signature was as unmistakable as his "lyricism," which transcended the boundaries of such typically "male" genres as the Western (JOHNNY GUITAR, 1954) and the gangster film (PARTY GIRL, 1958).[5] As one of the Hollywood directors most often dogged and defeated by the studio system, he was also one of France's favorite* auteurs maudits *(along with Sam Fuller).[6] Yet even after scores of disappointments ("you have no idea how I had to fight to achieve even fifty percent of what I wanted to do"), years of self-exile from America (he left the USA for AMÈRE VICTOIRE/BITTER VICTORY [1957] and again during the shooting of THE SAVAGE INNOCENTS in 1960) as well as the rows with producer Samuel Bronston over KING OF KINGS (1961) and 55 DAYS OF PEKING (1963), which brought on a heart-attack that forced him to abandon commercial filmmaking, Ray admitted that "if you find the right sort of people you are better off in Hollywood than in the jungle of independent production."[7]*

What follows was an attempt, after attending the Nicholas Ray retrospective and the director's special lecture in January 1969, to register the impact of some twenty films, and to understand Ray's work as a coherent whole, both in its thematic structure and its development, its style and its ideology.[8] *There are thus no individual plot-synopses, only the Nicholas Ray "super-text": a single entity or organism constantly evolving and mutating.*

Nicholas Ray

The debate around the "*auteur*" theory, when first introduced to the English-speaking world in the 1960s through Andrew Sarris or the essays in *Movie* magazine, rightly stressed the need to go beyond a mere cataloging of a director's themes. In themselves these are usually little more than signposts on the way towards an understanding of an *auteur*'s work, often not that different from the conventionalized conflict situations as codified in Hollywood genre formulas. What therefore interests me in Ray are not so much the themes in themselves, but the larger patterns in which these themes appear in his films, and the developments or variations they undergo in the course of his career. Furthermore, I want to make some tentative suggestions of how these themes relate to his typical *mise-en-scène*. Ray's importance as a film-director is essentially on the level of his *mise-en-scène* and not on the level of ideas, as he himself admitted: "I'm not a very intellectual fellow, though it's taken me a long time to accept this."

But even with the themes, one can usefully ask certain questions. For example, why does the violence in Run for Cover (1955) differ from that in Johnny Guitar, or what is the significance of the fact that the loner-turned-delinquent adolescent—so central in Ray's early work—moves more and more to the periphery, until in Party Girl the young Cookie La Motte (Corey Allen) is no more than a pastiche, an almost clownish counterpoint to a conflict that is clearly focused elsewhere, that is, on the adult couple. Again, how do the early (adolescent) couples differ from those of The Lusty Men (1952) or Party Girl, and what exactly happens to the loner in the later films, and what does the inversion of certain themes in, for instance, The Savage Innocents (1960) indicate about Ray's changing vision of "life," "wilderness" and "nature," modifying both his own and Hollywood's binary divide between nature/culture?

Solitude and Violence

The early, mostly adolescent heroes are easily identifiable: they live in a world of pride and distrust, aggression and violence, which imprisons them as much as it protects them. This is the position of Nick (John Derek) in Knock on any Door (1949) and Davey (also John Derek) in Run for Cover, Danny (Sumner Williams) in On dangerous Ground, and Plato (Sal Mineo) in Rebel without a Cause. Insofar as adults react to threatening situations with the same kind of blind, instinctive aggressiveness, they too are adolescents: the screenwriter Dixon Steele (Humphrey Bogart) in In a lonely Place or Jim Wilson (Robert Ryan) in On Dangerous Ground. At the outset, their aggressive isolation makes them unfit for a social role: Steele is suspected of a murder which he did not commit, and Wilson is about to lose his job on the police force because once too often he has beaten up a suspect. Their violence is the violence of frustration and inner discord. Thus, their experience of society is negative, their response revolt. In the face of an imperfect life and difficult choices, they tend to run and precipitate themselves into far-flung places of violence and crime rather than confront their own inner selves.

The outlaw in Ray—as indeed in so many other American films—embodies an existential refusal. But it is also the expression of an existential confusion: not only do Ray's rebels panic; their aggression is often sheer self-aggression bordering on bad faith. This comes across well in a scene in Johnny Guitar, when Turkey (Ben Cooper), trying to show his love for Vienna by proving that he is a man, shoots up a couple of glasses in the bar. Suddenly Johnny appears, shoots the gun out of Turkey's hand, firing away until his gun is empty. Vienna, furious, tells them off and they both stand there, like schoolboys after a stupid prank: their violence demonstrates their immaturity, their unfitness for the love they crave from the women they love.

Thus, the stances the protagonists display in their isolation are intense, but at the same time the postures are false ones, for they often manifest the inverse of what they actually feel: Plato in REBEL WITHOUT A CAUSE kills his animals because he is unable to express his love for Jim (James Dean) and Judy (Natalie Wood), Dixon Steele nearly kills a careless driver because he cannot bear the strain of a mature relationship with Laurel Gray (Gloria Graham), Davey in RUN FOR COVER joins the bandits because he feels humiliated by Matt's (James Cagney) kindness, and Jesse James (Robert Wagner) in THE TRUE STORY OF JESSE JAMES becomes an outlaw because of his sense of dignity and justice. Ray's characters are fundamentally unfree because their actions constantly belie the needs that give rise to them. This is why they so often have to go "outside" or "away" to find their identity, why Wes (Arthur Kennedy) in THE LUSTY MEN leaves his steady farm job and joins the shifty rodeo-riders, ironically, in order to settle down and "have a place of his own." Likewise, Jim Wilson in ON DANGEROUS GROUND has to leave town, and drive into a strange, snowbound landscape in order to find himself. At the heart of the Ray hero's dilemma is often a permanent, but highly significant indecision about the true motives of his action and the place of his revolt. Introspection, in the manner of European characters facing similarly existential dilemmas, never seems an option.

This is because the early Ray heroes' solitude is above all an emotional experience: they feel wronged, isolated, misunderstood and they are afraid of themselves as much as of others. Their revolt is unfocused, diffuse and instinctive. It is in this that they differ from the later protagonists. With JOHNNY GUITAR and RUN FOR COVER, Ray seems to become increasingly critical of his violent adolescents: whereas in the early films the corruption of their sensibility, their penchant for violence and their slide into crime appear justified by the image presented of a thoroughly malevolent world or a corrupt society, where escape is the only answer (e.g. THEY LIVE BY NIGHT, 1948), this response to life becomes the sign of a fatal flaw in the later heroes—already hinted at in KNOCK ON ANY DOOR—but only fully explored in RUN FOR COVER, where the hero turns criminal mostly out of self-pity and a morbid sensitivity. The title "run for cover" is symptomatic and represents a recurring situation in Ray: many of the protagonists have secret hideouts, privileged places where they seek protection not only from society but also from self-scrutiny. The bungalow in THEY LIVE BY NIGHT, Danny's shed in ON DANGEROUS GROUND, the deserted house of Plato in REBEL WITHOUT A CAUSE, the Aztec ruins in RUN FOR COVER, the gang's hideout "on the other side" of the waterfall in JOHNNY GUITAR: all places where the protagonists seek a home and safe haven, only to discover that ultimately these are prisons. The break with the habitual environment, the rupture with society, instead of bringing a moment of self-recognition, becomes an expression of weakness: afraid of losing themselves in a hostile world, they escape further and further into their own private worlds, beyond which there is a void: Danny, eventually driven out of his shed, can only climb up a barren rock, from where he falls to his death; Davey dies in the Aztec ruins; and in JOHNNY GUITAR, the earth literally bursts asunder and forces the Dancing Kid (Scott Brady) back into his hideout where he is finally killed by Emma (Mercedes McCambridge). Thus, the hideout, the retreat betrays the hero because he has deceived himself about his self-sufficiency. In REBEL WITHOUT A CAUSE, his twofold betrayal is elevated into a metaphysical symbol: first the rival gang invades the deserted house to drive Plato out of his enchanted world, and then he is forced to seek refuge in the planetarium, metaphor of an indifferent universe, where he is eventually shot by the police.

It is this psychological situation of "run" and "cover" which organizes Ray's cinematic use of isolated buildings (e.g. Vienna's saloon "in the middle of nowhere"), enclosed spaces (the courtyard in IN A LONELY PLACE) and of rooms, interiors, doors and windows. For it is characteristic of the Ray hero—and indicative of his divided nature—that he never seems to recognize himself in a given place, and yet constantly tries to establish a private world, or map out a territory which is recognizably and proprietarily his. The violent reactions to an environment, as for example Jim's fit of violence in his father's house which ends with him bursting through the veranda door (REBEL WITHOUT A CAUSE) or Davey smashing the mirror with the chair with which he is supposed to prop himself up (RUN FOR COVER): these scenes always signal the refusal of the hero to recognize and to accept the image of himself which the setting and decor reflect.

Friendship and Maturity

As Ray's portrayal of society becomes more complex and differentiated, so the relation between the main protagonist and those who surround him develops into the central ambivalence of the films. In Ray's best work, therefore, the violent individualists are invariably counterbalanced by characters whose similar emotional make-up and experience nevertheless permit evolving in a different direction. The relationship between such complementary figures is either that of friendship and complicity (Jim and Plato in REBEL WITHOUT A CAUSE, Davey and Matt at the beginning of RUN FOR COVER), of dependence and mutual obligation (Nick and Morton in KNOCK ON ANY DOOR, Wes and Jeff [Robert Mitchum] in THE LUSTY MEN, Thomas Farrell [Robert Taylor] and Rico Angelo [Lee J. Cobb] in PARTY GIRL) or of an intense and ambiguous fascination, such as the brief scene between Jim Wilson and Davey in ON DANGEROUS GROUND, Jim and Buzz (Corey Allen) in REBEL WITHOUT A CAUSE, Capt. Leith (Richard Burton) and Major Brand (Curd Jurgens) in BITTER VICTORY, and of course, Walt Murdoch (Christopher Plummer) and Cottonmouth (Burl Ives) in WIND ACROSS THE EVERGLADES.

With these relationships, Ray seems constantly to underline the possibility of a fundamental choice in life, a choice, however, which articulates itself in the films as a wide spectrum of specific attitudes, ranging from total rebellion to total submission. Friendship, dependence and fascination are the human forms in which these options are tested. In the early films, the dividing line is much more neatly drawn: for example, in KNOCK ON ANY DOOR the lawyer Morton (Humphrey Bogart) defends Nick out of a mixture of obligation, professional interest and personal sympathy. But the two men never find a real understanding of each other. Morton's defense rests on a false assumption of innocence, and Nick ultimately despises Morton for having buckled down to the establishment as an easy compromise. In PARTY GIRL, it is the Morton character that becomes the central hero, but by then the theme has turned full circle, so that the "easy option" turns out to consist of a life of violence and criminality.

There is a crucial scene in KNOCK ON ANY DOOR which dramatizes the mutually irreconcilable positions: Morton and his wife take Nick and Emma (Alleen Roberts) to a restaurant. As they drink a toast to the young couple's future, the camera moves behind the characters, to frame Morton and his wife looking at Nick and Emma who are engrossed in each other, while in the background a waiter is pouring brandy over a steak and then setting it alight. The scene is shot in a way that underlines the essential division. The couple are visually isolated, they are in a world of their own, set against the flames of an ambiguous intensity, while the lawyer's perspective is rigorously identified with ours: mere spectators of a fate which one can interpret, but from which both the lawyer and the spectator are equally removed.

In a film like RUN FOR COVER, on the other hand, the respective positions of the two main protagonists appear as complementary: rebellion and acceptance have a mutually educative function. The theme is that of an adolescent who has to grow into a society, which is despicable, because of moral cowardice and conformism as well as endemic violence. In Ray, society appears always as the group, the gang or posse, hunting the individual, whether guilty or not. Ray underlines this division visually: a river, a sandstorm, the fence of a corral always seems to form a divide and force the characters to find their answers outside society. Even in the final scene of Run for Cover, Matt, having returned the money, has to go through the crowd. As the camera cranes up, he crosses the barrier, and walks away with his wife. The film does not advocate submission, though in the fate of Davey, Ray strongly affirms the need to "grow up," to reach a personal identity by coming to terms with society, however much it has wronged you. The hero has to sublimate the violence, which is the natural response to an inhuman situation. Ray recognizes the role of the rebel only insofar as he is capable of "learning," of eventually mastering his temper and interiorizing his revolt. Otherwise, violence becomes weakness, the sign of self-pity and the outcome of hypersensitivity. Where Ray's political liberalism shows itself most clearly is in the endorsement of a social contract: even a badly organized society is no excuse for a wholly a-social stance. "Maturity" in Run for Cover appears as the morality of enlightened self-interest, but it is important to see also the critique, which is implied in the presentation of Matt, especially in his role as Davey's "father." His attempt to mold Davey after his own image, to impose upon him an ordered, serene—and self-complacent—existence (a recurrent impulse in Ray's father figures) merely drives Davey further into the world where he accepts the bandit as his true father. The point about Matt is made explicit in the final showdown where Davey saves Matt by killing the bandit. But because he had already lost faith in Davey, Matt mistakes the gesture and shoots Davey. Refusing to allow for Davey's "otherness" and give it scope, Matt—as in a sense he does throughout the film—prevents him from living by his own code and thus taking responsibility. In a less pointed way, Matt prefigures Ed Avery (James Mason), the tyrannical father of Bigger than Life.

The Rebel and Society

After Run for Cover the central characters appear more and more as figures that seek appeasement and reconciliation, as against the violent self-assertion of the earlier protagonists. In Rebel without a Cause, for example, the violent loner is someone on the margin, while Jim's problem surpasses that of simple revolt. For him—and other subsequent heroes—the difference from the world around becomes a difference of moral awareness and not merely of sensibility. Jim is the first hero to admit explicitly the values of self-reflection and self-discipline. The ideal of a reconciled existence is most apparent in a later film, Party Girl, but already Johnny in Johnny Guitar is a rebel who wants to "come home," and who accepts that the homecoming necessitates the reliving of a buried past. From the opening scene where Johnny watches impassively while the stage-coach is being robbed, to the moment where he cuts the rope round Vienna's neck, his trajectory is one of progressive involvement and—in accord with the rules of the genre, and yet carefully prepared by Ray's own uniquely particularizing portrait of Johnny—of assuming personal responsibility.

This desire to find a place to rest is a constant feature in Ray, but dramaturgically, it is also the source of a continued tension: the conjunction of violence and solitude in the heroes' psychology places them in a highly ambivalent relation to the society in which they live. For the revolt of the Ray characters against the world around them is fundamentally flawed at the outset. As the aspirations that nourish their violence are contradictory, their course of action pushes them in two directions at once. They reject society in the name of an obscurely apprehended inner world—hence their hypersensitivity, as well as their outsider arrogance—yet because of their need for communication and "opening up," they are at the same time desperately trying to integrate themselves, adapt themselves, and accept "life as it is," that is, to submit to the existing social mechanisms by living a "normal" life. Ray's comment on what he found both fascinating and troubling about James Dean bears this out: "He could never resolve the conflict between needing to give himself, and the fear of giving in to his own feelings; he had a vulnerability so deep that it was almost disturbing."

One can find this dual pull in all the angry individualists in Ray's films whose ultimate aim seems to be to live a happy family life, or at least to establish a durable bond. This is the case of Bowie (Farley Granger) and Keechie (Cathy O'Donnell) in THEY LIVE BY NIGHT, of Wes in THE LUSTY MEN, of Jim in REBEL WITHOUT A CAUSE. But the rift that forecloses these modest ambitions is clearest in THE JAMES BROTHERS. Jesse James' career as an outlaw ironically culminates with his buying a respectable property and becoming an esteemed member of the community. But the acceptance of "life as it is," the return to normality implied by his sudden disappearance, has the opposite effect: it feeds extravagantly into the romantic myth of the outlaw. While seeking peace and integration in society ("Home Sweet Home" reads the embroidery), it is the negative image of his own revolt (his "fame" as a bandit), which catches up with him in the figure of Bob Ford. The rebel pays the price—not for his rebellion, but for his desire to live a normal life, incognito and unspectacular.

In this respect, the apparent progression towards reconciliation, maturity and acceptance in Ray's films must be understood as still set against the contrary tendency within the heroes to live their revolt to its paroxysm. In BIGGER THAN LIFE and WIND ACROSS THE EVERGLADES, this basic dichotomy in Ray's vision is given full expression. For there, the hero-villains live their isolation as a quasi-metaphysical revolt against creation itself, and their violence becomes elemental and Dionysian: both Avery and Cottonmouth try to impose on the human world an a-moral, "natural" order—not a "return" to nature, but a defiant and self-destructive pact with nature.

Generally, the Ray heroes are inextricably caught in their revolt against society. Either they attempt to escape from society altogether and retreat into a world of tranquillity—in which case they themselves are doomed, and their actions become suicidal. Or their revolt reveals itself as an attempt to revalidate degraded ideals, upheld (but betrayed) by the social system itself, and then their reconciliation is bought at an exorbitant price: Jess has to die for Wes and his wife in THE LUSTY MEN, in the same way as Plato dies for Jim and Judy in REBEL WITHOUT A CAUSE. These rebels try to live the explicit values of their society, while their very natures—or their alter egos—belie any possibility of permanent reconciliation. The secret of the Ray heroes is that they are poised between an unliveable individualism and an equally unliveable conformism.

This tension is most obvious if we take a closer look at the nature of violence in Ray's films. As already mentioned, violent rebellion is almost invariably a sign of weakness and impotence in Ray's characters: through violence, they also seek punishment, and therefore submission. Contrast the violence of the Ray hero with that of the Fuller hero, and the difference is striking. Fuller's characters, especially in films like THE STEEL HELMET, RUN OF THE ARROW or SHOCK CORRIDOR infringe the social norm, overreach themselves as do those of Ray, but they experience the moment of trespass as a moment of freedom, for it permits them to live unambiguously the contradictions inherent in an objective situation, rather than to act out their divided selves.

In Ray, then, the contradictions are dramatized psychologically—as subjective, internal. The violent outbursts of Davey in RUN FOR COVER, the chicken run in REBEL WITHOUT A CAUSE, or JOHNNY GUITAR emptying his gun in Vienna's saloon: these are typical Ray situations; the emphasis is always placed on the moment of total helplessness, of inner despair that follows such fireworks of intensity. The reason is easy to see. Fuller's heroes, whatever they experience, are enviably free from feeling guilt. Ray's heroes are so obsessed by it that their violence has a tendency to become masochistic—directed as much against themselves as against others.

The fact that there is an element of guilt in the rebellion of the Ray heroes helps one to understand the particular position of BIGGER THAN LIFE in Ray's work. Ed Avery, the film's hero and imbued by Mason with a truly tragic "flaw," is the first adult rebel who tries to confront this guilt, by questioning explicitly the cultural norms, social mechanisms and even religious values that foist upon the individual a belief in the virtues of maturity and acceptance of a higher order. For in BIGGER THAN LIFE the ideological demands of the symbolic order, as embodied in education, democracy and the negotiated resolution of conflict, which we find in a good many of Ray's films as the implicit horizon, is here denounced not by a youthful rebel, but by an otherwise fully integrated adult, whose vision is both justified and warped, whose character is both heroic and discredited. Avery, to whom a gradual addiction to cortisone reveals the insufferable pettiness of his personal life, inverts the dynamics of Ray's habitual moral journeys. His revolt against the ideals of education, against the institution of the family, against the democratic values of liberal America is like a mirror held up to the reconciled adults or grown-up adolescents at the end of The Lusty Men, Run for Cover or Johnny Guitar. Here, the very process of education appears as a form of sinister manipulation, hand in glove with conformism and bigotry, designed to stifle and suppress every vital impulse and to prevent social change. Avery, by now as dangerous to himself as he is to others, is not merely a victim of a medication whose side-effects have not been fully understood: the cortisone gives him a fatal "clarity" that makes adjusted adults appear as the sad product of a society that believes in the absolute value of sublimation, and admits vitality only in the form of socially sanctioned goals, such as procreation.

There is a scene, rather like the one in Run for Cover already mentioned, where Avery smashes the mirror of his bathroom cabinet to get at the cortisone. The drug is here not only the promise of relief from physical pain but also the certainty of a purer and more lucid vision. Thus, the mirror reflects both his true image and his false one: true, insofar as he is a paterfamilias, has a social role and responsibility and is therefore morally answerable for his actions, but false because this adulthood has made him so much less than his true potential, depriving him of his passion, his vision and his enthusiasm. Bigger than Life takes its Nietzschean thematic into a very specific American context, which also documents its historicity. Made in 1956, it reflects the dilemma of the liberal intelligentsia traumatized by totalitarianism and now fearing not only nuclear destruction, but the corrosive effects of witch-hunts and McCarthyism. Honest in its ambiguity, Ray admits that revolt against society, when consequential, can manifest itself as the immoral and violent assertion of an individuality whose fascist overtones mirror that of the forces it opposes. Thus, when the Ray hero becomes (too) lucid, his vitality appears as either mad or criminal, the two sides of destructive self-destruction. A (natural) desire for social change breaks itself on the fault-lines of an over-refined, hypersensitive individualism that perceives the world not merely as grossly imperfect, but as totally meaningless and absurd.

Bigger than Life pushes the Ray dilemma to its impasse. In it, the guilt-ridden rebel grows into a pseudo-fascist superman. Alternatively, to accept "life as it is" means to find oneself in the prison of a repressive conformism. The final scene of the film is one of the most nihilistic moments in Ray's work: Ed Avery wakes up from the demented fit during which he tried to kill his own son; at first he persists in seeing as the sun of his mad vision the naked neon light glaring above his hospital bed. But finally, he recognizes his wife and son. Ray first cuts in a low angle shot of the ceiling and then a high angle shot of the family huddled round the bed: two shots which define precisely—and balance precariously—the claustrophobic life ahead and the narrow limits of his newly won sanity, in a Hollywood happy ending that is indeed a "bitter victory," and appropriately the title of another of Ray's films.

However, it is in Wind across the Everglades and The Savage Innocents that the problematic limits of "human nature" are given further exploration and a new definition. Despite production difficulties which make Wind across the Everglades look "like a rough cut"—in Charles Barr's apt phrase[9]—and despite the extensive second-unit work on The Savage Innocents, one can see Ray in his late work moving in a significantly different direction. As I have tried to show, Ray's films become more and more explicit about the ambiguity in their heroes' opposition or rejection of the world: Wind across the Everglades has no central hero but examines the fascination that two men of totally different conviction feel for each other, each of whom violently protests against a degraded society, while being himself a flawed and degraded rebel. Against Walt Murdoch's aesthetic revolt Ray sets the a-morality of Cottonmouth. Cottonmouth, thoroughly contemptuous of organized society, proud to be living by the harsh law of nature, is implicated in that society by the very form his revolt takes. A poacher, who makes his living from shooting exotic birds for their fashionable feathers, he is the instrument of that decadence and frivolity against which Murdoch, a wildlife officer and conservationist, tries to take action. Yet Murdoch's instinctual revolt is based partly on ignorance, partly on naivety, or worse: on the misconception that nature needs to be preserved as the beautiful pleasure garden of man. Penetrating deeper into the Florida swamps, the violence and cruelty of the natural world appals him. Nevertheless, he puts up the sign "This is a Sanctuary"; his defiance is touching in its impotent idealism, for he strikes out in the name of patently inadequate humanist values. It is only the actual encounter with the world of Cottonmouth (first seen by him upside down in the viewfinder of his camera) that gradually makes him aware that he, too, is attempting to impose a false order on the natural world.

During an extended drinking bout, Murdoch realizes how alike he and Cottonmouth are: they aspire to a Dionysian liberation, which—ultimately—is denied to them by both society *and* nature. Their journey together merely proves the irony of their revolt: the impossibility of ever imposing themselves on "life." The everglades, symbolizing an implacable ecology as well as unpredictable elements—are there to remind them of the hubris of a civilization trying to take over the natural world, whether through a Cottonmouth or a Murdoch. But Cottonmouth and Murdoch are the first Ray heroes to become aware of a possible liberation from the social preoccupation and psychic drives which generally make the heroes' revolt so dubious. Although Murdoch, too, pursues his goal of a sanctuary to the brink of insanity, he comes to accept its irrelevance as he sees Cottonmouth die, become as much a part of the natural (dis-)order as the magnificent dead tree-trunks around him.

Shot in the same year as WIND ACROSS THE EVERGLADES, PARTY GIRL looks back to some of the earlier films, notably KNOCK ON ANY DOOR. By comparing the two films one notes the distance that Ray has traversed in the handling of his core preoccupations. While still recording the victory over a certain (external) milieu as a victory over a morbid (interior) sensitivity, PARTY GIRL recognizes—as does WIND ACROSS THE EVERGLADES—the possibility of freedom only in the active encounter of partners of equal strength and passion. But the real greatness of the film is the way Ray's use of colors translates to perfection the slightest developments of the action into visual-sensuous presence. In more than one sense, it concludes Ray's American studio period: the very traditionalism of its conflict (a crooked lawyer torn between his love for a singer who wants him to go straight and his underworld boss who extracts his price) and its genre identity (as a classic gangster film, albeit in flamboyantly gaudy Metrocolor and glorious Cinemascope) give PARTY GIRL a perfection, which WIND ACROSS THE EVERGLADES does not possess. A favorite of the partisans of "pure" *mise-en-scène*,[10] PARTY GIRL's central relationship is an appealing reminder of the delicacy with which Ray can depict two people, whose mutual bond is not (only) physical attraction, but a recognition of their essential vulnerability, in a world whose risks and dangers they have consciously chosen.

If one wants to know how Ray develops the more existential vision of the human condition beyond the nature/culture divide, which announces itself in WIND ACROSS THE EVERGLADES, one has to turn to THE SAVAGE INNOCENTS. Here, once again, the traditional connotations of Ray's theme of the loner who can live neither with nor without society, find themselves inverted. THE SAVAGE INNOCENTS, recounting the life of an Eskimo couple (Anthony Quinn and Yoko Tani) and their contact with Western civilization, is the anthropological mirror of Ray's American obsessions. In the *pensée sauvage* of the Inuits, not only dress, food and rituals, but violence and solitude are objective facts of existence. The blood that colors the blue arctic sea in the opening scene is that of a purposeful violence, necessary either to preserve life, or, as in the killing of the missionary, necessary to preserve customs and rites which alone make life bearable. Similarly, the habitual conflict between men and women, between young and old, still constitutes an essential element of Ray's vision of human life. But in THE SAVAGE INNOCENTS such conflicts are elements in a natural order, embedded in a regime of necessity that makes psychology redundant. Dramas of survival find their resolution in a world without choice or change and therefore without tragedy. One of the recurrent Ray situations, the sacrificial death which allows a couple to live with a new awareness of exposure and mortality (RUN FOR COVER, ON DANGEROUS GROUND, REBEL WITHOUT A CAUSE) is taken up in THE SAVAGE INNOCENTS and given a natural significance: the old woman dies peacefully and resignedly, because she knows that her death is necessary for the younger couple's physical survival.

Though it is with WIND ACROSS THE EVERGLADES that Ray's anthropological vision most decisively transforms his traditional themes, one would have to go back to HOT BLOOD (1956) to trace the precise outlines of Ray's interest in the exotic, between genuine anthropological curiosity for the "otherness" of a traditional community (here: an extended family of Gypsies or Roma, forced to arrange a marriage) and the excuse it gives the director for a Cinemascope riot of color and a spectacle of voluptuous sensuality (Jane Russell as the hot-blooded Shrew whose eventual Taming is more a matter of Ray's *mise-en-scène* of some wonderful dance numbers than due to the reluctant bridegroom—Cornel Wilde—impressing either her or us with his masculinity). It took the move away from America, whether undertaken by necessity or by choice, to consolidate Ray's broadly ethnographic or multicultural perspective. KING OF KINGS (1961) and 55 DAYS OF PEKING (1963) are both, and perhaps because of the interferences, rather than in spite of them, confrontations with different cultures at least as interesting as THE SAVAGE INNOCENTS. Using the canvass of the epic, and fully aware that these were the dying days of the classic Hollywood studio system, Ray appears to be looking less for a grand statement on the folly of human ambition, the persistence of poverty and injustice or the hubris of Empires, and instead strives for a visual harmony into which the dramatic conflicts of the individuals can finally insert themselves: a harmony-in-diversity which has always been the controlling principle of his *mise-en-scène*.

Ray's *Mise-en-Scène*

Nicholas Ray was trained as an architect. He studied under Frank Lloyd Wright, and this influence can be detected in his films in a number of ways. One of the stylistic marks of a Ray movie, for example, is the subtle but nonetheless highly effective use of spatial relations to set out the dramatic import of a scene, or to give thematic accents to a situation. Time and again, it is the bold geometric lines of a setting that prints the image on one's mind, like the iron drawbridge in PARTY GIRL, the carved branch dividing Ida Lupino's room in ON DANGEROUS GROUND, or the metal cages and space dividers at the police station in the opening scene of REBEL WITHOUT A CAUSE. The uncertainty of purpose, the insecurity of place, so typical of the Ray hero, is constantly translated into the complex, even labyrinthine arrangement of nonetheless distinct visual segments. This is also evident in the way the *mise-en-scène* makes use of doors, partitions and staircases: they act as the pivots of Ray's physical world in which they trace the lines of an always-precarious communication. Such architectural features invariably emphasize the emotional links underlying the antagonisms between one character and another, yet they equally structure an inner world in which the protagonists have to make their choices. In JOHNNY GUITAR Vienna locks herself up in her upstairs room, while commanding her men to keep the roulette wheels spinning in the empty saloon: a gesture, neatly symbolic of the kind of order and regularity she is trying to impose on her existence. Eventually, she is forced to come down the stairs to meet first Johnny, then Emma—and with them those parts of her self, her past and her emotions which she had chosen to deny. In REBEL WITHOUT A CAUSE, it is on the stairs that Jim has the most violent clash with his father, confronting his own sense of humiliation and impotence, at the same time as the stairs dramatize the urgency of his escape. The staircase in BIGGER THAN LIFE has a similar, and even more pivotal function in the story.[11]

Generally, what is involved in these and numerous other instances of architectural *mise-en-scène*, is not only an intuitive appreciation of the horizontal line (making him a master of the Cinemascope format), but also a complex and extremely subtle use of the principles of balance, sensed by the spectator's body even more than apparent to the eye. It is often as if Ray was expressing emotional tensions by transforming them into physical sensations, and the audience is keyed to a conflict by the way equilibrium is withheld and manipulated to clarify a theme or advance the dynamics of the story. Especially in the early films one notes a kind of precipitous or precariously poised use of the cinematic frame to create a psychological universe of extreme instability—of character, of motive, of action and reaction. Yet the *mise-en-scène* can be both amplifying and contrapuntal. It underlines moments of tension with a purposefully a-symmetrical organization of visual elements, what might be called a *mise-en-scène* of calculated disorder and strain. There is a scene, for example, in JOHNNY GUITAR, where at a dramatic climax (Johnny is trying to force a showdown with the Dancing Kid over Vienna) the characters are cut in such a way that—in apparent defiance of spatial verisimilitude or continuity rules—their individual glances all point in different directions of the frame, as if their very eyes were straining to explore the tight emotional situation in which they are enclosed.

At other times, the effects of *mise-en-scène* are contrapuntal in relation to the story-line. Not unexpectedly for an American director working in the studio-system during the 1950s, the majority of Ray's films follow a very classical linear pattern of story-structure (there is a central hero, a pursuit or quest or journey, leading to an eventual resolution). Yet a closer look at Ray's narrative patterns or plot development gives the impression that the veritable lines of force in his films tend towards a rather more open approach to the "ideology" of progress inherent in the linear form. For instance, a typical Ray ending—the therapy of a couple through an expiatory death—represents a variation on the cathartic resolution of conflict, central to almost all the genres of the American cinema. The variation, however, is of special importance, because it has to be seen against the values which the linear form most commonly implies: the underwriting of initiation, maturation and the transformation of external conflict into inner awareness and hence appeasement; values of which Ray—and not only since BIGGER THAN LIFE—seems to have become increasingly critical. What we see in the later films is a remarkable ability to retain the dynamics of the linear form, while never ceasing to probe it by his unbalancing use of color, angled frames, gestures and décor that subtly clash, which make his films obey gravitational laws of their own—a physical experience even before one is able to reflect on its wider significance.

Structurally, Ray's films often proceed by modulating one-two-three patterns of human relationships, whose thematic elements are the solitary individual, the couple and the triangle (the latter usually made up of two overlapping couples, result of natural or elective affinities: male/female, male/male, as in THE LUSTY MEN, RUN FOR COVER, HOT BLOOD or BITTER VICTORY). Characteristically, Ray makes great use of the spatial possibilities inherent in the "geometrical" organization of his protagonists' emotional bonds, to pursue a dialectic which finally—as I shall try to show—both dissolves and validates the linear progress of the plot.

One of Ray's favorite ways of starting a story is to make the solitary hero introduce, through his movements, gestures and actions, this sense of imbalance and disequilibrium from which flows the initial dramatic momentum. The opening ten minutes of THEY LIVE BY NIGHT, his first feature film, illustrate the principle in exemplary fashion. To underline Bowie's difference from the gang, and to mark the beginning of his reflexive turn, the camera isolates him, either through the composition of the frame (Bowie staying behind the billboard, as the others make their way to the garage) or through the repeated juxtaposition of group shots and medium shots of the young man. At the same time, one is conscious of an absence, for the numerical discrepancy (one against four), the difference in age, accentuate Bowie's isolation to a degree which would become intolerable if it were not counter-balanced. The shot of Bowie meeting Keechie (with the pump as a visual axis) resolves this prolonged period of a-symmetry and stress into a direct and simple visual harmony, lifting temporarily an ambiguity, which had forced itself into one's very perception of the visual field. Similarly, there are several occasions in Ray's work where the protagonist is morally isolated from a group, and invari-ably this isolation is also felt as spatial, as a question of physical scale and proportion. An opposition, an unresolved conflict thus lingers on beyond the moment of clash, while an emotional attraction or fascination is often sensed in advance by a dynamic relation of visual planes, as in the scene already discussed where Walt Murdoch sees Cottonmouth upside down in his camera (WIND ACROSS THE EVERGLADES).

This abstract, stereometric dynamic comes into play especially in films featuring the typical Ray couple, aggressive-defensive, passionate and shy, needy and proud, and thus always moving in a kind of gravitational field that is dominated by collision and polarity. Again, Ray underlines how partners are on different "levels": note the complex dramatic architecture of the apartment block in IN A LONELY PLACE, where in addition, Dixon Steele and Laurel Gray are almost never pictured at the same (visual) height, which becomes an essential part of their tragedy. Or think of the kitchen in KNOCK ON ANY DOOR, with its boiler and gas-pipes, a maze of conduits and obstructions in which the couple is hopelessly trapped. Another striking example occurs in JOHNNY GUITAR: during the famous dialogue between Vienna and Johnny ("Tell me a lie, tell me that you've waited all these years"), Vienna appears in the opening of the door behind Johnny, as if set in a picture frame. Near and yet infinitely removed, she is a presence conjured up by Johnny's solitary, yearning meditation.

It is within such architectures of longing and despair that Ray most potently captures basic human conflict situations. The effect is often emphasized by the use of color, as in PARTY GIRL, where Thomas Farrell and Vickie (Cyd Charisse) are sharply separated from the general "ambience" of Rico Angelo's party not only by the way they seem constantly placed near the edge of the frame, but also by the colors they wear—black and red (in a setting predominantly cream, yellow and gold). Distinguished from each other, the colors combine to give the sense of complementary personalities.

Most typical, however, of Ray's films is that the conflicts between the individual and the group, or between two individuals, are so often mediated through a triple beat or triadic progression. Although the precise emotional qualities vary from film to film, the Ray triangle is constant in its structural dynamism: at its most general, it indicates tension within affinity, or change within symmetry. In those films where a triangular relationship plays an important role (by my count, at least eight), it corresponds to a synthesis of the characters' aspirations: security, balance, two-way communication and space for individuality: all beyond polarity and self-division. However, these triangles, though seeming to represent the ideal, are invariably shown to be unnatural, and fundamentally unstable. Under the pressure of circumstances they dissolve and disintegrate into the forces that gave rise to them: often enough, the sense of isolation, fear, incomprehension and constraint. Where the linear plot comes to be associated more and more with a world permeated by flux, rush and transience, the triangle represents a striving for peace, respite and order. In some films, the triangle is emblematic of life, of action, even of hope, opposed to the circle indicative of a false harmony. For example, the rodeo world in THE LUSTY MEN, into which Jeff, Wes and Louise (Susan Hayward) insert a difficult, though dynamic triangle, or the saloon in JOHNNY GUITAR, at first dominated by the roulette wheels, and later "redeemed" by a number of triangular relations. In a way one feels that these obsessive and problematic triangles relate to a key situation in Ray's work, confronted most transparently in REBEL WITHOUT A CAUSE. There we see the protagonists momentarily fulfil an aspiration towards which so many Ray protagonists tend to gravitate. As soon as Jim, Judy and Plato have escaped from their homes and won an almost dream-like freedom in the deserted house, they immediately crystallize their feelings towards each other into the roles of father, mother and son. What here is the explicit theme (the "nuclear" or primary bonds) reverberates through the other films in a more or less muted form: the breakdown of the bourgeois family as a stable human organization. Perhaps it is Ray's vision of a kind of "holy family" which makes him return so constantly to the same configuration.

For even where these implications are less apparent, the triadic pattern is associated with survival and the search for some permanent value. In 55 Days at Peking, the triangular relationships between the different foreign powers, represented by Charlton Heston (US), Ava Gardner (Russia) and David Niven (Great Britain) come to stand for the will to resist and to survive the siege, juxtaposed to the even more frequent images of the circle—the water-wheel, the Imperial Palace, its circular ornaments, a plate which rolls on the floor—associated with the Boxer Uprising, mortal threats and imminent imprisonment. The most delirious use of the triangle occurs no doubt in Johnny Guitar, where all the important human relationships are triadic: Johnny-Vienna-Dancing Kid, Johnny-Vienna-Turkey, Emma-Vienna-Dancing Kid. The final showdown of the film, like a crazy ballet, is entirely organized in terms of a rapid succession of triangular positions, emphasized by the topographical pyramid formed by the hideout, with the waterfall as its base. The first figure has Johnny and the Dancing Kid on either side of Vienna, who is waiting further up at the door of the house. This is itself mirrored by the way Emma advances towards Vienna. The subsequent shot shows the two women appear at either side of the house, while Dancing Kid advances towards it from behind a rock. He is shot by Emma, and the bullet hits him in the middle of his forehead. As he falls to the ground, Ray frames him from above, his legs apart, and his feet forming a perfect triangle with the men of the posse, lined up below.

This geometrical structure is significant for the development of the themes in Johnny Guitar, as it validates the various stages of the action by resuming the emotional configurations and preparing the surviving couple, Johnny and Vienna, for their symbolic purification beneath the waterfall. The use of color, especially in the clothes, indicates the shifting roles and changing positions. Johnny is wearing the clothes of the Dancing Kid, and Vienna is in Turkey's bright yellow shirt—the legacy of two sacrificial deaths, with which they enter their new life.

At the end of The Lusty Men, as the couple walk into the sunset, a new rider comes into the rodeo. The unexpected introduction of a "third term" creates a momentum in which any sense of finality or achievement is once more suspended. The same is true of the "old man" walking to the planetarium at the end of Rebel without a Cause (played by Ray himself). In each case, the seeming repose and resolution appears merely as a transient instant of a precarious balance. Ray conveys in such scenes a harmony beyond acquiescence, for it includes the doubt of its own possibility. His heroes rebel against the structures of a social system without ever entirely breaking with it. His *mise-en-scène* detaches itself from the subordination to the plot-mechanism without ever entirely destroying the form upon which this detachment is brought to bear. In the last instance, it is perhaps this ability to articulate, in terms special to the cinema, a point of view, at once inside (the system) and outside (its limits on personal expression) that makes Ray's cinema so uniquely loved and so vitally important.

4
Sam Fuller's Productive Pathologies: The Hero as (His Own Best) Enemy

In the summer of 1969, at the British Film Institute in London, I saw a dozen or so films by Samuel Fuller, put on by Peter Wollen, in preparation for a major retrospective at the Edinburgh Film Festival later that year. Fuller was no stranger to me: I had seen THE STEEL HELMET, CHINA GATE, FORTY GUNS, MERRILL'S MARAUDERS and THE BARON OF ARIZONA (with Arab subtitles!) at the Cinémathèque in Paris the year before, and became quite obsessed with what I thought was one of the cinema's natural dialecticians, someone who not only could keep two contradictory thoughts simultaneously in his head, but actually put them in mine, by the sheer improbability of what he put on the screen.

I opted for SHOCK CORRIDOR as the film I wanted to write about for the Edinburgh booklet,[1] but also decided we should devote to Fuller a special issue of the Brighton Film Review, which I had been editing since my return from Paris in September 1968. We did so, late in 1969, publishing five lengthy film reviews, among them one on THE CRIMSON KIMONO.[2] At that time, Phil Hardy was on our editorial board and contributed a review as well. He would, the year after, write his own book on Fuller that has remained one of the standard works on the director.[3]

In 1975, Bill Nichols asked permission to include my essay on SHOCK CORRIDOR in his textbook anthology, Movies and Methods. Nichols wrote brief commentaries to all the texts he included, and in my case, contextualized the essay within the then still vigorously debated auteur *theory. He contrasted Wollen's structural-thematic approach with my own attempt to highlight stylistic features of the* mise-en-scène *as the entry point into the oeuvre of a director. I take the liberty of reproducing parts of Nichols' commentary:*

> *Whereas Peter Wollen's "Introduction" [to Sam Fuller] particularly stresses the thematic preoccupations distributed throughout Fuller's work, Thomas Elsaesser's piece on SHOCK CORRIDOR also brings a range of stylistic considerations into play. Fuller's cinema, however, is a polarized world full of intense conflict, where as Elsaesser puts it "the logic of rational inquiry becomes the logic of madness". There is little sense of the moderation or mediation that informs the work of John Ford or Howard Hawks. Characters are pushed and push themselves to the brink, where they risk the discovery that identity is madness. Fuller's stylistic extremes of very long takes, elaborate tracking shots, abrupt close-ups and spare, penetrating dialogue are elements which further examination correlate quite specifically with his thematic concerns.*

Fuller, along with Hawks, Ray and von Sternberg, is a Hollywood director for whom extensive critical analysis only followed in the wake of the auteur *theory.*[4] *Previously, his films were buried in the midst of scores of undifferentiated B-movies and back lot potboilers. His apparent political conservatism ("apparent" in Elsaesser's view of his concerns, but overt in his films' immediate impact) did not recommend him to critics looking for socially conscious films that were also liberal. His flamboyant and seemingly undisciplined style did not recommend him to critics looking for psychological depth or literate artistry. Fuller belongs solidly in the world of kitsch and popular culture, which is in no sense a judgment against him, but a warning signal that evaluative assumptions evolved out of the tradition of High Art and Social Purpose will not do.*

The analysis presented here extends the high but brief praise which Andrew Sarris accorded Fuller in The American Cinema: *"It is the artistic force with which his ideas are expressed that makes his career so fascinating. . . . It is time the cinema followed the other arts in honoring its primitives. Fuller belongs to the cinema, and not to literature and sociology." In fact, I would argue he belongs to all three, and it is the* auteur *critics who helped us discover that fact.*[5]

SHOCK CORRIDOR (1963)

One of the most distinctive features of a great number of Fuller heroes is their willingness—indeed their compulsion—to expose themselves to situations so intense that they are charged with contradiction. The Fuller hero, as it were, comes to life only under conditions of extreme physical or mental stress; he seems, and often is, on the verge of hysteria, and his mode of action betrays a kind of electric, highly explosive energy, which suggests that what is external is also internal, and that he is divided mainly against himself.

Paradoxically, the impression is that his apparent mental and emotional instability is precisely what makes him strong in will and action. I am thinking of figures like the THE BARON OF ARIZONA, Zack in THE STEEL HELMET, O'Meara in RUN OF THE ARROW, Tolly Devlin in UNDERWORLD USA, and even Merrill in MERRILL'S MARAUDERS: all live impossible situations, and knowing they cannot win, they nevertheless act with a kind of conviction, a kind of instinctive immediacy as if they were engaged in an incessant flight forward, committing themselves to a situation in whose perverseness they seem to rejoice, because they intuitively accept it as the fundamental condition of their existence. These figures always go beyond their limits. They venture into alien territory, with a kind of devoutly cynical and grimly nihilistic satisfaction. If the motto of SHOCK CORRIDOR is taken from the Greek dramatist Euripides, who in 425 BC wrote *Whom God wishes to destroy he first turns mad,* Fuller leaves little doubt that this "God" is also inside us, is part of us.

Contrary to the classical American adventure hero who experiences the external world as a challenge to the resources and the strength of his heroic individualism (the protagonists of Raoul Walsh, for example), Fuller's heroes respond to the complexity of the "real world" with a sense of inquisitiveness which often gives way to obsessive fascination. They show a scrupulous respect for the concrete uniqueness of any situation, as if—in the very strangeness of it—they recognized an aspect of their own divided selves.

However, the unfamiliar realms into which they enter are not chaotic (as is the universe into which Hitchcock lets his characters slide), but on the contrary, an evolving world of highly significant antitheses. As the action unfolds, contradiction and confusion generally shape themselves into a pattern of complementary opposites. We think of Zack cradled in the arms of the Buddha to defend himself, or of O'Meara finally shooting Driscoll in RUN OF THE ARROW. Why complementary? I think, because we have to imagine Fuller's characters as being fundamentally divided, split personalities, who experience a kind of symmetry between the situations and dilemmas imposed upon them from without, mirroring the contradictory nature of their own secret drives. It is this quality "within" which seems to form their invisible bond with the concrete circumstances and which enables them to act in what are otherwise "absurd" situations. The result is a profound ambivalence vis-à-vis their environment, in which they are at once accomplice and outsider: secretly in league with its chaos and confusion, they live this confusion consciously in the role of the traitor.

Although at first sight the dilemmas imposed on Merrill, Zack, O'Meara spring from given external situations, the logic of their actions is that of a strictly internal, existential purposiveness: the irresistible urge to go behind enemy lines, or to desert to the enemy altogether, are actions undertaken in order to discover the shape of a secret, or to accomplish a purpose, whose ultimate relevance concerns only the hero himself. At a certain point in a Fuller movie the convergence of external and internal necessity becomes axiomatic: what makes the heroes act so violently is the fact that they experience the world around them as the intolerable repercussions of an intolerable inner dilemma.

In this sense, almost all of Fuller's heroes are—to a greater or lesser extent—pathological: hysterics, neurotics or psychopaths. At the limits, there is, beneath their single-mindedness, their cynicism, their obstinacy, their megalomania, a latent, but powerfully purposive schizophrenia. Similarly, almost all of Fuller's films are "war" films, insofar as war is symptomatic of the chaos and disorder in society, and because war makes the absolute nature of an external necessity appear in its purest form.[6] Parallel to the action, we therefore witness a process in which this external necessity (the mission, the goal) is validated existentially (a search for self-knowledge). For what do these characters care about Communism, the war in Indochina or Korea, the American Civil War, the Sioux nation other than the fact that these ideologies or identities invariably permit their fight to become, after the encounter with "the enemy," a question of rescue or survival, perdition or redemption?

Indeed, the moments where the Fuller heroes are most completely under the contradictory pressure of a concrete situation are the only moments where they can live an authentic identity. This, I believe, is one of the reasons why the theme of so many Fuller movies is that of transgression and trespass—because only in this form can the protagonists live out their internal divisions. Fuller testifies to a fascination with "otherness" unequalled in any other of the great American directors. And this is not so much a concern with the outcast, the criminal, the socially under-privileged (though it may occasionally appear as such, as in PICKUP ON SOUTH STREET or UNDERWORLD USA); rather, otherness tests the existential or cultural alternatives to American and Western civilization. His heroes have the ability to expose themselves to the clash, the shock of radically different systems of values, and *act* out of a profound inner need, not merely "objectively" or disinterestedly, but with an intense subjective involvement.

Fuller, almost obsessively, returns to certain cultural opposites: Asia versus USA, Communism versus American Democracy, Black, Asiatic, Red Indian versus White. To all these opposites, Fuller puts questions: but these questions emanate from a specifically American context, and are ultimately addressed to America itself. They are dramatic self-reflections. This is obvious, for example, in the interrogation of the Korean prisoner in THE STEEL HELMET, or the conversation of the mercenaries in CHINA GATE. It is clear, therefore, that there can be no question of Fuller's heroes wanting or needing to be "objective" about, say, Communism, or their hatred for any specific group, creed or color. Indeed, I would claim that they *have* to be violently anti-Communist, racist, sexual maniacs, etc, in order to encounter the "other" on a sufficiently intense emotional level, in order for Fuller to find the definition of the American psyche across its own "others," that his cinema is after. To complain of his bias, and to expect the kind of Olympian objectivity of a Preminger or a Lang is to misunderstand completely the didactic-provocative nature of Fuller's cinema.

How is all this relevant to SHOCK CORRIDOR? It seems that SHOCK CORRIDOR gives us the mirror-image of the Fuller heroes as outlined above. In it, the submerged parts of their personality are brought to the surface. SHOCK CORRIDOR is Fuller's testament film in that it is, in a way, his own comment on his previous work. For my particular purposes, SHOCK CORRIDOR clarifies the relation of internal and external necessity, and unambiguously establishes the fascination with the "other" as a fascination with the self. The story comes from one of Fuller's favorite milieus, the one he himself grew up in: journalism, preferably of the sensationalist, muck-raking kind. Johnny Barrett, a newspaper reporter out to win glory for himself by garnering the Pulitzer Prize, hits on the idea of going undercover and simulates sexual abnormality, in order to be committed to the state mental hospital, where a murder has taken place. Successful in gaining entry, he mingles with the inmates, befriending the ones he suspects of having witnessed the crime, hoping to solve the case, which he can then write up as his story—little realizing that he might win the prize, but in getting there, lose his mind.

Whereas in the films cited above, the heroes' active identity is achieved by living disorder at its most intense under the pressure of necessity (resulting in an obsession, a maniac determination), SHOCK CORRIDOR turns the hero inside out; we see Johnny Barrett's obsession as rooted in a crisis of identity on a personal as well as on a cultural level. Johnny, trying to "make it" in society, has to go through the hell of his own self where he encounters the negative image of that society. Therefore, he is Fuller's most explicit hero, and in his fate is mirrored the inner dimension of most of them. Superficially, Johnny resembles many other Fuller heroes: committed by his job as a journalist to a precise purpose, he is prepared to brush aside all moral considerations and emotional ties, practicing the kind of (a-)morality which makes the Fuller war-hero so formidably efficient. But outside the war-situation, the "mission" inevitably changes its nature, and Johnny's objective in finding out the truth about the Sloan murder is undisguised in its intensely personal meaning.

The opening scene is a masterpiece of cinematic economy; the pan, by gradually revealing three different ontological dimensions (Johnny's schizophrenia, acted out under the approving glance of Swanee, the scam being watched in disgust by Cathy, Johnny's girlfriend) indicates the three layers of reality: the subjective/objective, the false/true, the insane/sane. At the same time, the camera describes, as it were, a spiral of decreasing involvement, which is, however, also one of increasing reflection and sanity. At the center is Johnny, filled with an intense desire to get to the truth—a-moral, irresponsible, on the way to becoming insane. On the periphery is Cathy, waking up to the implications, and equally intense in her disgust. From that moment on we know that Johnny's fate is inevitable.

Between the two stands a doctor and a newspaper editor—both socially sanctioned guardians of sanity and truth—colluding in a scheme of deceit and madness. By showing the "establishment" implicated and compromised in an act of madness and hubris, Fuller not only defines the general significance of the situation, he also gives an added moral force to Cathy's position outside. Stripper and nightclub singer, she is on the margin of society, but this position enables her to preserve a clear, humane and morally responsible perspective. In the two kinds of intensity of Johnny and Cathy we have two important aspects of the Fuller protagonist: put at the center and liberated from an external necessity, his divided self explodes into a boundless and possessed egomania; struggling at the periphery, exposed to the contradictions which the external world imposes, his (or her) perspective is often the only sane and possible one (the parallel is the role Constance Towers plays in THE NAKED KISS).

Johnny's penetration into the world of insanity is—visually—a progress towards fragmentation, in which the movement towards truth is intercut with one of subjective revelation (the frequency of tracking shots alternating with flash close-ups). The corridor becomes the supreme symbol of that urge, the geometrical line to infinity, which is also a void. In its symbolism Fuller has perfectly combined the internal and external dimension of the drama, because we cannot fail to see how the urge to penetrate to the truth gradually turns into a violent and vertiginous descent into Johnny's own self. The general thematic implications of SHOCK CORRIDOR thus become apparent: an obsession with objective truth in human affairs, the attainment of absolute certainty is itself a perversion, and can even be the expression of a deeply apocalyptic and suicidal drive. In Johnny's case, the energies of reason no longer serve the discovery of a meaningful reality, but become themselves the drives of a frenzied progression towards an abyss, culminating in the destruction of reason itself: Fuller's frames and editing style dramatize how the logic of rational inquiry becomes the logic of madness. This is nowhere more clearly in evidence than in the scene where Johnny is visited by Cathy, and surrounded by the most extraordinary scenes of misery and suffering, of which he seems entirely oblivious, he merely repeats again and again how near he is to solving the case.

Whatever the value of SHOCK CORRIDOR as an image of modern America, one of its interesting aspects is surely the way in which Fuller intimates that some of the most conscious and rational impulses of American society powerfully demonstrate the profoundly irrational nature of that society. I think, therefore, that it would be wrong to see the mental hospital simply as the reflection of some of the major social problems which haunt America: the threat from Communism, racism, the Atom Bomb. Fuller goes deeper by showing how the conscious side of America in its drives, its values and ideals is complemented by an "irrational" side which belongs intimately to these conscious attitudes—just as in Johnny he shows the deeply irrational side in the motivation of his ultra-rational, cynical (war-) heroes.

Johnny achieves what other Fuller heroes merely seem to strive for: the paroxysm of violence as the revelation of an existential truth. For in the pursuit of the Sloan murder, Johnny is groping for his own identity. As he advances, he meets more and more images of his own self and his desire to escape from his own contradictions: Stuart, Trent, Boden—all of them reflect Johnny's obsessions and his inquiry, his interviews once more evoke the situations which brought about their insanity. Each of the three witnesses—through Johnny's questions—is forced to relive his predicament: the loneliness, the isolation, the incomprehension which lies at the heart of their madness is also at the bottom of Johnny's megalomaniac desperation. The need to encounter the "other" which pushes so many of the Fuller heroes into the field of action, rebounds, turns inward and destroys the self. Johnny is exemplary of the Fuller hero, in that he is active only so long as he is a *latent* schizophrenic: his strength derives from his inability ever to live out his full identity. Thus identity, not only in war (the terrain of so many Fuller films), but also in modern America, is always close to madness.

One scene is particularly telling in this respect: when Johnny loses his voice trying to talk to Boden, Fuller contrasts the relaxed, free movement of Boden's speech, now that he has escaped from his isolation and is capable of communicating with Johnny's mounting anxiety and inward anger at not being able to ask the vital question. The discovery of the name of the murderer coincides with the finishing of the portrait—a portrait in which Johnny finally recognizes himself as he really is. It is the moment where the objective truth about Sloan reveals its necessary affinity with the subjective truth about Johnny. His voluntary course of action has assumed the form of a necessary destiny (the world of Euripides is after all not as far as one might have thought). The "relevant" truth, the moral identity, which Johnny had disguised under his rational pursuits, once established, immediately breaks the hero and propels him into madness.

In a sense, the killing of Sloan, perpetrated by Wilkes to stifle the voice of reason and humanity (Sloan wanted to denounce the illicit practices of the attendant) is paralleled in Johnny's pursuit of his desires, regardless of the suffering he inflicts on Cathy—ultimately having to "kill" their relationship in order to achieve his goal. Thus the final encounter with Wilkes becomes profoundly symbolic: Johnny here meets his alter ego, and the fury with which he attacks Wilkes is the suicidal fury of his own irrational pursuit. In the grotesque chase the pursuit of truth attains its paroxysm. The moment of final lucidity is at the same time the moment when the inherent madness of the enterprise explodes with full force, and when the wholly irrational nature of Johnny's drives bursts upon the spectator with a violence and intensity that makes its emotional logic irrefutable: the accumulated energy of frustration finds its issue in pure violence, in an apocalyptic crescendo where all the contradictions discharge themselves like the lightning does in Johnny's rain-soaked nightmare. Sometimes the price extracted in order to win, Fuller seems to say, renders the prize quite worthless to the winner.

However, such violence, born of frustration and contradiction, is typical of Fuller (see Zack shooting his Korean prisoner in THE STEEL HELMET, or Tolly Devlin's clenched fist) for it dramatically underlines the way the Fuller hero invariably overreaches himself and finds fulfilment only in excess and transgression.[7] What a terrible irony in Johnny's fate, as the paroxysm of action ends in total irreversible inaction, as his fixed idea conquers his body and condemns it to catatonic paralysis. The scene in Dr. Christo's office completes the opening one in Dr. Fong's: the simulation has become reality, and the desire for freedom has led to tragic constraint, epitomized in Trent's sarcasm about a catatonic patient looking like the Statue of Liberty.

In such a claustrophobic universe (there is not a single exterior in the whole film) the only escape is through the Eastman-color of nightmare, as the three witnesses to the murder, each rendered mad by one of America's major insanities, live their hallucinations on celluloid. The fact that these hallucinations are location material shot on 16 mm for some of Fuller's own projects—realized (HOUSE OF BAMBOO) and unrealized—make them doubly significant. For they are obviously linked (especially in Stuart's case) to the themes of Fuller's previous work. Placed in the context of SHOCK CORRIDOR, Fuller's preoccupation with Asia, Communism and racism becomes somewhat clearer in their significance: these themes represent the values of the "other," the secret longing and temptation by which the American psyche defines itself, and expiates its own crimes, while affirming desire for a freedom beyond reason and sanity. Note that in Stuart's defection to Communism, it becomes quite clear that Communism is not an ideological option, not even primarily a political one, but an existential one, which can take on quite different historical forms (in Stuart's case: the Korean war). But it could also be the American civil war, which reminds one of O'Meara, in RUN OF THE ARROW, who keeps fighting the same war over and over again. At the bottom lies a specifically American drama of solitude and self-love, of hypocrisy and bigotry and, in the case of Fuller's heroes, the desperate need to escape into a reality beyond the perpetual conflicts of America itself. In Stuart's defection the claustrophobic oppressiveness within American society is openly accused. One could quote of Fuller's films what Herbert Marcuse said of American society: "the Enemy is not identical with actual Communism or actual Capitalism—rather, it is . . . the real spectre of liberation."[8]

The Enemy, so fundamental a notion in Fuller's work, reveals himself in SHOCK CORRIDOR to be *within* the hero, for this hero bears all the scars of the society which has produced him. Madness is the state of unliveable truth, because it alone permits the extremes to persist side by side without reconciliation or mediation. The schizophrenic, traitor to reality, is the true hero of America, because he alone is "representative" by taking upon him the cross of contradiction. Thus, the courage—and, one supposes, the danger, too—of the Fuller hero lies in his desire to live the contradiction without concession, to make a bid for freedom and "liberation," irrespectively of the cost: violence, solitude and madness.

THE CRIMSON KIMONO (1959)

THE CRIMSON KIMONO, made four years before SHOCK CORRIDOR, does rely, up to a point, on the very same narrative structure: an inquiry into a murder is internally doubled by a quest for personal identity in the protagonist. Both films have thematic constants, relevant to the Fuller oeuvre as a whole, such as race and identity, or the tension between psychic and physical violence, yet the differences are telling enough to make any detailed comparison arbitrary and labored. Fuller's particular genius as a director cannot be adequately gauged by a strictly thematic analysis, although such an analysis clearly belongs to the homework of any conscientious critic. Nevertheless, it is not a director's themes that make his work important but what he makes of them—though often the evidence of a thematically consistent body of work (in the American cinema at any rate) is already proof of an artistic personality capable of imposing itself on conditions of industrial mass-production that are incompatible with individual self-expression. Thus, talking about "themes" often becomes a shorthand way of talking about a director's vision, his style and his artistic or moral concerns.

Sometimes, one can be a little more explicit, especially when it is a matter of guarding against the excessive zeal of thematic analysis. The two Fuller films mentioned above are unlike each other, thematic and structural evidence to the contrary, and it is this apparent contradiction that makes their joint discussion valuable. For their difference is not one of greater maturity—as if THE CRIMSON KIMONO was in some sense the confused forerunner of SHOCK CORRIDOR. The difference is (as always) in the *mise-en-scène*, which in the two films corresponds to a difference in purpose, movement and direction. THE CRIMSON KIMONO resolves the central conflict of its hero by progressive objectification and externalization, insofar as Joe's personal problem, namely his divided or mixed racial identity, is being finally clarified by a confrontation with the divided city, with (American) Los Angeles coming to acknowledge "Little Tokyo" (Los Angeles' Asian quarter) as a separate but integral part of itself. Insofar as it is a recurrent Fuller situation, namely that the hero has to learn to see his internal division as an external condition before he is able to live (with) it, THE CRIMSON KIMONO and SHOCK CORRIDOR are mirrors to each other, along the dividing lines of internal and external, friend and foe, individual and the collective.

Hence my reference to the *mise-en-scène*: in THE CRIMSON KIMONO the stress is on a-symmetry, centrifugal forces, with the plot full of red herrings, dramatic non-sequiturs, and an editing technique that makes both narrative and space progress in fits and starts: stylistic choices that all underline in some sense the difficult trajectory of the protagonists.[9] In SHOCK CORRIDOR, whose movement goes in the inverse direction—where a journalistic-forensic inquiry reveals itself as a progressively more personal, more intensely obsessional quest—the *mise-en-scène* exploits the concentric compositions, the strict, linear development of the story, funneling its energies along the ever-narrowing passage of an interminable hospital-cum-prison corridor.

THE CRIMSON KIMONO features two LAPD policemen, Charlie (Glenn Corbett) and Joe (James Shigeta), roommates and comrades from the Korean war, who are assigned to track down the murderer of a nightclub dancer. Their investigation leads them to Christine (Victoria Shaw), a bohemian artist, who once painted the dead girl in a red kimono, and is now willing to assist them in their detective work. As Fuller himself sums up the plot:

> Charlie, the white cop, falls for Christine first. But she prefers Joe, the Nisei [Japanese-American]. He suppresses his warm feelings for the girl because he doesn't want to betray his best friend. Furthermore, Joe is neurotic about his racial background, believing that his growing love for Christine has brought out long-buried racist hatred in his buddy. The situation explodes at a kendo sword-fight exhibition, where the two friends go at each other violently, almost getting Charlie seriously injured. With Christine's help, Sugar Torch's killer is tracked down. It turns out to be a woman who mistakenly believed her boyfriend was seeing the stripper on the sly. Joe sees a parallel between the killer's crazed behavior and his own mistaken reaction about Charlie. The two buddies are able to finally talk openly about their shortsightedness. However, their love for Christine has permanently damaged their friendship.

The picture closes at the Nisei Festival in Little Tokyo as Joe and Christine embrace in the middle of a group of Ondo dancers.[10]

Before it comes to this conventional happy ending, racism and jealousy are played off against each other several times, aggravating the officers' mutual standoff and seriously jeopardizing their assignment. One gets the sense that Fuller relished criss-crossing the dramaturgical lines between his protagonists, until every position is skewed, or thrown off kilter, by its opposite.

There is a shot, early on in CRIMSON KIMONO, which epitomizes rather well the dramatic purpose of Fuller's a-symmetric *mise-en-scène*. After Christine has given her identikit sketch of Hansel, the suspected killer, to the policemen, we know she is in danger. We see her in her apartment framed in a medium shot. Suddenly, exactly aligned with the camera, a gun appears in the foreground, pointing at the telephone. The compositional logic is compelling, since we sense immediately that as soon as the phone rings and Christine picks up—completing the visual symmetry of the scene—she will be shot. The film, as it were, can only continue, because this kind of symmetry is ultimately frustrated. But we have to feel the temptation of symmetry, before we are rescued from its consequences.

THE CRIMSON KIMONO starts with a blonde stripper, "Sugar Torch," being shot after her act, as she is running along a busy Los Angeles boulevard, half-naked, her screams all but drowned out by the noise of the passing traffic. Not only does this scene set the atmosphere for the whole film, it also strikes an essential thematic chord—the individual fate played out in the very heart of collective indifference. For the opening shot of this scene is a leisurely pan across Los Angeles at night, coming to rest and craning down on the neon sign advertising Sugar Torch's act. The garish white of the neon lights is picked up in the girl's blonde hair and white body, and the flickering of the sign has its ironic echo in her screams of fear. This is Fuller at his most concise and crisply understated, violently yoking together disparate, cruelly contradictory elements in a single visual or dramatic conception.

Two other pursuits punctuate the story. One at the end, inverting the opening scene, with the murderess being herself chased and finally killed. She, too, dies alone, in the center of a swirling group of Japanese dancers with fantastical masks. The other chase, somewhere in the middle, has Joe and Charlie, the two cops, pursuing a massive Korean whom they finally corner and manage to knock out in a monstrous fight. What stays with the viewer in this scene is not the realization that, in terms of plot and theme, the scene is all but gratuitous, but the spectacular yet also desperate way the Korean, with the bulk, force and energy of a bull, charges through the flimsy, precarious world of the Asian quarter, knocking over plywood boxes, bicycles, pots and pans, tearing down partitions, overturning billiard tables and wrecking restaurant kitchens. As it draws the protagonists bodily into the Nisei world, the action introduces the audience, in the most dramatic and economic way, into the relevant setting and environment, visually as well as emotionally. As much as the psychology and politics of race, it is the topology and physical presence of two contrasting worlds that make Joe's subsequent emotional predicament—a Caucasian woman, in love with him, a Japanese—appear authentic, highlighting why Christine is attracted to him, rather than Charlie: his diffidence and delicacy, which is also the civility and restraint of his ethnic community. By contrast, the Korean is something of an alter ego of Charlie, more assertive and macho than Joe, but also less beset by (self-)doubt.

It would be futile to demand that Charlie's potential jealousy and Joe's identity crisis ought to be linked more "organically" to the murder hunt (for which the love triangle proves to be such a distraction), because this would be asking for SHOCK CORRIDOR, which, as indicated, has an altogether inverse movement, when it aligns inner and outer world, in order to mirror and reflect each other. Joe's identity crisis is peripheral precisely because for Fuller it is the prismatic slant that illuminates the center. And to argue, as one critic has done, that the dichotomy between the US and Japan was "artificially created" because Joe's feelings of racial inferiority are merely imagined, a self-delusion, is to miss a crucial point of the film altogether: namely the contrast between an (imagined) racial conflict and the visual—as well as musical—evidence of two cultures, whose ways of life (and values) are so different that (real) racial conflict can never be entirely excluded. What could be more extraneous to the world of Sugar Torch or Mac, the drunk mural painter, than the quiet, solemn and solitary memorial service in the Buddhist temple and cemetery, observed by Fuller with such scrupulous attention to every detail of the ritual? Throughout the film this dichotomy is maintained: a subjective intensity is juxtaposed to an objective world, indifferent or hostile (Los Angeles), serene or seemingly uncomprehending (Little Tokyo). They exist side-by-side, or even one inside the other, but there is no promise of fusion, and maybe there should not be.

Therefore, on the question of race, Fuller is neither a liberal nor a racist. By relegating the very question to the level of Joe's hysterical overreaction, he makes it part of a certain emotional context, which in the film is associated with "American" Los Angeles. Joe, having served America as a soldier and sworn the oath of allegiance as a citizen, knows how much he is ultimately part of this world. Precisely because he has lost his innate contact with the "old country," because he has no attitude towards the Japanese in America, the potential jealousy of a rival can wrong-foot him racially, leaving him in ethnic limbo, and leading him to rationalize his feelings in racist terms. In this light, Fuller's radicalism appears at once more lucid and more judicious: Emotional insecurity makes one a racist—in this case, an "inverted racist"—and not pride in one's race, ethnicity or cultural identity.[11]

THE CRIMSON KIMONO draws a distinction between "race" (here, the rationalization of emotional insecurity) and "culture" (the complex mixture of traditions—Japanese nuns, white woman making Japanese dolls, white policemen playing kendo, Nisei policeman playing piano, etc.), and it is this distinction, complemented by a subjective/collective dichotomy, that provides the real underlying tension of the film. In this sense, Fuller is a demystifier of racial stereotypes, and his aim is nowhere more apparent than in the kendo fight itself, one of the highpoints of the film, as he himself pointed out.[12] What it does right away—under the uniform protective clothing that both Joe and Charlie are wearing—is to take away any physical or racial markers of identity. As the identical facemasks conceal, they also reveal what for Fuller is common to all human beings—the "honest" expression of intense emotions. In the heat of the contest, we—as audience—do not know who is the aggressor, since in terms of plot-motivation at this point, it ought to be Charlie. As it turns out, it is Joe, and thus Fuller, with one scene, dismantles a false racial dichotomy. It is at the level of basic emotions that all men are equals: "normal, jealous hate."[13] This notion is fundamental to Fuller's idea of identity (as indeed it is to his idea of the cinema)—namely, that human beings assert and affirm themselves through their emotions, their bodies and psyches *in action*. As such, the "racial hatred" issue must be treated in a "tilted" way, and Fuller twists it, by making sexual jealousy its non-identical twin. What Roma, the jealous wife, says of herself at the end, as she is dying ("so it was all in the mind") is evidently true of Joe, but with the difference that Joe can come to see what is in the mind and what in the world. The fact that he is the one who had to shoot Roma indicates not only the complementary nature of their respective delusions, but—employing a frequent trope in the genre—the hunter and hunted are kindred spirits, each seeking redemption, and purging transgressions with an act (or gift) of sacrifice. Or as Mac, the hard-bitten muralist says, in typical Fuller fashion: "Love is like a battleground, someone has to get a bloody nose."

Joe's "bloody nose" is to learn to accept his Japanese heritage as an extension of his person and not as either an intolerable straightjacket or a matter to be treated with casual indifference. Through the décor in the apartment (which in the crucial scene with Christine has a cluttered, discordant look—emphasized by the peculiar screen on the piano, at one point framed almost in close-up, radically dividing the image), Fuller's *mise-en-scène* assigns to Joe an identity as the split self he is initially unwilling to admit to. Only thanks to Christine, who—as we are clearly made to understand—is attracted to his "Asian" sensibility and artistic temperament, does he find access to that submerged part of himself, though it means going through the private hell of conflicting loyalties and nearly losing (indeed, killing) his best friend. In the closing shot, with the painted faces staring at the dying woman, the Nisei festival becomes a potent sign, not of exoticism or ethnic otherness: it is the tragic mask of a common human fate, echoing the face mask of the kendo armor. But the difference and distinctness of the two worlds is also emphasized. Solemn and sustained, it becomes the counterpoint to the lovers' kiss: Joe is ready to enter into a more complex, but freer existence.

5

Cinephilia: Or the Uses of Disenchantment

The Meaning and Memory of a Word

It is hard to ignore that the word "cinephile" is a French coinage. Used as a noun in English, it designates someone who as easily emanates cachet as pretension, of the sort often associated with style items or fashion habits imported from France. As an adjective, however, "cinéphile" describes a state of mind and an emotion that, on the whole, has been seductive to a happy few while proving beneficial to film culture in general. The term "cinephilia," finally, reverberates with nostalgia and dedication, with longings and discrimination, and it evokes, at least to my generation, more than a passion for going to the movies, and only a little less than an entire attitude to life. In all its scintillating indeterminacy, then, cinephilia—migrating into the English language in the 1960s—can by now claim allegiance of at least three generations of film lovers. This fact alone makes it necessary to distinguish between two or even three kinds of cinephilia, succeeding each other, but also overlapping, coexisting and competing with each other. For instance, cinephilia has been in and out of favor several times, including a spell as a thoroughly pejorative and even dismissive sobriquet in the politicized 1970s.[1] In the 1960s, too, it was a contentious issue, in Andrew Sarris and Pauline Kael's controversy over the *auteur* theory, when calling your appreciation of a Hollywood screwball comedy by such names was simply un-American.[2] It was the target for derision, because of its implied cosmopolitan snobbery, and the butt of Woody Allen jokes, as in a famous self-mocking scene outside the Waverly Cinema, New York in Annie Hall.[3] Yet it has also been a loyalty badge for filmgoers of all ages and tastes, worn with pride and dignity. In 1996, when Susan Sontag regretted the "decay of cinema," it was clear what she actually meant was the decay of cinephilia, that is, the way New Yorkers valued the movies, rather than what they watched and what was made by studios and directors.[4] Her intervention brought to the fore one of cinephilia's original characteristics, namely that it has always been a gesture towards cinema framed by nostalgia and other retroactive temporalities, by pleasures tinged with regret even as they register as pleasures. Cinephiles were always ready to give in to the anxiety of possible loss, to mourn the once sensuous-sensory plenitude of the celluloid image, its architectural envelope the movie theater, and to insist on the irrecoverably fleeting nature of a film's experience.

Why then, did cinephilia originate in France? One explanation is that France is one of the few countries outside the United States which actually possesses a continuous film culture, bridging mainstream cinema and art cinema, and thus making the cinema more readily an integral part of life than elsewhere in Europe. France can boast of a film industry going back to the beginnings of the cinema in 1895, while ever since the 1920s, it has also had an avant-garde cinema, an art-and-essay film-club movement and in each generation France produced notable film directors of international stature: the Lumière Brothers and Georges Méliès, Maurice Tourneur and Louis Feuillade, Abel Gance and Germaine Dulac, Jean Renoir and René Clair, Jean Cocteau and Julien Duvivier, Sacha Guitry and Robert Bresson, down to Leos Carax and Luc Besson, Cathérine Breillat and Jean-Pierre Jeunet. At the same time, unlike the US, French film culture has always been receptive to the cinema of other nations, including the American cinema, and thus was remarkably free of the kind of chauvinism the French have since been so often accused of.[5] If there was a constitutive ambivalence around the status of cinema, such as it existed in countries like Germany, then in France this was less about art versus commerce, or high culture versus popular culture, and more the tension between the "first person singular" inflection of the avant-garde movements (with their sometimes sectarian cultism of metropolitan life) and the "first person plural" national inflection of French cinema, with its love of stars, genres such as *polars* or comedies, and a vaguely working-class populism. In other words, French public culture has always been cinephile—whether in the 1920s or the 1980s, whether represented by the art historian Elie Faure or the writer André Malraux, by the television presenter Bernard Pivot or the socialist Minister of Culture Jack Lang—of a kind rarely found among politicians, writers and public figures in other European nations. A respect for, and knowledge of the cinema has in France been so much taken for granted that it scarcely needed a special word, which is perhaps why the particular fervor with which the American cinema was received after 1945 by the frequenters of Henri Langlois' Paris cinémathèque in the rue d'Ulm and the disciples of André Bazin around *Cahiers du Cinéma* did need a word that connoted that extra dimension of passion, conviction as well as desperate determination which still plays around the term in common parlance.

Cinephilia, strictly speaking, is love of cinema: "a way of watching films, speaking about them and then diffusing this discourse," as Antoine de Baecque, somewhat stiffly, has defined it.[6] De Baecque judiciously includes the element of shared experience, as well as the need to write about it and to proselytize, alongside the pleasure derived from viewing films on the big screen. Cinephilia meant being sensitive to one's surroundings when watching a movie, carefully picking the place where to sit, fully alert to the quasi-sacral feeling of the nervous anticipation that could descend upon a public space, however squalid, smelly or slipshod, as the velvet curtain rose and the studio-logo with its fanfares filled the space. Stories about the foetal position that Jean Douchet would adopt every night in the second row of the Cinémathèque Palais de Chaillot already made the rounds before I became a student in Paris in 1967 and saw it with my own eyes, but I also recall a cinema in London, called The Tolmer near Euston Station, in the mid-1960s, where only homeless people and alcoholics who had been evicted from the nearby railway station spent their afternoons and early evenings. Yet there it was that I first saw Allan Dwan's SLIGHTLY SCARLET (USA: 1955) and Jacques Tourneur's OUT OF THE PAST/BUILD MY GALLOWS HIGH (USA: 1947)—two must-see films on any cinephile's wish-list in those days. Similarly mixed but vivid feelings linger in me about the Brixton Classic in South London, where the clientele was so rough that the house lights were kept on during the feature film, and the aisles were patroled by security guards with German shepherd dogs. But by making a temporary visor and shield out of the *Guardian* newspaper, I watched the Anthony Mann and Budd Boetticher Westerns—BEND OF THE RIVER (USA: Mann, 1951), THE FAR COUNTRY (USA: Mann, 1954), THE TALL T (USA: Boetticher, 1957), RIDE LONESOME (USA: Boetticher, 1959), COMANCHE STATION (USA: Boetticher, 1960)—that I had read about in *Cahiers du Cinéma* and *Movie* magazine, feeling the moment as more unique and myself more privileged than had I been given tickets to the last night of the Proms at the Royal Albert Hall. For Jonathan Rosenbaum, growing up as the grandson of a cinema-owner from Northern Alabama, it was "placing movies" according to whom he had seen them with, and "moving places," from Florence, Alabama to Paris to London, that defined his cinephilia,[7] while Adrian Martin, a cinephile from Melbourne, Australia has commented on "the monastic rituals that inform all manifestations of cinephilia: hunting down obscure or long-lost films at suburban children's matinees or on late-night TV."[8] The "late-night TV" marks Martin as a second generation cinephile, because in the days I was referring to, there was no late-night television in Britain, and the idea of watching movies on television would have been considered sacrilege.

Detours and Deferrals

Cinephilia, then, wherever on the globe it is practiced, is not simply a love of the cinema. It is always already caught in several kinds of deferral: a detour in place and space, a shift in register and a delay in time. The initial spatial displacement was the transatlantic passage of Hollywood films after World War Two to newly liberated France, whose audiences avidly caught up with the movies the German occupation had embargoed or banned during the previous years. In the early 1960s the transatlantic passage went in the opposite direction, when the discourse of *auteurism* traveled from Paris to New York, followed by yet another change of direction, from New York back to Europe in the 1970s, when thanks to Martin Scorsese's admiration for Michael Powell, Paul Schrader's for Carl Dreyer, Woody Allen's for Ingmar Bergman and Francis Coppola's for Luchino Visconti, these European masters were "rediscovered" also in Europe. Adding the mediating role played by London, as the intellectual meeting point between Paris and New York, and the metropolis where art school film buffs, art house audiences, university-based film magazines and New-Left theorists intersected as well, Anglophone cinephilia flourished above all in the triangle just sketched, sustained by migrating critics, traveling theory and translated magazines: "Europe-Hollywood-Europe" at first, but spreading as far as Latin America in the 1970s and to Australia in the 1980s.[9] On a smaller, more local scale, this first cinephilia was—as already implied—topographically site-specific, defined by the movie-houses, neighborhoods and cafes one frequented. If displacements there were, they mapped itineraries within a single city, be it Paris, London or New York, in the spirit of the Situationists' *détournement*, circumscribed by the mid-week movie sorties (in London) to the Everyman in Hampstead, the Electric Cinema in the Portobello Road, and the NFT on the South Bank. Similar maps could be drawn for New York, Munich or Milan, but nowhere were these sites more ideologically fixed and more fiercely defended than in Paris, where the original cinephiles of the post-war period divided up the city's movie theaters the way gangs divided up Chicago during prohibition: gathering at the MacMahon close to the Arc de Triomphe, at the Studio des Ursulines in the 5é or at La Pagode, near the Hotel des Invalides, each cinema hosted a clan or a tribe that was fiercely hostile to the others. If my own experience in London between 1963 and 1967 was more that of the movie-house flâneur than as member of a gang, the first person inflection of watching movies by myself eventually gave rise to a desire to write about them, which in turn required sharing one's likes, dislikes and convictions with others, in order to give body to one's love object, by founding a magazine and running it as a collective.

However spontaneous, however shaped by circumstance and contingency, the magnetic pole of the world's cinephilia in the years up to the early 1970s remained Paris, and its marching orders retained something uniquely French. The story of the *Cahiers du cinéma* critics and their promotion of Hollywood studio employees to the status of artists and "*auteurs*" is too well known to need recapitulating here, except perhaps to note in passing another typically French trait. If in *La Pensée Sauvage*, Claude Lévi-Strauss uses food to think with; and if there is a time-honored tradition in France—from the Marquis de Sade to Pierre Klossowski—to use sex to philosophize with, then it might not be an exaggeration to argue that in the 1950s, the cinephile core of French film critics used Charlton Heston, Fritz Lang and Alfred Hitchcock, in order to theologize and ontologize with.[10]

One of the reasons the originary moment of cinephilia still occupies us today, however, may well be found in the third kind of deferral I mentioned. After detours of city, language and location, cinephilia implies several kinds of time delays and shifts of temporal register. Here, too, distinctions are in order. First of all, there is "oedipal time": the kind of temporal succession that joins and separates paternity and generational repetition in difference. To go back to *Cahiers du Cinéma*: the fatherless, but oedipally fearless François Truffaut adopted André Bazin *and* Alfred Hitchcock (whom Bazin initially disliked), in order to attack "le cinéma de papa." The Pascalian Eric Rohmer (of MA NUIT CHEZ MAUD [FR: 1969]), "chose" that macho pragmatist Howard Hawks *and* the dandy homosexual Friedrich Wilhelm Murnau as his father-figures, while Jean-Luc Godard could be said to have initially hedged his bets as well by backing *both* Roberto Rossellini *and* Sam Fuller, *both* Ingmar Bergman *and* Fritz Lang. Yet cinephilia connects also to another, equally deferred tense structure of desire: that of a lover's discourse, as conjugated by Roland Barthes: "I have loved and love no more"; "I love no more, in order to better love what I once loved"; and perhaps even: "I love him who does not love you, in order to become more worthy of your love." This hints at a third temporality, enfolding both oedipal time and the lover's discourse time, namely a triangulated time of strictly mediated desire.

A closer look at the London scene in the 1970s and early 1980s, under the aspect of personal friendships, local particularities and the brief flowering of film magazines thanks to funds from the BFI, would indicate the presence of all these temporalities as well. The oedipal time of "discovering" Douglas Sirk, the dissenting re-assessments of neo-realism, the rivalries over who owned Hitchcock: *Sight & Sound, Screen* or *Movie*. The argument would be that it was a delayed, deferred but also post-lapsarian cinephilia that proved part of the driving force behind what came to be known as *Screen* theory. The theory both covered over and preserved the fact that ambivalence about the status of Hollywood as the good/bad object persisted, notwithstanding that the love of cinema was now called by a different name: voyeurism, fetishism and scopophilia. But naming here is shaming: nothing could henceforth hide the painful truth that by 1975 cinephilia had been dragged out of its closet, the darkened womb-like auditorium, and revealed itself as a source of disappointment: the magic of the movies, in the cold light of day, had become a manipulation of regressive fantasies and the place of the big male escape from sexual difference. Yet would the torn halves ever be brought together again? Laura Mulvey's call to forego visual pleasure and dedicate oneself to unpleasure, while not always heeded, was nonetheless, within the feminist project that took its cue from her essay, remarkably productive, perhaps precisely because of its ambivalence.

The Uses of Disenchantment

These then, would be some of the turns and returns of cinephilia between 1960 and 1980: love tainted by doubt and ambivalence, ambivalence turning into disappointment, and disappointment demanding a public demonstration or extorted confession of "I love no more." Yet instead of this admission, as has sometimes happened with professional film critics, leading to a farewell note addressed to the cinema, abandoned in favor of some other intellectual or critical pursuit, disappointment with Hollywood in the early 1970s only helped renew the legitimating enterprise at the heart of *auteurism*, converting "negative" or disavowed cinephilia into one of the founding moments of Anglo-American academic film studies. The question why such negativity proved institutionally and intellectually so productive is a complex one, but it might just have to do with the time shifting inherent in the very feeling of cinephilia, which needs the ever-present possibility of disappointment in order to exist at all, but which only becomes culturally productive against the knowledge of such possible "disenchantment," disgust even, and self-loathing. The question to ask, then—to the cinephile as well as to the critics of cinephilia—is: what are the uses of disenchantment? Picking the phrase "the uses of disenchantment" is, of course, meant to allude to the book by Bruno Bettelheim,

The Uses of Enchantment, where he studies the European fairy tale and its function for children and adults as a mode of story-telling and of sense-making. What I want to borrow from Bettelheim is the idea of the cinema as one of the great fairy-tale machines or "mythologies" that the late 19th century bequeathed to the 20th, and that America, originally inheriting it from Europe, has in turn (from the 1920s up to today) bequeathed to Europe under the name of "Hollywood," from where, once more since the 1980s, it has been passed to the rest of the world.

By turning Bettelheim's title into "dis-enchantment" I have also tried to capture another French phrase: that of "déception," a recurring sentiment voiced by Proust's narrator Marcel whenever a gap opens up between his expectations or anticipations and the reality as he then experienced it. It punctuates *A la recherche du temps perdu* like a leitmotif, and the gap which disenchantment each time signals enables Marcel's mind to become especially associative. It is as if disappointment and disenchantment are in Proust by no means negative feelings, but belong to the prime movers of the memory imagination. Savoring the sensed discrepancy between what is and what is expected, constitutes the semiotic act, so to speak, by making this difference the prerequisite for there to be any insight or feeling at all. Could it be that a similarly enacted gap is part of cinephilia's productive disenchantment? I recall a Hungarian friend in London who always awaited a new film by Losey, Preminger or Aldrich "with terrible trepidation." Anticipated disappointment may be more than a self-protective shield. Disenchantment is a form of individuation: it rescues the spectator's sense of self from being engulfed by the totalizing repleteness, the self-sufficiency and always already complete there-ness that especially classic American cinema tries to convey. From this perspective, the often heard complaint that a film is "not as good as [the director's] last one" also makes perfect sense: disappointment redeems memory at the expense of the present.

I therefore see disenchantment to have had a determining role within cinephilia, perhaps even going back to the post-WWII period. It may always have been the verso to cinephilia's recto, in that it lets us see the darker side, or at any rate, another side of the cinephile's sense of displacement and deferral. In the history of film theory a break is usually posited between the *auteurism* and cinephilia of the 1950s/1960s, and the structuralist-semiotic turn of the 1960s/1970s. In fact, they are often played off against each other. But if one factors in the temporalities of love and the trepidations of possible disenchantment, then Christian Metz and Roland Barthes are indeed key figures not only in founding (semiologically inspired) film studies, but in defining the bi-polar affective bond we have with our subject, in the sense that their "I love/no longer/and choose the other/in order to learn/once more/to love myself" are the revolving turnstiles of both cinephilia *and* its apparent opposite, semiology and psychosemiotics. Disenchantment and its logic of retrospective revalorization hints at several additional reversals, which may explain why today we are still, or yet again, talking about cinephilia, while the theoretical paradigm I have just been alluding to—psychosemiotics—which was to have overcome cinephilia, the way enlightenment overcame superstition, has lost much of its previously compelling power.

Raymond Bellour, a cinephile (almost) of the first hour, and a founding figure in film studies, is also one of the most lucid commentators on cinephilia. In an essay entitled—how could it be otherwise—"Nostalgies," he confessed that what fascinated him most about the American cinema was the fact that "[right from its invention] America immediately recognized in this machine for the reproduction of reality the instrument it needed in order to invent its own reality. Its power was to instantly believe in it."[11] If America instantly believed in the cinema's reality, then this seems to me a most felicitous insight about Europe's relation to Hollywood, since clearly, we in Europe were incapable of such an act of faith. For it is around this question of belief, of "croyance," of "good faith" and (of course, its philosophically equally interesting opposite "bad faith," when we think of Jean Paul Sartre's legacy) that much of French film theory and some of French film practice, took shape in the 1970s. French cinephile disenchantment, of which the same *Cahiers du cinéma* made themselves the official organ from 1969 onwards, also helped formulate the theoretical-critical agenda that remained in force in Britain for a decade and in the USA for almost two. Central to the agenda was to prove that Hollywood cinema is a bad object, because it is illusionist. One might well ask naively: what else can the cinema be, if not illusionist? But as a cinephile, the pertinence of the problem strikes one as self-evident, for here, precisely, the question of belief arises. If you are an atheist, faith is not an issue; but woe to the agnostic who has been brought up a believer: he will have to prove that the existence of God is a logical impossibility.

This theological proof that Heaven, or cinephilia, does not exist, is what I now tend to think *Screen* theory was partly about. Its radicalism can be most plausibly understood, I suggest, as an insistent circling around one single question, namely how this make-belief, this effect of the real, created by the fake which is the American cinema, can be deconstructed, can be shown to be not only an act of ideological manipulation but an ontology whose groundlessness has to be unmasked—or on the contrary, has to be accepted as the price of our modernity. It is one thing to agree that the American cinema is illusionist, and to define what "believing in its reality" means. For instance, what does it mean to take pleasure in being witness to magic, to see with one's own eyes and ears what the mind knows to be impossible, or to experience the uncanny force of cinema as a parallel universe, peopled by a hundred years of un-dead presences, of ghosts more real than ourselves. But it is some-thing quite other to equate this il-lusion or suspension of disbelief with de-lusion, and to insist that we have to wake up from it, have to be dis-enchanted from its spell. That equation was left to *Screen* to insist on.

But what extraordinary effervescence, what subtle intellectual flavors and bubbling energy the heady brew of *Screen* theory generated in those early years! It testifies to the hidden bliss of disen-chantment (which as Bellour also makes clear, is profoundly linked to the loss of childhood), which gripped film-makers as well as film theorists, and did so, paradoxically, at just the moment, around 1975 when, on the face of it, practice and theory, after a close alliance from the years of the nouvelle vague to the early work of Scorsese, Paul Schrader or Monte Hellman, began to diverge in quite different directions. It is remarkable to think that the publication of Stephen Heath's and Laura Mulvey's famous articles coincides with JAWS (USA: Steven Spielberg, 1975), THE EXORCIST (USA: William Friedkin, 1974) and STAR WARS (USA: George Lucas, 1975–77)—films that instead of dismantling illusionism, gave it a fourth dimension. Their special-effect hyper-realism made the term "illusionism" more or less obsolete, generating digital ontologies whose philosophical conun-drums and cognitive-perceptual puzzles still keep us immersed or bemused. Sadly, for some of us, the time came when students preferred disbelieving their eyes in the cinemas, to believing their teachers in the classroom.

Cinephilia, Take Two

It is perhaps the very conjuncture or disjuncture between the theoretical tools of film studies and the practical film experiences of students (as students *and* spectators) that necessitates a return to this history—the history of cinephilia, in order to begin to map the possible contours of another cine-philia, today's cinephilia. For as already indicated, while psychosemiotics has lost its intellectual lustre, cinephilia seems to be staging a comeback. By an effect of yet another act of temporal displace-ment, such a moment would rewrite this history, not only creating a divide, but retrospectively obliging one to differentiate more clearly between first generation cinephilia and second generation cinephilia. It may even require us to distinguish two kinds of second generation cinephilia: one that has kept aloof from the university curriculum and kept its faith with *auteur* cinema, with the cellu-loid image and the big screen, and another that has found its love of the movies take very different and often enough very unconventional forms, embracing the new technologies, such as DVDs and the internet, finding communities and shared experiences through gender-bending *Star Trek* episodes and other kinds of textual poaching. This fan cult cinephilia locates its pleasures neither in a physical space such as a city and its movie-houses, nor in the "theatrical" experience of the quasi-sacral space of audiences gathered in the collective trance of the big screen film performance.

I shall not say too much about the cinephilia that has kept faith with the *auteur*, a faith rewarded by that special sense of being in the presence of a new talent, and having the privilege to communicate such an encounter with genius to others. Instead of discovering B-picture directors as *auteurs* within the Hollywood machine, as did the first generation, these cinephiles find their neglected figures among the independents, the avant-garde and the emerging film nations of world cinema. The natural home of this cinephilia is neither the university nor a city's second-run cinemas, but the film festival and the film museum, whose increasingly international circuits the cinephile critic, programmer or distributor frequents as flâneur, prospector and explorer. The main reason I can be brief is not only that my narrative is trying to track the interface and hidden links between cinephilia and academic film studies. Some of the pioneers of this second generation cinephilia—the already mentioned Jonathan Rosenbaum and Adrian Martin—have themselves, together with their friends in Vienna, New York, San Francisco and Paris, mapped the new terrain and documented the contours of their passion in a remarkable, serial publication, a daisy-chain of letters, which shows the new networks in action, while much of the time recalling the geographical and temporal triangulations of desire I already sketched above.[12]

Less well documented is the post-*auteur*, post-theory cinephilia that has embraced the new technologies, that flourishes on the internet and finds its *jouissance* in an often undisguised and unapologetic fetishism of the technical prowess of the digital video disc, its sound and its image and the tactile sensations now associated with both. Three features stand out for a casual observer like myself, which I would briefly like to thematize under the headings "re-mastering, re-purposing and re-framing."

Re-mastering in its literal sense alludes, of course, directly to that fetish of the technical specification of digital transfers. But since the idea of re-mastering also implies power relations, suggesting an effort to capture and control something that may have got out of hand, this seems to me to apply particularly well to the new forms of cinephilia, as I shall try to suggest below. Yet re-mastery also hints at its dialectical opposite, namely the possibility of failure, the slipping of control from the very grip of s/he who wants to exercise it. Lastly, re-mastering also in the sense of seizing the initiative, of re-appropriating the means of someone else's presumed mastery over your emotions, over your libidinal economy, by turning the images around, making them mean something for you and your community or group. What in cultural studies came to be called "oppositional readings"—when countering preferred or hegemonic readings—may now be present in the new cinephilia as a more attenuated, even dialogical engagement with the object and its meaning. Indeed, cinephilia as a re-mastering could be understood as the ultimate "negotiated" reading of the consumer-society, insofar as it is within the regime of universalized (or "commodified") pleasure that the meaning proposed by the mainstream culture and the meaning "customized" by the cinephile coincide, confirming not only that, as Foucault averred, the "control society" disciplines through pleasure, but that the internet, through which much of this new cinephilia flows, is—as the phrase has it—a "pull" medium and not a "push" medium.[13]

One of the typical features of a pull medium, supposedly driven by the incremental decisions of its users, is its uncanny ability to *re-purpose*. This, as we know, is an industry term for re-packaging the same content in different media, and for attaching different uses or purposes to the single product. It encompasses the director's cut, the bonus package of the DVD with its behind-the-scenes or making-of "documentaries," as well as the more obvious franchising and merchandizing practices that precede, surround and follow a major feature film release. The makers of THE MATRIX (USA:

Andy & Larry Wachowski, 1999) or Lord of the Rings (USA: Peter Jackson, 2001–3) already during the filming have the computer game in mind, they maintain web-sites with articles about the "philosophy" of their plots and its protagonists, or they comment on the occult significance of objects, character's names and locations. The film comes with its own discourses, which in turn, give rise to more discourses. The critic—cinephile, consumer guide, enforcer of cultural standards or fan—is already part of the package. Knowledgable, sophisticated and expert, this ready-made cinephilia is a hard act to follow, and harder is it now to locate what I have called the semiotic gap that enables either unexpected discovery, the shock of revelation or the play of anticipation and disappointment which I argued are part of cinephilia take one, and possibly part of cinephilia *tout court*.

This may, however, be the jaded view of a superannuated cinephile take one, unable to "master" his disenchantment. For there is also *re-framing*, referring to the conceptual frame, the emotional frame, as well as the temporal frame that regulates the DVD or internet forms of cinephilia, too. More demanding, certainly, than selecting the right row in the cinema of your choice for the perfect view of the screen, these acts of re-framing require the ability to hold in place different kinds of simultaneity, two different temporalities. Most striking about the new cinephilia is the mobility and malleability of its objects, the instability of the images put in circulation, their adaptability even in their visual forms and shapes, their mutability of meaning. But re-framing also in the temporal sense, for the new cinephile has to know how to savor (as well as to save her sense of identity from) the anachronisms generated by total availability, by the fact that the whole of film history is henceforth present in the here-and-now. Terms like "cult film" or "classic" are symptomatic of the attempt to find ways of coping with the sudden distance *and* proximity in the face of a constantly re-encountered past. And what does it mean that the loved object is no longer an immaterial experience, an encounter stolen from the tyranny of irreversible time, but can now be touched and handled physically, stored, replayed and collected, in the form of a videotape or disk? Does a movie thereby come any closer, become more sensuous or tangible as an experience? In this respect, as indeed in several others, the new cinephilia faces the same dilemmas as did the old one: How to manage the emotions of being up close, of "burning with passion," how to find the right measure, the right spatial parameters for the pleasures, but also for the rituals of cinephilia, which allow them to be shared, communicated and put into words and discourse. All these forms of re-framing, however, stand in yet another tension with the dominant aesthetics of the moving image today, always seeking to "un-frame" the image, rather than merely re-framing the classical scenic rectangle of stage, window or painting. By this I mean the preference of contemporary media culture for the extreme close-up, the motion blur, wipe or pan, and for the horizon-less image altogether. Either layered like a palimpsest or immersive like a fish-tank, the image today does not seek to engage the focusing gaze. Rather, it tries to suggest a more haptic contact space, a way of touching the image and being touched by it with the eye and ear. Contrast this to the heyday of *mise-en-scène*, where the art of framing or subtle reframing by directors like Jean Renoir, Vincente Minnelli or Nicholas Ray was the touchstone of value for the cinephiles of the first generation.

Cinephilia take one, then, was identified with the means of holding its object in place, with the uniqueness of the moment, as well as with the singularity of sacred space, because it valued the film almost as much for the effort it took to catch it on its first release or its single showing at a retrospective, as for the spiritual revelation, the sheer aesthetic pleasure or somatic engagement it promised at such a screening. On all these counts, cinephilia take two would seem to be a more complex affair involving an even more ambivalent state of mind and body. Against "trepidation in anticipation" (take one), the agitation of cinephilia take two might best be described by the terms "stressed/distressed," having to live in a non-linear, non-directional "too much/all at once" state of permanent tension, not so much about missing the unique moment, but almost its opposite, namely about how to cope with a flow that knows no privileged points of capture at all, and yet seeks that special sense of self-presence that love promises and sometimes provides. Cinephilia take two is therefore pain-fully aware of the paradox that cinephilia take one may have lived out in practice, but would not finally confront. Namely that attachment to the unique moment and to that special place—in short, to the quest for plenitude, envelopment and enclosure—is already (as psychoanalysis was at pains to point out) the enactment of a search for lost time, and thus the acknowledgment that the singular moment stands under the regime of repetition, of the re-take, of the iterative, the compul-sively serial, the fetishistic, the fragmented and the fractal. The paradox is similar to that put by Nietzsche in *Thus Spake Zarathustra*: "doch alle Lust will Ewigkeit" ("all pleasure seeks eternity"), meaning that pleasure has to face up to the fact of mortality, in the endless repetition of the vain attempt to overcome it.

Looking back from cinephilia take two to cinephilia take one, it once more becomes evident just how anxious a love it had always been, not only because we held on to the uniqueness of time and place, in the teeth of cinema's technological change and altered demographics that did away with those very movie-houses which were home to the film lover's longings. It was an anxious love, because it was love in deferral and denial: already in the 1960s we preferred the Hollywood films from the 1940s to the films made in the 1960s, cultivating the myth of a golden age that some cine-philes have since transferred to the 1960s themselves, and it was anxious in that it could access this plenitude only through the reflexiveness of writing, an act of distancing in the hope of getting closer. It was, I now believe, the cinephile's equivalent to the sort of *mise-en-abyme* of spectatorship one finds in the films of early Godard, such as the movie-house scene in Les Carabiniers, where Michel-Ange wants to "enter" the screen, and ends up tearing it down. Writing about movies, too, was trying to seize the cinematic image, just as it escaped one's grasp. Once the screen is torn down, the naked brick wall that remained in Godard's film is as a good a metaphor for the disen-chantment I am speaking about as any. Yet cinephilia take two no longer has even this physical relation to "going to the movies," which a film as deconstructive, destructive and iconoclastic as Les Carabiniers still invokes with such matter-of-factness. Nowadays we know too much about the movies, their textual mechanisms, their commodity status, their function in the culture industries and the experience economy, but—equally important, if not more so—the movies also know too much about us, the spectators, the users, the consumers. The cinema, in other words, is that "push" medium which disguises itself as a "pull" medium, going out of its way to promote cinephilia itself as its preferred mode of engagement with the spectator: the "plug," in Dominic Pettman's words, now goes both ways.[14]

Cinephilia take one, I suggested, is a discourse braided around love, in all the richly self-contradictory, narcissistic, altruistic, communicative and autistic forms that this emotion or state of mind afflicts us with. Film studies, built on this cinephilia, proceeded to deconstruct it, by taking apart two of its key components: we politicized pleasure, and we psychoanalyzed desire. An impor-tant task at the time, maybe, but not a recipe for happiness. Is it possible to undo the damage and once more become innocent? Or to reconstruct what, after all, cinephilia take one and take two have in common, while nonetheless marking their differences? The term with which I would attempt to heal the rift is thus neither pleasure nor desire, but memory, even if it is no less contentious than either of the other two. At the forefront of cinephilia, of whatever form, I would argue, is a crisis of memory: filmic memory in the first instance, but our very idea of memory in the modern sense, as recall mediated by technologies of recording, storage and retrieval. The impossibility of experience in the present, and the need to always be conscious of two temporalities, which I claimed is funda-mental to cinephilia, has become a generalized cultural condition. In our mobility, we are "tour"ists of life: we use the camcorder in our hand or often merely in our head, to reassure ourselves that this is "me, now, here." Our experience of the present is always already (media) memory, and this memory represents the recaptured attempt at self-presence: possessing the experience in order to possess the memory, in order to possess the self. It gives the cinephile mark two a new role, maybe a new cultural status even, as collector and archivist, not so much of our fleeting cinema experiences as of our no less fleeting self-experiences.

The new cinephilia of the download, the file-swap, the sampling, re-editing and re-mounting of story line, characters and genre gives a new twist to that anxious love of loss and plenitude, if we can permit ourselves to consider it for a moment outside the parameters of copyright and fair use. Technology now allows the cinephile to re-create in and through the textual manipulations, but also through the choice in media and storage formats that sense of the unique, that sense of place, occasion and moment so essential to all forms of cinephilia, even as it is caught in the compulsion to repeat, and its place is cyberspace. This work of preservation and re-presentation—like all work involving memory and the archive—is marked by the fragment and its fetish-invocations. Yet fragment is here understood also in a special sense. Each film is not only a fragment of that totality of moving images which always already exceed our grasp, our knowledge and even our love, but it is also a fragment, in the sense of representing, in whatever form we view or experience it, only one part, one aspect, one aggregate state of the many, potentially unlimited aggregate states by which the images of our filmic heritage now circulate in culture. Out there, *the love that never lies* (cinephilia as the love of original, authenticity, of the indexicality of time, where each film performance is a unique event), now competes with *the love that never dies*, where cinephilia feeds on nostalgia and repetition, is revived by fandom and cult classics, and demands the video copy and now the DVD or the download. While such a love fetishizes the technological performativity of digitally remastered images and sounds, it also confers a new nobility on what once might have been mere junk. The new cinephilia is turning the unlimited archive of our media memory, including the unloved bits and pieces, the long forgotten films or programs into potentially desirable and much valued clips, extras and bonuses: proving that cinephilia is not only an anxious love, but can always turn itself into a happy perversion. And as such, these new forms of enchantment will probably also encounter new moments of dis-enchantment, re-establishing the possibility of rupture, such as when the network collapses, the connection is broken or the server is down. Cinephilia, in other words, has reincarnated itself, by dis-embodying itself. But what it has also achieved is that it has un-Frenched itself, or rather, it has taken the French (term) into a new ontology of belief, suspension of disbelief and memory: possibly, probably against the will of the "happy few," but hopefully, once more for the benefit of many.[15]

II
Genius of the System

6

The Persistence of Hollywood, Part I:
The Continuity Principle

The Cinema is Dead, Long Live the Cinema

The cinema is dead, the cinema has never been so popular; the cinema has disappeared as a public sphere, the cinema has never been so ubiquitous. Audience figures in the US and in many European countries have rallied from their historic lows in the 1980s and are holding steady, but in India and Asia they have sometimes more than doubled in the past twenty years. Neighborhood cinemas and art houses are closing, but cineplexes and multiplexes are being built in and around most major cities, often in combination with vast shopping malls and next to giant entertainment and leisure centers.

To these apparent contradictions, one can add that in the year of the cinema's centenary in 1996, Susan Sontag had declared the cinema irreversibly decaying,[1] echoing the 1980s, when staunch supporters of the "New Hollywood" had anxiously asked themselves "who killed Hollywood?"[2] A decade earlier, in the 1970s, it was Jean-Luc Godard who had pronounced the cinema dead ("fin du cinéma"), mixing relief, anxiety and despair, notably about the fate of French cinema, always deemed a reliable index for all of cinema. In other words, for at least the last thirty years, it has been widely assumed that demographic factors, new entertainment media and a combination of megalomania and mismanagement among the Hollywood studio executives meant that the bell had tolled on an industry as well as an art.[3]

There were good reasons for thinking that Hollywood the dream-factory had become, like ship-building in Scotland, coal-mining in the Ruhr or car-manufacture in England, an obsolete industry. Due to the rise of television the family audiences stayed at home, teenagers preferred rock music venues and discos to Westerns or musicals, and eventually, the big film studios were sold off to property speculators, undertakers and oil-tycoons. The competition between Europe and Hollywood—almost as old as the cinema itself—had even briefly shifted in favor of Europe: audiences over twenty-five, if they decided to go to the movies at all, generally preferred art cinema and (American) *auteur*-films over commercially motivated mainstream productions.

This preference was also reflected in the scholarly writing about the cinema, beginning in the early 1960s and making its entry into the university by the mid-1970s. In fact, as suggested in previous chapters, the study of cinema as an academic discipline was built on what now turns out to have been the premature burial of Hollywood: academic film studies in the 1970s were a paradoxical mix of nostalgic celebrations of past glories and impatient calls for a radical break, whose deconstructive passion still registered an intense sense of loss, as it conducted its thorough post-mortem on the American cinema.

The "death of the cinema" and the loss of innocence—not of the movies, but of us, its cinephile critics—was turned into a sharp ideological critique of Hollywood: its illusionism masquerading as psychological realism, its voyeurism masquerading as spectacle, its gender inequality masquerading as romantic comedy. Against the background of the cinematic "new waves" between the 1950s and 1980s in almost every country,[4] the film theory imported from France "deconstructed" Hollywood, regardless of whether a film was directed by John Ford (YOUNG MR LINCOLN), Alfred Hitchcock (SUSPICION), Orson Welles (TOUCH OF EVIL) or George Lucas (AMERICAN GRAFFITI). Hollywood became the incarnation of a system that passed off as pleasurable a world put up for ocular possession through its images: images, furthermore, seen through the distorting lens of sexism and the narcissistic mirror of patriarchy and the male gaze.

Why Hollywood—a Question that Persists?

Given this evidence, Hollywood should by rights no longer exist, at least not as an object of serious academic study. And yet it does, more than ever: what is it, then, that has allowed the American cinema to recover from its crises and confound its critics, as much in the present as it did in the past? Is it the high-tech of sound and image production, is it the stars and their celebrity glamor, is it the skill and know-how of its storytelling, with its serial variations on familiar adventure-stories, fairy-tales and heroic myths, or is it mostly the amounts of money invested? No doubt, all of the above applies, but in what relation to each other, and with what causal force of each of the determinants (given that these qualities or properties have been present throughout, and therefore cannot account for the doomsday scenarios of imminent demise)?[5]

That money has been a key factor is undeniable: both the money that goes into the making of a blockbuster production—often sums inconceivable to ordinary mortals—and the money that is clocked up—first over the single opening weekend, then once the prints circulate around the globe, and finally as DVDs and downloads, on television or on other distribution platforms—is of such a magnitude that it keeps any potential competitor at a respectful distance. When popular formulas are recycled as sequels or prequels, such as INDIANA JONES (1981–2009; dir: Steven Spielberg), SHREK (2001–10; Andrew Adamson et al.), ICE AGE (2002–6; R: Chris Wedge, Carlos Saldanha), or when they live to see another day as franchises: JAMES BOND (since 1962 and still going strong), the BATMAN series (since 1980; Tim Burton et al.), HARRY POTTER (since 2001; Chris Columbus et al.) and THE LORD OF THE RINGS (2001–3; Peter Jackson), then it seems undeniable that the creative forces which Hollywood the talent-factory undoubtedly possesses, tend to lend themselves most happily to being harnessed to Hollywood the money (making) machine.

But the money factor is not all there is. In 1972, at the first height of the crisis, I asked myself "why Hollywood?" and offered an answer of sorts: the linear, goal-oriented narrative, the sublimation of human desire and the drives into purposive action, the spectrum of genres and their division-of-labor complementarities, the formal resources of *mise-en-scène* marshaled to create unity out of diversity and seeming contradiction: they all seemed to point to a "classical" art form, intimately connected to both ancient drama and the bourgeois novel. This pedigree of universal genres, generations of craftsman technique and individual talent working together to create a major art of quasi-mythological self-representation and modernist self-reflexivity—remarkably in tune with its moment in time, that is, with social upheavals and the nation's history—was, as indicated, under siege and on the defensive. By making an appeal to my erstwhile cinephile comrades-in-arms, I was ignoring neither their political critique ("bourgeois individualism," "patriarchy") nor the economic arguments ("multi-national capitalism," "cultural imperialism") put forward by those who refused to see either the artistry or the mythology for the money and the ideology. It just seemed to me that art and money, creative collective achievements and great concentration of economic power had often gone hand in hand, whether in Egypt at the time of the Pharaohs, the Athens of Pericles and the philosophers, the Catholic Church at the turn of the first millennium, or Rome, Florence and Venice in the days of the Borgia, the Medici and the Doges.

In 2011, revisiting this question of "why Hollywood," I am both less defensive and less confident that I still have the right answer. To begin with, the argument for seeing Hollywood as a "classical" art, capable of great formal complexity, reflexivity and lasting beauty, has been made—more convincingly by others than myself.[6] Second, the critical condemnation of mass-entertainment as mass-deception is now more part of post-68 intellectual history than a burning issue. Even when not seen as a quaint prejudice from another age, the academy as much as society at large has recognized in the products of popular culture legitimate forms of aesthetic expression and even granted popular music, television and the movies the power to mobilize "progressive" energies. The battle between high culture and popular culture has, for the time being, been decided in favor of the latter, not least by recognizing the point just made, namely that high culture achievements since the 16th century were as much dependent on money and power and driven by self-display and propaganda as commercial art and popular culture—spearheaded by the cinema, radio and advertising—has been in the 20th century.

At any rate, the debate is no longer framed in these terms, which, however, does not mean that it is over. The critique of Hollywood now belongs to a conservative rather than a progressive discourse: are we "amusing ourselves to death," as Neil Postman asserted, or is "Hollywood and Popular Culture waging War on Traditional Values of America" as Michael Medved averred?[7] A "postmodern" view would put it more ambiguously or ironically: Hollywood films are the fakes we love to make authentic, the virtual worlds we like to inhabit, the fantasies that fascinate us even as they make our hair stand on end. As the mind-expanding drugs we do not want to do without, they are not subject to the same reality-test as, say, advertisements or political discourse, and if they were, it would be "reality" that is found wanting, rather than the movies.

But this easy play with paradox may also have had its day: now liberals as well as conservatives are more concerned with the very existence of a public sphere, molded so relentlessly by "the media": among signs of increasing polarization, of political niches and religious sects fragmenting the fabric that holds together allegiance to the nation with loyalty to the secular state, there is now the worry that the media purposely intensify these divisions by segmenting their respective "markets" while stoking controversy for controversy's (and the ratings') sake. The cinema is no longer the medium of greatest concern, no more than it is the choice for the family audience. Having become the projective surface of a youth audience perpetually in the larval stages of mutation and transition, it seems hardly in a position to counter the fraying of the social contract, or make a convincing case for being part of what constitutes the "common good."

Yet precisely for reasons of its global audiences, and the universalism upon which its appeal is predicated, Hollywood often tests the values professed in (American) public life more critically and more acutely, legitimating the points of view of the rebel, the outsider, the marginal and the misfit, and putting them in a permanent if oblique dialogue with the consensus. The late work of Clint Eastwood—from MYSTIC RIVER, via MILLION DOLLAR BABY to GRAN TORINO—would be a good example of such a complex engagement with controversial and unconventional public issues of the nation, the community, private morality and the outsider, by a Hollywood insider and couched in generic Hollywood formats that are resolutely "classical."

On the other hand, the sheer economic prowess of Hollywood financially and its presence in so many of the world's entertainment "markets" (music, television, toys, computer games, magazine publishing) has made it increasingly apparent that we also need a deeper analysis and a better history of Hollywood's political economy, with or without the particular ideological agenda that drove such critiques in the 1970s. The gaps in these areas have given rise to a number of different scenarios, ranging from the various theories of cultural imperialism ("McWorld," "Cocacolonization") and the history of cooperation between the US State Department and the film industry ("trade follows the movies," "America's soft power") to differentiated accounts of how the global markets in audiovisual products and services are being managed and controlled via the multinational conglomerates situated in Los Angeles, New York, Toronto and London ("Global Hollywood," "Screen Traffic," "Hollyworld")[8] as well as the new synergies between Hollywood, the military and the computer software industries ("the military-entertainment complex," "the electronic baroque").[9]

Elsewhere in this volume, I outline several factors that I think begin to explain both the ruptures and continuities in the historical development of Hollywood, stressing that even the "death" of Hollywood is a "cyclical" prediction, usually indicating a major change in either the mix of media technologies sustaining and surrounding the cinema, or in the legal-institutional frameworks that embed Hollywood so deeply in American society and the fabric of its national self-perception. These factors are multiple: they are irreducible to a single explanation, and yet, my main thesis will be that it is the constantly shifting, inherently contradictory combination of "product" and "services" Hollywood provides, which it finances and turns into profit, that best accounts for the economic cycles, the peaks and troughs, as well as the nature of the creative input from producers, directors, screenwriters, sound-designers, cinematographers and visual and audio effects specialists.

Yet on these questions of how to explain Hollywood—whether to emphasize the continuities and recurring patterns, or to highlight the significant turning points and changes—the scholarly field is sharply divided: there are those for whom it is "business as usual," and those who see a significant break, not only with the emergence of the blockbuster and the "package deal" (generally recognized as short-hand terms for a range of transformations in the "product/service" equation), but with the entire system that sustains Hollywood filmmaking as both an economic-industrial and a symbolic-textual practice. The "rupture" faction tends to speak of "new economy," "neo-classical" or "post-classical" Hollywood, while those who insist on the continuities stick with "Hollywood" and "classical cinema."[10] Hollywood's global pre-eminence, too, has given rise to spirited debate. There are those for whom this question is part of a larger one, which goes beyond Hollywood's cultural imperialism, and touches on the 20th century as the "American Century,"[11] on the nature of the United States as an "Empire,"[12] while being both engine and vehicle of "globalization," that is, affecting and affected by the increased and accelerated circulation of goods, services, human labor, bodies and lives.[13] There are those who try to analyze the particular "culture industry" which is Hollywood, but from the "cultural geography" perspective of place and placelessness, as much as from the socio-economic vantage point of "post-Fordist" industrial practices of outsourcing and the vicissitudes of finance capitalism.[14] And there are even some who take the longer, quasi-anthropological view: asking what contribution or difference the hundred years of cinema and Hollywood have made to the "progress" of mankind—"why does the cinema exist?" alongside the question "why Hollywood?"[15]

In the by now substantial literature devoted to both Hollywood and to cinema as a phenomenon that defines the 20th century, several sets of arguments tend to recur, besides the case for and against Hollywood hegemony: the importance of place, and the "clustering" of talent, skill, amenities and facilities in one particular location; synchronicity between the peaks of American power in the 20th century and Hollywood's own cycles of world success; the extent to which globalization and new technologies impose a different dynamic of feedback and amplification between Hollywood, its audiences and its overseas markets; the manner in which the cinema affects, intervenes, models and re-formats the human body and the senses.[16]

Among these—often divergent and even contradictory—ways of examining the puzzling question of the persistence, periodic revivals or fundamental robustness of Hollywood, the present collection of essays concentrates on five: one, Hollywood as a cultural phenomenon of transnational and global dimension, highlighting the critically, theoretically and emotionally ambivalent reception in Europe via the *auteur* theory (France and Britain); two, Hollywood's paradoxically effective-efficient mode of representation, its way of telling stories that is highly abstract and formulaic, as well as supremely physical and sensuously specific, combining a universalizing deep-structure with a particularizing surface texture; three, given the United States' economic hegemony and political supremacy, the contributions made to Hollywood by foreigners, outsiders and eccentrics is remarkable; four, the salient features of the transitional period in Hollywood's recent history, when both "authorship" and "system" experienced major realignments and redefinitions; five, the adaptability and resilience of this representational mode and the industrial-institutional frameworks that sustain it, in light of the changes between "classical" and "post-classical" Hollywood.

The first part of this chapter passes in review the question "why Hollywood?," while the second part opens out in the direction of the more "anthropological" approach, where, as just indicated, the answer to be sought is less "*why* Hollywood cinema?," nor "when is Hollywood *cinema*?" (as opposed to Hollywood being merely one element within US audiovisual entertainment), but something more like "why is the cinema (still) *Hollywood*?," not just for the world's mass audiences, but also for those interested in cinemas other than Hollywood). The answer will be sought in the particular forms of reflexivity, recursiveness and self-reference that Hollywood has always manifested, in the many films explicitly set in Hollywood and about "the picture business," from WHAT PRICE HOLLYWOOD (1932) and A STAR IS BORN (1937) to SULLIVAN'S TRAVELS (1941) and SUNSET BOULEVARD (1950), from SINGIN' IN THE RAIN (1952) and THE BAD AND THE BEAUTIFUL (1952) to THE PLAYER (1992) and WAG THE DOG (1997), in the auto-reflexive films (perhaps too exclusively credited to the *auteurs* featured in the essays here assembled), but also as strategies of self-regulation and audience-address, as ways managing a whole array of dynamic interfaces and feedback loops which can be analyzed either economically, from the perspective of struggles over power and control between producers and audiences, or semiotically, as control over meaning and interpretation, and ranging between what I have called "access for all" and "world-making."[17]

The Continuity Principle

To anticipate on the point about audiences: it is important to remind oneself that ever since the early 1920s, Hollywood has been not just a (national-international) industry, but also the world language of moving pictures, whose narratives, iconography and modes of narration were developed initially very quickly, but then refined and stabilized themselves over decades. Momentum for change and adaptation, and momentum tending to inertia and equilibrium either alternate in cyclical fashion, or they show signs of quasi-Darwinian evolution: long periods of stasis, interrupted by brief bursts of cataclysmic transformation. One consequence of thinking of Hollywood cinema in these terms is that periodization becomes a problem, as does identifying the determining forces that bring about change, when it does occur: federal legislation, victory in the Second World War, technological innovation, different business models and accounting practices, internal shifts of power between producers, talent agents and stars are among the contenders for driving change on the side of the industry, against the power of demographics, state censorship, age-related trends in fashion and taste, patterns of consumption and life-style on the side of its (domestic) audiences. The wildly differing nature of the forces just enumerated are a good indicator, in that they accurately reflect what it is that makes Hollywood such a difficult but also fascinating topic of research and object of study, even if one is not a cinephile or a movie fan: namely the irreducibly dual status of Hollywood motion picture-making as at once an art form and an industry, a secular mythology and a business model, a service provider and a propaganda instrument, a universally popular medium and a particularly rewarding—albeit risky—generator of (financial) profit, (cultural) prestige and (social) power.

On the other hand, "change" in Hollywood has often been in the service of keeping things the same. "Continuity" is thus an overdetermined word in the Hollywood vocabulary, because it helps to describe, but also to disguise the many discontinuities, breaks and antagonisms that not only char-acterize its "mode of signification" (its filmic language of "realism" and "continuity editing") but also its "mode of production" (its organizational structure and division of labor, around analytic modu-larity and re-assemblage). "Continuity" stands behind this mass medium whose secret it is to be both extremely stable and highly adaptable, and it is through the contradictory dynamic of its different "continuity-systems" that Hollywood wields part of its political-ideological power, to complement its economic-industrial power.

However, Hollywood is not a monolith, either in its historical development, or in its internal functioning. It is the ongoing drama or spectacle of how so many divergent forces are held together, are forced together or are made to fuse together, that I want to signal with the term "continuity." Some of the discrepancies are of quite a fundamental nature; others are troublesome mainly to the academic analyst. Among the first, one apparent disparity or contradiction is, as indicated above, whether one should think of Hollywood quite generally as providing "goods" or "services." If the former, is the product "material" or "immaterial"; if the latter, what are the relations—and inner tensions—between the different "branches" of the film business: production, distribution, exhibi-tion? How is this question of goods versus services affected by such new technologies of commodifi-cation as the DVD, by new attractions, such as IMAX or D-3-D or by such new forms of distribution and exhibition as the Internet download and the streaming video to a mobile phone?

A case in point: if Hollywood movies are part of a service industry, what exactly are its uses, benefits and applications? Hollywood's global reach affects both internal and external power rela-tions; it may tilt them, as we shall see, by giving its global spectators a different, more active role in the differently situated feedback circuits. But the effect might also be more indirect. Thus, one of the services Hollywood is providing, thanks to its ubiquity and universal appeal, is a certain *sociability* and *connective tissue*: when people meet for the first time, or in chance encounters in a train or on a plane, sooner or later, they talk about movies.[18] The popular mainstream cinema, its stories and stars have become a kind of lingua franca, a sort of "common currency" with which young and not so young people communicate with each other, share experiences and get to know each other. A movie (along with the movie-standard HBO-output of US television) lets people find out about each other's likes and dislikes; it is a test of someone's sense of humor, basic values and attitudes to life. Not least because one's reaction to a film is something personal, even intimate, it is a kind of barom-eter, and yet at the same time, it can create a sense of belonging and of sharing: "American popular culture tends to be popular when people interact with others from around the world and seek markers of global identity."[19]

A related paradox of the cinema as a cultural force today is that an extremely self-centered and narcissistic interest in the moving image on the big screen exists side by side with the equally explicit social dimension which I just alluded to. Much of Hollywood is about "me": questions of identity, coming of age, role modeling and role reversal. This has to do not just with the age bracket of the target audience, but with a legitimate and necessary interest in ourselves. The social dimension reflects an equally legitimate and necessary interest in seeing and testing ourselves within the world of others. While a film often enough acts as a sort of flattering mirror image to our idealized selves, the activity of "going to the cinema" involves us in communities: loyal communities of fans and followers, instant communities across language barriers and geographical boundaries, and imagined communities across shared fantasies and aspirations. Going to the movies has become a way of participating in public space and using the cinema as a site of pleasures for which the film itself may be merely one element among others, rather than the sole "attraction," yet without the big screen, the heart would have been ripped out of the communal experience.[20]

There is another paradox: although we know that the cinema does not deal in reality, it can sometimes touch us as one of the most real and intense experiences of all the realities we are likely to encounter. The moving image has a special kind of power to carry us along, and it is still the case that mainly Hollywood seems to possess the secret of the magic formula: emotion comes from motion and the movies move us. American cinema is a bodily experience and a sensory-kinetic encounter, as much as it is a quest, rite of passage, an uplifting, moral (or depressingly cynical) journey. European and Asian films, too, can generate intense experiences. But why so few of them lend themselves to the same kind of shared physical experience is a question I can merely note in passing.[21]

A further aspect where product and service are complementary, but also in conflict, is notoriety and ubiquity: one of the most notable features of Hollywood film culture is the sheer visibility of the cinema, but also the way in which certain films have become more than a film. Movies, both contemporary and classic, are the reference points and metaphoric registers in all manner of public and personal contexts, their (often eponymous) protagonists becoming iconic figures or proverbial examples of vice or virtue, if one thinks of "Dirty Harry" (1971), "The Godfather" (1972), "Tony Montana" (from SCARFACE, 1983), "Hannibal Lecter" (from SILENCE OF THE LAMBS, 1991), or "The Joker" (in the BATMAN films, 1989 onwards). Films are not just a way of spending time watching beautiful or ruthless people do nice, evil or dangerous things: their fully realized, fleshed out and detailed milieus have become emotional environments, mental worlds and imaginary habitats in which to live and breathe and where one encounters others. The cinema is no longer a window onto the world, as it has tended to be in its first century; it now behaves more like a door or portal to other, parallel, totally impossible but also thoroughly familiar worlds. Is this a service, allowing us access through the mind and the senses, or is it a product, in the sense of creating a material-immaterial abode for restless spirits and homeless bodies? These worlds are self-enclosed and self-sufficient, yet by virtue of the universality of their visual language and narrative grammar, they are paradoxically open to all and accessible at all times.

In this respect, the most problematic but also most telling aspect of the potential disconnect between products and services is the status of the film as a commodity. Where once one paid for the pleasure of a seat and a view, in order to enjoy a crafted and regulated segment of time, the videocassette and subsequently the DVD have given the consumer the physical object, now containing the locked and stored piece of time, irrespective of seat and view, that is, occasion and event. It has not only shifted the balance between public and private, between the cinema as forum for public debate and the cinema as a private passion or even furtive vice; it has also brought films into closer comparison with the music CD and the printed book, signaling a different relation to ownership and possession and not only to memory, the moment and presence. A blockbuster release still trades on its time- and location-advantage in order to gain a window of attention and accumulate recognition value, but its commercial value accumulates and is increasingly determined by its extended presence in other (no less reified) forms.

Another a-symmetry or bifurcation may thus have opened up which film history has begun to reflect and to conceptualize: that between the history or "life of the cinema" and the history or "life of films," with the latter entering into a period of paradoxical mutation. At the same time as the cinema began to become the academic discipline of "film studies," by treating films as authored texts, analogous to literature and the other arts, the cinema experience has increasingly tended towards the status of "event"—manifest most strongly in the emergence of the blockbuster, known in the business as "event-movie," with all that this entails. Film-as-text and film-as-event stand in considerable conceptual tension to each other, but both apply to Hollywood. As several of the chapters in this volume will show, spectacle and narrative are not as inimical to each other as has sometimes been alleged, nor can they be fully integrated with each other. The linear, one-directional flow of the narrative feature film that is so typical of classical Hollywood cinema nonetheless also has properties that are the very opposite of flow, responding more to an iterative or fractal principle of organization: one of the great virtues of Hollywood films especially during the studio era was that you could "enter" the performance or screening almost at any point, and immediately "orient" yourself in its world, which is to say: find your way in the story, among the characters and settings—exactly as one might orient oneself in a building or house, and not at all in the way one is carried along by a piece of music or forward-rushing narrative. Today, on the other hand, as narratives have become more complex, more "modular," with separate strands or storylines, loosely connected or branching off into forking paths, it becomes more difficult to "enter" in mid-action, as it were, but also, to "take it in" in one sitting. Instead, the audience is encouraged to re-see the film, to repeat the experience, but this time under the controlled and controllable conditions of the DVD, where the viewer can freeze, rewind, fast-forward or consult the various supplements, bundled together under the generic term "bonus material" and provided as "extras": with the consequence that the extras and bonuses can take over the film as the primary object of attention, reversing the relation once more, at the expense of the "text" and in favor of contexts, paratexts, sub- and intertexts.

The onus would be on film studies—the subject born out of a love of, as well as disenchantment with the cinema, as I argued in a previous chapter—to try and understand these paradoxes that hide not only inside the persistence of Hollywood and its dominance on the world market,[22] but also within its continuity principle, understood in the double sense: as "continuity editing," the body of techniques by which to render invisible the inherent discontinuity of time and space, and to establish a causal coherence out of succession and contiguity, but continuity also as "the show must go on" resisting change while implementing change; living with disruption and contradiction, while weaving them into a coherent whole; adapting to new technologies, while keeping the experience the same; practicing amnesia while celebrating one's history. Under similar circumstances, other national cinemas (or rather, other national film industries, notably in Europe), have fared so much less well, even though presumably possessing just as much talent, and in principle at least, just as much money (if profits could be made with movies). Turned around, one can say that while cinema has been produced in almost every country in the 20th century, it is nonetheless the American art par excellence, like tragedy was for the Greeks, the medieval cathedrals were the expression of both Europe and the Catholic Church, or the still life, the portrait and paintings of domestic interiors were the peculiar art of the Dutch Golden Age. It is what justifies the adjective "classical" to be attached to Hollywood, and to concur with André Bazin about the "genius of the system."[23]

7

Why Hollywood?

Let us destroy cinematic form, so that falling snow is once again falling snow.
(anon., Canada, 1970)[1]

Aesthetics and Ideology

Once the case against Hollywood is no longer made by citing the producers' economic stranglehold imposed on stars and directors with studio-contracts and package deals, nor on the grounds of censorship and prohibited subjects, or of monopolized distribution methods squeezing out the independents, then perhaps it should be phrased as an objection based on genuinely aesthetic principles. The appeal cited in my motto above implicitly tries to do this by challenging the way physical reality (and ephemerality) figures in the traditional Hollywood studio movie. By implication—possibly punning on the name of an avant-garde filmmaker—it contests an entire approach to the representative and mimetic properties of the cinematic image, as these have been understood, with on the whole increasing but not unlimited sophistication, by Hollywood filmmakers during the last fifty-five years of film history.[2]

That a critique of Hollywood's film language can be a meaningful polemical exercise is not in question. Jean-Luc Godard was scarcely the first director to make films which are also commentaries on their own genesis and which offer a critique of the tradition he both inherited and challenged. Yet the "destruction" of certain formal conventions does not by itself make the cinema an instrument of social change, or a weapon in the political struggle. At the same time, one can recognize that a particular form may contain assumptions which are neither purely aesthetic nor ideologically neutral. An aesthetic critique of the Hollywood cinema, for instance, poses two problems of a general nature. First, what is the "reality status" of the image which the film, by virtue of its form or genre, itself implies; and second, what is the relation between a given artistic form (in the case of Hollywood: fictional realism) and the kind of truth it implicitly asserts or explicitly articulates? That both these aspects are relevant to a critique of Hollywood is obvious, when one considers how often it is despised for being a dream-factory, and thus judged inauthentic on aesthetic grounds, and on the other hand, how it is attacked for its ideological mystifications, and thus judged inauthentic on the grounds of (extra-aesthetic) reality or history. My argument will be that the "reality status" of

Hollywood cinema is almost invariably marked in the films themselves as being "non-objective," and that the realism to which Hollywood is committed is an emotional and subjective one, not a phenomenological one, open to site-inspection. In other words "falling snow" in a Hollywood movie (say, in John Ford's CHEYENNE AUTUMN) is also "snow falling": observed by someone, to whom it matters, and we as audience understand why it matters; its perceptual presence is both motivated and meaningful.

The problems raised by a formal or aesthetic attack on Hollywood picture-making are therefore not without interest. Yet what yesterday's critics who argued in the name of high culture (deploring Hollywood's crass commercialism and rank sentimentality) and today's ideological critics (who denounce Hollywood's formal conventions as reactionary propaganda) have in common is, I suspect, that neither group has been unduly concerned with trying to understand Hollywood as a cultural phenomenon in its own right. This would seem to be, however, a precondition of judging its aesthetic merits as well as its social function.

The Classical Tradition

When in the following, I speak of the American cinema and try to define its classical tradition, I refer above all to films made between the 1940s and the early to mid-1960s. This may be an arbitrary restriction, and although imposed partly by my own personal preferences, I nonetheless feel it to be a representative period. It comprises Hollywood at a time when the major technical innovations—sound, color, cinemascope—had for the most part already become assimilated as integral parts of the expressive capacities of its filmmaking, while the industrial organization was still that of the studio-system. For the period under consideration, the filmic language evolved in the late teens and early twenties by D.W. Griffith, Cecil B. de Mille, Erich von Stroheim and F.W. Murnau still retained its validity as the syntactical basis, whatever modifications it underwent in the 1930s and early 1940s in terms of sound-effects, montage and camera-movements (such as the use of dolly, crane-shots and deep-focus photography in, for instance, CITIZEN KANE or GONE WITH THE WIND). This tradition embraces on the one hand the best work of second-line directors, such as William Wellman, Don Siegel, Allan Dwan, Jacques Tourneur, William Wyler, Delmer Daves, and among the great directors, includes the films of John Ford, King Vidor, Raoul Walsh, George Cukor, Vincente Minnelli, Otto Preminger, Douglas Sirk, Joseph Losey, Nicholas Ray, Anthony Mann, Bud Boetticher or Samuel Fuller.

The list may be long, but it is not infinite. There comes a point even in the American studio product, where aesthetic seriousness or artistic purpose is no longer discernible, though even below that level, there are still a huge number of films with moments not devoid of interest. At the other—top end—of the scale, I consider that Joseph von Sternberg, Orson Welles, Alfred Hitchcock, Fritz Lang and, to a lesser degree, Howard Hawks have produced films which, for a variety of reasons, fall outside the mainstream as I see it. This does not mean that PSYCHO, FURY or RED RIVER are incomprehensible within the framework of the traditional American cinema, far from it: yet what makes these films so exceptional lies more in the directors' individual personalities, their vision of the cinema, than in the technical and expressive means which they share with others. One might say that the great directors within the tradition have created and formulated the standards for their fields and genres. Thus, for example, Ford, Mann and Boetticher dominated the Western in the 1950s; Minnelli, Kelly and Stanley Donen gave shape to the musical; Walsh specialized in the adventure film and made some of the best gangster movies; Leo McCarey, Frank Capra, Frank Tashlin and George Cukor, have defined the potential of sophisticated comedy; Preminger, Cukor, Sirk and Minnelli together explored most successfully the melodrama in color and cinemascope.

The other group, except for Hawks and Lang, have created their own genres, and with them, their own standards.[3] But they all have in common a far more explicitly intellectual, analytic approach to the medium, in which the classical tradition is reflected obliquely, or reformulated altogether. This, however, does not mean that their films are better than those produced by the mainstream, nor that their films are good by virtue of their "breaking the rules." Rather, in order to do justice to their work, one has to shift one's critical perspective, as one has to, in each case, for European directors such as Luis Buñuel, Godard, Ingmar Bergman or Michelangelo Antonioni. It is inevitable, therefore, that my generalizations deal with only a tiny minority of the overall production of Hollywood, and yet the point is that even the exceptional film is still representative of the system, while even the most mediocre product still shares the formal assumptions and partakes in the professional practice of the masterpiece. Even if as little as one percent of Hollywood's total output deserves close critical discussion, this would still leave—on a year in, year out basis—more consistently great films than one could claim for the production of all other filmmaking countries taken together. This is a singular achievement in any art.

A fundamental challenge the critic of the American cinema encounters is to find criteria by which, first, to describe a certain, on the whole remarkably homogeneous and consistent practice of this cinema, and thus to describe how American films "work"; and second, to find criteria by which nonetheless to evaluate individual instances of this practice, that is to say, to be able to differentiate among a vast body of films, on the basis of distinctions that are inherent and pertinent. As a result, there have been a limited number of essentially related approaches among serious film-critics in the last ten years to the Hollywood cinema. Briefly, these focus on the question of authorship, of who "in the last resort" is responsible for the aesthetic qualities and formal coherence of a film; coupled, but also dialectically juxtaposed to the question of authorship as the function of genre, that is, in what sense and to what extent American mainstream films are dependent on the established conventions and the iconography of certain genres: the Western, the gangster movie, the musical, the war-film, comedy, melodrama. Third, in line with the argument with which I began, critics have been trying to define what kind of unique visual language the American cinema represents, and how it uses cinematic images in a formalized discourse. Only with these issues clarified does it make sense to ask in what social and cultural context the American cinema operates—does it "reflect" social reality or "mystify" it, and what does it mean to say that it presents a "purely emotional" appeal to its audience?

Obviously, it is impossible here to go into all these questions in detail, or even to summarize the debate as it now stands. What I would like to do, is to reformulate some of these questions in terms of minimal conditions which seem to me to apply to the vast majority of Hollywood films, and which would allow one to determine more clearly a movie's formal qualities and aesthetic merits. I am aware that this may sound like an attempt to define a normative aesthetic, where everything that does not fit the proposed categories is rejected. This is not the intention, even though the classical Hollywood tradition is clearly in some sense "normative." I can only hope that by dealing with a particular period, and a body of films already recognized as historically representative, I am not unduly speculative about the future of the American cinema in general, nor trying to construct an ideal film. However, my view is that a "good" film is a form of visual narrative that possesses coherence, inner consistency and a purpose, all of which can be discovered, described and assessed. In other words, if a film is meaningful, it can be shown to be so, and its style will be a matter of relating means to meaning. Where the relationship can be shown to be neither necessary nor consistent, ideological criticism will have leverage, but so will aesthetic judgment. Yet as Roland Barthes pointed out: "the import of a work of art is that it puts sense in the world, not a sense." The question is, therefore, how do we discover what kinds of sense an American movie puts in the world, when it complies with the formal criteria of a classical work, such as dramatic unity, compositional coherence and a demonstrable relation of stylistic means to subject matter? Basically, I am trying to find out what elements contribute towards overall aesthetic unity in a Hollywood picture of the period under discussion; what use does it make of phenomenal reality in its symbolic system; what types of aesthetic pleasure or satisfaction does it offer; what ideology does it embody, and how does it validate this ideology rhetorically?

A Psychological Cinema: Drama, Novel or Music?

The American cinema is organized along fairly precisely calculated lines, which are evidently economic and industrial, but to a significant degree also social and cultural. I am here only concerned with the latter, though all are evidently interrelated. Two things characterize this American cinema most distinctly: first, it is an exclusively narrative cinema, that is, its primary concern is with telling a story and representing in fictional terms certain human situations and experiences. Its structural constants are dramatic conflict and narrative progression, leading via complication to a formal resolution. Without these, no Hollywood movie would ever leave the cutting-room.

Second, it is a psychological cinema, based on both representing and on arousing emotions. One might also say, borrowing Brecht's terminology, it is Aristotelian and not epic. Yet what it means in its simplest form is that a Hollywood film can, and does for one-and-a-half to two hours, hold an audience's undivided and empathetic attention. Louis B. Mayer allegedly judged films by whether his bottom started to ache before the lights went on again or not. In his habitually crude way, the chief of MGM thereby indicated that a good movie, one that he was putting his money in, should activate certain psychological processes—of identification, of emotional engagement, psychic participation or imaginative projection; furthermore, that these processes constitute part of the aesthetic meaning of a film, and fall within the control of those who make it. These are elementary points, but they are easily forgotten. To what extent this psychological-narrative structure characterizes the American cinema ideologically as a bourgeois cinema is something that is currently the object of vigorous discussion. One of the consequences which I draw from the fact that the traditional Hollywood movie is narrative and psychological is that it excludes certain other categories of filmmaking, and thus renders largely irrelevant such aesthetic criteria as have been formulated for the documentary, the didactic tract, whether scientific or political, the home movie, whether shown to friends or in a cinema, ciné-vérité and experimental cinema. To demand of Hollywood that it is Snow is thus a category mistake.

Once one has defined what kind of cinema it is not, perhaps one can agree about the critical terminology which might be most appropriate to the object under consideration. For example, I believe that neither the phenomenological vocabulary of André Bazin nor the concepts of structural anthropology or linguistics and information theory can be applied directly. If one has to choose a certain terminology, I would say that, given the dual characteristics of narrative and psychology, literature and music still seem the most appropriate arts to compare the classical cinema with. What historically and sociologically corresponds perhaps closest to the aesthetic experience and artistic form of the greatest Hollywood movie in the 1950s and 1960s is—all proportions guarded—the narrative fiction, as exemplified by the 19th century novels, whether romantic, realist or naturalistic. Regarding the depiction of character, the relation of people to their environment, the dramatic devices and plot-construction, the American cinema owes a great deal to the work of Walter Scott, Honoré de Balzac, Charles Dickens, Leo Tolstoy and even Emile Zola. In other respects, however, notably its overall structure, its semantics, its duration in time, its emotive effect and dramatic line, its elements of audience participation, the movie approaches rather more romantic and post-romantic music, for instance that of Hector Berlioz, Anton Bruckner, Franz Liszt, Frédéric Chopin or Richard Wagner. This analogy is obviously not intended as a value judgment, implying that Frank Capra's MR. DEEDS GOES TO TOWN equals Balzac's *Les illusions perdues*, or that a Preminger movie is worth a Bruckner symphony. I merely want to draw attention to some aesthetic features of the American cinema which hitherto have been neglected in the general debate.

The most relevant implication of the parallel with music is the shift from manifest content of a film to an appreciation of the non-figurative, non-referential aspects of a film, where the subject-matter can be seen as only one element in a more varied concert of elements formalized into a discourse. That the classical cinema is a formalized discourse has been recognized by almost all film-criticism, even where the underlying assumptions differ. Parker Tyler, for instance, concluded that despite its manifest inadequacies, the literary analogy best serves this recognition: "What is actually needed by film-criticism, sadly enough, is a handbook in which film craft is 'translated' into literary craft, so that at least a lucid linguistic system can enable one to 'read' the ABC of film craft correctly and not by semantic 'equivalents.'"[4] Similarly, when speaking of the "conventions" of a genre, we are alluding to a film's stylization and codification of dramatic elements and visual details, and thus to a pre-existing system. It seems to me, however, that this impression of a systematic practice extends beyond, and indeed across the genres, as a general characteristic of the American cinema, at once exceeding the traditional arts that one might invoke by analogy and redefining the basis—economic, technological, ideological—in which such "conventions" are grounded in the cinema, and which do not to the same degree apply to the fine arts or literature. Partly owing to its nature as a capital-intensive industry, Hollywood has always aimed at a certain optimum degree of conformity to dominant economic practices in its methods and means of production. Writing a script seems often a question of assembling in different, but recognizable combinations a given number of common or near-identical elements—of subject, situation or character—not unlike the engineering blueprint of industrial production. But this affects mainly the structure, not necessarily the significance of the finished film. More importantly perhaps, the codification of stylistic elements implies that a given action sequence, besides playing its denotative role in the progressive unfolding of the narrative and its connotative role in building up a character's psychology, can also have a more or less precisely specified "melodic" function, giving the narrative its inner tensions, distinctive rhythm and energy reverberations. It will depend on the spectator's own sensibility whether he can distinguish between the fleet-footed rhythm in a Minnelli film and the heavily orchestrated rhetorical flourishes of a David Lean.

The analogy with literary fiction, on the other hand, can also draw attention to the middle-of-the-road character as a mediating consciousness in many a Hollywood film, a stand-in Everyman, who functions rather like the protagonists in the historical novels of Walter Scott, Dickens or Stendhal, with whose baffled observer status the reader is meant to identify, in the face of such momentous events as the Border Wars, the French Revolution or the Battle of Waterloo. A character like O'Meara in Fuller's RUN OF THE ARROW, Eddie in Minnelli's COURTSHIP OF EDDIE'S FATHER or Bowie in Ray's THEY LIVE BY NIGHT have an "eccentric" perspective on the events in which they are involved, forcing the audience to keep two viewpoints simultaneously in mind. One could invoke Georg Lukács' distinction between "narrate" and "describe," defining the former as typical for Balzac or Tolstoy, in contrast to Zola:

> we experience events which are inherently significant because of the direct involvement of the characters in the events and because of the general social significance emerging in the unfolding of the characters' lives. We are the audience to events in which the characters take an active part [which is why we] ourselves experience these events.[5]

Similarly, Hollywood storytelling qualifies as "narration" because, however ordinary the protagonist's social status or intelligence, the spectator is given access to events through a character's consciousness, however partial or limited this might be.

Both the musical and the novelistic analogy, however, ought not to be taken too far. They help prevent too literal an interpretation of a Hollywood movie in terms of its story-line and subject-matter ("description") or its referential realism (the "reality status" of the image), drawing attention not only to the subjective dimension of narrated action, but also to such formal features as the dramatic patterns of symmetry or repetition, as they emerge from the successive conflicts between characters, the creation and manipulation of visual space, the rhythm of the action, its action set-pieces and climaxes in relation to its *temps morts* (an extreme, and therefore perhaps not altogether typical example of the classical mode is the dramatic rhythm of Peckinpah's THE WILD BUNCH, which presents a succession of dramatic anti-climaxes). Other significant elements are complex camera-movements, composition and framing—Fritz Lang's tracking-out from a close-up to a medium shot which relates a detail to its setting or startlingly recontextualizes a character to his environment; the way Nicholas Ray signalizes an inner conflict of a character by unbalancing the architectural composition of the frame; Otto Preminger's pans that lose a central character in a space too vast for his control or comprehension; Fuller's track-in-track-out sequences like the reloading of repeater rifle; Anthony Mann's and Budd Boetticher's crane-shots, or Sirk's use of vertical camera movements to indicate a moral context of rise or fall. Each of these directors has a particular, though in its means often quite standardized and not necessarily innovative manner of dramatizing and at the same time interpreting a situation—unobtrusively giving a comment that is, above all, integrated into the narrative action itself. Finally, there is a director's handling of the "persona" of a star which inflects meaning by creating difference: Hawks' and Ford's remarkably distinct use of John Wayne, for instance, or Billy Wilder's directing of Marilyn Monroe in SOME LIKE IT HOT, which manages to both undercut and reinforce pre-established expectations, in order to convey better the innocent knowingness of her shrewd naivety. All these elements are implied when one speaks of a director's *mise-en-scène*. It follows from this that the style of the film, understood to include its *mise-en-scène* defined as that which controls how a film signifies by its form, is logically prior to, but also inseparable from what is being signified and communicated: meaning follows form which comments on the content.

Authors and Genres

It also means that as a critical audience, we have to attain a certain level of abstraction in our viewing habits, and to learn to see significant units where previously one might have had the impression of mere repetition, psychological obtuseness, lack of verisimilitude and random accumulation of action. On the other hand, this is a dangerous recipe to advocate, because there is indeed repetition, simplistic characterization and stock dramatic clichés in the classical cinema, not always redeemed or redeemable by *mise-en-scène*. Just because one can name the director, not every B-feature by Michael Curtiz, Burt Kennedy or Roger Corman must therefore have the kind of controlled pace and subtle dramatic rhythm of a Ford, or the diversity of visual invention and layering of meaning of a Hitchcock or Lang. Such excesses of the *auteur* theory are only avoidable if the hunt for consistency of themes in a director's work is supplemented by a careful investigation of the thematic constants across the genres in the American cinema as a whole, and if the zeal for detecting an individual directorial style is matched by a thorough knowledge of the "zero-degree" of Hollywood directorial style, and if the search for a film's meaning is more evenly spread over criteria other than themes and their generic variations, and lastly, regarding *mise-en-scène*, if not everything that is merely unusual or startling, is immediately claimed to be profound.

Although I have invoked a certain level of abstraction I might add that this does not mean an "intellectualization" of the American cinema, but rather the reverse, namely a way of talking intelligibly about precisely the non-intellectual aspects of American movies and their aesthetic significance. As a general rule, in order to judge what an American movie is worth, one ought to have some idea of the relation in which style and form stands to subject and themes, which of course implies that one can also recognize those instances—even in good films—where a theme is only partially visualized on the screen, or a conception only imperfectly translated into action. In this context, it is pertinent to ask oneself whether a good film need necessarily always have a personal style. *Auteur* critics in the past have often accepted this as axiomatic, though it creates the well-known problem of the good film made by an otherwise undistinguished director. Instead of talking about a personal style which belongs to a particular director, one perhaps ought also to be able to speak of a film's specific style, which means that a film will invariably reflect a specific approach of the *mise-en-scène* to its theme, that is, show evidence that the material has been worked out in specifically cinematic terms. Such cinematic specificity may sometimes be drawn from the conventions of a genre, reflect the flair of a particular studio and crew, be owed to the felicitous dialogue or well-plotted structure of the screenplay, but it will always need a competent director, though not necessarily a directorial personality, which is why the French have added the designation of *metteur-en-scène* to complement the categories and differentiate him from the *auteur*.

Richard Fleischer's Violent Saturday is an excellent example of a film which triumphs by its minimalism, transparency and economy of the generic means: a certain visual efficiency imposes itself far more strongly than Fleischer's potential for being considered an *auteur*. Indeed, the attraction of the 1950s B-picture as a distinct practice is the extraordinarily terse and compact way in which restrictions of budget or pared-down décor do not prevent them from telling their story. As such they are object-lessons in the art of a certain functional cinematic narrative, and demonstrate how in Hollywood sheer technical competence—often by a skilful use of editing techniques and montage effects—could body forth its own style, characters and moral codes. The sense of fatalism, of inevitability and of apocalyptic despair which characterizes the *film noir* thriller in the late forties and fifties, with its aura of black romanticism, pervasive corruption, and its drive for self-destruction, is perhaps as much the consequence of a montage-based type of visual logic (whose causality operates on the "post hoc ergo propter hoc" principle of action as process-progress, focused on essentials also through tight shooting schedules), as its glistening back-streets at night, fawn raincoats and sinister looking men in hats seem a hangover of German Expressionism tempered by the virtues of American reportage. If a director endorsed the material constraints as part of the assignment of a project, the conjunction of low-rent genre and high-productivity nonetheless put a great number of pre-defined or ready-made elements—formal, pictorial, thematic—at his disposal. The strictly limited set-up left him free to exercise his talents of observation, of visual imagination, giving his images a flexible frame of reference by their poetry of the unexpected detail. Working in Hollywood has meant for the director in the classical mold that instead of expressing individuality through personal themes, he could express personality through disguising it in universal themes.

For much of Hollywood history, it was the genres which provided the artistic form without which the story was often nothing but a verbal message. Genres forced directors to reflect upon the specific language of their medium, and to develop a code whose virtues were efficiency, formal elegance, precision and simplicity. They developed an aesthetic functionalism whose aim was perfect legibility, and only second, the individual flourish. Yet it seems in retrospect that because a studio-produced Hollywood movie in the 1940s and 1950s combined what are essentially "technocratic" values of an engineering aesthetic with a basically humanist, liberal narrative tradition, certain moral and social concerns have always been implicitly affirmed, as the felt presence of a cultural sensibility often of great subtlety and intuitive truth.

One effect of a new generation of directors coming from television, is that the screenwriter's pleasure of devising a complex plot, such as that of The Big Sleep or Out of the Past, which the director would give a sober, pared-down and matter-of-fact visual treatment, seems to have been lost. Owing to the small-screen image—or perhaps to the influence of the *auteur* theory itself giving directors an inflated self-image that requires "self-expression," the relation seems to have been inverted, and basically simple plots receive a baroque and ornate elaboration, without there being the dramatic or thematic necessity for such flashy stylistic touches. Since the mid-1960s, mainstream films seem to strive after effect with the use of the zoom lens, split-screen, slow-motion and soft-focus. Where once a director sought psychological depth by concentrating on the natural dynamics of the action, the director of Bullitt now has the camera placed on the floor in order to shoot a scene through Steve McQueen's legs.

The extent to which the studio-system and the work within genres, imposed on the director stylistic restraint which nonetheless gave him an identity as an *auteur* can perhaps most clearly be seen in the career of Joseph Losey. After he left Hollywood, Losey took ten years to develop a directorial style both personal and specific, working within the genres (of British cinema) at the same time as he helped transform them. During this time he made films in England that were unmistakeably constructed and shot in the manner of a Hollywood movie. From The Sleeping Tiger to Blind Date and The Criminal, Losey was working on films in which he could express himself only in the oblique, but nonetheless highly effective stylization of a genre-director. Since The Servant and Eve he seems to have paid the price of inventing an English *auteurism* as well as reap its rewards, for he has been experimenting with new modes of cinematic expressivity in a way a Bergman or Buñuel never had to experiment, however important the changes that have occurred in their view of the cinema as well. Losey's career is unique and yet symptomatic. Many Hollywood directors, who during the last decade have, by choice or by necessity, become independent, seem today like exiles in their own country, cut off from the cinema they knew, and forced into the perilous realms of experiment. Only few have, like Losey, avoided shipwreck, survived and made it to new shores. Even such an old hand as Otto Preminger, who epitomized the independent producer-director after the break-up of the studio-system, when he made films like Anatomy of a Murder, Exodus, Advise and Consent, appears to have temporarily lost his bearings with Skidoo! or Such Good Friends—films intended to please new audiences, but placed in an exhibition no-man's land.

The Classical System: Aesthetic Unity and Formal Coherence

From the position which I have taken, the question of artistic value in the classical system revolves to a large extent around the notion of aesthetic unity and formal coherence—as do, in a way, the questions of authorship and genre. There seem to be several ways in which the classical Hollywood movie contrives to be coherent. Most importantly, it is through the unity of action. Because of its nature as a narrative genre, the American cinema creates a universe which is governed by a certain fundamental dramatic logic. Like the woof of a carpet, an Aristotelian dramatic logic holds together the fictional world, and allows other thematic and moral patterns to emerge. To put it schematically, Hollywood rigorously respects and adheres to a first-level verisimilitude, in which any change of time, of place and action, as well as of a protagonist's goal or purpose is internally motivated, and communicated to the audience through a cinematic language primarily destined to follow, as closely as possible, the dramatic, causal and psychological exigencies of the action. As Walsh has said, there is only one way in which to shoot a scene, and that's the way which shows the audience what's going to happen next. Any consideration of the value of the *mise-en-scène* must in consequence be based on recognizing the primacy of the dramatic continuum over other factors (such as directorial self-expression or stylistic self-display), since whatever point—moral, intellectual, emotional—the director cares to make, he will have to ensure that it does not violate the transparency of his story-line. We can see at once the place and importance of the aesthetic virtues outlined above, namely efficiency, sobriety, elegance and simplicity as the condition sine qua non of classical Hollywood movie-making: they alone provide a film's formal coherence, precondition of any expressive or thematic potential.

This does not mean that every film needs to have a chronologically linear narrative continuum—the more and more elliptical handling of the narrative in certain recent American films, flashback and voice-over narration, and the anti-dramatic narratives of directors influenced by European cinema disprove it. Yet whenever the illusionist logic of the temporal-spatial unity is altogether abandoned, the individual image radically changes its status, and both its syntagmatic (narrative-linear) place and its paradigmatic (metaphoric-parallel) use are fundamentally altered. While European directors of the nouvelle vague, such as Godard, or the surrealist Luis Buñuel have thrived on the break-up of the single time-space continuum or never felt the need to adhere to it, for the American cinema, this rupture in the first-level coherence of its fictional world upsets the communicating vessels between internal and external reality, threatening the link between body, drive and action.

To put it paradoxically, one might say that in the American cinema, it is the apparent autonomy of the events and situations vis-à-vis the characters, the illusion of a real world "out there," which allows a Hollywood director to use story and intrigue psychologically for the rendering of an otherwise inaccessible or inarticulate subjectivity, and "abstractly" for the elaboration of a meta-language or critical commentary. As Erwin Panofsky pointed out in his essay on "Style and Medium in the Motion Picture,"[6] the radically different conception of cinematic language by comparison with literary language makes it possible for a bad story to furnish a good film and vice versa (which was also a key point in the argument against the "cinéma à papa" of the *Cahiers du cinéma* critics).

A second type of unity, closely related to the dramatic unity of action, is the unity provided by the conventions of the genre. Traditionally, critics often proceeded from the notion that genre is first of all a descriptive category which producers and audience share, such as the Western or the musical, and whose function it is to serve as a classification of production, thereby creating a relatively stable horizon of anticipated pleasures.[7] Alternatively, genres emerged when critical attention focused retrospectively on a body of work which had previously not been seen under this particular generic heading. Such was famously the case with *film noir* (which originally was not an industry or consumer category, but imposed itself as the result of critical interventions).[8] Yet since genres are also the conduits for stereotyping both socially acceptable and transgressive behavior, notably via a specific iconography or recurring narrative situations, genres are the most obvious ways the cinema addresses its audience's ideological and historical identities, and thus their prejudices and preferences. Genres, in other words, negotiate the cultural codes as well as the shifting norms and values of a given community.[9] However, if we look at the thriller or the horror film, for instance, we see that each genre not only possesses its own distinct iconography and a cinematic-thematic stock of situations, characters and roles to draw on, but an added element that holds the genre together, namely the unifying force of suspense. This special case of the dramatic continuum—special, in that suspense manipulates causality and anticipation in very distinct ways—operates occasionally at the expense of plausibility and realism, or rather, establishes its own conventions of verisimilitude, that is, of what is plausible in a given generic world.

Perhaps one of the most audacious films of this kind, which manages to persuade an audience of a dramatic inevitability by means of suspense, is Don Siegel's INVASION OF THE BODY SNATCHERS, where the final and crucial transformation of the girl into a zombie is in contradiction to the supposed body-substitution which had previously motivated the film, for if a person could change simply through excessive fatigue and nervous exhaustion, what is the need for all the giant pods? Yet we are convinced by it, because of Siegel's handling of the suspense, which literally suspends both narrative logic and disbelief, in order to convey the more powerfully a different order of logic—here, the powerfully subjective logic of existential fear—for which the pseudo-rational explanation is only a vehicle, almost the mechanical conveyor-belt of our involvement. And this is of course Siegel's thematic aim: to discredit a certain scientific positivism and its attendant bourgeois conformism, in the name of a passionate appeal to elemental emotions connected with anxiety and the dread of invasion or penetration.

The Hero, His Central Drive and the Happy Ending

What such a film as Siegel's does retain, however, despite its expressive formal stylization and structural plot-implausibilities, are two elements, both very important in the American cinema: the behavioral realism of the actors, and the ordinariness of the main protagonist, already alluded to above in another context. This ordinariness exemplifies a third kind of unity, namely that of the hero, his motives and drives. Perhaps most, and certainly some of the most memorable Hollywood movies made during the 1950s derive their persuasive rhetoric and sense of coherence from the way the dramatic focus is concentrated on a single person. Thus, the most common and unfailing manner of structuring a film is to have a central protagonist with a cause, a goal, a purpose—in short, with a motivation for action that sustains the dramatic interest of a film, and that preferably gives him an unflagging emotional charge. We think, for example, of the heroes in Anthony Mann's Westerns, propelled as they are by their sense of justice, their urge for vengeance. Or—as a significant contract—of Boetticher's Randolph Scott characters, whose slow-burning emotional and moral impulses are so deeply buried and sublimated into a cool, detachedly ironic stoicism, that they surface as a wholly abstract—on the level of the *mise-en-scène* strongly geometrical—set of motifs, which structure the action of, say, COMANCHE STATION into its curiously circular form.

The hero's central drive not only furnishes his identity, enhanced as it is by the physical presence of an established star. It also ensures the predominantly uni-linear (and this can, of course, include circular) movement, at the basis of the essentially "closed" developmental arc of the typical American movie, where a personal initiative, a subjective, instinctual choice so often materializes as an objective necessity (through the mechanism of crime, guilt, revenge, injustice), finally to overtake the hero as his personal fate and destiny.

This is a situation typical of the films of Fritz Lang, and we find it in three of his most famous American films, FURY, YOU ONLY LIVE ONCE and THE BIG HEAT. All these films start from a personal, subjective sense of injustice and moral outrage which triggers off a machinery that determines and dominates all the hero's subsequent actions. Lang, however, uses this stock dramatic device also critically, at the meta-level, in order to dismantle the ideology of personal initiative and private morality in a mass-society, while still giving his heroes the tragic dignity of a unique existence.

In general terms the presence of a central protagonist means that a vast variety of plots and a diversity of directorial themes can nonetheless have a common structural denominator and a near-identical dramatic function. Hence the persistent impression that protagonists in Hollywood movies always have a kind of dogged energy and unwavering determination: not to give up in the face of adversity, to better their lot, to believe in the future, in justice or personal happiness—which has frequently been ridiculed and interpreted as evidence of a facile and intolerably shallow optimism, a bogus craving for the happy ending. This view of the classical cinema's narrative structure is, I would argue, an untenable simplification, both in terms of Hollywood's ideology and the function of the happy ending.

Rather, one ought to recognize that the happy ending is a structural constant and a given, functioning like a coda in a musical context. At the same time, it is the trope of resolution in a rhetorical discourse, and to that extent, a primarily formal device, which by itself can be said to be ideologically neutral. Once the subject-matter is no longer seen as the only or even the most significant part of the story-line and its rhetoric-emotional function, it becomes apparent that there exists an important interrelation between the diversely motivated drives of the heroes—whether it is greed for money, thirst for adventure, social ambition, hate, vengeance, dreams of power—and the dramatic principle of action, reaction, complication and resolution in the American cinema. For, as even the most cursory analysis of the narrative structure of American movies of the 1950s would show, a variety of socially and morally defined aims nevertheless rely for their aesthetic embodiment on an identical or significantly similar emotional substratum, governed by the articulation and distribution of psychic energy. One of the most significant implications of this—and one that ought to give rise to more detailed discussion than I can give it here—is that moral choices in the American cinema manifest themselves in terms of aesthetic values, such as symmetry or balance, and that ethical dilemmas are elaborated not on the basis of intellectual argument, but entirely by means of the psychological pressure-point of desires and needs, and energy-expenditure. This factor has some importance if we want to get a clearer picture about the ideological function of the American cinema.

Practically, two considerations impose themselves. First, we note that in the majority of Hollywood films during the classical period, the living out of an emotional impulse or psychic drive is accompanied and paralleled by a deepening of moral awareness, a growth and progress in the hero's consciousness, such as the audience can infer it across action, setting, symbolic objects and iconography. Through the psychic energy available in the person of the protagonist, and thus through his essentially unreflected and often explicitly non-intellectual mode of perceiving and experiencing social and human reality, American movies conduct a kind of education of sensibility, a clarification of basic emotional responses which is of enormous cultural significance. The dramatic pattern of the Hollywood movie is an accumulative one: from simple impulse to an experience of complexity. What a character has to come to terms with in so many movies, is the impossibility of instant gratification and the consequences of deferral.

This inhibition and deferral, as we know from Freud, is one of the primary cultural acts, and constitutes also the creative principle par excellence. American movies show how the emotional potential of a character and his feelings have to disperse themselves, have to engage in and be lost in the labyrinth of the real world. Alternatively, in order to escape from a hostile or unresponsive world, the protagonists are impelled to construct an imaginary world, an anti-reality which is tested against the forces and pressures of the real world. But this "sublimation" of a desire for action is at the same time the driving force towards the spectacle, which of course, in its most grandiose form, is the cinema. Hollywood has taught America the collective virtues of sublimation and deferral, of controlling the individual's creative and destructive impulses—always in the name of community values, the nation's collective interest, or of global survival. Yet, significantly, it has transmitted this message in a code which secures Hollywood's continuation. And that is also its greatness: like every art, its first and last reference is to itself. Like every genuinely cultural myth, its form is contradiction, its meaning, however, tautological.

Violence Unbound

If one were pressed to define by a single aesthetic feature the difference between the 1950s and the Hollywood films of the late 1960s, it would probably be the increasingly dislocated emotional identity of the central protagonists, and the almost total absence of the central drive and its dramatic mechanisms. Instead we have the comedies of Jerry Lewis, which draw from the distortions, the spasms, the interrupted flow of the emotional impetus their most subtle and disturbing effects. Or, as in Sam Peckinpah's The Wild Bunch and many other, lesser movies, we have heroes who shrug their shoulders and laugh uncontrollably for no apparent reason, only suddenly to break into unmotivated and wholly irrational violence—evidence of a "desublimated" energy which is no longer translated into clearly identifiable moral and social objectives or bodily coordination. Individual violence, for example, in Ray or early Losey, represents complex psychological and cultural "values": it might be a necessary step in the hero's education or self-knowledge (as in case of the hero of In A Lonely Place), or it provokes, in Losey's The Lawless, Siegel's Invasion of the Body Snatchers or Lang's Fury, the collective and institutionalized violence of the forces of law and order or of the bigoted community to show itself openly, threatened by the outsider.

As with the dual (subjective and objective) reality-status of the image, American directors seem to have lost interest in this dual perspective on violence, treating it either as a purely aesthetic quantity, or as the cheerfully or cynically admitted acting out of an aberrant national pathology. What in Arthur Penn's Bonnie and Clyde is still couched in a form that understands itself as a half-critical, half-apologetic spectacle of violence, becomes in Butch Cassidy and the Sundance Kid the blithe opportunism of self-display. Indeed, we seem to have come full-circle: if the classical cinema's self-restraint was able to translate aesthetic principles of unity and formal procedures of symmetry, it would seem that the aestheticizing tendencies of the modern mainstream cinema are also responsible for the classical cinema's decline, revealing ideological nihilism and artistic despair. For where Hollywood's great films of the classical tradition were above all critically perceptive was in their ability to depict the emotional undercurrent of a particular social condition in terms of an individual's crisis, which in American culture is almost invariably coded as physical violence. But by obsessively insisting on the irremediable contradiction between desire and fulfilment, between private frustration and the fantasies of glory, between the forces of the imagination and restrictive social behavior, they turned even the happy ending into a tragic insight: the existential rift between seeming and being, heritage of European Romanticism and the puritan ethic, could not be healed other than in restating it in the most uncompromising terms. Today, these essential contradictions are being blurred by a cult of the aesthetically pleasing, as if the energy was purely external, a matter of mechanical reflexes or pyrotechnics.

Obviously, if this is to be more than a casual observation, it would need an analysis that takes in the changes of the Hollywood studio-system and the American cinema's relation to its audiences. It points to a complex process of mediation and transmission, for on the one hand, such formal changes in style and narrative would "reflect" changes in American society and its predominant mood and dominant self-understanding—changes to which Hollywood has reacted with uncanny speed, showing that it still has its finger on the nation's pulse, even if this is now the pulse of a much younger generation. On the other hand, it raises problems of narrative structure and dramatic form which only few directors have recognized, and none has yet satisfactorily resolved. Kazan's The Arrangement is a typical example of a film that tries to confront the problem of what one could call "the unmotivated hero," whose life-project or driving conflict falls into its disconnected parts, with the narrative patched together by the negative force of entropy, which in the hero shows up as emotional stress and the total withdrawal from all kinds of gratification. Yet the film's analytic-reflective mode of narration remains unsatisfactory, precisely because Kazan cannot resolve the aesthetic problem of still wanting to find a principle of unity which would hold the film together on the level of motivation. The same might be said of Penn's Mickey One. Easy Rider, by contrast, relies on a perfectly conventional dramatic structure, with the motif of the journey—which, in the true tradition of Hollywood's *film noir*, can only lead to death—underscoring the goal-oriented motivation of the heroes by default.

What makes the film interesting is that it signalizes this goal-orientation more or less as explicitly nostalgic, as a journey into the national past, and thus having the best of both worlds. And just as in the classical movie, the hero learns something from his quest about himself and about the world, so Billy and Captain America learn the inevitable lesson of failure—that they cannot live among the hippies, that straight society rejects them, and that the American South is (still) murderous: that, in short, "we blew it." Given the ideological climate of contemporary America, with anti-Vietnam protesters failing to persuade the Silent Majority and a stagnating civil rights movement, such an admission may seem the sign of a new (political) realism. In terms of the ideology of cinematic form, however, the sacrificial deaths of the heroes, engineered by a deus ex machina, spell a more mystifying and confused message than a classical movie of the 1950s—obsessed with a similar presentment of failure—would ever have proposed. In an oddly retrograde move, Easy Rider, for all its Harley Davidson machine energy, ends by affirming a stance of youthful self-destruction which Nicholas Ray's movies once took as their starting point.

8

Narrative Cinema and Audience Aesthetics: The *Mise-en-Scène* of the Spectator[1]

Starting life as a BFI-seminar paper, "Narrative Cinema and Audience Aesthetics" was my attempt in 1973 to lay out a third way between the polemical auteurism of Movie, and the new structuralist ortho-doxies of Screen. By focusing on the experience of the viewer and the perceptual and physiological situa-tion of the cinematic event, I was, however, less influenced by French phenomenological debates, or by Jean Paul Sartre's L'imaginaire, than I was steeped in the then popular Freudo-Marxism of the Frankfurt School, which I tried to adapt to what I knew of structural linguistics and Freudian literary criticism, somewhat naively promoted by me as an alternative to Jacques Lacan. Although the Freudian energy-cathexis model here on display was rather crude (its echoes of American ego-psychology were construed as a reprehensible rearguard action when compared to the new school of Althusser-Lacanian theory presented at other BFI seminar sessions),[2] I have retained a certain fondness for the piece, because even in its prolix formulations and incompatible theoretical paradigms I recognize many themes that have remained important to me over the years.[3] For instance, the reference to Roman Jakobson's communica-tion model is clearly not worked out, but what I think I wanted indicate with my emphasis on the "phatic" dimension and the references to cognition as "recognition" is not that different from Christian Metz's concerns in his last work on enunciation from 1991,[4] when he attempted to explain around (linguistic) indexicality, deictic and anaphoric modes of reference, how films create their own complex memory of themselves, and bind us into the meaning-making process.

"Narrative Cinema and Audience Aesthetics" also wanted to raise the question of cinematic time in relation to signification, by suggesting that "narrative," rather than being a non-negotiable "given" of cinema, or the arch-enemy of "progressive cinema" also functions as regulatory mechanism for managing and articulating time, and not only as a means for conveying information in an orderly progression, or naturalizing ideology. This seems once more to be relevant and topical, because it gives one kind of answer to an issue become urgent with digital images and the waning of the interest in "narrative" as the sole way of engaging the spectator. The classical cinema, too, is a way of "perceiving time," situated between the micro-level of pure duration (extending from the Lumière films to Andy Warhol and surveil-lance cameras), and the macro-level of the contemporary blockbuster as a cultural, mythopoetic time-machine.[5] So while the energy model locates the essay in the historical moment and the place where it originated (written in London in 1973, after "Why Hollywood" and before "Pathos of Failure: Notes on the Unmotivated Hero") it, too, does belong to my attempts to work out the nature of classical narrative,

adding to the goal-oriented hero, and the linear drive structure of the action, also the blocking of affect (and its managing through narrative) on the side of the spectator. I argue that one can identify distinct types of emotional engagement and affective disarticulations across each of the major filmic genres. At the same time, because I was already interested in the specific dynamics of the cinema experience after classical Hollywood, it became a piece that—with retrospect—can be read as much in the spirit of Deleuze as of Freud, around the "crisis of the action image," shifting the question of meaning to affect, "embodiment" and what I called "the viewing situation," here theorized more or less explicitly in non-specular terms, that is, avoiding the spatial geometrics of the so-called "cinematic apparatus" (with its attendant idealist problems around illusionism/Brechtian theories of anti-illusionism that became so crucial in the 1980s).[6]

Viewing Conditions

Theoretical interest in the cinema has recently tended to focus on notions such as "Brechtian distan-ciation," "anti-illusionism," "identification" and "audience-address."[7] The feeling that the cinema ought to raise the consciousness of the spectator, demystify social reality and instruct him about (political) action has become an analytical program about the ideological function of the cinema. In a broader sense, this is a discussion about the cinema as an institution within a certain society and as a rhetoric within a certain range of public discourses. But it also involves another issue, namely how the cinema challenges these discourses of both society and art, by aesthetic and rhetoric processes that are specific to the cinematic medium and at the same time flow from its peculiar mode of reception. How do formal and aesthetic structures interact with and determine individual consciousness, and more specifically, how can we picture this interaction in a concrete way as taking place in the primary reality of the cinema, namely the bodily, emotional and intellectual experience of watching films?

In order to give an answer, what perhaps has to concern us is not only what happens on the screen, but what happens between the screen and the audience. We should try to describe more closely than has hitherto been the case the physical, material and psychological conditions under which a film relates to the spectator, and analyze the implications these conditions have for audience perception, emotions and intellectual response. What I would like to explore in this paper, then, is the nature of the cinematic experience, the viewing conditions, and ask whether they impose specific constraints on the spectators' capacities of comprehension, of apprehending "meaning" in a film (and thus also determine what constitutes "meaning" in a film). My hypothesis will be that the viewing conditions operate as a "limit," and define in a psychological as well as an ideological sense the efficacy of a film as an experience, and by the same token, they also affect the tensions and inner dynamic of an art form whose purpose it is not only to capture a (mass-) audience's attention, but to "move" this audience: an aesthetic effect usually relegated to the realm of the inartistic and more at home with propaganda, but in the cinema peculiarly constitutive of the art and medium itself.

The experience of watching a movie immerses the spectator in a temporal sequence. The cinema, despite the importance it gives to the spatial organization of the image (and even of sound), is an art which depends for its articulation on time: a slice of time, usually between one and a half and two hours, is marked off by a strong caesura at either end (lights down—projection of film—lights up), giving the spectator a sense of closure and enclosure more radical than either watching television is able to produce, or a play at the theater and listening to a concert, not to mention the infinitely weaker sense of closure when picking up or putting down a book, or the virtually "open" time experi-ence of looking at a picture or a piece of sculpture. It would appear that in the cinema we are subjected to a particularly intense organization of time, experienced within a formal structure which is closed, but in a sense also circular: we are "captured" in order to be "released," willingly undergoing a fixed term of imprisonment. However, this suggests that while we are watching a film—any film—a pressure (the pleasure of anticipation, the discomfort of expectation, even the anxiety about possible disappointment) is generated which by its very nature has a strong psychic component and which would seem to demand some form of "management," by way of projection, energy transformation and emotional release.

At the same time, it is easy to see that this pressure is both real and artificial, both fictional and factual, both an "illusion" and physiologically present. It is under our control, because we induce it at will, every time we buy a ticket at the box-office, but we also hand over control, because we want to be captured and taken (somewhere else). The film experience is repeatable like a laboratory experiment, and yet the viewing situation is quite unlike any situation encountered in "real life." The question is whether the energy, emotion or pressure inherent in the film as event and existing logically prior to any particular film, does not necessarily impinge on the actual film, regardless of whether this film is aware of this energy and sets out to accommodate it in its visual-dramatic articulation or not. Perhaps one would here find a clue to why the popularity of a given film is still such an unpredictable, erratic affair, as if with each film a particular bond was being forged that has to do with an exchange of energy more than with a flow of information. When this exchange does not occur, the film does not "take place" as an event. It suggests a reciprocal relationship between film and audience: a film not only immerses and absorbs an audience into its (fictional) world, there is also a counter-current where the spectator has to immerse the film into his (psychic) world, brought to the threshold of consciousness and bodily sensation by the complicated dynamics emanating from the viewing situation itself.

The consequences are significant: communication between film and audience may depend vitally on the way this field of force establishes itself, and it may be that neither meaning nor pleasure are possible if the energy-flow from the spectator finds no appropriate channel. Expressing it in terms of communication theory, and using Roman Jakobson's terminology, the viewing situation provides the "phatic" aspect of the communication process, and rather than being a static situation, it is in fact a channel, where energy flows in both directions.[8] Could it be that whenever this channel is blocked, a form of psychic resistance develops, which—whatever the story, stars or setting—makes it impossible for a film to "work"? Assuming the phatic element in the cinema to be more directly concerned with psychic (but also physiological) energy than in any other artistic medium (except perhaps music), one would expect it to be a determining factor also in the meaning-making process. The phatic conditions of spectatorship would thus be part of the semiotic basis on which a film generates meaning, while the film experience—as a tightly organized time experience—in turn engenders in the spectator certain mental and emotional predispositions that keep this phatic channel "open." Being enclosed in a darkened room, cut off visually from the surroundings and exposed to a state of isolation, the spectator looks for a visual focus—and finds it in the rectangle lit by the projector, the screen, which can function as a point of orientation. But he is also looking for a time-focus, which becomes a kind of escape or safety valve for the aggression and anxiety mobilized by the viewing situation.

This latter need might explain the importance of narrative in the development of the cinema, for the intensified demand for orientation, direction and focus is exceptionally well served by the narrative cinema's emphasis on causal sequence and a central protagonist, while the transformation of duration into flow or rhythm is accomplished by classical editing, with its discontinuous articulation of a coherent visual and aural field. In the narrative cinema, the spectator cannot but project emotional energies onto the images on the screen. There is perhaps less room for Bert Brecht's cigar-smoking sports-fan or Walter Benjamin's "distracted examiner" in the cinema than the advocates of distanciation and anti-illusionism would wish for.

Furthermore, one is watching movies not at the pace one chooses, and in the random order one normally observes the "world outside," but in a sequence selected and combined by someone else. This (hypothetically) increases the spectator's lack of freedom, which montage and action, controlled by the director, and the irreversibility of the film-strip running through the projector convert into a sort of purposive captivity, giving imprisonment a positive turn, whenever the artificial rhythm thus imposed (the film's "heartbeat") locks into the spectator's physiological disposition (the audience's "heartbeat"). On the other hand, such a visual rhythm (the editing, the *mise-en-scène*, the pacing) can itself be very disorienting, especially when markedly at variance with one's bodily perception of physical motion or one's mental perception of narrative progress. In some types of films (e.g. of the European cinema) this force field at play is perhaps neutralized by the spectator's ability to construct his own time-space continuum as a perceptual hypothesis of self-presence ("I am here, now, watching a film") which reduces the degree of anxiety caused by the sense of un-freedom and dependence, the passivity and state of receptivity to which he is exposed. But this requires a special effort and the willingness to be in two temporalities at once: that of the film, and that of the viewing situation. However, where a spectator does not succeed or is unwilling to entrust a film with his own state as a captive subject, one might expect a sort of paralysis of the mind and of bodily motor-forces. Such a paralysis, however, produces heavy defenses and resistance, of an emotional, ideological and intellectual kind. In other words, the fact that the spectator is pinned to his seat and only has the screen to look at, may cause emotions to arise which demand to be compensated and taken in charge: the film has no option but to be a time-and-energy manager. It may be that "style" is initially perceived by the spectator on this level, determining reception of a film's ideational content, plot and themes. Identification and emotional participation would become less a matter of the fictional characters or the story, and more an integral component of the viewing situation: *mise-en-scène*, narrative and point of view structure, whatever else they are, are also means by which the film manipulates, controls and directs the defenses mobilized by the ever-present threat of motor-inhibition in the viewing situation.

Hollywood's Psychic Matrix

Thus, an essentially psychological handling of time and space in the cinema enters into the formal articulation of the filmic material in ways that make it not just a provocation to say that the primary material of the cinema is neither celluloid nor the spectator's ideological consciousness, but the viewing situation itself, which functions as a sort of matrix of latent affect. As already hinted at, the presence of such a matrix makes a strong case for a certain type of cinema, not only based on narrative, working with fictional situations, but favoring spectacular, action-oriented narratives, which work with "illusionist" means and set out to manipulate audience responses. Before arguing this more specifically in relation to Hollywood cinema, I want to offer a sort of negative proof for the existence of this matrix, by mentioning what might be called the fall-out of a failed defense-management. Whenever the energies latent in the viewing situation are not staged or represented by a film, or where the tensions of expectation are not objictified into the narrative terms of conflict, suspense, complication and resolution, an audience seems to produce its own defense-management, often by way of its "active participation," such as reacting with restlessness, becoming aggressive, voicing protective laughter and other audible comment, or conversely, with suppressed boredom and claustrophobia, to the point of "walking out." It might explain why, besides good films, there are "good" bad films, but also why watching a "bad" bad film can be such a disproportionately depressing experience. It suggests that such a film is not only at odds with the psychic matrix and therefore fails to make phatic contact with its audience, but also requires an additional investment of psychic energy on the part of the spectator in the defense-management of the viewing situation. No doubt, the oral cravings habitually associated with the cinema experience—the ingestion of food and drink—are equally part of this defense-management. A film, one could say, never encounters a "neutral" audience, but a tissue of expectations, which have as their materialist basis an energy aggregate of the psyche, the body and of the motor body-system.

Phrased like this, my model of the functioning of narrative in the context of the viewing situation might appear crudely mechanistic and offer a severely reductionist account of the film experience. But emphasis on these physiological aspects of the viewing situation does lead to further speculation, and offers a possible insight into the vexing question of the function of "realism" and "mimesis" in the cinema. For instance, the one element which is mimetic in even the most unrealistic genre film is the physical movement of the actors, and as we know, the Hollywood acting codes strongly reinforce mimetic response. Who doesn't feel his feet itch after seeing 42ND STREET or SINGIN' IN THE RAIN and start twirling an imaginary gun in its holster after watching RIO BRAVO? Yet instead of judging the American cinema's emphasis on body, motion and gesture by the canons of verisimilitude and the criteria of phenomenological realism, and relating it to the ideational or referential part of the "message," it seems to make better sense to see the Hollywood style of acting and its framing of the body as contributing primarily to the establishment of phatic contact and the maintenance of cathexis.[9] Consequently, Hollywood realism has little to do with either literary realism or illusionist representation in the theater or in tableau or easel painting, for it belongs in the first instance to an aspect of the communication process specific to the medium film, or rather, specific to the conditions of its reception: the motor inhibitions.

It once more indicates that "modernist" arguments against "illusionism" might be mis-directed, at least when they are accompanied by a call for anti-illusionism. Rather, the mimetic function of the moving image does not belong to representation at all, and is primarily of a psychological-physiological kind, where it becomes an aspect of the spectator's bodily presence in the cinema, rather than a matter of visual perception, whether "real" or "illusionist." As E.H. Gombrich has shown in his "Meditations on a Hobby-Horse," realism for the infant at play is often determined by function and use (the stick that serves as a hobby-horse) and "realism" as an effect is in any case not a one-to-one matching, but a complex process of "consistent" or "purposive" reading, in view of some particular goal or end. Realism in the cinema would be, so to speak, not only in the eye but also in the body of the beholder. Such an interpretation could account for the fact that one can tolerate a good deal of motivational improbability in the characters, lack of plausibility in the situations, elliptical story-telling and other discontinuities, provided that phatic contact is maintained and that there are sufficient elements which allow for the possibility of "consistent reading" on another level of articulation, be it acting, editing or the placement of the human figure in space.

If what I have asserted about the pre-existence of such a psychic matrix is correct, constituting a primary, albeit "negative" level of articulation in a film, it needs arguing that it does not only affect a film's possibilities of communicating with an audience in general, but can also be shown to play a role in the visual articulation itself, that is, in the style and types of narrative of the films most suitable for the cinema's dominant viewing situation, the artificially closed, psychologically active time experience in the spectator. This matrix, so my argument would run, is transformed into a syntax thanks to narrative, but the accumulation and management of energy impulses and their transformation into dynamic patterns is the task of cinematic style and constitutes the aesthetic dimension of a film, its specificity as a practice of the medium and its forms. Style in this sense also defines the relationship of the filmmaker to his material, indicating the scope within which the director as author can generate meaning and convey it, not intellectually, but bodily. Perhaps it is therefore useful to approach a Hollywood film as the type of aesthetic object which is the result of a series of transformational processes: transformation of psychic impulses into action sequences, of action into emotional responses, of emotional responses into "consistent readings," of consistent readings into plots or larger structural units, and of plot into continuous phatic contact as well as ideational or ideological "meaning." Evidently, this is not a hierarchical progression, but an interpenetration and coalescence of simultaneous processes. From the point of view of an aesthetics of the Hollywood film, whenever transformational processes of this kind can be shown to be present in a systematic form, one can speak of a work possessing aesthetic coherence, and one can identify its different "levels of discourse" as being connected by mutually sustaining correspondences and equivalences, such as the "translation" of subject-matter into style. In the second part of this essay, I want to look more closely at two aspects of this type of coherence in the American cinema, namely the ability of plot and *mise-en-scène* to function as two crucial transformational agencies, the engines, so to speak, behind the syntax also becoming matrix, as well as vice versa.

Realism and the Dynamics of the Plot

It is well known that the narrative tradition developed by Hollywood is based on strongly profiled, "archetypal" plots: symmetrical in overall shape (linear or circular, marked by repetition), they are generated by an alternating rhythm of conflict, climax, resolution. Western and gangster films almost invariably feature narratives of pursuits, quests, treks and themes centered on the ambition to arrive, make it, get to the top, or to avenge, control, conquer. Even in psychological dramas and melodramas one finds a similar plot-dynamic and the same thematic conjunction of impulse and its blockage: articulated as guilt and regret, as the need to expiate or atone, to rein in or adapt the self, by purging or working through anti-social impulses and libidinal forces. The spectator is usually introduced to the protagonist at a point when he is faced with a dilemma, or confronted with a situation of tension, friction, mystery and contradiction. The subsequent action fleshes out either the direct consequences of this dilemma or its genesis (via a flashback structure), and in an action-reaction process, the implications are progressively revealed, until a final resolution returns us to a state of appeasement. These formal configurations engineered through plot and protagonist are evidently important structural constants in the American cinema. But they also strongly reflect the dynamics of the psychic matrix: because of their schematization, the plots provide a possible way of regulating psychic pressure, and on this level, they could be seen as the primary vector of energy, a macro-structure of cathexis, projecting and objectifying libidinal and aggressive drives. This would help to account for the emphasis of the Hollywood tradition on action, violence, eroticism, the predominance of energy-intensive heroes, the graphs of maximum investment in virility and vitality, phallic models of identity and self-assertion, instinctual drive-patterns, the accent put on voyeurism and fantasy projection, as well as the premium placed on spectacle, sex, adventure. Being efficient vehicles for charting a course of energy expenditure and management, these action-based plots compensate very directly the spectators' motor inhibitions, and allow for the discharge of anxiety feelings by converting primary emotional arousal into more ideationally motivated conflicts or intellectually validated tensions. Action and reflection in the American cinema do not oppose each other; on the contrary, they mutually necessitate each other, as twin aspects of engaging the spectator as physically sited in time.

It is, in other words, the action-based, dynamic realization of these stereotypical plots that makes them capable of extensive and almost infinite "thematization," that is, they can take on all manner of meanings (moral, social, affective, intellectual), absorbing in the process a great deal of ideational subject matter and representational substance—about American society, the American family, the nation and the national past. But this subject matter is not only overt, that is, the crisis of the nuclear family in the melodramas of the 1950s, the political topics in Capra's movies, the Warner gangster pictures and their references to the Depression, or the same company's socially progressive prison movies. More important is perhaps the fact that the dynamics of action allow these plots to be "about" anything, precisely because the matrix as syntax permits different kinds of semantics to organize themselves into aesthetically coherent patterns that are also "meaningful" to the audience at the physiological level of the film experience. In this respect, the plot is a closed system, for the Hollywood feature film manipulates and transforms the very condition it has called into being. Film and film-experience are thus highly self-referential, they echo each other, and the "world outside" comes in only at one remove, inflected and shaped by the intra-psychic and physiological constituents of "being at the movies."

Another aspect of how the strongly articulated plots reflect the viewing situation is the conversion of chronology into causality, in accordance with the principle *post hoc ergo propter hoc* (one thing after another becomes one thing because another), making sequence suggest a cause-and-effect relation, while emphasizing the irreversibility of the film experience, in itself dramatized especially in the thriller and *film noir*: time is always running out on the hero, and an aura of fatality or entropy shapes the course of events. The one-way temporality of the viewing situation here actualizes a social theme and accommodates a cultural metaphysics, giving intuitive credibility, for instance, to the gritty stoicism of the flamboyantly anti-social criminal or outsider, but also to more "existential" interpretations of this genre, or its link with German Expressionism. It suggests that it might be possible to construct a theory of genres not only around iconography and setting, but once more factor in the viewing situation, so that besides a symbolic or allegorical interpretation of Westerns, gangster films, melodramas and comedies in terms of current social issues or the contradictions engendered by capitalism, these genres specifically respond to different aspects of the pressures and actively manage the constraints which the psychic matrix mobilizes in the spectator.

Mise-en-Scène

However, the strong plot is only one element that serves to establish phatic contact with an audience and produces a form of energy cathexis. Just as important is the manner in which information is exchanged in patterns of discontinuity, which because of the narrative's dynamic nature, play a vital part in the processes of transformation mentioned above: by energizing the narrative articulation, discontinuity itself builds up patterns, suggesting totalities and contexts of meaning which are effective precisely because they are based on gaps and elisions. Intellectual structures of meaning, for instance, seem to become affectively important in the cinema only when they are communicated as "rhythm" or alternation, which means that the discontinuities in filmic articulation ("continuity editing") and of plot sequencing (what is "left out" in the story-chronology) become major sources of narrative energy, the discontinuities acting as the release-mechanisms for "switches" between various levels of discourse as well as for different modes of involvement (suspense, empathy, thrill, tears).

If we look at the history of Hollywood from the 1940s to the 1970s, we can see that the strongly accentuated action-adventure-romance plot has been the basis for some of the most sophisticated stylistic and narrative elaborations. For instance, the cut on action or reverse-field (shot-counter shot) editing have become standard models of organizing the visual field as at once a dynamic space and conveying a subjective view not only in Hollywood films. The German director G.W. Pabst already in the 1920s acknowledged his debt to Hollywood when he outlined as one of his directorial principles: "every cut is made on some movement. At the end of one cut somebody is moving, at the beginning of the adjoining one the movement is continued."[10] He is echoed by a "Cinema Novo" director like the Brazilian Ruy Guerra, who stated in an interview in 1972:

> All my camera movements, except in very special cases, are on the characters. In other words, if there are two characters, the camera would never pass from one character to another through

empty space, the camera has never a life of its own, it is always linked either to a human field of vision or a movement.[11]

These principles are part of what is generally known as classical *mise-en-scène*, and *auteur* criticism has made this one of its key domains. But in this sense, all *mise-en-scène* is transformation, and all transformation is "distanciation." The deployment of stylistic elements "manages" story-material, by modeling an action or giving shape to an interchange, by imposing a form, but also detaching itself from it. The work of directors like Hitchcock, Lang, Sirk, Cukor, Losey, Fuller is proof that the relationship of story to style and style to meaning has never been simple, for these *auteurs* have each created specific ways of transforming their story-material into motion and flow that "manages" and accommodates the viewing-situation, maximizing the energy-patterns arising out of it, while abstracting from the action also an argument and commentary.

However, what characterizes the directors we now think of as "classical"—from Ford and Lang to Minnelli and Preminger, from Welles to Ray or Sirk—is that besides their feel for these energy-patterns and their cathartic-cathectic function in relation to character-psychology and the staging of violent action, they are also capable of using *mise-en-scène* as almost the opposite, namely to attenuate the affective-aggressive potential inherent in the phatic dimension of the film-experience, by transforming spectator-projection into double vision: shaping an exteriorizing eye, aimed at action, affect and consequence, and creating an inner eye, that places an interior, "subjective" vision within the action itself, capable of reflection, or more accurately, of seeing itself seeing. This transformation of action into subjective vision accomplished by the *mise-en-scène* is the point at which a critical discourse takes root, "placing" protagonists and "contextualizing" objects at the same time as it "shows" them. *Mise-en-scène* in this sense is the capacity for generating hesitation and ambivalence about whose field of vision we share, created by the mobility of the camera in relation to a scene, and the inevitable assumption of a point of view vis-à-vis the action which this fluid camera and practices such as shot-counter shot editing maintain, whereby the image not only codifies a certain spatial configuration, but serves as the metaphoric expression of a (state of) consciousness and its comment on the action or setting.

In the American cinema, the production of the image as a direct, perceptually saturated and densely textured record of a situation or action, and at the same time as the subjective extension and materialization of an inner world, has given rise to the theme of vision itself as the meta-subject of many films, irrespective of genre: notably in the thrillers of Lang and Hitchcock, but also through a genre like the musical in Minnelli, the melodrama in Sirk, the Western of Ray, or the psychological drama in Losey and Preminger. This, too, is of course, part of the management of the viewing situation: the double aspect of the image as representation of an action and emanation of a consciousness (at once participating in and distanced from the action) is not only one of the fundamental ways in which the *mise-en-scène* transforms *histoire* into *discours*, it is also the staging of the spectator's own situation, his own "doubling" on the screen.

In its function as a reservoir of stylistic devices subservient to the materiality of the viewing situation as much as to the material density and specificity of the represented world, *mise-en-scène* allows the filmmaker to establish a dialectical relationship between these "materials" and their formal articulation. The typical structuring features of classical narrative, for example repetition, parallels, contrasts, juxtapositions, spatial organization as social metaphor, the use of visual or aural leitmotifs, and the possibilities of the sound-track in itself generating spatial presence can all be seen to work at both levels: making the world "out there" seem substantial and real, while making the space "in here" seem present and real.

Yet what I have called the phatic aspect of communication is also accommodated by the *mise-en-scène* at another level, that of "recognition" and surprise (or suspended recognition), the latter acting as a stimulus towards renewed energy-investment and increased participation. Recognition in the American cinema can take a variety of forms: recognition of stereotypes, of genre-conventions and iconography; recognition of plot-situations or of typical drive-patterns; recognition of the actors and stars across their previous roles; recognition of allusion to other movies; recognition of a director's style and themes. All these moments of recognition, depending on different degrees of familiarity or critical awareness, have an affective component that feeds into the matrix of expectations and anticipations coexisting and fusing with the more primary matrix of the viewing situation itself. Like the latter, this matrix of generic or cinephile expectations—the cultural dimension of the film-experience and the habitual side of "going to the movies"—can be frustrated or gratified, shifting the level of participation from the emotional to the intellectual and thus accounting for the diversity of the cinema's appeal, but also its addictive or compulsive element. The film experience as a physiological state of excitation is what the Hollywood cinema both elicits and appeases, and by appeasing it, once more elicits.

Illusionism and Fictional Reality

None of these forms of recognition or its attendant regime of frustration and gratification seem to depend on and produce the illusion that what is being represented is mistaken for "real" in the way one might be mistaken about a person's anger or love being "real" or merely simulated: one of the functions of imaginative literature and fictional narrative in the cinema is precisely to shift this problem to another plane—namely where we know what we read or see is "real" on the level of articulation, and "unreal" on the level of the referent. For fictional realism, however we define it, is not concerned with the reproduction of substances, but based on an analogy of functions, that is, it furnishes a system of symbolic representations. Thus, for instance, the cinematic image produces representation for symbolic use, and this primarily by virtue of being able to imitate or represent motion: any kind of imaginative participation takes place only under dynamic conditions, and in the cinema this first-level dynamism is furnished by the movements of the characters and the camera. The fictional-dynamic framework therefore allows us to construe all movement as significant, by interpreting it as purposive, directional and motivated. In this context it is of less importance whether we think of the "motivational" impulses as emanating from the locus of intentionality we normally call the director or as behavioral-psychological clues manifested in the characters. Regardless, in other words, of where we locate motivation or how construe purpose, it is the endeavor towards "consistent readings" within the fictional framework (an endeavor heavily relying on recognition) that provides the basis for stimulating active participation, and thereby providing for identification, understanding and cognition, even if this cognition is inevitably a function of recognition rather than the break with recognition associated with a "raising of consciousness," or the acquisition of new knowledge, said to require anti-illusionist distanciation.

According to the dynamics of my original model, if expectations are instantly gratified, the level of audience participation will be correspondingly low, because the viewing situation would be reduced to its situational dimension, missing the vector of temporality and managed duration. The spectator will be bored, feeling the pressure of the psychic matrix, unable to project himself through participation and anticipation onto the screen. If on the other hand, expectations are partially frustrated and partially gratified, they may generate an energy that re-orients the spectator towards another level of discourse: temporary frustration itself acting as a relay in the process of exchange. If the spectator is permanently frustrated, the aggregate energy will no longer be available for cathexis, and the spectator lapses into irritation, aggressiveness and boredom. In other words, at both ends of the spectrum of responses, boredom and aggression await the film, the limits of its existence as experience. If the Hollywood cinema has undoubtedly colonized the ground of managing the viewing situation in all of its manifestations most successfully and consistently, it is nonetheless possible to envisage the model also working for more "difficult" films. Here the assumption would be that spectators seek to "retrieve" or "recover" their emotional investment in the film-experience (not to mention their investment of time and money), by making an extra effort towards re-orientation. The more experienced spectator will usually be able to derive increased participation from having been able to tolerate a certain degree of frustration without "desublimation," arriving at another level of cathexis, for instance, by identifying with the director, and using the phatic energy blocked by the film itself in order to construct a more distanciated form of participation. Thus even in the European or avant-garde film, there is still a close relationship between the motor-inhibition of the viewing situation, the need for projection, the presence of movement on the screen, the stimulation of emotional participation, and the frustration of participation through discontinuity, ellipsis and other formal attributes of the narrative. What was earlier said about realism here applies to anti-realism: the spectator requires an effort towards consistent reading, he picks up whatever fits his own plotting of meaning, and he seeks confirmation of himself and his presence in order to rescue the film experience as event. At the limit, even the non-narrative film relates the spectator in a dynamic way to the unfolding of the filmic sequence, although rather than cathecting on the basis of action and plot, physiological involvement and psychic participation will be regulated by the fictional nature of filmic representation, the "suspension of disbelief" now understood not as an aspect of illusionism or identification, but as a process that opens for the spectator the possibility of relaxing the defensive mechanisms active in normal life and to entertain feelings, states of being, fantasies, anxieties, desires normally repressed or censored. To this extent, it is the non-narrative film that most approximates the Freudian dream, prior to secondary elaboration. The particular achievement of the classical Hollywood tradition, on the other hand, has been to bind—partly because of maintaining a very controlled phatic contact with its audience—non-individual fantasy material and popular mythology into a discourse, often about these fantasies and mythologies.

To sum up. My argument has been that the narrative cinema is not merely the effect of a particular ideology. It finds its rationale just as much in the specific nature of the cinema experience, here identified with the psychic matrix of its viewing conditions—managing anxiety of motor-inhibition and the engulfing darkness, and managing duration by shaping and articulating time. This double management is accomplished in a paradigmatic manner by the classical Hollywood cinema, thanks to its plot and by *mise-en-scène*, each distancing and engaging the other in a dynamic process that is not "form" transforming "content" or style embellishing theme, but the two sides of a single purpose: the transformation of the materiality of the viewing conditions into the film-experience.

Hollywood narrative cinema thus engages the spectator on any number of issues, whose thematic or ideational scope is unlimited but whose plot articulations, patterns of energy and narrative resolutions are determined by their interaction with more primary patterns constitutive of the cinema as a particular institutional space and as a particular psychic/physiological time-experience. As long as the cinematic experience is defined by such an interaction of historically given elements as the darkness of the movie-theater, the placing of the projector at the back of the auditorium and the fixed rectangle of the screen, narrative appears to be the most complex and difficult, but also the optimal mode of filmic signification: it enables the spectator to make contact with his physical self by stimulating access to levels of fantasy material normally closed, while neutralizing his defenses against the threat of motor-inhibition; and it does so by giving the viewer a sense of self-presence in the viewing situation that no other aesthetic experience appears to equal. Hollywood always makes sure we know we're in the movies, when we're at the movies.

9
Film as System: Or How to Step Through an Open Door

Film Studies and Textual Analysis

One of the major objectives of close textual reading is to address the problem of cinematic significa-tion: how does a film create meaning?[1] The question could be phrased in the form of a series of paradoxes. There is the fundamental contradiction between stillness and movement, between the perception and reception of a film as motion (and thus as kinetic bodily experience), and the mate-rial reality of the celluloid strip, made up of separate individual still photos. What used to be called "persistence of vision" and is now identified as the phi-effect—allowing the human eye to perceive continuity where there is rupture and interruption—is only made more mysterious by the action of the Maltese Cross, without which we would only see a blur as the images pass through the projector aperture. A discontinuity is made continuous, for a mechanical device to slice this continuity into regular segments, and only then can the eye and brain compute the images again as a world in movement and motion.

The paradox extends to the fiction effect: on the one hand, the narrative action starts *in medias res*, without the felt presence of a narrator setting the scene or introducing the characters, and on the other hand, the impression of the story developing its own momentum is once more produced by means of discontinuous and discrete entities: individual scenes, which themselves consist of segments, with each segment furthermore divided into individual shots, and the shots built up from hundreds of individual frames. These paradoxes have an allegorical significance, not just in respect of "grounding" of cinema in an optical trick, but in pointing to a pervasive principle of modernity: the dialectical relation of analytic and synthetic in our relation to visible and tangible phenomena, of taking apart and building up; yet the cinema, by these very same principles, always brings together a "real" world and a "virtual" one.

Consider the following: as an industrial, technological product, film is a commodity, created on the basis of a complex and sophisticated division of labor and tasks, with a high degree of specializa-tion in each of its branches of production. But its textual basis is usually a story, derived from sources as various as a novel, short story, newspaper item or original screenplay. These sources are converted into the shooting script, itself a historically evolved practice, adhering to strict rules. In one sense, the shooting script is comparable to a blueprint for an engineering project, on the basis of which tasks are allocated, schedules distributed and budgets worked out. Thus, it reflects the "industrial" nature of mainstream filmmaking, with a crafted and manufactured product as the end result. But the shooting script is also derived from the so-called "well-made" play of 19th century theater practice, from which the screenplay takes a number of conventionalized forms, such as three-act division, scene-construction or plot-points, as they are laid down in advance (and taught in screenwriting manuals), while nonetheless allowing for the most extraordinary versatility and ingenuity in the "filling in" or "fleshing out" of the "bare bones" dramatic architecture.[2]

There are thus several sets of tension: between industrial production methods and artistic or artisan forms of creative work; between the continuous flow of images, with their "impression of reality," and the discontinuity of the material basis of these images. A similar tension between heterogeneity and homogeneity also applies to the sound track. It, too, gives the illusion of continuity while in actual fact, sound-fragments are normally spliced together to produce the impression of a persistent and always present sound ambience. Sound is separately recorded, in order to be matched, mixed, dubbed and so on. It undergoes a considerable amount of work and processing, because it serves a complex set of functions in respect of narrative and the image. In order to make either sound or image convey distinct meanings, both have—in most cases—to be first separated into discrete units and broken down into individual elements, before these are once more combined, in an order or sequence that follows certain rules. A similar analytic-synthesizing process of breaking down the phenomenal world and recombining it pertains to many other aspects of the filmmaking process: set design and scenery building, costume design and art direction, and even an acting performance follows the same taking apart-putting together principle. Taken together, these rules have been studied many times: for the fiction effect and narrative continuity go by the name of "editing" and "montage," and used to be designated as a "grammar" (of film editing). Others prefer to speak of the semiotics of filmic signification, and critics trained in literature refer to "close textual analysis," also called a "hermeneutics" interpreting a poetics.

Textual analysis thus tries to explain the functioning of the film as a coherent and continuous experience. It implicitly asks: how is it that a film suggests a world that is seamless, always already there, continuous beyond the film's frame and the film's time, while at the same time it tells a story, builds up a narrative, develops an intrigue, a drama with beginning, complication, climaxes and resolution? Following on from this, textual analysis is concerned with another question: how does a film create the impression of a world "out there" (of which we are merely the invisible witnesses) when all the while the film itself only exists for our benefit, "in here" (in and for our minds), cunningly disguising that its sole aim is to address us?[3] One could say that these questions involve two kinds of logic: the logic of the actions in a film, and the logic of the spectator's position in relation to these actions. Traditionally, the logic of the actions has been discussed by asking whether film possessed a language (with a subject-verb-object) or, as indicated, a "grammar." In which case, the theoretical basis underlying textual analysis would be some version of linguistics. This did indeed happen in the 1960s, and the result was a reorientation of film studies as a theoretical discipline, its transformation into "film semiology."[4] Largely due to the work of Christian Metz, the question of whether film is organized according to the same principles as is language—for instance, with a vocabulary (semantics), and a grammar (syntax)—has been given the answer "yes-and-no."[5] While this may seem an unsatisfactory answer to most ordinary mortals, film theorists have actually learnt much about film from this ambivalent answer, even for textual analysis.

Nonetheless, scholars tend to agree that Metz's approach via structural linguistics has been an incomplete or even misleading way of looking at the problem of how films create meanings. They have moved on to other approaches, for instance, by choosing a cognitivist approach.[6] Others have merely criticized the particular language model used by Metz (i.e. his reliance on Ferdinand de Saussure) and have begun to look towards other theorists of language systems (e.g. C.S. Peirce,

N. Chomsky, G. Lakoff) in order to better understand cinema as a special form of semiotics, as well as possessing its own mode of enunication or location/address.[7]

At the same time, theorists and critics were also looking to narrative theory as perhaps the more promising starting point for the analysis of signification in the cinema, rather than the more specialized approach via language theory. Thus, the extensive involvement of film analysis with semiology, linguistics, transformational grammar and the study of metaphor in the 1960s and 1970s was complemented by an equally extensive discussion of cinematic narrative. Literary theories of narratology, of narration, point of view and focalization (as formulated by Roland Barthes, Gerard Genette, Tzvetan Todorov and Jonathan Culler) were drawn on by scholars like Seymour Chatman, Marie-Claire Ropars, David Bordwell, Edward Branigan and François Jost, in order to understand how a filmic text obtains its cohesion, and whether such effects of cohesion as time-space continuity constitute a distinct "signifying system."[8] Already at the time of semiology's heyday, Metz's notion of the *Grande syntagmatique* was an attempt to give a sort of classification of narrative elements and sequences in fiction films. While the *Grande syntagmatique* may now seem largely inadequate (not least judged so by Metz himself), the many critiques of Metz have given rise to a host of competing propositions, in order to come to terms with the rich range of meanings inherent in the moving image, and the types of constraints necessary in order for images to "tell a story" coherently, while simultaneously "involving," "affecting" or "engaging" the spectator.[9]

For this second question, namely how films address, involve and position the spectator, narratology has provided one of the several entry points. In order to describe what is sometimes called the enunciative level as distinct from the narrative level, scholars have borrowed from both structural linguistics (Emile Benveniste) and Freudian psychoanalysis to explain not only the "reality-effect" of classical narrative, but also the "subject-effect," that is, the kind of direct identification which puts the spectator as if "inside" the action. The psychoanalytic approach has proceeded from the assumption that a film necessarily involves us in the position of voyeurs (with the director, across the characters/actors inevitably playing an exhibitionist game with us). Furthermore, psychoanalytic critics have also argued that the cinema's "reality-effect" and "subject effect" involve a particular form of suspension of disbelief, or "disavowal," characterized as typical of fetishism (according to Octave Mannoni's formula "I know, but all the same"). The psychoanalytic approach has been most thoroughly thematized by feminist film theory. It is associated with the names of Laura Mulvey, Teresa de Lauretis, Kaja Silverman, Tania Modleski, E. Ann Kaplan, Annette Kuhn, Linda Williams, among many others.[10]

Scholars, not convinced by psycho-semiotics, have preferred to examine theories of "narration," and—borrowing from Gérard Genette—have tried to elaborate a model of filmic narration which dispenses with the notions of enunciation/identification, or voyeurism/fetishism as well as with the distinction between "narrative structure" and "identification," replacing both by the concept of "narration." Narration can deal with all these processes, once it is seen as an act of ordering, hierarchizing and prioritizing the way information, coming from sound, images, dialogue, editing and so on reaches spectators and is processed by them. There is no need to invoke the unconscious, because the result of narration, understood as the control of the variable flow of information, gives both an impression of structure (of the patterns inherent in the work) *and* an effect of comprehension and identification (subject-effect, whether gender-specific or not). Hence the greater emphasis put on levels of narration and instances or modes of narration ("narrators" [Branigan], "restricted" vs "omniscient" narration [Bordwell]).

In a more common-sense usage, narration might be seen as the process by which the relationships between the impression of "out there" and "in here" is being negotiated, manipulated and controlled. One could add that textual analysis tends to assume—for methodological, and therefore more or less purely pragmatic or procedural reasons—that meaning is located "out-there" in the text. Calling a film a "text," for instance, is evidently already a somewhat counter-intuitive and arbitrary procedure, because a text is something composed of words, something one reads, while a film is viewed by the eye or experienced by the ear, that is, it is above all a sensory-perceptual event.

Whether intentional or not, text and textual analysis refer us, as indicated, to the study of litera-ture. It serves as a reminder that film studies originally arose historically from within departments of literature and languages, and thus owes a methodological debt to the study of literature. And while film studies arose at the height of French structuralism, it also retained strong links with the Anglo-Saxon tradition in literary studies called "practical criticism" or "close reading." This tendency regarded novels, plays, poems as "free-standing," self-contained works, as objects. In the famous phrase of Cleanth Brooks, citing the English Romantic writer John Keats, a poem (and by extension, any work of literary art) is like a "well-wrought urn," that is, a self-sufficient object of beauty which you can handle, which you can pick up, you can turn around and inspect from all sides. This is how textual analysis sometimes also treats a film: cut loose from its conditions of production, cut loose from its creator(s), and also cut loose from its condition and history of reception, its spectators and audiences. In which case, it is probably quite fitting that an urn is the sort of receptacle in which you keep the ashes of your dear departed after you have cremated them. It may even justify the thought occasionally crossing film students' minds, namely that textual analysis is a way of turning a living film into a corpse, and not only a corpse, but a heap of ashes.

The Classical Hollywood System: Excessively Obvious Codes?

On the other hand, textual analysis is different from interpretation. The purpose of close textual analysis in this sense is not necessarily to arrive at a new or startling interpretation of a film or a sequence of a film, but rather the opposite: to explain what David Bordwell has called "the excessive obviousness" of a Hollywood film based on a classically constructed film-scenario, and what Raymond Bellour has called the interplay of "the obvious and the code," in a famous essay on a scene from THE BIG SLEEP.[11] What both writers allude to is the fact that we can all understand a Hollywood film, we can all react to it, and in a sense, we are all experts. According to the screenwriters' manuals, we can even learn how a film is put together: we can study its "building blocks" and structural prin-ciples. Indeed, a Hollywood film usually gives us its instructions for use, and as I shall argue, it often comes with its own "manual," as it were. But just as, in the end, it is much more difficult to write a film that "works" (i.e. finds a public, becomes a classic), it is also not at all easy to describe how exactly and why a Hollywood film "works" (i.e. is internally constituted, manages to produce an impression of "realism," and affords pleasure even on repeated viewings).

What is of interest, then, for textual analysis is the functioning of film as a system: how meaning is an effect of a set of relations and their mutual interdependence, and how this system is complex in its means, but (deceptively, excessively) obvious in its effects. Attention therefore needs to be focused on the narrative and figurative processes typical for and standardized in the American cinema: a system that historically speaking, has remained extraordinarily stable from about 1920 to at least the 1970s, that is, for about fifty years, if not much longer. Bordwell and Thompson, for instance, have frequently affirmed that they think the classical cinema is still intact and practiced today.[12] While this is a controversial statement, there is also much evidence to prove their point, when one thinks of the extraordinary success of the films by a "classical" contemporary filmmaker such as Steven Spielberg.

The most common way of proceeding with a segmentation of a Hollywood film, in order to understand the regularity, unity and coherence of a classical film, is thus perhaps to start by focusing on the narrative, and to define this narrative above all by different "units of meaning," such as the logic of the actions: what characters do, and why they do it, what goals or aims they pursue, what obstacles they encounter and so on. Other "units of meaning" might be emblematic clusters (i.e. moments or images particularly rich in suggestions), symmetries and repetitions (recurring motifs and situations), the openings of films (see below), and spatial or architectural motifs, such as "doors" or "stairs," "windows" or "mirrors."

Three Types of Narrative Logic

Narrative would seem to be a kind of logic—with a temporal, a spatial and a causal component (the latter taking the form of question-and-answer, or "where?"–"here!" also called a film's erotetic system). Any given film's ordering, interlacing or sequencing of these components specifies the overall relation of the parts to the whole, and thus predicates certain hierarchies of relevance, certain arrangements of functions. Briefly, for mainstream film analysis we can distinguish three types of narrative logic that have been widely used.

The first one could be called the Aristotelian model (which is also the one Bordwell uses, since his "poetics" is practice-oriented, and the Aristotelian model is also the one found in all the screen-writer's manuals: its main features are the three-act division, with its "plot points," "turning points" and subtexts).

The second one I shall call the morphological model, in honor of Vladimir Propp, who developed such a morphological "grammar" for the Russian folk tale. His method at a certain point found much favor among film analysts (especially Peter Wollen), but also criticism (notably Bordwell).[13]

The third one I shall call the structuralist model, best known through the work of the anthropologist Claude Lévi-Strauss, who elaborated the logic of narrative on the basis of myths—and clusters of myths, and again, his model was hugely influential in film studies, mainly via the exemplary film-sequence analyses of Raymond Bellour, but also in Peter Wollen's structuralist reconfiguration of *auteur* theory.[14]

What all three models have in common is that they proceed by segmentation, by first trying to determine the principles of division, and identify the significant units or pertinent parts which make up a narrative. And in order to be able to divide a narrative into these constituent parts, they tend to make a distinction between macro- and micro-analysis, of how the whole is divided, and how the parts are articulated, and what relations—of homology, or of (fractal) repetition—might exist between the micro- and macro-level, or the individual segments and the whole. Some argue that each segment in a Hollywood film is a complete mini-narrative; that a Hollywood movie is like a worm that you can chop up and it still survives in all its vital functions, which is meant to explain why it is so easy to follow a Hollywood film, at whatever point you happen to "enter" into its story.

The Aristotelian Model

The Aristotelian model works at the macro-level according to a division into acts—three acts, four acts, or five acts (like drama, the well-made play). And indeed, Bordwell and Thompson never tire of pointing out how precisely the classical Hollywood narrative conforms to a three- or four-act division, an assertion repeated by the manuals:

> What is narrative ('a sequence of action ordered in time and space'), and what is Hollywood narrative? The scriptwriters' manuals borrow their models from drama, the Aristotelian division, or from the short story. Three or four act division, development of character, transformation, the initial situation, the complication, the resolution, the consequences of the resolution.[15]

A more sophisticated model of understanding the macro-structure of a film is the one provided by Bordwell in *Narration in the Fiction Film*, where he talks about the double plot-line of the classical

Hollywood film, the plot-line of the adventure and the plot-line of romance, and how these two are intertwined, cross each other and become the terms for each other's resolution.

The Proppian Model

One reason that Hollywood cinema is successful and has survived so long is because it has developed a way of telling stories, a form of narrative, which aims at being free-standing, self-explanatory, self-sufficient (which does imply an ideological corollary, namely that it pretends to universality, based on prioritizing not only the "American way of life," but what one could call the American way of thinking about life). But cognitively and from the point of view of successful communication with an audience, this has an inestimable advantage: if it is free-standing and self-sufficient (what Bordwell has called "obvious"), it means that it can be understood everywhere, you do not need to "learn" it, you do not need to be told who these characters are, what goes on in their heads, where this film is set, other than by a universal short-hand, a sort of minimal tool-box of cultural cues or clichés. European films, for instance, are almost the exact opposite: they are enigmatic, you never know what motivates the characters, if you do not know a particular country's history or geography, you may never pick up the meanings and references. The Hollywood cinema, on the other hand, is made up of dramatic clichés, set pieces and narratological units, which function almost like detachable parts, like organic cells—and each cell is a mini-narrative, so that even with only a few of these cells, you can (as it were) reconstitute the rest: like DNA, or a morphology, like the dinosaurs from JURASSIC PARK—or like the cut up worm just mentioned.

What is meant by this somewhat unsavory metaphor is that I can switch on the television, and when a Hollywood film is showing, even though I might have missed half the film, within minutes I know where I am, can place myself "inside" the film, am hooked and can follow the story. This, I think, is one of the secrets of the American cinema's success: it is in this sense wholly portable, movable, because each segment, each unit, carries with it at the micro-level enough elements of the macro-structure. A good way to study this, as I shall try to show, is to analyze the openings of Hollywood films. They are often the whole film in a nutshell, and they tend to give the viewer not only a sense of what will be the problem, the disturbance, the lack or absence and thus the motor of the film, but also how to read the film, its particular textual system: a Hollywood film has to lay out its problem in the first ten minutes, if it is to work as an epic-narrative experience, but it encodes or encrypts this problem in all of its sequences, like a watermark in a bank-note. Vladimir Propp provides a possible model for both this worm-like structure, and the watermark encryption of classical narrative, because of the very simple set of functions he itemizes, and the principle of repetition and redundancy that he allows for. His assertion is that, although these functions have to come in a certain order in a narrative, some can be cut out and omitted, leapfrogged, as it were, in certain tales, while others come in series, for emphasis. As Lévi-Strauss, building on Propp, subsequently elaborated, the high degree of redundancy built into oral or popular narrative (i.e. repetition, inversion, isomorphism), is functional, because it compensates for what gets "lost in transmission."[16]

The Lévi-Strauss Model

Claude Lévi-Strauss became famous for his analysis of what he called "wild thinking"—*La pensée sauvage*—that is, the concepts used by certain oral cultures to narrate their myths of creation, or the stories that rule their social life. This wild thinking turns out to follow an often very precise logic, built not out of abstractions but with the blocks of a concrete materiality, and developed on the basis of complex, modular classification systems. Like other body-, family- or kinship-based schemata (such as those worked out by George Lakoff in his example drawn from Australian Aborigines classification,[17] or, in a more facetious-fantastic register, Jorge Luis Borges' "Chinese encyclopaedia," cited by Michel Foucault[18]), such wild thinking works in a seemingly meaningless way, but—depending on perspective and purpose—can also be shown to be surprisingly sophisticated and resourceful, once one is able to "crack the code" of the semantic clusters and syntactic arrangements into which they are organized via the mythic narratives. These analogies obviously do not translate in one-to-one fashion into the narratives and mythologies of Hollywood, nor does "wild thinking" correspond to the surface/depth structures to be discussed below. In Borges (as in Lévi-Strauss), surface and depth appear interchangeable, interwoven: which only underlines that surface and depth refer themselves to an organizing metaphor prioritized by Western cultures but by no means universal, proving that peoples, cultures or groups develop new modes of classification and sorting criteria, usually in light of different priorities, or more recently, thanks to different technologies.

Nonetheless, there are some benefits for film scholars in Lévi-Strauss' model, insofar as he provides an ideological-cultural explanation for both the encoding of the mythic message and for its efficacy or objective. The ultimate goal of telling stories, their social motive and motor, as it were, Lévi-Strauss avers, is to resolve a contradiction, and to deal with double binds. Somewhere he gives the example of the North American Indians, at the time of the arrival of the first European settlers, which posed for them not only a physical threat, but a metaphysical dilemma. Their religion forbade them to kill living beings, unless they kill them for food. So what do they do when they are attacked by whites and want to defend themselves? Become cannibals and eat them? No: they kill them and then scalp them. Why do they scalp them? Because a scalp for the Indian is the "crop of war": in other words, the semantic metaphor, and corresponding physical act allows for a saving shift, whereby they can claim to have killed for food after all, except not like buffalos, but like maize or grain, which they harvest from the fields and store.

The example may be anthropologically unsound, and no less fantastic than Borges' Chinese Encyclopaedia, but it illustrates well Lévi-Strauss' contention that myths constitute an imaginary resolution to real contradictions.[19] It is this formula that I think can be applied to Hollywood film narratives, which insofar as they are comparable to myths, also function in this manner, as the "enzymes" dissolving "dirt" from, or as algorithms, running self-repairing software programs on, the larger social belief system. In Lévi-Strauss, this is no easy matter. His analysis of the Greek myths clustering around Oedipus, the House of Thebes and its various (transgressive) family members, shows how many myths—as so many logico-mathematical moves, in the form of equations, such as A: B = −A: −B,—are needed, in order to resolve their inner contradiction in the form of narrative fictions. A heuristic step, when confronted with Hollywood films, might thus be to ask: what is the nature of the transgression or the contradiction that this film wants to resolve by way of its story? Or put slightly differently: If one follows Lévi-Strauss, one would also ask oneself: "what is the 'real contradiction' for which the film narrative thinks it provides the 'imaginary resolution'?"

Raymond Bellour was such a follower of Lévi-Strauss, and he made central to his practice of textual analysis (notably of Alfred Hitchcock's THE BIRDS, Vincente Minnelli's GIGI, and D.W. Griffith's THE LONEDALE OPERATOR)[20] not only the overall question of the imaginary contradiction, but also certain formal resources, to track their resolution, namely the many different kinds of symmetry, such as repetition (everything seems to come in threes), of mirroring, of doubling, of splitting and reversal, of echoes and parallels, typical of the classical Hollywood film. In a sequence of THE BIRDS, for instance (Melanie crossing Bodega Bay to deliver a pair of love birds), he shows the different kinds of symmetry and alternations at work which structure the scene in terms of moving camera/static camera, Melanie looking/Melanie being looked at, and close shot/long shot, and in

Gɪɢɪ he takes a whole film, and meticulously demonstrates how its individual sequences are organized in an exactly symmetrical shape, so that the whole film folds into itself, like an intricate origami figure, but also folds outward from relatively simple units, which are like themes and variations in music. Not only is the film structured like a poem, in that each sequence rhymes with another sequence, often individual sequences turn out to have the same structure as the film overall, in other words, repeating itself at different levels, like the morphology of a plant, or like the fractals of the Mandelbrot set that we so often see computers generating out of very simple forms and programs.

Bellour argued that the Hollywood narrative film progresses and comes to a closure by what he calls the "repetition-resolution" effect. In other words, for him the excessive and insistent symmetry of the classical film is in fact not mere ornament or "formal play," but does valuable, indeed essential "work." This work one might describe in two ways. First, it seems that it is this repetition resolution which "reconciles" or makes imperceptible the two different levels I provisionally called the surface level and the deep level. While on the surface, a thriller or action film impresses us with its relentless forward drive, its cause and effect, blow and counterblow, question and answer linearity, "underneath," as it were, nothing moves at all, and instead, what we have is simply a repetition of the same elements or the same constellation over and over again, as if the film was moving in circles, or as if the central character was hitting his or her head against a brick wall.

Bellour has a name for this—he calls it the "symbolic blockage" (cf. his analysis of Hitchcock's Nᴏʀᴛʜ ʙʏ Nᴏʀᴛʜᴡᴇsᴛ)[21]—but we could also remind ourselves of the example I gave from Lévi-Strauss, the double bind, the imaginary resolution to the real contradiction: the real contradiction would then be the metaphorical brick wall or symbolic blockage, and the surface action, the impression of brisk forward movement.

Summary: The Oedipal Logic

While these three models show some significant difference, they also display remarkably consistent traits, when one asks what it is that drives storytelling, what gets things going, and in what direction or with what purpose. In the Aristotelian model, it is the conflict between the hero wanting something, and the world, his society or the Gods, putting obstacles in the way of this wanting something. In Propp's morphological model, the motor driving the story is a lack, a missing object or person that the protagonist has to restore to its rightful place, like returning the princess to her father (the king), or getting the magic ring back from the evil dragon.

The Lévi-Straussian structure has often been called the "Oedipal" logic of the classical narrative film, meaning very simply that the center of a Hollywood film is mostly a male protagonist worrying about what it means to be/or become a man, worrying about his male identity, subjectivity and worrying even more about female subjectivity and sexuality. An important variant on this Oedipal logic is what one might call the melodramatic logic—where the main protagonist is a woman, and the film charts the formation of female identity, subjectivity-sexuality—or its impossibility. In this Oedipal story it is a transgression, of having knowingly or unknowingly broken a law, which then produces terrible consequences.

We could also summarize these modes as revolving around either a disturbance via an intrusion, or a matter of closing a gap, filling a lack, returning the missing object. An even more basic schema would be to say that a narrative structure is complete when it consists of a triple structure: equilibrium/disequilibrium/equilibrium (proposed by Todorov).

To sum up this part of the chapter on narrative: Bordwell's definition or Aristotelian method of the well-made drama, implies the screenwriter's manual formula of the three-act structure, plus introduction and coda; furthermore, Hollywood films have a double plot structure (action-adventure and romance-love story); they have a character-centered, goal-oriented causality, and display certain types of narration, differentiated according to the degree and kind of information flow: narrative is either "restricted" or "omniscient." To these characteristics one could add the typically Hollywood attention to the surface structure, understood as a linear, one-directional movement forward, which helps disguise that other structure, the depth structure that is circular, repetitive. The motor of the Aristotelian model is a problem or task, which the hero has to solve, against all odds. The other models indicate what makes the motor stall . . .

Wollen's definition or the Proppian method implies that actions are mere moves in a more abstract game; that characters are functions rather than individual autonomous agents, and that the motor is a constitutive lack. A more sophisticated elaboration of the Proppian model is Greimas' semiotic square, which could be the basis for a cognitivist approach, revolving around "logical" categories or syllogisms, organized by contradiction, complementarity.[22]

Bellour's definition as well as Lévi-Strauss' method of myth analysis implies a series of more or less autonomous segments; the overall direction is towards the resolution of the romance plot (or what he calls "the problematic of the formation of the [heterosexual] couple"),[23] and the protagonists are attributes that are bundled, not rounded characters. Bellour mostly pays attention to the deep structure, mentioned above, understood as circular and reversible.

Thus, to repeat: the object of textual analysis is not, in the first instance, to provide an interpretation, that is, to give a new or unusual reading of a film or a sequence. If at all, it wants to explore the inner workings of a feature film—any feature film: the choice could ideally be more or less arbitrary or contingent—because it wants to take apart the story-telling, image-making and sound-producing machinery ("the film [as] system," the film as process) which is the classical Hollywood cinema, directing attention to the obviousness of a classically constructed film, the fact that we can all understand it, all react to it, all be entertained or scared by it.

Surface Structure—Deep Structure—Morphology

I have deliberately concentrated in my examples on aspects of macro-analysis, and I have chosen a form of segmentation that varied between the specifically filmic (the treatment of sound and image, of space, camera movement and visual composition) and the non-specific and cognitive (metaphors and categories like inside-outside, arrival/departure) or of roles—the heterosexual couple, for example. I could have, and perhaps should have also said something more about the micro-analysis of a film, the problem of segmentation at the level of the sequence or the shot. This is an area that film semiotics has spent a good deal of effort on, namely to define the smallest units of meaning in a film (very important for the language analogy), and to see if the same kinds of alternations, oppositions and repetitions structure the apparently continuous and smooth flow of the images.

However, what the double plot structure model does not quite address is the fact that in the Hollywood film, we can speak of three levels, each of which is organized and structured in particular ways—let's call them the surface structure and the deep structure, or the overt and the covert logic, or (to give this division a certain psychoanalytic turn) we can distinguish between the "rational agent logic" and the "logic of desire." The third level would then be one that one might identify by its energies, its intensities, its fluidity and instability: it could be called the "Gestalt" logic, or we could call it the "figural" logic or "body-logic."

The surface structure is linear, mono-directional, causal; the deep structure is recursive, typified by repetition, it is often circular, and the body-logic is regulated more by motor-sensory energy, by colors and shapes, by aggregate states and conversion-rates, by surface touch, by haptic space, by the visceral and the somatic, as opposed to the semiotic.

These three levels can stand in a marked tension to each other. To give an example from BRAM STOKER'S DRACULA: as a rational agent, Jonathan Harker leaves Mina because he has been given an important business assignment, and he also hopes to make a lot of money so that he can provide Mina with the kind of life-style of her friend Lucy. But parallel, or underneath this rational agent motivation, there is the logic of desire—or anxiety—which impels Jonathan to leave Mina because he is afraid of her sexuality, so that the business assignment acts as a rationalization of a desire, namely not to get married to her, which is to say, not to have sex with her (just yet). And side-by-side to it, is the logic of blood and "bleeding," of contamination and inflammation, of fluids and their dispersal, of energies accumulated before they are released or discharged.

The "Film Work": between Film as System and Film as Process

In the approach I have chosen to demonstrate this Hollywood system at work, certain terms play a major role, such as repetition, alternation, symmetry, dissymmetry, reversal, difference, splitting and doubling, condensation and displacement. In a whole range of studies devoted to the classical Hollywood narrative system these have emerged as key concepts, and while originating from quite different fields of endeavor they can be shown to work together in the filmic process in order to unify, harmonize, or smooth over the discontinuities at the level of image and sound by giving the impression of coherence, narrative progress and spectator participation. The major prototype for this kind of investigation in literature has been Roland Barthes's *S/Z*, the study of *Sarrasine*, a short novel by Honoré de Balzac, in which Barthes distinguishes and differentiates between a number of codes, and whose working together weaves the story's textual substance, its body, density, realism, suspense and so on, in a process which Barthes either called "braiding," or spoke of as the articulation of the different "voices" of the text, that is, not characters and protagonists but the registers and functions of their actions and their presence in the text.

Films draw on a variety of pre-existing and pre-established conventions common to other narrative arts, in setting up and unfolding their system which allows them to tell a story in the most economical and rapid way—economy and rationality being a major characteristic of classical storytelling in film. But they also utilize means that are unique and peculiar to the cinema, not least in the manner in which the viewing situation (the spectacle in the darkened room) and the viewing status (the film doesn't acknowledge that I am watching/the film addresses only me) involves the spectator in a highly contradictory and ambiguous attitude, which one might characterize as that of fiction par excellence (the suspension of disbelief) but which one might also call, using a more psychoanalytic vocabulary, a condition of disavowal, and of double identification. For many of these considerations, the openings of films take on a privileged role, being in a sense both a miniaturization or compression of the film, and that which sets up the terms of the enigma, posing a question, a dilemma, a paradox, to which the film as a whole will appear to give the answer.

To exemplify the processes involved in an opening sequence and also give some idea of the efficacy with which it prepares the stage for story comprehension and spectator involvement, while at the same time presenting (in a different form or code) the whole film in a nutshell, scholars have often turned to the analysis of dreams. Film as a form of (day-) dream has been one of the most widely used metaphors in the history of the cinema, but in film studies, thanks to psychoanalysis, it has taken on a much more specific meaning. In particular, scholars have found in Sigmund Freud's groundbreaking study of dreams the methodological tools or concepts also useful for film. Especially suggestive has been Freud's notion of the so-called dream-work, with its typical psychic process and goals, which are: condensation, displacement, distinction between manifest and latent content, infantile fantasy material, considerations of representability, secondary elaboration, and wish-fulfilment.

Two well-known articles by Thierry Kuntzel on THE MOST DANGEROUS GAME and Fritz Lang's M are good examples of such a systematic investigation into a film opening from a classically psycho-analytic perspective. I shall try to work without a specialized vocabulary as much as possible, and if at all, encroach only upon the territory of rhetoric and semiotics, in order to describe the operations whereby the unity of a sequence or a shot is decomposed and recomposed, altered and used up in the unfolding of a narrative sequence.

After what has been said so far, I can be brief about the methodological presuppositions and the general principles of narrative analysis entering into the question of a film's textual system. But broadly speaking, we should distinguish between the macro-analytical level, which all narratives share, regardless of the medium and the material support (i.e. oral, written, film narratives, strip-cartoons, allegorical painting, etc.), and the micro-analytical level, where one would be looking for the minimal units pertinent to the analysis of the cinematic discourse (the size of the shot, camera-movement and camera-perspective, composition of the image, the transitions from shot to shot, the relation between sound and image, etc.), that is, those elements, techniques and processes which are specific to film. For the macro-analytic analysis, Lévi-Strauss has provided some of the more useful categories, not because they are necessarily "true," but because his analyses of myths adhere to a rigorous formalism. They have also given some indication of the socio-cultural function of narratives: how narratives construct and articulate kinship relations (and thus address the question of sexual difference), how they deal with contradictions (what logical categories are involved), and finally, their importance for economic relations (the systems of exchange and equivalence implicit in narratives).

On the question of micro-analysis, the most influential work can be found, apart from Thierry Kuntzel, in essays by Christian Metz, Raymond Bellour and Stephen Heath, all of whom have conducted analyses of specific sequences or individual films, in an effort to provide exemplary and generalizable models of textual readings of films. All of them have come to rather similar conclusions, which may either reflect the homogeneity of the Hollywood classical system, or indicate common problems in their methodological assumptions.

Opening Sequences

Opening sequences of classical films, I have claimed, are rather like manuals. They are the first encounter you make with your new purchase when you open the box. Manuals belong to the package, but they are also at one remove from the package: part of the purchase, but not part of the object. Thus, while the opening of a film usually establishes background, place, time as well as introducing the main protagonists, it also functions as a meta-text, so to speak, introducing us to the film's system, how it wants to be read and how it needs to be understood.

I have picked three examples of opening scenes from feature films made in the 1930s, plus one from the 1940s. They are all comparable in terms of the technological and organizational structure of the film industries that produced them. Apart from the already mentioned M, by Fritz Lang, made in 1931 in Germany and THE MOST DANGEROUS GAME, by Irving Pichel and Ernest B. Schoedsack, made in 1932 by the company that produced KING KONG the same year, I have chosen ANGEL (directed in 1936 by Ernst Lubitsch, and starring Marlene Dietrich, both émigrés from Germany) and Howard Hawks' classic 1946 Warner Bros. film THE BIG SLEEP.

In order to discuss all these opening scenes within one coherent set of assumptions, I have chosen a number of common characteristics, which seem to govern the construction of classical cinema's opening scenes. These are adapted from the two articles by Thierry Kuntzel already cited: entry or transgression, transfer or substitute, cluster or constellation, enigma or problem, name or title, condensation and displacement.

Entry (into the Film, Entry into the Fiction, Entry into the Characters)

Doors (passages, camera-movements forward, primary and secondary identification, punctuation marks, segmentation, points of reversal, thresholds, secrets beyond the door, mysteries, forced or forbidden entry). The notion of passage: a space is delineated by a door, but it may just lead to other doors (the many passages leading inwards and then outwards again, as in THE MOST DANGEROUS GAME), the door into Frau Beckmann's apartment in M (which, via the door of the cuckoo clock, leads to the outside of the School, via the sound bridge of the chimes and the bells). Doors do not reveal, but act as passages (they are privileged moments of narrative transit). In ANGEL, we have several doors, marking a number of distinct spaces: the revolving door of the Imperial Hotel, the door of 314 rue de la Tour, the two doors for entrances and exits of the Grand Duchess Anna's reception room. In actual fact, the two central characters pass through these spaces, rather than inhabit them. Anna's salon is not so much a meeting place for Marlene Dietrich and Melvyn Douglas, as it is a passage: to the restaurant, to their love affair. As Kuntzel points out, in THE MOST DANGEROUS GAME, the door marks the spectator's entry into the film, in the credit scene, and then, via the character of Joel McCrea, and the repetition-in-difference of the hand entering the picture to activate the door-knocker, identify with the main protagonist, indeed make him the main protagonist.[24]

Doors as limits, doors as signs of transgression: in M the door marks a rigid division of inside/outside, an occasion for the camera to change sides, which later on becomes itself simply a system of difference, no longer dependent on the door as its signifier, its visual support. The front door of the Salon in ANGEL is barred to everyone not familiar to the Grand Duchess, but it becomes transparent to the camera, which first prowls along the outside of the house, following in a parallel trajectory the Grand Duchess' progress inside, and then suddenly via the camera and sync sound, we are allowed to join in on the conversation: aware of our inferiority to the characters, we become privileged over the characters who have to wait in the anteroom, while we are already inside, thus setting up a fairly complex structure relative to the spectator's position of knowledge vis-à-vis the characters.

Transfer, Displacement, Substitute

The question of the position of knowledge brings us to the issue of "who" and "what" the spectator identifies with, and how this is brought about. We have seen that in THE MOST DANGEROUS GAME, it is the hand, that is, a part-object, which strongly encourages us to put our selves in its place, rhetorically speaking it is a synecdoche, operating by allowing us to infer the person by the part. A different process governs narration in M, where the film opens on a static high-angle shot of the courtyard. Once a complete round of the nursery rhyme has eliminated another little girl, the camera begins to move and slowly circles or rather spirals round the children until it picks up the movement of the woman carrying the laundry. It follows her up the stairs, and when Frau Beckmann opens the door, the camera makes a rapid forward movement, before reversing angle, and staying behind with Frau Beckmann in the kitchen, as it were. The camera thus has a movement of its own, independent and non-identical with any of the characters, and yet, by a threefold mimetic process of equivalence (or doubling, as Bellour would say), it associates itself successively with the circle of children, the washer-woman and Frau Beckmann. Here the transfer is extremely fluid, and is not so much determined by part-objects as it is by substitute characters: the girls substitute for Elsie, the washer-woman substitutes for mothers in general and then for Frau Beckmann in particular: the fiction has finally settled on the main protagonist of this sequence.

In the case of ANGEL, we have, apart from the splitting of the camera-position into the (socially) excluded and (voyeuristically) included spectator, two rather prominent examples of another structure of involvement, where the camera's point of view is delegated to the character in the fiction via the close-up of an object, in the form of a glance-object shot. When Marlene Dietrich opens her handbag in the hotel lobby we get a close-up of the bag and its buckle. It is not the case that she is now scrutinizing the contents of the handbag and we have her point of view; instead, the close-up connotes a situation of collusion and participation in which the spectator is implicated: we share her intention of concealing her identity.

This shot is repeated, a few seconds later, when she pulls the visiting card out of the bag, letting us see the address. The close-up thus gives us access not to the field of vision of the character, as in the point of view shot of the front door of Count Zaroff, or the apartment door of Frau Beckmann, but to the character's intention, her secret plans, her thoughts, which we infer via the object thus brought to our attention, but primarily via the camera's active role in the flow of images. The transfer is from camera to object, but the meaning of the shot has nothing to do with the object as such, because the object is itself a stand-in, a substitute: for the character's motivation (she is about to go to this address) and for the place itself: the next shot shows us the number on the front door—except that it is not her but another character, played by Melvyn Douglas, who is about to enter: another substitution. The action progresses by involving us with the protagonists, successively and by transfer, using the film's objects metonymically for its action spaces, and its characters metaphorically via substitution and equivalence.

The Constellation, or Emblematic Cluster

In an opening scene or sequence, we often find a privileged image or composition, which in a sense gathers together diverse and heterogeneous elements in a single configuration, whose meaning will only become fully apparent in retrospect. It thus functions rather like an emblematic picture, as a condensation of the various narrative motifs, as well as implying a temporal structure of anticipation and suspense. In THE MOST DANGEROUS GAME, as Thierry Kuntzel points out, there are a number of such constellations, chief among them the door-knocker, with its representation of a centaur, carrying a woman, and pierced by an arrow in his chest. It represents, in stylized and figurative form, three central oppositions (or enigmas) which the narrative sets itself the task to resolve: the relationship between man and beast, the relationship between hunter and hunted, aggressor and prey, and finally, the relationship between sexuality and death—all three enigmas being crucially centered on the woman: as prey, as game, as prize. The figure of the centaur condenses the three central male characters: Ivan, Zaroff's servant; Zaroff himself; and Rainsford, the hero.

In M, this emblematic composition is the shot of the poster, with the girl's ball bouncing off the billboard, and Peter Lorre's shadow falling across the image. Here we have less a process of condensation and more a constellation of displacements: from Elsie we move to the ball, from the stranger to his shadow, from his person to his voice, from voice off to voice on, from the physical body to the printed word. Lorre himself enacts this matrix of displacements when he says to Elsie: "what a pretty ball you have," meaning "what a pretty girl you are." In this emblematic scene, then, the Lorre character is three times removed as it were, and three times signified by these displacements: the shadow, the voice, the poster. His body-voice-presence is systematically translated into the (mere) signs of that presence.

This is important because this splitting and substituting of the subject by its representations is ultimately the only access that the film gives us to the murderer: who he is, why he does what he does. He sees himself, in his final speech before the underworld bosses, as his own Double, haunted by the Other within himself. In the rigidly binary and oppositional field that the film creates, he is in fact a void, the space that the opposition gangster/police at the thematic level and the separation of elements of filmic process generate. In this sense, he is produced by the gaps that open between the film's system of alternation and its system of substitutions, but he is also the product of the discourses of the others, the descriptions, the definitions, the clues and motives that others attribute to him. Finally, he is for everyone a mere pre-text, a stand-in, a conveniently concrete object to be hunted and eliminated, the scapegoat whose disappearance—like that of the child Elsie—does not seem to interest either the police or the gangsters per se, but only in relation to something else: for the gangsters to get the police off their backs, for the police to get the politicians off their backs.

The Enigma

Narratives, according to Todorov's formula, can be characterized, at their most basic, as structures, which begin with a steady state, an equilibrium, a balance. This balance is disrupted by an intervention, an irruption (the explosion on board in The Most Dangerous Game, the non-return of Elsie from school in M) which it is the task of the narrative to neutralize, redress, eliminate, so that finally, an equilibrium is re-established which resembles the initial one, but with significant differences. This interruption can also be presented as an enigma, a puzzle. In M the enigma is not the question of who is the murderer of Elsie or the other girls, nor even whether the police will get the murderer before the underworld, nor exactly what the criminal's motives might be, but something more intangible at first sight, indicated perhaps when we note that in M a crucial ambiguity is established between who is the hunter and who is the hunted, the positions being infinitely reversible. This, as we have seen, characterizes the narrative enigma and paradox also of The Most Dangerous Game, whose story develops by reversing the roles twice over, although as Kuntzel has pointed out, despite these reversals what remains intact and unquestioned is the status of the woman: her position remains outside, irrespective of who is the hunter and who the hunted.

In Angel the enigma is already associated with the woman's identity: who is she, where does she come from, where does she disappear to? The opening scene itself is based on a number of questions concerned with this enigma, and an equally elaborate system of concealment of the answer, a tantalizing series of recognition and mis-cognition scenes, a shift of naming and un-naming of mis-attributions and re-attributions, all centered on the question of who is this woman, itself a displacement of the question: "what is woman?" As cinema audiences, we know the answer to the first one in advance: it is "Marlene Dietrich." Typical of the game Hollywood plays with the spectator, we have a film whose enigma is the star persona of the actress, whose reputation as a star, precisely, is built around the notion that she is an enigma—as a person, as a woman, as an actress—comparable in this only to Greta Garbo.

M is unique, insofar as its enigma is not centered on an identity as much as on the construction of an identity out of absence. For instance, in Frau Beckmann's kitchen, the plate, the chair, the napkin stand for Elsie, but in such a way that their presence signifies her absence. This relation presence/absence structures the entire opening scene, mapping itself onto the opposition kitchen/staircase, interior/exterior, as the presence of somebody outside (the children on the stairs, the news vendor doing his round) promises the return of Elsie, yet in the event only serves to confirm her absence. This extends particularly to the use of sound in its relation to image. Frau Beckmann, for instance, replies to the washer-woman: "as long as you can hear the children, they are at least safe." Whereas the washer-woman associates the murder metaphorically with the children's rhyme, Frau Beckmann's relation to the song is metonymic, accepting one (the song) for the sign of the other (the children's safety), thus endorsing a system of substitution which is the film's main form of dramatic irony, and indeed part of its enigma.

The Name, the Title

In each of the examples chosen, a major ambiguity hinges on the word, or a word, contained in or making up the title. In ANGEL the identity of the character is given, but by way of an answer to the enigma of the opening scene this is a non-answer, initiating ambiguity rather than settling it. The title credits are followed immediately by the shot of an aeroplane: this is itself a punning reference to the title, a joking literalization of angels coming from heaven. This shot is followed by one of a woman's face, unrecognizable because of a huge hat, shading most of her face. We follow the direction of her gaze, and cut to a shot of the Arc de Triomphe, immediately succeeded by a printed title: Paris, as if we hadn't already recognized it. This in turn is followed by a shot of a revolving door, itself a pun on the Arc de Triomphe with its star-shaped avenues going off in different directions, like the different wings of the revolving door, thus miniaturizing the Arc in the door, after the Arc had already been miniaturized by the bird's eye view (or should we say the Angel's gaze?) from the plane. These first three or four shots establish the name, the title, even the place as a kind of sliding signifier. Or perhaps we should say revolving signifier, insofar as it names somebody by not naming her, as becomes evident in the scene in which Melvyn Douglas gives her the name Angel, frustrated at her persistence in withholding information about her. Second, the opening shots inscribe two other kinds of splits and divisions in the film: that of perspective and point of view (via the relativity of size), and that of over-explicitness and reticence (over-explicit in relation to Paris, reticent in relation to the identity of the central character).

In THE MOST DANGEROUS GAME, the male protagonist is, as Kuntzel remarks, the only character who is given a Christian name and a surname, thus privileging him, making him the hero, by an over-explicitness of naming. In ANGEL, it is the other way round. Furthermore, we should note that both types of division establish a reversibility and symmetry constructed around a binary axis—in one case the axis is that of information (over-explicit/reticent), in the other case it is perspective. In a film, which will construct an impossibly complex and volatile (because constantly overturned and reversed) triangular sexual relationship, reversibility and instability are thus introduced in an apparently quite unrelated and irrelevant context, once more indicating the displacement and metatextuality that so often operate in film openings. Also, the fact that the significant and pertinent codes or structural relations permeate even the most insignificant features, help prepare the spectator for the film's specific system of generating oppositions, and draws from them its signifying power. In THE MOST DANGEROUS GAME, the ambivalence clusters around the word "game"—polysemic insofar as it can mean something you play—what Zaroff calls "outdoor chess," to do with gambling, taking risks, as in the case of the owner of the ship, taking the risk of going through uncharted waters, or of the man on board who plays cards by himself. But also game in the sense of wild animals being hunted, introducing in the condensation of the two meanings the central obsession of Zaroff, who wants to increase the danger of the hunt by pursuing not animals, but human beings. On the other hand, while "game" in this sense seems to refer to man, meaning male, a displacement occurs between the two adjacent signifiers contained in the term human being, namely man and woman, so that the most dangerous game might indeed be woman, because it is she who is the prize, the triumph, the trophy in Zaroff's words.

Most complex in relation to name and title is, however, M. What does it actually stand for? Murderer, Mothers, or is it a reference to Lang's previously most famous films—DR MABUSE, METROPOLIS? Does it have a connection with the capital M on the poster promising a reward? Does it stand for Mark in the sense of "marking": does the chalked hand brand him or identify him? Is it a reference to the puppet in the shop window, the little man on a string (*Hampelmann* in German), whose legs form the letter M when one pulls the string? Does it stand for Mann or Mensch or Everyman: as in the many references to "Beckmann," "der schwarze Mann"? We have here in a title not only an enigmatic mark as such—an abbreviation, or a code word, but a sign in which the signifier as well as the referent are uncertain, sliding. Is it a letter, a name, a figure (multiple meanings of the signifier, visual pun if you like) or does it apply to Lorre, to the police (the ambivalence of branding and identifying), to the mother? Maybe it is the author's signature, a kind of private reference and in-joke?

Condensation/Displacement: Metaphor/Metonymy

In decomposing the image-material to draw from it its narrative potential, classical cinema works very heavily with relations of similarity and difference, by employing the rhetorical possibilities inherent in the difference/similarity axis represented by metaphor and metonymy, which is at the same time a way of generating narrative momentum, and demanding psychic investment from the viewer, precisely "work." Both Kuntzel and Metz have looked at the scene in M which signals to the viewer the death of little Elsie, and in particular at the chain of signifiers and how they are interwoven: the ball and the balloon. These two objects stand in a complex relation to both Elsie and the murderer, through the symmetry of belonging to/given to on one axis, and looking like, resembling on another axis. Both objects are part-objects, but they become operative in the narrative through the common denominator of absence: they figure Elsie in her absence and as absence.[25]

The Opening of THE BIG SLEEP

Can these common characteristics of opening scenes be located in the beginning of a film where seemingly not much happens? Before ending this chapter on the semiotic constraints at work in ANGEL, I want to examine the opening of THE BIG SLEEP: a rather ordinary "warming-up" scene, where characters just impart and exchange information; talking heads mainly: a sort of zero degree of classical narrative. It also does not seem to have a follow-up beyond its expository purpose, and rather oddly, one of the chief protagonists of the opening, the General, never features again in any of the scenes.

Entry

There is a notable emphasis on doors, as they organize, divide and articulate the space(s) both physical and narrative. In this respect the film draws attention to itself, it becomes self-referential, because the doors mark also our trajectory as spectators, "entering" into the fiction. The topography of the mansion (left to right, downstairs-upstairs; hero moves from left to right and then returns from right to left via upstairs; elision of exit/entry to next location via fade out/fade in) becomes a mental map that very unobtrusively but nonetheless very efficiently helps us orient ourselves within the narrative and "places" the protagonists in relation to each other. The self-referentiality extends to the use of what film scholars have termed the "erotetic" principle of question and answer, how one scene provides the "answer" to the implicit or explicit "question" left hanging or posed in the previous scene. For instance, consider the calibrated, incremental way in which Marlowe is introduced: first we see a thumb on the doorbell, then we have a voice, before we see a "body," followed by a young woman coming down the stairs (Carmen) asking: "who are you" and "what are you—a prize fighter?" asking, in other words, questions we would like to ask: now *she* is acting as our stand-in, after Marlowe had been *our* stand-in initially when gaining access to the Sternwood mansion.

Rhyming Effects, Textu(r)al Density and Repetition

There are, at the macro- and micro-levels, many unobtrusive elements that can help us understand just why a Hollywood film, already at the scenario stage, is such a labor-intensive (and thus expensive) enterprise. Consider the symmetry of the opening scene as a whole. It is divided into three parts of equal length, and each is marked by a written sign/card/plaque. There is the brass name plate ("Sternwood") at the beginning, echoed by the metal plaque "Public Library" at the end, but punctuated in the dead center of the sequence by a close-up of a business card that reads "Arthur Geiger/Rare Books." We thus have symmetry/division, distributed across "the name and the book," but also spelling out the duplicity which each of these signs implies, hinting at a "secret beyond the door," and in the wider sense, pointing to the "corruption" of signs across the film as a whole, here in the opening already repeating itself in different variations.

A similarly elaborated textuality can be found at the verbal level, where a number of metaphoric clusters, sliding signifiers and (bad) puns ensure a richly woven fabric of allusions that condense some of the main themes and indicate the dynamics of the (male-female-family centered) relationships. Particularly noticeable is the use of clichés and stereotypes, around drink and alcohol, that are both aptly literalized and invigorated by their interconnectedness: when Marlowe says to the butler about Carmen that she is "old enough to be weaned," he not only makes us notice that sorely missing in this family is a mother (-figure), inadequately substituted by an avuncular butler. The phrase also prepares us for Marlowe's aggressive come-on to Mrs Rutledge, when he dryly observes that she is having her "lunch out of a bottle," indicating that both women, despite their sexual promiscuousness and air of sophistication, are profoundly child-like. But the slangy witticisms also pick up General Sternwood's own remark, namely that his age obliges him to indulge in "drink by proxy," as he encourages Marlowe to pour himself another whisky to cope with the heat in his greenhouse/conservatory, in which the orchids are an excuse for the heat, but also a potent signifier in a chain that goes from orchid to flesh to blood to sex to heat, in order to spell out pretense, decadence and corruption, a metaphoric chain underlined by the overt symbolism of the proper names that combine paternal severity (General "Stern"wood) and filial promiscuity (Mrs "Rut"ledge) in one continuous, if contradictory line up.

A closer look at the overall architecture of these metaphorical clusters confirms how much of this opening is structured around significant absences, themselves centered on the "family" as the core unit of "normal" societal cohesion and personal identity. We could summarize this relation of deviance to norm by saying that the opening scene revolves around (fading) Dynasties, (rutting) Daughters and the (unfulfilled) Desire for a Son. There is the doubly deficient family (a father who is too old to be a parent, and a mother who is mysteriously missing), creating a gap around the maternal signifier, filled by the butler ("you ought to wean her"), and another gap around the son the General never had, a place at first filled by Shawn Reagan, who betrays his elective father, and then offered to Marlowe, who politely refuses.

This apparently so banal scene thus revolves around "serious" dynastic issues: about the well-known aristocratic-bourgeois dilemma of too many daughters and no male heirs, as well as about authority and succession (here: the enigmatic function of the butler Norris, who is "foreign" [English, i.e. associated with the aristocracy] and stands in for the maternal element, but also has powers of attorney and can sign cheques, the supreme patriarchal right). In this respect, Marlowe's physical trajectory from door (opening) to door (closing) is intervaled by a sequence of interruptions symmetrically placed, which while taking the form of question and answer, also prepare the (eventual) resolution (of the film as a whole: the formation of the couple). The question is: will this be the return of the (prodigal) "son" who comes through the door, scrutinized by the "mother" and the "father," and which daughter will he choose? So the sequence of encounters that Marlowe has:

door/Butler/Carmen/Butler/General: General/Butler/Rutledge/ Butler/door, prepares for the answer, because it effects in the reverse order of its repetitions the significant "substitution" of the female, namely Mrs Rutledge for Carmen, but also the approval of the "father" and the disapproval of the "mother."

Embedded in this macro-structure with mythical resonances is another structure, which mobilizes historical knowledge and cultural codes, cunningly deployed. This not only refers to what has just been said about British butlers, but extends also into the area of the American civil war, and the background to America's Irish immigrants, their relation to the homeland, and the homeland's relation to Britain. Sternwood's discussion of Shawn Reagan and Marlowe's acquaintance with him mobilizes the different tropes of rebellion and insubordination: Sternwood is a Southern, that is "rebel" general; Reagan fought in the IRA before becoming a gangster, and Marlowe was fired from the police force for "insubordination"—all three men are bound together by their rebellious nature, unwilling to accept "castration," a trait emphasized by the mirror-relation between Reagan and Marlowe, who according to Marlowe, were on opposite sides but alternated between swapping bullets and swapping drinks, the pun and linguistic zeugma underscoring their equivalence in respect of the General's symbolic masculinity and dynastic ambitions.

Here, then, as in all classical films, two plot strands are intertwined: that of the hero as detective, charged with an investigation, and that of the "substitute son," charged with continuing the Sternwood dynasty, which means that Marlowe is immediately inserted into an Oedipal scenario, whose negative version we are told is Shawn Reagan, whom the General "treated like a son." The fact that General Sternwood never comes back in the film thus does find at least a symbolic justification: he is the embodiment of the Oedipal principle per se, but in a self-avowedly transgressive form ("Anyone who fathers children at my age, deserves what he has coming") so that a higher instance of the Transgressive Law (Marlowe) can take over from him, and at the same time, the General "dissolves" into all the other instances of "corruption" and paternal abuse that the film parades and explores.

"Woman Trouble" and the Fairy Tale as Deep-Structure

Howard Hawks' "camera at eye level" also means that the hero is at eye-level with the action: however much confusion and digression there is, as spectators we keep our feet planted on the ground, because this topsy-turvy world is ultimately "grounded" in the (male, investigator's) eye-level perspective (where little information is available to us which is not also available to Marlowe). But, as I have tried to show, with its intricate rhythm of balance and imbalance, hiding and revealing, surface-structure detail and deep-structure generality, the opening of THE BIG SLEEP can also be seen as following the logic of disavowal, that is, initiating a major shift in emphasis from the opening to the film as a whole, which not so much exemplifies the "lesson" of the opening scene as it reverses it either mirror-fashion or by displacing the crucial conflict to another register (see also SINGIN' IN THE RAIN, SUNSET BOULEVARD, or THE POSTMAN ALWAYS RINGS TWICE for other examples of how an opening may stand in a tension of disclosure/disavowal to the rest of the film).

This points to the fact that THE BIG SLEEP is also marked by what theorists such as Colin MacCabe or Stephen Heath have analyzed as the fundamental imbalance of the classical system, in particular, the excessiveness and instability of its "geometry of representation," here concentrated on the skewed "architecture of the looks" between male and female protagonists. Furthermore, it is a film where "the woman" appears as the trouble in the system. The film seems full of digressions, compared to the information that the plot requires, but as it turns out, most of this "redundant" information is about women, or rather, about how Marlowe is seen by women, how he displays himself to women, how he is motivated by women. Such an emphasis on male desire and male anxiety means that "woman trouble" becomes the motor of this perfectly functioning narratological machine, where there can be no interruption or pause, and where the minor details and detours are relentlessly re-integrated, retrospectively re-motivated, but—as David Thomson shows,[26] in his analysis of the scene with Dorothy Malone in Geiger's bookstore—with just enough bravura to stand out as set-pieces in their own right.

Considered as a *film noir*, THE BIG SLEEP conforms to the general model of telling a (sexist) love story, where the battle with the femme fatale tends to take over when the detective story begins to have motivational holes. This "inconsistency" is structural when we recall how, according to feminist critiques of the narrative economy of Hollywood, "woman" is that which "troubles" the Oedipal system and thus the detective plot, at once pointing to and hiding the fact that the hero is ultimately "investigating" himself. The nature of the erotic digressions in THE BIG SLEEP, however, is such that each encounter with a femme fatale seems to motivate the next encounter, but the viewer never entertains doubts about the outcome of any of them, because the principle of repetition has been so firmly set up and lodged in the viewer's mind in the opening scene: *all* the females in the film (eventually) fall for Bogey, the ultimate *homme fatale*.

But the film works this out in a system of carefully calibrated parallels and incremental differences that range from female dishonesty (Carmen) and deception (Mrs Rutledge) to (in the subsequent scenes) complicity (at the Acme Bookstore) and duplicity (Agnes). These are matched by the full spectrum of sexual arousal that their behavior elicits in Marlowe, from fatherly indulgence to out-and-out sadism, via first the symbolic (but explicitly staged) and then the actual (but ostentatiously off-screen) sexual act, paralleled by a plethora of double entendres, indirections and euphemisms, come-ons and teases.[27]

ANGEL: A System of Semiotic Constraints

In ANGEL we have a system, which is constructed to name, but also to protect an absence: that of the identity of the female heroine (I am/I am not; I want to/I don't want to). The film builds up an extraordinarily dense and complex network of negations, denials, disavowals and reversals. It does so, primarily, on the basis of repetition and alternation, structured by a rigorously binary code of splitting and doubling: I have already mentioned the repetition of the close-ups on the hand-bag, or the repetition of the revolving door motif. But consider the following shots: we first see Melvyn Douglas get out of a taxi; we have seen Marlene Dietrich enter the hotel, but we see her leaving it in order to get into a taxi. Douglas speaks English to the cab driver and he only pretends not to understand; Dietrich speaks English to the cab driver, he doesn't understand and she switches to French. The two scenes are put in alternation with each other, and they rhyme with each other, because they are built similarly, but they also mirror each other by reversing not only the direction of the movement, but the transfer of languages. In one case the cab driver speaks both, in the other the customer speaks both. The receptionist in the hotel looks at the name Dietrich gives on the register and then at the name in the passport, his gaze wandering in disbelief and then in recognition from one to the other. When Dietrich returns to ask is anything the matter he disavows both those gazes and replies: everything alright, nothing the matter, making himself the accomplice and colluding in the deceit, at about the same time as the camera makes us an accomplice with the close-up. At the Grand Duchess' salon, the game of repetition, reversal, symmetry and alternation is continued: Douglas (Mr Horton) is made to wait because he is a friend of Captain Buckley; Dietrich, because she says she is an old friend, is not received. Douglas dutifully waits, but Dietrich does not even wait for an answer. The shifting meanings and referents of the word "friend" are further punned on in one of the subsequent scenes, when the Grand Duchess says to Douglas, after expressing the wish to see the Louvre and so on: "are you sure you're a *friend* of Captain Buckley?"—a question which she answers herself at the end, when Douglas confesses that he has a date with the mystery lady: "you *are* a friend of Captain Buckley"—a displacement of accent, such as Freud analyzed it for the structure of jokes. Likewise, the signifiers "Louvre," "Eiffel Tower," "Notre Dame"—while like the Arc de Triomphe redundantly signify the high-culture of Paris—have a different signifying function: they are indeed symmetrically reversed when Douglas says them to the Grand Duchess, from whom he wants to get away (once he has recognized she *is* the Grand Duchess), compared to what they mean when Dietrich uses them, when she wants to get to know Douglas. Douglas came to see the Duchess, but when he sees her ("I recognized you instantly") he doesn't want to see her. When he realizes that he has been mistakenly thinking Dietrich the Grand Duchess, he is delighted at the mistake: he wants to see the Duchess and he doesn't want to see the Duchess—a shifting of signs and referents, which parodies Dietrich's indecision, namely "I am in Paris"/"I'm not in Paris," and "I wanted sensible advice"/"I don't want sensible advice," or the ironic reply that Dietrich gives when the Grand Duchess says to her "why haven't you written to me? I always like to keep in touch with my friends"—and she answers: "precisely."

The point I am trying to make is twofold. One: the entire opening scene is constructed around a verbal and visual system aimed at multiplying the uncertainties, the arbitrary relations between signifier and signified, by exploiting the plurality on the side of the signifier (puns, double entendres) and the plurality of the signifieds (ambiguity, irony, reversal of context), thus showing the reversibility of the relations and situations on the level of visual and verbal language, and condensing thereby the "theme" or "plot," namely the heroine's dilemma about which man to choose, when they are both equally desirable.

Second: the examples show, I think, how the signifying economy of the classical Hollywood system functions, where an extremely limited number of elements, situations or events are subjected to the most rigorous permutations and combinations, to yield very complex structures, whose logic is indeed quite abstract, and could be formulated as an algorithm, somewhat on the lines of Greimas's semiotic square.

Lubitsch's Mode of Narration as the Ethics of his Storytelling

The opening of ANGEL also gives us a way of resituating both surface and deep structure, in the way the figural operations play through the different repertoire of making continuity out of discontinuity while at the same time "thickening it" by way of figuration. But all this takes place on the surface, the sliding signifiers and visual puns; we do not need to assume that there is "depth" of something "hidden." Take once more the credits: Angel, followed by the shot of a plane (linking credits and first shot by way of a visual pun, activated via "inner speech," that is, dependent on a verbal/visual combination). The plane also acts as an establishing shot, leading to a cut-in: the cabin window which cues the face to turn and look out: reverse angle cut to what she sees as we see her (the axis seeing/seen as a continuity device: the Arc de Triomphe from above. Superimposed: "Paris," then a fade in/fade out to the revolving door of the hotel, which makes the continuity via a purely visual pun, the similarity of the Arc from above and the revolving door. The procedure is basically designed to create continuity out of discontinuity, but by displaying quite different ways of doing so (connoting that we are in a film that is self-consciously "narrated," which is a signifier of the "sophisticated" in the generic name of "sophisticated comedy").

Yet at the same time, the opening of ANGEL works on the principle of giving us too much information and not enough information. Thus the narration, while punning and self-conscious, is already introducing us to the major feature of narration in this film, namely that it tells us too much and too little, that it conducts a kind of narrational-cognitive striptease, hiding and revealing, saying and not saying, being over-explicit and too reticent.

This mode we can describe as one in which contradictions can coexist, and indeed intensify a certain emotion, a certain subjectivity, rather than leading (as in real life) to misunderstanding and blockage of communication. For instance, in GIGI, as discussed by Raymond Bellour, there is the famous sung duo "I remember it well" between Maurice Chevalier and Hermione Gingold, where they are the romantic couple that once was across a realization of perfect harmony built on total misunderstanding, since she contradicts everything he asserts about their former love-affair, and he replies "oh yes, I remember it well," that is, the two at one and the same time negate and affirm their divergent experiences in peaceful harmony. Likewise, in ANGEL, Marlene Dietrich can both be in Paris and not in Paris, can seek advice and not seek advice, be Mrs Brown and not Mrs Brown and so on.

The film plays this game, insofar as its first two segments are symmetrical in relation to Marlene Dietrich disappearing suddenly in both, once out of the door, the other out of the park. But it underscores the point in the opening of the second segment, because it opens with the violinist playing for them at dinner, and when he is finished, she says: "that's a beautiful tune, what is its name?" he replies: "it has no name, I've just invented it for you." Repetition also with Melvyn Douglas tipping the taxi driver (reluctantly), then tipping the musician in the restaurant, and then tipping (delightedly) the old lady with the bouquet, even though she lures him away enough for him to lose Marlene Dietrich who has disappeared (like an angel), while the camera lingers on the face of the old woman, giving us a chill of mortality and the inevitability of old age.

For as Marlene Dietrich says in the private dining room in the restaurant, "we've gone though our story very fast. I meet you at five, ten minutes later I agree to dine with you, and here we are after a romantic dinner, getting terribly serious." This moral-emotional point "doubles" the fact that these two opening segments are indeed the film in a nutshell, the *mise-en-abyme* of the film as a whole. Furthermore, the Angel descends from the sky to ground herself on the earth, getting more and more constricted and "private" until she feels caged and imprisoned by the man's passion and possessive urges. She has to keep her mystery. So, there is linearity in the narrative trajectory while repetition works on the texture and the surface, in order to suggest "depth." At the same time, there is a contradiction, in that this is clearly no angel, but a femme fatale, and furthermore, we know the answer to the insistent question "who are you?" is namely Marlene Dietrich, so that the textual operation and the extra-textual stand in a relation of contradiction to each other, but a contradiction which is not one, and instead, makes a further case for linking the outside of the film to the inside of the film, as the credits had already done with the word "Angel." Now the name of the star is evoked (with all that this star connoted by way of femme fatale, enigma and remote mystery). We thus have a kind of bracketing effect where Marlene Dietrich is bracketed with ANGEL, and Angel is bracketed with coming from the sky to Paris (where the real Marlene Dietrich was soon to settle, for the rest of her life).[28]

As a postscript to the postscript one might add that the opening shot is also a possible reminder of the opening scene of TRIUMPH OF THE WILL (Arc de Triomphe/Triumph of the Will), the party political propaganda film for the Nazi party made by Leni Riefenstahl in 1934, where Hitler emerges from the clouds and we share his bird's eye view of the city of Nuremberg. One's reply would be: yes, but what a difference! In Riefenstahl we have one full signifier following the other (plane, shadow, Wagner, crowds surging, everyone knows the Führer, everyone expects him). In ANGEL, no sooner do we have a "full" signifier than it is emptied again by way of the pun or by its negation—hence my phrase of the cognitive striptease. It is the ethics of Lubitsch's game of hiding and revealing, of opening doors, only to shut them in our faces, rolling out the carpet, only to pull the rug from under us.

This, then, is what textual analysis could be good for. You buy a new appliance—say, a television, or a hairdryer—and as you open the box, the first thing you find is a manual. Maybe, the Hollywood cinema is like this box you unwrap, and the opening of the film is like the manual, with textual analysis no more than someone explaining the manual. Perhaps next time, when unpacking the box, knowing how to read the manual will simply give you more pleasure and a longer life out of the "appliance." But film is also different, and this, too, close analysis can teach us: you cannot finally tell where the "out there" becomes the "in here," you don't know whether you open a door and come inside, or whether you are already inside and have just stepped through an already open door.

10

Gangsters and Grapefruits: Masculinity and Marginality in THE PUBLIC ENEMY

> The infamous grapefruit scene caused women's groups around America to protest the on-screen abuse of Mae Clarke. . . . For years afterward when dining in restaurants, fellow patrons would send grapefruit to actor James Cagney, which—almost invariably—James Cagney would happily eat.[1]

THE PUBLIC ENEMY, made in 1931 by Warner Bros., produced by Darryl F. Zanuck and directed by William A. Wellman, is remembered as one of the "classics" of the gangster genre. It is usually named along with Howard Hawks' SCARFACE and Mervyn Le Roy's LITTLE CAESAR as the third of a "cycle" made in the 1930–31 season, purportedly shadowing the Al Capone trial which took place in Chicago during the same period. One of the reasons why these three films have attained legendary status (out of an estimated thirty titles made across the relatively brief life-span of this gangster cycle) may be their unusual combination of generic prototypes with male stars. They all have rise-and-fall narratives, with colorful, flamboyant and ethnically stereotyped macho psychopaths, played by actors whose professional background did not necessarily predestine them for such roles: James Cagney, Paul Muni and Edward G. Robinson respectively.[2] In the case of THE PUBLIC ENEMY, the film's identification with Cagney is especially strong:

> PUBLIC ENEMY [is] a particularly brutal account of the rise and fall of a monstrous gangster. Cagney delivers one of the most famous performances in film history as the snarling crook who—in one of the film's most famous scenes—smashes a grapefruit into the face of Mae Clarke.[3]

Yet Cagney was trained as a dancer and entered Hollywood via vaudeville and musicals, usually teamed with Joan Blondell, who also co-stars in THE PUBLIC ENEMY as Mamie, Mae Clarke's girlfriend. David Thomson astutely summarizes the contradictions and duplicities embodied by Cagney:

> No one could move so arbitrarily from tranquillity to dementia, because Cagney was a dancer responding to a melody that he alone heard. . . . He made his first great impact in PUBLIC ENEMY . . . in which Cagney smacked Mae Clarke in the face with a cut grapefruit and ended in a ballet of hysterical expiration dead on his mother's doorstep. It was the gleeful smartness

in Cagney's playing that made PUBLIC ENEMY so influential and that induced the public's ambivalent feelings towards the criminal classes.[4]

Who Speaks: *Auteur*, Actor, Studio or Society?

It can be argued that THE PUBLIC ENEMY is one of those relatively rare cases where an acknowledged masterpiece is not also identified with an acknowledged *auteur*, even as the director, William Wellman, has a certain standing, though not to be compared with that of Hawks, Ford or Raoul Walsh.

Still, according to the *auteur* theory, THE PUBLIC ENEMY ought to be a Wellman film, but rarely is it seriously treated as such. More often, as indicated, it is identified by its genre or studio cycle (Warner Bros.' gritty realism prior to the Hays Code, and the studio's backing of Roosevelt's New Deal). Such labeling confirms the paradigmatic role THE PUBLIC ENEMY played in setting out chief tropes of the gangster film right up to the present (for instance, an IMDB review compares it to THE GODFATHER and GOODFELLAS, and another notes its citation/appearance in Coppola's COTTON CLUB). If its cultural identity is first and foremost that of the archetypal gangster picture, it may ultimately be Cagney who qualifies as the *auteur* of THE PUBLIC ENEMY. This feeling is born out when one looks at the long line of Warner directors who have further utilized, fleshed out or refined the Cagney persona from THE PUBLIC ENEMY onwards for the rest of the decade. Besides Wellman (2), we find Archie Mayo (3), Lloyd Bacon (3), Howard Hawks (2), Roy del Ruth (3), Michael Curtiz (3), William Keighley (3) and Raoul Walsh (2) who all signed for Cagney vehicles during the 1930s. With THE PUBLIC ENEMY, in other words, a case can be made for the actor as *auteur*. In support, one could cite Richard Dyer's theory of stardom.[5] There, he proposes to see the Hollywood star as a "bundle of relations" or "values" which are contradictory if taken separately, but whose contradictions are reconciled in the image of the star. The star thus does useful ideological work in "naturalising" contradictions that mark the social fabric of a given community. As has already been hinted at, it is the over-the-top gestural excess and generic crossing that Cagney brings to the role of Tom Powers, which have secured the film an enduring place in filmgoers' memory. In the literature on Cagney, both Robert Sklar and Patrick McGilligan have made such a case for Cagney as "*auteur*," based on the contradictory associations that his role seems to unite, notably that of the "dancer gone wrong."[6]

However, what interests me about THE PUBLIC ENEMY is almost the opposite of arguing the case for either the director or the star to be considered as the film's *auteur*. Even the studio, Warner Bros., for whom both Wellman and Cagney were contract employees, has, as we shall see, as good a claim as anybody to authorship. And taking the studio argument a step further, it is the "system" which here functions as the author, albeit in a different and maybe even negative sense to the way we usually think about authorship. What makes me want to revive some of the issues of authorship and recall its traditional opposition to the system, is that THE PUBLIC ENEMY is a case where the "classical" system, as it was to become conventionalized during the sound period, can be studied in *status nascendi*. At the same time, the film shows signs of being a hybrid, whose deviancy or transitional status raises a number of historical and methodological considerations, which touch on my central topic: does Hollywood represent the genius of the author or genius of the system?

Given that THE PUBLIC ENEMY is so strongly associated with a particular cycle and a particular studio, the tension that I claim exists between its classical status and its deviant identity also implies a more general point, namely the social or ideological function of genre cinema. The latter question, while much discussed in the early days of film studies, when sociology or social psychology tended to be the disciplines called upon to make sense of the movies, has somewhat fallen into disrepute. For a time, it was superseded by first, Claude Lévi-Strauss' version of structural anthropology, and then by the more directly Marxist-inspired ideological critiques of Hollywood's textual system. The revival of

Hollywood in the form of blockbusters with strong generic identities or pedigrees, has rekindled interest in the issue of genre, that is, Hollywood's role in shaping the social imaginary through the manipulation or recombination of stereotypes.[7] If the debate has shifted away from "realism" and the reflection model of social relevance, we may now have a better grasp of the discursive, affective and mediatized realities present in mainstream movies—and their function as cultural memory or as the sites of contest for dominant and conflicting "representations."[8] Yet ideas about their precise argumentative or rhetorical operations—so central during the brief period of film semiology and textual analysis—have given way to polemical, but often tautological arguments about Hollywood genres stereotyping minorities.[9]

My aim in this chapter is partly to revive the debate about Hollywood as a formal and thus formally analyzable system, and partly to pick up the question of Hollywood's function, now phrased less in sociological or ideological terms, and more from a broadly anthropological angle. First, I want to remind myself of the strengths and weaknesses of the "anthropological" model for understanding generically coded narratives in the 1970s, that is, structuralism. Second, I will note the deadlocks the model reached when trying to mediate between the organizing and regulating forces of genre on the one hand, and the cohesive, self-referential and expressive forces implied in authorship on the other. Third, I hope to pose once more that quintessential Lévi-Straussian question: who speaks to whom and about what in trans-personal narratives, which are nonetheless originating from somewhere, addressed at someone and located in specific moments of time? Finally, I want to know why is it that every critic and commentator feels obliged to mention the famous or infamous grapefruit scene? Why is it so shocking, why is it so well remembered, why has it all but consumed the rest of the film in the dictionary-and-handbook store of movie-lore, trivia and common knowledge?

Historically, in other words, THE PUBLIC ENEMY stands at three distinct conjunctures: the change of film technology and film form we associate with the introduction of sound; the change of public attitude to the gangster, prohibition and corruption in local politics after the introduction of the New Deal; changes of censorship and self-censorship in the film industry in the course of a new self-understanding of the role Hollywood assumed as a significant social factor and political player not only in the United States, but as a global force: shaping ideals, identities, consumption habits and life-styles.

Methodologically, THE PUBLIC ENEMY also stands at a point of intersection of different registers. First, as argued above, it is of interest for the debate around authorship and genre, a debate which all but defined the initial phase of British film studies in the late 1960s and early 1970s. Influenced by a whole decade of *Cahiers du cinéma*'s championing of Hollywood *auteurs*, but increasingly interested by structural linguistics, Peter Wollen was probably the first to ask himself explicitly on what basis it might be possible to combine an *auteurist* approach to Hollywood films with a structuralist reading of the same body of work. His essay on the *auteur* theory in *Signs and Meaning in the Cinema*, followed by monographs by several of his colleagues at the British Film Institute (Jim Kitses' *Horizons West* on the Western, and Colin McArthur's *Underworld USA* on the gangster film), plus Geoffrey Nowell-Smith's study on *Luchino Visconti*, made up a critical movement that later came to be known as the "Cine-Structuralists."[10] Their use of Vladimir Propp's work on folk-tales, together with Claude Lévi-Strauss' "The Structural Analysis of Myth", was in turn critiqued or rather, put to the test by among others, Brian Henderson and Charles Eckert in the United States.[11] Both made significant contributions to the methodological debate, while shifting the parameters from *auteur* versus genre to genre structure versus socio-historical conjuncture, reflecting a similar shift that had taken place within the *Cahiers du cinéma*, signaled by the publication of the collective text on (John Ford's) YOUNG MR LINCOLN.[12] While they gave an overtly Marxist inflection to Lévi-Strauss, Henderson and Eckert also applied to Hollywood genre cinema the Paris anthropologist's dictum of myth as a form of utterance by which a community talks to itself about itself, in order to find an "imaginary resolution to real contradictions." Henderson, focusing on the question of race, published an influential essay on John Ford's THE SEARCHERS, while Eckert, taking class and gender as his key discourses, took up the gangster film once more, and paid attention to one of its sub-genres, involving women and the working classes.[13] MARKED WOMAN, a prototypical example of the "Fallen Woman" cycle, another Warner Bros. gangster-related genre from the early to mid-1930s, provided Eckert with a test case for the usefulness of Lévi-Strauss. While fully engaging with the historical, political and topical background that sociological readings of the American gangster film habitually draw on, he gave credit (and critique) to earlier attempts to read genre cinema in terms of binary oppositions, notably Robert Warshow's essays on "The Western," and "The Gangster as Tragic Hero."[14] It is therefore tempting to conduct an Eckert-style reading of THE PUBLIC ENEMY in order to disengage some of the salient features of his analysis, while also bearing in mind the somewhat paradoxical conclusion he eventually reached. Namely, that whereas a Lévi-Straussian reading brought to the fore several distinctive features of the film that he would not have been able to decode or make sense of otherwise, he had—by the end of his close textual analysis—become so convinced of the trenchant critiques made of Lévi-Strauss within Anglo-Saxon anthropology that he had to conclude the method to be irredeemably flawed.

Useable results from a flawed theory may not be the best starting point for reviving either the structuralist or psychoanalytic enterprise, but it is my expectation that precisely this paradox might give us an entry point not only into the identity and authority of THE PUBLIC ENEMY (the relation of coherence and incoherence it displays), but into the coherence/stability or incoherence/adaptability of Hollywood as both a (closed) structure (system) and an (open) process (field of forces), each contributing to the 'meaning' an audience might extract from a film. In this respect, I hope that THE PUBLIC ENEMY lends itself to testing assumptions about what might be called the "political unconscious" of the Hollywood cinema, treating "cultural artifacts as socially symbolic acts," but also ask *who* or *what* speaks in a film, and to whom or what does it address itself?[15] What, in other words, is the "center" of the classical system? Does it have to have a center at all? Is it a text, internally structured in particular ways, or does it constitute a discourse, in which several centers—or perhaps better: focal points of disturbance—interact and intersect with each other?

Such points of systemic (or ideological) disturbance are easy to identify in THE PUBLIC ENEMY: they have to do with *masculinity* and sexual identity (Tom Powers' relation to women, to his mother and to other men), with *ethnicity* (almost a "given" in the gangster film: and here focused on "Irishness") and its relation to either side of the law (the Irish make up both the police force and the criminal underworld), and finally, there is the issue of *authority* and the symbolic order (family, kinship, patriarchy). To put it more schematically, one could argue that the film, while on one level telling an ambiguous morality tale of how a hoodlum comes to no good but has fun on the way, on another level, it addresses itself to young (ethnic) males trying to sort out social identity, by rehearsing their relations with fathers, authority figures, the law on the one hand, and sort out their sexual identity, by rehearsing their relations with women—mothers, schoolboy crushes, good-time girls, fiancées and wives.

To anticipate the results of my reading of the film in this conjuncture of history, method and mythological matrix: what seems symptomatic about THE PUBLIC ENEMY is that in respect of the super-genre of male initiation/male socialization, one of Hollywood's recognized "anthropological" functions, the film displays a curious failure of socialization and identity formation. Put most banally, this failure is manifested in the fact that, unusually for Hollywood, the film does not have a happy ending. Tom Powers does not reform, the promised truce between the rival gangs is defaulted upon, and Tom's brother Mike is both too naive and too late with his good intentions. Of course, it can be argued that from the point of view of "society" Tom's brutal demise is a happy ending, because the gangster is punished, and the world is rid of him. But it is not the law that defeats him, and thereby restores the symbolic order: rather, Schemer Burns, head of the competing gang, manages to kill Tom Powers in his hospital bed. The reign of lawlessness, graft and gangsterism has just moved from one hoodlum to another, making it a hollow victory for society. And yet, I shall argue, the very terms of the failure of socialization manifest a logic of their own, which may account for the fact that the ending, shocking though it is, is nonetheless experienced as a satisfying closure. It is intuited as "right," not at the level of morality and the symbolic order, but at a poetic or mythic level, distinct from that of the surface narrative.

History: Gangsters in the Streets, Gangsters on the Screen

To recapitulate the salient features of the story, by reproducing a brief plot summary, taken from the Internet:

> Starring as Tom Powers, a police officer's son who becomes a petty criminal and later a crime lord, Jimmy Cagney pulls out all the stops and delivers an electrifying performance. Tom is first shown as a delinquent boy, along with his friend Matt. The two boys are schooled in petty crime by their fence Putty Nose. By this time, WWI has broken out and Prohibition is not far behind. Tom and Matt go into the liquor business. Tom's elder brother comes back from the war and refuses to join in a drink with Tom and their Ma at the old homestead. "I know what's in that keg. Beer and blood. The blood of men". The next morning takes place the infamous grapefruit scene where Tom rubs a grapefruit half in the face of his moll, Kitty (Mae Clark). Tom goes from one exploit to another. He catches up with his old mentor Putty Nose, who left them holding the bag earlier. Tom shoots him to death. By this time, a gang war has broken out, between Paddy Ryan's gang and Schemer Burns' gang. Tom and Matt get ambushed by a machine-gun. Matt goes down but Tom gets away. He robs a couple of .38s from a pawnshop and has it out with Burns' gang. Tom wins the gunfight, but is severely wounded. His family visits him in the hospital, and he reconciles himself with his brother and mother. But Schemer Burns has one last trick. He kidnaps Tom, swathed like a mummy in bandages, from the hospital. Paddy offers to quit the rackets if Burns will return Tom. Return Tom he does, but bullet riddled and standing at his mother's front door, still wrapped like a mummy. Brother Mike answers the door and Tom falls face first, dead, onto the floor.[16]

The summary accurately conveys some of the film's overt narrative action, indexing turning points as the story develops along its surface structure of cause-and-effect. But in the re-telling, the author has also considerably linearized, streamlined and smoothed out the actual film's rather more elliptical and even enigmatic succession of episodes and set pieces. In a more neo-formalist vocabulary, the summary gives us the story more than it reproduced the plot.

The film, for instance, is remarkably specific in its historical indicators. It starts with an intertitle, announcing "1909," then moves forward in increments: 1915, 1917, 1920, 1929. The 1909 segment, for instance, shows Tom, Matt and his sister as children, together with Tom's father and mother. Later segments also open with significant dates, such as the end of WWI and the return of Mike, Tom's brother, as a de-mobbed soldier from Europe. In a montage sequence, we are made aware of the introduction and effects of prohibition, and also the moment when it is repealed and lifted. As Richard Maltby has argued, in an essay on THE PUBLIC ENEMY:

> No one who saw LITTLE CAESAR or THE PUBLIC ENEMY in 1931 saw them in a cultural vacuum. Embodying the metropolitan civic corruption that had been tolerated in the 1920s, the gang-ster had been an acceptable representative of anti-Prohibition sentiment in the popular press

until 1929, but in the cultural catharsis of the early Depression he became a scapegoat villain, threatening the survival of social order and American values. This shift in public sentiment was most conspicuously charted in changed press attitudes to Al Capone, who had ceased to be the celebrated "Horatio Alger lad of Prohibition" long before his conviction for tax evasion in October 1931.[17]

Maltby also points out that the solemn admonition in the rolling titles at the beginning of the film should not to be too quickly dismissed as a sign of Hollywood's double standard: making THE PUBLIC ENEMY out to be a contribution to combating gangsterism as a menace to society, while at the same time glorifying the swagger and panache of the working-class hero:

> Like many 1930s crime movies, THE PUBLIC ENEMY begins with an explicit statement of authorial intent: "It is the intention of the authors of THE PUBLIC ENEMY to honestly depict an environment that exists today in a certain strata [sic] of American life, rather than to glorify the hoodlum or the criminal." This declaration of civic responsibility is usually regarded as an empty, cynical gesture intended to appease critics concerned at the movies' "subversive" effects, but such an interpretation simplifies the complex and contradictory cultural position occupied by Hollywood's representations of criminality in the early Depression.[18]

Yet the figure of the gangster has a relatively long history in the American cinema prior to the Warner Bros. cycles, stretching at least from Griffith's MUSKETEERS OF PIG ALLEY (1912) and Maurice Tourneur's ALIAS JIMMY VALENTINE (1915), to Lloyd Bacon's BRASS KNUCKLES (1927) and Josef von Sternberg's UNDERWORLD (1927). Charles Eckert, in the article already cited, distinguishes two lines of descent for the gangster in movies, almost antithetical: first, there are the criminals played by John Gilbert, Walter Huston, Monte Blue in the 1920s. They are Anglo-Saxon, polished in speech and bearing, dressed in the formal attire of the wealthy. Often they were the alter egos of the financiers and businessmen, also insofar as their henchmen and sidekicks were the low and proletarian characters, were sometimes the only indication of the criminal association, but also pointing to the class-prejudice governing such short-hand representation. It is a line that resurfaces in some of the *films noirs* of the late 1940s, where the detective has to uncover the criminal element beneath too much politeness among the men, and the "rotten to the core" corruption beneath too much beauty among the women. The other pedigree of the gangster goes back to Sternberg (and I would add Griffith): represented by George Bancroft in UNDERWORLD, he is decidedly of lower-class origin and thus a direct precursor of such bruisers as Victor McLaglen, with the same ethnic tilt towards the Irish immigrant community as we find in Griffith's BROKEN BLOSSOMS. Cagney, Robinson, Muni, Raft, on the other hand, have in common that they are short, slight men whose violence is verbal and psychological as much as physical, and with the exception of Cagney, their ethnic identity is "Latin." What emerges from these genealogies are, however, not so much sociologically useful or representative data, but the confirmation of one of Robert Warshow's key points, namely that the gangster in Hollywood cinema is an artificial figure, at once a composite of several, potentially incompatible traits, and a simplified version of actual, urban outlaws and their criminal organizations, pared down or reduced to some kind of archetype/stereotype.

In many ways Warshow's essays anticipated major insights of the structural method: the gangster is portrayed as a tragic hero, a figure bodied forth by the American dream, wedded to its underside: the urban nightmare of slums, poverty and an unforgiving as well as unbridled fight for survival. Warshow saw in the gangster the contradictions of capitalism (at first summoning desire for self-advancement, by an appeal to the entrepreneurial spirit of American ideology, and then restricting it by the barriers of class, ethnicity and state coercion) as well as those of patriarchy. The typical gangster hero's narcissism and eccentricities, his tics, his manic traits / the need for control / his childishness and romantic rebelliousness, as well as the alternation between cynicism and sentimentality indicate unresolved issues of paternal authority and masculine identity. Finally, in the stereotypically troubled relation of law and individual, society and the subject, the gangster does not seem to be a social or historical phenomenon, as much as he embodies a particularly "pure" and abstract way of figuring a different dilemma altogether. What is kept ambiguous in Warshow's rather lyrical evocation of this typical but to him also tragic American figure is the question whether the Oedipal paraphernalia of the hero's dilemma provide the basic code through which other, more specifically social and historical conflicts can be represented. Or, on the contrary, are the socio-political conflicts more a displacement, a rationalization of the unconscious fantasy, the existential dilemmas, the psychic fears and phobias we associate with (Oedipal versions) of adolescent manhood?

Maltby's more rigorously historicist investigations do in fact specify the type of gangster represented by Tom Powers. First of all, he is not modeled on Al Capone:

> The conventional critical identification of THE PUBLIC ENEMY with LITTLE CAESAR and SCARFACE as the trilogy of "classic" early 1930s gangster movies has encouraged a reading of its plot as if it portrayed the rise and fall of a gangster in Capone's image. Unlike LITTLE CAESAR or SCARFACE, however, THE PUBLIC ENEMY does not depict the acquisition, exercise or loss of power. Tommy Powers remains more hoodlum than gangster, occupying a subordinate role in the bootlegging business, not an organisational one, obeying instructions rather than giving them, and untroubled by any ambition to escape the neighbourhood.[19]

Maltby goes on to track the outlines of the story to:

> a composite biography of a neighbourhood criminal gang such as Chicago's Valley gang, led by Patrick 'Paddy the Bear' Ryan until his assassination in 1920. His protégés Terry Druggan and Frankie Lake became the first gangsters to distribute beer on a large scale in Chicago after Prohibition, providing Capone's mentor John Torrio with a model of successful collaboration between bootleggers and respectable business. By 1924 bootlegging had made them millionaires.

Many of the episodes and especially some of Tom Powers' character traits seem to derive from other notorious Chicago criminals:

> Tommy inherited his "sunny brutality," his impulsiveness and lack of organisational prowess from press accounts of Northside gang leaders Dion O'Banion and Hymie Weiss, who were depicted as figures of local colour rather than as Capone-like businessmen. The beer wars between Capone and the Northsiders were most often represented as a conflict between two systems of social organisation, Capone's mercenary capitalism against O'Banion's dependence on loyalty, friendship and affection.
>
> The movie borrows freely from the "factual" accounts of the O'Banion gang's exploits, incorporating several incidents from newspaper reports of the lives of O'Banion, Weiss, and Louis "Two-Gun" Alterie. Most famous of these was the 1923 death of Samuel "Nails" Morton in a riding accident, and the subsequent (apocryphal) execution of the horse by either O'Banion or Alterie. After O'Banion's assassination in 1924, Alterie vowed revenge by proposing a publicly staged shoot-out with O'Banion's killers, akin to Tommy's attack on Schemer Burns' headquarters. Weiss was notorious for his evil temper and impulsiveness, and reports that he once pushed an omelet into a girlfriend's face were cited as the source of THE PUBLIC ENEMY's infamous grapefruit incident. His assassination in the first "machine-gun nest" murder in October 1926 was recreated in the killing of Matt Doyle (Edward Woods).
>
> Like other crime movies of the period, THE PUBLIC ENEMY omitted any substantial or detailed representation of what sociologists at the time described as the "unholy alliance

between organised crime and politics," in favour of their representation of the spectacle and melodrama of criminal performance.[20]

At this point it might be helpful to ask oneself what is the function of genre in this "unholy alliance"? Is it to establish a level of communication where historical reality and symbolic representation intersect in a manner that is readily decodable by the spectator? Or is it to disavow the links to—as in this case—a mesh of very specific local socio-graphics and historical circumstances? The contrast between Maltby's reconstruction of the historical-topical matrix and the textual work of the film might provide the entry point into our second set of considerations, namely those concerned with method.

Method: Genre and Gender

What are the functions of genre, according to the conventional wisdom of film studies? For the film industry, genres serve standardization, and make possible a certain division of labor. For the viewer or consumer, they provide recognition, and thus are a way of regulating the expectations that an audience brings to a film. In all these respects, genres have a normative function, irrespective of how "transgressive" the behavior its typical protagonists display. It is at this point that the relation between narrative and genre becomes relevant, if we accept that popular narratives, of the kind encoded in myths and fairy-tales (and by extension, in generically stable film-narratives) are called upon to resolve ideological contradiction, or compensate by processes of substitution. How do they do it? According to the structuralist model, by generating out of their referential material a number of elements that can be arranged in terms of oppositions, parallels, repetition, contrary and complementary pairs. Furthermore, narrative and genre work together, by a dynamic which, borrowing from Freud's analyses of dreams, has been called "condensation" and "displacement." Eckert defines condensation as "a process whereby a number of discrete traits or ideas are fused in a single symbol. Each component is usually an abbreviated reference to something larger than itself."[21] He defines displacement as "the substitution of an acceptable object of love, hate, etc., for a forbidden one."[22]

This structuralist approach is the one chosen by Eckert, in his analysis of the relation of the gangster genre to the social reality and political ideology of the United States in the 1930s, when he starts his essay by stating that "every ethos [by which he means ideology?] presents itself as a unified body of polarized conceptions."[23] Eckert goes on to summarize a basic insight of Lévi-Strauss to the effect that a dilemma (or contradiction) stands at the heart of every living myth, and that this dilemma is expressed through layered pairs of opposites, which are transformations of a primary pair. The impulse to construct the myth arises from the desire to resolve the dilemma; the impossibility of resolving it leads to a crystal-like growth of the myth through which the dilemma is repeated, conceived in new terms, or inverted—subject to semiotic operations that might resolve or attenuate its force. In the gangster and crime films, we often start off with a depiction of "real" conditions, but once the alternating pattern has been set up, the narrative can be taken over by melodramatic oppositions. This is certainly the case with THE PUBLIC ENEMY, where after the first few minutes of documentary material shot in Chicago's goods yards, slaughterhouses and industrial terrain, the camera moves to a working-class neighborhood, eventually settling on the entrance of a saloon. As soon as the two boys emerge, the action shifts to their home, and the first major confrontation of Tom with authority, in the figure of his father, coming out of the house to call him in for physical punishment with a leather belt—defiantly received, because routinely expected, by the young Tom.

The question then, is, what is the "ethical dilemma" of a given film? We have to find our way through the transformations to the crucial conflicts. According to Eckert and others, those in the Hollywood films of the 1930s had to do with class and gender in particular, often expressed in the oppositional pair big city/small town, urban/agrarian. In MARKED WOMAN (Lloyd Bacon, Warner Bros., 1937), the film scrutinized by Eckert, the oppositions are displaced. He points out that in one of the songs we find a structural opposition between "witty" and "right," which Eckert reads as a doubly metonymic displacement, in need of de-coding and transformation. Accordingly, witty and right are a condensation/displacement of two separate oppositions: that of right and wrong, and that of dumb and smart/witty. Both have been layered or superimposed in order to yield the composite "right" and "witty," a composite that functions as a compromise because it disguises contradiction.

By analyzing the song, Eckert recognizes how the film shifts from an economic or class (rich/poor) dilemma to an ethical dilemma (right/wrong), of which the country/city dilemma is a further transformation. The oppositions are presented in the melodramatic terms of conflicting emotional states: anger/apathy, despair/sentimentality, where social criticism resolves itself into passive contemplation. In other words, the song constructs an emotional attitude for the viewer, it turns the film's ideological oppositions into a particular form of narration or address by which to implicate the spectator. In this context, displacement becomes "the substitution of an acceptable object of love, hate, etc., for a forbidden one." The "work" of the song, and by extension of the narrative, has been to substitute for the class conflict that cannot be named, a set of oppositions than can be named, often by initiating a play with regional difference, ethical choices or as in the example of MARKED WOMEN, the smart/dumb opposition. Thus, the *force* of a specific opposition is attenuated while the *form* is retained. This process is both an act of censorship and of transformation: one might say, censorship *as* transformation (or vice versa).

The position of women within these oppositions is touched upon but not altogether fully appreciated by Eckert. From his description it is clear that they bear the brunt of the unresolved opposition, but it is their gender position across all these divisions that allows them to function as the transformational agents. Instead of the film giving us either an analysis of poverty or of the position of women (as commodities bought and sold), we get the conflict gangster/the law into which the dilemma of the women is inserted. From the point of view of the women, the gangster focuses the "patriarchal" issues, by forcing them into the clear exploiter/exploited opposition. But the film only indirectly targets prostitution, and is more concerned with the precarious position of women between "too old" and "too young" to survive in the world of male authority and sexual predators.

Once we accept that the gangster is himself a composite or contradictory social formation (a "product of condensation"), the first-level (or surface-level) conflict (between the heroine and her pimp, who is responsible for the corruption and death of her younger sister) needs to be deconstructed on the side of the women, as much as on the side of the law. Yet the gangster is also an "empty" sign, in the sense that every social ill could be projected on him: he could become the scapegoat, the one in whom all the faults could be personalized and psychologized, but he could also be the center of all sorts of (social, psychic) agency, the one through whom the Law—even patriarchal authority and heterosexuality—has to redefine itself. This composite nature of the gangster's persona is perhaps best illustrated by the recurrent stress on his deviant "psychology": he is egotistical, narcissistic, acquisitive and obsessed with control—the Freudian anal-sadistic type. At issue, however, is less the acquisition of money, but of power—of which money and sex are the socially visible, conventionalized signs (rather than, say, influence on officials or politicians, as in the *films noirs* of the 1940s). Little Caesar's motto is: "Be somebody," Tony Camonte in SCARFACE has "The World is Yours" flashed in front of him from a neon billboard, Cagney, in WHITE HEAT, famously shouts "Ma—top of the world" and Tom Powers' name could not be more explicit. Yet as Eckert points out, the gangster is a pared down, partialized version of the capitalist: his sadism becomes an end in itself, his need for control makes him insane and self-destructive. By splitting the rationality of acquisitiveness from the psychology of ambition and hubris, the gangster signals a dramatically linear figure—the overreacher, overshooting all goal-directed behavior, rather than a sociological prototype, who happens to be maladjusted. Gangsters can thus be inserted into melodramatic schemes more easily than businessmen. They allow both for condensation (the social motifs) and displacement (the archetype), and thus facilitate the dramatization of conflict: they can be their own worst enemies. As I argue elsewhere in this book, the drama of the American capitalist is depicted in CITIZEN KANE, not in THE PUBLIC ENEMY or LITTLE CAESAR: "his cruelty reflects his alienation and loneliness. He can have Xanadu but not Rosebud. This pernicious conception is designed to placate the dispossessed."[24] But, besides enforcing respect through violence, sexual deviancy is also an important motif in the gangster, turning up in both SCARFACE and THE PUBLIC ENEMY, and suggesting that this aspect of the gangster's pathology also has a structural function—destabilizing one sort of normativity (i.e. heterosexuality), in order to stabilize another contradiction.

THE PUBLIC ENEMY: Logic of Actions/Logic of Desire

If we now return to THE PUBLIC ENEMY and begin to apply to the film Eckert's version of classic structuralist analysis, we can indeed fairly easily identify certain pairs of opposites that suggest a matrix of conflicts and issues, which have to be unpacked and translated in order to elicit the appropriate set of social or historical referents. However, this is not my primary goal. Instead, I want to examine how the film is internally structured by certain oppositions which in turn stabilize and hold together an otherwise very loose collection of episodes, but which at crucial moments also destabilize the narrative, in order to make room for a different dynamic to manifest itself.

Instead of itemizing the pairs of oppositions, as Eckert had done, I want to go through the film by showing how the oppositions are braided, and emerge in the course of the action, focusing—as already indicated—around an unstable male identity, which uses the social (class), ethnic (Irish) and gender (homo/hetero) oppositions to work out not so much the inherent contradictions of the "gangster" as composite figure, but the male/female tensions inherent in James Cagney, the "dancer gone wrong"—making the film, in other words, an anthropological-ethnographic biography not of the individual James Cagney, but of the Cagney persona, used and deployed by Warner Bros., the studio that created this persona.

On the narrative surface level, THE PUBLIC ENEMY falls to pieces: it is episodic, disjointed, either faltering or a series of set pieces. But, on the symbolic level, it is absolutely coherent. We can see this in the film's opening sequences, which present a condensation of much of the film which follows: "beer" is presented as a motif, coded in terms of: working class/ethnicity (it is the democratic beverage); the Salvation Army/Temperance/Prohibition; and the making of money/business out of the desire/needs of others. It also introduces the theme of the family ("Family Entrance"), of male friendships and of women (Matt's rebuff by the girl entering the saloon leads Tom to say to him: "that's what you get for fooling with women").

The opening sequence, consisting of documentary footage, is edited both on a contrasting montage principle (business district, downtown with traffic/the slaughterhouses) and for continuity from the city as a whole to the particular neighborhood. Emphasis is placed on ethnic difference/ same communal pursuit, organized around the beer motif: unity despite diversity/unity through diversity ("e pluribus unum").

Another opposition becomes dominant as the opening scenes transition from documentary to fiction—between work and leisure. However, both terms receive the same assembly-line treatment: what the workmen do to the cattle in the stockyards is repeated in the mechanical movements behind the bar filling the pails with beer. The point at which the fictional world takes over from documentary is when camera movement is motivated by character movement: the two boys leaving the saloon move towards the camera, and the camera reframes in order to center them. Girls enter the frame from off-screen, and the scene ends with them disappearing inside and the saloon swing door hitting

Matt (which completes the scene with a rhyme: the males exit, the females enter). The verisimilitude of fiction is created through the formal play on symmetry and alternation.

The following scene, in the department store, depicts the characters' anti-social behavior, split between the energy and wit it imparts to the narrative: the chase, and how the boys outwit the floor-walker; the customers, and how they make brilliant use of the technology of modern life (the escalator); we learn how the boys treat the urban landscape as a playground (using the escalator rail as a fun-fair chute), and the anti-authoritarian gesture that lies behind their behavior. They knock the hat off a gentleman, but there is also already the fear of and fascination with women (a lingerie scene, where the boys stare at bras, was shot but then was censored out of the film). It depicts childishness and irresponsibility, but also the darker side of childhood.

The next scene fully introduces us to Tom's pathology. He makes Matt's sister trip up on her skates, so as to see under her skirts. The desire to look is immediately self-censored by expression of denigration and contempt (Tom: "It's only a girl"/ Matt: "She's my sister"/ Tom: "what does that matter!"). And at the end of it, there stands the figure of the father as the Law. The cause: the desire for women, the effect: punishment by the Law. Key to the film is this ambivalence towards women: curiosity and fear, attraction and repulsion. Later on, from the scene with Jean Harlow, we almost infer that Tom is impotent (a motif in the gangster film taken up by BONNIE AND CLYDE). At the same time, there is indifference to the Law: Tom says to his father in a mocking voice, just before his father gives him a thrashing, "how do you want them [i.e. the trousers] this time, up or down?" Authority (the paternal law), Education (Tom says about his brother Matt: "he's learning to be poor"), Patriotism (the ethnic-working-class attitude in the film is similar to that of African-Americans whose "patriotism" is tempered by their origin as "slaves," that is, who see themselves as involuntary immigrants) are all treated as virtues to be debunked. They never enter the semantic value circuit: they are ridiculed, so as not to be marked as valid or important oppositions.[25]

The film is dominated by other themes and oppositions: right and wrong, the ethos and moral code, social class, gender and identity are redefined into a) rich/poor (flouting the Law makes you rich/being a law-abiding citizen keeps you poor, and b) male bonding/male betrayal: right is defined as sticking with your friends (Paddy O'Ryan says to Tom: "you gotta have friends"), wrong is double-crossing them (Putty Nose). Male friendship replaces paternal authority. Putty Nose appears as the good father (reward rather than punishment), but he is weak, deceiving and double-crossing. Which goes to show that not all males are equal: another vital distinction is introduced between brothers and friends. Brothers are rivals (for the mother's love), friends can share women, or do without them. In fact, class-conflict is displaced into family feud and Oedipal conflict (discussed below), when the Tom/Mike opposition becomes the displaced continuation of the father-son conflict. While never made explicit, Tom and Mike's father has disappeared in and through the botched robbery: we only see the arm of the dead policeman, the first of a series of symbolic (substituted) parricides in the film, but the body's identity is never made explicit. The closest we get is at the funeral of Larry, Tom's accomplice killed in the raid. In a strict opposition through repetition, Larry's mother sobs "he was a good boy," followed by a cut to the men saying "he was a no-good boy," an exchange where the dead Larry serves as displaced reference to the surviving Tom, retroactively making the murdered policeman the stand-in for Tom's henceforth absent father.

The Tom/Mike (brothers as rivals) opposition is, however, also the symbolic site for the oppositions lawless/law-abiding, street-smart/educated, working class/middle class, egotism/patriotism, where it is the first terms—applying to Tom—that retain the positive connotations, so that Mike is made to look foolish and stupid. Challenged by Tom why he is enlisting, all he can say is: "when your country needs you, she needs you." The sibling rivalry is thus over-determined, having to articulate all these other conflicts—which is a typically economic way of organizing story-material, even if not conducive to realism. Classical Hollywood invariably puts narrative economy before realism (or manages to present narrative economy as realism), and in this case the script makes Mike (the brother) marry Matt (the friend)'s sister, Molly. This schematism (M, M, M) in the figure constellation strengthens not only the story's tight nexus of mirroring correlations, but it also "keeps" the lethal conflicts "within the family," as so often in fairytales or Greek tragedy.

Friends, however, are not only the reverse of brothers; they are alter egos, doubles of the self, ready to explore alternative possibilities, but also canceling both competition and the threat of otherness. Tom says on several occasions: "I'm always alone when I'm with Matt," and there is a notable similarity of gesture and speech, building up a choreography of being in synch between the two that ensures there is never one without the other. Matt, the friend, mirrors and complements Tom, the hero. Matt likes women, he is a ladies' man and "the marrying kind"; Tom is contemptuous of women, sadistic (the skates incident, the grapefruit scene), unable to form a permanent relationship with either Kitty (Mae Clark) or Gwen (Jean Harlow). Mike, the brother, is the opposite of Tom, and provides his contrasting foil. A patriot and a hard worker, he loves his mother, but successfully transfers this love to another woman, his future wife. Tom cannot cut loose from his mother and transfer his sexual desire/ affection to another love object (Gwen comes closest, but only by cradling him like a little boy).[26]

The close interweaving of Tom/Matt and Tom/Mike into complementary and contrasting pairs is necessary in order to generate the conflicts that actually produce a narrative out of what, at another level, is a stalemate. To put it differently: a narrative is also the vehicle that gives shape, body and promise of resolution to conflicts which are internal to the hero, stemming as much from his psychic disposition as they are external, located in society. If, as indicated earlier, in THE PUBLIC ENEMY these conflicts circle around, probe and obsessively repeat the male ego's affective ambivalence towards women, then this ambivalence divides the hero more than it divides society, and it is the inner division that becomes the motor for the story's development and trajectory. As with almost all of classical cinema, inner divisions have to be externalized in order to exist; they are embodied in the secondary characters, whose function it is to act out alternative stances, to test the more transgressive options, and to give expression to each side of a dilemma or an ambivalence.

Causality and Narrative Motivation, Oedipal Logic and the Hysterical Text

Given these clusters of characters, grouped around the central protagonist, with their formal arrangements into binary oppositions, complementary pairs and mirroring doubles, it would not be too difficult to conduct a structuralist analysis of THE PUBLIC ENEMY, in which the general contradictions of the gangster, as discussed above, and the specific contradictions of prohibition (as a set of laws that helped to create the crimes of which they were meant to be the prevention), are condensed into kinship relations and compressed into a succession of good and bad father-figures. However, while this gives the film an overall motivational coherence, by holding it together at the symbolic level of the classic Oedipal tale, what also needs to be explained is the choppy manner of its telling. Gaps and minor anecdotes turn the normally lock-step logic of cause and effect into a series of loose episodes, set-piece numbers and bravura vignettes, which could be attributed to the "documentary" impulse and "gritty realism" for which Warner Bros. films of the period were justly famous. But there could also be a more internal reason for this disjointedness, revealing an alternative or supplementary logic, one that might explain why this initiation story fails to initiate, and why this rise-and-fall story gives us at best an intimation of poetic justice, while denying us the satisfaction that the moral order or social justice have been restored.

I mentioned earlier that the synopsis I took from the Internet straightened out and smoothed over the episodic plot. Here, then, is a synoptic re-telling of the film, focusing on Tom's successive encounters with father-figures, following the scene with his natural father of punishment and defiance.

- The boys' first big job is a robbery at the Fur Trading Company, which they botch, when Tom, terrified by the sight of full-size stuffed grizzly bear, starts discharging his revolver and thereby alerting the police. It is Putty Nose, their fatherly friend and "fence," who puts them up to it, giving the boys their guns, only to betray them when things go wrong. The scene illustrates the ambiguity of paternal authority: in place of punishment and defiance within the law, outside the law, there are fathers who may em-"power" the hero, but also abandon him.
- Released from prison, Tom substitutes Paddy Ryan for Putty Nose. Paddy, respectable brewery owner, pretends to be representative of the law, but flouts it flagrantly. His elevated social position is an index of Tom's rise, but Paddy's double standards put him on a par with Putty Nose's equivocation and betrayal. Tom exchanges Paddy for Nails Nathan, the flamboyant gangster who has it all: money, status, women, respectability (race horses). How will Tom cope with this ideal father, how will he become a man? He takes a girlfriend (Jean Harlow), but they are "just good friends."
- Detour and displacement: instead of Tom marrying, Matt is celebrating his wedding party. Faced with losing his friend to a woman, Tom persuades Matt not to go home with his bride and consummate the marriage, but instead, to come with him in order to finish some business. Tom makes it a straight either/or choice: Matt decides for the friend and against the wife-to-be.
- The "unfinished business" is Putty Nose, spotted by Tom at the wedding party. They follow him home, confront him, and make him sit at the piano. Tom asks him to sing again the song he used to play when they were boys: "Mrs Jones, big and fat, slipped on the ice and broke her . . ." at which point Tom kills Putty Nose. The camera pans away just before the shot is fired (a technique Howard Hawks also used in SCARFACE), turning the gun shot into an off-screen sound, covered over by the piano: an image-sound substitution that furthermore draws attention to the missing word in the song.
- The scene is brutal in its casual cruelty and sadism, but also extremely compressed in its semantics. Not only does the gap in the song stand for a sexual innuendo, the name "Putty Nose" appears as a homophobic slur, connecting with a number of other moments that mark Tom's sexual ambivalence towards men (most explicit in the scene with the tailor). Tom's male bonding either involves putting down women, as in the song (whose repetition takes the victim back to the scene of the betrayal for which he now pays with his life), or of deserting women, as in the case of Matt.
- Tom's masculinity strengthened by the revenge killing of Putty Nose, he once more tackles his "shyness with women" at a date with Gwen in her white-on-white boudoir. As she cradles him in her lap, lowering his inhibitions by calling him her little boy, the phone rings: Nails Nathan has been killed, thrown off his horse. News of Nails' death prevents consummation, making the Father ominously present in his sudden absence, barring access to the woman and causing a coitus interruptus: Tom is never seen again with Gwen, as the scene mirrors the wedding party, when Matt leaves his new bride to join Tom in order to kill Putty Nose. This time, Tom rushes out and avenges Nails by killing the horse—a sequence of events that borders on the comic, were it not for the inner logic of the episodic structure that in this instance suggests a reversal of cause and effect, while the parallels establish a retroactive sequence: killing the horse substitutes for not killing Nails (the Oedipal condition of becoming a man), indicating that the killing of Putty Nose (not being a "real man") failed to fortify Tom's manhood.
- After the death of Nails Nathan, Paddy Ryan re-emerges as the substitute father-figure. He takes Tom and Matt's guns away, and locks the "boys" up at his home with his wife Jane: ostensibly to hide and protect them from the rival gang. But Jane makes sexual advances to Tom, showing herself to be scheming and deceitful, predatory and promiscuous. In order not to be

swallowed up by her, Tom leaves the safe house, followed by Matt, who promptly gets killed, thus making his death the woman's fault. Misogyny once more joins homophobia: it was Putty Nose's male companion who betrayed their hideout, having befriended Paddy's wife.

- At a pawn shop, Tom manages to acquire a gun, referring to it as his "jewellery": suggestive not only of sexual connotation, but condensing male and female attributes and hinting at his unstable or troubled sexual identity. He tries to shoot it out with the rival gang of Schemer Burns, but gets severely wounded, ending up in hospital. Kidnapped by Schemer Burns' men, Tom is returned in exchange for Paddy Ryan giving up his turf. Trussed up like a mummy, Tom comes home as a corpse.

The narrative I have been reconstituting in these scenes and episodes does not contradict the one in the more conventional plot synopsis, such as the one cited earlier, but neither does it entirely complement it. Causal chains link distinct thematic strands, and character motivation travels across several separate, possibly incompatible routes: There is, first of all, the linear chronology from 1909 to 1929, covering World War I, Prohibition and the dawn of the New Deal, against which is pitted the trajectory of the rise (clothes, cars, dames and night-clubs)—and fall (shoot-outs, hide-outs, depredation and death) of a working-class hoodlum with roots in the Irish community. Sustained by the logic of gang warfare, with its logic of blow and counterblow, action and reaction, betrayal and revenge, it is a story that should move with a relentless forward drive, not letting up until the final scene.

Yet as indicated, this is not quite the way THE PUBLIC ENEMY unfolds, and instead, a counter-current of deferral and displacement, obsession and repetition also is at work. One drama that unfolds inside the tit-for-tat turf-war story is a family melodrama, where a mother, become widow, has to keep the peace between her two sons, each a rival for her love, each in every other respect the other's opposite, so that Tom can accuse Mike of "hiding behind Ma's skirts," to which Mike retorts that Tom is "hiding behind machine guns."

Beneath this competitive game of sibling rivalry, however, there plays another drama: the one I have been concentrating on, and located within the main protagonist himself. It is a drama that instead of being about a "Public Enemy" should be called "My Private Enemy," because it speaks to Tom Powers' struggle with his own inner demons: insecurity over his sexual identity and masculinity tossing him between the (symbolic) killing of the father and the incestuous desire for the mother. Each takes on forms that border on the grotesque, but the scenes are, for the most part, staged with such an astonishing degree of raw emotional ambivalence that they become once more credible: the violence in action and visual clues, in verbal language and explicit symbolism being somehow "in character."

Sexualized metaphors and imagery abound in the film: lewd songs, guns that are "jewellery" and suggestive gestures at the crotch while telling a tailor to "leave plenty of space."[27] But pivotal scenes, too, reveal their sexual connotations. For instance, the fatal appearance of the stuffed grizzly bear is staged like a *vagina dentata*, when wide-open jaws suddenly appear as Tom parts the furs hanging from racks in the store. Or consider the bold stroke by which the beginning of Tom Power's story and his miserable end are made to rhyme, across a slippery verbal and visual pun, yet one that aptly condenses the film's central motif: the fear and desire of woman. As already mentioned, it is after emerging from the beer-hall door marked "Family Entrance" that the boys—their upper lip sporting a beer-foam moustache, as if to mock their pretence to manliness—experience "what happens when you mess with women." At the end, when the mother makes the bed in expectation of her "baby boy coming home," Tom returns to the family entrance in more senses than one: he literally falls on his face through the family door, but all wrapped up as he is in bandages like a swaddled new-born, he is metaphorically returning to the womb, that other family entrance, as if to suggest that his death undoes his birth, an analogy underscored by the mother's oddly contented sigh: "in a way, I'm glad it happened." One can now perhaps understand how the anti-climactic and morally unsatisfactory ending at the narrative level, finds in the "family entrance" a symbolic closure at the poetic level of the (bad) pun.

Such is the affective ambivalence of these scenes (to which the Cagney persona—gangster gone dancer, and dancer gone gangster—powerfully contributes) that the fragmentary narrative exceeds the "Oedipal trajectory" it so clearly follows.[28] One could call THE PUBLIC ENEMY a "hysterical" narrative,[29] to acknowledge the repetition compulsion at work; but hysterical also in the way the unresolved inner conflicts threaten the causal coherence of the sequence of events, as if the protagonist as psychopath had somehow transmitted his emotional instability to the narrative itself, making it choppy, episodic, over-the-top and unpredictable. In which case the impression one has of a narrative full of gaps and discontinuities, of digressions and detours would be nothing other than the film's way of speaking of all that it knows it must say but cannot say and still manages to say. It would add to the question of "authorship" and "genre" ("who speaks, and to whom and about what?") a further dimension: that of a film becoming a "body with symptoms," in this case, behaving like a hysteric, not only in the sense of "unmanageable emotional excesses," but insofar as the symptoms are sexual in nature and origin.[30]

Conclusion: The Grapefruit Scene

I can now return to the grapefruit scene.[31] My reading of the film as a hysterical narrative would make the scene the very epitome of this hysteria, giving the most direct expression to the latent aggression against women that not only pervades the film, but structures its thematic crux and powers its irresolvable dilemma. Furthermore, it does so once more by virtue of a verbal pun with sexual connotations, because it is easy to see the grapefruit half as the material equivalent of a "sour-puss," or at any rate, as a brutally direct "in your face" reaction/defense action of the threatened male, fighting the woman with an especially graphic symbol of her own sexuality, another *vagina dentata*, at once grotesquely disfigured and punningly refigured. It is our simultaneous awareness of its scandalous inappropriateness (at the surface level) and its scandalous aptness (at the deep structural level), which makes the scene both shocking and unforgettable.

The grapefruit scene is thus a particularly "successful" condensation of several culturally sensitive motifs and strands of affective ambivalence that otherwise could not articulate themselves, but which were essential to the symbolic logic animating the film. Defiance of male authority and deference to male camaraderie (under the taboo of homosexuality), coupled with a defiance against women and deference to maternal authority (under the taboo of incest) were all suspended and rendered ambivalent by the fear and desire of being smothered and re-absorbed by a resurgence of primal maternal solicitousness. More generally, however, insofar as THE PUBLIC ENEMY is a hysterical film, it not only associates this composite figure of the American gangster with several crises of masculinity. By refusing to align the Oedipal trajectory with either male initiation or the restoration of the symbolic order, THE PUBLIC ENEMY would indicate that before they could become classical, certain genres of Hollywood cinema had to be hysterical, developing a "pathology" that in cases such as the gangster film (but also melodrama) memorably provided their own poetics of hysteria and excess.

III
Studio and Genre: *Auteurs Maudits*, Mavericks and Eminent Europeans

11
Transatlantic Triangulations: William Dieterle and the Warner Bros. Biopics

Warner Bros.' two biographies of Eminent Frenchmen, THE STORY OF LOUIS PASTEUR (1935) and THE LIFE OF EMILE ZOLA (1937), have been widely recognized as symptomatic examples of the genre and intriguing evidence for the tensions inherent in transatlantic film-politics during the 1930s.[1] The two films do indeed merit close analysis for the several layers they reveal in the ongoing Hollywood dialogue with France, and vice versa. In what follows I want to propose that the layering is equally an effect of the "institution cinema," in this case the classic studio system in its early sound phase, and to put forward the argument that such filmic representations of the cultural and national "other" as one finds in both films, are—while undoubtedly addressed to an *international* or transnational public—also mediated by different discourses of *internal* self-presentation, self-regulation and self-representation.[2]

A few background observations first. The two films are part of a sextet of biopics, all directed by the German William Dieterle. The others are: THE WHITE ANGEL (1936, about Florence Nightingale), JUAREZ (1939, about Mexico's independence from France and the Spanish Crown), DR EHRLICH'S MAGIC BULLET (1940, about the German inventor of a cure for syphilis), A DISPATCH FROM REUTERS (1940, about the German-Jewish telegraph operator who founded the first international news service). Five of them feature men, three star Paul Muni and two Edward G. Robinson, both previously known for their roles in gangster films. Dieterle in Hollywood made other films with specifically "European," indeed "French" settings: MADAME DUBARRY (1934, with Dolores del Rio), possibly a sound remake of Ernst Lubitsch's MADAME DUBARRY of 1919, but with a different screenwriter; BLOCKADE (1938), a cloak and dagger story set during the Spanish civil war; and perhaps most famously, THE HUNCHBACK OF NOTRE DAME (1939), after Victor Hugo, and starring Charles Laughton—still considered the best adaptation of the famous novel. In *Quinlan's Illustrated Guide to Film Directors* (1999), for instance, one can read:

> Considering that the 1939 version of THE HUNCHBACK OF NOTRE DAME is just about my favourite film, it is a bitter pill to swallow that its German director, William Dieterle, also made a fair percentage of outright clinkers. . . . But in his Warner years, Dieterle's dark, Germanic nature was in full flight and he made some weird and wonderful variations on standard genres there, before becoming immersed in the studio's passion for biopics.[3]

Relevant to an understanding of this transnational conjuncture and its role in "the studio's passion for biopics" are first, a studio-centered discourse of self-presentation: the films were part of the Warner Bros.' long-term strategy to modify the studio's public image in the mid-1930s.

Second, there is a star-centered discourse: Paul Muni wanted to have, after the successes of SCARFACE and I WAS A FUGITIVE FROM A CHAIN GANG (both 1932), a greater say in the choice of his roles, and a different star image.

Third, at stake was the director's own attempt to change his image, and to move from professional contract worker to "European-style" producer-director.

Fourth, the films involve an intra-German émigré political debate about the role of "great men" or "leaders" in the course of historical events, with (indirect) implications for US foreign policy (isolationism vs interventionism). The two most prominent émigré writers—Thomas Mann and Bert Brecht—were involved in this debate, and Dieterle, who knew them both during their Hollywood years, puts himself somewhere in the middle.

While none of these discourses can claim to have "causal" or "determining" force, their reconstruction is useful, I would maintain, because it supports an ongoing debate about the retrospective rewriting of the historical or cultural meaning of symptomatic works of cinema, as well as providing proof of the transnational dimensions of even the most international of "national" cinemas, namely Hollywood which, in addition, has always had a "special relation" with France as both a specific location (from "Gay Paree" to "An American in Paris") and a symbolic-semantic cluster of reference points (the Cannes Film Festival, for instance), while its relation to Germany has mainly been to siphon off directorial and other talent, both large (Ernst Lubitsch, F.W. Murnau) and small (Henry Koster), both voluntary (E.A. Dupont, William Dieterle) and refugee (Fritz Lang, Max Ophuls).

Self Regulation as Self-Reflexivity

Anyone who speaks of the Hollywood studio system in the early 1930s has to address two major changes: one was the conversion to sound, and the other was the implementation of a number of regulative measures, or industry guidelines which culminated in the redrafting of the Motion Picture Production Code, better known as the Hays Code, adopted in 1930 but not fully enforced until 1934. The American film industry, as we know, is a very complex organization, having evolved over many years and comprising any number of potentially damaging sources of conflict, rivalry and competition, while also relying on cooperation and synergy in just about every area of its functioning. In such a situation, self-regulation becomes one of the top priorities for the system's robustness, in order to ensure its survival. As the anthropologist Hortense Powdermaker already observed in her fieldwork in the late 1940s, Hollywood has a very high degree of tribal cohesion, which is accompanied by image-consciousness and self-policing.[4]

Warding off external interference by closing ranks and adopting strategic responses has proven to be the key to an understanding of how the studio system—like other forms of clustering[5]—so successfully mediated between outside social demands, coming from various lobby and pressure groups, and internal responses—be they economic, managerial, creative or personality-based. Self-regulation, considered as an economic as well as an ideological premise, works like a membrane: communicating external pressures to the studio-system, but filtered because figured in its own terms: the demands become translated into practical decisions, operational directives, personnel management, self-presentations and last but not least, textual representations (the kinds of narratives and images that end up on the screen). Unlike the sociological "stimulus-response" model, or the direct bracketing of production and consumption with the box-office (so that only successful films are deemed to be socially significant), giving priority to self-regulation acknowledges the internal organization of the film industry as a material factor of change. Bordwell, Staiger and Thompson's

The Classical Hollywood Cinema[6] is perhaps the best-known study of the studio system which makes self-regulation and the principle of functional equivalence its cornerstone assumption and guiding heuristic principle.[7]

Self-regulation may also be one of the keys to another feature typical of mainstream commercial filmmaking (and not only since the days of postmodern or post-classical cinema): the high level of self-reference and intertextuality, as evidenced in the crossovers of genres, the typecasting and against-type casting of stars, the endemic remakes, the targeted confusion of public and private lives of stars and personalities by the Hollywood publicity machine, and the general tendency to translate other art forms, entertainment media, cultural values into the terms of its own system. As the critic Robert Warshow pointed out,[8] the American film industry in many of its utterances and pronouncements, credibly talked about itself as if it was talking about society at large: it is one of the characteristics that defines a hegemonic institution, and Hollywood has often—and certainly in the 1930s and 1940s—behaved as a state within the state.

This slippage from film reality to social reality was particularly true of Warner Bros.' B-picture production, which in the years 1931–33 became the target of much textual interference: from local censorship boards, from educators and the Churches, usually in the form of a demand for censorship. At Warner Bros., the operational constraints were such that distinctions between A and B features (due to their different modes of circulation: B-films for rapid circulation in a vast number of second-run cinemas, as opposed to A-films, the more visible and more highly promoted prestige films) that this distinction structured many of the internal hierarchies of executive decision making and production planning. Historically, most studios maintained a diversified production policy precisely because it allowed them to let the different kinds of exhibition spaces determine the shape of the material supports (the films). B-films provided a substantial source of revenue and thus required not only tight supervision, but also a very skilled roster of personnel. If the industry agreed to the Hays Code so readily, it was because it wanted to retain control not only over the unity of its products, but also the social spaces and audiences which these products penetrated.

When looking at the output of Warner Bros. in the years after 1934, one can detect a pattern of risk-management and diversification-strategy: the vertical strategy encompassed A- and B-productions (translating into genres and cycles), but studio output was also horizontally diversified by way of its source material: newspaper stories, stage musicals, prestigious theater productions, films with a radio or other media-intertext; best known in retrospect is the studio's investment in domestic social issues (the "New Deal" brand of Warner Bros. products: films about unemployment, juvenile delinquency, prostitution and organized crime). But the studio was also active in spotting international issues: European fascism, Spanish civil war, Latin America. With this, Warner product could be present in very diverse social milieus and occupy broad ideological terrain.

If each of these "issues" also translates into "access to audiences," guaranteed via ownership or control of first-run film theaters, publicity and other distribution channels, such extra-textual factors nonetheless share with the films themselves the material/immaterial, economic/textual status of the images as "representations," often successfully dissimulating the boundary between the economic and the textual. It was this transformation of external demands into "images" and "representations" which acted as the buffer: against the State intervening on the economic side, in order to affect, for instance, distribution and exhibition (the anti-trust action); against the banks, in the form of finance capital, intervening on the production side, by determining cash flow (the importance of stars to rescue near-bankrupt studios); against social institutions (Church organizations, civic pressure groups) trying to intervene on the textual level (censorship). By contrast, other entertainment and information media (newspaper, radio, stage theater, at least until the arrival of television), affected the film industry by reinforcing the self-regulation reflex. Hollywood tended to co-opt competing media, by turning them into intertexts in the films themselves or by including them economically, buying out performers and buying up intellectual properties. One could therefore say that self-regulation (as a way of guarding autonomy and protecting against outside intervention) also acted as a powerful stimulus to intertextuality, intermediality and reflexivity and self-reference already in classical Hollywood.

The Warner Biopic and the Bid for "Culture"

One reason why Dieterle, as a European, and Warner Bros. as a major studio (having been at the forefront of the implementation of sound) make for such an instructive case in the 1930s is that Warner Bros. found itself at the cutting edge not only of the latest film technologies around sound, but also at the sharp end of the various forms of outside intervention. Its gangster films and social issue films caused well-publicized controversies, being accused of promoting gratuitous violence, immorality and bad language. But as Lea Jacobs shows in her study *The Wages of Sin*, about the "fallen woman" cycle (made by Warner Bros. and other studios), which served as a focal point for much of this public criticism of the film industry, self-regulation and self-censorship could work to sometimes paradoxical effect. "Because industry self-regulation functioned as a sort of machine for registering and internalizing social conflict, it provides an extraordinarily fruitful means of contextualizing film analysis and for studying the rules governing representations of female sexuality in the 1930s."[9]

I will not be offering a similarly detailed reading of the cycle of biographies, or of THE STORY OF LOUIS PASTEUR, but the general principles of contextual film analysis that emerges from such studies are, *mutatis mutandis*, also valid, when one looks at the biopics which Warner Bros. made from 1936, even if their referents seem at first sight so remote from contemporary American reality: the Dieterle biopics I named—from THE STORY OF LOUIS PASTEUR (1936), THE WHITE ANGEL (1936), THE LIFE OF EMILE ZOLA (1937), JUAREZ (1939), DR EHRLICH'S MAGIC BULLET (1940), to A DISPATCH FROM REUTER (1940)—are all distanced either in time or geography from America in the 1930s, and that is one of their salient points. Yet "socially" significant evidence need not be exclusively sought in the pro-filmic material: certain constellations around the central figures in the biopics give clues to the inscription of the social: depending on how the social is to be defined. Read in terms of class, for example, a film like LOUIS PASTEUR can be usefully compared to HEROES FOR SALE, if only because the latter—a typical Depression film about war veterans on the slide—and the former (a historical drama) both focus on inventions or discoveries that interfere with vested interests. While Tom Holmes capitalizes on his skills and markets a successful improvement to the washing machine, the discoveries of Louis Pasteur have to prove themselves in opposition to the prevailing ideology and even to be protected from the market in order to be of social benefit.

The paradigms are similarly structured around public responsibility and private enterprise, even if the terms appear inverted. Scientists or inventors are in these films as symbolically overdetermined figures as are gangsters, not in any strictly sociological sense, but owing to the conflicting social value systems at stake in their actions: free enterprise in conflict with the law and public interest, or corporate capitalism inventing its own forms of philanthropy, while social welfare falls to the State: in each case, they are the figures of a problematic mediation.

Such a reading raises, but does not answer the question of what integrative function the different mechanisms of self-regulation might have had on the text, in order to produce a number of typical narrative images and condensations strong enough to found a genre: for the biopic did establish such an image not only for itself ("worthy, but dull," "slow, but penetrating"), but also for its star (Paul Muni's Pasteur, Zola, Juarez), its director (William Dieterle, the humanist, representative of the better Germany) and the studio (successfully answering its critics by winning Oscar nominations and cultural capital with each of its biopics). In this way, the conjunction of director, producer, star and studio could be seen as a compromise formation emerging from quite heterogeneous and structurally distinct factors, in which a genre can act as a counterforce to the internal threat (a star restless with his roles) and the external threat (the public protest against Warner's violent crime films), thereby redefining the basis on which one particular Hollywood studio could rebrand itself via a different self-representation.

If this sounds a little too convoluted, here is a more conventional narrative about the "origins" of the Dieterle biopics. Early in 1933, in a move to counter the adverse publicity its highly successful but violent films had attracted, Warner Bros. decided to upgrade the cultural appeal of their production. They cast around for a suitable property, and through the offices of Henry Blanke, a former personal assistant to Ernst Lubitsch at Ufa who accompanied him to Hollywood in 1922, and then worked for Warner Bros., first heading their production in Germany (1928–30), then their foreign productions in Hollywood (1930–31), before working as producer or production supervisor under Hal B. Wallis from 1932–61, Warner Bros. began negotiating with Max Reinhardt over the filming of A MIDSUMMER NIGHT'S DREAM, already a successful theatrical extravaganza at the Hollywood Bowl. Reinhardt was greeted in Hollywood with something of the same reverence for the "artist" which eight years earlier had been bestowed on Murnau.[10] Blanke knew Reinhardt through Lubitsch, and because of the media attention focused on Reinhardt in the United States, the film was preceded by its already marketable "image," and while not a particularly spectacular box-office success, A MIDSUMMER NIGHT'S DREAM generated enough publicity and prestige to be awarded an Oscar for the cinematographer (Hal Mohr), precisely at the time (May 1934) when the Hays Code had been redrafted and given "teeth": it was thus an excellent investment for Warner, the gain in terms of "image" compensating for the lack of box-office.

The Director as Image Value

Dieterle for his part had come to Hollywood in 1928, thanks to Blanke, and after Warner Bros. had offered him a contract via their German First National operation. The studio's reasons for wanting Dieterle, and Dieterle's reason for accepting the offer, were in some sense quite fortuitous and a-symmetrical. Dieterle had debts he was glad to leave behind (his theater company went bankrupt: even a prison sentence might have awaited him, had the Warner offer not bailed him out), and Warner needed someone fairly menial, but nonetheless a seasoned professional to direct German language versions in Hollywood under Blanke's supervision. After the brief spell of multi-language versions was over, Dieterle was able to stay on, and he established himself quickly as a successful contract director mainly with B-pictures.

When Max Reinhardt came to Hollywood, Dieterle seemed a good choice as co-director, not only because he spoke German and had behind him a long career as a movie actor and theater director in Berlin. He also had a quite distinguished career as a director in Germany, with half a dozen commercially very successful films, among them GESCHLECHT IN FESSELN, one of the most sympathetic treatments of homosexuality in Weimar cinema.

Encouraged by the critical success of A MIDSUMMER NIGHT'S DREAM, Dieterle began to redesign his directorial image: in order to advance to the status of an A-picture director, he reconstructed himself as a Germanic Director, taking up the kind of sartorial eccentricity which such notable "Viennese" as Erich von Stroheim and Josef von Sternberg had made popular.[11] Dieterle's trademark was a pair of immaculate white gloves which he wore whenever on the set. It now began to feature in the publicity material. But far from having a genteel or aristocratic background, Dieterle, rather like Stroheim, was actually self-taught and had grown up in a working-class or artisanal family. Nor, of course, was he a political refugee. In Hollywood, the gloves which Dieterle wore for a skin allergy, paradoxically connoted a "cultural" value which the publicity department was able to use for the promotion of the image they needed for A MIDSUMMER NIGHT'S DREAM: Viennese charm and sophistication combining with immortal art, thanks to Warner Bros.' respect for culture, and their patronage of famous émigrés. At first, Dieterle's attempts to become permanently associated with European *Kultur* failed. The projects he proposed to Wallis—another Shakespeare play: TWELFTH NIGHT, then Georg Büchner's play about the French Revolution, DANTON'S DEATH—were turned down: the studio clearly did not want him to continue in this vein. Box-office considerations played their part, but also their assessment of Dieterle as a contract director:

> To be a big success you must first have the ingredients for success, and in the picture business this means a good story. [After A MIDSUMMER NIGHT'S DREAM], well, I thought I was in for a real good assignment. Then they gave me a story, and it was really terrible. I said "No", and they gave me a two-week vacation. I was having a great time when I got a wire which said, "Come back immediately. We have a wonderful story". Well, it was the same script, *Dr Socrates*, only sweetened up: it had been rewritten for Paul Muni.[12]

Dieterle did direct DR SOCRATES (1935), and it proved to be a blessing in disguise, whatever the merits of the script, because it became his first collaboration with Paul Muni, the go-between to better assignments. DR SOCRATES, directed by Dieterle and starring Muni, himself of central European origin, thus paired two Warner Bros. malcontents on a low-priority studio-property. Muni, who did not think of himself as a movie star, had insisted on being taken off the topical films and working-class hero parts. Essentially an actor with stage training, he was afraid of being typecast, and sought subjects where his talent for mimicry and impersonation could be showcased. Wanting screen roles more in the vein of his Broadway success *Counselor at Law*, DR SOCRATES must have seemed to Muni an acceptable compromise: playing a young idealist doctor ostracized by the small-town community in which he worked, he gets caught up in the world of crime out of sheer humanitarianism. In retrospect, the role (an idealist among bigots) looked forward to the biopics, while the character, setting and iconography harked back to I WAS A FUGITIVE and BLACK FURY: DR SOCRATES coheres perfectly as a Paul Muni vehicle, even though Dieterle thought the material "terrible" and its plot is indeed extremely incoherent, unsuitable as the prototype of a new genre or for significant social statements.

Dieterle had decided that only producer-director status in one of Warner Bros.' special unit productions, such as those of Howard Hawks and William Wyler, could get him more control over his studio image, and thus over studio resources. It was working with Muni on DR SOCRATES which made him see the possibilities of a package around a property that had been passed back and forth several times: THE STORY OF LOUIS PASTEUR came to Dieterle via Blanke after Robert Florey had had an option on it in 1934. However, it needed the support of Paul Muni to persuade Hal Wallis to take it on, and delegate it to Dieterle, for whom it was the first time he was involved in a project from the start and present at script conferences: "It was paradise. It was the beginning of the second phase of my career in Hollywood."[13]

From "Realism" to "Authenticity"

THE STORY OF LOUIS PASTEUR was an enormous hit. Years later, Jack Warner (who had done much to block the property as it was passed back and forth between story-departments and producers) was awarded for it a medal of the French Légion d'Honneur on a subsequent visit to Paris: the studio had successfully created an image larger than the film. Indeed, the combination or "mix" of elements was such that it could form the basis of a series. The marketing of biopics, too, represented a shift in strategy by the studio. While playing the high culture card for one part of its audiences (the French setting), the studio discovered a way of combining its reputation for social concern with an altogether less controversial "realism" than that which had troubled the Legion of Decency.

Distinctive about the publicity at Warner Bros. for its biopics was an emphasis on historical accuracy, on the quantity of research materials, the extensive inspection of original locations, the quality of the professional consultancy: for DR EHRLICH, the research department established the exact date when gummed labels first came in use, and no lesser person than the vice-consul of Mexico acted as the technical adviser on JUAREZ.[14] What gritty realism was to the topical picture became historical authenticity to the biopic: the trademark for a genre.

As a genre in its own right, the biopic has a mixed parentage. Film biographies of characters from history were made famous by Lubitsch with his fictional and comic treatment of MADAME DUBARRY (1919) and ANN BOLEYN (1920). Not only did they help establish the reputation of the German cinema in the twenties, they were also imitated by émigré directors such as Alexander Korda (THE PRIVATE LIFE OF HENRY VIII, GB 1933) and Dieterle himself: his first filmed biography was LUDWIG DER ZWEITE (1930), in which he also played the lead. Another generic intertext altogether are the scandal sheet and pulp revelations of the private lives of the rich and famous, which found their way into the pseudo-biographies that structure the narrative of the gangster films.

By turning this latter genre (LITTLE CAESAR, THE PUBLIC ENEMY, SCARFACE) inside out THE STORY OF LOUIS PASTEUR sets up both a different generic space and recalls other Warner genres, thus rewriting the studio's own past, while not breaking with it. THE STORY OF LOUIS PASTEUR, for instance, opens in the decor and dramatic atmosphere of a horror film; we see a Second Empire interior, heavy drapes billowing in the wind from an open window. A man enters, unaware that he is being watched by someone lurking in the shadows. Suddenly a shot, and the man, now recognizable as a doctor, slumps over the table and collapses—in much the same dramatic way as a gangster film like SCARFACE set its violent tone, where in the opening scene a man is killed by Tony Camonte (Paul Muni), as he sweeps out his restaurant after a party. The intertext of leading actor and his traditional genre is written into the first of Muni's biopics as a signpost for audience orientation well before he makes his entrance in the film.

The biopic thus represents a *threefold compromise formation*: in terms of generic codes, it reworks and rewrites motifs from the studio's other cycles; as a strategic response to censorship, it substitutes narratively motivated violence for supposedly gratuitous violence; in absorbing the "authorial" ambitions of particular studio personnel, such as its stars, it stabilizes its internal organization. Although a limited and perhaps special case, the biopic suggests that the call for censorship addressed to Warner Bros. films was answered not so much by direct self-censorship, but by a sort of textual displacement of exhibition values and "attractions": from gritty realism to historical authenticity; from sexual display to European culture and sophistication as display; from domestic social issues to international politics.[15]

Bertolt Brecht and the Biopic

For quite a different view of the ideological discourse of the biopics one could turn to Bertolt Brecht:

> William Dieterle with his filmed biographies of Zola, Pasteur, Juarez, Ehrlich has inaugurated a gallery of great bourgeois figures. [His . . .] extraordinary characters allow the actors [Muni and Robinson] the depiction of personalities, which constitutes a considerable advance, [since] the representation of ordinary people as personalities seems impossible to realize within the Hollywood cinema; even Dieterle's interesting experiments in this area encountered resistance.
>
> The element of conflict in these bourgeois biographies derives from the opposition between the hero and dominant opinion, which is to say the opinion of those who dominate. The type is that of Ibsen's *Enemy of the People*. Bourgeois society is already eyeing the increase of productive forces as if it was a cancer. . . . Zola, himself a bourgeois, turns against the bourgeoisie in order to

address mankind. Pasteur is shown as the Galileo of medicine; he too risks being put in prison. . . . An example of the difficulties [that Dieterle encountered]: the studio wants to do a biopic of the Life of Mme Curie because of the scene where the Curies, who conducted their experiments in great poverty, refuse to sell their radium patents to industry, in order that the world as a whole may benefit from them. Several scripts later, each costing a lot of money, the studio is still not satisfied until it is discovered that it is precisely this scene that spoils it all: the Curies' refusal of a million dollars is altogether too unnatural; it ruins the credibility of the entire film.[16]

Brecht isolates two symptomatic elements: first, in the biopic the central conflict has to do with a division within dominant liberal ideology itself, produced by the rapid increase of productive forces under capitalism which bourgeois society, particularly in its judicial, medical and scientific discourses, is no longer able to contain. Second, he highlights the tension inherent in a story that dramatizes contradictions while at the same time confining and resolving them within the terms of ideological and motivational verisimilitude. In Brecht's view, "personality" functions as the discourse that unifies an ideologically incoherent narrative around a coherent motivational core (the concept of psycho-logical credibility), but he overlooks that the cinema can impose coherence by personality, because the star image unites contradictory attributes, and functions as a mode of address, a way of inscribing a unified audience in a text, even when (especially when) it deals with potentially divisive topics. But Brecht's first point may further help to understand a film like Louis Pasteur as part of a discourse in which the industry talks about itself as if it was talking about society.[17]

What is the function of narrative in a Hollywood studio film? At Warner's as indeed at other studios, the importance of the story for producer or director lay in the resources and organizational assets which could be accumulated around it: this was its technical and financial aspect. A certain type of story was allocated a certain budget, which in turn determined the importance of the production and the status of the director. In terms of the industrial mode of production generally, however, the script had to be able to articulate the narrative in such a way as to fit into the already established division of labor and the separation of functions, from casting and work schedules to set design, music scoring and editing. The priority at Warner Bros. was the organization of production time, with managers charged to ensure full utilization of the production facilities. According to Dieterle, for instance, Zanuck was the type of producer who, even without a story, could produce a script, and Curtiz was the kind of director who, even without a script, could shoot the requisite number of scenes per day:

Under Zanuck we sometimes had to start a picture with only ten pages of script. A film should have a unified all-over conception. If I don't know the ending how can I motivate the beginning? What does it mean? Where does it lead to? Oh, the fights we had sometimes. . . . It was the system. We had to shoot 4–5 pages of script a day and those poor fellows, the writers had to produce so many pages a day from 9–5 whether they had an idea or not. They had to deliver or lose their job. If a director wasn't fast enough, or gave them too much trouble, they replaced him, usually with Mike [Curtiz]. Mike did everything. He could finish a picture at 11 and at 1pm start a new picture. He was extraordinarily talented. He did not always know what he was doing, but he had such an instinct for film, he could do it. I couldn't. If I didn't have my script I was helpless.[18]

The productive forces at Warner's were clearly in conflict with bourgeois notions of the organic work, or what Dieterle calls "a unified all-over conception." The form of the product pre-existed its content, and a narrative style could develop which was based on divisibility: action-oriented, below average shot length giving priority to editing rather than complex set ups and allowing for the sort of textual *bricolage* necessitated by filming out of sequence, or without a completed script. For Dieterle, to get an A-picture assignment meant therefore also that the script would determine the allocation of production facilities rather than the availability of facilities determining the script.

It is possible to see in THE STORY OF LOUIS PASTEUR and other biopics the textual traces of the conflicts between the divisions of labor within the studio production system on the one side and the "unified overall conception" on the other. There are generic traits typical of Dieterle's biopics which seem to reproduce within the fiction the difficulties of the fiction: the hero's struggle, for instance, to retain intact his or her vision, invention, humanitarian ideal, against the social forces that attempt to appropriate it: a self-representation of the bourgeois artist, the man of genius—a figuration of Dieterle himself in his struggle with the studio-system? Dieterle did rewrite his career in the light of his self-identification with the (success of the) biopic: this, however, would be to reduce the textual operation to an anecdotal function. Instead, what is important to retain is the emphasis in the films on the "unified conception" (biography: the meaning of a life becomes identical with, because rewritten, the meaning of a work) and the emphasis on "personality" as that which transcends the contradictions which Brecht names: that between the organization of the productive forces and their personalization or psychologizing in the fiction. Hollywood's mythology of the mogul, the tycoon, its legendary figures in and out of films can be seen as the attempt to give human—if necessary, monstrous—shape to impersonal historical or abstract economic forces.

Blanke, for instance, saw the role of producer as someone who can "weld and rivet the loose ends."[19] Which is to say, reverse the divisibility of the production process, and give the product an appearance of unity for consumption. It is in this context that one can understand Brecht's other point: the tendency of the central character in the biopic to address himself no longer to his own class but to humanity at large.

This, I think, is a crucial textual feature in the films. One of the main contradictions of the biopics as ideological self-representations of American capitalist society in general or the studio-system in particular, is that the subjects whose biography the films narrate are *idealists*, which is to say, the very nature of their mission implies working either in isolation (writer, politician in exile), or under conditions of artisanal production (inventors, doctors, scientists), rather than as parts of a corporate hierarchized enterprise such as the studio-system. By contrast, the economic discourses of earlier Warner cycles (gangster film or Depression musical) register in a more overtly metaphoric fashion the historical shift in American industry and the film industry from entrepreneurial to corporate capitalism (e.g. the small-time gangster getting "wise" and "organized").

"Spontaneous Crowds"

The biopics represent a more indirect encoding or "working through" of this historical process. The "sheer force of personality" creates a unified mode of address capable of articulating but also reconciling the ideological divisions within the bourgeoisie itself, to take up Brecht's terms. However, instead of being merely worked over by the narrative, in the manner of myths ("the imaginary resolution of real contradictions"), Hollywood displaces ideological incoherence in the direction of spectacle and the show, capitalizing on the unifying and uniting force of the "riveting" performance: the star image mediates between society and the text as much by the imaginary coherence of its addressees, as by any formal narrative homology.

Dieterle's biopics reconcile the private with the public by engineering situations that allow the hero to present himself, with an impassioned speech or plea to a court jury (EMILE ZOLA), to a crowd of his followers (JUAREZ) or to journalists; all of them different instances of intra-diegetic audiences which function as delegate of us, the spectators. By electrifying an audience or by addressing a skeptical and hostile gathering, the hero bypasses the "system" and temporarily at least suspends the validity of the institutions and their discourses. As far as I can ascertain, this intra-diegetic public sphere is a significant feature of the cinema in the 1930s in general; with the coming of sound, a new dimension of public life is opened up to cinematic representation. The courtroom, the election platform, the market place or even a cattle auction can come to stand for the democratic process itself. The disagreements which Brecht had with Fritz Lang over the function of spontaneous crowds and the hostages in Hangmen also Die (1943: Brecht wanted to call it "Trust the People") are an instructive example of an ideological conflict over different versions of popular democracy.[20]

Dieterle's films in this respect appear to typify a system of address inflected by the cinema's changing role as a forum of public debate within the context of fulfilling a specific ideological task: making good the claim of Hollywood to speak with a voice representing the whole nation, indeed "the world", thanks to its ability to create an imaginary consensus audience. In particular, the desire to represent in the biopic an individual who is both within and outside given ideological discourses, who belongs to his age and in some sense transcends it, affects the process of enunciation itself. The famous Cahiers du cinéma article on Young Mr. Lincoln (1939) had located this effect as unique to the representations of Lincoln as founder of the nation. But Dieterle's biographies, and notably Juarez, show some of the same strategies (is Juarez anti-French?). "The newly named emperor Maximilian and his wife Carlotta arrive in Mexico to face popular sentiment favoring Benito Juarez and democracy. Abraham Lincoln supports Juarez and asks the French to withdraw support for Maximilian. Carlotta goes to France to plead with Napoleon, to no avail."[21] (Juarez always carries a portrait of Lincoln in his luggage.) In The Story of Louis Pasteur, for instance, the primary opposition—the individual against society—is first recast in terms of a limited or local conflict (here: scientific interests against the vested interests of the medical profession). Closure and resolution, however, are achieved by a kind of mise-en-abyme of different social fields (the sphere of the family, the medical profession, the government and international relations), which are layered concentrically and resolved consecutively.

Within the family, narrative closure is assured by the formation of a couple. Pasteur's daughter marries the former assistant of Dr. Charbonnet, enemy of Pasteur in the French State bureaucracy. However, the resolution is only apparent, because the child born from this union has to be delivered by a doctor who does not believe in Pasteur's theories about the causes of childbed fever, and is only persuaded to observe the new hygiene rules on condition that Pasteur recants publicly. The conflict with the medical profession thus takes on the form of a wager: Pasteur's biological survival (family offspring) is played off against the survival of scientific truth.

As it turns out, this, too, is a pseudo-dilemma: it merely provides the motivation for the dramatic reversal in the closing scene. Pasteur's devoted wife cajoles the frail and discouraged scientist to attend a public lecture disproving his findings, but in actual fact, it is a ruse to make him accept the honor of membership into the Académie Française. The narrative resolution is thus guaranteed by reconciling him with the medical profession: he is accepted into the ranks of the institution, which had done everything to block his work. This would seem to undo and take back Pasteur's opposition, obscuring the original issue: pure science vs vested interests. It is therefore telling that Brecht should refer to Pasteur as "the Galileo of Medicine": his own biopic for the stage, The Life of Galileo, can be seen as a kind of dialogue with Dieterle's biopic, which it both imitates and subjects to a materialist critique. In its dialectical structure, Brecht's play juxtaposes rather than metaphorically doubles private life and work, and opposes the "idealist" transcendence of the conflict between pure science and the uses that society makes of its discoveries, a radical non-equivalence: self-interest, "truth," political reason and commerce are in Brecht totally antagonistic fields allowing for neither narrative closure nor a unified spectator-position.

In Dieterle, the specifically filmic terms of the narrative resolution are those of a public spectacle in front of a diegetic audience that includes the members of Pasteur's own family. While in the narrative, the divergent discourses of personal self-esteem and public acknowledgment, scientific truth and social medicine resolve themselves by being placed en-abyme (science inserts itself in the family via son-in-law and grandchild), spectacle coherence is only possible across the terms of another discourse altogether: that of the enactment of a performance and a public ritual, whose function, however, it is to secure the double inscription of the spectator. Pasteur, the audience's main figure of identification, is both protagonist and spectator of his own public recognition. The spectator identifies simultaneously with two subject positions: that of the surprised Pasteur and that of the diegetic audience in the fiction, metonymically represented by Pasteur's wife.

Personal Style or a Historical Subject Position?

Although I have not been able to verify this with a larger corpus of films, it would seem that the forms of self-reference and *mises-en-abyme* of spectatorial address which I have identified in biopics like THE STORY OF LOUIS PASTEUR, THE LIFE OF EMILE ZOLA or JUAREZ could probably be distinguished from other or earlier Warner genres by different kinds of spatial construction and a different sense of continuity. For example, scenes in the biopics are very often staged frontally, which reduces the illusion of spatial depth (raising the possibility of comparison with the Warner musicals); second, noticeably sparing use is made of the point of view structure, and thus the suturing process does not always place the spectator on the side of the chief protagonist (reserving this for a dramatic climax, as in THE STORY OF LOUIS PASTEUR). Instead, lives often appear as if already set in the picture frame of history.

These effects of staging and *mise-en-scène* have earned Dieterle a reputation for slow and ponderous direction, lacking the elegance and drive of classical continuity editing. Whatever the criteria may be for calling Dieterle's style "elephantine," "leaden," "clumsy," they unfortunately do not consider the possibility that this *mise-en-scène* is itself historically and ideologically determined: by attributing it to Dieterle as a personal style (or lack of it), one conveniently overlooks that in other films he was as versatile as any other Warner contract director. THE LAST FLIGHT (1931), JEWEL ROBBERY (1932), LAWYER MAN (1933), FOG OVER FRISCO (1934) show him capable of visual elegance, of fast-paced direction in the Warner manner, for what these epithets are worth.[22]

The differences between, say LAWYER MAN (a B-picture, where the legal setting is only interesting for an oedipal analysis of the narrative, not for its civic connotations) and JUAREZ (an A-picture with political references about American isolationism and the Spanish civil war) point not only to a shift in paradigm or genre, or a different target audience, but within the social field that the Studio occupied from around 1938, also to Hollywood consciously creating an image of public and ideological responsibility: this time less in order to ward off textual interference like censorship, but economic interference (the anti-trust suit) displacing itself to a world political or historical canvas in the narratives and to a self-consciously civic mode of address.

The style of the biopics, therefore, may have corresponded to what one might call a particular social imaginary: that of synthesizing different spectators by redefining the space which the cinema as an institution occupies in public life and consciousness—part of the industry's way of talking to the Justice Department by endorsing the Administration's foreign policy and addressing the box-office audience as civic subjects. Dieterle's *mise-en-scène* could then be seen as a mode of cinematic address, which has itself a transcending function. The spectator identifying not only with the main character (humanizing genius) but with the audience that the hero is addressing himself to (removing him from ordinary humanity): the suspicious doctors, the doubting peasantry, the anxious family, the French Academy, the Mexican People; all of them, as it were, juries of men and women good and true, and representative of unity in diversity that only the hero (and therefore the cinema) has the power to spellbind, persuade and rally.

The fact that in Dieterle's biopics most of the heroes are non-American facilitates audiences being addressed as humanity in general rather than in terms of vested interests and classes. Humanity becomes the term for all those who can be gathered in a movie theater: this would seem to be the condition under which Hollywood can talk about politics. With a biopic like JUAREZ the studio not so much endorsed a specific international policy or took sides within the spectrum of opinion represented by the government of the day, but competed within the public arena, by reproducing some of the subject effects hitherto occupied or identified with other public media, notably radio.

This form of address, on the other hand, strikes us today as un-cinematic perhaps precisely because we no longer share the same historical subject position, nor does the cinema situate itself in the same arena of public debate as it did then. A fuller understanding of the subject inscribed in the biopics and of the economics that have inflected the texts might well require a look at the mass medium which the cinema in the mid- and late 1930s had begun to displace in almost all spheres except for news. The historically vanished intertext of the biopic might be live broadcasting, and the relevant intertext to Muni's acting or Dieterle's direction would then be something like President Roosevelt's fireside chats, going straight to the Nation, bypassing the press, and straight into the homes, bypassing Congress or political parties.[23]

From Civic to Universal Address

The biopic is a genre of special interest if it can be understood as trying to inscribe the spectator as an individual (the classical subject-position of American cinema) and as a member of a collectivity, a civic audience (a more specific, historical mode of inscription), held together by the force of personality (in this case the authenticated historical individual represented by the performer as specialist in morphing and metamorphosis, such as Muni, rather than the star who is always identical with himself).

The confrontations between Hollywood and civic bodies in the early 1930s and the judiciary in the late 1930s outline the historical moment where Hollywood itself recognized its function as a universalizing, representative discourse, thanks to the very real economic power represented by the film industry. In this sense the discourse of the biopic is only one form of dramatizing this process of the cinema competing as a mode of civic "direct address" before it is secure in the universality of its audiences. The films of Frank Capra from the same period, for instance, could provide an instructive parallel.[24] Yet this obsessive inscription of the community as addressee becomes in turn obsolete, precisely to the degree that Hollywood's own status as dominant discourse becomes uncontested: by the time of WWII, it can address the individual as universal.

In other genres, the dominant economic position of the film industry in relation to other and earlier mass forms of entertainment expressed itself by their appearance in the films, like prisoners triumphantly put on show by a conquering army. The dialectic of neutralizing interference by internal self-regulation meant that the competing media and the institutions with which the cinema might enter into conflict (state and federal agencies, the legal system, different lobbies) were often either taken into the narrative as symbolic figurations (metaphoric presence) or appeared as cultural values which the cinema could appropriate for itself (metonymic presence): the adaptation of famous plays or classics of literature, best-sellers, Broadway hits.

Genre, authorship, *mise-en-scène* and studio style: these are traditional areas of investigation whose relation to each other is neither homological nor strictly speaking, oppositional. They articulate themselves in a case like the Dieterle/Warner Bros. biopic at different levels, as a collage of motives, or even fortuitous coincidence, as heterogeneity. But does this mean that they have no social meanings, and can only be discussed as separate fields of inquiry? To analyze them as if they were would be to submit to an unreflected empiricism and positivism, which treated the phenomena at the level of their own self-image. The imaginary unity, which the various processes of self-representation of the institution cinema strive to achieve at their point of reception, is precisely the result, the work of the discourses, not their natural state. In the biopics the code that ensures unity is ultimately congruent with one of the most naturalized paradigms of all: that of a Life. That this paradigm is itself dependent on textual as well as social and biological processes is evident from a symptomatic title: not the LIFE, but the STORY OF LOUIS PASTEUR.

What the present essay has tried to outline is how a directorial, generic and studio-based discourse—each with its tendency towards self-representation, self-regulation and autonomy, its different modes of seeking to establish equilibrium, autopoesis and imaginary coherence—articulate themselves in a conflicting arena, but one that can be reconstructed by empirical scholarship and is thus historically locatable.

Are there any lessons we can draw for a more general project about émigrés in Hollywood? In the study of émigré culture there have been at least three paradigm shifts in recent years: one is to see even the period of the 1930s and 1940s, usually treated as *sui generis* because of the political, racial or ideological factors that forced emigration, embedded also in the larger history of transatlantic film migration and the different kinds of talent transfers in the film industry, which have been continuous throughout—even if subject to certain fluctuations both in their peaks and in their distribution across the world's filmmaking nations. The second paradigm shift is to emphasize the role of contingency in the careers and fates of individual émigrés, while noting the different kinds of role they played in Hollywood, including an often unrecognized political part, extending beyond and developing sideways from the usual left-right dichotomies. The third paradigm shift is to acknowledge that the film industry cannot be regarded as isolated from the other mass media, with which it competes and on which it depends: notably radio, the gramophone and music industry. Although this is not the place to address all these aspects in full, I believe that the case of William Dieterle and his biopics of Eminent Europeans offers instructive instances of each of these paradigm shifts: he was not an émigré-exile in the political sense of having to leave Germany because of Nazism, but his and his wife's engagement for political and racially persecuted refugees—and not only from Germany— was exemplary. His career, as I have tried to show, was marked by flukes, abrupt changes and happy accidents that might disqualify a director from becoming an "*auteur,*" and yet the struggle to create a coherence, a personality and a life/work are everywhere in evidence, culminating in, precisely, the biopics. Finally, the mode of address, the gathering of audiences, the investment in creating a political space is part of a very American way about politics and the mass media, but its inspiration and enduring political interest is manifestly European. For even more so than the nationality of the protagonist, whose biopic I have been concentrating on, the political values are also unmistakably French: part of the dialogue over democracy, republicanism, populism and the people, taking place between France and the US for nearly 250 years. Hence the configuration of my title and the different levels at which the three components, France, Germany and America articulate, or rather, triangulate themselves and implicate each other.

12

Welles and Virtuosity: CITIZEN KANE as Character-Mask

Authorship and Orson Welles

Given the fact that films are for the most part industrial products, made and circulated for profit, the question of authorship—of who or what originates a work and gives it the authority of meaning and value—has always presented special problems.[1] The "*politique des auteurs*" of *Cahiers du cinéma* in the 1950s tried to cut the Gordian knot, but it had a double polemical edge: within a conservative, craft-oriented film industry in France, the "policy" wanted to create a space for new talent to gain access to working in the cinema as directors. But as a "theory" it also wanted to provide a way of discriminating among the mass of Hollywood product, setting criteria for singling out aesthetically significant films. Finally, its effect was to give names, faces and personalities to the Parisian love affair with 1940s and 1950s Hollywood cinema. Since then, the question of authorship has been many times reinterpreted and reformulated, cast aside and recast.[2]

What I want to retain from this discussion when looking at Orson Welles are two points. First, the original *auteur* theory was developed to apply principally to directors working more or less successfully *within* the Hollywood studio system (as opposed to making films in an art cinema, independent or avant-garde context). As a consequence, the theory implicitly subscribed to what one can call the "classical" notion of the artist, as opposed to its romantic variant. While the latter is deemed to break the rules in order to be able to express his [sic] innermost self, the classical artist accepts the traditional forms (of drama, of poetry) or the canons (of painting or sculpture), because his talent thrives on the knife-edge balance between freedom and constraint. The dialectic allows him to give new life to old conventions, revitalize the stereotypes, enter into dialogue or competition with his forebears, or even create a pastiche of traditional subjects and themes in ways that will make them seem fresh and new.

Second, the *auteur* is as much a set of stylistic and formal traits/marks in the films themselves, discovered or extracted retrospectively by the critic from the work in view of establishing principles of coherence, as it names the biography, the creative force and artistic individuality of a particular person in "real life," outside the films. In the case of Welles, neither of these meta-critical caveats and historicizing assumptions around the film director as *auteur* quite seem to apply. On the contrary, he is mostly remembered as implacably hostile to Hollywood and the "system." The "wonder boy from

Kenosha" (Bazin), he is the director of genius whose career was wrecked and blighted by having to work within the constraints of the studios, someone whose films (THE MAGNIFICENT AMBERSONS, TOUCH OF EVIL) suffered irreparable damage at the hands of studio executives, while many of his most cherished projects (DON QUIXOTE) were either endlessly delayed or never made, because the industry blacklisted him for being profligate, "difficult" and box office poison. But Welles was also in love with Hollywood, famously calling it "the biggest electric train set a boy ever had!," and thus he does not altogether fit the romantic stereotype either.[3] Nor does the argument from reception—the retrospective emergence of common themes and existential pre-occupation—quite hold. He was an *auteur* from the beginning, precisely because of the force of his personality and colorful biography, amplified into legend also by his many acting roles and media appearances. His public persona possessed such a reality outside his films that it could fairly be said to have "consumed" many of his films.[4] He is both more than the sum of his films—the larger than life personality, the familiar gravelly voice—and less than his films, being chiefly (and perhaps unfairly) remembered as the director of one film only, albeit an undisputed masterpiece of the cinema, CITIZEN KANE. This is the paradox about Welles: a director who said and did it all in his very first film, becoming an embodiment of "the cinema" while spending almost another half-century at once fighting and fostering the myth of himself as his own worst enemy. It is as if in order to rescue his one enduring achievement, his life had to become the masterpiece which circumstances and character prevented his other films from becoming, at least in the public mind.

If critics have identified and distinguished several more phases of the *auteur* theory, the two just briefly outlined are probably the best known versions: one, the creative self-expression in the medium of film, and as such a production-oriented model, giving pride of place to issues of intentionality, agency and origin. The other, arguing from the retrospective principle of coherence of the films by a single director for a reception-oriented approach, looks for significant patterns: repetition of themes, stylistic traits, mannerisms—whether taken as the sign that the director was able to impose himself on the material, that is, on story, studio, stars, the industry, or as the meaning-making effort of the attentive spectator. Yet since any claim that Welles—because he does not fit either—is really not an *auteur* would be patently improbable, one may need to add a further definition. One could, for instance, argue that coherence, besides connoting totality and wholeness, should also be regarded as the force of resistance, of a self-consistency against "the system." In which case, one would praise Welles as an *auteur* who consolidated himself most peremptorily by the principle of non-coherence, chance and even "failure." More than the iconoclastic disruption of "the norm," it is the inapplicability of norms in general that singles him out as an *auteur*, whose "style" or signature manifests itself a) through textual effects (marks of excess, form in excess of subject); b) through formal devices that draw attention to themselves (the formalist "baring the device"); and c) through a certain autoreferentiality (or modernist "self-reflexivity"). Added to this, but separate is the star image of the *auteur*, as personality (extra-textual), performer (both within and outside the films) and all-round talent. Welles pioneered this understanding of the term (perhaps self-consciously taking over the mantle of Erich von Stroheim and Josef von Sternberg from the 1920s and early 1930s). It is more closely aligned with European notions of the artist-director (Bergman, Fellini, Antonioni, Godard), but was in the 1970s increasingly applied also to American directors of a younger generation (Martin Scorsese, Francis Coppola, Paul Schrader), whose role as self-advertisers and superstars, however, relates them to the media hype and personality cult surrounding actors, popular music stars, television performers and sometimes politicians. Even leaving aside his frequent sojourns in Italy, France and Spain in later life, it therefore makes sense to see Welles belonging to the international art cinema as much as to the American cinema or Hollywood, which makes him an *auteur* also in quite a different sense.

For in the art cinema, the *auteur* is constructed within a different conceptual matrix or semantic field: the *auteur* can be a recognition factor for several different distinctions between Europe and

Hollywood: *auteur* versus genre, *auteur* versus star; but s/he can also stand for (neo)realism against working in a studio-setting (aligning realism against the more commercial idea of genre); the *auteur* can stand for high art (in the paradigm art versus industry); and finally, the *auteur* can represent a national cinema—not least because European national cinemas saw themselves in competition with Hollywood (even among their own domestic audiences whose preference tended to be for American movies), and expected film directors to embody the conscience of the nation—to the outside world. But an art cinema *auteur* can also present himself as a literary artist or composer, as Welles often did in interviews:

> With me, the visual is a solution to what the poetic and the musical form dictates. . . . People tend to think that my first preoccupation is with the simple plastic effects of the cinema, but they all come out of an interior rhythm, which is like the shape of music or the shape of poetry. . . . I believe in the film as a poetic medium . . . . poetry should make your hair stand up on your skin, should suggest things, evoke more than you can see. . . . And the interior conception of the author, above all, must have a single shape.[5]

Citizen Kane is such an important test-case for authorship because Welles is both: an artist-*auteur* as defined for the Hollywood studio system and as current within the art cinema, flaunting "showmanship" as much as the vocabulary of high art, while his romantic-Byronic side and his affinity with the Elizabethan "overreacher" ensure that he is also a film author who straddles all the categories. Moreover, he is the author who at once fills and voids the categories, his presence and persona anticipating a posteriority of fame, even as they self-mockingly undermine his own pretensions to immortality.[6]

Citizen Kane's History: Authorship and Industry

Orson Welles was twenty-five when he made Citizen Kane in 1940. He had come to Hollywood the year before, already a very famous man, and his contract with RKO was envied by the industry, making Welles the target of professional jealousy and gossip from the day he arrived. In New York he had been celebrated as America's greatest and most promising theater director, comparable to the legendary Max Reinhardt in Berlin in the 1920s.

Welles was born in 1915 in Kenosha, Wisconsin in the American mid-west. His father was an inventor, a globetrotter and playboy, with a penchant for the theater, fairgrounds, saloons and magicians. His mother—in love with another man who asked the young Orson to call him "Daddy"—was an accomplished pianist and a society lady. She died when Orson was eight years old, the same age as Charles Foster Kane when he is taken away from his mother and comes under the guardianship of Thatcher. Orson at first toured the world with his father, but after the latter died, he, too was given a guardian and sent to a private school, where he wrote plays, became an expert magician and took up painting. He had what amounted to an aristocratic upbringing, which became the basis for the scale of his artistic ambitions, the larger than life image of himself as a kind of Renaissance prince, skilled and gifted in all areas of human knowledge and creativity. At the age of fifteen he co-authored a manual for teaching Shakespeare's plays in schools, at sixteen he became a professional actor, while on a study trip in Ireland, already then specializing in the parts of old men. When twenty-one he had his own radio show in New York and ran one of the most important New York theater projects, the Mercury Players, with John Houseman (later producer at MGM, notably of musicals and the films of Vincente Minnelli). Welles made headlines with his 1938 radio-broadcast adaptation of H.G. Wells' *The War of the Worlds*, which he presented as news bulletins about an invasion of New York by Martians. So realistic were the sound-effects and so authentic the style of reporting that the broadcast sparked off a state-wide panic, giving spectacular proof of the mobilizing efficacy of this particular mass medium, used by Welles as if he was competing with—parodying and pointing a warning finger to—the use that Joseph Goebbels made of radio in Germany around the same time.

It was no secret that Welles wanted to go to Hollywood, and he could afford to consider offers from several studios, including Paramount, where a rather instructive memo circulated praising his virtues and potential, but also worrying about the probity of his "manliness."[7] Welles took his time, for he was intensely aware of his newly won fame and acclaim. When RKO (in the person of Harry Schaefer) finally signed Welles on, the studio made him an astonishingly generous offer, hoping to secure the services of a recognized talent.[8] RKO wanted a star, and in this respect it was the studio, the industry itself which marketed the director as an *author*, well before he had made a single commercial film.[9]

Why did RKO make Welles such a lucrative offer? According to Charles Higham, the studio was in financial difficulties and desperate for a new talent and a change in direction.[10] RKO got more than they perhaps bargained for: both the production and the release of CITIZEN KANE were surrounded by scandal and controversy, only partly under the control of the studio. There were leaks to the press, rumors of libel suits, threats and counter-threats, mainly orchestrated by journalists and gossip columnists like Louella Parsons, in the employ of the press-lord William Randolph Hearst, the historical figure that Charles Foster Kane was said to resemble most.[11] The film was an immediate critical success, but it did very badly at the box-office. From his first film onwards, then, Welles, again like Stroheim and Sternberg before him, was apparently at odds with the Hollywood studio system. His reputation of a boy wonder was quickly turned into the notoriety of the *enfant terrible*. After another film for RKO, THE MAGNIFICENT AMBERSONS on which Welles lost the right of final cut, while scenes were re-shot by another director, Robert Wise, his studio contract was terminated, and from then onwards, until the end of his career, all of Welles' films were made on an ad hoc basis, under great financial and organizational difficulties, often as international and European co-productions.[12]

The opposition "director" versus "studio" has often been pictured as a clash of personalities, on the model of producer Irving Thalberg reputedly "destroying" the career of Erich von Stroheim. This was not the case with Welles, either at the time of CITIZEN KANE or subsequently, if only because his producer-protector Schaefer lost his job as well. On the other hand, Welles—whether out of self-protection or as a way of dealing with the challenge of making a major film at such an early age and with so little insider experience—developed a considerable talent for antagonism, along with his charm. François Truffaut suggests as much, when he argues that a spirit of contrariness informed everything that Welles did in the cinema, and that the logic of his life and his work was that of a systematic, and systematically cultivated perversity—citing the parable of the scorpion and the frog crossing the river, as told by Welles in MR ARKADIN—CONFIDENTIAL REPORT.[13]

But this cannot have been the main reason for the question of authorship around CITIZEN KANE to simmer all through the 1960s and come to the boil in 1971 with the vehemence that it did. What is no doubt relevant historically is that Welles belonged to the generation of bright young men from New York who were attracted to and employed by Hollywood in the early 1940s, and who came from a very sophisticated theatrical milieu. At the same time, another group had also moved West with the coming of the talkies, identified with journalism and short fiction, rather than Broadway. Many of them were Jewish, and they brought not only urbanity and wit, but sarcasm, a touch of nihilism and unsentimental toughness to screenwriting. It was one of the periods where Hollywood was able to absorb a good deal of Europeanized, New England intellectual sophistication. And CITIZEN KANE is one of the best examples of this. Generically it is in the tradition of the newspaper film (made in the same year as Howard Hawks' HIS GIRL FRIDAY, after the play by Ben Hecht), but Welles' film also has echoes of other 1930s genres, as I shall try to show. Regarding the script's witticisms and elegance, CITIZEN KANE is a 1930s film rather than a 1940s melodrama. But in other ways it is precisely a 1940s film, belonging to another generation. As the critic Richard Corliss once pointed out, the youthful aspects can be traced back to the co-scriptwriter who was twenty years older than Welles, while the gloomy side of the film, steeped in death, decay, decline and failure is that of the twenty-five-year-old Welles. Corliss actually called CITIZEN KANE "the *Hamlet* of film."[14]

The legend of Welles' genius, based as it is on the exceptional, but for his detractors isolated and even accidental achievement of CITIZEN KANE, does somewhat obscure how many other issues— from the traditional opposition of East Coast and West Coast artists to the different versions of the *auteur* theory—are the backdrop of the notorious debate that flared up when Pauline Kael published first an article and then her book-length polemic *The Citizen Kane Book*, challenging the authorship of Welles in the making of CITIZEN KANE. Polemical, deliberately provocative and less reliably researched than one would have expected from a writer from the *New Yorker*, she claimed that CITIZEN KANE was actually the work of the scriptwriter, Herman J. Mankiewicz, whom Welles had cheated of his full credit. Furthermore, whatever Mankiewicz did not contribute should go to the credit of the film's cameraman, Gregg Toland, one of the most inventive photographers ever to have worked in Hollywood, and certainly in his own profession a star when he agreed to work with Welles.[15]

Charitably interpreted, the core of Kael's argument is not so much the status of either Welles or of CITIZEN KANE, but the nature of the cinema, and of a film as aesthetic and cultural object. Kael holds a conjunctural view of the cinema, and an intertextual one (as well as perhaps an old-fashioned "romantic" one, in the sense alluded to above). To this extent, Kael may be right in saying that CITIZEN KANE is a "superficial" masterpiece, rather than an intentional one, but she was committing an intentionalist fallacy when she located in the screenplay the source of authorship. However, the reason she mounted the attack in the first place, and why it created such a storm, had as much to do with her feud with fellow-critic Andrew Sarris over "authorship" in general as it was inspired by an animus against Welles in particular.[16] Besides much else, the controversy involved a sort of category mistake, where authorship as artistic originality (with the accompanying charge of plagiarism and dishonesty) fights on the terrain of intellectual property claim (the Hollywood battle over "credits"). It thereby pits itself against the French understanding of authorship as stylistic signature, visible in the details (in the manner of the 19th century art historian Giovanni Morelli), from which the critic could reconstruct not just personal mannerism, but a "vision." Although Kael the populist may not have subscribed to the tacit assumption that only individual, non-industrial forms of artistic production can have aesthetic value, the disputed authorship of Welles as the director of CITIZEN KANE took on the rancorous contours of an "either-or" battle also because of an ultimately false opposition between individual versus collective authorship. Whether one thinks of the director as the leader of an industrial team or as the conductor of an orchestra, neither analogy satisfactorily defines cinematic authorship—nor does the fact that Hollywood screenwriters have always tended to feel if not underpaid then undervalued. Finally, quite apart from the merits of this individual case (where much speaks for Welles as author not only in his role as director, but also as co-scenarist), the nature of the writer's contribution to a motion picture is still a bone of contention. It cannot be resolved textually, while authorship in the sense introduced by the French critics in the 1950s and transferred to the United States in the 1960s was less a basis for historical analysis of industry practice than it served as a hermeneutic tool, which allowed film to be taught in universities alongside literature and art history, before its success as a mark of distinction in turn made it a successful marketing device.

The Importance of CITIZEN KANE

Most of what I want to say, therefore, addresses itself to Welles as the author of CITIZEN KANE, in the spirit of trying to answer why CITIZEN KANE is and has remained such an important film, still regularly topping the polls as the best film ever made. My own argument can be broken down into five sections, of which the first one—the relation of author/director to industry/ Hollywood—has just been discussed, but to which I want to return right at the end. The second section is about Welles' handling of genre and generic intertexts, the third reviews his contribution to cinematic technique and technological change. The fourth reason of CITIZEN KANE's enduring interest for critics and scholars is its narrative construction and implicit challenge to notions of film form, while finally, the very fact that it has engendered so many debates makes it not only a classic and a canonical masterpiece, but also invites speculation as to its contextual dimensions, hidden implications or unintended consequences.

To start with perhaps the least obvious feature of CITIZEN KANE: its potential as a particularly rich source for American studies and cultural theory. There are, as already indicated, textually and extra-textually, so many references to other media, such as the press (Chicago newspaper history, the Hearst press and politics), to the theater and opera (Broadway, the back and forth of Welles himself between New York and Hollywood, with its opposition "intelligentsia" versus "show-business"; the links with Ben Hecht, John Houseman, or Welles' reliance on former Mercury Players like Joseph Cotton and Everett Sloane) that an evocation of American cultural history has always seemed a necessary backdrop to telling the history of CITIZEN KANE. Less important at first glance to the film, though not the man, are the links with radio. Rick Altman, for example, argues that "*Citizen Kane* constitutes the first effective meeting place of the century's two most powerful media, broadcasting and film."[17] He demonstrates how Welles employs various devices from radio on the soundtrack of CITIZEN KANE.[18]

Among the arts on which Welles impinged when he came to Hollywood was also literature, both as a body of canonical texts that could be adapted, and as a forever deferred ambition, to fashion in the language of the cinema what had eluded the writers of his generation: to create the "Great American Novel." How obliquely he approached this objective can be seen in his avowed aim to direct as his first film an adaptation of Joseph Conrad's *Heart of Darkness*. The figure of Kurtz, the colonialist and administrator who goes "native"—and his relation with the man sent to investigate his disappearance—becomes a recurring constellation in Welles (including in CITIZEN KANE). It can be read psychologically as well as politically, and it was to find echoes in many subsequent American rescue scenarios both literary and cinematic. Yet Welles' lifelong fascination with Shakespeare and the Faustian themes of power also turn out to be very American themes. It is notable to what extent CITIZEN KANE became the classic formulation (in the medium of cinema) of an American cultural obsession: the function of "personality" as a driving force in US society and politics. America's wealthy public figures, its self-made men and millionaire tycoons from an earlier period (the Rockefellers, Vanderbilts, Morgans, Duponts) became not only icons and mirrors of the United States' self-definition as a "free nation." Their ambitions as patrons of the arts, accumulators of cultural trophies and philanthropic benefactors to the nation were less clearly recognized as heralding a new kind of societal power, wielded indirectly and often of more importance than the holding of political office.

CITIZEN KANE was originally to have been called *The American*, then *Citizen USA* and these rather awkward titles point to the symbolic and—if we think of John Dos Passos—literary antecedents of Welles' film and its themes, which to some extent were European, although from another age. In fact, with his theatrical and literary background Welles took up the challenge to transpose the Elizabethan tragic potentate—Marlowe's overreachers *Tamburlaine* and *Dr Faustus*, Shakespeare's *Macbeth*, *Richard III, Coriolanus, King Lear*—into the new medium by blending the figure with motifs (besides those taken from Joseph Conrad) from Henry James and American literature of the Gilded Age: archetypically in Scott Fitzgerald's *The Great Gatsby* and *The Last Tycoon*, but echoed also in early Ernest Hemingway (the theme of male hubris, the doomed macho hero, the "Latin" settings of Cuba, Spain, Mexico) and William Faulkner (*Absalom Absalom, The Wild Palms*).

Thus, Citizen Kane is right in the mainstream of American fiction. It appears as an attempt, no doubt deliberate on the part of Welles, to make this literary imagination (which is more or less contemporaneous with the film) fertile for the cinema. If Welles set out to make the American cinema intellectually and culturally as reflexive and self-critical as the literature of the period, Citizen Kane would have been the premature, but for this very reason, subversively influential hour of birth for an American "art cinema." Ironically, Martin Scorsese acknowledged this when he said: "The one key element we learnt from Welles was the power of ambition. In a sense, he is responsible for inspiring more people to be film directors than anyone else in the history of the cinema."[19] Certainly, one can see what Scorsese meant when one recalls how much a self-invented overreacher of the New American Cinema like Francis Ford Coppola owes to Welles, in both posture and themes.[20]

But Citizen Kane has several very densely woven cinematic intertexts, although the film's more precise relation to other Hollywood genres hovers between pastiche, homage and satire.[21] For instance, Citizen Kane's cross-references to the Warner Bros. biopic (as practiced by the German William Dieterle and admired also by Bert Brecht) would deserve to be more fully examined.[22] Citizen Kane is also in many ways a gangster film (the motif of the investigation, the rise-and-fall), as well as a political thriller (of a rather more European inspiration), while its opening can be read as a spoof of a 1930s Universal horror film. Across these genre echoes, Welles looks back over the Hollywood of the 1930s, reviewing the history of its stances and styles, and providing a summary of its forms. But Welles' film is also of its time, with the core conflict being typical of melodrama. In its knowing reference to overpowering mothers and remote fathers, it stages a self-consciously Oedipal story, which Welles himself qualified as "dollar-book Freud."[23] The melodrama mixes with the showbiz story of the backstage musical (though here with a more tragico-farcical ending than the comedy ending of the Warner Bros. backstage musicals of the early 1930s). If, as already mentioned, there are the links with the Warner Bros. newspaper stories, then Pauline Kael is no doubt correct when she argues that Citizen Kane is the last of the Thirties journalists' films. But Welles' pastiche of the genre also highlights a crucial shift: he takes the gritty newspaper genre and turns its wise-cracking nihilism and superficial brilliance into politics and backstory, though not by opposing to it a new depth and seriousness, but by giving "surface" another twist with a baroque formal extravagance of ornament, technique and style.

Citizen Kane, despite its generic cross-references, its look back at Hollywood history, nevertheless sets itself up self-consciously as watershed, a dividing line. This is due, first and foremost, to flamboyantly displayed cinematic special effects, making it an anthology piece of until then (in American films) rarely used filmic techniques, such as staging in depth, or particularly striking sound montages (which Welles called "lightning mixes"). Because it is such an impressive but also handy compendium of film techniques and cinematic effects, Citizen Kane has become a textbook example, an eminently teachable film, from which almost all the major techniques of filmmaking, such as montage, continuity shot, deep focus, use of extreme close-up, narrative space and story ellipsis can be illustrated. Its use of trick shots, process shots, scale models, stock shots is impressive, and has been much commented upon, not least for taking its cue from such unlikely predecessors as King Kong. Besides the innovation of the lightning mixes, the film also boasts one of the most ingenious and inventive sound-tracks, where music, sound, silence, grain of voice, accent, echo, close microphone recording are developed both to underline and to counterpoint the image track.[24]

Welles' boldness and ambition has often led critics to claim that Citizen Kane was formally and technically innovative. This is, strictly speaking, not true, and scholars have been at pains to detail in what ways none of the devices and techniques used to such striking effect in Citizen Kane are in themselves new or invented for the film by Welles.[25] Its innovative thrust lies partly in the cultural gesture of its director, to demonstrate the possibility of a sophisticated, elegant, but above all intellectually complex cinema right at the heart of the dream factory. It was a gamble which at the time did not pay off, either for RKO, or—as indicated—for Welles. Yet where the gamble did pay off is that formally and technically, CITIZEN KANE represents a synthesis, not only of the literary themes of the previous fifty years, but of the various styles, techniques developed by Hollywood, but even more by its rivals from an earlier decade: prominent amongst them, so-called German Expressionism and Russian montage techniques. So many tricks of the trade are here combined, and displayed so flamboyantly and theatrically, that they amount to a very youthful gesture of self-confidence and daring. It is as if Welles and his technicians had wanted to draw a balance sheet, by concluding with an exclamation mark a decade of sound cinema, and two decades of classical Hollywood story telling. This makes it a very eclectic work, but one where the borrowings are synthesized in such a concentrated and impressive way that most of the techniques and devices spark and shine as if for the first time. In this sense, the studio did get what it needed: the film raised a technology debate in the industry, and by posing as an amateur, Welles had supposedly inspired and conspired to unite very diverse talents and expertise in the studio.[26] By all accounts he challenged seasoned specialists like Toland, but also other technicians, to overreach themselves, to implement within the studio-system part of the myth of the Renaissance guild, the workshop and craft-center preceding capitalism and the division of labor. Welles saw himself as the ring master.[27]

This, if nothing else, qualifies him as a director and justifies his authorship. In this context, it makes more sense to discuss the astounding wealth of anthology scenes in the film not in terms of originality or invention, but to attribute them to Welles' conscious attempt to explore and exploit to the limit certain new resources of the Hollywood technology, the gains in film technique as well as the acquired achievements of, say, black-and-white photography, at the very moment when color would become viable for studio-produced movies.[28] It is interesting to note that Welles himself never put down Hollywood the industry the way his admirers often expected him to do in interviews. Quite the opposite: he regarded Hollywood as the most advanced center of filmmaking and by this did not merely mean that the equipment was advanced. For him these advances could be used by a filmmaker, but he also highlighted the fact that at a certain point, the development of the productive forces even in the cinema could come into conflict with the relations of production, as Marxists had been wont to argue. Could it be that Welles deliberately aggravated this tension, risking conflict with audience expectations and the front office, while giving his technicians a freedom they were not accustomed to in the slow process of the studio system, turning new technical possibilities into stylistic choices that could connote stable meanings, universally understood? Welles was a director-author who pushed the limits on several fronts simultaneously, while CITIZEN KANE emphasizes filmic technique as a special effect in its own right to a point that had not been done in Hollywood since the early days of the cinema, making it appear as if CITIZEN KANE is really an avant-garde film in the guise of a classical Hollywood narrative. This is the line taken by Peter Wollen, though Welles is not an Eisensteinian formalist interested in narrative. His formal strategies have to be seen in relation to what the film is about, and in this respect, his formalism ought to be called "excessive": not in the sense that form and content are not matched, but rather in terms of the conflict between a particular conception of the artist (as all-round creative personality) and a mass-medium which at every level is heavily technologized and industrialized in its *means* of production, as well as conventionalized and generic in its *mode* of reception.

Welles and Narrative: The Scholarly Debate

Perhaps because it is such a deliberate watershed, the film has also given rise to a good deal of controversy: briefly stated, there are two main arguments. First, there is the question of authorship, that is, whether it is indeed Orson Welles who can claim to be the author of CITIZEN KANE, already discussed; and second, the question of narrative and cinematic forms: whether CITIZEN KANE is, film-historically speaking, a forward-looking or backward-looking film, also already touched on. The further question would be: from its own historical point in time, did it represent a dead-end, brilliant but a stylistic dead-end nonetheless, or can one see in it the shape of an entirely different kind of cinema, even if this cinema was retrospectively prescient (in the sense that it now seems the premature birth of an American art cinema, i.e. the "New Hollywood" of Scorsese and Coppola thirty years before its time)? From our own perspective, now—after even the New Hollywood has proven to be short-lived and was smothered by blockbuster Hollywood—has CITIZEN KANE remained a classic, because it is an "open text" needing to be the touchstone of every new theoretical paradigm, but also keeping alive the aspirational hopes of every new generation of filmmakers?

The earlier critical crux had been centered on its narrative structure, one of the most complex and intricate in classical Hollywood, while still observing most of its formal laws and generic conventions: was CITIZEN KANE a genuinely modernist work, questioning its own conditions of possibility, or a contrived, self-consciously performed piece of showmanship and magic, merely twisting and re-jigging a modern, but conventional biopic storyline? The novelist Jorge Luis Borges called it "a labyrinth without a centre" (presumably meant by Borges as a compliment). And indeed, as the different testimonies succeed each other, there is a sense of disorientingly swift changes of moral perspectives canceling each other, without actually building up to a three-dimensional picture of either the man or his motives. Modernist in the Faulknerian sense, CITIZEN KANE's narrational perspectivism and relativism has been hailed as an inspiration for films such as Akiro Kurosawa's RASHOMON and Alain Resnais' LAST YEAR AT MARIENBAD.[29] Pauline Kael's debunking argument, on the other hand, with its declared aim to make the former newspaper man Herman J. Mankiewicz the true author, values the film for its sophisticated but solid storyline of a quest for the secret of a biography lived larger than life but turning on small secrets.

Most scholarly contributions to the CITIZEN KANE debate take position on one or the other side of this divide, either showing the contrast between the apparent discontinuity on the surface, and the deeper coherence of motifs, or making the case for why and how the way the elements fit together, even at the surface. The favorite image is of course that of the jigsaw puzzle, which because it features so prominently both in the visuals and the narrative, becomes the *mise-en-abyme* of how the film itself represents the discontinuous nature of its own narrative construction.[30] Three types of fragmentariness find in the jigsaw pieces their visual metaphor: the time structure consisting of flashbacks, question-and-answer dovetailing across temporal gaps, and overlapping time-frames; the montage structure of a life pieced together from personal possessions, testimony and hearsay, gossip and headlines; and finally, the multiple points of view on a single story, where vested interests clash and truth is not only relative and subjective, but can be manufactured and made to order.[31]

CITIZEN KANE has been the Mount Everest for many an eminent critic. From André Bazin to Francois Truffaut, from Andrew Sarris to Pauline Kael, from Peter Wollen to David Bordwell, from Noel Burch to Laura Mulvey: two if not three generations of iconic founding figures of film studies have risen to the challenge and provided deeply informed, thought-provoking and surprisingly divergent views on the film and its narrative, so that for Truffaut, for instance, it does not follow a literary model but has a musical form; for Bordwell, it is a unified narrative despite the jigsaw puzzle, because a mimetic representation of consciousness, and thus a study in psychology; while for Wollen, the narrative is modernist discontinuous and heterogeneous, despite the coherence of the themes and the linearity of the investigation.

However, the first sustained and in many ways still most influential defense of CITIZEN KANE saw it as a breakthrough: not towards an avant-garde cinema of reflexivity or formalist deconstruction of illusionist narrative, but towards "realism" and a significant step in the evolution of cinematic language. This position was itself a watershed in film theory, because it created a synthesis between the "genre" view of the film's themes and motifs, and the formalist view of its means and devices, by arguing that the complications of Welles' narrative were a necessary development of the cinema in achieving a greater degree of psychological depth, in which external action and motive were complemented and complicated by the internal movement of consciousness and memory, without either undermining the codes of verisimilitude or sacrificing density of detail and specification, the sense of place and of the weight of objects that Hollywood excelled in producing, even in the artificial studio setting.

This theorist of the "realist" position on CITIZEN KANE was, of course, André Bazin. In his influential article, "The Evolution of Cinematic Language," published in 1958 (though written between 1950 and 1955), Bazin chose CITIZEN KANE as a key witness in his argument against Russian, and especially Eisenstein's montage theories. Bazin coined the now famous opposition between filmmakers who chose the image over reality (montage) and those who chose the reality over the image. It was the latter which had won a decisive victory in CITIZEN KANE because Welles' and Toland's use of deep focus in combination with the sequence or continuity shot as practiced in France by Jean Renoir and Hawks or Ford in Hollywood, gave an entirely new dramatic sense to a scene as a present reality in process, of temporal and spatial coherence, allowing the spectator an entirely different sense of involvement and participation.

Bazin argues that, in the American cinema up to the mid-1930s, the "classical" way of editing a film was to assemble it from more or less short sequences which were put together in such a way as to suggest the illusion of continuity in space and time across the cuts, which were thus rendered "invisible." The technique was to exploit the human eye's natural tendency to supply missing visual information as well as the spectator's tendency to accept as coherent and continuous a discontinuity which did not disturb the logic of the action or block the desire to know what happens next. Hollywood had by the early 1920s established a set of rules: the 180 degree rule, the eye-line match, the reverse field shot and so on, which greatly enhanced the smooth transition from shot to shot. With Welles' film, Bazin maintains, the situation had changed:

> It was this fashion of editing, so admirably suitable for the best films made between 1930 and 1939, that was challenged by the shot in depth introduced by Orson Welles and William Wyler. The influence of CITIZEN KANE cannot be overestimated. Thanks to the depth of field, whole scenes are covered in one take, the camera remaining motionless. Dramatic effects for which we had formerly relied on montage were created out of the movements of the actors within a fixed framework.[32]
>
> CITIZEN KANE is part of a general movement, of a vast stirring of the geological bed of cinema, confirming that everywhere up to a point there had been a revolution in the language of the screen.[33]

Yet any actual viewing of CITIZEN KANE makes it evident that rather few of the scenes are in fact "plan-sequence" or continuity shots of the kind identified by Bazin, and among them, one ought to distinguish quite clearly between continuity shots and deep focus shots. There are, on the other hand, many more examples of montage, even of Eisensteinian montage of collision, shock and attraction. This does not in itself invalidate Bazin's argument (which is historical, evolutionary rather than oppositional, categorical), for Bazin is essentially concerned with establishing another crucial point, namely to demonstrate that the technique of a film, the style it uses, the cinematic devices it employs are chosen in relation to its subject matter. In other words, Bazin is interested in the relation of themes and subject matter to style and technique in the cinema.

In the case of CITIZEN KANE, Bazin can still maintain that Welles is the greater realist, because he uses neither sequence shots nor montage as stylistic bravura pieces but in order to get as close as possible to the reality of what he is portraying: be it the dynamic interchange of a group of people, all of whom have a stake in the action, have their own point of view (as in the celebration of *The*

Chronicle taking over *The Inquirer*), in which case the sequence shot when combined with deep focus lets us watch these different aspects of the action simultaneously and in the most aesthetically satisfying, which is to say, economical manner. On the other hand when it is a matter of penetrating into the various layers of the character's consciousness and even unconscious, to probe his personality, his passion and motives, then montage effects rapidly establish the different layers or contradictory associations.

The logic of this argument is to look at the complex narrative structure of Citizen Kane and discover the various principles that unify these structural and stylistic choices. We need to make explicit the motivation and reasoning behind the style of a given scene, and to link the cogency of this reasoning not only to the director's control of the material, his authorship, but also to the mind and motivation of the central character. Such an interpretive strategy will highlight two aspects: the overall coherence of the film, and its status as the study of a character and thus a psychological film.

Just such an interpretation is offered by David Bordwell's essay on Citizen Kane. Bordwell is able to discuss and disentangle the intricate narrative structure by designating the film as being about the nature of consciousness. The shifting points of view, the manipulation of the audience's knowledge, the various strategies of relativizing what is being said, stress for Bordwell the essentially subjective nature of filmic narration in general and of Citizen Kane in particular: "The inquisitive camera movements, the angled compositions, the 'lightning mixes' of sound and image—these suggest subjective attitudes and the workings of narrators' memories."[34]

Yet this interpretation already contains within itself several critical challenges. First of all, in line with André Bazin's argument, Bordwell stresses the basically ambiguous, enigmatic nature of the film. But he then goes on to provide an impressive list of answers to these enigmas, thus resolving, in his own terms, quite satisfactorily, the puzzles that are supposed to characterize the film.

The second challenge to Bordwell's solution can best be approached if we look at Welles' treatment of sound. Welles had had more experience in sound recording through his radio work than most other directors. His sound techniques (analyzed in detail by Altman) make Citizen Kane one of the most important sound films ever made. Sound and image are often treated as if they were completely autonomous, and they constantly juxtapose each other, in order to enrich the texture of the film and grip us with different sensory stimuli simultaneously. This in many ways suggests that the narrative structure of the film is taken from examples in music, of leitmotif and counterpoint (as argued by Truffaut), and owes less to literary theories of psychological realism than critics have assumed, although one could maintain that the modernist novel is itself heavily influenced by musical form (James Joyce, Thomas Mann, Faulkner).

In this respect, André Bazin's argument about realism is rather perverse, for there seems to be a genuine problem in treating Citizen Kane as an advance in realism, unless we drastically define and redefine realism; as Bordwell does, by talking about "consciousness." Welles' film introduces a new level of sophistication in the handling of sound montage (his lightning mixes), where the sound from one scene is carried over to the next, that is, often across a cut in space or time, building aural bridges as it were. This not only draws attention to itself as a narrational device, it introduces an extra-diegetic narrator, as distinct from the narrator-investigator within the film, but it also allows the film attain a certain level of formal abstraction—without making the film itself an abstract or formalist film. But, so one could argue, if one pushes Bazin's or Bordwell's interpretation all the way, one finds oneself right in the middle of the modernist dilemma.

And it was the critic and theorist Noël Burch who, in "Propositions" (an article written in 1974 with Jorge Dana), attacked Citizen Kane on precisely these grounds, namely that if one follows Bazin and gives priority to the subject matter (whether this is defined as the nature of consciousness, or the question of power and personality in American public life), and one then treats the style as the themes' adequate or optimal expression, one ends up with a film whose conventional subject matter is merely dressed up with modernist tricks and technological gadgetry. Burch, too, starts by indicating that the film on the one hand makes heavy weather of its enigmatic structure and then proceeds by giving all the standard answers.[35]

Burch's conclusion is that the film is essentially an exercise in rhetoric, and thus does in no sense represent a break in the history of the cinema or constitute an avant-garde work, in the way that for instance, Carl Dreyer's GERTRUD constitutes an avant-garde narrative film for Burch: "It is the *iterative* nature of the set of *parti pris* activated by CITIZEN KANE which ensures that their combination results only in a style which dissimulates the functions of the codes."[36] And: "we would cite as evidence the enormous influence that CITIZEN KANE exerted on post-war commercial cinema, as against the repression to which truly innovatory works like those of Dreyer have always been subjected."[37]

Burch's procedure is the exact inverse of Bordwell's. Where Bordwell is trying to bring out the coherence, the overall unity of the film, Burch attempts to find points of rupture, of dissonance, the triumph of formal articulation over subject matter in the autonomy of the play of cinematic codes. Burch does not find this in CITIZEN KANE, which is to say, he negatively confirms Bazin and Bordwell: Welles has made a classical film, or a classical modern film, as opposed to a genuinely modernist film.

It is this conclusion which in turn seems to disturb Peter Wollen, who—fully aware of the ramifications of these arguments—wants to make the case for CITIZEN KANE as a truly modernist work, even though Welles may not have intended it that way. And Wollen sets out to demonstrate his case by a twofold twist. First of all, he argues that those who admire the film for its technique are wrong, once more pointing out that it is not an innovative film in this respect. But Wollen then goes on to criticize those who, like François Truffaut, conclude that what has become obsolete are the flashy effects, and what stays are the complex intertwining of themes. To them, Wollen replies:

> CITIZEN KANE, we can now say, was a milestone along the road that led, not to a re-invigoration of Hollywood, or a novelistic complication of narrative, or the unfolding of the realistic essence of film, but towards the expansion and elaboration of a formal poetic which would transform our concept of cinema entirely, towards film as a text that is a play with meaning rather than a vehicle for it.[38]

Where do we stand then? In one sense, all I wanted to do is to indicate in what sense CITIZEN KANE became a crux for film studies, and how the kind of textually constructed "authorship" alluded to at the beginning of this chapter focused on Welles as a test case for questions of aesthetic coherence versus symptomatic gaps and fissures. What the discussion brought out is that there is indeed an unresolved discrepancy between apparent subject matter and apparent style. I say apparent, because I think before one has actually grappled with the issue, it is not at all clear what the "subject" of CITIZEN KANE is and what functions its stylistic devices serve. Wollen, by junking the "content" has perhaps made the job too easy, taking the film out of its historical place in order to extract from it what might be regarded as a clutch of none too revolutionary formal devices. Or rather, these devices lose much of their interest when they are de-historicized and decontextualized in this manner.

To sum up, let me state what I think are the paradoxes that might provide the basis for further research: first, the film posits itself as an enigma and then gives a whole series of rather melodramatic solutions to this enigma. Perhaps the dissatisfaction critics have experienced about these solutions ought to make one look again at the enigma. One way to do this would be to say that CITIZEN KANE on the thematic level, but also on the stylistic one, is concerned with the processes of hiding and revealing, probing and foreclosing, investigating and repressing. Yet this corresponds on another level—the level of narrative structure—to all kinds of doubling effects, echo-effects, repetitions, leitmotifs, circular devices, so that one might formulate the following question: what is the relation of the unresolved enigma on the thematic level, and the staged evidence of symmetries on the structural and stylistic level?

Therefore, it probably will not do to dismiss the themes of the film as easily as Wollen does, or Burch. Perhaps we ought to ask, and this would lead us also beyond Bazin and Bordwell, not what the nature of consciousness that we are presented with is, but what is the nature of this particular American mind, the tycoon. The obsession of the film with this aspect may lead one to seeing it as a dramatization of its own origins: the film industry creating the myths about the exceptional individual. Finally, there is the fact that Welles himself interprets Kane. Is it a self-image or an alter ego? Welles has always maintained that he morally disapproved of the characters he portrays, the megalomaniacs, the protean figures, with their monstrous monumentality. But why did Welles choose these parts, from his very early youth onwards? What is this relation between self-image and alter ego, this love-hate relationship with power and personality, with genius and destructiveness?

Historically, I argued, the place of CITIZEN KANE can be described as the clash of two milieus: the theatrical, "high-cultural" one, and the journalistic wisecracking-cynical one.[39] Theoretically, it is about narrative authority, while politically it is about power. On each level, the film is vertiginously self-referential, not only in the very general sense of giving us a demonstration of the classical cinema's own basic mechanism, of which Welles' narrational procedures and the central device of the enigma are representations. The self-referentiality also confirms why the film is so eminently teachable and so much taught in film courses, and just as the film progresses by a constant process of hiding and revealing, so that the reporter and investigator is very knowingly a stand-in of our own curiosity, an aspect doubled by the names of the newspapers: *Inquirer* versus *Chronicle*, seeing and probing versus documenting and recording; Welles plays with and invokes the themes of the cinema itself. Is not the enigma the cinematic text's minimal condition of its own production? Even the author, as the locus of intentionality, of motive and origin is, as we saw in one version of the *auteur* theory, a function of the text's mechanism of hiding and revealing.

Welles and Virtuosity

If Welles' film is a textbook film, then, it is so also because its formal brilliance and virtuosity is itself symptomatic of a historical and cultural shift. Orson Welles the virtuoso, the man of many parts and many faces, the master of a baroque excess in the *mise-en-scène*, capable of self-dramatization but also of self-irony is also a chronicler and inquirer of virtuosity, and of a society which needs the belief in personality and virtuosity as its own mirror.

In CITIZEN KANE, history as biography is shown to be unknowable, enigmatic and manipulable at the same time. The film is a series of negations ("cynicisms") about America: the American claim that fame is proof of achievement, and the American claim that history is made by great men. Welles offers a new critique of the traditional conflict between the idealism of the American dream and the materialism of its actual manifestations. Central to American culture and its self-definition, where accumulation of a quantifiable kind ("power") is inversely proportional to creating and sustaining affective bonds ("love"), this historical and humanist conflict has often been the subject of American fiction, but also of the American cinema.

The fascination with the film is thus also connected to the fact that the enigma of Charles Foster Kane is that of not only the cinema's own mode of production within capitalist society, but of power per se, in this case the power attained through public opinion and the mass-media. Since wealth in capitalist societies is collectively produced but individually appropriated, the great man, the tycoon is, as it were, the character mask of capitalism's very own enigma, of how money breeds money, and more money brings ever more power. Kane is after all, as Thatcher puts it, "a man brought up by a bank," capitalism with a human face if you like, but also with the monstrosity behind the face.

CITIZEN KANE in this sense is a critique and exposure of this cult of the personality as it manifests itself in biography, authorship and the celebration of virtuosity.

Virtuosity is the rhetoric of art and artifice in protest against the rhetoric of material wealth and material power. It is the artist's protest against the millionaire. The problem of the film is how to trace the social significance of its stylistic and artistic virtuosity. The desire to do everything himself, the Shakespearean ambitions of the Renaissance man: this trait Welles shares with an earlier generation of directors already mentioned (von Stroheim, von Sternberg), and it is typical of a certain sensibility which could flourish in the US film business in the 1920s and 1930s, but is no longer tolerated or even functional by the 1940s. These men criticize the fact that an immense material power is dedicated to trivial pursuits and satisfactions, by inverting but also by reproducing the fundamental imbalance and a-symmetry: they protest by creating everything from within themselves and take their stand against the supremacy of the ordinary, the triumph of the mediocre. Their "manipulation" of the material substance—human and inanimate—is part of a self-destructive pessimism that comes out of a lack of resistance that the material offers. There is thus something tragic about this precocious virtuosity, something funereal and imbued with the spirit of Mannerism.[40]

When Wollen says that CITIZEN KANE has thematically little to offer, that we can merely see it as a storehouse of new cinematic techniques, is he not cutting short the dialectic that is of interest here, namely how the cinema "inherits," that is, takes over, exploits and transforms a cultural thematic, such as the American success story, the rise and fall of Great Men? Perhaps the way to discuss this relationship in Welles' case is in terms of this virtuosity: both as a concise way of resuming and summing up the history of the cinema until then, and as an act of protest and refusal, across the many roles and functions he has played in his films. Welles has always cultivated the protean aspect, the showman aspect of his life work, while simultaneously priding himself on being the amateur and the perfectionist. But there is also his cynicism, nihilism and sadism as a filmmaker in relation to both his characters and the audience, the baroque sensibility, the filmic manipulator who uses the most outrageous montage effects ("believing in the image"), but also pioneered the dramatically charged long take ("believing in reality"). And to force the contradiction regarding his themes and heroes, power and corruption, friendship and betrayal, idealism and gross materialism: why did Welles always choose heroes capable of great moral evil—with whom he sympathized, whom he humanized by playing them himself—and at the same time profess his abhorrence and condemn them?

In one sense, CITIZEN KANE does tell a banal story always yanked into significance, chronicling a life consumed by the awed self-regard of its own actions, so that one is tempted to juxtapose to the social rhetoric of Charles Foster Kane's self-significance the habitual self-significance of Orson Welles, about whom his then wife Rita Hayworth is supposed to have said that he was impossible to live with, because he was the sort of man who needed applause for taking a shower!

Yet, almost all commentators have pointed out that the enduring strength of CITIZEN KANE, and the pleasure critics and film specialists get from it, is the sheer exhilaration Welles communicates about what cinema can do, its spectacular display of its own magic, surprise and cleverness. It, too, as so many classics, is a film about the cinema, and this in two respects: stylistically, as an exercise in virtuosity, and thematically, as both a critique and a celebration of power—in the realm of life and in the realm of art. This chiasmic construction of CITIZEN KANE points to the braiding of a contradiction which may explain why Welles focused on overreachers, figures tainted by Shakespearean hubris, but also recognizable from American history and myth.

Is the excess of the formal means in respect of subject matter finally the mark of authorship—or is the virtuosity a secret protest, the rage against the powerlessness of art in the face of so much concentrated and accumulated power in the hands of men raised by a bank? For the celebration of virtuosity could also be seen more dialectically, being Welles' own reply to the cult of personality in public life and show business, as well as to the abuses of such power in the realm of politics. Thus, one may need to distinguish two kinds of power: Power (economic, political) versus Power (over time and space, over the processes of meaning making). The tycoon versus the film director as author: for both, the supreme goal is controlling time and space, creating realities rather than interpreting them. In Citizen Kane it is as if Welles is simultaneously destroying and building a world (the simulacrum). The film starts with a dead inanimate world, a primeval world, a ghost world, before reviving these ghosts, animating the inanimate. Perhaps the most apposite conclusion is that Citizen Kane is finally more pastiche than satire: one that acknowledges such doubleness to itself and thus obliges us to acknowledge that this is the fate, but also the force of cinema: to be a pastiche of life, while consuming ever more "life" and to be parodying the postures of power, while becoming ever more its instrument, its emblem and embodiment. The triumph of the film director as *auteur* would thus fatally coincide with the failure of the artist as filmmaker, according to the axiom that cinema corrupts, but total cinema corrupts totally. Welles seems to have known it, and has—in both senses of the word—acted accordingly.

13

The Dandy in Hitchcock

Not only every generation, but every critic appropriates his or her own "Alfred Hitchcock," fashioned in the mirror of the pleasures or uncanny moments one derives from his films.[1] Most scholars have arrived at *their* Hitchcock by paying scrupulous attention to the work, the individual films, as is quite proper—the more so, since Hitchcock the man was an exceptionally private person. And yet, most are aware of the paradox that this private person also cultivated an exceptionally public persona quite apart, or so it seems, from his work. From very early on in his career he was a star, he knew he was a star, and he dramatized himself as a star.[2]

The question occupying me in this chapter is whether in this most self-reflexive of cinematic oeuvres we do not find a "portrait of the artist." Not, of course, of the historical individual—that can be left to the biographers—but of the type of creative being, bridging and maybe even reconciling the rift that in the past, before he became a classic, so often appeared in Hitchcock criticism: between the entertainer and the "serious artist." Rather than take the usual route of polarizing the two terms, I want to make my tentative answer hinge upon what I consider to be the enigma of Hitchcock's Englishness.

In the critical literature, there is no shortage of coherent images of Hitchcock. No need for me to present them in detail: the Catholic and Jansenist, the artist of the occult forces of light and darkness, the master-technician, the supreme showman and so on. In Britain, the crucial period of revaluation in the 1960s created two Hitchcocks: one in the pages of *Sight & Sound*, characterized by either disdainful or regretful dismissal of the American Hitchcock. The foil for it was a preference, nostalgically tinged, for the craftsman-stylist with an eye for typically English realism or social satire. The second was Robin Wood's Hitchcock, who was polemically opposed to *Sight & Sound*. Robin Wood's Hitchcock emerged not only as a very serious artist, but one who in his American films had a consistent theme, almost a humanist concern: the therapeutic formation of the couple and the family.[3] Such a notion of Hitchcock the moralist was already anticipated and rejected by Lindsay Anderson when he wrote in 1949:

> Hitchcock has never been a *serious* director. His films are interesting neither for their ideas nor for their characters. None of his early melodramas can be said to carry a message, and when one does appear, as in FOREIGN CORRESPONDENT, it is banal in the extreme. . . . In the same way, Hitchcock's characterisation has never achieved—or aimed at—anything more than surface verisimilitude.[4]

Peter Wollen might be said to have developed *his* Hitchcock in opposition to both of these English constructs, apparently leaning more towards seeing him as a director who subverts the morality, the politics and the realism of his sources, in order to exhibit their narrative and structural mechanisms. "For Hitchcock it is not the problem of loyalty or allegiance which is uppermost, but the mechanisms of spying and pursuit in themselves."[5] But these mechanisms, as Wollen wisely adds, "have their own psychological significance. In the end we discover that to be a master-technician in the cinema is to speak a rhetoric which is none other than the rhetoric of the unconscious."[6] Since then, almost all the major readings of Hitchcock have followed and explored this path—often with spectacular success. The very force and cogency of this success, notably through Raymond Bellour's work, strongly persuading us to accept a definition of the American cinema and of classical narrative remade in the image of Hitchcock—makes me, perversely, want to look for a more limited, historical, more English and more "ideological" Hitchcock.

I take my cue from a few casual remarks by Raymond Durgnat, who has commented on Hitchcock's affinities with Symbolism and Decadence. Durgnat writes:

> Since the cinema is traditionally associated with the lower social grades, a man who delights in perfectly wrought film form is likely to find himself referred to as a master craftsman, and the full sense of his involvement with aesthetics is missed.... Hitchcock is as lordly as any Symbolist of *l'art pour l'art*.... A craftsman whose craft is aesthetics and who takes a deep pleasure in practising it as meticulously as Hitchcock does, is an aesthete.

And Durgnat points to a spiritual affinity with Oscar Wilde, calling Hitchcock "an epicure of suspense and terror" whose films bring to mind "titles of the Decadence: *Le Jardin des Supplices, Les Fleurs du Mal*."[7] It is this cultural sensibility and aesthetic temperament that I want to investigate a little further.

Is Hitchcock an aesthete in his work, and as Durgnat implies, was he a dandy in life? Let me remind you of some typical attitudes that are supposed to make a dandy. A dandy is preoccupied above all, with style. A dandy makes a cult of clothes and manners. A dandy has an infinite capacity to astound and surprise. A dandy is given to a form of wit which seems to his contemporaries mere cynicism. A dandy must be negative: neither believing in the world of men—virility, sports—nor in the world of women—the earthy, the life-giving, the intuitive, the natural and flowing. A dandy prefers fantasy and beauty over maturity and responsibility, he pursues perfection to the point of perversity. He is, to quote an authoritative study: "A man dedicated solely to his own perfection through a ritual of taste . . ., free of all human commitments that conflict with taste: passion, moralities, ambitions, politics or occupations."[8] And he despises everything that is vulgar, common, associated with commerce and a mass-public.

Now, granted, it is difficult to recognize in this description the familiar and portly figure, dressed in sober business suits; Catholic, devoted husband and father, the son of a grocer; the quiet, private upholder of domestic virtues par excellence. It is difficult if not incongruous to discern in the familiar silhouette the traits of a Baudelaire, or Oscar Wilde, or Proust, or Dhiagilev. Neither does there seem to be any connection, either directly or indirectly, with the British Pre-Raphaelites, or the Bloomsbury Group. None of the gregariousness, none of the in-group rituals, but also little of the elitism or the anti-democratic exclusivity of the European aesthetic coteries in literature or the performing arts.

But let us look a little further: sartorial dandyism, the cult of clothes. True, Hitchcock wore sober business suits, but he *always* wore them, in every climate, in his office, on the set, in the Californian summer, in the Swiss Alps or in Marrakesh. As John Russell Taylor remarks:

> When he was filming he would turn up punctiliously at the Studio every day disguised as an English businessman in the invariable dark suit, white shirt and restrained dark tie. In the 1930s the fact of wearing a suit and tie, even in the suffocating heat of a Los Angeles summer,

was not so bizarre as it has since become, but in a world where many of the film-makers affected fancy-dress—De Mille's riding breeches, Sternberg's tropical tea-planter outfit—Hitch's was the fanciest of them all by being the least suitable and probable.[9]

Quite plainly, Hitchcock was applying a most rigorous public gesture: the dandyism of sobriety.

The ritual of manners. It already annoyed Lindsay Anderson that Hitchcock, when he came to London, stayed at a luxury hotel. It smacked to him of Bel Air snobbery, contempt and a vulgar display of *money*. The point, however, was that Hitchcock *always* stayed at the *same* hotel, in the same suite at Claridges, just as at home, he always had dinner at Chasen's. Affecting a superstitious nature, a fear of crossing the street or driving a car was part of the same public gesture: to make out of the contingencies of existence an absolute and demanding ritual, and thereby to exercise perfect and total control, almost as if to make life his own creation. It is a choice not so different from, say, Ronald Firbank's, a notable dandy of the 1920s, who, after moving to another part of London, decided to retain his gardener, but insisted that the gardener should walk, in a green baize apron and carrying a watering can, from his lodgings along Piccadilly and Regent Street to Firbank's new home in Chelsea.

Hitchcock's daily rituals, which he made known to everyone, are not only a rich man's indulgence of his own convenience, they touch one of the dandy's main philosophical tenets: to make no concessions to Nature, at whatever price. Hitchcock's life, which has been seen as that of "a straightforward middle-class Englishman who happens to be an artistic genius,"[10] seems in its particular accentuation, its imperviousness to both change and time more problematic, more enigmatic than merely the attempt to cling to the values of his native country, out of season, as it were. Nor is it simply the mask of a man whose painful shyness makes him adopt a role that everyone recognizes and therefore dismisses: for that, his work is too much obsessed with domination—of who controls whom by the power of the gaze, of fascination and its objects. More pertinent, then, is the suggestion that Hitchcock's life-style was a determined protest, the triumph of artifice over accident, a kind of daily victory over chance, in the name of a spirituality dedicating itself to making life imitate art. The revolt against Nature, of course, is one of the strongest traditions of European aestheticism and dandyism—from Baudelaire's *Paradis Artificiels*, via Huysman's *A Rebours*, to Oscar Wilde's *The Truth of Masks* and *The Decay of Lying*. From the latter comes the most well known defense of Hitchcock's use of back-projection, process-shots and studio-sets:

> The more we study art, the less we care for nature. What art really reveals to us is nature's lack of design, her curious crudities, her extraordinary monotony, her absolutely unfinished condition. Nature has good intentions, of course, but as Aristotle once said, she cannot carry them out. When I look at a landscape I cannot help seeing all its defects. It is fortunate for us, however, that nature is so imperfect, as otherwise we should have no art at all. Art is our spirited protest, our gallant attempt to teach nature her proper place.[11]

Hitchcock fully responded to Wilde's challenge when famously he said: "My films are not slices of life. They're slices of cake."[12]

As in his work, so in his life, Hitchcock excelled in turning a cliché inside out. Everyone is agreed that Hitchcock was a professional, an addict to work. Yet, part of the image of a dandy is that he disdains work. Hitchcock was able to cultivate both images simultaneously: that of perfection, and of effortless ease. A film is finished before it is begun: creation takes place elsewhere, in another scene, not in the process of filming. No commentator leaves out the description of Hitchcock on the set, sitting in his director's chair, appearing languid, his mind on something else, or simply looking bored. He made a point of never looking through the camera lens. "It would be as though I distrusted the cameraman and he was a liar.... I don't rush the same evening to see 'Has it come out?' That would be like going to the local camera shop to see the snaps and make sure that nobody had moved."[13]

This immobility is another important clue: the true work of the dandy is to expend all his effort on creating about his person the impression of utter stasis. One recalls the Sphinx-like profile he presented as his trademark, and in later life, his public appearance was designed to accentuate the statuesqueness of his massive body. Disarmingly, he turned himself into his own monument, aware of his own immortality. Of course, he carried it lightly, like the wax effigy with which he let himself be photographed and which, deep-frozen, appeared amongst his wife's groceries in the refrigerator. In a typical inversion of a Romantic motif—that of the Double—Hitchcock rehearsed his own death and lent it the semblance of life.

If his working methods show a disdain for improvisation, his films stand and fall by the degree to which they exhibit the intricacies of their design. While one can interpret this as a need for order, for control (and the domination of recalcitrant material is clearly part of the filmmaker's ambition to possess the world and fix it through the gaze), it is equally the case that in the quality and patterning of the scripts, Hitchcock manifested a most exuberant freedom and playfulness, a love of ornament, of which the much-vaunted realistic touches seem only the most obvious manifestations. Artifice, in Hitchcock, controls the shape of the films' dramatic structure, based as it is on always seeking out contrasts, counterpoints, ironies and reversals, thereby also appealing to a powerfully *intellectual* sense of abstract form.

In this regard, Hitchcock is a filmmaker's director, and one wonders whether the persuasiveness of a Proppian or Lévi-Strauss-inspired analysis of Hitchcock's plots stems in no small measure from the "musical" or contrapuntal temperament typical of an aesthete's sensibility, at least as much as from the archetypal, mythological nature of the communication set in motion by the cinema generally, considered as mass-art narrative. Paradoxically, this draws attention to a certain modernism in Hitchcock, which has to do with forcing as sharply as possible the line where the sensuous, the concrete quality of film appears as a disguise for the mechanical, the abstract, and *its* sensuality. Gavin Lambert has remarked that "many scenes and details from his movies could be titled like surrealistic paintings: Human Being Caged by Bird, Cigarette Extinguished in Fried Egg, and. . .Young Man Dressed as his Dead Mother."[14] Rather than relating this aspect of Hitchcock to an approximation of dream-like states, an argument can be made that sees him as a filmmaker of ideas, in much the same way as Duchamp was a painter of ideas, and with rather a similar cult of the sterile, of the degradation inherent in matter, as the essence of male desire and its manifestations in art.

If this seems rather fanciful, something like it has nonetheless been implicitly recognized before. Hitchcock's critics, for instance, have often been offended by what appeared to be his obsession with "effects," his purely external manipulation of fear, suspense and the audience's emotions—which he played, according to the well-known dictum, like other people play the piano. What, negatively, have been described as "gimmicks," tricks, are at the same time signs of a will towards abstraction, and a part of a modernist's conceptualization of the artist's material. One of the "gimmicks" that Hitchcock's realist critics objected to, for instance, was the scene in THE 39 STEPS (1939), when the woman's scream, upon discovering the body, is in effect substituted by the whistle of a train entering a tunnel. Or in a similar register, the electronic simulation of bird-cries and wing-beating in THE BIRDS (1963), the use of a violin at an abnormally high pitch in PSYCHO (1960), the look of surprise on the face of the real Mr Townsend in NORTH BY NORTHWEST (1959) which turns out to be due not to the photo that Cary Grant is holding out to him but to the knife in his back. Hitchcock's imagination seizes on occasions, emotions, at that point where within the human element the mechanical becomes visible, undoing thereby the anthropomorphism that the cinema so deceptively simulates.[15] One remembers the scene as described to Truffaut, that was to have gone into NORTH BY NORTHWEST: a discussion between the hero and a foreman as they walk along a Detroit car assembly line. We see a brand-new car being put together, and when it's finally completed and rolls off the end of the line, a man's body pops out. Not only does the mechanical here produce the human, it produces it *ex nihilo*, so to speak, and what it produces is a corpse. The scene has a special status in never having been filmed, and yet many times told: it is in itself a parable of cinema, the making of a Hitchcock film.

The principle at work here is that of negativity, where the human is bounded everywhere and contained by the mechanical, by death and by absence: all metaphors of the cinema at work in defying Nature. It can perhaps be best exemplified by repeating Hitchcock's own version of the *MacGuffin*:

> The word MacGuffin comes from a story about two men in an English train, and one says to the other: "What's that package on the baggage rack over your head?" "Oh", he says, "that's a MacGuffin". The first one says, "well, what's a MacGuffin?" "It's an apparatus for trapping lions in the Scottish Highlands". So the other one says, "but there are no lions in the Scottish Highlands!" And he answers, "then that's no MacGuffin".[16]

We know that the MacGuffin is the red herring, the thing the characters make much of, but which for the story is irrelevant, and for the audience no more than a bait. But looked at from another aspect, Hitchcock's story of the MacGuffin is the very epitome of a narrative process, the process of negation, of cancelling something out, what in the language of Derrida one might call an "erasure." Phrased by Hitchcock as a kind of pseudo-definition, the anecdote confirms, in a most theoretical way, Hitchcock's profound grasp of what he usually puts in rather simpler terms, like "I'm interested not so much in the stories I tell as in the means of telling them."[17] The MacGuffin, considered as a structure, turns on a contradiction: "that's a MacGuffin"/ "that's not a MacGuffin." And it does so by operating a switch of identity and transferring the terms' denotation. The MacGuffin is, in Hitchcock's pure cinema, the "pure signifier," to which no signified corresponds. Without stretching the point, one might speak here of the logic of transference itself, of the dynamic of substitution and erasure. In a film like Strangers on a Train (1951), this logic can be observed in its most abstract form at the same time as it is firmly embedded in the narrative itself. As critics have remarked, the "theme" of transference of guilt, the exchange of crime, the doppelganger-motif is actually realized in terms of a series of verbal and visual puns, centered on the notion of crossing, crossing over, double-crossing, criss-crossing: visually, the film opens with feet crossing the frame diagonally, then the shape of a double cross formed by the railway tracks, and finally, the crossing of legs, where the two protagonists accidentally meet. On the verbal level, you have the play on the moral implication of crossing someone, running across someone, being cross with someone and double-crossing someone: all in all, a remarkable case of "inner speech," as it was defined by the Russian Formalists in the 1920s. Not to mention, the crossed tennis rackets on Guy's cigarette lighter, or the audience going cross-eyed during the vital tennis match. This is presumably why the film does not end with Bruno's death on the merry-go-round: by repeating the opening scene in the train, and the opening line, "Say, aren't you Guy Haines?" the film seems to cancel itself by establishing the diagrammatic abstraction in a kind of double mirror, where the mathematical figures of the double (parallel) and the diagonal cross emerge as the true obsession of the film. As Hitchcock said to Truffaut: "isn't it a fascinating design? One could study it forever."[18] Similarly, an early film, like Number Seventeen (1932), much underrated by critics looking for realist touches, is entirely constructed around transfer, switch and substitution in an abstract cancellation of the signified, reminiscent of that other master of pure cinema, Fritz Lang.

This "conceptual" quality of Hitchcock's imagination, which one might, with perhaps too slight an emphasis on its many implications, describe as a love of paradox, is worth noting, because the issue of Hitchcock's morality has so often been debated. If for Rohmer and Chabrol the master-theme is the transference of guilt, if Robin Wood found his therapeutic theme in the moral ambiguities of choices opening up at every turn, if we can find Lévi-Straussian antinomies and binary oppositions generating and traversing every text, if the secret of Hitchcock's enunciative process is a principle of alternation, we are clearly dealing with something which in its structural dimension considerably undercuts a specific moral impulse that is supposed to inform the work. Rather, it is the insistence on form itself that constitutes an essential part of Hitchcock's morality.[19]

One evident implication, surely, is that Hitchcock's art is the art of surface, intimately connected with the notion of effect on the one hand, and with the sensibility of the dandy on the other. One might phrase it as itself a paradox: Hitchcock cultivates surface as the true profundity of the cinema, and it would be shallow indeed to call him the moralist of appearance. There is in his films a complete devotion to surface, which should not be mistaken for a mere interest in technique, and it might be more appropriate to say that technique is only the very inadequate name applied to a cinema dedicated to the rule of contiguity and metonymy. Whether it's the accidental brush of feet in STRANGERS ON A TRAIN, the crossed trajectories in a hotel lobby of NORTH BY NORTHWEST ("Paging Mr Kaplan") or the converging paths when Karen Black appears suddenly out of nowhere and forces Bruce Dern to stop in FAMILY PLOT (1976)—in every instance, the narrative is generated out of a veritable "splicing together": the fortuitous encounter of the unlikely with the improbable. The somewhat facile generalization that in Hitchcock evil does not lurk *behind* a door but is there, in broad daylight, and comes out of a blue sky, might be rephrased by saying that montage, in Hitchcock (as in Eisenstein) is the very sign of a categorical refusal to give the cinematic image any kind of transcendental value. And it seems entirely appropriate that film scholars, digging deeper in his films, should discover structures that reveal an ever greater simplicity, where the elements become more mathematical, more musical, more schematic. It is therefore one of the incidental virtues of Raymond Bellour's work that it emphatically brings us back to the surface in Hitchcock, where what we need to know can be grasped by an attention to segmentation, the interplay that arises from the precision with which the filmmaker controls, for instance, the size of the shot, the direction of the gaze and the motility of the camera.[20]

By outlining some of Hitchcock's particular characteristics as a filmmaker of surface and contiguity, I am suggesting that the chance encounter, the collision of apparently unrelated destinies, as in NORTH BY NORTHWEST, or PSYCHO, or STRANGERS ON A TRAIN, leads us not necessarily into the realm of moral and metaphysical essences, but also constitutes a denial of essence, an aesthetic delight in what, from a different vantage-point, is always a catastrophe: identity as merely the violent suppression of random gestures and exchanges. In Hitchcock, action always takes precedence over character, which is why his narratives offer themselves for structural or morphological analysis.[21]

Such partiality for the contiguous is an important clue to Hitchcock's humor, and more specifically, his irrepressible penchant for playing the practical joker, the perpetrator of countless hoaxes: I shall not attempt to recall here the stories, anecdotes and legends, kept in circulation not least by Hitchcock himself, whose point invariably seems to be to confound a certain naive literalness with lessons in "lateral thinking." There is the story of Hitchcock serving blue food at dinner, because one of his guests had, on a previous occasion, made a crack about the master's devotion to "cordon bleu" cooking. It would be worthwhile to study in detail the principles underlying Hitchcock's wit, his verbal playfulness, his penchant for epigrams: it relates closely to the predominance of paradox and dramatic irony in his plots, and the principle of erasure through double transfer which I briefly analyzed as the structure of the MacGuffin. To give an example of Hitchcock's verbal dandyism, let me cite an anecdote that James Stewart liked to tell about work on the set:

> Hitchcock actually has very little regard for the spoken word. . . . He pays no attention to the
> actual words—he's done all that, finished all that, months before. He's an absolute villain to

script girls and people that have to follow the lines. So when the script girl says to him, "Mr Hitchcock, Mr Stewart didn't say anything like what's in the script", he'd say, "It sounded alright; *grammatically* it was alright."[22]

The need to startle and to baffle an audience is of course part of any showman's artistic make-up. But the practical joker displays a particularly violent ambiguity: he attracts and holds an audience, in order to distance himself the more definitely from any community with it. He recalls, in this guise, Baudelaire's *saltimbanque*—the mountebank, the circus artist, the jester of modernist literature and painting— often a figure of pathos, as he stands apart from the crowd, yet bears the burden of their amusement. To the unconscious disloyalty of the audience corresponds the practical joker's betrayal of his victim's trust. We find, especially in Hitchcock's British films, a number of references to this ambiguous figure: the portrait of the jester, for instance, which plays such an important role in BLACKMAIL (1929), or the murderers in the 1930 MURDER! (playing a circus acrobat) and the 1937 YOUNG AND INNOCENT (disguised as a blackface minstrel), both of whom one hesitates to call villains, precisely because the pathos of their costume underlines their separateness and isolation from people enjoying each other's company. Separateness, distance, is the hallmark of the public persona which Hitchcock also created for himself with his television appearances. Not only did he stand apart, there was the manner in which he "presented" the TV shows, quite different from the personal appearances in the films: the host's presentations of *The Alfred Hitchcock Hour* displayed the more grotesque, clownish, aesthetically aggressive sides of his showmanship, letting these find expression and form in grand-guignol images of himself with a bloody hatchet buried in his bald pate, or carrying his own head under his arm.

The *saltimbanque*, on the face of it, seems to have little in common with the dandy, especially since we do find quite a number of dandies among the villains in Hitchcock's films. From Ivor Novello in THE LODGER (1926), Peter Lorre in THE MAN WHO KNEW TOO MUCH (1934), Robert Walker in STRANGERS ON A TRAIN, down to James Mason in NORTH BY NORTHWEST, Hitchcock's villains are often either sharp dressers or aristocratic aesthetes, often made "sinister" by stereotypically homosexual traits or hints of sexual perversion.[23] Yet some of Hitchcock's *heroes* are also practical jokers and even aristocratic rogues: Robert Donat in THE 39 STEPS, Cary Grant in the 1941 SUSPICION (and the 1955 TO CATCH A THIEF), not to mention Melanie Daniels who in THE BIRDS is introduced as a practical joker.[24]

The sensibility I am trying to sketch for understanding the Hitchcock persona, then, is clearly a composite one: a combination of the aesthete, the rogue and the mountebank. At the same time, it is precisely this somewhat unlikely combination that makes Hitchcock's dandyism specifically English and historically definable. For these attitudes can be seen to occupy, in the literary and artistic culture of the 1920s and 1930s, one side of a dialectic which opposes the values of Victorian and Edwardian public life—social responsibility, maturity, moral and artistic seriousness—with the values of a generation that was in rebellion against identifying art exclusively with seriousness, an attitude it considered philistine, suffocating and inartistic. Instead, it affected and cultivated, out of an equally serious commitment to art, a mode of irresponsibility, playfulness, unseriousness and sexual ambiguity that combined the stance of the Oscar Wilde dandy with a more aggressive brand of schoolboy humor and a wilful immaturity. Reacting to the "consensus humanism" of Edwardian England, because they saw in the cultural forms of seriousness and responsibility an ideology of power and social hierarchy digging itself in, after the debacle of the First World War, the dandies of the 1920s and 1930s, according to a popular study of the period, "shared a sense of humour, a humour developed to abnormal intensity, so that it takes over the psychic and social functions usually performed by the erotic or idealistic aspects of personality."[25]

This seems a pertinent observation also in relation to Hitchcock: if, however remotely, he belongs to this side of the cultural divide, then it may be possible to see his irony, his verbal wit, the apparent unseriousness and showmanship both in his persona and as it manifests itself in the structure and material of his films, as itself part of a more coherent project—that of a refusal, a rejection, a protest against a specifically English concept of maturity, dominant in the culture in which he grew up. We could then say, without merely stating a paradox, that Hitchcock's cultivated unseriousness has behind it the force of a moral stance. In any direct sense, Hitchcock is not a social critic: his morality resides in the complexity of his dandyism and what it entails ideologically. That it is a morality mediated by a culturally specific gesture of refusal makes the reading of his films in the manner of Robin Wood so problematic, because the values that Wood asserts in Hitchcock (maturity, moral growth, the therapeutic theme) are precisely the values upheld by the inheritors of the Grand Tradition against which the dandy in Hitchcock is in revolt. On the other hand, a purely formal or structural reading of Hitchcock tends to ignore the extent to which Hitchcock's anti-humanism, his cult of artifice and surface are the result of a moral and historical *parti pris*. That Hitchcock chose the dandy side of the British cultural character—a choice greatly facilitated by his move to Hollywood—shows another irony; for in Hollywood, the *dandy* turned into the *saltimbanque*: he chose a disguise that remarkably looked like it belonged to the other party—that of philistine Victorianism.

It does not seem entirely by chance, then, that one finds most of the English dandies from the 1930s but also after, choosing to live a kind of double life: both inside and outside the British Establishment. Many of the writers and artists among them moved into voluntary exile—California, France, Italy. Some of them deliberately betrayed their social class: W.H. Auden, Christopher Isherwood, Stephen Spender siding with the cause of the international proletariat, Oswald Mosley founding the British Fascist Party. Others, in apparently secure and even higher places, chose to betray their country. For among the dandies of the 1930s are Guy Burgess, George Blake, Donald Maclean and Anthony Blunt: all at various times spies or agents for the Soviet Union.

This peculiar complexion of the British dandy may well induce us to look once more at the preponderance of the spy, the traitor, the agent and the double agent in Hitchcock's work. In the image of the saboteur, the secret agent, the man who knew too much, the foreign correspondent, there is always in Hitchcock an emphasis on disguise and *mise-en-scène*. Now, a popular entertainer knows that spy stories will always find their public: but few filmmakers have given the thrill of playing double agent quite as consummate an embodiment in film after film as Hitchcock. One may well ask whether the man who in his public persona chose to "disguise" himself as a dandy and jester did not put into these thrilling villains a little piece of his own creative self, giving us a portrait of the artist not just as *metteur-en-scène*, but as the man who knew too much. Or, putting it slightly differently, the role Hitchcock, throughout his long years in California, pleased himself to perform was not, as many believed, that of unofficial ambassador. Instead, he was the secret agent of an Englishness more devious for being dead-pan, in a medium that happily knows loyalty and pays allegiance not to King and Country, but to the customer as King: His/Her Majesty the spectator. However, this loyalty, too, must not be taken altogether at face value. Hitchcock's films—splitting our gaze and dividing our attention, transferring our identity and switching our allegiance—teach us the subtlest and most beguiling form of treason: recognizing in the other a part of ourselves. Putting our ordinary selves under erasure, the dandy in Hitchcock makes us rediscover the morality of artifice. To quote the old saying "with such friends, who needs enemies": Rule Britannia—Cool Britannia: with such Traitors, who needs Royalists. . .?

14
Too Big and Too Close: Alfred Hitchcock and Fritz Lang

An English Director in Germany: Hitchcock at Ufa and Emelka

In 1925, a young British set designer takes on an assignment in Berlin for Graham Cutts (who was a little too fond of drink and women). The set designer spends his time watching German directors at work at the Ufa Studios in Neubabelsberg. The director whom he observes most closely is F.W. Murnau, just completing the film that is to make him world-famous, THE LAST LAUGH. The Englishman is especially impressed by a scene in which an entire train station, busy with morning commuters, is suggested by painted perspectives, lighting, and a "real" train carriage in the farthest distance of the shot. The "German influence" on Alfred Hitchcock, often talked about by himself and almost as often referred to in the literature, is usually said to have been as profound as it was made up of distinct elements.[1] Among them was the German studio style (i.e. filming in totally controlled environments, surrounded by highly trained professionals), the ambition and ability of wholly visual storytelling ("no intertitles"), and a mastery of complex camera movements (those, for instance devised by Karl Freund for Murnau's film, and generically referred to as the German's "unchained" camera).[2] Complex camera movements famously recur in many of Hitchcock's films throughout his long career, whether in THE LODGER and MURDER!, NOTORIOUS, ROPE, UNDER CAPRICORN, PSYCHO or FRENZY.[3]

Late in 1925, only months after the initial visit to Berlin, Hitchcock returned to Germany, this time as the director of an Anglo-German production, working for the München Lichtbild Kompanie, better known by its acronym Emelka. This production, THE PLEASURE GARDEN (1925), involved location shooting mostly in Northern Italy, about which Hitch himself has left a number of hilarious and self-deprecating accounts, mostly revolving around his sexual innocence and anatomical ignorance, that can scarcely to be taken at face value. The film's other claim to anecdotal status is that its producer, Michael Balcon, is famously quoted as having appreciated just how "American" the movie felt, implicitly predicting, it is suggested, the turn Hitch's career would later take.

Lang and Hitchcock in the 1920s

There has been some speculation about the contacts between Hitchcock and the other Olympian figure of Ufa in the 1920, Fritz Lang. If Hitchcock's testimony to François Truffaut is to be believed, he admired Lang. Especially to his French critics, the director often acknowledged that Lang was someone from whom he could and did learn. Lang was born in 1890, Hitchcock in 1899: there was thus a difference in age of about ten years—a lot for Hitch, then in his twenties. But what, if anything, did Hitch "learn" from Lang? He is said to have visited the set of METROPOLIS (started that same year, 1925, when Hitch was assistant to Cutts on THE BLACKGUARD).[4] In this respect, however, he was no different from literally hundreds of official or semi-official visitors to the METROPOLIS set during 1925/1926, so that it is unlikely that Lang would have taken notice of the young Englishman, nor was Hitch at that time (or after) interested in such futuristic films as METROPOLIS was then billed. It is safer to assume that, back in London, and probably rather later, Hitch saw DER MÜDE TOD at one of the London Film Society screenings in 1926 or 1927. As with Luis Buñuel, the impression the film made on Hitchcock was lasting. The famous shot of Ivor Novello endlessly descending the "down" escalator of a London subway station in DOWNHILL (1927) immediately recalls the Lang heroine endlessly ascending the stairs suddenly opening up in the Wall around Death's domain. At that time, Hitch may also have seen DR MABUSE DER SPIELER (1921), much admired by just about every European filmmaker of note in the early 1920s. Yet the film which the director himself later called "the first true Hitchcock film," THE LODGER (1926), while certainly showing "German" influence (we know that Hitchcock had seen Paul Leni's WAXWORKS, 1921, before he made THE LODGER) does not seem indebted to Lang, except perhaps in one scene or trick-effect: the superimposition of faces in the opening sequence, where the general public receive news of another murder over the radio, is a direct citation from DR MABUSE. What is typically Hitchcock about THE LODGER is the combination of London-fog gothic with a whole array of tongue-in-cheek visual, verbal and practical jokes, such as the famous rear windows of the newspaper delivery van, looking like the eyes of the masked Avenger; the verbal jokes in the intertitles like "wet off the press, hot off the wire"; or those Edwardian *diableries* where cheeky young men hide their faces behind cloaks to frighten the girls.[5] These generic idioms, as well as the typical Hitchcock penchant for of mock-serious banter, are pretty far removed from the Langian atmosphere of heart-pounding breathlessness, malevolent claustrophobia and ominous foreboding.

However, already THE LODGER and BLACKMAIL share with Lang's German films a fascination with interlocking and routine processes: the mechanics of crime, of the investigation of crime, and of the wheels-within-wheels machinery of urban life. In THE LODGER, the scenes of the newspaper presses, the delivery vans or the transmission of messages via modern technology and gadgetry could be said to "hark back" to DR MABUSE and "anticipate" SPIONE (1928), if these terms were not themselves almost as slippery as those of "influence," "homage" or "pastiche." Rather, the fact is that Hitch, besides a passion for processes and the procedural, was just as interested in extreme psychological states as was Lang, who had a lifelong fascination with the so-called "criminal mind." It points to a convergence at a different layer of their respective creative personalities than suggested by either direct influence or discipleship. This convergence is a philosophical one, at the core of their aesthetics as much as their ethics, and ultimately the reason for comparing them at all: their shared conviction that truth is a function of falsehood, rather than its opposite, and that even for falsehood, there is ultimately neither "ground" nor "beyond" from which to judge it.

Before elaborating on this, a few less philosophical but no less pivotal points of contact, as well as of divergence, should be mentioned. One relates to their modernist stance on myth and archetype. Both directors participated in the re-discovery of the presence of mythic patterns in human experience which we find in many of the great novelists and artists of the early 20th century (Joseph Conrad, James Joyce, T.S. Eliot, Thomas Mann, Franz Kafka, for instance). They also appreciated just how important archetypes were in establishing the cinema as not only a popular art, but as a permanent art. The tension between modernist and popular with respect to myth can nonetheless be seen in the ambiguity which both directors displayed about so-called "fairy-tales," such as DER MÜDE

TOD, which Lang in later years, tended to dismiss in favor of the kind of expressive realism he took to such perfection in M or DAS TESTAMENT DES DR MABUSE. Hitchcock, for his part, claims in the conversations with Truffaut, to have been attracted to German Expressionist cinema because of its closeness to the world of the Brothers Grimm fairy tales. But in the same Truffaut interview he also disparages the generic term fairy-tale, downplaying for instance the gothic elements of REBECCA, by calling it "just a fairy tale."[6] Yet, as Peter Wollen among others has shown, several of Hitchcock's films reveal a Proppian folk-tale structure (e.g. NORTH BY NORTHWEST, PSYCHO),[7] while even Lang's most folk-tale inspired films, such as DAS WANDERNDE BILD, DER MÜDE TOD or DAS INDISCHE GRABMAL, display a complexity of plotting strategies and a layering of instances of narrative authority which Hitchcock sought to achieve by quite other means, such as his sudden shifts in point of view and narrative perspective, fully established as early as BLACKMAIL, where within the space of four or five minutes of screen time, he can make the audience share the moral points of view of the heroine, the detective, the blackmailer and finally the relieved, but secretly guilty couple. While Lang in his later work gravitated to mythic narratives inspired perhaps by Euripidean tragedy ("hate, murder and revenge": from DIE NIEBELUNGEN to RANCHO NOTORIOUS), Hitchcock increasingly relied on the mythic resonances of romance.[8]

Another point of contact is the fact that their deeper understanding of cinema was formed in the "silent" period and that their work kept features of early cinema throughout. Especially evident is the D.W. Griffith legacy of how to link different action spaces by bold narrative ellipses,[9] showing a close understanding and appreciation of the American cinema, at a time when Europe still lagged behind. Together with the use of the dissolve and certain other peculiarities of editing, this deployment of space is part of a formal vocabulary established in the late 1910s and perfected in the early 1920s. More generally, by retaining the visual syntax of the silents throughout their careers, both directors, paradoxically, seemed to become more modern and more daring, the longer they stuck to its essential elements.

Their adherence, for instance, to the so-called "cinema of non-continuity"[10] (to distinguish it from the classical continuity cinema on the one hand, and the Russian montage cinema on the other) greatly contributed to Lang and Hitchcock making the transition to sound in such a brilliantly innovative, distinctive manner, in films like M, DAS TESTAMENT DES DR MABUSE, BLACKMAIL and MURDER! (of which Hitchcock directed also a German-language version).[11] The leitmotif use of sound and the emphasis on non-synchronized counterpoint, indeed the almost "material" way of treating sound as a physically separate element, forever seeking and failing to find its proper moral or psychic "embodiment" in the image, is a legacy from early cinema. Working with image, script, intertitles and the visualization of sound-effects, the directors intuitively but creatively applied montage principles to synch sound as well, making them avant-gardists of the talkies well into the 1940s.

Parallels and Non-Convergent Similarities: Hitchcock and Lang in Hollywood

Both Lang and Hitchcock found themselves in Hollywood by the late 1930s, Lang arriving in 1934, Hitchcock in 1939. Each was in fact a "trophy" of David O. Selznick's European shopping trips,[12] and each had the long-time acquaintance of Eric Pommer, with whom Lang had been working since 1918, to whose indefatigable co-production efforts Hitchcock indirectly owed his stay at Ufa in 1925 and for whose Mayflower Company he (rather unhappily) directed JAMAICA INN in 1939, his last picture in Britain for some thirty years. But despite these common producers (to whom one should add Walter Wanger), there seems to have been little actual contact, and I have found no reference to the two directors having met either professionally or socially in all these years of being in Hollywood.[13]

There is, however, evidence of jealously and rivalry, at least on the part of Lang: "Fritz hated Hitchcock because he felt that Hitchcock had usurped his title as king of suspense" is apparently what Gene Fowler jr., a close friend of Lang's during three decades, told Patrick McGilligan.[14] It must have been galling for Lang to observe the younger director on his seemingly unstoppable rise and rise during the 1940s and 1950s, while he, Lang, was noting with increasing frustration his own seemingly irreversible downward slide, after the false dawn of SCARLET STREET and the subsequent debacle of Diana Productions. The two directors' salaries in the 1940s reflected their respective status. Hitchcock, for a time a contract director at Warner Brothers, was making $250,000 per film, whereas the most Fritz Lang was ever paid for directing a picture in Hollywood was $100,000, and as McGilligan points out, that was the salary he paid himself as one of the stock-holders of Diana Productions, for SECRET BEYOND THE DOOR, a commercial fiasco. Lang's usual director's fee was $50,000, a pittance by Hollywood standards and embarrassingly little compared to that of even most of the leading actors in his films.[15] So the question of whether Lang and Hitch ever stood in a relation of master and disciple to each other must, in light of Lang's subjective feelings and Hollywood's "objective" salary-equals-status scale, be answered negatively. On a more metaphorical level, however, one might argue that Hitchcock may have been, in the eyes of Lang, the sorcerer's apprentice, haunting and surpassing with his skill, wealth and power the one who thought of himself as the master-magician.

This curious relation of haunting and echoing, surpassing and competing, mirroring and inverting can be given some substance, if one looks at a few of the films the two directors made during the 1940s and 1950s. For certain parallel concerns and complementary themes do emerge; or rather, one can conjugate their films across certain shared (or transferred!) generic preoccupations: there is the Hitchcockian theme of "The Wrong Man" which one can find also in Lang's FURY, YOU ONLY LIVE ONCE, BEYOND A REASONABLE DOUBT, the last with the Hitchcockian but also typically Langian twist that the wrong man was the right man all along.[16] In Lang, however, this constellation goes back to one of his earliest films, KÄMPFENDE HERZEN/FOUR MEN AND A WOMAN, made in 1921, in which a jealous husband lays all the clues himself that indict his wife of adultery, effectively engineering and initiating the very adultery he was so fearful of finding out.[17] The similar, though inverted logic of BEYOND A REASONABLE DOUBT where Dana Andrews makes sure someone "witnesses" the clues to a murder, in order to detract from the fact that he did in fact commit it, is itself reminiscent of a late Hitchcock variation on the "wrong man" theme, where Richard Blaney, in FRENZY, suspected of being the necktie murderer, turns out to be, if not the right man then almost as culpable, when he brutally batters the dead woman's body with an iron bar, "mistaking" it for the sleeping Rusk, the "real" murderer.

Both directors in the 1940s made anti-Nazi films: Hitchcock features Nazis as the villains in THE LADY VANISHES and FOREIGN CORRESPONDENT, as well as SABOTEUR and NOTORIOUS, while Lang's outstanding examples among his anti-Nazi films are HANGMEN ALSO DIE, MAN HUNT and MINISTRY OF FEAR (the last two set mostly in London). About MAN HUNT, for instance, the reviewer for *The Nation* wrote a comment that must have been balm for Lang's wounded pride: "The director, Fritz Lang, seems able to give a few lessons in the technique of suspense even to Alfred Hitchcock, and he has created out of a maze of improbabilities, inaccuracies, and poor performances a really exciting picture."[18]

MINISTRY OF FEAR, on the other hand, could almost be seen as a spoof British Hitchcock. Based on a Graham Greene novel, it might even have started out as Greene spoofing the John Buchan of THE 39 STEPS.[19] In the film version of THE MINISTRY OF FEAR, a typically *noirish* atmosphere and a self-consciously "Expressionist" lighting style were presumed to compensate for the improbabilities of the plotline. As McGilligan writes:

> Seton Miller [the writer of the screenplay and also the film's producer] had finessed a breezy
> adaptation of the Graham Greene novel, treating the story as Hitchcock might have—glossing

over the puzzling clues that didn't quite add up, the alarming leaps in continuity, the superficial characterizations. Everything was sacrificed to the style and momentum of a slick Hollywood thriller. Graham Greene detested the resulting film. So did Fritz Lang. It was his compulsory imitation of Hitchcock.[20]

Similarly, both directors made memorable melodramas in the paranoid woman's film: Hitchcock REBECCA (1940) and Lang SECRET BEYOND THE DOOR (1947). There, "homage" and "influence" might indeed be the appropriate words, though one-upmanship is also what comes to mind. In the Bogdanovich-Lang interview book, for instance, Lang says how tremendously impressed he was by REBECCA:

> You remember that wonderful scene where Judith Anderson talks about Rebecca and shows Joan Fontaine the clothes and fur coats and everything? When I saw this picture (and I'm a very good audience), Rebecca was *there*, I *saw* her. It was a combination of brilliant direction, brilliant writing, and wonderful acting. And—talking about stealing—I had the feeling that maybe I could do something similar in SECRET BEYOND THE DOOR.[21]

In the same book, Lang claims that he did not mind directors "stealing" from him, because he saw it as "the sincerest form of flattery," though this noble sentiment is contradicted by the fact that Lang never forgave Losey for remaking M—just as in turn Jean Renoir never forgave Lang for remaking LA CHIENNE (SCARLET STREET, 1945) and LA BÊTE HUMAINE (HUMAN DESIRE, 1954).

More recently, the suggestion has been made that the two directors had a contrasting investment in what are now referred to as "Cold War movies": NORTH BY NORTHWEST (1959), TORN CURTAIN and TOPAZ have usually been seen as typically anti-communist in both subject and treatment, while THE BIG HEAT (1953), BEYOND A REASONABLE DOUBT or DIE 1000 AUGEN DES DR MABUSE (1960) could be read as "liberal" films in an illiberal decade.[22] It raises the question of just how political these two directors were. In practical terms, as the Lang papers have shown, Lang in Hollywood was an anti-Fascist left-wing liberal, who gave generously to support refugees, and who was not afraid of signing protest statements that could have given him trouble with the studios.[23] Hitchcock, as far as I am aware, rather kept his political views to himself during the 1940s.[24] Arguing from the films, Pascal Bonitzer has made a case that Lang and Hitchcock are "political" filmmakers, in the sense that both were as suspicious of the masks of decorum and rectitude put on by dictatorships as they were wary of the "carnivalesque" rebel element in crowds, mobs and onlookers. METROPOLIS and THE LODGER, FURY and SABOTAGE, WHILE THE CITY SLEEPS and THE WRONG MAN are all distrustful of the energy and effervescence of the community when on the move.[25] This would bring us closer to the theme of falsehood and faking as ambiguous revelators of truth, already mentioned above, and so prominent in films otherwise as different as FURY is from NORTH BY NORTHWEST. Pushing the idea of a competitive transfer of genre and motif, it would be intriguing to pursue other non-convergent parallels, such as seeing WHILE THE CITY SLEEPS (1956), with its opening scream and its scrawled lipstick message "Ask Mother" as Lang's PSYCHO (1960), the underrated HOUSE BY THE RIVER (1950) as Lang's VERTIGO (1958), and THE BLUE GARDENIA (1953) as Lang's REAR WINDOW (1954), the latter not only because in both the villain is played by Raymond Burr.[26] To balance these potentially parallel tracks, one should, however, also point out some contrasts, or inversions. The centrality of the Mabuse figure in Lang is not matched by Hitchcock, whose reliance on making female characters the center of the story was adopted by Lang only rarely and not always successfully. A reputation, therefore, for one of Hollywood's most important genres, the woman's picture, was denied to Lang, in contrast to Hitchcock. What the thriller was for Hitch, *film noir* became for Lang: a genre he could give his own distinctive stamp to. Hitchcock felt comfortable with comedy, which cannot be said of Lang. Hitchcock was a showman, Lang was pathologically secretive, and more a schemer behind the scenes than a manipulator up front, such as Hitch in his personal appearances. Hitchcock used stars and made actors into stars, Lang always remained uncomfortable with the Hollywood star system, and often used (had to use?) uncharismatic or even wooden actors.[27]

Europe-Hollywood-Europe: Crossover Populists or Disguise (High Culture) Artists?

Both directors were profoundly European, and I would argue, accented their Europeanness by their move to Hollywood, insofar as it permeated their take on make-believe, showmanship and the realm of appearance and spectacle. This manifests itself, again rather paradoxically, in their attitude to popular entertainment and mass-taste. When working in their respective native film industries, they were committed to popular culture and mass-audiences in ways that were unusual for flagship *auteur*-directors of a national cinema. In other words, they had "taken seriously" the importance even for Europe of popular culture in the 20th century, at a time when being on the side of the popular still meant taking risks. Consider Lang, in the 1920s lambasted by the critics for lack of originality, charged with employing the most hidebound dramatic clichés, using folk tales and pulp material, cutting ideas for stories out of the newspapers, and generally pandering to comic book tastes. And recall the reviews Hitchcock received in Britain in the 1940s and 1950s, after he had left for the United States, from establishment magazines such as *Sight & Sound*. The notoriously dismissive notice on Vertigo by Penelope Houston was indicative of a wider attitude to American Hitchcock. It was against this dismissal that Robin Wood wrote his original book on Hitchcock, explicitly claiming for the director "serious artist status" by arguing the case of the universal artist, who can address a popular and a sophisticated audience, with references to Shakespeare and Mozart.[28]

But might even Lang have been tongue in cheek or played on a double register, when it came to negotiating the serious artist and the popular entertainer? The German Lang did try to hold on to the label "artist" when he let himself be seen in public or had society columnists take pictures of his domestic ambiance, but he relied on Thea von Harbou, notorious novelist of potboilers, to come up with the good scripts. The American Lang reputedly became enamored with things American, such as Cowboy shirts and square dancing, crime fiction, comics and city-grit. But he also had T.W. Adorno and his wife Gretel over for dinner, and maintained more than a professional relation with Bert Brecht and Hanns Eisler. Hitchcock was a serious collector of art, and knew about modern dance. They were crossovers, before the term existed, in their embrace of the popular in their work, coupled with their awareness of and active interest in modernism. It gives, I believe, an added dimension to their critique of appearances, their sometimes sadistic pleasure in always pointing out the false bottoms of their story situations. At the same time, as artists masquerading as entertainers, they both gave perfect impersonations of the bourgeois as gentleman, perhaps the better to put others off the scent as to their subversive conformism and their hyper-orderly subversiveness. The same crossover paradox holds for their relation to the cultural status of their story-material. Even as they appeared to become more indiscriminate in their use of pulp material, with Lang remaking The Indian Tomb and reviving Dr Mabuse, and Hitchcock seemingly abandoning the sophistication of the Cary Grant movies for the B-movie horror of Psycho and gothic horror of The Birds, both found defenders who passionately argued for the seriousness of purpose and the respect each director had for his lowly material. And it is this revaluation of their work in the 1960s that makes relevant the choice of comparing the two in the first place, by claiming a philosophical dimension. This radical revaluation, as we know, did not happen in the United States, nor in their home countries, but in France.[29]

Hitchcock and Lang in France in the 1950s and 1960s

While both directors—after the war and well into the 1960s—had critics who complained that their American films was not as good as their former European ones, their work began a dramatic new life, when French admirers claimed the exact opposite, namely that their American work was superior to what they had done in Europe.[30] This revaluation was, of course, part of the more general revaluation of the American cinema thanks to André Bazin and the *Cahiers du cinéma* critics, but none perhaps benefited more from this change in attitude than Lang and Hitchcock. Both directors became not just canonized but paradigmatic, they helped define what was specific about cinema. The term that came to signify them was "pure cinema." By adopting what the French meant by this idea, Hitchcock himself began to subtly rewrite his own filmmaking biography, giving substantial tribute to the German cinema of the 1920s in forming his own notion of the term. What do we understand by pure cinema, in relation to Hitchcock?

The French Hitchcock—besides insistently dealing with themes such as guilt and grace—was above all a filmmaker whose concern was for the primacy of vision, the deceptiveness of appearances. The self-reflexivity with which he endowed all his films, according to this view, indicates a deep commitment to the expressive as well as self-reflexive possibilities of the medium, to such an extent that the films ultimately had one topic only: the cinema itself. French Hitchcock, in other words, was less the universalist he later became for *Movie* and Robin Wood, more the high modernist of cinematic specificity.[31]

Lang, too, in the 1950s remained not only a German director with an American passport. Thanks, in part, to a seminal article on his style by Lotte Eisner that appeared in Paris in 1947,[32] his reputation began to undergo a sea-change, and he became for all intents and purposes a French director. Not in the sense that he "returned" to France from Hollywood like Jean Renoir or Max Ophuls. Rather, the reputation his films acquired in Parisian cinephile circles made his work—just like Hitchcock's—the very touchstone of a certain idea of what was cinema.[33] Eric Rohmer, Alexandre Astruc, Jacques Rivette, Jean-Luc Godard and François Truffaut were Lang's admirers among the filmmakers, and their respect was echoed in important articles on Lang as the master of *mise-en-scène* and of "pure cinema" in the otherwise rivaling journals *Cahiers du cinéma*, *Positif* and *Présence du cinéma* by Jean Douchet, Philippe Demonsablon, Michel Mourlet and Gérard Legrand.[34]

For Raymond Bellour, Noël Burch, Thierry Kuntzel, writing in the late 1960s and 1970s, Lang's work became exemplary not so much because it illustrated certain problems in film theory but because it helped define the agenda of what these problems were: questions of cinematic space, of figuration, of off-screen space and the cinematic imaginary, the relation of image to narrative, the importance of point-of-view.[35] To Burch, for instance, Lang was an avant-garde director, whose work exhibits strategies of formal permutation in the treatment of space, narrative and editing that, given other circumstances, might have taken the cinema in completely different directions: away from novelistic forms of story-telling, or illusionistic representation of action, to "abstract cinema."[36] One of the strongest claims for Lang's pre-eminence in this vein came from Bellour:

> For today, with Fritz Lang entering legend in France, far from America which never really fathomed him, and from his native Germany which was unable to reclaim him, the audiences flocking to the Cinématèque are coming more or less consciously to admire the man who, in his work, has envisaged film as the ultimate metaphor.[37]

In the works of Lang and Hitchcock, then, a key axiom of French *auteurism* could thus become manifest. The idea of the "ultimate metaphor" also implied that the more trashy the material, the more the film was the triumph of form over content, a tension that embodied the victory of the *auteur* over the studio system, and of the artist over the world of matter. Sometimes, the contrast was pushed to the point where incommensurability between form and content became the constitutive paradox underpinning and holding in place this idea of pure cinema. The elevation of the two directors as not only pantheon directors, but as creators totally in control of their creations, made them celebrated as implacable perfectionists. In the French context of the late 1950s, such perfectionism was no doubt also a projection, based on a transferential relationship with the idol, nurtured initially by critics about to turn directors themselves. They were therefore vitally interested in what it means to have control, to take control and to keep control in a business in which the director's decisions and intentions usually extend only to a small part of the production process in the machinery that is the film industry. The *auteur* theory in this respect is a control-freak theory, and both Lang and Hitchcock perfectly fitted the bill.

Hitchcock and Lang: Their Reputation Since

This extraordinary reputation of both directors underwent another change in the 1980s, when Hitchcock, as it were, was adopted by Anglo-American film studies. Partly thanks to the rise of psychoanalytic film theory, Hitchcock's extraordinarily complex female heroines and his tortured relation to his (blonde) stars, feminist film theory began to focus strongly on Hitchcock. From Laura Mulvey's "Visual Pleasure" article in 1975 to Raymond Bellour's Hitchcock essays in *Camera Obscura* in the early 1980s, from Stephen Heath's long piece on "Narrative Space" in *Screen*, to Mary Ann Doane's Hitchcock chapter in *The Desire to Desire* and Tania Modleski's *The Women who Knew too Much*, Hitchcock rapidly became the very epitome of Hollywood, and his films the paradigmatic examples of "the regime of the look."[38] Given the stress on sight and vision, and the notion that voyeurism/fetishism (the relation of seeing/seen) were the constitutive elements of filmic identification and subject positioning in general, French Hitchcock's modernism of "pure cinema" became "gendered" and deconstructed accordingly. Anglo-American Hitchcock was recast across the ideological critique of the dominant codes of classical Hollywood, with his work paradoxically both exposed and valorized by the anti-patriarchal agenda that took this post-*auteur* Hollywood as its object of study.

Not so in the case of Lang. Although Douchet and Bellour, among others, here fulfilled crucial mediating roles, because they wrote trenchantly and with great intellectual force on *both* Lang *and* Hitchcock, the Lang reinterpretation of the 1980s—such as it occurred in the Anglo-American world—focused predominantly on the revival of "*film noir*," notably in *Women in Film Noir*, edited in 1978 by Ann Kaplan (who was to go on to edit a source-book on Lang in 1981).[39] Another study, edited by Steve Jenkins, called *Fritz Lang: The Image and The Look* (1981), as well as a book in French by the Scotsman Reynold Humphries (1982), *Fritz Lang, Cinéaste américain* relied heavily on the French Lang of "pure cinema" and vision.[40] However, they attempted to deconstruct this "Lang-*auteur*" effect by demonstrating that the repressed term in Lang's American films concerned the position of women (see above, and Lang's "failure" in the genre of the "woman's film"). Notably in the *films noirs* (THE BLUE GARDENIA, THE BIG HEAT, WOMAN IN THE WINDOW, SCARLET STREET) the woman's shifting place in the social symbolic of patriarchy in Lang's films was at once the narrative motor and the reason for the impossible resolution. It explained that sense of the anti-climactic, unresolved, derisively ironic tone so often hovering around the endings of Lang's American films. Yet these books, however acute in their detailed readings, seemed—at the conceptual level—mainly to amplify, but not substantially modify the feminist discussions that had earlier focused on Hitchcock, and continued to do so throughout the 1980s. Also, for many years—possibly until the biography by Patrick McGilligan at the end of the 1990s—no Lang scholarship of a more historical, empirical or philological kind emerged that could be compared to the scholarly work on all aspects of Hitchcock's life, films, contributors, sources, influences and so on, which properly got under way after his death in 1980.[41] Obviously, there are few Lang films as popular as NORTH BY NORTHWEST, PSYCHO or THE BIRDS, and the Anglo-American neglect of Lang may have to do with his inevitable identification as the most prominent and problematic exponent of Weimar cinema, but the discrepancy of scholarly attention—up to the end of the century—was nonetheless striking.[42]

Another point why the Lang reception in Anglo-American film studies may have differed from that in France, was that whereas Hitchcock had found his Truffaut, whose sympathetic eye and ear gave the director a chance to fashion himself in the image of his admirers, Lang only found Peter Bogdanovich, whom he finally did not trust as a filmmaker, so that he used him as he had tried to use all his interviewers before and after, as reluctant messengers of his own preferred self-presentation. This was also the dilemma facing Lotte Eisner, who felt too close, and also too loyal, to make her questions more probing, and whose sensibility, in the end, was not "technical" enough to elicit the sort of close analysis that Truffaut elicited from Hitchcock, which appears in the Bogdanovich book only in brief flashes, such as the one cited above about REBECCA. In France, it is true, Lang also found Jean-Luc Godard who scripted a beautiful part for him in LE MÉPRIS and mock-interviewed him in a television feature called *The Baby and the Dinosaur*. Tom Gunning's critical and sympathetic study of Lang constitutes something of a summa of all these books and articles that place Lang's work at the heart of the 20th century. While Gunning thus gives Lang his due as *the* philosopher-artist-allegorist of modernity, alongside Walter Benjamin or Bertolt Brecht, the writer who perhaps could best do justice to both Lang and Hitchcock from a similarly broad cultural perspective, and with an equally acute, cinematically literate intelligence, is Raymond Bellour. His many articles on both directors tantalizingly promise such an analysis, and he even occasionally hints at the need for (and his temptation to embark on) it.[43] In the meantime, we must content ourselves with the biographical detective work of Patrick McGilligan, so far the only professional biographer in the United States to have undertaken extensive empirical and critical research on both Lang and Hitchcock.[44]

Sphinx and Satyrs from Slovenia: Ljubljana Hitchcock and Ljutomer Lang

There is another parallel, hitherto not commented on, to my knowledge, which involves the re-evaluation of both Hitchcock and Lang in the 1990s. This time it stands under the sign of Slovenia and its capital. The Ljubljana Hitchcock is the better known, by which I mean the post-feminist, New-Lacanian readings of Slavoj Žižek, Mladen Dolar, Alenka Zupançiç and Miran Bozoviç.[45] What is less well known is that there exists also a Ljubljana (or more precisely, Ljutomer) Lang. As early as 1984 two Slovene art historians and cinema scholars, Jure Mikuz and Zdenko Vrdlovec discovered documents (which they subsequently published in a book) relating to Fritz Lang's 1915 convalescence during the First World War in a rural villa in Ljutomer, Slovenia, as the guest of a Dr. Karol Grossmann.[46] There, Lang was keeping himself busy as a sculptor, making terracotta objects, garden ornaments and pottery figures, decorated with human or humanoid heads like gargoyles and satyrs, among them also self-portraits.[47] These fantastic, distorted and none-too-obliquely phallic figures that Lang produced between 1915 and 1916 in Ljutomer prior to any filmmaking, and now permanently on show at the Slovene cinémathèque in Ljubljana, are not as unconnected with the Ljubljana Hitchcock as they might at first seem.

In *Everything you Always Wanted to Know about Lacan but were afraid to ask Hitchcock* Žižek has given us the fullest version of the Ljubljana Hitchcock, but already in *The Sublime Object of Ideology* and *Looking Awry* there is a drastic re-casting of the feminist Hitchcock, re-coding and thus returning to sender the accusations of Hitchcock's cinema as "phallic." Translating the complaint literally into "that which sticks out," Žižek argued that despite all the Proppian, Greimasian and other "structuralist" accounts of Hitchcock's films, they are actually quintessentially post-structuralist. What makes them special and unique is that their structures hinge on a contingent, material detail, an object that functions like a blot, stain or blur: sometimes, though not always the one which Hitchcock himself has called The MacGuffin.

Generally speaking, therefore, objects in Hitchcock relate, on the one hand, to the nature of the enigma that triggers the narrative and keeps it going, and on the other, to what defines the relationship between the heroes' drives and their place in the social order. Objects, in other words, condense the subject's rebellion against the social order, as well as his or her impossible reconciliation with it, as manifest in the formation of the couple and the (impossible) heterosexual love relationship, both central to the ideological function of the American cinema, if one follows the psychoanalytic paradigm.

According to Žižek, one can go further and divide these objects into three kinds. First, there is the MacGuffin, the "pure" or "empty" signifier, the formal rupture, merely signifying in the most general and abstract manner that something is at stake, and thus that something needs to get the story rolling. It can be the secret clause in a contract, a reel of microfilm, a tune or a mathematical equation that needs to be memorized. It can also be a verbal-visual pun, endlessly passed back and forth, such as the "cross," "criss-cross" or "double-cross" that migrates between Bruno and Guy Haynes in STRANGERS ON A TRAIN from the moment Bruno crosses his legs and the tip of his shoe touches that of Guy. Second, there is the small but crucial object, what one might call the "giveaway object" that embroils the characters in each other's fantasies, and puts them at the mercy of a corrupt or powerless paternal authority. This giveaway object is an object of circulation or exchange, disseminating too much knowledge that must be contained, retrieved or returned: a key (in NOTORIOUS), a cigarette lighter (in STRANGERS), a wedding ring (in SHADOW OF A DOUBT), a tie-pin (in FRENZY). Finally, there are the massively mysterious objects, grotesquely disproportionate representations of unattainable fusion and hence annihilation. These are female objects or rather, female presences at once too close and too far, like the Egyptian goddess in the British Museum in BLACKMAIL, the birds in THE BIRDS, the giant human Statue of Liberty (in SABOTEUR), the Mount Rushmore Presidents' faces (in NORTH BY NORTHWEST), and the tanker at the end of the Baltimore street (in MARNIE). To the objects correspond three kinds of narrative: the romance (or fairy tale) plots of heterosexual initiation (the reluctant, screwball couples, often shackled to each other, as in THE 39 STEPS, SABOTEUR, MR & MRS SMITH). Then, there are the paranoia narratives, told from the perspective of the passionate female, caught between two differently unreliable, differently untrustworthy males, from THE LODGER, BLACKMAIL and SABOTAGE to SUSPICION, NOTORIOUS and NORTH BY NORTHWEST. And third, the narratives centered on an obsessive, ultimately murderous male, blocked by a maternal superego: Uncle Charlie in SHADOW OF A DOUBT, Bruno in STRANGERS, Norman in PSYCHO, Jeff in REAR WINDOW, Scottie in VERTIGO, Rusk in FRENZY.

If I here summarize Žižek's Hitchcockian schemas so extensively, it is for several reasons. On the one hand, Žižek's repositioning of Hitchcock as a postmodernist adopts a typically 1990s perspective on the debates in film studies between classical, *auteurist* and postclassical/postmodern cinema, summed up by Žižek as "conflict and resolution," "excess and subversion," "the authorless, impersonal yet highly self-referential text" respectively. But the twist is Žižek's claim that Hitchcock has since his death in 1980 increasingly functioned not as an object of study for, but as a mirror to film studies, and its contemporary obsessions. Commenting, by self-referentially double-backing on his own contributions to the unabatedly thriving Hitchcock industry in academia, he diagnoses the logic behind the various hermeneutic moves and shifts in reputation I have charted above as the blatant effects of transference. This transference has made of Hitchcock himself a monstrous figure, at once too close and too far, a (maternal) superego blur as much as a super-male Godlike "subject supposed to know."[48]

In other words, in this logic Hitchcock occupies the place not so much of the author analyzed, as of the (psycho)analyst, listening impassively to the interpretive talking cure. His famous silhouette getting to look more and more like those giant faces just mentioned, he is always already there: in place and in control, when the interpreting critic arrives with yet another definitive or diabolically clever reading (especially those of Žižek and his Ljubljana colleagues). The various stages of Hitchcock's reception from the 1950s to the 1990s and beyond, thus chart only partly the inner, autonomous dynamic of film studies, as scholars refine, redefine or overturn the reigning critical paradigms. What drives the Hitchcock hermeneutic mills would be an impulse altogether more philosophically serious, namely the desire to overcome, across transference and mirror doubling, the deadlocks of ontological groundlessness: from "pure cinema" to "pure deconstruction"—and beyond.[49]

Too Close and too Big: The Close-Up as Blot and Blur

Do Žižek's Moebius-strip contortions allow us perhaps to spin another turn also on the question of why it was Hitchcock and not Lang who was afforded this extraordinary Sphinx-like status? In the face of what Žižek calls the "unrestrained madness" of interpretation that has enveloped Hitchcock, why did Lang, despite the revival of *film noir* as everyone's favorite genre, not encourage the same transferential relationship for the film studies community that Hitchcock still does and that Lang briefly did for the French *Cahiers* critics of the 1960s? Or to reverse the question, what would it mean to give Lang the sort of reading that Žižek provides for Hitchcock, which is at once critical-hermeneutic, historical-symptomatic and meta-critical philosophical? Having undertaken something along these lines for Lang's German period elsewhere,[50] I here merely want to venture some further suggestions, beginning with the pragmatic question: what would correspond in Lang to Žižek's sinthome, that is, the peculiar relation of object-subject in the field of vision? What would be the Langian blur or anamorphic stain, that bit of the non-symbolizable real, on which the authorial coherence of the themes, in both their repetitions and variations, finally rests, according to Žižek and the New Lacanians? The question is interesting not only because of the discovery of Lang's Ljutomer sculptures with their bits "sticking out." Given how elaborate, geometrical and ruled by infinitely intricate symmetries the work of Lang is, such an over-elaboration of "structure" as one finds in his films would have to—if we follow Žižek—directly imply, or at any rate, "hinge on" a series of sinthomes. Which is to say, elements that in their facticity or contingency, their there-ness and thing-ness, defy all attempts to integrate them into the circuits of symbolic exchange: in other words, they, too, must "stick out."

In Lang, just as in Hitchcock, there are plenty of (magical) objects that have to be lost and found, that are telltale signs of obsession or betrayal (the hand-stitched cross that betrays Siegfried in Siegfrieds Tod, the arrow-shaped hatpin of Joan Bennett in Man Hunt, or the brooch owned by Arthur Kennedy's murdered wife and then spotted by him on Marlene Dietrich in Rancho Notorious). But the element of possible anamorphosis (both literal and metaphorical) that I want to focus on in Lang is his use of the close up, not least because it is another stylistic feature from silent cinema, retained and creatively deployed by Lang and Hitchcock throughout their careers. The close-up as a distinctive filmic technique has, of course, been exhaustively analyzed by critics and scholars such as Pascal Bonitzer, James Naremore, Jacques Aumont and Philippe Dubois. Barry Salt, Tom Gunning, Dominique Nasta, Yuri Tsivian among others have studied it from a historical perspective (how the autonomous insert shot of early cinema became integrated and narrativized, how close ups function in juxtaposition—the Kuleshov effect—or when set in a series, as in German cross-section films or Russian montage films). From a more aesthetic vantage point (regarding questions of scale, space, point of view), the close up has been commented on by just about every film theorist from Rudolf Arnheim and Siegfried Kracauer onwards, with writers from Bela Balázs to Gilles Deleuze analyzing in particular the notion of the "faciality" of close ups, whether depicting an actual face or not.

What is a close up: a metaphor, a metonymy or a figure of absence? If there has been no shortage of discussions around the close-up in classical Hollywood, theorists are far from unanimous. In the three options just given, the close up is seen in semiotic-semantic terms, oscillating between being a supplement of sense, a clarification of sense or causing a lack of sense, insofar as—in its insert mode—the close up destroys meaning and context, as it ruptures space, time and narrative.[51] Instead of choosing between these several possibilities, I want to invoke the definitions given by Pascal Bonitzer. He once aptly described certain close ups as the "fainting-fits" of representation (in Griffith), and on another occasion, argued that the close up is both a revolutionary and a terrorist in the field of cinema. A revolutionary, in that a close up reverses the hierarchies, and is opposed to realism, to good sense, to democracy and the classical. And a terrorist, because of its violence, and because it marks the highest point of ambivalence between beauty and horror, attraction and repulsion.[52]

Again, I cannot even begin to review these arguments in detail, or test how they refer to Lang and Hitch,[53] except to underline a distinction that I extrapolate from Bonitzer and the others mentioned. It is that between the close up as a formal, analytical figure (insert shot) provoking a detachment from the surrounding space and externalizing the point of view, and the close up as a potentially anamorphic figure (the extreme close up when faces or part-objects are depicted), provoking an uncanny effect, because of the ambiguous location of the implied gaze, often not marked as external and sometimes clearly "impossible" if meant to be internal.

My contention, however, would be that by comparing the close ups in Hitchcock and in Lang, now on the basis of Žižek's Hitchcockian taxonomies, the result might blur the distinction just made. On the other hand, it would bring Lang closer to the Ljubljana Hitchcock, because it redefines for Lang two other features noted by Žižek's classification of objects in Hitchcock. One would be that instead of having the MacGuffin as an empty signifier circulate through and drive the narrative, as in Hitchcock, a Lang film in its entirety might be built as a MacGuffin, in the sense of a construction doubly slung across a chasm and a void.[54] Another point would be that next to oversized statues such as giant nostrils carved into rock or impassively looking Buddhas (of which similar versions can be found in Lang, e.g. in DIE SPINNEN, MOONFLEET, DAS INDISCHE GRABMAL), or the giveaway objects, such as keys and lighter serving as the lure, the passage to the non-symbolizable real (also present in Lang, as we have seen, as symbolic tokens), there are the extreme close ups that chiefly represent the empty signifiers and disproportions of scale and size, traversing a Lang film in the way that objects do in a Hitchcock film. In Lang, the close ups, in other words, should be added to the list and types of objects, rather than shots, because they are often handled like material presences that function not as views, but intransitively, as objects.

This is especially evident in those close ups that, because of non-continuity structuring the visual field, seem more like insert shots. Rather than conforming to the plot-motivated, smoothly integrated close ups aligned along the axis of a point-of-view shot or a glance-object shot, such an isolation of details as we find so frequently in Lang is reminiscent of early cinema. Examples of carefully staged, ambiguous non-continuity are the famous shots of hands entering the frame, first analyzed by Jacques Rivette in the early 1960s.[55] They stick out by the oddly angled framing of the desk-top, the hand and the revolver in the opening scene of THE BIG HEAT—a shot either perceived as enigmatic, rebus-like, or as materially opaque to the point of illegibility. What in any case becomes evident is that if it is a point-of-view shot, it is the point of view of a dead man. Other examples would be the shot of Peter Lorre in M, looking in the mirror and distorting his face into a grimace. As the camera closes in, one loses the sense of orientation, feeling a sort of nausea, as the distorted features look at us with the same disgust that the child-murderer looks at himself. Other examples can be found in Fury and You Only Live Once, where a pointed gun or the smoke from a gunshot pointed at the camera not only threatens the spectator, but the coherence of the filmic space and the reality-status of the sequences that follow. One can usefully compare this to the final shot in Spellbound, when Leo G. Carroll aims his revolver at Ingrid Bergman, and then at the screen. This apparent point of view shot, followed by a blank frame, is so disorienting because it is a shot-in-the-eye shot, creating the impossible spectatorial vantage point. Hitchcock may well have remembered several films from the earliest period of cinema, for instance, as they occur in Williamson's The Big Swallow (1901), Edwin Porter's The Great Train Robbery (1902) or D.W. Griffith's An Unseen Enemy (1912): famous insert shots, from ambiguous or impossible points of view, "bending" cinematic space, or creating an "anamorphosis in time" as one is trying to "place" such shots in their logical sequence.

Perhaps the most perceptive comment made on the typical Lang close up, however, does not come from a French critic turned director, such as Godard, Rohmer, Rivette or Bonitzer, but from a novelist, speaking through one of his characters. Franz Pökler, the Fritz Lang fan in Thomas Pynchon's *Gravity's Rainbow*, is clearly drawn to the dynamic of fragment and flow, the violence and terror of the close-up that lies at the heart of several of Lang's German films. A scientist who during the last years of the Nazi regime worked on Hitler's secret weapon, the V2 Rocket system, Pökler is being de-briefed by his American captors shortly after the collapse in April 1945, when he begins to ruminate, recalling the Weimar years "through inflation and depression." "The *Zeitgeist* . . . came to have a human face attached to it, *natürlich* that of the actor Rudolf Klein-Rogge whom Pökler idolized and wanted to be like."[56] Rudolf Klein-Rogge, it will be remembered, was Lang's Dr Mabuse, his Attila the Hun in Die Niebelungen, Rotwang the scientist in Metropolis, and Haghi the master spy in Spione.

The most intriguing part of Pökler's testimony is not his identification with Klein-Rogge as such, but the way Pökler's comments evoke the extraordinary climate of violence that emanates from Lang's films, when there is in fact surprisingly little violence shown, at any rate in the German films. In the combination of close up and face, of close up *as* face, and the face as uncanny and violent, Pynchon's hero accurately grasps the disorienting, anamorphic quality of these moments in Lang, for instance when watching Die Niebelungen:

> Pökler kept falling asleep, waking to images that for half a minute he could make no sense of at all—a close up of a face? a forest? the scales of a dragon? a battle scene? Often enough it resolved into the features of Rudolf Klein-Rogge, ancient oriental thanatomanic Attila, head shaved except for a top-knot, bead-strung, raving with grandiloquent gestures and those enormous bleak eyes. . . . Pökler would nod back into sleep with bursts of destroying beauty there for his dreams to work on, speaking barbaric gutturals for the silent mouths.[57]

In his somnambulist, mesmerized state Pökler comes to instructive conjectures. Estranged through magnification or an unusual angle that makes him lose the coordinates of size, scale and perspective, the close-ups unsettle Pökler because they locate his eye at once too close and too far away, leaving his mind without appropriate cognitive mapping. They become materialized, illegible without being incomprehensible, until he manages to re-familiarize them thanks to the paternal—or as both Balázs and Žižek might argue, monstrous maternal—face of Rudolf Klein-Rogge, to which he responds mimetically, uttering gutturals like a baby. The impression of simultaneous violence and vulnerability comes from the nakedness with which the framing and editing exposes the act of representation as an interference, an incision similar to a surgical operation.[58] It is as if Lang's cinema was a constant reminder of the violence of exposure done to things made visible when representing them, to which objects respond by "looking at us," that is to say, by becoming faces, even if we cannot locate them as bodies in space. Rarely attributable to a character's point of view in the fiction, they install another look altogether. On the level of narration, these grimace shots suggest that only an externalized, non-psychological *mise-en-scène* can contain the fantastic world that, seen by the camera, exists right next to that of human perception, always ready to disown it.[59]

Beyond Distance and Proximity

What Pökler perceives in Lang's close-ups, then, is a hesitation between registers, chiefly those of distance and proximity. He "fantasizes" not only because he is either too close or too far, but because he is both at the same time. This inscription not only of multiple points of view and planes of vision, as in Cubism, but of multiple relations of scale on the same surface or three-dimensional object may have been what Ljubljana or Ljutomer brought to Lang as he was sculpting his figures in clay to while away his convalescence. These anamorphic depictions of faces, which one hesitates to call distortions, one literally encounters in DIE NIEBELUNGEN, first in Alberich's underground caves, and then at the court of the Huns, as well as in DR MABUSE's masks and Cara Carozza's stage props, and also later, in METROPOLIS, at the Yoshiwara night club, and in the Cathedral "Dance of Death" figures. In each case, the faces introduce an oblique angle, a gothic perspective and an uncanny point of view. Resisting the wish to be either contemplated or scrutinized, the look they return is one that changes the space their gaze encompasses, because it forces the mind to construct a different field of vision altogether—without quite knowing whether to include or exclude the viewing subject.

Thus, it does not matter whether theorized as the "absent one" of Lacan's Gaze, or whether one thinks of such shots more generally as momentarily suspending our habitual perceptual and cognitive adjustments when "perceiving" size, scale, volume and their relations to each other. What is crucial is that the close up in Lang's *mise-en-scène* does not simply regulate or conflate distance and proximity, it introduces a "beyond distance and proximity." In effect, it asks: who looks, and what looks back when one looks, and what happens in the gap of those moments of not knowing whether the look is a look or a blind look that sees through me?

Lang's editing and framing, in other words, become identified with a non-returnable look, the equivalent of the blank stare, but now not the blank stare *in* the film, as much as the blank stare *of* the film. This would ratchet up by one more notch the more familiar effects of retrospective revision of perception and understanding, through reframing of a fragment or a partial view, so familiar in the directors' *mise-en-scène*, introducing another of those anamorphic (cognitive) moments common to both. In Lang's YOU ONLY LIVE ONCE, for instance, there is a scene where we wait for the verdict of Henry Fonda's trial, and Lang cuts to the newspaper office, where the banner headline reads "Eddy Taylor Freed." The camera then tracks back to reveal two further banner headlines: "Eddy Taylor: Hung Jury," and "Eddy Taylor Found Guilty." As we are regretfully revising our relief and rectifying our initial mistake, the camera inexorably tracks forward until it frames "Eddy Taylor Found Guilty" and our hopes seem cruelly, even sadistically dashed. In Hitchcock, one thinks of the United Nations scene in NORTH BY NORTHWEST, where the real Mr Townsend seems to register shock upon seeing the photo that Roger Thornhill shows him, until we realize the real cause of his astonished expression: a knife in his back. Such an effect of reframing can also be aural. An example in late Hitchcock would be the trial of Richard Blaney in FRENZY, where a policeman on guard obligingly opens the swing doors of the courtroom, so that we, the absent audience, can hear the judge's summing up, only for the policeman to suddenly let go of the doors again, leaving us with the anxiety of probably missing the verdict.[60] Both directors are masters of such and similar effects, which can be aligned with what Žižek calls "the retroactive conversion of contingency into necessity,"[61] except that in Lang, even the dreaded satisfaction afforded by "necessity" is ultimately withheld. This, I would argue, has wider implications.

While the Hitchcock vision system, as has been claimed time and again, revolves around the point of view shot (or as here, the point of audition), sometimes initiated or concluded by a direct look into the camera, the moments which in Lang unsettle vision are those of the watcher watched. Thus, a shot is made uncanny by one's realization—often too late, one is tempted to add—that what one is looking at is also being seen by someone else, or has already been seen by someone else. This sense of being ambushed by another look is profoundly disturbing and disruptive. Because of an uncanniness rarely acknowledged by the film's action, its effect is somewhat different from the more ironic *mise-en-scène* of apparently similar scenes of the watcher watched in Hitchcock, where the viewer is often compensated with a humorous or erotic pay-off. Such is the case in the scene of The Birds when Melanie in the motor-boat has to duck in order to avoid being seen spying on Mitch, as Mitch focuses his binoculars on her, or the shot of Thornhill's car leaving the Townsend residence without his having convinced the police, taken from one of the villain's point of view, masquerading as the gardener, giving us the security of knowing that our hero was right after all.[62]

However, the Langian "watcher watched," for instance, in Dr Mabuse or Spione does seem to be related to two prominent and frequently cited features of Hitchcock's *mise-en-scène*: the elaborate tracking shots in or out (as in Frenzy), and especially the long tracking shots up or down. In Notorious, the camera gradually closes in on Alicia's hand clutching the key to the wine-cellar. There is the scene in Shadow of a Doubt, when the camera focuses on the niece Charlie's hand on the banister as she descends the stairs, or the scene where the camera suddenly cranes up into the ceiling of the public library, at the point that Charlie the niece finally has proof positive before her eyes about Charlie the uncle's identity as the serial murderer of merry widows. Equally well known are the sudden high-angle shots in Vertigo, and especially the Arbogast murder on the staircase in Psycho. Analyzing the latter, Žižek has drawn attention to these high-angle, God's eye point of view shots, as at once confirming the impossibility of viewer identification with either the detective or the killer, taking us "behind" all possible human perception and vision, rather than "beyond," as I argued for Lang. By placing us in the gap "between" any human field of vision, it generates an anxiety that hints at the unbearable experience of the absolute point of view. Gradually detaching what starts as a character's subjective point of view from any diegetically plausible perspective while refusing to cut, Hitchcock's camera makes us aware of an all-seeing and—in relation to any subjectivity—blind gaze, of which a character's inquisitive look or even punishingly aggressive point of view are merely the inadequate impersonations and mockingly ironic or murderously hysterical stand-ins.

While these scenes in Hitchcock are relatively rare and flamboyantly executed, they are more subdued and often barely perceptible in Lang, but once one becomes aware, all the more devastating. Beyond a Reasonable Doubt, While the City Sleeps and even Clash by Night have several such moments, which to the inattentive eye could be mere glitches in the continuity. By contrast, the scenes of watchers watched, and the retrospective revision of our trust (or suspicion!), when the camera reframes a scene and with it, reverses the very ontology of the frame we have been taking as reality, are irretrievably disconcerting. The shock of such forced attribution of retroactive causality constitutes the peculiar fascination of Lang's cinema, but it also accounts for its air of remoteness and even of calculated coldness. While we think we are stealing a (forbidden) glance at something, or being admitted to a world normally closed to us, Lang suddenly lets us know that this world only exists for our benefit, that it is only staged for our eyes. This effect, so similar to that in Hitchcock and yet so different, is finally less voyeuristic than feminist theory has led us to believe. True, it can be discussed under the heading of the possibly sadistic director-spectator relationship deployed by Hitchcock and Lang, never letting us forget that we are watching a film, rubbing our noses in our voyeuristic pleasures, and making us pay for them. But one could argue that it forces a cognitive readjustment, producing especially in Lang a queasy feeling of having been "had." Perhaps this is the key reason why the Lang interpretation frenzy has not taken off, in the way Žižek symptomatizes the academic Hitchcock industry. Lang's *mise-en-scène* (and thus morality) precludes the narcissistic doubling of the spectator's pleasure, whereby Hitchcock—transferential Big Other and Lacanian "subject supposed to know"—gives the spectator the illusion of collusion, of "being in the know."[63]

Vision and the Gaze: Beyond Reasonable Doubt

On the other hand, one might go back to the French "pure cinema" position, arguing that both Lang and Hitch have an allegorical relation to the spectator, and that this relationship is ultimately not only not "voyeuristic," but not even visual in the way film theory traditionally understands this self-reflexivity or the foregrounding of the viewing situation and the cinematic apparatus.[64] Lang's compositions and narrative concatenations of seemingly disparate, ambiguously coded shots bring the cinematic image up against its own limits, even where it does not posit the "impossible" point of view. Beyond distance and proximity become in fact a matter of "beyond" itself, as belonging neither to the possible relations of the self in narrative space, nor to a specific temporal relation of before and after.[65]

But what could lie beyond vision in this sense? Not pure cinema, but pure contingency ("blind chance") for instance. Both directors have often been accused of relying too heavily on implausibilities such as one finds in trashy literature. Lang, as we saw, was given a back-handed compliment for making one forget the "maze of improbabilities" in Man Hunt, and Truffaut chides Hitchcock for not having noticed what an improbable coincidence he built into I Confess, by making the priest be blackmailed by exactly the same man whom his sacristan kills, after robbing him.[66] It would seem that one reason Lang and Hitch liked to work with coincidences is that it allowed them right away to move to the allegorical level of their films. In this respect, I Confess could be regarded as the most Langian film in the Hitchcock oeuvre, perhaps because nearly every shot has this uncanny moment I just described, namely as if the image had already been seen by someone else, an effect helped by the fact that for much of the time, the setting is a church. The diegetic assumption that is constantly present is that "God" sees it all, folded, however, into the malevolently prying but also anxious spying look of O.E. Hasse, the sacristan and villain, fearful of his detection.

From this, one could once more conclude that the emphasis on vision drawing attention to itself is central. But alongside the deceptiveness of appearances, the wrong man, guilt and the Law's impersonations, there is always another reality, which may be no reality at all.[67] Although blind chance is always open to the Pascalian wager and leap of faith (as Chabrol and Rohmer have argued for Hitchcock), it could, in the more agnostic Lang, also amount to a fairly radical, epistemological (if not ontological) scepticism, and imply another turn of the screw applied to the deconstruction of ocular perception and the specular-ocular paradigm, more radical than the ideological critiques of illusionism or of the construction of sexual difference have maintained. Common to these two directors is their insistence that to see is not to know, nor is to be visible equal to being powerful. The powerful neither hide nor show themselves, they hide in the light, and thus they have to be combated by a similarly perverse exhibitionist strategy. Roger Thornhill at the auction, Hanratty at the speaker's lectern in The 39 Steps, Cary Grant in Notorious, leading Alicia away at the end. As Žižek has argued, all of them expose themselves, in order to get away, and they impersonate the enemy as camouflage. Similarly, Dr Mabuse in Lang was also a figure of over-exposure: for instance, in the scene where the informer is shot, Mabuse draws attention to him by a ruse. Man Hunt plays a similar game with Joan Bennett's silver arrow, pinned to her beret, and in While the City Sleeps, the structural reversal is that the hunter offers himself to the hunted first as bait. Light, sight and vision are thus, in another sense, merely the deceptive decoys of this other "ontology."[68]

What this suggests is that beyond appearances does not lie the "thing itself," but in the first instance, there lurks what the Lacanians have called the Gaze, fulfilling this double role of both protecting/constituting and exposing/deconstructing the subject. But since the "beyond/behind/inside" signified by the Gaze cannot be identified with the camera, the Gaze can also be related to a more properly metaphysical void, the blind spot around which any "system" turns, be it that of the subject (and gender) or of the social (and power). In this respect, it would be BEYOND A REASONABLE DOUBT that is Lang's PSYCHO (as two films of radical, ontological doubt), rather than WHILE THE CITY SLEEPS, which seems to have a superficial likeness to PSYCHO because of an almost identical shot of a female mouth/eye contorted by a scream. In the latter case, we are in the realm of vision/gaze, sexuality/death, in the former, ontological case, a more philosophical groundlessness is being addressed.

The "Machinery of Fate," for which Lang is so famed, is thus in one sense no more than the name for the retrospective effect of revising a false assumption, of being misled by a scene of foreshadowing, or of discovering that the planted clue turns out to have a double reference even underneath the false bottom. In another sense the machinery announces, after the regime of the look, the episteme of surveillance, which Lang was one of the first to extend, beyond voyeurism and exhibitionism, into the realm of impersonal ubiquity (DIE 1000 AUGEN DES DR MABUSE). But Hitchcock, too, if we follow Žižek, takes vision to the point where it looks as if "there is nothing there." He quotes Raymond Durgnat's possibly disparaging remark about Hitchcock's films being a fleet of submarines, "all periscopes without hulls,"[69] and turns it into a compliment, because it points to the peculiar agencies that barely surface among those free-floating mechanical eyes. Post-panopticism could be the name for this new formation, after both modernism and postmodernism, building yet another slim bridge between Hitchcock's look/gaze, and Lang's blind Mabuse with the thousand eyes. When reality can no longer be retrieved by an ideological critique of illusionism, the options that remain for going beyond "beyond" are not that many. They lead in the direction of either philosophical scepticism or the Moebius strip metaphysics of the Lacanian subject, strung out between the look and the Gaze, the latter now either the deferred hope of symbolizing that which cannot be symbolized, or firmly identified with the all-seeing blind eye of surveillance, which, rather like the Lacanian "Real," does not belong to the order of the visual at all.

Beyond "Beyond": Metaphysical Laughter and Olympian Irony

After vision and its vicissitudes, what knowledge, in Hitchcock's and Lang's view, does the cinema have to offer? I have suggested that in their films it is scepticism and radical doubt that underpins as well as undermines their respective positions of "mastery": master manipulator, master of suspense, master of impersonation and disguise, but also master of the ironic gaze and the cold eye. Their work could stand under the overlapping and superimposed title of two of their films: SHADOW OF A DOUBT, BEYOND A REASONABLE DOUBT—a cinema "Beyond the Shadow of Radical Doubt," which would add the possibility of another kind of mastery: mastery of the double negative.

This is also why a philosophy of film, coming after our all but abandoned theories of cinema, would need both Lang and Hitchcock, to think itself out of a blind corner and lift itself up by its own conceptual bootstraps. We need the absolute irruption that Lang represents with his *mise-en-scène* of moments that, briefly, unhinge even the obverse of vision and open up such cognitive gaps as can take the spectator to the brink of the abyss. Such bleakness, however, needs in turn to be mitigated by Hitchcock's offers of complicity, extended to the audience, that allow it to find its way back to the consolations of "romance," the age-old self-therapy of the community. But we also need Hitchcock's eagerness to shock, his willingness to rupture the social fabric with often gross effects that speak as much of lust as of bodily disgust, to be tempered by Lang's incomparably chaste demonstration of the violence and vulnerability inherent in all acts of representation, putting cinema, in the face of doubt, nevertheless in the service of life. And after a life spent living, thinking and breathing cinema, Hitchcock's metaphysical laughter and self-canceling irony can be heard loud and clear in his famous, probably apocryphal sentence "Ingrid, it's only a movie." For Lang, such wisdom of Olympian irony came late, and in a role made poignant by the fact that he was merely playing at being the director. And yet, Godard's LE MÉPRIS gave Lang one of the best lines of his life, and certainly the best epitaph for trying to think beyond scepticism and radical (as opposed to reasonable) doubt, when he quotes Friedrich Hölderlin's enigmatic, but also heroic self-therapy: "it is the distance of the Gods which proves that help is close at hand." I can think of no better definition of the metaphysics of the close up, as I have sketched it here for Hitchcock and Lang, to help us keep our love of cinema also as a faith in life.

15

Robert Altman's NASHVILLE: Putting on the Show

> NASHVILLE, that's the new Hollywood, where people are hooked on instant stars, instant music, instant politicians.
>
> Robert Altman[1]

The Loser as Winner

Robert Altman's career can stand as the epitome of the direction the American Cinema in the 1970s might have taken—but did not. After an especially "long march" from industrial filmmaking in Kansas City to *Bonanza*-type television work, a break on *Alfred Hitchcock Presents* and a worthy but unappreciated attempt at making an "outside the box" Hollywood film (THAT COLD DAY IN THE PARK, 1969), the enormous success of M*A*S*H (1970) promised Altman a degree of control that until then was barely thinkable within the American film industry. It seemed to predestine him to play a leading role in transforming the moribund studio system into a leaner, more dynamic and more responsive "New Hollywood" for the post-Vietnam era and generation.

Why it did not quite work out that way, either for him or for others of his talent, stamina and temperament, is a question that has kept film scholars preoccupied for the last two decades. There is a general consensus that the years between 1967 and 1975 formed one of the more crucial periods in the history of the American cinema, and that—for reasons as diverse and inconclusive as the influence of European New Waves, revisions in the Motion Picture rating system, the loss of the family audience to television, changes in the exhibition practice, the Zeitgeist of the anti-Vietnam protests and the rise of popular music—Hollywood produced a string of remarkably unconventional films and gave a number of remarkably gifted filmmakers breakthrough opportunities. There is less consensus whether this shift of gears and of generations was merely an interim phase, in the otherwise consistent historical development of a conservative, risk averse, but adaptable industry, or whether the interlude, however brief and serendipitous, altered the character of American cinema forever. The filmmakers sensed the desire for change and captured the mood of a disillusioned, perhaps more realistic America, but only some of them were able to turn their iconoclasm into the new mainstream. Consequently, there is little agreement about names and labels: New American Cinema, New Hollywood, the cinema of the "movie brats" and "mavericks," just as there is no clear definition of the resulting style: postmodern, post-classical or merely a minor modification of classical narrative and the canonical story-telling formats.

Altman, this much is certain, was a key player in all these games and battles, even if, in retrospect, it is still not clear whether he belonged to the "winners" or "losers" or, indeed, who time will declare the winners. During his lifetime, it often seemed as if Altman was among the losers, judged by the commercial failure of so many of his projects, and by the fact that his way of making movies did not become the template of Hollywood in the 1980s and 1990s. Yet, given that he was able to make thirty-three films in thirty-eight years, right up to the time of his death, of which some eight or ten have become classics, his record is impressive and his stature as one of the American cinema's great directors is assured.[2]

Putting on the Show

In light of these ambivalences, it is worth taking another look at NASHVILLE (1975), pivotal in that it is Altman's most ambitious film and certainly his best remembered, but also because it premiered the same year as Steven Spielberg's JAWS, the director and the film that—by common consensus—did transform Hollywood, reinvented the classical style, by capturing a different cultural moment and representing another America.[3] Altman tried to reinvent Hollywood, by perfecting his own (television) techniques, and certainly discovered a daringly original way of making large-cast ensemble films, of the kind in which Hollywood excelled in the musicals of the 1930s and the spectacular epics of the 1950s. But he did this in the idiom of the 1970s, and in a manner that redefined the core Hollywood virtue: the dynamic relation and creative tension between realism and artifice, "life" and "show." Nathaniel Rich, in a retrospective essay, pays tribute to Altman's "acrobatic" style in NASHVILLE and his knack for action-as-perpetual-motion, praising what one might call the film's *constructive instability*, as it "always feels poised on the brink of chaos, and it balances there until the final minutes, when an assassin's bullet sends it over the edge."[4]

Since it first screened thirty-six years ago, NASHVILLE has remained one of the most written about films in the canon of New Hollywood cinema. Articles too numerous to count, chapters in the many monographs devoted to Altman's works, Joan Tewksbury's screenplay with the writer's commentary, a blow by blow account of its making (*The Nashville Chronicles*), as well as extensive, in-depth interviews have left few questions unanswered and even fewer interpretive avenues unexplored.[5] What then, by common consent, makes for the originality of Altman's masterpiece? Overlapping dialogue, and the innovative use of multi-track sound (un)mixing are among the techniques most often mentioned,[6] as is Altman's eye for the telling incidental detail, made possible by a camera style that manages to "cover" several actions at once, while combining the unobtrusiveness of the fly-on-the-wall documentary with the authorial intentionality of the zoom. Beyond these technical and stylistic traits (which, of course, make for an ethic and a world view in themselves), NASHVILLE is seen as Altman's most perfect expression of his perplexingly paradoxical genius. A film quintessentially of its time[7] and uncannily prescient;[8] brilliantly relying on improvisation[9] and tightly organized in its narrative deep-structure;[10] a heartless satire of the shallow world of Country & Western and a deeply humane vision of an America at the crossroads; a film about the cancerous invasion of show business into politics and a film that merely uses politics and popular music to "get at" the petty tribalism of Hollywood. Altman's uneven box-office record made him the Hollywood insider's outsider, and he never quite resolved his own ambivalences concerning the movie colony. Hesitating between Malibu and New York for the best part of his life, Altman, with NASHVILLE, not just entered the art-versus-popular culture debate, but also reopened an older cultural divide, now not between Hollywood and Broadway, but between *Variety* and the *New Yorker*.[11]

In the early days of the film's impact and fame, I was myself among those who could not get enough of Nashville. Having made Altman the hero of a previous essay,[12] I wrote an article in 1977 for the French journal *Positif*, whose editors were also great admirers of Altman.[13] Although proposing some of the same antinomies and paradoxes that subsequently became the clichés of Altman criticism, I was more interested in another aspect, which had already caught my attention in the earlier attempt to define the New Hollywood: the way Altman, along with other directors, flamboyantly broke conventions of classical storytelling, while simultaneously reaffirming or reinstating so many others. This seemed especially true of his approach to genre, where, by reviving the musical, Nashville became something like an ode or elegy to the "society of the spectacle."[14]

Nashville as the Stage for a Family Melodrama

Nashville, which fits several possible genre designations,[15] is most robustly "Hollywood" when approached in the tradition of those backstage musicals whose action revolves around the trials and tribulations of "putting on a show." The stage being the eponymous city of Nashville, in the days preceding the Tennessee presidential primary; the show being John Triplette's (Michael Murphy) attempt to mount a pre-election rally in order to promote Hal Philip Walker, presidential hopeful and quite possibly sole registered member of the Replacement Party. The conjuncture of show business, sex and politics is as evident as in the Warner musicals, but there is in Nashville little of the foot-stomping verve and aspirational brio of the 1930s "New Deal" musicals. Instead of a concerted focus on the final performance, the energies are now "distributive": pointing downward and outward, and dissipating into shabby political deal-making, marital infidelities and lacklustre performances in front of ill-assorted audiences. Whereas in Footlight Parade or 42nd Street, the different individuals and their ambitions were blended and melded together by a ringmaster turned drill sergeant, to culminate in a firework of choreographed energy and a military singleness of purpose, the point about Triplette's show in Nashville's Centennial Park is how reluctantly the participants have assembled there, energized only by Haven Hamilton (Henry Gibson), after he has been shot and the star act has been carried off-stage. Until then, they were cajoled, persuaded, even bribed into performing on a political platform, not because they support this "New Deal" of taxing the property of churches and bringing politics into the family budget ("when your automobile costs more than what it cost Columbus to discover this continent, that's politics"), but because everyone has a personal motive that Triplette—helped by Del Reese (Ned Beatty), his local organizer—succeeds in synchronizing with his own plans and appears to further with his casually proffered promises. If Haven Hamilton is intimated a state governorship (which recalls both the unsuccessful Roy Acuff and the successful Ronald Reagan) and Barbara Jean (Ronee Blakley) attends because her husband feels the need to restore a tarnished image with her fans, Sueleen Gay (Gwen Welles) and Albuquerque (Barbara Harris) have long been waiting for a chance to perform, while Tom, Bill and Mary (Keith Carradine, Allan Nicholls and Cristina Raines) are persuaded to stay not least prompted by their internal jealousies and rivalries as a trio. In each case, their indifference to politics, whether those of H.P. Walker (a "small government" conservative in a liberal's "tax-the-rich" clothing) or of the local Southern Democrats, is heavily underscored by Altman, who intimates that the show as promotional tool for special interests—as hidden as the presidential candidate remains faceless—never connects with the personal motivations of the performers that eventually bring the rally into being.

These personal motivations, on the other hand, are not private, in the sense of preserving a sphere of intimacy, protected from the public realm. The characters use show business to test their self-worth and to become celebrities, but even more they need spectacle as a language, a context and a setting that gives the personal the flavor of the intimate, by the very fact that it is performed in public, where it is always on the verge of tipping into indiscretion or banality, shame or embarrassment. This flirting with failure—neatly captured in Barbara Jean's collapse in the middle of her triumphant homecoming and her lapse into incoherence when wandering off-message—is part of the promise and challenge of Nashville itself. Having to live up to its reputation as unofficial capital of White America's "soul," the home of Country & Western music, Nashville blends the pomposity of its replica Parthenon with the heartfelt hospitality of a Plantation mansion barbecue. The image which Nashville connotes and NASHVILLE promotes may be corny to the core, but it is one that Altman celebrates as much as he satirizes it: the South as a warm, friendly place where everyone belongs, where one has roots to return to and memories to cling to. It epitomizes a community bonded by patriotism, religion, conjugal love and above all, by once more declaring the patriarchal family as sacred, while deprecating party politics. But the show sold every night at the Grand Old Opry and packaged by day in the city's recording studios is political in precisely the way Hal Philip Walker understands it: first highlighting the discrepancy between reality and the image, it then offers the image as remedy.[16]

Altman's NASHVILLE is of its time and about its historical moment. It documents how a transfer of ideological tasks across the mainstream media was under way, from "Hollywood" and popular movies, to "Nashville" and popular music (with television both mediating and presiding over the transfer).[17] The director rightly sensed that within the culture at large, music by the early 1970s had taken over from the movies as the *lingua franca* of American society's most volatile energies as well as its most traditional values: in the case of Motown and "soul," to assert a "crossover" appeal that wanted to blur racial divides and blend sexual identities, and in the case of Nashville and "country," to reaffirm—after Vietnam and Watergate, and on the far side of civil rights, student protests or the women's movement—the family as the focal point in the national mythology of primary-instinct emotions and primary-color loyalties. However, songs like "My Idaho Home" or "For the Sake of the Children," no less than "I'm Easy" or "I Never Get Enough" are penned and performed by characters who seem to be in the music business—almost without exception—in order to escape from ties and obligations, broken hearts and bad relationships, traumatizing memories and unhappy longings negatively centered on the family. Hence the seriously ambiguous status of the songs in the film, confirmed by Keith Carradine and Ronee Blakley, key songwriter-performers in NASHVILLE.[18] Both have commented on the fact that Altman makes ironic-satirical use of songs written "straight," heart-on-my-sleeve, without any tongue-in-cheek. Ronee Blakley pinpoints the crucial dichotomy when she says that in "My Idaho Home" she was able to express in public and through the character of Barbara Jean something she could not tell her own parents in private. Subdued by a bullying husband whose role it is to keep her in an enforced childhood of dependence, fragility and infirmity ("I've been running your life for quite a while now, and I've been doing pretty well"), the secret of Barbara Jean's appeal is not only that she is everybody's doll and Nashville's sweetheart, but that so powerful a presence (on stage) can combine with so fragile a personality (also on stage). Choreographed around the need to perform "presence" in public, in order to exorcise a dysfunctional marriage in the present and disturbing memories of a past that must have been as traumatic as she claims it was bucolic—her stage acts punctuate the film and provide the subterranean motivation for the violent denouement, not least because the vulnerability and hurt she displays so defiantly are a real threat to the patriarchal order on which Nashville depends. Haven Hamilton offers a further conspicuous example of how the family has to be celebrated in song or on stage, because its reality is so precarious. He is the most patriarchal figure in the film, obsessively paying back-handed compliments to his son Bud in public, while Tom, the most "macho" of the younger generation, is manifestly incapable of a meaningful relationship in private, wooing his women in public with an intensely private love-song: in each case, it is as if the private sphere could be validated only when presented to an audience—in the confessional mode.

Indeed, NASHVILLE's mosaic of mini-narratives proliferates around the disintegration of the family as a viable emotional unit. Its resurrection as projected fantasy or "phantom limb" memory turns the "togetherness" of the family into the "altogether now"-ness of the spectacle. As a substitute or surrogate, "Nashville" offers the synthetic family of performer and audience, where domestic scenes of emotional indifference (Del Reese's home life), cruelty (Tom Frank's bed) and violence (Bill and Mary's marital spats) are exchanged for a song of heartfelt regret ("Since You've Gone"), a hymn to defiance ("We must be doing something right") and a gospel of acquiescence (". . . it don't worry me").

In other words, NASHVILLE's Country music numbers and stage acts serve to live out in public, as ritual, so many variations on the family melodrama, which Hollywood, twenty years earlier, played straight and in the tragic mode, rather than as musical and satire.[19] The women in particular—no feminist among them—rebel against pre-ordained gender roles: they escape from being wife, lover, mistress, daughter, niece: Albuquerque in perpetual flight from her husband; Sueleen Gay estranges her loyal boyfriend in order to sing on stage "Let me be the One" to an indifferent and hostile audience; Haven Hamilton's mistress Lady Pearl (Barbara Baxley) resists by insisting on her outsider-Catholicism, and L.A. Joan (Shelley Duvall), anxious not to be the niece of Mr. Green and his dying wife, escapes into the role of a super-groupie with one-night stands.

Once Altman establishes on every level of the action and in every relationship a similar double-bind that motivates the spectacle as compulsive ritual, he plays through the shifting configuration of constituent terms: performers, places, spectators. In order for the sense of togetherness to sustain itself, it has to be endorsed by an audience whose participation alone renders the illusion real and efficacious. NASHVILLE progresses by assigning to its players particular roles, fixing degrees of distance and participation, at once replacing hierarchies and reorganizing them. Jeff Goldblum's Tricycle Man embodies the flattening effect of the film's decentered circularity, as well as being the minimalist among the army of performers: a silent, mischievous Ariel figure on an Easy Rider chopper, he is both central and marginal, linking places and people, while staying on the sidelines and performing party-magic only for the minutely attentive. While the message of the spectacle is thus couched in the language of the nuclear family, the social "order" that corresponds to this disavowal of deterritorialized randomness presents itself as a fine gradation of poses and postures: from detached observer, mute spectator, faithful fan and groupie to frustrated would-be performer, star and superstar, flanked by the paraphernalia of supporting parts necessitated thanks to the logistics and technology of performance: attendants, body-guards, session-musicians, sound-technicians, photographers, journalists, impresarios, chauffeurs and hustlers. Given the possible vantage points from which the phenomenal revival of Country & Western music as the successor-rival to Rock and Soul could be viewed, it is remarkable how Altman balances his insight into the politics of this music and the extent of its commercialization with such close attention to the effects spectacle has on the sense of self, and on the distributive positions of audience and performer in social life. When power relations shift from real inequality to the a-symmetries and double reflections of the show, putting it on is not enough: "the show must go on," as the film's ending suggests, if both performers and audience are not to be pushed "over the edge."

Altman's *Mise-en-Scène*

To suggest that NASHVILLE belongs to the genre of the musical whose plot is motivated by the different logics of the show is to foreground an aspect that viewers might regard as quite minor, considering that the urgency and forward drive, typical of the genre, is here so singularly lacking. NASHVILLE's characteristic is the meandering plot and the serendipitous narrative, familiar from 1960s European cinema, following Michelangelo Antonioni's L'AVVENTURA (1960), Alain Resnais's

LAST YEAR AT MARIENBAD (1961) and several films of French nouvelle vague. This and other examples of "plotless" filmmaking in the 1970s briefly became the hallmark of the "liberal" wing among New American cinema directors, associated with the names of Bob Rafelson, Dennis Hopper, Jerry Schatzberg and Monte Hellman. But Altman's seemingly laid-back acceptance of contingency and chance in NASHVILLE and several of his previous films also manages to lay bare a contrast of attitudes with wider cultural resonance: between those who consider life as a project, to be designed and planned, whose progress has to be monitored and self-assessed, and those who treat life as an adventure, as the opportunity for encounters, possibly or preferably ones that will radically change both the direction and the meaning they give to existence. Consequently, a more or less fatal tension develops between protagonists whose behavior is goal-oriented—"pure" idealists like Brewster (BREWSTER McCLOUD, 1970) and Bill (in CALIFORNIA SPLIT, 1974), or "anachronistic" idealists like McCabe (of McCABE AND MRS. MILLER, 1971) and Marlowe (in THE LONG GOODBYE, 1973)—and those who relate to the world across quite another level of motivation, communicating with people on impulse or whim (often, the heroes' partners or antagonists, and above all, the women in their lives). Their behavior might seem random, but could also be called "entropic" and likened to the laws of particle physics. Although NASHVILLE is a carefully plotted film, with all the narrative pieces eventually fitting together, while mood and tenor are subtly modulated to prepare the denouement, one's first perception is that of randomness and accident, both literal and metaphoric, yet—proving the point about plotting—one does not feel either confused or overloaded.

Of the cast of twenty-four principal protagonists each is etched indelibly with the first encounter, and while their commerce with one another could be described as "molecular" (in the Deleuze-Guattari sense of implying "intensive potential"), their nomadic souls are also in "Brownian motion."[20] Like particles in an enclosed space they bounce off each other and ricochet; their contact, fleeting though it is, increases their disjunctive velocity. It is as if we sense the patterns, but our perceptual or even cognitive capacities fall short of grasping or naming them. Haven Hamilton's son Bud, for instance, seems to come into contact with L.A. Joan and Opal solely to launch these ladies in diametrically opposite directions. Like in no other of his films, the gambler's passion and aleatory instincts of Altman here find ample expression without needing to be enacted literally, as in CALIFORNIA SPLIT, and yet the pathos that can emerge from such chance encounters, as that of Sergeant Kelly and L.A. Joan in the hospital, carries the poignant irony of "bad timing" usually found only in full-blown melodrama.

For some, the risks of involvement, improvisation and interaction are such that remaining outside the flux of particles that energize themselves through mutual collision feels worse than to accept the synthetic community of "instant stars, instant music, and instant politicians." The character of Opal is a case in point: she is incapable of losing herself or "going with the flow." Her self-conscious perspective on America and on events prevents her from entering into the reciprocating tension of performer and audience. Confined in another kind of sensibility (or insensibility), Opal scans the visual field for depth of meaning of a rather more old-fashioned kind. She is—the satirical treatment of her shallowness notwithstanding—another of Altman's *idée fixe* idealists. Her pathetic ramblings in the school bus compound or in the car with Linnea during the freeway pile-up are in truth frantic and desperate attempts to extract from the surface of things, from their collage-collision, something like a valid metaphoric language: "vertical" custodian of meaning that to the literary mind ("from the BBC") is meant to survive the evaporation of truth in the performance.

Altman's roving camera movements, his probing zooms and shifting perspectives, along with the overlapping sound from multi-channel recordings, undoubtedly help to open up the narrative along the horizontal: the interplay of several media inputs activates different sensory bands and triggers chains of association which create the illusion of richly varied visual and densely textured aural surfaces.[21] But this should not be mistaken for a wholesale abandonment of the more linear, cause-and-effect sequence of actions and events of classical narrative. While the artfully loose string of incidents, typical of the musical with its "numbers," liberates potentialities in the protagonists that emphasize a readiness for taking risks in some, and revealing dangerous *idées fixes* in others—apart from Opal, mainly those who take no part in the world of the spectacle, like Mr. Green, Star (Albuquerque's husband), Lady Pearl who is obsessed with the Kennedys, and of course, Kenny, the loner with the guitar case—the inner logic of Altman's *mise-en-scène* in NASHVILLE nonetheless flows from the exigencies of the central paradox that his film explores so persistently: the spectacle is a festival of the body and the senses, but as a reification of time and space, it freezes social relations, paralyzes political action and suspends the individual in the permanent "now."

It is this two-sidedness that fascinates the director: the show as the celebration and realization of a new type of community: "instant," spontaneous, unstable, molecular, open towards possibility and chance, and yet also projecting a dysfunctional, neurotic, fragmentary mode of existence, one that pulverizes the very category of "experience" into isolated stimuli and ephemeral sensory shocks. Nashville, the place, is nothing but a succession of stages and mini-stages: permanent, like the Grand Old Opry; transitional, like the bars with their aspiring nightly acts; improvised, like the airport reception; or "accidental," like the mass pile-up on the freeway. Each time, as soon as movement comes to a halt, the scenes divide up and split into audience and protagonists; the show develops, blossoms, consumes time and space and transforms the world into a communal fairground, which is also a commercial enterprise and a social vacuum. In this, the film recalls Billy Wilder's ACE IN THE HOLE (1951), in a humorous key, when ice cream vendors or popsicle stalls appear as if out of nowhere, right in the middle of the freeway. The dynamic of incidents opening out into spectacle renews itself incessantly, and is nourished by the fortuitous presence of any two out of the triad: spectator, place, performer. Not only can every place become a stage if there is a public, but if there is an audience there will be performers willing to fill the hiatus of waiting: the drum-majorettes at the airport from the Tennessee twirling academy, or Albuquerque mounting a platform rig and singing inaudibly against the roar of engines on the race track. Speed, mobility and spectacle appear as the only modalities that afford the experience of feeling oneself "real."

In interviews, Altman was careful to both promote and sidestep the impression that his films are "improvised."[22] Rightly so, because improvisation as inspired impulse or formal variation of a given theme were certainly his *topics*, but they were part of his *method* only insofar as they helped him get closer to something that to him was "real."[23] When, much to screenwriter Joan Tewksbury's chagrin, he allegedly told the actors to "toss away the script,"[24] it was because he made sure they had internalized their part, that is, they knew their place and function in the unfolding Altman landscape, extended before the director's inner eye. This is perhaps why Michael Henry called the director of NASHVILLE an action-painter, treating the actors as so many colors or daubs on his "palette."[25] But one wonders whether Altman, rather than the Jackson Pollock of the New Hollywood, is not also second cousin to Jean Tinguely, master of the sculpted happening-machine, elaborately setting up conceits of mechanical parts that take on a life and a dynamics of their own: "In NASHVILLE more than any other film, what we did was sort of set up events and then just press the button and photograph them, pretty much like you would a documentary."[26] Through the logic of the happening, that category of the auto-generated, non-purposive event in which otherwise hidden energies are allowed to emerge, Altman becomes the ethnographer of spectacle in the very idiom of spectacle, letting a world transfixed by the treacherous substantiality of the image "document" its slippages between performance, person and personality, and thus enact its own "professional deformation." In other words, this paradox or dilemma is the "script," and the command to "toss it away" is Altman's ironic comment on the very impossibility to do so.[27]

A History of the Present: One-Dimensionality, Flatness and the Spaces in Between

The documentary or ethnographic method in NASHVILLE does not contradict Altman's dramaturgical concern with the clashes of different points of view, his love of oblique or impossible angles, the fragmentation and *mise-en-abyme* of his images: they all serve to establish how worlds function that consist mainly of mutually reflecting fantasies, at the intersection of people's imaginary projections. It is a theme abundantly evident in his films before and after NASHVILLE, from McCABE AND MRS. MILLER (1971) and IMAGES (1972), to BUFFALO BILL AND THE INDIANS (1976), HEALTH (1980) and COME BACK TO THE FIVE-AND-DIME, JIMMY DEAN, JIMMY DEAN (1982), which helps inscribe a continuity in his work, but also gives consistency to Robert Benayoun's claim of Altman as an "American moralist."[28] It places his films in an American literary tradition, as well as in a cinema pedigree we think of as both "classical" and "European." His self-confessed "obsession with reflections, images"[29] puts him in a line of descent from Hitchcock, Ophuls, Preminger, via Cukor, Minnelli, Sirk, to Billy Wilder, Frank Tashlin and Blake Edwards, all of whom are directors whose works have provided a running commentary on the United States as a country and a people living by the self-fashioning as well as self-deceiving iconography of its media. Altman's box-office problem—his seeming lack of popular appeal at the time each film premiered (if one excepts M*A*S*H from the early period and THE PLAYER [1993], SHORT CUTS [1993] and GOSFORD PARK [2001] from the final decade)—stems in part from the fact that his films can rarely be summed up in a sentence,[30] but also that they addressed, through wit and satire, an audience that had internalized celebrity and show business so completely that any version of reality inherently not in the mode of the show, or critical of the performance of self, lacks plausibility and conviction. Altman's satire is so deadpan or slippery because it has to operate without a position shared with the audience, from which it could direct its jabs. As a result, it appeared sour and misanthropic, leaving spectators at a loss how to take the tone.[31] The same applies to the protagonists: parallel to Carradine and Blakley's discomfort at seeing their songs used ironically, the C&W community at first distrusted the film, regarding it as mean-spirited and elitist.[32] With time, Nashville has come round to embracing NASHVILLE: nostalgia, narcissism and the film's cult status no doubt helping.[33]

Yet, in a wider sense, too, time has been on Altman's side. Reified to the point where it is the touchstone of the real, the spectacle is in the sphere of perception and self-perception what money is in the sphere of economics and the market: a great leveller, a force subjecting all other values to its own laws. It is in this sense, that (feminist) film theory regarded narrative and spectacle as hostile to each other. Narrative is an affirmation of progress and development, of energies inflected towards meaning and purpose, with an implicit acknowledgment of history as propelled by a *telos* or purpose; while spectacle in this respect is not only a form of looking and being looked at, of dividing the world into performers and spectators, but an arbitrary, contiguous distribution of energies, the suspension of goal and direction, the sacrifice of history in favor of the eternal recurrence of ritual, defined by a spatial configuration, where the horizon of aims and means collapses as they get caught up in the mirroring gazes of mutual self-confirmation. Altman, after giving America in NASHVILLE the history of the present (his "present" for the Bicentennial, as it were), set out in search of past American history with BUFFALO BILL AND THE INDIANS (his film immediately after NASHVILLE), to discover already back in 1885 only pre-arranged tableaux, staged scenes and fake images. His Buffalo Bill is the very type of hero unable to assume a role as performer without being constantly tempted into becoming the narcissistic spectator of his own *mise-en-scène*. Even the myth of the Conquest of the West, containing too much narrative (and a telos that by 1977 much of Hollywood felt obliged to discredit and repudiate), shrinks to the "one-dimensionality" of the wild-west-show.

But if action is reduced to the suspended animation of spectacle, this spectacle in itself need not be one-dimensional; layered by the multiple points of view that sustain its reality-effects, Altman in

NASHVILLE provides critical leverage, without becoming distant. Hence the fruitful ambiguity in his *mise-en-scène*: capable of suggesting a mental space—the abstract form of all these events, the inner theater of a collective mind, so to speak—he also depicts these events with the pure externality of a "mural tapestry."[34] In line perhaps with the reigning avant-garde orthodoxy of the period, *flatness* is Altman's aesthetic credo even more than one-dimensionality is his critical theory.[35] Enacting a kind of zero-degree of perspectival vision through the use of the zoom, he implies the possibility that film technology has intervened, if not in the mutations of human perception, then in the fine arts aesthetics. It suggests a hidden dialectic between high culture and popular media that once more marks the historical moment: the technical advance in sound recording, the increased mobility of video, contrasted with the stasis or stagnation in the apparatus of cinema. For the dialectic also extends to the relation between movies and music mentioned earlier: the more the movie's aural soundscape provides depth, layeredness and "perspective," the more the image-plane can content itself with pure surface and explore the spatiality of human interaction.

The abstract or cerebral aspects of Altman's *mise-en-scène* make NASHVILLE, in more than the sense indicated by the quotation heading this essay, a film about the cinema, but not necessarily in the usual mode of self-reflexivity. What is striking—perhaps even more so in retrospect—is that the cinema finds itself reworked in the idiom of music, insofar as it needs a cinematic imagination, in order to appreciate and comprehend the pattern of participation, performance and presence which sustains the spectacle.[36] The opening scene in the recording studio, the gala night at the Grand Old Opry, Tom Frank singing at the *Exit Inn*, and the final rally in Centennial Park are almost textbook exercises of how to dramatize space through the rhythm of seeing, looking, being seen. In each location, camera angles and editing punctuate and structure the event in order to "place" the viewer inside the show, involve him (Altman leaves no doubt about "the male gaze") by privileging his vision, only then to relegate him to the casual and peripheral witness that he also is. When Connie White (Karen Black) performs at the *King of the Road*, she says to the audience: "that's what I like about this place—I can't see you and you can't see me." She makes explicit what the film recalls at crucial moments: the hazards of being a spectator, and not just its pleasures. Sueleen Gay's striptease at *Trout's Club* is given neither soft-porn velvet glamor, nor the suggestion of hard-core brutishness: Altman, who shows the assembled male audience's deterioration into ogling and leering drunks without explicit didacticism, enforces the point of our discomfiture by placing his camera at the crucial moment in a most disadvantageous position, with the young woman's frail nudity blotted out by the bandstand. The cinema goer, as voyeur or uninvited guest, has to make do with a particularly poor seat at the show, because to flatter the spectator at this point would be to render invisible a key critical dimension of the film, which is the most palpable sign of Altman's authorial presence.

The sequence where Tom Frank sings "I'm Easy," the number that won Carradine an Oscar and a Golden Globe, is outstanding for its complex handling of emotional tensions as well as its architecture of looks. Composed of shots that take a physical space and make it erotic by the indeterminate gaze of Tom, as it intersects with the longing or radiant look of the four women to whom he seems to be individually addressing himself, the scene has such a lingering impact because of a further dimension, which inscribes a presence that is visually absent. For the point of intersection is the spectator rather than either Tom or the individual women. All characters involved look directly into the camera: the conventional sense of a real space "out there," in relation to which we are mere observers, does not materialize; the type of shot one most expects at such a dramatic moment, such as a reverse-field shot—returning the look, say, between Tom and Linnea (Lily Tomlin), to confirm the visual axis and generate the impression of three-dimensional space—is suppressed in favor of a visual openness that draws in the spectator and makes him the stand-in for the fictional character, rather than vice versa, as is the rule. Altman's multiple cameras insinuate themselves within a visual field that cannot be comprehended within a top-down, or male-female hierarchy: the scene demands a spectator-displacement in some ways as radical as in a play by Brecht, while being orchestrated by means of a *mise-en-scène* that is as classical (in its momentary transgression of the rules) as that of any of the Hollywood directors mentioned above.

If withholding the master-shot, the close-up or shot-counter-shot at the expected places creates a critical gap that involves the spectator emotionally via "perception and its dislocation," the show at the Grand Old Opry becomes a claustrophobic nightmare by the sheer surfeit and redundancy of spectatorial presences, layer upon layer. The promiscuity of audiences on-stage, off-stage and in the auditorium is already stifling, before the performers themselves begin to play at being spectators. Haven Hamilton is looking at the audience while the camera looks at his back, thus assuming the point of view of his entourage, sitting as audience on stage while in full view of the auditorium. Photographers are below-stage and up-stage, as emcees introduce the performers and then lead the applause; each new star brings on stage his/her own family or associates, while the camera picks out the faces of those who are to be the main protagonists in the final act of the drama. As a dizzy uncertainty about who is watching whom envelops the scene, a further Pirandellian twist is introduced with a cut to the hospital room, where the show has its irritated listeners in Barbara Jean and her husband Barnett (Allen Garfield), already engaged in a bad marital fight with Barbara Jean badmouthing her replacement Carol White, while having to endure Haven Hamilton's sentimental appeal to her fans not to forget that "she cried real tears" about not being able to perform at the show.

By contrast, at the final rally in Centennial Park, these various architectures of the look and of spectatorial displacement make way for a different architecture of make-believe. First, it is the camera, distant, hovering or zooming in, but each time, flattening out all sense of depth, that gives the event no more than surface texture. Second, such flatness befits a place whose landmark is a plaster-of-Paris replica of the Parthenon, a mere piece of stage scenery, originally built for another show, and which the citizens of Nashville had rebuilt in concrete and stone to commemorate their own presumption. This piece of self-conscious history of American image-making with borrowed plumes, Altman ingeniously appropriates for his film's final grand design, muffling its monumentality in a sea of faces and the mediocrity of the songs. Despite Haven Hamilton's protestations ("This isn't Dallas, this is Nashville") destined to become the scene of another national cliché—the "lone-nut" assassination—the Parthenon is also a sign that the spectacle in NASHVILLE was indeed a political category all along, not only because Triplette had managed to co-opt Nashville stars to collude in a political propaganda show, but because in Nashville, the very signs of history signal the "end of history," in the sense of Jean Baudrillard's simulacrum, where the copy's hyper-reality destroys the original by making it obsolete. Casting a wary eye at what was implied by "postmodernism" before the term had gained currency, Altman found a uniquely emblematic as well as enigmatic shot to encapsulate this message. When Hal Philip Walker is finally about to appear in a motorcade of black limousines, the camera zooms in on his arrival, but our view is conspicuously blocked by the very pillars of Nashville's monument to artifice. With the oversized symbol of the city's pretension of being "the Athens of the South" as an obstructing backdrop, this black Cadillac, possibly not even containing a presidential candidate of doubtful credentials, is an appropriate update of the Emperor's New Clothes, now in the automotive idiom that resembles a funeral.

NASHVILLE and *Vanitas*: Country Music's Funereal Baroque

As virtually every vista of transparent perception (the classic cinema's way of establishing the realism of its representations) is partially obscured by obstacles, by spectators' backs or a deliberately skewed and awkward camera angle, one realizes why Altman, in so many ways the most classical director among the New Hollywood generation, is also a harbinger of the post-classical, in a mode that makes him a bridging figure of transition, comparable in this respect perhaps only to Stanley Kubrick's equally pivotal role. Rather than a postmodern cynic or relativist, Altman shows himself in NASHVILLE possessed of that same Baroque sensibility of *vanitas* and melancholia, of mirror-mazes and *trompe l'oeil* effects that had served Kubrick from LOLITA (1962) and 2001—A SPACE ODYSSEY (1968) to BARRY LYNDON (1975) and THE SHINING (1980) to give his sceptical realism an unsettling edge of cosmic doubt. Despite the seeming openness and loosely joined narrative of NASHVILLE, Altman's final tableau is one of claustrophobia and menace, into which the shot from Kenny's gun bursts as if to break the spell that the spectacle of so much make-believe had cast over the people and the place. But this fatal shot, despite the brief shock it causes among performers and audience, and despite the grieving cortege that takes Barbara Jean's prostrate body off-stage, fails to deliver finality or closure, because it leads, in true Baroque spirit, merely to another spectacle. As a terrified Albuquerque grabs the microphone and with it her chance to become a star, present fear and past trauma reveal themselves as the true reasons why "the show must go on," on this stage, as well as on the one of national politics. As the song's refrain "it don't worry me" is quickly taken up by the crowd, the performer most in need of the spectacle is the audience itself, defiantly in denial. With a slow backward track, Altman extends an invitation of participation to those in the cinema seats, and an eerie feeling of something peeling off the screen overcomes the spectator when the heads in front of the movie spectator imperceptibly begin to merge with the backs of the chanting crowds in Centennial Park, prompting not the famous question, posed in Jean Renoir's THE GOLDEN COACH, "where does the spectacle end and life begin?" but rather: where does the show end and our collective death-in-life begin?

Such intimations of a Baroque *memento mori* beneath the rhinestone-and-taffeta glamor of Country music, of Nashville and what it stands for, clearly appeal to one side of Altman's Saturnine imagination, but the director himself has also suggested a less apocalyptic and more equivocal reading:

> that song [at the end] is double-edged. I think it's both a negative and a positive comment. In one way you can say Jesus, those people are sitting there singing right after this terrible thing happened; that shows their insensitivity. . . . You ever watch an automobile accident? People will sit there and gawk, then get back in their car, turn the radio on and finish their Pepsi-Cola. . . . So what you really have to wonder about is the reason for it or the lack of reason for it. We sit and demand such great answers in our drama but in our lives we'll accept anything.[37]

In NASHVILLE, we accept the paradoxes of the "instant" and the "moment" that is the cinema: most vividly "present" when "putting on the show," most thrillingly alive when poised precipitously close to death.

16
Stanley Kubrick's Prototypes:
The Author as World-Maker

Kubrick is like the black slab in 2001: a force of supernatural intelligence, appearing at great intervals amid high-pitched shrieks, who gives the world a violent kick up the next rung of the evolutionary ladder.[1]

A Filmmaker of Extremes and of Contradictions

Stanley Kubrick was a director of extremes. Extremes in his person: the "control freak" who had to interfere in every detail, down to the color of the ink people could use when writing to him; the "demented perfectionist" (Kubrick) who drove his employees into white rages or year-long diets of tranquillizers.[2] Against this reputation as a meddling maniac endowed with uncanny ubiquity, there is the image of the taciturn recluse who since 1963 had rarely left his walled-up fortress in rural England,[3] and the man who issued gagging orders to journalists as well as putting non-disclosure contracts on anyone who worked for him.[4] Yet this need for privacy and secrecy is again confounded by his habit of interminable transatlantic phone conversations to not only friends and intimates, but also early morning calls to prospective collaborators who had never met him.[5] The long-distance communicator of a thousand faxes[6] in turn is contradicted by reports of his vast kitchen-living room area, where people came and went all day, while a gregarious and witty Kubrick held court, giving extensive interviews to his biographer Michel Ciment.

Extremes also in his films, each of which probed the limits of some aspect of the human condition: sexuality and death, natural aggression and man-made violence, warfare and the military mind, the audible silence of space and the inaudible screams inside the nuclear family. Nothing less than deep philosophical issues, but often packed into banal, stereotypical or barely existent plots. Extremes, finally, in the critical opinions aroused by his films. Since the controversies sparked off by LOLITA, the drug-busts during screenings of 2001: A SPACE ODYSSEY and the media-scandal—at least in Britain—around A CLOCKWORK ORANGE (which eventually led to the director withdrawing it from exhibition), each film polarized the critics, making some of them unforgiving even beyond Kubrick's death. Next to an early and faithful admirer, such as Alexander Walker in London, he had, in New York's David Denby and Pauline Kael, two implacable and persuasion-proof opponents.[7] In his obituary of the director, David Edelstein could not help writing: "I'll despise Kubrick forever for associating

Beethoven's Ninth Symphony, 'Singin' in the Rain', and some of the most glorious works of Handel and Purcell with sadomasochism and man's inhumanity to man."[8] That all these critics were willing to grant Kubrick the distinction of having been a "visionary" or "dark genius" hardly lessened the confusion either about his status as a world-famous director or the meaning of his films.

Yet these colorful contradictions, accumulating around his person(a) and his working methods—especially because they are so predictably and ritually invoked—should give us pause. They are even a little irritating in their clichéd inevitability, unless one sees them as something other than mere perversity.[9] The extremes, for instance, point to the effort required in the latter half of the 20th century to control one's image, if one wished to remain (in and for the film industry) that totemic individualist par excellence, the director as *auteur*, and to retain the name of Artist in the wider public realm. Both opened the necessary space for Kubrick to build a very special "brand-name" and to keep its market value, under conditions when a new "Kubrick" took up to five years to appear, causing gaps much longer than the average cinema-goer's attention span. That an element of parody or pastiche should creep into such self-presentation is thus not so much a personal foible or character trait, as a structural given of "late capitalist" cultural production.

Kubrick's mythology of self-contradictions and extremes has furthermore to be seen in the context of his decision, taken around 1962, to become a one-man-studio, and to relocate this operation to Britain, a country at that time experiencing a modest revival of its indigenous filmmaking, both "new wave" (Tony Richardson, Lindsay Anderson, John Schlesinger, Karel Reisz) and commercial (the *James Bond* series, for instance, so successfully launched in 1963).[10] The move to Britain nevertheless did not dent Kubrick's resolve to be an American mainstream (rather than a European art cinema) director. This focuses attention on Hollywood itself, and on the changes that intervened in the studio system in the 1960s and early 1970s. The traditional studios, as is well known, went into steep decline, beginning in the late 1950s with the rise of television, but accelerating dramatically in the 1960s. Huge losses on prestige projects such as HELLO DOLLY, PAINT YOUR WAGON or DR DOOLITTLE had by the late 1960s led to widespread bankruptcy and the sell-off of assets, such as real estate and film libraries. Kubrick's own position did not remain unaffected, since MGM, the studio for whom he had produced and directed 2001, his most successful film, was one of the major casualties. MGM's demise forced the director, among other things, to abandon his long-nursed project to make a film about Napoleon.[11] The deal he was subsequently able to strike with Warner Brothers-Seven Arts, reputedly unique within the annals of Hollywood—complete freedom to choose his subjects, unlimited time and almost unlimited money to develop them, retaining total control over the execution, final shape and manner of distribution of the finished film—has to be seen within the context of the major transformations which American industrial filmmaking underwent in the period between 1968 and 1975.[12] While not contradicting the exceptionality of Kubrick's position, the Hollywood context relativizes its uniqueness. It helps, for instance, to locate the economic reasons and institutional circumstances that made such an arrangement possible, when comparing Kubrick to fellow filmmakers of his generation—most of whom during this crucial period produced box-office successes bigger than his—such as Arthur Penn (responsible for BONNIE AND CLYDE), Mike Nichols (THE GRADUATE), Robert Altman (M*A*S*H), Roman Polanski (ROSEMARY's BABY) or William Friedkin (THE FRENCH CONNECTION, THE EXORCIST).

Kubrick follows in the footsteps of the first generation of author-producers after the decartelization decision (the Paramount Decree of 1948), such as Otto Preminger and Alfred Hitchcock, and the establishment of actors as producers (Warren Beatty, Robert Redford or, of course, Kirk Douglas, for whom Kubrick directed SPARTACUS, after Anthony Mann was sacked). While Preminger went under, and Hitchcock managed to survive for a few more years, mainly thanks to the protective cover of Lew Wasserman at Universal, Kubrick, like Woody Allen, straddled the age divide, becoming one of the directors of the next generation (together with Martin Scorsese and Steven Spielberg), who established, via their own registered companies, a long-term professional relationship as well as a personal bond with one or two key figures in the newly re-conglomerated studios. For Kubrick at the now Kinney-controlled Warner Brothers, these key figures were the new and flamboyant CEO Steve Ross (also a close friend of Steven Spielberg, when one remembers that SCHINDLER'S LIST is dedicated to Ross), his then deputy, Terry Semel, and Warner's man in London, Julian Senior, with whom Kubrick had worked closely since A CLOCKWORK ORANGE. After the death of Ross, it was Semel at Time-Warner who became the recipient of Kubrick's all-hours-of-the-day-and-night phone and fax messages.[13] In addition, many of these American *auteurs* had a career-long association with a trusted executive producer. In the case of Woody Allen, for instance, it is Charles H. Joffe (continuously since TAKE THE MONEY AND RUN, 1969), and for Kubrick it became Jan Harlan, descendant of Veit Harlan, who also happened to be Kubrick's brother-in-law. Concurrent, and possibly also a consideration for Warner's, was the fact that the British film industry, while unable to mount significant productions itself after the brief boom period in the 1960s, did become a major infrastructural resource for the new Hollywood in the 1970s and 1980s, not only in the case of the apparently so "British," but in truth Italo-American *James Bond* film franchise, but for such typically Hollywood blockbuster production as STAR WARS or CLOSE ENCOUNTERS OF THE THIRD KIND.[14] It made Kubrick's apparent eccentricity of filming in London part of a sound Hollywood economic strategy, and put him in this respect level with director-producer-superstars such as Spielberg and George Lucas.

Kubrick's Authorship: Between One-Offs and Prototypes

If Kubrick's position was thus not quite as unique as the myth would have it, and much more embedded in the transformations of New Hollywood than his recluse "exile" existence suggested, the particular forms his "authorship" took deserve brief comment. For instance, as a way of valorizing American commercial directors, such as John Ford, Howard Hawks or Hitchcock, the *auteur* theory had peaked in the mid-1960s, and started being attacked by the time Kubrick the author came to prominence (in 1968, after 2001: A SPACE ODYSSEY). So much was heard about his "death" that, according to the structuralist doctrine of the time, the author was a mere effect of the text, quite unconnected to the biographical person or even the artist with a "body" of work.[15] Unlike Altman or Allen, the Kubrick recognition effect initially attached itself not to his person, or to his work as the evolving stages of an unfolding project, but was focused on individual films, as if they were one-offs: notably 2001: A SPACE ODYSSEY, which received scores of detailed studies, but only few of which analyzed the film in reference to Kubrick's preceding ones, which would have been the typical move of the *auteurist* critic.[16]

However, these one-offs can be seen in relation to another "crisis" of the Old-New Hollywood, namely that around genre. In view of the fact that traditional genres, such as the Western, the musical comedy, the epic and even the thriller no longer seemed to attract the "baby boomers," Hollywood was seeking new "formulas" to woo these different (younger) audiences, and was willing to experiment, with untried directors (Dennis Hopper, Bob Rafelson), untried actors (Jack Nicholson, Robert de Niro) and untried genres (the Road Movie, for instance). Kubrick's one-offs, it can be argued, fit into this strategy, and would thus become more like "prototypes." In other words, the perceived characteristics of Kubrick's working method, namely that from film to film, he moved to different themes and subject matter,[17] but also to different styles, forms and techniques, did have a strategic value also to his employer, as Warner Brothers, like every other studio, was casting around for the winning combination, which could revitalize and re-energize what in spite of these transformations, remained an essentially stars-and-genre based way of making mainstream cinema.

This distinguishes Kubrick once more from the European *auteur*, such as Fellini, Bergman, Antonioni or even R.W. Fassbinder or Wim Wenders, each of whom developed not only his own style and recurring thematics, but his own genre (often helped by key actors or stars: Marcello Mastroianni, Max von Sydow, Liv Ullmann, Monica Vitti, Hanna Schygulla, Rüdiger Vogler). By contrast, a Kubrick film rarely carries a key player over from one film to the next, and insofar as he can be associated with genres, these were once more Hollywood genres rather than *auteurist* genres. But even here, Kubrick's work shows interesting anomalies. He certainly pioneered a new kind of war-film with PATHS OF GLORY, and A CLOCKWORK ORANGE dramatically changed our idea of the Swinging London films (Richard Lester's films with The Beatles) or the pop-art-anarchic-mayhem strand of the 1960s British Film Renaissance (John Schlesinger's BILLY LIAR [1963], and Lindsay Anderson's IF . . . [1968], from which Kubrick took Malcolm McDowell), not to mention the changes A CLOCKWORK ORANGE rang on the genre of the musical. And there is almost universal consensus that with 2001: A SPACE ODYSSEY, Kubrick reinvented the modern science fiction film, taking it definitely out of the disreputable 1950s B-genre category.

But already with BARRY LYNDON, and then again with THE SHINING, the genre question becomes more complicated. To these (and other) films, Fredric Jameson has applied the label "meta-genre" films, whose typical mode is "pastiche":

> Pastiche seems to have emerged from a situation of two fundamental determinations: the first is subjectivism, the over emphasis and over-evaluation of the uniqueness and individuality of style itself—the private mode of expression, the unique "world" of a given artist, the well-nigh incomparable bodily and perceptual sensorium of this or that new claimant for artistic attention. But as individualism begins to atrophy in a post-industrial world, as the sheer difference of increasingly distinct and eccentric individualities turns under its own momentum into repetition and sameness, as the logical permutations of stylistic innovation become exhausted, the quest for a uniquely distinctive style and the very category of "style" come to seem old-fashioned. . . . The result, in the area of high culture, was the moment of pastiche in which energetic artists who now lack both forms and content cannibalize the museum and wear the masks of extinct mannerisms.[18]

Jameson goes on to argue that, evidently, pastiche in mass-culture is different from that in Thomas Mann or Joyce. But he sees the revival of B-film genres, the mimicry of past (high culture) idioms, such as classical paintings and costume drama, and the technologically manufactured (zoom lens, light sensitive stock, Steadicam tracks) cult of the self-consciously beautiful "glossy" image,[19] as symptoms either of what he calls elsewhere a "nostalgia for the present," or as a boredom with "the aesthetic" itself, ambiguously poised between symptom and critique of this very same facile perfection, wrought by the technologies of vision and imagining:

> Beauty and boredom: this is then the immediate sense of the monotonous and intolerable opening sequence of THE SHINING. [Kubrick's] depthless people, whether on their way to the moon [in 2001], or coming to the end of another season in the great hotel at the end of the world, are standardized and without interest. . . . If Kubrick amuses himself by organizing a counterpoint between this meaningless and obligatory facial benevolence and the ghastly, indeed quite unspeakable story the manager is finally obliged to disclose, it is a quite impersonal amusement which ultimately benefits no one. Meanwhile, great swathes of Brahms pump all the fresh air out of THE SHINING's images and enforce the now familiar sense of cultural asphyxiation.[20]

I shall come back to Jameson's modernism-postmodernism periodization scheme and the place he sees for Kubrick within it. But evidently, the dilemma or the dialectic of the one-off and the prototype within Hollywood itself that I tried to sketch, adds another historical-economic layer to Jameson's critique and with it, may give a different meaning to the peculiar temporality or a-synchronicity that emerges. What Jameson calls "nostalgia" I am more tempted to identify with a Freudian term: "Nachträglichkeit"—deferred action. For it looks as if the logic of Kubrick's reformulation of genres also implied a certain risk—that of having been "too soon" to benefit commercially from a "cycle," or having been "too late" in the life-span of such a cycle. Thus, if 2001: A SPACE ODYSSEY came "too soon" to reap the enormous financial windfall that came with the blockbuster marketing strategies, which Lucas exploited for the STAR WARS saga, and BARRY LYNDON (as a revised TOM JONES, Tony Richardson, 1963) missed out on the subsequent vogue for costumed classics adaptations on (BBC or PBS) television, one could argue that both THE SHINING (1980) and FULL METAL JACKET (1987) were completed when the crest of their respective waves (horror: THE EXORCIST [1973]; HALLOWEEN [1978]; Vietnam film: APOCALYPSE NOW [1979], PLATOON [1986]) had already peaked or broken. In fact, it is known that Kubrick, who usually nursed his projects for up to twenty years, abandoned or set aside certain films, because he sensed that they would have arrived after another prototype had become the defining blockbuster (this was the case with Brian Aldiss' story "Super-Toys Last All Summer Long," a.k.a. "Pinocchio" and "Artificial Intelligence," which Kubrick put aside after the success of STAR WARS, and the abandonment of "The Aryan Papers" (based on Lewis Begley's *Wartime Lies*), which would have been released after Spielberg's SCHINDLER'S LIST.[21] What one can say is that the prototypical aspects of Kubrick's work highlight, besides the oblique relation to authorship and genre, also an oblique relation to "influence." So many of his films met with indifference and incomprehension, and only later, with hindsight, revealed their place in a given generic history, as if there *had* to be a delay or a deferral, before the prototypical features became apparent, or the films imposed themselves as classics. In this sense, they are the opposite of the blockbuster with its sudden, immediate, but also ephemeral impact. "Kubrick's films," as one of his temporary collaborators put it, "seem to be out of time."[22]

Kubrick's Modernism or (his Critique of) Postmodernism

This feature of Kubrick's films—their a-temporality as masterpieces and unique works—in turn modifies the more industrial logic of the one-off and the prototype. It would, however, also indicate that Jameson is right in seeing Kubrick as essentially a "modernist"—but at the moment in time where cinematic modernism, too, became aware of its own "exhaustion" (if that is the right word). The fact that Kubrick the stylist is both technically innovative and generically eclectic, while his "themes" shift from film to film, makes him fit the model of the late-modernist artist who adopts particular styles as pastiche or mimicry. But the modernist line in literature that stretched from Gustave Flaubert to Thomas Mann via Joseph Conrad and James Joyce is not only characterized by the mask of genre pastiche. It also cultivates the narrational style of irony, or the studied neutrality and impersonality of an "absent God." As Flaubert put it: "the writer has to be in his work like God in his creation: nowhere to be seen and everywhere to be felt," to which Joyce famously added: "The artist, like the God of the creation, remains within or behind or beyond or above his handiwork, invisible, refined out of existence, indifferent, paring his fingernails."[23] Such references to Flaubert's impersonal style ("free indirect") and Joyce's multiple layers of citations, puns and riddles can put into a literary-historical perspective much of the irritation felt with Kubrick for seemingly never showing his hand. The whole debate, for instance, about Kubrick's supposed lack of a moral—but also lack of a narratological—point of view can be located in this cultivation of an absence, which would then not be a lack at all, but a precious pointer to the fact that in Kubrick—as, say, in the Anglo-Irish theatrical tradition derived from Joyce, such as Beckett or Pinter—the absence signifies a presence, the unseen is as important as the seen, and silences are more eloquent than words. This does not mean that Kubrick is feigning to possess some kind of supra-human objectivity. Rather, his effort to establish and sustain a position both inside and outside, polemically committed and ironically aloof, passionately human but also machine-like in-human is itself one of the keys to his identity and "signature" (Jameson) as a modernist.

However, one could also argue that Kubrick is, as Jameson implies, already a full-blown postmodernist, where instead of a carefully studied impersonality, the director impersonates, pastiches and mimics styles and poses, but in such a way that the parodic intent is often muted to the point of invisibility, and the irony seems so remote that the usual contract which parody has with the viewer—namely, that of complicity or eye-winking knowingness—has no shared space in which to establish itself. Jameson refers to this as blank irony, a deliberate flattening out, or even one-dimensionality, which makes certain culturally saturated, recognizable signs available for new contexts, such as the space vehicle spinning to the strains of the Blue Danube waltz (2001), of Beethoven and masturbation, "Singin' in the Rain" and rape (both in A CLOCKWORK ORANGE), the Road Runner and horror-hauntings, television-presenter Johnny Carson and homicidal mania (both THE SHINING).

In Jameson's scheme, as we saw, postmodernism is characterized by a clear recognition that "the uniqueness and individuality of style itself" has been overvalued. Already in 1960, Kubrick voiced a similar view, namely that the emphasis on being "original" in the movies is exaggerated:

> I haven't come across any recent new ideas in film that strike me as being particularly important and that have to do with form. I think that a preoccupation with originality of form is more or less a fruitless thing. A truly original person with a truly original mind will not be able to function in the old form and will simply do something different. Others had much better think of the form as being some sort of classical tradition and try to work within it.[24]

The statement balances the "classical" definition of Hollywood authorship—to be creative within an established tradition, rather than break with a form for the sake of originality—with an already postmodern disdain for or fatigue with "the new" for its own sake. To these features can be added the "invisible ink" aspect of Kubrick's authorial signature, marked by a refusal to invest his work with the semblance of individual biography or personal touches—a refusal which has earned him the attribute "calculating" from so many critics—and has also baffled audiences.

A second point of postmodernist style is the refusal of depth, the attachment to surface, and here too, one recognizes an often voiced complaint about Kubrick, namely that the glossy surface of his films not only repels contact, empathy and identification, but mirrors the glib moral judgments and facile symmetries in his stories.[25] Third, postmodernism is anti-psychological, and it is true that Kubrick in his films often destroys psychological motivation (notably in 2001, A CLOCKWORK ORANGE and THE SHINING), substituting instead such typically "postmodern" surrogates as magic, the supernatural, comedy or horror conventions, without a corresponding commitment to believing in any of them.

But if Kubrick is—in this as in other respects—a typical postmodernist, one might with equal justice argue that he already "overcomes" postmodernism—the only question being whether he does so from a modernist perspective or from a post-postmodernist point of view, in which his (absent) perspective has to be imagined as being located somewhere else—either in the "future," or outside these space-time coordinates altogether, and in some other ("third") political-discursive space. For instance, if critics have spoken of DR STRANGELOVE, 2001 and A CLOCKWORK ORANGE as his futurist trilogy, then his films about sexuality, couples and the family (LOLITA, THE SHINING, EYES WIDE SHUT) could be said to probe the contours of a post-bourgeois society, and his films about military or para-military institutions (PATHS OF GLORY, A CLOCKWORK ORANGE, FULL METAL JACKET) see masculinity from the perspective of highly problematic post-patriarchal "male bonding." And while he kept audiences shocked and the critics divided with his determined effort that each of his films should take up a burning and controversial issue, it seems clear that his aim was not only the strong response he usually received, but to ensure that the values espoused by his characters, in all their conflicting extremity, could not be attributed to him or be used to pin down his own moral point of view. The opposite of neutrality, this courting of a strong response, in the absence of identifying the author as their moral origin, points not to the postmodernist, but to the modernist. In particular, it would make Kubrick a modernist who does not wear either the mask of impersonality or of pastiche, but who cultivates a "cold persona," and more specifically in the case of Kubrick, a cold persona in the face of (or because of) some very hot subjects. It would indicate that the critics, who so often applied the label "cold" to Kubrick were on to something, but not to what this chilly mission was finally about.[26]

For what characterizes the cold persona? Rather than to the blank irony and pastiche discussed under postmodernism, it would refer to the dilemma of the human observer, who in the face of suffering, inhumanity and violence cannot act other than to armor himself with "coldness" for protection, self-protection and camouflage.[27] The notion was developed to typify the post-traumatic literary response to World War I in otherwise such politically opposed figures of German modernism as Bertolt Brecht and Ernst Jünger, whose "Expressionist" angst turned into the perhaps no less troubled, but outwardly expressionless "cool" of the New Sobriety.[28] While Brecht dismantled his animalistic "Baal" into the socio-technical cyborg Galy Galy in *Mann ist Mann*, Jünger's *Storms of Steel* combined the point of view of the militarized-technological eye (the precision optics of war photography and the vision machinery of the motion picture camera) with the dispassionate-dissecting eye of the entomologist, itemizing and describing society, in peace and war, as he would beetles, ants or a butterfly. With reference to the former, Kubrick's Alex from A CLOCKWORK ORANGE turning into his "Private Pyle" from FULL METAL JACKET would be the analogy to Brecht's Baal/Galy Galy transformation, while in the case of Jünger, one can trace an affinity with Vladimir Nabokov's particular cool, whose own entomological fascination would in turn, via LOLITA, take us also to Kubrick. For him, one has to add as part of the "cold persona" the point of view of the no-longer human, the extra-terrestrial (2001—Hal the Computer), but also the not-yet human, as in the hominid ape in 2001, as well as that of the child (Danny, in THE SHINING).

The perspectives of the extra-terrestrial and of the child might be starting points for exploring more closely the enigmatic relationship that existed between Kubrick and Spielberg. Spielberg acknowledged influence and precedence when he said of Kubrick: "he copied no one, yet all of us were scrambling to imitate him." Even without comparing details or speculating about the differences between Kubrick's A.I. and the film Spielberg eventually made, in memory of and as homage to the director, their fundamentally different personas can be gauged when remembering how Spielberg systematically and obsessively reinscribes everywhere—including in his extra-terrestrial figures—the "child" in search of the good father (E.T., EMPIRE OF THE SUN, JURASSIC PARK, A.I.), while Kubrick's "children" have to find their way, lose their way or retrace their steps all by themselves, in a (dangerously, but also daringly) post-oedipal universe.

Second, with the cold persona in mind, one can return to the question of Kubrick's "influence" also in the sense of his films as delayed or deferred prototypes, because what now comes into view is a whole range of directors who—mostly associated with postmodernism—appear to have adopted not so much the cold persona, but extracted or subtracted from it a different "cool." They, too, try to stay cool in the face of hot subjects, but they invest their cool with precisely those traits of personality, individuality and idiosyncrasy that the modernist Kubrick had taken out of it. I am thinking of David Lynch (the entomological point of view in BLUE VELVET), of David Cronenberg (the vantage point of the virus in SHIVERS, the perspective of cold surface metal in CRASH, or of the mutant organisms in THE NAKED LUNCH and EXISTENZ), but also of David Fincher's Tyler Durden in FIGHT CLUB. And last but not least, Quentin Tarantino, whose heroes in RESERVOIR DOGS and PULP FICTION might be said to be self-consciously "cool" versions of Alex and his Droogs from A CLOCKWORK ORANGE.

The Regime of the Brothers

The argument would be that A CLOCKWORK ORANGE, possibly even more than 2001 or THE SHINING is Kubrick's most enduring, but also perhaps most enigmatic prototype film, less for giving rise to a particular genre and its cycles, as for this persona and its psycho-social constellation.[29] Ostensibly a film about individual freedom and the state's right to engineer goodness in its citizen, the film can today most usefully be read as a defining statement about the crisis of masculinity so often invoked, whether elaborated psychoanalytically, around the post-oedipal "culture of narcissism" (C. Lash), the "enjoying superego" (S. Žižek) and the "regime of the brother" (J. Flower-McCannell), or anti-psychoanalytically, around "discipline and punish" (M. Foucault) and the "control society" (G. Deleuze). In each case, what is implied is the demise of the efficacy of the symbolic order, represented by classical bourgeois individualism and its patriarchal identity-formation, in regulating the male's entry into society. What makes Kubrick's contribution so special within this rather broad horizon of cultural critique and analysis, is how accurately he has located the fault-lines and breaking points, the ambivalences and irreducible aporias of these shifts in gender-roles and symbolic functions, notably the socio-political formation of the all-male group, impersonating the father's prohibiting function, without accepting the law of castration. To recapitulate briefly how the psychoanalytical argument might go, by recalling the three paradigmatic scenes with which A CLOCKWORK ORANGE opens: the scene of the Irish tramp in the underpass who defiantly says to his aggressors that he no longer wants to live in this world, because there is no respect for law and order; the scene where Alex and his gang enter the home of a writer, tie him up and in front of his eyes, cut up and gang-rape his wife; and the scene where Alex wakes up the next day, to see his social worker sitting on his father's bed. He berates and threatens Alex, but mainly in order to blackmail him into granting sexual favors.

While these acts and reactions are in each case the consequence of Alex's behavior, who has been displaying the kind of unbridled violence he and his gang are capable of, they can also be read as their retro-active "causes," responsible for Alex's (lack of) socialization. In this sense, Alex's subsequent journey is determined by another gang: not the rival youth gang of Billy-Boy whom Alex's Droogs cheat out of their prey, but the gang of "obscenely enjoying" superego fathers, starting with the social worker and continuing through the prison warder, the government minister, even the prison chaplain and the abused writer who becomes himself a moral crusader. Most revealing in the present context is probably the figure of the writer. Also called Alex(ander), he is transformed from a left-leaning liberal into a rabid advocate of law-and-order. Having to helplessly witness the rape of his wife casts him in the role of the humiliated father, which according to Žižek, is one of the key conditions for the post-Oedipal male to emerge. This graphic scene, combined with the direct address to the camera, is a defining moment of modern cinema, shattering not only the "illusionist" space of classical cinema, by calling attention to the ordinary voyeurism that goes "unpunished" every time we go to the movies. It also names one of the most unstable power-relations in the social symbolic: that of the son, no longer rebelling against the father, but still capable of humiliating him, and thus demonstrating his own inability to enter into the symbolic order, other than through feelings of shame, and its obverse, exhibitionist violence.

The impotent father-figures, representing the symbolic order and the law, on the other hand, flaunt their extreme libidinal investment in exercising this law. Against Alex's rights as a citizen, here defined as the right to do evil and then face just punishment, the State now plays the role of the enjoying super-ego. As Žižek has so often pointed out, this reverses the Kantian categorical imperative, by putting the subject into a double bind. No longer is the individual free to "choose" the personal good, in view of its compatibility with the general good: when goodness is imposed on the individual by the State, it may be good, but it is no longer ethical. Conversely, if the symbolic order extracts pleasure out of knowing itself to be "good," it may be representing the general good, but it does not act ethically. The response of Alex, mirroring the "enjoyment" of the super-ego fathers, may itself become the more authentically ethical act.[30]

The appropriate Foucault reference to the universe of Kubrick's films and its particular socio-political inscription would be Gilles Deleuze's "Postscript on the Societies of Control," where, following Foucault, he outlines a number of key sites of modernity that have started to mutate in the late 20th century:

> Foucault['s] disciplinary societies . . . reach their height at the outset of the twentieth century. They initiate the organization of vast spaces of enclosure. The individual never ceases passing from one closed environment to another, each having its own laws: first the family; then the school ("you are no longer in your family"); then the barracks ("you are no longer at school"); then the factory; from time to time the hospital; possibly the prison, the pre-eminent instance of the enclosed environment. [. . . Now] we are in a generalized crisis in relation to all these environments of enclosure—prison, hospital, factory, school, family. The family is an "interior," in crisis like all other interiors—scholarly, professional, etc. The administrations in charge never cease announcing supposedly necessary reforms: to reform schools, to reform industries, hospitals, the armed forces, prisons. But everyone knows that these institutions are finished, whatever the length of their expiration periods. It's only a matter of administering their last rites.[31]

One can see how A CLOCKWORK ORANGE responds very precisely to the crisis identified by Deleuze, and especially its notion of institutional enclosure, which in the film extends to the enclosure of the body itself via the Ludovico treatment, hinted at by Deleuze, and certainly prominent already in Foucault. At the same time, the idea of looking at disciplinary practices not as part of an anti-authoritarian moral critique, but from the perspective of what is in the process of replacing them, makes FULL METAL JACKET even more of a follow-up of A CLOCKWORK ORANGE, by detailing the discursive and physical violence necessary to both insert males into social institutions (here, the Marines), and to break them out of the "regimes of brothers" with their mutual dependence via shame, complicity, humiliation and the sharing of guilty secrets (as happens in both A CLOCKWORK ORANGE and FULL METAL JACKET).

But as Kubrick also points out, when at the end of FULL METAL JACKET, we hear the "Mickey Mouse Club" theme tune, the move to control societies has a purpose well beyond new kinds of warfare and combat: it signals a broad range of changes of psychic ("psychotic") processes, setting free different kinds of "energies" once tied up in the disciplinary regime of the classical bourgeois state, and now needed to regulate the processing of sensory stimuli and the professional flexibiliza-tion demanded by post-industrial societies of its "productive" members, as well as of those whose socially most useful task is consumption. The ambivalences attached to the portrayal of Alex, confusing audiences and so resented by the critics, can be seen as the necessary corollary of Deleuze's dictum about:

> the ultra-rapid forms of free-floating control that replace the old disciplines operating in the time frame of a closed system. There is no need to invoke the extraordinary pharmaceutical productions, the molecular engineering, the genetic manipulations, although these are slated to enter the new process. There is no need to ask which is the toughest regime, for it is within each of them that liberating and enslaving forces confront one another.[32]

Les Extrèmes se Touchent

So, the extremes, with which I began, do seem to meet after all, and in the work, they even describe a trajectory of sorts. For while Deleuze's control society furnishes an apposite description of what links

A CLOCKWORK ORANGE to FULL METAL JACKET and both to THE SHINING, one can—in the light of Kubrick's last film EYES WIDE SHUT—add another dimension, where Žižek and Deleuze complement each other, and are at the same time given a further twist or reversal. EYES WIDE SHUT is first of all a film about fantasy, or rather, the devastating effect of having a fantasy and of not having a fantasy. It strikingly confirms Žižek's claim: you have to have a fantasy (a "symptom"), in order to function at all in everyday reality or in a human relationship, lest you be overwhelmed by the Real. In this reading, EYES WIDE SHUT would be the story of Bill Harford, a man who has no fantasy to sustain his (sense of) reality. In contrast to his wife, who has "healthy" sexual fantasies to support her role as caring mother and loving, sexy wife. Bill is thus the victim of other people's fantasies, or as Deleuze famously said: if you are living in someone else's dream, then you are *foutu*—lost, "fucked." And so he is, several times over, having to seek out the fantasies of others, where he promptly and abjectly loses himself—be they those of his wife, those of the two women, or those of the "enjoying" super-fathers (his "friend" Victor Ziegler as much as Sandor Szavost, the lewd, pimping costume lender). Bill, almost begging to be admitted to their fantasies, ends up in the most terrible forms of enclosure at the orgy. Here it is (sexual) fantasy itself that is the institution "disciplining" the male, while Kubrick makes the viewer aware of the "naked" violence that frames not just this fantasy enclosure, but all "institutionalized fantasy," as we know it from the entertainment industries and experience economies. In EYES WIDE SHUT, violence and fantasy become the recto and verso of each other, as had already been the case in A CLOCKWORK ORANGE. This film—prototype and key film, it would thus seem, also for Kubrick's own subsequent work—can now be re-read across EYES WIDE SHUT as already outlining the twin boundaries of the control societies and their post-oedipal identities: violence and fantasy are equally "complete," sealed worlds, neither promising freedom nor release, because they are as self-referential as they are self-policing.

This self-policing self-referentiality points straight in the direction of Hollywood—the old Hollywood of censorship and the Hays Code, with which Kubrick conflicted in his early work, such as LOLITA; the new Hollywood of the 1970s, with its apparent "freedoms," which Kubrick tested with A CLOCKWORK ORANGE; and the blockbuster Hollywood of the 1990s, whose strategy consists of dividing the "real world" into a series of self-contained zones, each one isolated from the others, and yet each supplied with the same "fantasy worlds." The strategy has its analogy in politics and warfare: when television reports about a conflict area, its coverage follows strict generic rules, permitting some kinds of discourses ("terrorism," "peace-keeping," "civilian casualties") and excluding others (the causes of poverty, the class structure or ethnic divides, the role of foreign investment or local corruption). Similarly, a tourist hotel during the off-season, or a fashionable domestic interior of an artist-writer, a President's War Room also have their generic boundaries, next to which, as Kubrick showed in film after film, lie as many kinds of madness as there are decors to trigger them. In this way Kubrick is able to relate the fantasy worlds of Hollywood movies to the real worlds of "zoning"—in suburban London, or downtown Manhattan, in bombed-out Hue or Parris Island—where genres provide the interface of these different enclosures, thereby also giving a clue to the paradox of his own recluse existence that encompassed the expanse of infinite space.

Kubrick, in other words, was the director of serious extremes, because they alone capture our lived reality. His persona and life-style finally allegorized not just Hollywood, but the "worlds" it has helped to put into the world.[33] If the prototypes he created were too unique for Hollywood mass production and rarely achieved mass-consumption, their deferred action may still propel those who are willing to be kicked up (or down?) the evolutionary ladder.

IV

Genie out of the Bottle: The Return of the System as *Auteur*?

17

The Pathos of Failure: Notes on the Unmotivated Hero

Journeys and Genres in the New American Cinema

Looking at THIEVES LIKE US and remembering THEY LIVE BY NIGHT, wanting to compare JEREMIAH JOHNSON with RUN OF THE ARROW, JUNIOR BONNER with THE LUSTY MEN, or thinking of THE NAKED SPUR when watching DELIVERANCE may simply be the typical pastime of someone who has seen too many movies; nonetheless the similarities are also another reminder of how faithful the classical American cinema is to its basic themes and forms.[1] One can safely venture, for instance, that the new Hollywood of Robert Altman, Sidney Pollack and Alan J. Pakula, or of Bob Rafelson, Monte Hellman and Hal Ashby is as fond of mapping out journeys as were the films of Nicholas Ray, Sam Fuller or Anthony Mann in the 1950s.[2] And yet, it is equally evident that this motif has nowadays less of a thematic or dynamic function: journeys are no longer the same drive- and goal-oriented moral trajectories they once were. And although still serving as an oblique metaphor of the archetypal American experience, they now foreground themselves and assume the blander status of a narrative device, sometimes a picaresque support for individual scenes, situations and set-pieces, at other times they are the ironically admitted pretext to keep the film moving. One wonders whether Two LANE BLACKTOP, FIVE EASY PIECES, THE LAST DETAIL, CALIFORNIA SPLIT (to name but a few) will come to be seen as apt examples of a shift, no doubt historically significant, that makes the existential themes of one generation of filmmakers no more than reference points to be quoted by the next—and to be used perhaps in order to scaffold a cautious, but differently constructed architecture of film narrative.

For if the themes remain the same, the attitudes and thereby the forms could not be more different, and there is evidence that in the films just mentioned an aspect of experimentation and meta-cinema is hidden, of the kind familiar only from the masters of classical *mise-en-scène* and from cinematically self-conscious European directors. What follows is an attempt to speculate in what sense some mainstream American films of the 1970s might be considered "experimental," in the sense of reflecting on the meaning and ideology of forms, especially where these forms are so embedded in a tradition—that of classical Hollywood—as to be self-evident and invisible.

The perversity of the enterprise must be admitted from the start. Not only is my choice of films selective. My argument is also self-contradictory, in that it both asserts a seamless continuity with this tradition, and posits a break, the latter by fastening on an element that seems excessively esoteric in the context of this American cinema of the 1970s, whose virtues are its down-to-earth realism, its unostentatious detachment, while still managing to convey the customary accuracy of observation, the palpable physical presence and emotional resonance of setting, spectacle and action. My claim is that the break occurs at another level: for me, the significant feature of this new cinema is that it makes an issue of the motives—or lack of them—in its heroes. My second claim is that this has implications for the narrative form and thereby for how one sees these films, both in relation to classical Hollywood cinema and to its apparent opposite, the European cinema of the 1960s. The contradiction—or tension—lies in the combination of the unmotivated hero and the motif of the journey, that is, the recourse on the one hand, to a motivation, ready-made, highly conventionalized and brought to the film from outside, and on the other, the lack of corresponding motivation on the inside, on the part of the protagonist's inner drive or palpable conflict. On the part of the director (or the community on whose behalf he speaks), this discrepancy would appear to correspond to a kind of malaise already frequently alluded to in relation to the European cinema: the fading confidence in being able to tell a story—with a beginning, a middle and an ending. But is the unmotivated hero in fact the same phenomenon as the self-conscious awareness of the status of narrative and fiction so noticeable in Chabrol or Buñuel, Godard or Antonioni?

To put the issue in perspective: the so-called classical narrative was essentially based on a drama-turgy of intrigue and strongly accentuated plot, which managed to transform spatial and temporal sequence into consequence, into a continuum of cause and effect. The image or scene not only pointed forward and backward to what had been and what was to come, but also helped to develop a motivational logic that functioned as an implicit causality, enveloping the hero and connecting him to his world. Whether Hitchcock thriller or Hawks comedy, one was secure in the knowledge that the scenes fitted into each other like cogs in a clockwork, and that all visual information was purposive, inflected towards a plenitude of significance, saturated with clues that explained motiva-tion and character. Out of conflict, contradiction and contingency the narrative generated order, linearity and articulated energy. Obviously, at a deeper level, such a practice implied an ideology: of progress, of forging in the shape of the plot the outlines of a cultural message, understood and endorsed by Hollywood's audiences as the lineaments of a pragmatism in matters moral as well as metaphysical. The dramaturgy on the other hand, posited figures who were psychologically or emotionally motivated: they had a case to investigate, a name to clear, a woman (or man) to love, a goal to reach.[3] Ideologically, therefore, the classical cinema has a fundamentally affirmative rather than critical attitude to the world it depicts. A kind of *a priori* optimism is located in the very structure of the narrative about the usefulness of positive action. Contradictions are resolved and obstacles overcome by having them played out in dramatic-dynamic terms or by personal initiative: whatever the problem, they seem to say, one can *do* something about it.[4]

Such implicit confidence is less easy to find in the films of the 1970s that pick up the motif of the journey. On the contrary, the casual way it is usually introduced specifically neutralizes goal-directedness and warns one not to expect an affirmation of purposes and meanings. Taking to the road comes to stand for the very quality of contingency, and a film like Two Lane Blacktop is symptomatic in this respect: there is only the merest shadow of an intrigue, the action provocatively avoids the interpersonal conflicts potentially inherent both in the triangular relationship and in the challenge personified by the Warren Oates character, and finally, the film toys with goals (the race to Washington) in an almost gratuitous, ostentatiously offhand way. On this level, Hellman has made, and doubtless intended, an anti-action film, playing down an intrigue that might goad the spectator into involvement, and putting off a plot that promises to generate a psychologically motivated causal web of action and romance.

Hellman is not alone in this. The change one can detect, I think, is that the affirmative-causal-consequential model of narrative is gradually being replaced by another, whose precise shape is yet to be determined. This is why the films I am here discussing have a transitional status. Their liberal, but critical outlook, their unsentimental-distanced approach to American society makes them reject personal initiative and purposive affirmation as a viable ideology. But this rejection has in turn also rendered problematic the dramaturgy and film-language developed by classical Hollywood within the context of a can-do culture. Obviously, the changes have also something to do with the altered conditions of production. Television has not only affected the economic structures of filmmaking, it has also brought ideologically less representative groups into the cinemas, notably the young who now see the cinema as an escape from television, rather than as its inferior predecessor. And since independent producers and directors are now more relentlessly under pressure to tailor their films to the ideological assumptions of prospective audiences than they were in the days when a studio could cushion even a string of failures by a production schedule planned on an annual basis, it is not surprising to find films reflect stances of dissent typical among minority groups, such as the youth audience, or college-educated spectators. Compared with the 1940s and 1950s, the commercial cinema now has such a tenuous economic hold over its audiences that it is in practice forced to seek them out, capture them either by an intensity of emotional involvement that is unavailable to television—a dramaturgy of suspense, horror, spectacle and violence—or by an anticipation of currently favored emotional anti-stances, such as world-wise cynicism, or the detached cool of a certain machismo. Cop-thrillers, slasher-films or disaster-movies cater for the first type, road-movies with rebels and outsiders are a useful outlet for the second.

The problem that emerges from seeing recent American films is that directors seem unsure of how to objectify into plot, or articulate into narrative this mood of indifference, this post-revolt lassitude which they, rightly or wrongly, assume to predominate in their audiences. The trend, where it is not towards the defiantly asserted lack of direction and purpose, as in the road-movies just named, manifests itself in stories that do not have a linear plot structure, and in situations that live from a kind of negative, self-demolishing energy. For in one sense, the American cinema still understands itself as governed by a realism of place and setting, while elaborating this setting metaphorically. The give-and-take between the documentary texture of a location, and the existential allegory it may have to carry is as strong as ever in Hollywood, and a film that is not simply feeding off the television genres of the 1950s often conveys (like much of the best American fiction) a central image that powerfully reverberates as an icon standing for the present state of America. Thus, one finds recent films favor locations that convey such emblematic overtones: the open prison in SUGARLAND EXPRESS or THE MEAN MACHINE, the dance hall on an ocean pier of THEY SHOOT HORSES, DON'T THEY, the movie house of THE LAST PICTURE SHOW, the rodeo-circuit of JUNIOR BONNER. What the heroes bring to such films is an almost physical sense of inconsequential action, of pointlessness and uselessness: stances which are not only interpretable psychologically, but speak of a radical scepticism about the typically American virtues of ambition, vision, drive, themselves the unacknowledged—because firmly underpinning—ideological and narrative foundations of the classical Hollywood action genres.

Two Sides of the Hero: Extreme Violence and the Lack of Motivation

This becomes the more evident when one looks at what one might be called the conservative or "Republican" films of the 1970s—the cop-thriller or vigilante film, for instance, which now presents a desublimated version of the moralized violence typical of the drive-oriented hero that used to feature in similar films from the 1930s to the 1950s. The neurotic streak in this tradition, such as the Cagney characters of THE PUBLIC ENEMY or WHITE HEAT, the Hawks characters in overdrive

(SCARFACE, HIS GIRL FRIDAY, ONLY ANGELS HAVE WINGS) or the Fuller and Ray heroes blemished by uncontrollable violence (SHOCK CORRIDOR, STEEL HELMET, ON DANGEROUS GROUND, IN A LONELY PLACE) possessed either anarchic grace in their romantic hubris or a moral complexity of compulsion and ambition that made them symbolic of the contradiction in the American ideal of personal achievement. By contrast, a Clint Eastwood in DIRTY HARRY or a Charles Bronson in DEATH WISH, both so purposive and determined, so firm and single-minded, nonetheless appear powered above all by the negative energy of resentment, frustration and spite, seeking to vent a destructive rage under the guise of a law-and-order morality. These coldly determined heroes featured in excessive, violent plots are the reverse side of the unmotivated heroes in the liberal films: both typify the predicament of mainstream cinema, when it is representing in narrative-dramatic form the contradictions in American society, while having as its language only the behaviorist code of direct action and raw emotion, devised for an altogether different philosophy of life or masculine ideal. But if violence, whether physical or emotional, is the defensive gesture of the self-alienated male in a society he no longer understands and over which he has no control, then the affirmative mode of the cop-thriller, and all other forms of strongly dramatized narratives, are evidently also a subjective, compensatory reflex, responding to a felt lack, but violently closing a gap and overcompensating an absence. The image of the non-committed hero, on the other hand, the one who keeps his cool (who seems at first wholly depoliticized and alienated) might well be the vehicle of a perspective from which American society, in its present state of crisis and self-doubt, can be seen more analytically and less hysterically.

Such a more objective, historicizing realism can be found in the type of hero depicted by actors like Jack Nicholson (FIVE EASY PIECES), James Taylor (TWO LANE BLACKTOP), Randy McQuaid (THE LAST DETAIL) or Elliot Gould (CALIFORNIA SPLIT). As Mark Le Fanu notes:

> The numb, dull stubborn inarticulacy of the heroes of the 1950s, Marlon Brando and James Dean . . . has become a kind of passive and ironic aimlessness, symbolised by the hysterical five-minute burst of laughter of a Randy McQuaid in THE LAST DETAIL, or else the kind of stoned, endlessly inarticulate verbalising one gets in Robert Altman's movies, where the fragmentation of American society is seen not so much in terms of a hero, but literally, in the promiscuous chance encounters of the crowd.[5]

But a cinema that could be considered progressive in this context would have to be more than symptomatic: one would be looking for signs that the director had thematized in the very structure of the narrative an awareness of the problem. The question comes down to how the scepticism about motives and justification in the hero, and the doubts about an experience of social and political life where reality is pasted over by ideological fictions, are translated into a form of film narrative free from the externally imposed causality of a dramaturgy of blow and counterblow. Again, to cite Mark Le Fanu:

> [In films like Terrence Malick's BADLANDS, Dennis Hopper's EASY RIDER, Jack Nicholson's DRIVE HE SAID, Sam Peckinpah's PAT GARRETT AND BILLY THE KID or John Huston's FAT CITY], the spectacle of history is presented for all its dangerousness as a calculated "spree," as a kind of dumb and violent odyssey which never gets anywhere. A sardonic view of history as "failed lives." Elsewhere, it is a *night to remember*, where the adolescent hero gets drunk or gets laid, a last night of innocence before the daylight of history and the subsequent unsettling events of the last twenty years force themselves on his consciousness (see for instance, the sense of bewildered regret that marks Hal Ashby's THE LAST DETAIL, George Lucas' AMERICAN GRAFFITI, Peter Bogdanovich's THE LAST PICTURE SHOW). . . . The Hero aims to lose himself in a kind of concentrated zeal, like the shuddering shoulders of James Taylor, as he forces his

car through the gears in the closing shots of Two Lane Blacktop, while the screen blisters into oblivion (it is the definition of epiphany to be timeless).[6]

Is there, then, a particular mode of representation that validates such doubt and hesitation without either encasing them in the categories of symbolism or stifling them with spectacular effects? In other words, one is asking for a *mise-en-scène* that can differentiate and take a critical stance, within the classical narrative model, rather than against it. What evidence is there today that the New American Cinema is finding an appropriate *mise-en-scène*?

Among the directors whose involvement with the dynamic-affirmative model dates back to the 1950s and early 1960s, Aldrich and Peckinpah (both of whom have a more than casual interest in "violence") show most clearly that they are affected by the crisis of motivation. Bring Me the Head of Alfredo Garcia is an interesting study (within the now familiar Peckinpah thematic) of a hero who this time has no past to romanticize (as in The Wild Bunch, or Junior Bonner) and who is therefore more radically unmotivated than any previous Peckinpah character. When he does finally find a cause, it is made clear that to Benny (Warren Oates) the use of violence comes almost as a form of moral rearmament, ambiguous but devoutly desired, as such violence often is in Peckinpah (e.g. in Straw Dogs). However, in Alfredo Garcia Peckinpah is both fascinated by a zero-degree of motivation and still too attached to the apocalypse of violent acting out to conceive of any narrative other than a cathartic one.

Lack of motivation is even more explicitly the subject of Aldrich's The Mean Machine, a movie whose complex narrative conception appears in the realization more awkward than elegant. It is as if Aldrich, as much in desperation as disgust, had broken his film into several disjointed pieces. One can unscramble at least three strands pushed into each other, as if after a freeway pile-up. In the first, the Burt Reynolds character gets out of bed, savagely mauls his girlfriend, drives her sports-car across a half-opened bridge-leaf, dumps it in the river and then stands at the bar waiting for the cops to pick him up. The violence is excessive, the motivation for it non-existent. One feels that neither movie nor hero can go in any direction whatsoever, and one wonders whether one has seen the last fifteen minutes of the previous film, or the pre-credit scene to a flashback movie that never follows. What does follow is another film, which superficially belongs to the classical genre of the prison film, where the hero rehabilitates himself by organizing the sports team, turning anti-social convicts into loyal team-mates. Aldrich twists the genre out of shape, and the rehabilitation does not mean release, but converts the sentence into an indefinite one. However, the real twist is that inside the second film is a third one, which by rights is not a movie at all, but a Saturday-afternoon TV-baseball game complete with PR-man, coach and cheerleaders. So flat and predictable is this section that one suspects Aldrich of giving us an object lesson about the impossibility of (still) making action films: unmotivated heroes, morally bogus genres couch potato audiences—three times he is showing us drama without consequence, three variations on a (sad) theme. A stretch of dialogue midway through the film verbalizes the situation once more: we know there is something obscure in the hero's past that concerns his motivation. His friend keeps asking "Why did you do it?" Finally, Burt Reynolds relents and gives an explanation, a sob-story belonging to the conventions of the rehabilitation genre. But before we have recovered from its painful, embarrassing pathos, Reynolds starts to grin and admits that he has been having his friends on. He just does not know why he "did" it; maybe for the money? In Aldrich's film, the salient fact is that whatever it was that was important, it happened too long ago. This in itself is a telling metaphor of the film's motivational predicament: if characters have no moral history that can plausibly explain their behavior, action becomes the spectacle of gratuitousness. What makes disaster movies like The Towering Inferno or The Poseidon Adventure seem anachronistic in this light, is that they assume the catastrophe is still about to happen, and that what is needed in order to prepare for it is to rehearse it, when it is clear that disaster has already struck.[7]

Another form of self-conscious knowingness practiced by New Hollywood directors is to resort to remake, parody or pastiche: Peter Bogdanovich, Altman, Roman Polanski. Bogdanovich's reconstruction of the last days of a small-town movie house in THE LAST PICTURE SHOW celebrates the now past Saturday nights at the movies as if they had been more part of nature than the pond where Ben Johnson used to go fishing. Polanski's CHINATOWN, a beautifully poker-faced pastiche of the *film noir* is on the other hand as contemptuous of its detective hero as Altman is in THE LONG GOODBYE, except that Polanski's lack of respect for him appeases itself in the meticulous craftsmanship of the reconstruction of his fall. Altman's parody of the Raymond Chandler hardboiled hero (in THE LONG GOODBYE) and his reprise of the Depression-era gangster story (THIEVES LIKE US) would appear to mark him out as the director with the most "European" sense of fictional impasses, reminiscent in fact of Godard's early (A BOUT DE SOUFFLE) and Truffaut's films of the mid-1960s (LA SIRÈNE DU MISSISIPPI). In THIEVES LIKE US the heroes listen as compulsively to radio-shows and want to read about themselves as avidly in the newspapers as the heroes of BANDE À PART or BAISERS VOLÉES were caught in the seductively narcissistic mirror of sensing themselves characters in an already told story. Altman, possibly taking his cue from Penn's BONNIE AND CLYDE, develops the mythopoetic magic of the American cinema's own past through the double mythomania of newspaper and radio-serial, but then, choosing a 1930s setting, is he not himself helping to build up a myth? Maybe so, but the movie also wants to impress by its unromantic, anti-glamorizing sobriety, and in this it is as much anti-BONNIE AND CLYDE as in another way it is anti-THEY LIVE BY NIGHT.

Altman is one of the New American Cinema's directors who is still prepared to cite a cinematic language that clearly belongs to the epoch of the classical *mise-en-scène*: the symbolism of objects through thematic use in the narrative. One would have thought that it belongs too obviously to a cinema of purposive development and positive meanings to be of use in any other form than as quotations. THIEVES LIKE US features a patchwork quilt that is given all the grand rhetorical orchestration that Shirley MacLaine's "sweet-heart" pillow had in Minnelli's SOME CAME RUNNING (a film whose symbolic objects Godard remembers in both LE MÉPRIS and PIERROT LE FOU). Kechie's patchwork quilt is charged with special meaning in an early scene when she covers the injured Bowie and then slips under it herself when they make love for the first time. The importance of the quilt is emphasized when she explains that it was made by her grandmother and is her sole personal possession, evidence that she, too, once had a family. It then reappears when the two have their decisive quarrel and has its thematic apotheosis when Bowie, now a corpse riddled by police bullets, is wrapped up in it and dumped, mud- and blood-spattered, into a puddle. The price Altman pays for using such obvious dramatic symbolism is a stylized poignancy rather too overt not to disrupt the somber, unemphatic ending, but it is in line with other formal devices (the repetition of the line from *Romeo and Juliet*, for instance), whereby Altman seems unsure just how self-consciously he can treat the genre he has chosen to pastiche.

The Pathos of Failure

The penchant for depicting this kind of pathos goes deeper in the New American Cinema. "We blew it": one remembers the resigned and melancholy admission of Captain America from EASY RIDER. For all the traditionalist plot elements and stylistic uncertainties, EASY RIDER still functions, along with BONNIE AND CLYDE, as the one popular and commercially successful alternative to the affirmative stance. Not just because it is a film about heroes without a goal who take "drive" out of the psychic realm and onto the road, and who take "trip" off the road and into the mind, but also as a paradigm of the open-ended loose-structured narrative, so frequently imitated since. The heroes are still motivated, though, even if this motivation now harks back not so much to classical Hollywood as to classical American fiction: thematically, EASY RIDER revives the perennial motif and structural device of American literature, from J.F. Cooper's *Leatherstocking* to Mark Twain's *Huckleberry Finn*, about the male couple ganging up to escape civilization and women. In fact, the double male lead—the buddy couple—now predominates so much (from MIDNIGHT COWBOY, BUTCH CASSIDY AND THE SUNDANCE KID, THE STING to CALIFORNIA SPLIT and THUNDERBOLT AND LIGHTFOOT) that one wonders whether it has not become *the* genre of the New American Cinema, lending itself to the depiction of both conformist and of dropout attitudes. The permutations reach from Ashby's THE LAST DETAIL to Spielberg's SUGARLAND EXPRESS, the latter particularly interesting, if one thinks of it as a BONNIE AND CLYDE-story that ends up as a love-story of the all-male couple. As the young policeman taken hostage befriends and is in turn befriended by the male kidnapper, we realize just how reluctant an accomplice he is in his wife's hi-jack trip to recover her baby.

Over all the movies that take to the road on quests that are escapes and escapes that are quests, there hangs like a haze the sweet poignancy of defeat. At the end, when the heroes face the patriarchal law, whether in the shape of Southern rednecks, mean-mouthed farmers, hick patrolmen or gas station attendants, scowling women and bragging middle-aged men with fast cars and high-powered rifles—all those who were already there before our young men came on the scene and who win out and survive, as they invariably do—then the characters' wry self-abandonment and lassitude registers with the particular pathos reserved for "beautiful losers." The cool mockery, the detached satire which such films direct against the America of the Silent Majority fades out on a wave of self-pity.

If one sees this in thematic or ideological terms, the New American Cinema here shows its most symptomatic side. Caught between having to codify a different image of America from that of Hollywood, while still validating it emotionally in the way the classical cinema had been able to translate a reality into image and an image into feeling, the new directors opt for a kind of realism of sentiment that is faithful to the negative experiences of recent US history, but often at the price of sentimentality. True, the movies catch the moral and emotional gestures of a defeated generation, but this strategy—since it is concerned with depicting a mood rather than probing its causes or historical circumstances—gives both heroes and the world that dooms them an element of sentimental mystification and starkness of contrast which must finally affect the intelligence of the observation and therefore the value of this new, de-dramatized realism. The problem is not dissimilar from that presented by the "happy ending" in the melodramas of the 1950s: how can it be seen as ironic (and thus distanced by a double reference), without losing the emotional impact that provides closure and catharsis? In THIEVES LIKE US the pitch of the emotional response at the climax is counteracted by a deliberately flat, emotionless coda, which dismisses the audience into a welter of mixed feelings, ranging from ironic detachment about the futility of the characters' modest ambitions to shallow anger about their victimization. Altman's film in this respect thematizes a dilemma felt by other directors, several of whom have opted for such an epilogue (e.g. AMERICAN GRAFFITI), which sets out to balance or neutralize the dramatic charge previously accumulated. By foregoing the dramaturgy of interpersonal conflict, suspense and enigma in favor of episodic story-structure and paratactic ("and—and") plots, the films stylize the heroes' aimless despair into the pathos of failure. Dramaturgically, this answers the pressing problem of how to end an indeterminate narrative: pathos provides the emotional closure to an open-ended structure and retrieves affective contact with the audience.

Thus, whatever ideological doubts one may have about the seemingly unqualified emotional sympathy enjoyed by the heroes of THIEVES LIKE US, SUGARLAND EXPRESS or AMERICAN GRAFFITI as victims of society or history, one needs to bear in mind that under cover of such simple but effective hold over the spectator's involvement and identification a new type of popular film narrative is trying to cope with the technical problem of how to depict the unmotivated hero. European directors—from Jean Marie Straub to Jacques Rivette, from Luis Buñuel to Alain Tanner—experiment with different kinds of narratives, not generated by any of the conventional dramatic supports such as melodramatic conflict, investigation of an enigma or crime, journey and goal (although as films like La voie lactée or Le charme discret de la bourgeoisie show, Buñuel for one is more than ever committed to the picaresque journey motif). While they are inventing new kinds of episodic or situational narratives (as in Rivette's Céline et Julie s'en vont en bateau) in the comforting knowledge of an appreciative metropolitan-intellectual audience, the pressures on reaching a wider public and thus the constraints on experimentation in the commercial cinema are obviously very different. Where French directors in particular like to allow the narrative substance of their films to whittle itself out of existence through an ever-more sophisticated play of multiple fictional strands, parallel worlds and tantalizing plot fragments, such possibilities are not open to an American director faced with a similar dilemma of representational realism: his remains an audience-oriented cinema that permits no explicitly anti-narrative fictional construction. Consequently, the innovatory line in the New American Cinema has not followed the conceptual abstractions of the New Wave with their slipping in and out of fiction and the documentation of fiction, but progress is made by shifting and modifying traditional genres, motifs and themes, while never quite shedding the basic Hollywood convention of the single diegetic world, be it to facilitate audience recognition or for structuring the narrative. In search of a new realism, directors such as Robert Altman and Monte Hellman, after periods of undertaking non-commercial ventures (Brewster Mccloud, The Shooting) can be seen to return to more traditional subjects and themes that are, as it were, already acculturated and cinematically sanctioned. Nor can they afford to suspend the narrative momentum altogether, however de-dramatized. But they do manage to hold the thin line between locating a new image of America while keeping in touch with the visual and emotional rhetoric of their culture, and thereby also keeping open the lines of communication with a mass public. The price of making American history (the West, the gold-rush, the history of the American Indians, the Depression, the plight of farmers or migrant workers) once more relevant to a new generation seems to be a sort of "miserabilist" realism, to which corresponds the basic emotional stance of defeat: of the sons and the young, by the fathers and the forces of the Establishment.

American History and Nostalgia Movies

In this connection, perhaps the much maligned "trend" of the nostalgia movie should be regarded under a double aspect. Certainly, Paper Moon and American Graffiti are testimony to a symptomatic search for a more unproblematic, innocent past, free from the guilt of knowledge and the responsibility for redressing the evils of the past. But the quest for a lost national Eden, perhaps more overtly apologetic in films like Summer of '42 or The Way We Were in which pointedly non-political individual experience is rather shamefacedly celebrated against the background of a political period, also allows for a succinct and poignant thematization of the absence of consequence and history, in today's self-understanding of America. This feeling of having come to the end of something, in the wake of the brief period of 1960s revolt is, I have tried to suggest, one of the ideologically determined features of the New American Cinema today and therefore part of its realism. But this terminal point or plateau position also gives directors the opportunity to scan a historical and geographical American landscape (besides the Depression era, it is the early 1950s as lived in small-town rural communities that has attracted attention) for clues of what one might call the new verisimilitude of the American image and thus a new iconography of place alongside a new emotional topography. This is not a matter of a pristine visual experience, nor of documentary objectivity, more the pursuit of a gestural and physical world that connotes historicity and is cultur-ally resonant, without being overtly symbolic or sensational-spectacular. In contrast to the perfected glamor, the aestheticism of self-sufficient perfection as (often somewhat facilely) attributed to

Hollywood, especially directors such as Altman, Rafelson, Hellman are emotionally charging with beauty and dignity the rough and the squalid, the unattractive and the plain, the imperfect and the incomplete.

Altman in particular, in his genre pastiches McCABE AND MRS MILLER, THIEVES LIKE US, THE LONG GOODBYE and CALIFORNIA SPLIT is not afraid to use the pathos of loss, across historical patina and a sentiment of nostalgia, in order to transform settings, objects and decor into signs and icons: from a mid-century mining town in a snowstorm, to the first Coke bottle and the memento of a heart-shaped purse. Unlike the patchwork quilt in THIEVES LIKE US, which figures as a symbolic object whose meaning is used—and used up—by the narrative, the objects just mentioned only refer to themselves, while raising expectations of a pay-off on the level of positive meanings which never quite constitutes itself, except as enigmatic potential or benign pastiche.

In his experimentation with a reality, untainted or overdetermined by the symbolic accretions that have made so much of the American urban and rural landscape into cinematic clichés, Altman seems to admit the status of the image as inescapably coded sign, but its sign character can be exploited by focusing emotional resonance on its palpable facticity. Plot, genre convention and intrigue henceforth function in an inverse sense; instead of providing the continuity and logic of the narrative that guarantees the coherence of a secondary level of symbolic meaning, they are the secondary meaning, alluding with their hollowed-out ruins of an intrigue back to a time when stories still had strong plots: what is left of classical narrative in Altman has become the vehicle of communicating with the audience across a memory, offsetting the better his own films' discrete visual moments, voided of metaphorical or mythic significance. In the absence of any positive motivation of either hero or plot, the pathos of failure becomes the zero-degree of all the moralized emotions, which the dynamics of desire and violence supplied to the classical narratives of John Ford, Nicholas Ray or Howard Hawks.

Contemporary Subjects and Settings

In a sense, it is easier to test the possibilities of this new low-key, matter of fact and almost documentary realism in a period film, or when subverting the pre-formulated expectation of a particular genre, be it Western or detective film, because genre and period assure a provisional structure of empathy and recognition. But similar tendencies can be observed in other directors, and they extend beyond the nostalgia pictures or the remakes of old genre-films. For instance, films with a contemporary setting, such as FIVE EASY PIECES or TWO LANE BLACKTOP are generated out of the same desire for an image of America that becomes palpable not because of the interplay between moral symbolism and a generically coded plot, but because of a renewed pleasure in solid specificity, in realized physical presence, whatever dramatic clichés or conventional motifs the films cite in order to make this realism acceptable. And again we find the same pathos as in the nostalgia films that charges the image with the (negative) emotion of perceived gap and disappointed expectation, while nonetheless neutralizing any moral urgency and drive-oriented energy to do something about it.

Significantly, Rafelson, Hellman, Spielberg and others choose a "rural" America for their fables of temperate futility. Recognizable by its stretches of barren roadside, its drive-ins, petrol-stations and small-town main-streets—the kind of scenery precisely nowhere and everywhere in America, and therefore furnishing an important element of abstraction without being itself abstract. It is a scenery that, on the one hand, has the sanction and precedent of *film noir*, that other high period of an almost documentary realism in the American cinema, but this time, without the black romanticism of mood or the heavy machinery of fate and destiny knitting together character and incident. On the other hand, today's low-key, de-dramatized *noir* films are ultimately not so different in their insistence on the emotional stance appropriate to Hollywood's gritty realism—negativity, a defensive cool, the somewhat sentimental gestures of defeat. One way of explaining the similarity is to say that, like *film noir* (a response to suburbia, by fetishizing the city) the new realism is itself a defensive stance: is not the focus on rural America something of an anthropological perspective, taken by an urban culture of corporation men, on an America where nothing ever seems to happen, where time has stood still and where a people survives that apparently has no history? One remembers the encounter of the businessmen on vacation in DELIVERANCE with the banjo-playing mentally retarded boy. In the very understatement of the scene is hidden an anxious wariness for clues as to what it was that made the United States of the "heroic" 1940s and 1950s so appallingly what it is today. It is as if only such secluded places, with their ominous silences and treacherously innocent-looking nature, could give an explanation for the violence, the paranoia: as if, finally, only rural hamlets could explain urban ghettos and suburban hysteria. A favorite image, put to good effect in THIEVES LIKE US, is to show a fine silence at dawn in an idyllic landscape suddenly torn apart by a furious exchange of gunfire (also used by Penn in BONNIE AND CLYDE and Spielberg in SUGARLAND EXPRESS).

Faced with such allegorical re-enactments of morning raids on the Black Panthers or Kent State incidents, one wonders how long directors can go on codifying in such oblique ways the experience of revolt and the history of a protest movement, whose impulses towards change aborted. Where it does not lead to a pathos of loss, as in THIEVES LIKE US or the paranoia of sadistic rape and murder, as in DELIVERANCE, memories of the radical sixties now seem transfixed in stunned moments of inconsequentiality, such as George Segal piling up his chips at the end of CALIFORNIA SPLIT, or Gene Hackman sitting in his demolished room in THE CONVERSATION. Today's heroes are waiting for the end, convinced that it is too late for action, as if too many contradictions had canceled the impulse towards meaning and purpose. In TWO LANE BLACKTOP everything goal-directed appears simply neurotic, uncool, a compensation for frustration, like the fantasies of GTO, the Warren Oates character, about being faster, better, more virile than the boys with the souped-up Chevy. In AMERICAN GRAFFITI the action, the constant stream of cars circling the town's main-street, revolves around an "empty" center: the mythical DJ whose disembodied "Wolfman" is nothing more mysterious than a lonely man sitting amongst a lot of technology in his radio-mast, eating sandwiches. Clearly in a period of historical stasis, these movies reflect a significant ideological moment in American culture. One might call them films that dramatize the end of history, for what is a story, a motivated narrative (which such movies refuse to employ) other than an implicit recognition of the existence of history, at least in its formal dimension—of driving forces and determinants, of causes, conflicts, consequence and interaction?

A Double Negative

However, there is another point: if, as I have suggested, the pervasive pessimism of the New American Cinema in the 1970s, is not only a personal statement of their authors' sense of social and political failure, but also the limiting conditions, the formal constraints of a new kind of cinematic realism— the price, so to speak, for being exploratory and tentative—then the strength of a film like TWO LANE BLACKTOP lies in the way that, sheltered by the structure of the journey motif, it quietly steers towards a sort of abstract grace, a narrative poise and a documentary minimalism unknown in the Hollywood canon except perhaps in the work of Jacques Tourneur. Released from the fable and from the need to engineer the drama into a didactic shape, the images develop an energy that charges representation with something other than symbolic overtones or metaphoric meaning: one is, remotely, reminded of the studied literalness in Paul Morissey's films for Andy Warhol, but Hellman's film is free from the claustrophobia so carefully controlled in FLESH or TRASH. Whether the cancelation of the dramatic impulse and the search for another cinematic rhythm, made up of underplayed gestures and coolly observant looks, will suggest less problematic downbeat endings than the negative emotion of male melodrama which I have here called the pathos of failure is difficult to predict: the freeze-frame nowadays connotes nothing other than the indecisiveness of the director and the suspension of his narrative on just this point. In Two Lane Blacktop, by its own logic, the drive, and thus the film, could go on indefinitely: that is its beauty as a composition of pure movement. The ending—in order to work—quite clearly, must have the status of a "device": Hellman motivates his hero, the James Taylor character, in the end quite conventionally when underneath his cool he reveals an obsession with the young woman he cannot possess, and thus is faced with a situation (as the hero of his own Hollywood action-adventure movie) that he cannot get a grip on. This impulse is allowed to live itself out, albeit destructively: he takes ever greater risks and finally meets his nemesis. At the same time, seeing how Hellman has hollowed out and flattened the action genre, the ending is aptly "meta-cinematic" and self-reflexive: Hellman lets the image burn itself out in the projector in extreme slow-motion, a metaphor both for the hero's erotic obsession and for the impasse of the film's form.

The fact that this ending is borrowed from Skolimowski's Le Départ, also a film about racing and impossible quests, throws an interesting sidelight on the no doubt complex interchange between European and American filmmaking today. Tentatively, however, one might assume that both, aware of essentially similar problems, proceed along different routes. Against multiple fictions and double diegesis, the American directors prefer to literalize their cinematic language, de-dramatize their narratives, to strengthen the inner dynamism of their scenes: the momentum of action gives way to the moment of gesture, and the gesture can take on the numinous truth of revelation. A new form of *mise-en-scène* seems in the making in America that could mean a revaluation of both classical Hollywood and the European heritage. In that case, the unmotivated hero and the pathos of failure will be the double negatives that might well result in a positive.

18
Auteur Cinema and the New Economy Hollywood

For many critics writing in the 1980s, when Hollywood once more began to conquer the world's screens with its blockbusters, the American cinema they loved and admired—the cinema of the great studio directors as well as that of independent-minded *auteurs*—had entered its terminal decline. Not only was the industry that produced these new event movies different: so were the people who made them, the shoot-them-up plots that obsessed them, the special effects that enhanced them, and the money that drove them. Article after article mourned the "death of cinema" and poured scorn on those who had "killed Hollywood."[1]

The retrospective vanishing point from which these critical obituaries were written was located in the early 1970s. Especially the years between 1967 and 1975 became the Golden Age of the "New Hollywood," beginning with Bonnie and Clyde (Arthur Penn, 1967), The Graduate (Mike Nichols, 1967), Easy Rider (Dennis Hopper/Peter Fonda, 1968) and ending with Roman Polanski's Chinatown (1974), Martin Scorsese's Taxi Driver (1975) and Robert Altman's Nashville (1975). Coincidentally or not, these were also the years of the most violent social and political upheavals the United States had experienced for at least a generation, and probably not since the Depression in the mid-1930s. Between the assassination of Martin Luther King in April 1968, and Richard Nixon's resignation in August 1974, America underwent a period of intense collective soul-searching, fueled by open generational conflict, and no less bitter struggles around what came to be known as "race" and "gender." The protests against the Vietnam War, the Civil Rights movement and the emergence of feminism gave birth to an entirely different political culture, acutely reflected in a spate of movies that often enough were as unsuccessful with the mass public as they were audacious, creative and offbeat, according to the critics. The paradox of the New Hollywood was that the loss of confidence of the nation, its self-doubt about "liberty and justice for all" in those years, did little to stifle the energies of several groups of young filmmakers. They registered the moral malaise, but it did not blunt their appetite for stylistic or formal experiment. They put aimless, depressive or (self-) destructive characters on the screen, but the subject matter was often bold and unconventional, in settings that were strikingly beautiful, even—especially—in their unglamorous everydayness. A whole new America came into view, thanks to the work of Monte Hellman, Bob Rafelson, Hal Ashby, Joseph McBride, Peter Bogdanovich, Jerry Schatzberg, Terrence Malick, James Toback, Dennis Hopper: there, one came across rural backwaters, motels, rust-belt towns and Bible-belt communities, out-of-season resorts and other places of Americana, whose desolation or poignancy had rarely been conveyed with such visual poetry, enriched by oddball characters, a love of landscape and a delicacy of mood and sensibility, even in scenes of violence or torpor.

This American cinema of the 1970s is sometimes referred to as the decade of the lost generation (or of "lost illusions"), at other times recognized as the first of at least two "New" Hollywoods, though perhaps the one without which the other—the 1980s cinema of Francis Coppola, Steven Spielberg, George Lucas, Robert Zemeckis, Tim Burton—could not have come into being. Such an assertion, however, risks provoking immediate protest, because where the historian detects continuities, the critic sees unbridgeable gaps of talent and integrity. The scholarly debate has tried to find, beyond the critical divides, a new understanding of the phenomenal—and in light of the many "death of cinema" predictions during the 1970s and 1980s, also unexpected—box-office revival of Hollywood in the 1980s and 1990s requires a revision of how we see the American cinema of the 1970s. No longer (only) as the endpoint of the classical studio epoch and the all-too-brief flourishing of an American *auteur* cinema in the European mold, but as the period that allowed an astonishing array of talent, of contending and often even contradictory forces within US movie-making to come to the fore. The late 1960s and early 1970s are a genuine period of transition, as momentous in some ways as that in the late 1920s and early 1930s, when the coming of sound changed the structure of the film industry even faster than the film forms could follow, breaking open genres and styles, and in the process producing hybrids or, unexpectedly, a new prototype or cycle. Similarly in the 1970s: one can see several forks in the road, leading in directions (regrettably) not taken, and too many talents gave up in frustration, or were sidelined and subsequently fell silent. But the historical distance also makes evident the sheer scope of what was possible, by trial and error, by happenstance or unsuspected affinity: the unlikely blend, for instance, of avant-garde and exploitation, or the fusion of rock music and movies, both of which changed the traditional genres, just before new technologies of sound and image also began to have an equally great impact, and once more altered the course of the Hollywood revival.

Digital technologies did mark a watershed in the mid-1980s, but they were certainly not the only and maybe not even the decisive forces. Other—economic, managerial, demographic and "global"— factors that subsequently turned the Hollywood cinema into the gigantic world-wide entertainment machine of blockbusters it is today, also began to make themselves felt in the 1970s, often in the same places, and occasionally even promoted by the same people that were at the forefront of what was then hailed as the New Hollywood. Whether one regards their crossover as compromise, opportunism or even betrayal, it is undeniable that Francis Coppola, Martin Scorsese, Steven Spielberg, George Lucas, Jack Nicholson, Warren Beatty or Robert de Niro (among others) have so stamped the public image of American cinema over several decades, that their choices, moves and gambles set an agenda of sorts which at least in part determined the dynamics behind the shifts from one New Hollywood to the next. In other words, their presence in the early 1970s also prepared what was to follow, for good or ill, which suggests that there is reason to reassess the 1970s in the light of the 1990s and beyond, and to provide, whatever one's aesthetics and cinephile preferences, also a "revisionist" account next to the retrospective one: both serving, when taken together, as part of the archaeology of the present.

Such a revisionist account may take the form of a "canonical" story, in which the changes that have taken place in American cinema between the 1960s and the 1980s are now so apparently well understood that they fit into larger institutional frameworks of Hollywood history, while also corresponding to larger models of economic transformation and business practice under conditions of post-industrialism. In this canonical story, spanning the late 1940s to the late 1980s, the directors and the films of the years 1967 to 1975, for instance—the emergence of an American *auteur* cinema, the early years of the so-called movie brats, the many talents that perhaps shone too brightly and hence too briefly—mark at best the exception. At worst, they are merely the blip in that otherwise logical and largely unproblematic history of the continuities of the American cinema almost since its beginnings. What counts are the Paramount decree in 1948 and the rise of television, the changes in the rating system in 1968, the Time Warner merger in 1990, rather than the unfulfilled promises of a Bob Rafelson, Terrence Malick and Monte Hellman, or the early successes of an Arthur Penn or Peter Bogdanovich.

But there is another "revisionist" story, more small-scale and local, but as much part of the history of classical cinema, of "New Hollywood," of American independent cinema and developments behind the label "post-classical." This story would set out to record distinct moments in time that overlap, run parallel or are contiguous, rather than form a continuous, more or less unbroken, line. The history of the New York avant-garde and that of (New) Hollywood barely touched, but once in a while made sudden contact, in the person of Dennis Hopper, for instance, as Jonathan Rosenbaum has pointed out, or in the brief encounter that Jim Hoberman once staged for Don Siegel and Clint Eastwood with Andy Warhol and Joe Dalessandro, when he compared COOGAN's BLUFF with LONESOME COWBOYS (both 1968).[2] There is the change of generations, where directors Robert Aldrich (b. 1918), Robert Altman (b. 1925), Arthur Penn (b. 1922) and Sam Peckinpah (b. 1925) all made films that count as New Hollywood. Their careers overlap with those of a younger generation (Martin Scorsese, b. 1942, Brian de Palma, b. 1940, George Lucas, b. 1944, Paul Schrader b. 1946), whose own role in this *auteur* cinema is both crucial and ambiguous. Equally typical for the 1970s is the role of godfathers like Orson Welles (for Bogdanovich, Jaglom, arguably for Malick and more indirectly, but also more decisively for Coppola), Hitchcock (for de Palma and Spielberg), Michael Powell (for Scorsese) and Roger Corman (for just about everybody else). Many temporalities are thus present simultaneously in the apparently single chronology of 1967 to 1975, tracing the different timelines, and also showing where they break off or suddenly resurface.

These several cinematic genres and topographies just mentioned—avant-garde, mainstream, art cinema, exploitation—map themselves across geographical divides, such as New York and Los Angeles, Paris and New York, with an occasional detour via London. More broadly speaking, Europe and/versus America are, from the critical point of view, the tectonic plates and poles of mutual attraction in the seismic shifts that shook the American cinema during that period, before the transfers and crossovers became global (Asian cinema, Australian cinema) in the 1980s, and the transformations pushed by certain commercial and technological innovations (video recorder and video-store, special effects and digital imaging) began to favor multinational and corporate players on the global stage.

The Canonical Story

But first of all, once more a look at what I have called the canonical story. Earlier, I suggested that for many film historians, the New Hollywood of the late 1960s now appears as an interesting, but otherwise intermediate episode: a happy accident to some, a symptomatic aberration to others, but at any rate, a moment of hesitation, while the juggernaut of the corporate entertainment business changed gears, taking a few years to get back on track, during which Europe could foster (and finance) its various New Waves, while America afforded itself (by panicky studios heads briefly bankrolling television upstarts and industry outsiders) the New Hollywood. It was Tom Schatz who summarized most concisely what was to become the canonical story:

> [The] movie industry underwent three fairly distinct decade-long phases after the War—from 1946 to 1955, from 1956 to 1965, and from 1966 to 1975. These phases were distinguished by various developments both inside and outside the industry, and four in particular: the shift to

independent motion picture production, the changing role of the studios, the emergence of commercial television, and changes in American lifestyle and patterns of media consumption.[3]

In line with the more economic emphasis of such a perspective, the canonical narrative tends to give space to the film industry version and underlines the institutional factors, rather than telling the story from the directors' point of view, which favors a Portrait of the Artist. Or the journalist, who develops a wider analysis around an individual film and spots significant social trends in genres and cycles. Although contrasting with the often polemical tone of the critics, whether partisan or participating observers, the canonical account nonetheless contains many elements that were first proposed by critics.[4] For instance, Pauline Kael had already identified some of the crucial shifts in her review of BONNIE AND CLYDE in 1967, still considered the first full-blown manifestations of the New Hollywood, with its triple agenda of self-obsessed youth, aestheticized violence and a distrust or contempt for all forms of established authority. The December 1967 issue of *Time Magazine* officially announced a "renaissance" of American cinema, and identified complex narratives, hybrid plots, stylistic flourishes and taboo subject matter as its hallmarks. Beverly Walker, writing in 1971, flags several other components. In an article entitled "Go West Young Man" she takes that other landmark film, EASY RIDER, as her point of departure for a discussion of the changes within the film industry.[5] Apart from also mentioning subject matter with youth appeal and a low budget, she points out that established actors became engaged in moviemaking; that record companies and other American media industries began investing in films; and that finally, new production companies, such as BBS, smaller and more flexible, were set up to produce these movies.

Walker also notes that by 1971 the brief renaissance was already over, with producers and studios retrenching. She points to the resurgence of genre-filmmaking, with new directors having to "go the porn-horror-violence route" if they were to secure the (low budget) financing which the EASY RIDER formula had pioneered. The directors of this first New Hollywood in fact faced some of the same problems as their European counterparts, even if on a different scale: there too, getting finance for a second film was contingent on the box-office (or festival) success of the first. And even where the first film had been a critical success, if the second found little or no distribution, it often terminated a promising talent's career. In Hollywood, the old industry norms were quickly re-established, with control over distribution and exhibition outlets becoming once more the factors that counted, not the director's artistic control: he or she had to do-it-yourself, as in the case of Tom Laughlin's four-wall exhibition methods for his BILLY JACK (1971), or claw back control by becoming producers, as in the case of Coppola, Spielberg or Lucas, three of the leading names of the second New Hollywood.

The film historians who since the late 1980s have studied the American cinema of the 1970s— besides Tom Schatz, I am thinking of Janet Staiger, Kristin Thompson and David Bordwell, Douglas Gomery, Robert C. Allen, Janet Wasko, Tino Balio, Tim Corrigan, Jon Lewis, Richard Maltby and David Cook—have put the salient features of the New Hollywood already named by Kael, Walker and others in a broader historical framework, usually combining economic, industrial, demographic and institutional factors. The result is a composite, but there is general agreement on the outlines, and often even the particulars, of the story of Hollywood's fall and rise between the late 1950s and the early 1980s. Some historians give more prominence to the agents-turned-producers (Lew Wasserman, David Geffen) and to the rise of the package and the deal-makers (Barry Diller, Steve Ross, Sumner Redstone), than to actors, writers or directors; they discuss the shifts in media ownership and the business management practices brought in after the several waves of take-overs and mergers affecting the (assets of the) major studios (Kirk Kerkorian, Ted Turner, Rupert Murdoch); and they underline the changes in the institutional-legal frameworks under which the

American cinema operated, the dates of which I already mentioned: the disinvestiture imposed on the studios by the Paramount decree of 1948, changes in the industry's self-censorship (abandonment of the Hays Code, the revision(s) of the rating system) in the late 1960s, the relaxation of the anti-trust laws during the Reagan presidency, culminating in the abandonment of the Treasury's case against the Time Warner merger in the early 1990s. The net result of focusing on these developments is to argue that by the mid- to late 1980s, Hollywood had effectively undone the consequences of the post-war decartelization, and had—in somewhat different forms, and in a quite different media environment—de facto re-established the business practices once known generically as vertical integration, that is, the controlling ownership of the sites (studios) and means (stars, personnel) of production, (access to) all the relevant platforms of delivery and distribution and (programing power over) the premier exhibition outlets.

Closure in the canonical story of the renaissance of American cinema is thus provided by a return to the beginnings, the re-establishment of the status quo ante, in good classical Hollywood narrative terms. In many ways the canonical story claims that, by the end of the 1980s, it was business as usual. Hollywood had once more demonstrated its deeply conservative character, where the fundamental forces at work confirm that the American cinema is remarkably (or infuriatingly) stable: a self-regulating organism, whose strength, or indeed, whose "genius of the system," in André Bazin's famous words, "lies in the richness of its ever vigorous tradition, and its fertility when it comes into contact with new elements."[6] This may be too blithely optimistic an account for those who think the American cinema died around 1980, and too coarse-grained for those, who—noting some of the more subtle, but nonetheless substantial changes—think it justified to use the terms "post-classical" or "neo-classical." However, adaptability, the absorption of foreign elements, the appropriation of talent and incorporation of innovative techniques were already part of Bazin's definition of the classical.[7]

Crossover *Auteurism*

The question raised in the minds of some historians is whether the non-classical, romantic, European, baroque aesthetics, as well as the antagonistic, critical and countercultural energies manifest in the first New Hollywood were a genuine, if short-lived and aborted alternative, or whether the misfits, rebels and outsiders were necessary for the "system" to first adjust and then to renew itself. This application of the push-pull model, too, may be too neat—or cynical—an opposition, but as I shall argue, it is an option worth thinking about. What the reference to the industrial, managerial and legal frameworks of the American mainstream movie business in any case does provide is a foil against which more text-immanent, deconstructive or self-reflexive and allegorical analyses of individual films can be read. To signal a few of the connections that are often being made: the New Hollywood links with European art cinema; the contacts with the (New York) avant-garde; the hybridization of genres; the "allusionism" and self-referential dimension of pastiche and irony; the role of an earlier generation of "Godfathers" of New Hollywood, or the impact of Roger Corman; the political dimension of Vietnam and the Nixon years; the macho codes and troubled gender relations; the implications for narrative structure and story motivation; and finally, the dimension of post-Fordism (John and Henry), and the hegemonic force of the Hollywood Empire established, as it "struck" back against European, avant-garde or independent cinema, with its carefully timed event-movies.

In what follows, I want to thematize one aspect of the "micro-history" of American *auteur* cinema in the 1970s, namely the different "crossovers" involved in its several moments of transfer, transition and backtrack. Crossover above all, in the directors' many filiations to distinct traditions within American filmmaking, including those to the generation that preceded them. But crossover also, in the meaning we attribute to the various levels of analysis (historical, political, institutional) usually invoked in order to explain the moves and maneuvers from Old Hollywood to New Hollywood, and from New to New Economy or Contemporary Hollywood.

The European Crossover and the French Connection. What cannot be stressed often enough is just how crucial, but also contradictory the idea of an *auteur* cinema was, and why it should establish itself in America at this point in time. Some explanations are well known: first of all, there is the influence of European cinema of the 1950s and 1960s, and especially the combined impact of the French nouvelle vague and their reassessment of (classical) Hollywood cinema, via *Cahiers du cinéma* and its *politique des auteurs*. Emblematically this link is preserved in the now quasi-mythical story of Robert Benton and David Newman's script of BONNIE AND CLYDE having been written for François Truffaut, and then offered to Jean-Luc Godard. Other explanations stress the role played by the newly founded film departments at NYU, UCLA and USC, where future directors were trained not only in filmmaking, but took classes in cinema studies. They read Bazin, rediscovered Ford, Hawks, Walsh, Lang, and emulated Hitchcock or Welles, once primed by Manny Farber's writings and Andrew Sarris' *The American Cinema: Directors and Directions*, before publishing essays on *film noir*, or Master's Theses on *Transcendental Style in Film: Ozu, Bresson, Dreyer* (Paul Schrader). Then, there are style features and filmic techniques with a specifically "expressive" charge, such as freeze-frame, the zoom or slow motion. Whether these are "European" imports in films such as THE GRADUATE, THE WILD BUNCH or BUTCH CASSIDY is debatable (they could also be seen as a technology transfer and a crossover from television), but in the cinema such devices were initially felt to be un-classical (and maybe even un-American), since they drew too much attention to themselves, allegedly lacking story-motivation and blocking transparency and therefore spectatorial identification: major sins in the classical Hollywood rule-book that have since become, if not virtues, then certainly well-understood conventions.

Taken together, European influence, film school training, a re-evaluation of American directors, and expressive style give body to the idea of the *auteur*, understood as the personality manifesting itself in a film or oeuvre through the singular "signature" or the authentic "voice." Peter Bogdanovich, for instance, appropriating the idea for his own generation, projected it back on the grand old masters of the classical American cinema, whom he interviewed in the late 1960s and early 1970s: "in all the films I really liked, there was a definite sense of one artist's vision, a feeling of the director's virtual presence within and outside the frames we watched: often you could recognise the personality from picture to picture, as you could various paintings from the same hand." And in support, he quotes Howard Hawks, who provides him with the title of his book: "I liked almost anybody [in Hollywood] that made you realise who in the devil was making the picture. . . . Because the director's the storyteller and should have his own method of telling it."[8] What is perhaps elided is the difference between the romantic conception of the artist-*auteur* (of the New Hollywood) and the classical artist-*auteur*, a difference discussed in several of the other essays above.

Important aspects of the Europe-Hollywood story not discussed here are, for instance, the literary influences. But the role of Rudolf Wurlitzer in getting the script for TWO-LANE BLACKTOP published in *Esquire* as advance publicity for the movie or Paul Schrader's well-known obsession with Dostoevsky, Sartre and Camus do not establish quite such a strong link between cinema and literature as the adaptations and the collaboration between writers and filmmakers during the same time (and somewhat earlier) in the European cinema, when one thinks of Alain Resnais (Jean Cayrol, Marguerite Duras, Alain Robbe-Grillet), Wim Wenders (Peter Handke) or of an American in Europe, such as Joseph Losey (Harold Pinter).

The European connection also goes the other way, when one recalls just how many European directors actually went to the United States from the late 1960s onwards, often on the strength of the reputation they had built up in the meantime among New York cinephiles, but also because Hollywood, in a well-known practice, was keen to put under contract foreign talent with box office potential. Working for the American market, their names could also be exploited overseas. Not everyone, however, had the staying power of a Roman Polanski, a Milos Forman or, a little later, Louis Malle. Michelangelo Antonioni's ZABRISKIE POINT (1968) has remained the classic case study of all that can go wrong for both parties in this marriage of European *auteur* and Hollywood studio. Alexander Horwath once pointed to a counter-example when he argued that the brief sojourn of the French *nouvelle vague* in America also produced two under-rated—perhaps because so self-reflexively documentary—films about the mutual attractions and misunderstandings between Paris, New York and Los Angeles: the ironic and sharply observed LION'S LOVE by Agnes Varda, and her husband's, Jacques Demy's more playful, melancholy MODEL SHOP (both 1969). Not until the 1980s, when Wenders, an equally sensitive and cinephile soul, briefly left Germany for his Zoetrope adventure in San Francisco (HAMMETT, 1983), would there be such a hopeful if ultimately unhappy encounter between European *auteurism* and the New Hollywood.

The Crossovers with the Avant-garde and Exhibition. In an important essay tracing the influence on the mainstream of the European nouvelle vague—the key films are LAST YEAR IN MARIENBAD, SHOOT THE PIANO PLAYER and BAND OF OUTSIDERS—Jonathan Rosenbaum also discusses the links between New York avant-garde and mainstream movies. But for him the impact of the films of Kenneth Anger and Andy Warhol, for instance, had more to do with subject matter—homoeroticism, sex, drugs—than style, so that these films, like similar ones from Europe, mostly prepared the general public for changes that were then reflected in the new rating systems, which in turn underlines the capital importance of exhibition.[9] Noting how many of the films from the 1970s we now consider the period's artistic highlights never had an American release, Rosenbaum argued that the so-called art houses in Europe in the 1970s began to promote the blending of hitherto distinct film cultures. Retrospectives of mainstream directors elevated to *auteur* status, avant-garde films, art-cinema or independent directors' work were all shown in the same venues. In the US, such spaces did not exist, so that the films either ended up in what Rosenbaum aptly calls a "rather specialised no-man's land," or they had to wait until retrieved from limbo by the class-rooms of the academy, not altogether appropriate for experimental films, for instance, since "it tended to remove [them] from the social spaces of ordinary or makeshift movie theatres and relegate them to safer confines of various institutional venues."[10]

What here justifies the tone of regret is the value placed on the actual experience of cinema. The base note is the recollection of films as they came alive in a particular location, the sensation of the images projected onto a screen, viewed alone or with someone special across a possibly vast and darkened auditorium. But almost as relevant is the outside: the built site, the movie front or façade, the location on a particular block or street. The preference was for the neighborhood or small-town movie house (as in Bogdanovich's THE LAST PICTURE SHOW, 1971), frequented during the years of their slow decline into seediness, or their rebirth as art houses (as described in Rosenbaum's autobiographical *Moving Places*). A picture show still meant the big screen, and maybe even, as in Bogdanovich's first film TARGETS (1968), the drive-in cinemas.[11] The New Hollywood, which for its makers just as much as for its admirers so definitely belongs in the cinemas, often found little or no distribution, and eventually happened on late-night television or in film classes: it makes these movies, in the best possible sense, once more manifestos of "cinephilia," the love of cinema, and not just of films.

Crossovers between the different sites, where spectators now encounter movies, and even more so, crossover between different storage media and media-platforms are one of the major features of the second New Hollywood. This is why exhibition is often the key change that is tracked in the canonical story.[12] The forced separation of the studios from their prime exhibition outlets through the Paramount decree, which also made block-booking illegal, initiated the experiments with roadshowing, four-walling and other attempts at attracting special attention for what became a film-by-film business.[13] But beginning in the mid-1970s (with the marketing of JAWS as the break-through case), distribution-exhibition started once more to take the lead over production, so much so that the system eventually stabilized itself around saturation booking, coordinated release dates and the targeting of public holiday weekends. A further consequence (or is it cause?) of the new type of event-movie (commonly referred to by the curiously anachronistic and in the meantime oxymoronic term blockbuster) was that secondary exploitation now happened in the ancillary markets: television, toy-shops, video game arcades, clothing and fashion outlets, consumer electronics, theme-parks and, since the 1980s and 1990s, video-cassettes and DVDs. Not only does exhibition wag the production dog (and thus also the *auteur*), the primary exhibition outlet—the cinema (movie palace or multiplex)—is itself wagged by the secondary markets of the broader entertainment industries and the experience economy, by becoming their advertising billboard.

In these changes from production towards marketing, the first New Hollywood occupied perhaps a more ambiguous place than the lament over lack of exhibition suggests. Besides Spielberg's and Lucas' well-ventilated role as crossover figures in the mid-1970s, there is the case of EASY RIDER. It made industry history by its highly favorable ratio of production cost to box-office earnings, as well as by establishing once and for all the youth appeal that motion picture mass entertainment henceforth had to have, and which included the sound-track as an integral marketing tool. Another case study was Tom Laughlin's campaign for getting his BILLY JACK to carefully targeted audiences, which also showed the industry the way towards advertising-led, media-blitz promotion techniques. These marketing and exhibition practices, in other words, supported by new delivery systems and the digital technologies of sound and image reproduction turned the big screen picture into something that superficially seems the same and that has yet changed utterly. As David Thomson once remarked when he called the 1970s "the decade when movies mattered," it is also because it was the last decade without the video-recorder. In the 1980s, there are still big screens—in fact, they are now often even bigger than they used to be in the 1960s and 1970s—but their function has doubled: site of an intensified experience, they are also a blockbuster's "screen test," first inflating the images, before they shrink and disperse, percolating through a multitude of media outlets, all the way down to the video-rental store, at once the morgue, the supermarket and the permanent museum of our film culture.

The Generational Crossover. It (almost) goes without saying that these *auteur*-directors—the old ones whom Bogdanovich was interviewing, as well as the new ones he introduces alongside himself in the opening pages—Henry Jaglom and Warren Beatty—are *male*. However, the male values on display are suitably multiple and ambivalent. The *auteur* concepts as interpreted by American filmmakers left room for the rugged individualist, but also for the anxious loner, for the compulsive womanizer, the hard drugs user, as well as the flamboyantly gay avant-gardist. There are long-haired heroes of the counter-cultures and inner city losers, caught in cycles of self-destructive violence. In some cases, the directors also played the leads in their films (Dennis Hopper, Peter Fonda, Tom Laughlin, Jack Nicholson), and in others, a handful of male actors (Warren Oates, Jack Nicholson, Robert de Niro, Harvey Keitel) are fictionalized stand-ins or ironically idealized alter egos (for Hellman, Rafelson, Scorsese). That there is another male dimension to this *auteurism* has already been mentioned in connection with Peter Bogdanovich: the generational "thing," the typically oedipal mix of admiration, emulation and rebellion shown towards an earlier generation of directors, to whom the label "Godfathers of the New Hollywood" would seem to apply.[14]

Such (Oedipal) Godfathers can be understood within the template of auterism European style, when we think of how Eric Rohmer, Jacques Rivette and Claude Chabrol called themselves Hitchcocko-Hawksians, how Godard stylized himself as Fritz Lang's "assistant" in LE MÉPRIS (1963) and as "son" ("ciné-fils") of Roberto Rossellini, and how Truffaut balanced his need for father-figures between the somewhat antithetical figures of André Bazin and Alfred Hitchcock, Jean Renoir and

Orson Welles. As already hinted, Coppola, Scorsese, Schrader, de Palma and others also picked elective paternities, including Spielberg when—repaying the compliment, as it were—he asked Truffaut to play the fatherly French scientist in Close Encounters of the Third Kind (1977). Coppola, in turn, could be said to have become Godfather to a subsequent generation, including European directors, when he distributed in the US the films of Werner Herzog and Hans Jürgen Syberberg, or invited Wenders to direct a movie for his Zoetrope company. I have already mentioned how unhappy an experience this proved to be for the German director, so much so that he felt impelled to make a movie about it. The State of Things (1982) is a film about filmmaking made back-to-back with Raoul Ruiz's The Territory (1981) in Lisbon, for Portugese-French producer Paolo Branco, featuring another adopted Godfather-*auteur*, the veteran Hollywood maverick Sam Fuller, making a film-within-the-film. But a truly inspired piece of casting on the part of Wenders was to give the role of the lawyer of Coppola's (fictional) stand-in to Roger Corman, since Corman in a sense played for Coppola the Godfather part that Coppola played for Wenders (not forgetting that Paolo Branco was a European Corman to both Wenders and Ruiz).

The Corman Connection

The historical crux here is the role of Corman in the story of the New Hollywood. The Corman legend and legacy fits the Godfather paradigm, but nonetheless opens up another genealogy. Maitland McDonaugh has plotted the convoluted undergrowth of "exploitation" filmmaking, with its mixture of grind-house, sweatshop and the various archipelagos of creative freedom, experiment and even exuberance that existed in this domain.[15] Her essay soon tracks down this most improbable source of the New Hollywood, geographically much closer to hand, and aesthetically more subterranean than that of European art-cinema. At the center is not an *auteur*-artist, but an entrepreneur, not a single masterpiece, but a stream of low-budget B-pictures, made at the margins of the studio system, but nevertheless mimicking it; made not on the expensive, labor-intensive real-estate of Culver City or Burbank, but on abandoned industrial terrain and disused railroad property behind Venice Beach.

Corman's production companies AIP (American International Pictures, owned by Samuel Z. Arkoff) and New World Pictures (co-owned by Corman and his brother Gene) made biker movies and women prison movies, jungle movies and monster movies. Most of them may have been forgotten, but he is respectfully remembered by the whole generation of young ex-film graduates, the movie brats, to whom he gave a chance as cinematographers, script-writers, sound technicians, editors, actors and second unit directors. As McDonagh has shown, the names of the people who worked for Corman, indeed were often "exploited" by him, reads like a Who's Who of New Hollywood: among the directors, Martin Scorsese, Francis Ford Coppola, George Lucas, Peter Bogdanovich, Bob Rafelson and Monte Hellman, and among the actor-directors Dennis Hopper, Peter Fonda and Jack Nicholson, among the actors Bruce Dern and Warren Oates, and among the writers Robert Towne and John Milius.

But Corman and his lurid adaptations of Edgar Allen Poe stories, his cheap horror films or youth movies had another function relevant to our argument. If in the late 1960s, it was he who supplied the dying neighborhood flea-pits, the drive-in cinemas, the bottom half of double-bills in the disreputable end of the teen-market, he was also, in the 1970s, the American distributor of Ingmar Bergman, Federico Fellini, Francois Truffaut, Joseph Losey, Volker Schloendorff and Alain Resnais. Thus, thinking through the issue of exhibition sites mentioned earlier, one is led to another form of crossover. For Corman provides also a link between the declining second-run cinemas and their (occasional) re-emergence as art houses. Already mentioned in the passage cited from Beverly Walker about the "porn-horror-violence route" is the suggestion that the US notion of the art house was of strategic importance for the 1970s *auteur* sector not least because of a fruitful confusion between different kinds of transgression, taboo-breaking and deviancy. With their reputation for "adult movies" (in the years prior to the abandonment of the Hays Code and changes in local censorship and the industry's own rating system), the art houses were home to some of the strangest encounters between European *auteur* cinema and commercial productions, whether from the maverick mainstream, from off-Hollywood B-picture genres, or from the sex- and blaxploitation sector. By providing both stage and outlet for New Hollywood, European *auteur* films, as well as exploitation movies, New World Pictures and the art house circuits invented the idea of the cult film or the "cult classic," labels later taken over by the successors of all second-run movie houses: the inner-city basement, commercial strip or suburban shopping mall video store, mythical breeding ground of Quentin Tarantino's mercurial talent.

In other words, even though Corman did not exactly embody the European concept of the *auteur*, any more than he was an avant-garde artist, his operation was such a vibrant and improbable hybrid that the Corman connection may be the closest the 1970s came to supplying an authentically American pedigree for the *auteur* theory as it "went West" and found itself practically and unselfconsciously applied in a volatile industry situation. His version of autonomy-within-the-system even provides a clue to how the second New Hollywood evolved out of the first: if one re-centers American *auteurism* from New York and Paris to Los Angeles and San Francisco, then—leaving aside for a moment differences of scale, as well as ambition—it may not be altogether fanciful to see the Godfather Corman pass the baton to the Godfather Coppola, before the Zoetrope enterprise overreached itself and had to be "rescued" by the bankers and the corporate suits, a lesson not lost on some of Coppola's fellow-alumni from the Corman Academy, UCLA and USC, who met the suits halfway.[16] Spielberg, Lucas, Milius could be more circumspect and prudent, not least because of the combined example of Corman and Coppola. In different ways, they blended the *auteur* with the entrepreneur, when they began making common cause with the new studio managers, the dealstrikers, talent agents, advertising executives and marketing men. If this may be no recommendation for their artistic integrity, it nevertheless, I would suggest, opens up an intriguing perspective when examining the shifts from one New Hollywood to the next.

Crossovers in the Modes of Production. For another defining feature of (the second) New Hollywood in the canonical story is the debate over the mode of production which characterizes the "renaissance" and its aftermath. If one argues from an *auteurist* perspective, there seems to be a clear opposition: the old Hollywood studio-system worked according to a recognizably industrial model, which—so the 1960s' eventually ruinous overproduction seemed to prove—collapsed of its own weight and inflexibility. It was superseded by the more nimble, small-is-beautiful, artisanal mode of American independent film production, for which the producer-writer-director, negotiating with the studios on a film-by-film basis, or a production company dedicated to its creative talent seemed to be the pragmatic mode of organization. The ideal(ized) model, in the 1970s, was BBS (founded by Bert Schneider, Bob Rafelson and Steve Blauner) which produced EASY RIDER and TWO-LANE BLACKTOP. The exact relation of the one-man independents to the studios, and to distribution awaits examination in more detail,[17] but it has been noted that several major studios themselves took risks and hired considerably younger and sometimes untested heads of production, most famously perhaps Robert ("the kid stays on the picture") Evans at Paramount (producing Coppola's GODFATHER films [1972–74], Polanski's ROSEMARY's BABY [1968] and then the same director's CHINATOWN [1975]).

Despite elements of crossover between Old and New Hollywood, the gap between New and New New, with regard to production, seemed to become wider and wider as the decade wore on. In most directors' biographies (Penn, Peckinpah, Rafelson, Ashby, Hellman, Bogdanovich) the pattern of rapid decline or of patchy alternation between so-called commercial and more personal projects is by and large remarkably similar, however different their biographical circumstances. It even includes the more mainstream figures such as William Friedkin, Alan J. Pakula and Bob Fosse, whose films could also be considered harbingers of the genre-based blockbusters of the 1980s. The exceptions among the generation born before 1940 are Robert Altman, whose production company Lion's Gate might fit the BBS model, and Stanley Kubrick, who moved to England and even more than Altman became a one-man studio. Despite ups and down at the box-office, their work remained very consistently "*auteurist*," and above all, they were "survivors" with a steady output of films (though this is more true of Altman, protected by Alan Ladd Jr. at Fox, than of Kubrick who required much bigger budgets). Kubrick, however, is remarkable in another sense, in that, belonging to the *auteurs*, he nonetheless had an inordinate influence not so much on the first New Hollywood as on the second, insofar as each of his films from DR STRANGELOVE (1964) and 2001: A SPACE ODYSSEY (1968) onwards was a kind of prototype (of the science fiction film, of ultraviolence, of the costume film, the horror film) that others could adapt into a blockbuster formula. That Spielberg should be the one to direct and produce the long-nursed, but in the event posthumous Kubrick project A.I. (2001) emblematically pays tribute to this fact.

For the canonical story, the typical feature of the New New is the package deal, put together by agents-turned-powerbrokers, or the star-turned-producer, rather than a project initiated by either the director or by a producer working closely with the director (BBS, Robert Evans). The package deal thus not only superseded the studio-system's way of making movies, with its fixed production facilities, personnel under contract and pre-planned release schedules. It was also inimical to the *auteur* cinema, since the director may very well not have been the key element of the package, although in the case of Kubrick, and later Spielberg (or briefly, Quentin Tarantino), a "director as superstar" did represent a production value in his own right. In this respect, the director in the New Economy Hollywood is part of the marketing, which means that s/he is neither unrecognized, as might have been the case in the darker days of the studio-system, nor the admired *auteur* of the 1960s. Instead, s/he figures as an entrepreneurial brand name, who very often has to become a celebrity and media star, on a par with the leading actors, in order to maintain his/her box-office value.

In Praise of Pilot Fish

There is, however, another way of looking at the changes in the modes of production that took place around the mid-1970s, which modifies somewhat the oppositions just sketched. Taking a broader view, one can think of the classical Hollywood studio-system with its vertical integration as following the Fordist principles of industrial production, centered on a fixed production site, an in-house division of labor (the assembly-line) and producer-units. In such an environment, the product's outlets (the first run cinemas) and the final consumers (the family audience) are relatively stable and known quantities, while competition among different producers is regulated in the form of a cartel or trust. By contrast, the New Economy Hollywood mode of production, based (at the production end) on the package deal and driven (at the exhibition end) by more market-oriented, targeted campaigns to capture the fickle tastes, the unpredictable behavior and the floating age-and-gender balance of the ever more youthful cinema audiences, would qualify as an essentially post-Fordist model of industrial production. Its economic and managerial organization is that of conglomerate ownership, as it evolved across the two major waves of mergers and takeovers, the first in the early 1970s (by companies seeking diversification), and the second in the late 1980s (by companies seeking synergies). The diversified nature of conglomerate ownership necessarily leads to decentralization, sub-contracting and outsourcing, which would be a more technical description of the package deal. Murray Smith, referring himself to an article by Michael Storper, identifies the blockbuster era thus as post-Fordist, integrating the film industry into the bigger picture of post-industrial trends in the developed world towards service-industries, when manufacturing became more responsive to new patterns of consumption that split the mass-market into fluctuating cycles of demand, "boutique" tastes and niche markets. Smith, however, also adds a proviso, namely that the analogy may not be entirely appropriate, if one concedes that the classical cinema was less Fordist in the 1940s and 1950s than other industries, while also allowing for the possibility that Hollywood of the 1980s and 1990s is less post-Fordist than it appears, since production has always been a function of distribution, which has remained very centralized, both prior to and since the Paramount decree.[18]

It is this glass half-full/glass half-empty argument over the degrees of Fordist or post-Fordist organization in the film industry between 1950 and 1990 that give the cinema of the 1970s its proper place: as a distinct moment, and nevertheless, part of several ongoing but contradictory processes. The West Coast genealogy of American *auteurism* I have sketched above (where, at the limit, Corman's family/academy/factory not only mirrors the studio-system but also parallels and inverts the East Coast family/academy/factory of Andy Warhol), as well as the production methods of post-Fordist outsourcing as practiced by Corman's New World Pictures and Coppola's Zoetrope point to elements of the New Hollywood that the New New Hollywood would learn from (with Lucas' Industrial Light and Magic or John Lassiter's Pixar becoming rich and famous as highly specialized suppliers). Corman and Coppola were research-and-development units for—inadvertent or intentional—prototypes, but they were also do-it-yourself mini-versions (low-tech in Corman's, high-tech in Coppola's case) of various kinds of industrial post-Fordism. The same could be said, in different degrees, about Altman, Kubrick, Scorsese who, as it were, outsourced themselves in relation to the Hollywood studios' newly consolidated function as world-wide distributors. They developed prototypes for movie or television mass-production (the television series spin-off like *M*A*S*H, Happy Days* [after Lucas' AMERICAN GRAFFITI] or *Alice* [after Scorsese's ALICE DOESN'T LIVE HERE ANYMORE], and the systematic planning of sequels and prequels in the wake of STAR WARS). In this version, Corman would not so much be the Godfather within the oedipal paradigm of surrogate family and elective paternity. Rather, his production methods would be an ad hoc but also parodic version of post-Fordism, with sub-contracting and the exploitation of non-Union labor power both assuring his relative economic success as well as confirming his outsider status and pariah role within the Hollywood establishment.[19]

As an alternative (or sub-category) of post-Fordism, economists like Storper and neo-Marxists like Asu Aksoi and Kevin Robins have identified a two-tier industrial dualism, where the independents or small-scale entrepreneurs act as both "shock absorbers" and "pilot fish,"[20] which corresponds roughly to the push-pull model I mentioned earlier, and is reminiscent of the relation between the hackers in the earlier years of the computer industry, whose attacks on IBM accidentally or strategically helped "debug" the corporate giant's software. Applied to the film industry of the late 1960s and 1970s, the pilot fish model would specify that the old studios/new corporate conglomerates sought to renew themselves by "attracting risk capital and creative talent which [they could] then exploit through their control of distribution,"[21] or in the hacker analogy, the *auteurs* would have been the ones whose prototypes (but also failures) helped debug the Hollywood production system, as it slowly but inevitably moved from Fordist to post-Fordist modes of financing, marketing and asset management.

However, the transitions between the Old, the New and the New Economy Hollywood, according to this model, were not simply gradual or a matter of degree. The twists and turns would preserve their element of struggle, of antagonism and irreconcilable difference. The push-pull analogy (i.e. the mutual dependence between antagonistic forces) allows for the possibility that the protagonists involved in this story were often not in control of the parts they played (William Goldman's famous adage about Hollywood: "nobody knows anything," or the drug excesses chronicled by Peter Biskind), and that the story followed the law of unintended consequences. It also helps explain how and why there were so many crossovers and slippages: on the one side so many talents wasted, and on the other, so many talents "sleeping with the enemy." Put differently, but again, hopefully not too cynically, the *auteurs* drew their self-understanding from identifying with the ideology of the European artist (or the freewheeling spirit of the Corman operation and the various counter-cultures), while at another level they also played the role of the pilot fish: helping the white whales (or, more appropriately, sharks) of the blockbuster-era navigate the beach-area safely and profitably. So, in a sense, both factions could agree: long live the pilot fish.

Counter-Cultural Agendas

The "cynical" part of the argument would be its implications for the idealism of the period, the aesthetics of the films and the politics of their makers. For an additional issue concerns the value placed on the socially critical, or counter-cultural engagement of the films, as well as of the directors and writers: the paradox is that the American *auteurs* did not have to be of the left in the European sense of the term, or even liberal in the US sense (though many were). They could flaunt their love for the wide open spaces of the American West, and indulge in anti-modernist sentiments about cities, which Middle America might also have endorsed. But the landscapes and settings of New Hollywood show the ravages of an exploitative civilization, at the same time as they still hold out the promise of an unspoilt nature, glimpsed, as it were, out of the corner of the eye. Above all, there is the notable bias for the underdog, the outsider, the outlaw, the working man or disaffected middle-class protagonist, whose ideas of happiness and freedom imply emotional bonds that are lived outside the nuclear family, and for whom the romantic, heterosexual couple is not the end-point of the narrative, but doomed from the start, as in the many criminal couple films made in the wake of Bonnie and Clyde, such as Thieves Like Us or Badlands. Given that individualism and freedom are, in the American context, values prized in the vocabulary of the right as well as the left, the ideological makeup of New Hollywood has several dimensions, and the parties to the debate argue not infrequently at cross-purposes.

For instance, the counter-cultural crossover, staged between the law and the outlaw changing places or confusing the sides they are on, in Easy Rider, Sugarland Express, The Wild Bunch or McCabe and Mrs Miller, sometimes also form the bridge between high culture and popular culture. This encounter as well as clash is encapsulated in Jack Nicholson's Bobby Eroica Dupea, the protagonist of Five Easy Pieces, who leaves behind his middle-class home and college education, to do shift work as an oil-rigger, and who leaves Beethoven's piano sonatas behind for improvised jazz and blues. That he gets caught up with a waitress, whose elocution may be faulty and table-manners leave something to be desired, but whose emotional intelligence and sheer humanity knock spots off his blasé nihilism, is more than the attraction of opposites: it completes the hero's political, as well as his sentimental education. Generally, however, it is the twin strands of movies and rock music that braid the ideological texture of the protest movement and its sense of promise as well as pride, and thus define a major element of the period's political authenticity. *Auteurist* cinema and rock each had their distinct voice during the 1970s, but as never before or since, they entered into an exchange, a contest and occasionally even into a dialogue about what it meant to be American when one has reason to be ashamed for what is being done in its name, or when anger and despair about one's country were the only honest ways of being a patriot—the Bruce Springsteen way.[22] Some critics have argued that even the New Hollywood has done right by rock, among them also Wim Wenders, who wished the movies were as good as the music. He once said that when listening to Creedence Clearwater Revival, he saw in his mind's eye nothing less than a John Ford Western, so that he thought the only tune appropriate to 1970s Hollywood was Ennio Morricone's "Once Upon a Time in the West," as heard from Charles Bronson's harmonica.[23]

If the political event that inaugurated the protest movement was the Vietnam War, on which BONNIE AND CLYDE offers only oblique comment, there is general agreement that it was the election of Ronald Reagan as president in November 1980 that brought the New Hollywood along with the counter-culture to a close. David Cook in *Lost Illusions* makes Reagan's election explicitly the terminal event of his account of the decade:

> In fact, the election . . . marked the loss of two illusions fabricated during the decade that preceded it. First was the illusion of a liberal political consensus created by the antiwar movement, the Watergate scandal and the subsequent resignation of Richard Nixon . . . . The second illusion, intermingled with the first, was that mainstream American movies might aspire to the sort of serious social or political content described above on a permanent basis. This prospect was seriously challenged when the blockbuster mentality took hold in Hollywood in the wake of JAWS and STAR WARS.[24]

Thomson and Cook were preceded by Robin Wood's *Hollywood from Vietnam to Reagan* and Andrew Britton's article for *Movie*, "Blissing Out," which probably coined the term "Reaganite entertainment," subsequently invoked by several commentators.[25] According to this version, the counter-cultural, "progressive" politics of the first New Hollywood were replaced in the 1980s by films and cycles whose primary function was "reactionary," defined as a cunning mixture of repression and reassurance, with story-lines that were not only politically conservative and flag-wavingly patriotic. They also unapologetically affirmed the virtue of being dumb. As characterization became simplistic, conflicts puerile and psychology pared down to a minimum, the movies gave more and more space to spectacle, muscle-bound action and mindless destruction.

Without going into the polemical value of this periodization, there are two aspects relevant to my general argument. First, the issue of spectacle hints at another major so-called innovation of the second New Hollywood, besides financial management and exhibition practices: the increasing role played by technology and new kinds of special effects, as well as genres that put these special effects dramatically on display: the monster film (JAWS), the horror film (THE EXORCIST), and the sci-fi epic (STAR WARS). American cinema in the 1980s became identified with certain genres and their cross-over blends: besides the sci-fi fantasy, the body horror film and the action-adventure, it was the neo-noir porno-thriller and the time-travel nostalgia film which caught the critics' attention. This return to genre filmmaking, and especially to the big screen treatment given to formerly B-picture, exploitation and television genres was in contrast to the New Hollywood's quite troubled and even, some would say, tormented relation to genre, where the road movie, the anti-Western, and the cops-and-robbers stories gone horribly wrong predominated. The critical, counter-cultural stance was manifest in the preference for unconventional story-material and for apparently incoherent or meandering narratives that contest or simply ignore the goal-oriented, affirmative, plot-driven movies with their neat resolutions and sense of closure. Genre mutations have always been regarded as among the hallmarks of the 1970s, and in a sense, this aspect of American cinema—so apparently hostile to the *auteur*-ethos—confirms the permanence and cohesion of Hollywood across social changes and industry transformation. But genres and their capacious adaptability are also an index of how open mainstream filmmaking has always been to the national moods, or to the permeable political meanings given to the myths and typically American themes that genres are said to encode or transport.

To say that New Hollywood films skirted some of the traditional genres, or brought to the fore the twilight elements in the Western, for instance, is thus merely to underline that their oppositional energies still worked within the system rather than in outright opposition to it. The mutations have inspired critics to offer strong, political readings of certain movies or even whole cycles. Horwath gives such an assessment, and one could cite Robin Wood's analysis from 1976 of the horror film, which correlates the rebirth of the genre to profound changes in the American family.[26] One of the most sustained political readings of the decade under the heading of genre has been given by Jim Hoberman. In an essay entitled "NASHVILLE versus JAWS" he contrasted two ways of dealing with American political history in the 1970s, one by a quintessentially New Hollywood director, and the other "working through" the national malaise in an equally typical New New Hollywood manner.[27] Hoberman astutely notes the asymmetrical convergence of these two films, once one sees them generically, as variations on the themes of the disaster movie. If NASHVILLE is clearly about the complete loss of faith in the political establishment after Watergate and the Nixon resignation, to have it analyzed as a disaster movie comes as an illuminating surprise. JAWS, on the other hand, can easily be seen as a disaster movie in the tradition of B-films about monsters, invading aliens or inexplicably malevolent calamities befalling a community, as a consequence of human tampering with nature. Hoberman's close mapping, however, of the politics of the *unmaking* of both Richard Nixon (Watergate) and Edward Kennedy (Chappaquiddick), while cross-referencing it to the politics of the *making* of the film, provides a powerful reading of the Hollywood mainstream in respect of the nation's agenda at any given point in time. That the blockbuster serves this agenda by seemingly dealing with something altogether different and timeless (in the case of JAWS, primordial fear of "the deep") underlines what might be called the collusion or "conspiracy" (Fredric Jameson) that exists between Hollywood and American reality.[28] All it requires is to see the US under the dual aspect of a politics of shared myths and of shared mass media, in the push-pull of mutual dependency, even under antagonistic conditions, such as activist dissent or generational conflict.

It is this trade-off between the spectacle of politics and the politics of spectacle that was one of the hardest lessons Europeans had to learn about America during the 1980s. As a consequence, whereas US film critics blamed Reagan(omics) for the (death of the) movies, the rest of the world tended to blame the movies for Reagan's populist simplifications. Especially Europeans looked at the actor-turned-president Ronald Reagan and his myth-mongering across the lens of an ultra-conformist film industry. So much so that the perception of the United States was shaped by a White House whose political agenda—with its "Evil Empire" and "STAR WARS" initiative—was set by the season's blockbusters. Besides STAR WARS, Hollywood provided feel-good movies about the American Dream (ROCKY), and revisionist historical memories that turned even the war in Vietnam into a successful rescue mission (RAMBO). It was partly these growing polarities between Europe and America that also intimated a widening breach within America itself, between the values of the counter-culture and those of the neo-conservative US government. So irreconcilably different did the Hollywood of STAR WARS, Stallone or Schwarzenegger appear from NASHVILLE, Nicholson or even Paul Newman that the first New Hollywood suddenly discovered greater affinities with the old, classical Hollywood than it had with the second New Hollywood. Not only did the latter supersede it; it appeared to have wiped the slate clean, by either being "in denial" of what had gone before or deliberately misunderstanding the virtues of the classical.[29] But if critics like Wood and Britton offer among the bleakest visions of the movies of the 1980s, the better to let the films of the 1970s shine brightly, there is also the danger that the 1970s become a sort of fetish-period, the "last" permitted site of pleasure, before the American cinema turns (once more) into the no-go area for politically committed intellectuals which it used to be prior to the French-inspired *auteur* theory. Once again, the continuities are almost as conspicuous as the breaks.

The Action Hero in Trouble, or the Child is Father to the Man

So far, there is one antinomy which characterized the period that has hardly been mentioned. The 1970s were the beginnings of feminism or rather they intensely prepared the revolutions in male-female relationships. But here, too, the oppositions may not be as stark as usually argued, when pointing an accusatory finger at the relentlessly male, if not outright "macho" flavor of the New Hollywood, both in the films, and among the community that made them.[30] The contributions in the last part of the book offer a possibly more productive way of looking at the gender issue, as well as at the fate of the counter-cultural energies, in the wider context of the post-Fordist economic changes alluded to above. Some of these aspects can be put under the heading of "action-image," and the male action hero, whose apparent "return" in the 1980s in the shape of Stallone and Schwarzenegger should be seen also as the symptom of a crisis, and not merely as the affirmation of a new virility. If one adds the ambiguous protagonists played by Burt Reynolds, Bruce Willis and especially Clint Eastwood (for each DIRTY HARRY there is a PLAY MISTY FOR ME), the male action hero may not be diametrically opposed to psychopaths like Travis Bickle in TAXI DRIVER, testosterone time-bombs like Jimmy Angelelli in FINGERS, or Hamlet figures like Bobby Dupea in FIVE EASY PIECES. However, whereas the latter enact the politics of male identity mainly across the symptoms of imminent disaster and disarray, the former boldly or brutally overcompensate, repressing the knowledge that somewhere on the way to annihilating the enemy, they, too, had lost the plot. I once tried to suggest in my essay on the "Unmotivated Hero" (Chapter 17 in this volume) how the "symptom" and the "cure" were mutually dependent on each other, around what I called the "pathos of failure," that is, the inability of the New Hollywood protagonist to take on the symbolic mandate that classical Hollywood narrative addressed to its heroes: to pursue a goal or respond to a challenge. Paul Schrader once aligned this shift with the America-Europe divide when he remarked that in American movies people solved a problem, while in European films they probed a dilemma. The incapacity for purposive action is clearly related to the counter-culture's distrust of authority, which in turn sets free anarchic energies that are as destructive as they are creative. Implicit in our view of the New Hollywood is the possibility that its malaise about traditional American public institutions was matched by an appetite for self-exploration and personal experiment that, paradoxically, helped to "modernize" Hollywood from within as much as changes in ownership structures and distribution practice modernized it from without. Thus, if the private hang-ups, drug-abuse and predatory sexual behavior of the movie brats are graphically documented in Peter Biskind's account, the upside to the downside should also be recorded. Their general willingness to take risks, to follow hunches and intuitions, even the brinkmanship should be booked as assets, and not merely seen as morally irresponsible behavior that deservedly provoked a conservative backlash on the part of the new industry bosses.

The new behavioral norms of males—the mix of sensitivity and cock(iness), for instance—are discussed by Adrian Martin in James Toback's FINGERS, while the tactical virtues of "dirtiness" and "indiscipline" have been identified by Drehli Robnik.[31] Both show the masculinist ethic in crisis: at once excessive and deeply troubled, but also potentially "useful" as a set of adaptive strategies in a new kind of social and psychic economy. Others have looked at these ragged patterns of response as a "working through" of the dislocations caused by the Vietnam War, and recognized in them the traumatic after-shocks to self-image and self-esteem. Christian Keathley, for instance, has identified a "post-traumatic cycle" whose examples cut across the straight left-right, counter-cultural-conservative ideological schema usually invoked for plotting the fault-lines of the American cinema in the 1970s and 1980s.[32] In this sense, these male obsessions are also a kind of reverse mirror, in which one detects in often distorted form the changing role of women and the rise of feminism, so infrequently represented in the 1970s. A closer, retrospective look at the male-female relations and at the macho mores of the 1970s films could provide a better appreciation of the ambiguous role that this late flowering of anarcho-individualism played, in the sphere of consumption and life-style, and as an aspect of speculative and high risk-capitalism. The notable inarticulacy and non-communication among the men and women in 1970s films, where there is little shared intimacy and where the formation of a family-founding heterosexual couple (mandatory in classical Hollywood narratives) is nowhere in sight, may give us a clue to the turmoil in gender-relations to come. But the damaged or hysterical machismo would also have to be read against that other feature of Hollywood in the 1980s, namely the growing importance of women in industry positions, as producers and in public relations, besides their more traditional roles as screenwriters and editors.[33] The broader shifts taking place not only brought in agents and deal-makers, it also re-targeted marketing to the new audience segments, among which women, and especially young women began to feature as a core group of spectators.

Thus, another feature of 1980s Hollywood would gain in political significance—even if its analysis is open to different kinds of explanation—namely, the resurgence of mainstream movies featuring children as protagonists. The popularity of STAR WARS, E.T., CLOSE ENCOUNTERS OF THE THIRD KIND, GREMLINS, HOME ALONE and BACK TO THE FUTURE showed that more was at stake than the prolonged adolescence of one or two directors, or even the demographics of a younger audience. The films that were to come to dominate the 1980s and 1990s, such as the many fairy tale or adventure stories even outside the Disney orbit featuring young boys, show a curious tendency to endow them with a deeper knowledge than the adults. They are also entrusted with cosmic missions and communicate with non-human powers, as if they were being groomed for "inheriting" the universe, albeit that of fantasy and of self-enclosed worlds. Following the different manifestations of non-normative masculinity in Hollywood, one arrives at a somewhat confusing profile of options. Besides the "unmotivated hero" of the 1970s, there is the action hero of the "combat films" as obliquely communicating alter egos; next to the "outlaw couple" movies are the "buddy movies" (prototypically Robert Redford and Paul Newman in BUTCH CASSIDY AND THE SUNDANCE KID, THE STING) with their flipside, the "male rampage" cycle of LETHAL WEAPONS (Mel Gibson and Danny Glover). Likewise, there may be a subterranean connection between the psychopathic protagonists of the 1970s and the child hero of the 1980s, insofar as the anti-authoritarian impulse within the counter-culture could be said to actually produce these different kinds of masculinity in crisis, rather than "reflect" them. They perform not only as a protective defense, projected onto feminism's purported demands, but play through so many possible responses to what one might call the post-Fordist phase of patriarchal masculinity. This phase would require a degree of deterritorialization of the male body and a disarticulation of its traditional training for single-minded linear action, in order to become a "rapid reaction" body, full of paranoid and hysterical energies, easily mobilized and even more easily deployed against self and others. In other words, action as reaction, and agency uncoupled from choice. Kubrick has traced this new kind of unstable but effective psychotic mobility in FULL METAL JACKET, camouflaging it somewhat by confining it to the (anti-)Vietnam genre, but there are many other examples one could cite, all the way to FORREST GUMP, where hyperactivity and catatonia appear as the two sides of the same medal, readying the male for new kinds of multi-tasking.

Such a line of analysis could complement Gilles Deleuze's more formal distinctions between different types of images. Notably his idea of a "crisis of the action image" might in the present context of the New Hollywood be associated with these crises of masculinity, whether "post-traumatic" and tied to the aftermath of Vietnam, or as a change in the culture's demands on the male body in a post-industrial, post-manual labor economy, as discussed above. Conversely, by seeing such crises through Deleuze's deliberately non-gendered taxonomy of different kinds of action, affection and perception images, the topics of race, gender, body so prevalent in debates about contemporary Hollywood would be extended to include another horizon of reflection. A wider field of investigation could open up which brings the non-coordination of the motor-sensory system highlighted by Deleuze and the disintegration in the post-Fordist labor and organizational hierarchies under a similar heading, offering another clue to the "identity" of 1970s Hollywood. The triple beat of action, perception, affection image would allow us to track—in a way that is not binary but still preserves an element of conflict—the consecutive stages of Old, New and New New Hollywood, with the films of 1970s perhaps especially sensitive to the disarticulation of action, the disorientation of perception and the modulations of affect.

Action, perception, affection: The Deleuzian schema, applied to Hollywood of the 1970s, brings us back to the purported European influence, but now mediated by a specifically American crisis—the war in Vietnam, the corruption of the offices of state, the changing nature of post-industrial society—which would then correspond to the no less or even more traumatic experience of Europe after WW2 and the Holocaust, reverberating, according to Deleuze, in neo-realism (Rossellini, Antonioni), the nouvelle vague (Godard, Rivette) and the New German cinema (Wenders, Fassbinder). The "traumatic" consciousness, so often posited as the exclusive concern of European art cinema, reappears as also a dimension of the American cinema, though not necessarily folded into an inner void, but projected outward onto a hyperkinetic surface, turned into percussive sound, or exteriorized, self-voided as in Martin's account of FINGERS. Likewise, politics becomes not a question of committing to particular goals, values or ideological positions, but of bodies subject to degrees of intensity and affect that color their actions and give contours to gestures, irrespective of whether they lack motivation, in conventional terms, or are driven by its obverse, a paranoia which suspects plots everywhere, in a vain attempt to get at "the inner workings of power" (Fredric Jameson). Vain, perhaps, because power, if we follow Foucault and Deleuze, does not manifest itself in the form of top-down hierarchies or conspiracies, capable of being pictured as concentrically organized around an inner core (as in ALL THE PRESIDENTS' MEN, and nostalgically invoked by Oliver Stone in JFK). Instead power is dispersed, transversal, interstitial: the correlative in the political realm of the affection image in the somatic realm. There, according to Keathley, the protagonists of the post-traumatic cycle, from MIDNIGHT COWBOY and MEAN STREETS, to THE CONVERSATION and SHAMPOO are "trapped"—the inability to act being the first condition of the body having access to a different organization of the senses. Or is it the other way round: the affection image as the first condition of the body *being accessed* by a different "organization"—of the military, the state?

New Economy Hollywood—Home of Flexible Pathologies?

This more dystopian conclusion offers itself when one looks at reinterpretations of the counter-cultural war films from the 1970s, such as Robnik's analysis of M*A*S*H, KELLY's HEROES and THE DIRTY DOZEN. Such films take a high level of systemic breakdown for granted, apparently in order to draw from dysfunctionality new energies of ad hoc alliance and informal "teamworking," needed for unconventional tasks or missions. It would demonstrate the push-pull model (the mutual dependence of antagonistic forces) in the sphere of affective labor, by giving, for instance, the psychopath (as well as other marginalized, pathologized or criminalized existences, including "hippies") a potentially valuable function in periods of transition, or in emergency situations. The key to this function might be that these protagonists display or can be mobilized to display not only rapid reaction, but *random reaction* behavior. Capable of sustaining periods or phases of randomization, they are not hampered by an outmoded motor-sensory body-schema, and thus correspond to what Robnik sees as the ideal prototype of somatic organization in post-industrial society generally: "flexibilized affect" as the motor of societal change at the micro-level of power, fantasy and desire. "It is not about making the misfits fit, but of making them refit the machinery." In other words, harvesting and harnessing the counter-cultural energies (including their anti-social excesses) for new kinds of work, especially in those sectors where, according to Hardt and Negri, economic and cultural phenomena can no longer be distinguished. The randomized networks and informal teams would then be the mirror-image—or the cold light-of-day materializations—of those once hoped-for idealized communities of non-hierarchical communication and cooperative participation dreamed up by hippies and flower-power activists. These, of course, foundered not only because of state repression and capitalist exploitation, but also on the issue of gender (the couple and the "impossible" sexual relation representing the last bastion of resistance to randomization), and on the nature of power in complex social systems.

Perhaps we can now return to our initial question with a revived sense of its paradox: why are the 1970s by some critics seen as the unique and special highpoint of the American cinema, and by others as more like a brief interlude in an overall development of self-regulation and self-renewal which has allowed Hollywood not only to survive but to reassert its hegemony in the global business of mass-entertainment? It is, of course, "art" and "commerce" that once more appear to confront each other in implacable incompatibility. What makes the cinema unique is that it is an art form owing its existence to the particular interplay of capitalism and the state, at any given point in time. Perhaps more than any other creative practice, then, the cinema's potential and performance, its identity and vitality are closely aligned with the changing relations between these forces, as the capitalist economy and the bourgeois state are continually competing with each other over legitimacy and sovereignty in the public realm ("modernization"). The task falling to the cinema—as the economy's symbolic realm in the sphere of consumption, and as the state's symbolic realm in the sphere of bodies and senses—would be to keep open another site of investment in change and in "modernization": hence the suggestion that one way to understand the American cinema of the 1970s is finally as not so much a period either of radical innovation or of mere transition, but of crossovers, which is to say, one that mixes the signs in order to make all kinds of slippages (or reversals) possible. Hence also the insistence on asking what post-Fordism or post-industrialism might mean in and for the American film industry, and what the equivalent of such a post-Fordism might be in the male *auteur*, his (re-action) hero and his psyche. The implications have been to re-locate this 1970s American cinema from the East Coast to California, and to attribute to the unique community which is "Hollywood" the perverse status of an art-and-commerce avant-garde. Like all avant-gardes, this one may well have been at war with itself, but it also formed a tribal entity. Evidence for both, the tribal cohesion and the movie wars, may be the shattered biographies. But evidence can also be found in the films themselves, many of which now seem surprisingly legible also as allegories of the very "modernization" processes and "flexible" psychopathologies of which the movie community appears to have been both agent and victim. This will be the theme of another collection of essays.

19

The Love that Never Dies: Francis Ford Coppola and BRAM STOKER'S DRACULA

Post-Classical Hollywood

When looking to define post-classical Hollywood, one could do worse than take the 1980s American cinema's most maverick of charismatic producer-director-*auteurs* as example, and among his varied oeuvre, pick one of the more hybrid films. Francis Ford Coppola's BRAM STOKER'S DRACULA was allegedly a "commercial" and therefore less "personal" project (in the language of *auteurism*), helping to restore the director's battered industry reputation, after the collapse of Zoetrope and the disaster of ONE FROM THE HEART.[1] But it could also be regarded as a professionally confident, shrewdly calculated and supremely self-reflexive piece of filmmaking, fully aware that it stands at the crossroads of major changes in the art and industry of Hollywood: looking back as well as forward, while staking out a ground all its own.

Post-classical filmmaking of the kind represented by BRAM STOKER'S DRACULA is unthinkable without the "New Hollywood," a label referring, above all, to the economic revival of Hollywood filmmaking since the mid-1970s.[2] Its beginnings date back to the world-wide success of Steven Spielberg's JAWS, George Lucas' STAR WARS, and Coppola's THE GODFATHER.[3] Three elements make up the "New Hollywood": first, a *new generation of directors* (sometimes called the "Movie Brats"),[4] second, *new marketing strategies* (centered on the blockbuster as a distribution and exhibition concept),[5] and third, *new media ownership and management styles* in the film industry.[6] One could add *new technologies of sound and image reproduction*, ranging from digitized special effects to Dolby sound, and *new delivery systems*, but it seems that the second—the new marketing strategies, also known as "High Concept"[7] filmmaking—was in many ways the most crucial. If the cinema was to survive, so common wisdom has it, it needed to attract audiences brought up on television and popular music, who identified with the broader attitudes and values of "youth-culture" (non-conformism, rebelliousness, sexual freedom, fashion-consciousness and conspicuous consumption). The signs, images and sounds of this youth-culture have, since the mid-1950s, dominated much of domestic and public space, at first in the USA and subsequently taking over the urban landscape of the everyday also in the rest of the developed and developing world. Hence the argument that the New Hollywood's greatest challenge was the industry's uncertainty about an identifiable audience.[8] Even before the arrival and rapid diffusion of new consumer-oriented reception technologies like satellite broadcasting and the home VCR, the one commodity classical Hollywood could be sure of—the family audience—had begun to regroup around television. But with the cable-satellite-videotape revolution granting viewers a hitherto unknown freedom over the uses of the audio-visual product, it made even this audience "invisible" to the statistical targeting which formed the basis of the film and television industry's traditional marketing strategies. Timothy Corrigan, borrowing a term first used by Robin Wood,[9] went so far as to claim that this produced "illegible texts."[10]

That it was Hollywood and movie making which appeared to "resolve" this crisis, rather than television (still grappling with the implications of "desperately seeking the audience")[11] is one of the more startling features of the 1990s. In order to understand at least some of the factors, one has to cast one's eye sideways as well as back and include, along with these technological and demographic changes, the renaissance and international marketability of at first European (the *nouvelle vague* in France, the New German Cinema) and more recently, Asian *national art and/or cult cinemas* (Taiwanese, Hong Kong and New Chinese cinemas) whose critical reputation seems invariably built around star-directors. Taking its cue from these diverse trends in popular culture, Hollywood, too, began promoting "name" directors as superstars, often film-school graduates with a cult movie or a surprise success to their credit. After the roller-coaster years of box-office failure for costly *auteur* projects in the late 1970s—the most notorious being Michael Cimino's Western epic HEAVEN'S GATE—but also record profits earned by outright commercial productions in the wake of JAWS, the major Hollywood companies oscillated between giving new talent a chance and backing more conservative ventures. But the significance of the new breed of filmmaker (the line runs from Martin Scorsese, Paul Schrader, Brian de Palma to David Lynch, Quentin Tarantino, Abel Ferrara) rests also on the influence that the European cinema and its critical traditions (such as "*auteur* theory") have had on the American cinema's own understanding of itself. For instance, the mixing of genres, the mania for citation and self-referencing so typical of contemporary cinema can be traced to the French *nouvelle vague*, its admiration for the Hollywood of the 1940s and 1950s, and the use of film citation in the works of François Truffaut, Jean-Luc Godard, Jacques Rivette or Claude Chabrol.

Yet this vanguard role of Europe is complex and ambiguous. Ever since the European cinema came of age in the 1920s, and once more after 1945, Hollywood has been the implicit reference point of European national cinemas, whether commercial in orientation or *art-et-essai*. Rival to some, the Hollywood film was the admired model to others. In both cases, since much of any European nation's film culture is implicitly "Hollywood" (because this is what most people see when they go to the cinema), none of the relations of rivalry and emulation can be seen as purely negative.[12] More important in the present context, however, is the fact Hollywood is itself far from monolithic. The "New Hollywood" of Coppola, Scorsese or Altman: is it "new" in opposition to "old" Hollywood (the different as same: Coppola playing at being a reclusive mogul like Howard Hughes or an "*auteur maudit*" like Orson Welles), or is it "new" in relation to Hollywood assimilating its own opposite (the same as different): Arthur Penn borrowing from Truffaut, Altman's films influenced by Godard, Woody Allen's by Ingmar Bergman and Fellini, Schrader by Dreyer and Bresson, while Scorsese is an admirer of Michael Powell and Jerry Lewis, the latter possessing an *auteur*'s reputation only in Europe?

In order to account for the play with quotations, with genre parody, clichés and pastiche in post-classical cinema (and by extension, to point to the complex hopscotch logic of Europe's evaluation of American cinema / New York's evaluation of Europe / Hollywood's response to New York), we need to go beyond "influence." To picture this relationship, a number of paradigms offer themselves, including that of "self-colonization" and "elective paternity."[13] Noël Carroll has proposed the term "allusionism,"[14] basing his thesis on the premise that filmmakers and audiences grew up together, as it were, that they shared a common *film experience* which shaped their *social experience*. Robert Ray offers a differently angled picture, partly to explain why the New Hollywood is successful, even though its primary audiences seem both younger and more diverse. For him, success has to do with a double inscription of audiences, where the viewer is simultaneously addressed as a naive and an ironic spectator, as an innocent and a knowing one. Ray sees here the effect of television, purveying a certain kind of film culture:

> Television, with its indiscriminate recycling and baroque deployment of the American cinema's basic paradigms . . . has perpetuated the most conservative incarnation of those codes. As a result, we may be on the verge of witnessing the creation of mass audiences with a truly double system of consciousness, by turns (or simultaneously) straight and ironic.[15]

This double register has many names: Fredric Jameson, in a different context, has called it "blank irony," that is, unmarked, deadpan or neutral.[16] It can be related to the pervasive cultural feeling of nostalgia, itself a constitutive element for a sensibility which, in the words of Gore Vidal, "remembers the future and dreams the past." Such a definition of nostalgia makes it the simultaneous co-presence of the desire for the myth and a cynicism about its efficacy. Sociologically, one could say that blank irony is merely the broadest common denominator among diverse audiences, reconstructed as subjects capable of being in two places at once: for instance, we all have had a childhood, we all remember our childhood and we all would have liked childhood to have been something we like to remember.

The extraordinary economic rallying of Hollywood around the late 1970s thus needs to be seen in terms of subjectivity as well as demography, against a common background of an attunement of the culture to youth audiences of whatever age, which gave a focus to the infusion of talent. It provided the industry with exceptional growth potential as well as bequeathing to it a nerve-wracking volatility, while the introduction of so many new technologies called for a different managerial and financing logic (what has been called the move from "industry" to "business").[17] After the near-bankruptcy of all the major film studios, Hollywood appeared once more full of life, having mutated and shape-shifted out of all recognition. Curiously de-centered and re-centered by the series of studio acquisitions on the part of multinational corporations (starting in 1962 when Universal was bought by MCA, followed in 1966 when Paramount was bought by Gulf and Western, United Artists by Transamerica Corporation [1967], Warner Brothers by Kinney Services [1969] and MGM by the Las Vegas billionaire Kirk Kerkorian [1970]), the balance of power had shifted, making movies a minor element of the global entertainment industry, and the entertainment industry itself merely one part of multi-national corporate planning, focused on oil, transport, car-parks and real-estate.[18]

Under orders from their respective international parent conglomerates (Rupert Murdoch's Australian New Corporation took over 20th Century Fox in 1986, Sony bought Columbia Pictures from Coca Cola in 1989, Pathé Communications purchased MGM-United Artists in 1990 and the Japanese conglomerate Matsushita acquired MCA and Universal in 1991), most producers were looking for ways not so much of targeting different audiences, but of targeting audiences differently. Increasingly, in this post-studio system period, each film became a media event, exploiting different star qualities or spectacle attractions, whether a mechanical shark in JAWS, a musical score (the STAR WARS theme), or an ingeniously designed logo in BATMAN. Perhaps misleadingly known as the blockbuster formula, this event concept is built on costly production values, heavy advertisement and strategically chosen release dates. Borrowing the formal features of "platform shareability" and "content repurposing" (merchandising, spin-offs, sequels) from the music and advertisement industries, the blockbuster movie is based on a very quick cycle of commercial exploitation, by which a film is simultaneously started in thousands of cinemas the world over, and has to take millions of dollars in its first weekend's release—usually a public holiday—in order to reach the necessary universal audience that alone can guarantee a profitable return on the explosively rising production costs and marketing investments.[19] The marketing in turn is essential in order to give the film the recognition value needed to get coverage in press and on television, and also to ensure that its initial cinema release is followed by a saturation of even more profitable secondary markets like video-releases and computer games.

Citizen Coppola

In such changing contexts of entrepreneurship, technological innovation and the culture of youth and nostalgia, the career of Coppola occupies a symptomatic space. His gifts, his successes, but also his tragic mistakes shed light on more than his own work, making the man and his myth a particularly striking example of the different options between classical and post-classical Hollywood, as well as between modernist and postmodern authorship. As a film director, Coppola sees himself clearly in the American tradition, comparable to D.W. Griffith or John Ford, but this does not prevent him from identifying with Orson Welles, the great outsider of the American cinema par excellence, and the opposite of classical Hollywood's studio-directors.[20] However American he is, though, Coppola also belongs to America's "European" heritage, being a second-generation Italian immigrant, with strong emotional and family roots to Southern Europe, and a keen sense of a past either real or "dreamt about," and of futures either possible or "remembered."

Coppola's ambition has always been of Shakespearean proportions. Famous and wealthy at an early age, after the success of THE GODFATHER, he built up his own studio, Zoetrope, and wanted to make it in every way the prototype for filmmaking in the 21st century.[21] At the same time, the shape and thematics of (Orson Welles') CITIZEN KANE are everywhere in Coppola's films: from the Brando character in THE GODFATHER, and the Brando figure in APOCALYPSE NOW to the more recent BRAM STOKER'S DRACULA and MARY SHELLEY'S FRANKENSTEIN. Beverle Houston, referring to Welles' heroes, once called them "power-babies": men obsessed with control, and highly skilled in the devious ways of wielding it, but in some sense crippled by an immaturity, a thirst and a craving for attention reaching back to childhood, intemperate, insatiable and unmeasured.[22] These configurations in Coppola's fictional characters have colored the myth of his person: hence his reputation as an overreacher and a gambler, a man who takes immoderate risks, leaving a trail of destruction as likely as fabulous success and spectacular achievements, referring us back to a long line of American entrepreneurs, and culminating in the figure of Howard Hughes, the recluse mogul, whose ambition was that of a Renaissance prince but who ended up a crank, wearing Kleenex boxes instead of shoes for fear of virus infections.

New Hollywood when embodied by Coppola is rewriting the "old" as the "new" also in another sense. The very classicism we now associate with Hollywood and its golden age, its canonical directors and masterpieces were mostly named and defined not in the USA but by the nouvelle vague, precisely by the generation of critics-filmmakers like Godard, Truffaut, Chabrol, Rohmer, who in turn became a double influence on the American cinema, by telling a new generation of Americans what and who was important in their own cinema, and by inspiring them to be innovative in style, story-telling and sensibility. Yet by the 1980s, it was Coppola who rendered an inverse service to a younger generation in Europe, most notably from the New German Cinema. His Zoetrope Studio imported Wim Wenders (who made HAMMETT there), and Coppola made possible the distribution of Werner Herzog's films, as well as of Syberberg's HITLER A FILM FROM GERMANY. Fitting into the pattern, too, was Coppola's decision to bring to the States Kevin Brownlow's magnificent restoration of Abel Gance's NAPOLEON, for which he asked none other than his father, Carmine Coppola, to compose a score and conduct it with a live orchestra. Aguirre, Hitler, Napoleon—European over-reachers, failed world conquerors, studied with nonchalant but hardly casual interest by an American movie mogul, building up media power that seemed poised to take on the world, yet sufficiently

European to be also fatally in love with this ambition's failure: elements of a mythology perhaps too potent to resist. Does this not suggest an ironically self-referential relation of Coppola also to Dracula, and across the myth, to history as a horror film?

Technique and Technology: The Horror Film

Typical of the New Hollywood is thus a self-conscious use of old mythologies, genre stereotypes, and the history of the cinema itself. Especially striking is the revival of genres which—in the 1950s—were regarded as B-movies: the sci-fi film, the "creature-feature" or monster-film, and the many other variations on the horror film. B-picture conventions, when taken up in the 1980s and 1990s introduced into mainstream cinema the sort of ruptures in realism (understood as narrative coherence, unified characters, goal-directed story structure) that European filmmakers had brought in the 1960s to their own modernist art cinema practice. Unlike the full-blown (literary) modernism of Alain Resnais or Michelangelo Antonioni, however, the sources and techniques that split open the new Hollywood narratives came mostly from the American cinema itself, its minor genres and debased modes. Robin Wood perceived the connection quite accurately, when he argued that:

> [t]here are two keys to understanding the development of the Hollywood cinema in the 70s: the impingement of Vietnam on the national consciousness and the unconscious and the astonishing evolution of the horror film. One must avoid any simple suggestion of cause-and-effect—the modern horror film evolves out of PSYCHO; feminism and gay liberation were not products of the war; the history of black militancy extends back for generations.... The obvious monstrousness of the war definitively undermined the credibility of "the system."[23]

But was Wood not perhaps too optimistic when he suggested a convergence of all the political energies coming from the different liberation movements? Nor is it evident that the "horror of Vietnam" is what lies behind the phenomenon Wood notices, namely the resurgence since the 1970s of the horror film as a mainstream genre (from HALLOWEEN to the NIGHTMARE ON ELM STREET cycle, from THE FLY to SILENCE OF THE LAMBS) and as a visual code (of violent effects, body shocks and spectacular spilling of blood) in genres as diverse as adventure films (JAWS: a typically old-fashioned creature-feature), science fiction (the ALIEN trilogy), war films (APOCALYPSE NOW), erotic thrillers (FATAL ATTRACTION), and even family comedies (HOME ALONE).

Ever since the coming of sound, when the Dracula and Frankenstein stories starring Bela Lugosi or Boris Karloff fixed many of the genre's basic tropes, horror films permitted deviations and transgressions of the representational norm. In contrast to maintaining a coherent diegetic world and the rule of narrative causality, horror films almost by definition disrupt the cause and effect patterns of such classical devices as shot/countershot, continuity and reverse field editing, in order to create a sense of mystery, of the unexpected, of surprise, incongruity and horror, misleading the viewer, by withholding information or keeping the causal agent, the monster, off-screen as long as possible.

In this play with spatial relationships, around what is and what is not visually present, sound has always played a particularly important role. But while in classical continuity cinema, the sound-image synchronization perfectly reproduces the question/answer pattern of linear narrative, because we naturally identify a sound by picturing its source, the horror film emphasizes the presence of sound, in order that the absence of its source becomes localized by the mind more vividly—and more like a phantasm.[24] Thus, the horror film's generic device of breaking the neat synchronization of sound and image by keeping the sources of sound invisible and off-screen, also helps to destabilize the primacy of the diegetic story world over the extra-diegetic or non-diegetic world. Without resorting to super-natural forces or extra-terrestrial beings, the skilful use of sound can draw sharp attention to the characters' as well as the viewers' limited and partial perspectives. It is as if the formal resources of sound in the horror film as genre signal all kinds of other social or political "horrors," yet the starting point would not be senseless slaughter, social injustice or human evil, calling for the horror film genre as its most appropriate "reflection" or adequate "representation." Rather, it may be the other way round: in Vietnam films, for instance, the jungle becomes the epitome of the horrible not because drug-taking conscripts face a determined and ruthless enemy. Instead, it is because the films draw on the familiar horror genre trope of the "monster in the swamp"—nowhere to be seen, but when heard, effective action comes too late—that they succeed so well in "rendering" (the bodily sensations of danger in the face of) the Vietcong.[25] In other words, with the horror genre, we are no longer in the episteme of "realism" or "reflection," but encounter the cinema experience as first and foremost a bodily one, and thus an end in itself, rather than a means to an end, political, representational or otherwise. Many of these cinematic techniques, adopted from the horror genre and explicitly drawing upon visual disorientation and the loss of time/space certainties figure prominently in Coppola's APOCALYPSE NOW,[26] but also in the visual and sound effects of BRAM STOKER'S DRACULA: in what could be called a *tromp-l'ouie* [hearing] effect, for instance, Jonathan Harker, while exploring the Count's labyrinthine chambers, hears the sound of liquid splashing upwards, before he is raped by a gang of female Draculas, emerging from beneath him.

Rewriting and Self-Reference, Palimpsest and *Mise-en-Abyme*

The reasons for choosing BRAM STOKER'S DRACULA to examine the classical/ post-classical divide are thus partly based on considerations of genre, and the curious reversal that seems to have taken place between technology and referent, motivation and technique. This repeats, within the text, the slippage between director, character and media intertext I alluded to with the fanciful metaphorization of "Coppola/Kane/Dracula." Furthermore, if New Hollywood in the economic sense (the revival of the fortunes of the US film business discussed above) and the post-classical in the textual sense (a high-concept visual impact movie, preferably in the thriller mode)[27] share the vigorous re-figuring of the text and its limits, of the product and its market, we might define the new (postmodern) episteme as one which *joins economic with textual excess.* Consequently, a 1990s film about Dracula, figure of excess par excellence, as well as boundary-creature and boundary-crosser, invariably alerts one to the possibility of different forms of audience engagement, different ways of being "inside" and "outside" when it comes to identification and participation. Riding on the new audience demographics with their split mode of address is a post-classical treatment of often very classical narratives, a new treatment of sound and of the image, or at any rate, of the hierarchies between them. My argument would be that Coppola's BRAM STOKER'S DRACULA is symptomatic because in it the classical, the post-classical and the postmodern find distinct articulations. Indeed, part of the ambiguity of response or irritation this has generated among the critics[28] seems negatively to confirm the slippery, self-referential and self-mocking pose the film strikes in respect to its own place in movie history. Yet this deliberate hybridity evidently appealed to the volatile audiences Hollywood is chasing, perhaps not least because the film features an agelessly youthful hero who remembers a future, while living in a past which is yet to happen. What Pierre Sorlin has suggested about film history in general[29]—namely that since there can be no history without singularity or absence, films do not have a history, given that they are fully "present" every time they are screened—thus refers quite accurately not only to Count Dracula, but to our postmodern position vis-à-vis classical cinema: because of its undead nature, the cinema finally does not have a history (of periods, styles, modes): it can only have fans, clans and believers, forever gathering to revive a phantasm or a trauma, a memory and an anticipation.

This last point is pertinent to BRAM STOKER'S DRACULA also in another respect. In the press release and in interviews, Coppola made much of his faithfulness to the novel, but the script is actually based on a book by Leonard Wolf, *The Annotated Dracula.*[30] Even the sources, then, confront one with a commentary on a commentary, whose *mise-en-abyme* structure can be celebrated as the film's particular authenticity, itself only heightened when one realizes how replete with citations to other films Coppola's adaptation of Bram Stoker's novel is: at the last count, no fewer than sixty titles, and besides the thirty-odd Dracula films, this still leaves a dense intertextuality, though perhaps not as eruditely pedantic as Stanley Kubrick's BARRY LYNDON, where Omar Calabrese confidently identified 271 individual paintings.[31] To name a few of the films in BRAM STOKER'S DRACULA: Louis Lumière's ARRIVAL OF A TRAIN, Jean Epstein's THE FALL OF THE HOUSE OF USHER, Jean Cocteau's LA BELLE ET LA BÊTE, Akira Kurosawa's THRONE OF BLOOD, Walter Hill's THE LONG RIDERS, Werner Herzog's HEART OF GLASS, in addition to Herzog's NOSFERATU, itself a remake of Murnau's famous film by that title. We are thus offered a highly self-referencing text in relation to movie history, but also with respect to technology, in particular, the technologies of recording, visualization and reproduction: diaries, phonographs, dictaphones, peep shows, the *cinématographe* all play prominent and narratively important parts.[32]

Allusions to paintings, too, are almost as conspicuous as films and recording instruments: for instance, the Count's portrait pointed out by him to Harker as a picture of his ancestor Vlad is, as we know (though not Harker), a portrait of himself. In the posture of the figure and the composition, it alludes to Albrecht Dürer's famous self portrait, which was itself a "Self Portrait as the Young Christ," making the portrait in Dracula's castle a citation, as well as a *mise-en-abyme* of this citation around the trope of "the self as other." Also present is one of the most famous paintings in the Western canon, the *Mona Lisa*, precisely invoked in the scene with Mina/Elzbieta over absinthe in the café: as Mina "remembers" Transylvania, the Sylvan landscape of da Vinci opens up behind her, hinting at the film's pastiche of a painterly classicism, in the service of a postmodern subjectivity of "colonized memory" and "trauma," while—as so often in this film—drawing attention to the signifier, with a visual/verbal pun on the word "Transylvania" (beyond the woods).

Finally, the fact that Coppola has made a special point of importing and distributing the films from European directors he thinks important also finds an echo in DRACULA: not only does Dracula come from continental Europe and is "imported" (to the Anglophone world), the scene of Dracula's voyage to England on board of the *Demeter* has an astonishingly exact parallel in a scene from Abel Gance's NAPOLEON, where the emperor, banished to Elba, makes a triumphant and sinister return to mainland France, during a fearful storm, at the same time as the Convention in Paris visibly tosses and turns in agony and indecision: in Coppola's film it is the swinging and swaying of London Zoo and Renfield at Carfax Abbey, which is in empathy with the heaving and tossing of the *Demeter*.

Altogether, the film poses as a kind of palimpsest of a hundred years of movie history: the year Dracula comes to London is 1897, and the reason he gives for his trip (to the hapless Mina) is that he had heard about a new marvel of science: the cinematograph. What more fitting, then, than the idea that Dracula should seduce Mina at the movies, illustrating how a vampire film today qualifies as at once prototypical for movie history and for postmodernity. The theme of repetition and seriality, of cliché and stereotype, of reworking and re-turning (as crucial to postmodernism as to the very idea of popular culture) applies materially to both the vampire myth and its perennially favorite status as a movie subject at least since F.W. Murnau's NOSFERATU from 1921. Insofar as Dracula is almost another word for an ambiguous nostalgia, it remains the archetypal movie motif, for the very theme of the undead lies at the heart of the cinema's power, also as a cultural presence. One only has to think of old stars still alive, interviewed on television, looking at their earlier selves on the silver screen. Is not each his or her own Dracula, trying to reincarnate themselves, charm once more, and unable to rest quietly in their retirement graves, become the ghost at the feast of yet another retrospective? The very peculiar tragedy of photography and the cinema—that they appear to be defying time—is as deeply embedded in Dracula as it belongs to the literary thematic of, say, Oscar Wilde's *Picture of Dorian Gray* and Edgar Alan Poe's *The Oval Portrait*.

If the word "palimpsest" seems a rather literary term when applied to film, risking to remain a mere metaphor, it is nonetheless appropriate in ways which I hope will provide a novel perspective on how to re-read the "classical" and the mythological in BRAM STOKER'S DRACULA within its "post-classical" circulation of modes of address, media-forms and merchandized commodities. The changes, for instance, that Coppola and his script-writer introduced, notably with respect to Van Helsing's presence both inside the narrative as Dracula's nemesis and outside the narrative as the omniscient narrator/framer of the tale—his double function only marked by the recognizable voice of Anthony Hopkins, and thus another aural pun, so to speak—hint at a de-centering not only of body and voice, but of "text," "subtext" and "intertext," preparing the merger of Mina and Elzbieta, on which Coppola's narrative turns, in order to unite Dracula with his ultimate love, the one that has always been his. Literally remembering the future, his errant itinerary across the centuries has no other goal than to recapture what he had already had, when a single, fatal moment of "bad timing" deprived him of its possession.

Fin de Siècle Cinema: Classical, Post-classical or Postmodern

The echoes of Oscar Wilde and Edgar Alan Poe in the basic theme of the undead bring one back to Bram Stoker as a writer of his time. It suggests that the term postmodern is not altogether that remote from the pre-modernist: for what one can identify in the cluster of motifs with which this pot-boiler seduces the reader might be more properly be called "decadence," or "fin-de-siècle." And if we look at BRAM STOKER'S DRACULA—mindful of its intertextuality with respect to painting—we do indeed recognize in the figural work of Coppola's *mise-en-scène* a filmic equivalent of meandering motifs à la Aubrey Beardsley, or the monsters of Gustave Moreau, surging forward in the female vampires who are Gorgons and Medusas, snake women with writhing heads and dilating eyes. Mina herself, in the end, decapitating Dracula, is reminiscent of Salomé, one of the quintessential motifs of the French and European decadence: if the 1890s knew all about sexual ambiguity, then they share with 1990s the uncertainty of gender, eros and representation. Coppola seems to have taken his date of 1897 rather seriously, and we can reflect on the peculiar contiguity of fin-de-siècle painting and the birth of the cinema, which he brings together in Mina's seduction, where the scene shifts to the typical *chambre separeé* of the Naughty Nineties, yet instead of Moulin Rouge dancers, one can recognize a movie show of the Lumière London Polytechnic program across the frosted windows.

The point to make, however, concerns less the self-conscious citations of period detail, lending yet another layer of "authentic" movie patina to Bram Stoker literary *décadence*. Rather, such references as there are to pre-Raphaelite pictorialism in BRAM STOKER'S DRACULA can also be understood as giving the director a historically secured vantage point for something altogether more tentative: to put into play several distinct systems of representation, whose coexistence and frictions in the film help to define what might—in retrospect, so to speak—have been at stake aesthetically, as well as for media technology and audiences in the shift from classical to post-classical. Here the notion of the palimpsest seems also apposite, for in BRAM STOKER'S DRACULA, the classical is preserved in its very over-writing, just as other oppositions, such as Hollywood/Europe, are sustained in a non-binary way. In this sense, the film conducts a kind of deconstruction of the linear narrative/monocular perspective system of representation which film studies has identified with the classical. Dominated by a "character-centered causality," this model of narrative, faithful to broadly Aristotelian principles (unity of time, space and action) is organized according to a clear cause and effect chain which relentlessly motivates the action, and displays a high degree of "character consistency" (meaning that the protagonists normally do not do things out of character, unless the genre permits it, and they do not change physical shape or appearance other than in tales of magic and the fantastic).

By contrast, post-classical cinema could be said to have introduced two major changes: in many mainstream or popular productions of the 1990s, the narrative progression has become quite involuted, with complex temporal schemes binding the segments: to mind come time travel films such as BACK TO THE FUTURE, PEGGY SUE GOT MARRIED, TWELVE MONKEYS or multi-strand narratives as in PULP FICTION and SHORT CUTS. The second change concerns "character consistency": here, too, contemporary films can be quite radical: one thinks of John Malkovitch in IN THE LINE OF FIRE, of Arnold Schwarzenegger and his antagonist in TERMINATOR II and TOTAL RECALL, the aliens in ALIEN, the play with dual personalities in Lynch's TWIN PEAKS and LOST HIGHWAY, or the undecidability of who is replicant and who human in BLADE RUNNER. Similar "deviations" are present in BRAM STOKER'S DRACULA: the temporality, while apparently linear, jumps some four hundred years after the opening, and—as already indicated—is internally quite complexly interwoven via the different levels of recollection and memory in Mina, and the count's omnipresence and undeadness. In addition, Dracula manifests himself in a startling multiplicity of guises, only few of which are anchored in the myth itself. Instead of character consistency, post-classical cinema confronts the viewer with shape shifting serial killers, voraciously vigorous vampires or time traveling terminators, while still trying to negotiate the concepts of identity, person, agency. This may have been another reason why critics did not like BRAM STOKER'S DRACULA, complaining that the plot was confusing, the allusions gratuitous, or arguing that at a deeper level, the film had destroyed the potency of the myth, with Coppola driving a final stake through all the Dracula films.[33]

The combined impact of these changes in chronological time schemes and character-identity can be observed in the fate of another feature of the classical cinema, the double plot structure, where an adventure plot and a romance plot are at once distinct from and intertwined with each other. The first is often a quest, an investigation, the pursuit of a goal, while the second is always centered on the formation of—needless to say—the heterosexual couple, with the latter strand (the formation of the couple) usually providing the terms of closure. The post-classical plot is able to take greater liberties and "gets away with it." For instance, endings in post-classical films are often so open, so ambiguous (cf. BASIC INSTINCT, TWELVE MONKEYS) that one can no longer really speak of a "formation of a heterosexual couple," and even where the final situation is not ambiguous, it is positively menacing (as in SILENCE OF THE LAMBS) and open-ended enough to allow for a sequel. BRAM STOKER'S DRACULA is in this respect also a symptomatic example, in that it *deconstructs the classical by excessively instantiating it.* The plot involves the formation of two couples: the Jonathan Harker/Mina couple and the Dracula/Mina couple are at once superimposed and displaced in relation to each other, thanks to the time shift that allows the characters to exist in two temporalities at once. Character-consistency, faithfully observed in the classical mode, can—as indicated above—be transgressed in the classical model's minor genres, such as horror, science-fiction and fantasy. Here, too, the post-classical does not oppose the classical, but emphatically re-centers it, precisely by making the marginal genres the dominant ones, pulling an unusual time structure, a novel sound practice or an expressive visual style into focus and dead-center, without thereby neutralizing their unsettling aberrance. As for narrative-visual closure, BRAM STOKER'S DRACULA provides a particularly bold example of the classical "to excess": its ending is already embedded in and enfolds itself into the opening in the most startling manner.

One will recall that this opening—added by Coppola—is set in 1497, after the fall of Constantinople. Going into battle for Christendom, Count Vlad defeats the Ottomans, but loses his bride Elzbieta, who commits suicide after receiving a false message of the Count's death. Cursing God, the Count vows himself to the quest for Elzbieta, thus condemning himself to the unnatural, non-human existence arrested between life and death. Coppola thus gives his Dracula a quite unambiguously "classical" motivation, but he does so in a visual configuration that suspends the narrative's trajectory. For the sequence ends with the establishment of a double absence: that of Elzbieta's inert body, and of an unmatched shot of Dracula looking upwards. The gap here opened up is only filled in the final scene, once more in the chapel of Dracula's castle, when in the place of Elzbieta's prostrate body we now see the dying Dracula, about to be released into mortality, and eyes cast heavenwards. As Mina cuts off Dracula's head, we are allowed to see what Dracula is/had been looking at: the dome of the chapel with the painted ceiling, showing Dracula and Elzbieta united. With it, the point of view shot of the opening is sutured, allowing for a perfect visual rhyme, though not in the mode of "repetition/resolution,"[34] but by way of an elaborate relay of gazes, across the delay not only of the film's narrative completion, but of the viewer's realization that the opening scene had been seen *from the point of view* of the ceiling picture, inscribing the formation of the couple, Dracula's gaze and desire, but also the viewers' point of view during the opening scene in the mode of a future anterior of "what will have been," giving us the fulfilment before the promise, already at the outset, and catching our look in the gaze of an Other.

Such a baroque spatio-temporal-specular "bracket" around the film forcibly draws attention to the status of perspectival space in the post-classical cinema. Euclidian geometry and Renaissance vision, or rather, the resulting architecture of looks (between the characters, between spectator and screen, between camera and characters) is said to constitute the visual regime of the classical paradigm, and holds—as psycho-semiology has taught us—the subject "in place," by way of voyeurism and specular identification. It is this regime that the scene just quoted seems to be putting into infinite regress, as it deconstructs the cinema's specularity by highlighting it so dramatically via the missing reverse shot and the optative realized in its temporal delay. BRAM STOKER'S DRACULA subsequently does not abandon the familiar geometry of representation and its implied "play of gaze and glance."[35] Rather, the specular becomes the surplus and the supplement of another mode, grounded in a different kind of image. Often, there is, it seems, no frame to an image, nor does one always know exactly where and how a shot ends and another begins (for instance, the steadicam tracking shot that indicates Dracula's presence, suddenly seems to explode, as a gunshot "blows" away Quincy, the Texan). At other times, space contracts and expands, as in the scene where Dracula visits Mina, and suddenly Van Helsing bursts in: from being in an intimate bedroom, we are all of a sudden in a baronial hall, and Dracula becomes first a bat-gargoyle hanging from the ceiling, and then a huge looming figure in a carapace and armor. The term to which I therefore want to contrast "specularity" is engulfment or "immersion," in order to indicate how such a non-specular, body-based pliability of the image might modify the terms of the viewer's subject-position. For what we seem to be witnessing is the "decomposition" of the image as representation, and the screen as a bounded frame, in which case, the representational mode of post-classical cinema would indeed resituate both classical painting and photography. It would also explain why Coppola invests instead in the pictorialism and representational codes that are the precursors of abstract art, namely symbolist painting, Expressionist color schemes, art nouveau ornament.

The key technical means, or figural trope used in order to achieve this end is superimposition. There is superimposition in classical cinema, too, but used mainly to indicate either shift in time and/or space, or to signal interiority, that is, the character's thoughts. But in a post-classical film such as BRAM STOKER'S DRACULA, superimposition is freed from these connotations, no longer functioning as boundary marker. A key example is the parting scene between Jonathan Harker and Mina, with the couple in the garden placed in the foreground, so as to create an exaggerated perspective to the rose-garden and the fountain at the far end. All of a sudden, a peacock's feather forecloses our view of the lover's kiss, until the "eye" of the feather opens up like an iris shot in an early film, though in fact transforming itself into the tunnel through which speeds the train that is already taking Jonathan away from Mina. What makes these metamorphoses partake in the new solidity and material consistency of the image are, paradoxically, the sound effects of the scene, with the cry of the peacock modulating into the whistle of the train, before becoming the plaintive voice of Mina reading the letter Jonathan has written to her on that train.

This new material density of the non-perspectival, figurative image is, however, itself an illusion, for its consistency is guaranteed less by any tactility of perception, and more by the semantic-cognitive effects put into play, illustrated by the visual and aural puns, such as the peacock's eye or the train's whistle. Another instance would be the pun on AB(SIN)THE in the seduction scene between Dracula and Mina, which starts with a close up of the drink being poured, forming a vortex that shapes into an eye, not unlike the bathwater/plughole/eye transformation in the shower-scene of Psycho. Coppola plays on eye, glass, drink and bottle: startling changes of perspective put the mind on high alert, for the attack on vision and perception in these scenes inevitably reminds one of the even more ferocious assault on the eye in Luis Buñuel's Un Chien Andalou. Coppola repeats the effect later in the scene, when the ring with diamonds which Dracula is offering to Mina/Elzbieta seems to graze her eye, here building up, however, to the romance cluster of associations that lead from eye to stars to diamonds to tears, for Dracula, having gathered Mina's tears from her cheeks, can now, with a magician's gesture, open his palm and reveal that they have turned into diamonds.

Vision as Immersion: Beyond Narration and Perspectivism?

With all these visual puns and double entendres, some of which are gross or grotesque, such as the fade that makes the slicing of a red side of beef by Van Helsing rhyme with his decapitation of Lucy, one is unsure of how "Coppola" (i.e. the narrating instance) wants to be read: does he mock the viewer or does he mock his characters? Is it irony (blank or red-blooded), parody or pastiche? Is it deadpan humor, or sick humor? What is the mode of engagement, what is the interpersonal tone and address, or is it a kind of queasy complicity that here substitutes for voyeurism and fetishization, the classical model's modes of identification? This is part of the irritation that the film provokes, because its tone is unreadable in classical terms. What from the point of view of cinematic modernism or European art cinema might be a "foregrounding of the device," would from the vantage point of classical cinema appear merely as a gratuitous "showing off," the "bad taste" of B-movies, or even confusing the viewer by obstructing narrative progress and transparency. Yet from another vantage point, such gyrations of tenor and tone invoke an altogether different viewing experience and viewing habit: not of the cinema, nor even television, but *the viewing experience of the screen as a monitor*, as a flat surface, upon which, in a visual-video overlay, any number of elements can be called up simultaneously: graphics, images, script, text, sound, voice, in other words, a whole array of media signals. What Coppola (now perhaps less as *auteur* and cinematic heir to the traditions of Ford or Hawks, but as founder-owner of Zoetrope studios, and erstwhile recipient of research and development funds from the Sony Corporation) seems to be examining is the multi-media viewing experience, now writ large (i.e. for the large screen), though—if we believe the publicity department's assertion that the film contains no digital special effects—done as an "authentic pastiche" of the thrusting enthusiasm and craftsman's pride associated with the early cinema's inventor-bricoleur-pioneers![36]

And just as the cinema of the first decades developed sophisticated spatial arrangements, favoring subtler forms of spectator participation, sometimes at the expense of narrative, so Coppola's film can be seen to suspend narrative in favor of spatial play or aural perspectivism, though these moments of pseudo-primitivism are themselves elaborate semantic puzzles, crafted in order to engage narrative on its own terrain, by deconstructing its logic of agency, motivation, temporality and the causal chain. Yet Bram Stoker's Dracula, despite its shock effects, does not thereby treat the viewer to the video game emplotment of "shoot them, kill them, chase them, thrill them." Its own mode proposes a kind of articulation where consequence, motive and implication are still vital, but where nonetheless a different form of participation and engagement obtains—one that I have tentatively named "engulfment," aware that the term is perhaps tailored too specifically to Bram Stoker's Dracula, while the principles implied are evidently intended to be valid for a larger body of films, because symptomatic of the wider changes sketched above under the heading "New Hollywood" and "post-classical cinema." Immersive engulfment is meant to indicate a distinct mode of consequence, of implication and interrelation, signifying at once an attenuated kind of causality, while also signaling something more dangerous, because no longer capable of being kept at the sort of distance that engagement primarily via the eye and mind assures. Instead of the bounded image, immersive engulfment works with the ambient image, in which it is sound that now locates, cues and even narrates the image, producing a more corporeal set of perceptions; instead of voyeurism and fetishistic fixation, there is spatial disorientation; instead of the logic of the "scene," it is semantic clusters, mental maps, spatial metaphors that organize comprehension and narrative transformation.

Finally, the term immersive engulfment also signals changes to the way one might think about narrative and causality in a social or political context. Against the basically agonistic/antagonistic principle of Aristotelian poetics, or even the structuralist model of binary oppositions and logical transformation (Lévi-Strauss or Greimas), the more embodied nexus of the post-classical implies power-gradients and feedback loops that can encompass relations of "contamination," but also those of involuntary attraction: of memory and trauma, of anticipation and the *après-coup*, of dependence and interdependence, of addiction, of the host and the parasite, and all of them suspending and yet "sublating" the Hegelian master-slave dialectic to which the Dracula myth is often associated, for "Dracula rises when history is in crisis."

In light of this, one can understand how the myth of Dracula does double duty for Coppola: not only insofar as it allows a reversal of the classical paradigm (where the story's transparency makes the technology invisible and inaudible), in favor of a re-materialization of the filmic signifiers via techniques that are often adapted in BRAM STOKER'S DRACULA from early cinema and "decadent" visual culture. Where other postmodern directors might make a fetish of the new technologies, and in their films test-drive, so to speak, the recent developments in sound (Dolby), frame (special video-effects of overlay and morphing), and image (Steadicam), Coppola seems more ironically detached, perhaps melancholically conscious of haunting the present by having been a pioneering Godfather in almost all of these fields. Also, the Dracula myth already literalizes this different causality of contamination and interdependence, as well as the particular causality of media events or, more specifically, the blockbuster phenomenon. The pervasiveness of these media epidemics, at all stages of the body politic and the public sphere, with their peculiar absorption of the past into the present and their virus-like multiplications, seem to have become emblematic for the instabilities of the post-binary, post-antagonistic, post-Cold War world (dis-)order.

Against this one might hold the irritation that Coppola has "betrayed" the myth by appending a frame tale, which trades a deeper truth for the politically correct move of historically locating and unambiguously identifying Dracula with Vlad the Impaler, possibly alluding to the so-called "clash of civilizations" when Orthodox Christianity "saved" the West from Islam and the Turks. Similarly, one might accuse him of having turned Dracula's sexuality from one of indiscriminate polymorphously perverse lust, into the dimensions of a romance story about star-crossed destinies, unnecessary suicides and a "love that never dies," when the vampire ought to stand for a lust that never dies! Anything else, it is said, emasculates the potency of the very notion of the undead, sacrificing the psychic economy of Eros and Thanatos on the paltry altar of a heterosexual *Liebestod*.

Yet such differences cannot be settled without the considerations that have informed this chapter: namely, that the film proposes various paradigms, leaving it up to the viewer whether to be engaged as (already) a post-classical viewer within the classical mode, or (still) as the classical viewer within the post-classical mode. One conclusion might be that the perspectival metaphor which has dominated film studies for so long will have to give way to a different metaphoric cluster: the one suggested for BRAM STOKER'S DRACULA, not surprisingly has alluded to "trauma" and "contamination," but it might equally well be some other "figurative" space, like that of the "visceral" and "body horror." It is precisely because a film like Bram Stoker's Dracula offers itself not only to very different readings, but is able to combine the viewing experience of the big screen and the small screen, the monitor and the video-arcade that it belongs to the new Hollywood, to the history of the cinema and to its after-life. In this respect at least, Bram Stoker's Dracula is an "authentic" enactment of the myth: the true Dracula of cinema—once more risen from the grave of the (much debated) "death of cinema" and the (box-office) "death of Coppola" to haunt us all—hopefully for quite some time yet, because who does not want the cinema to be *the love that never dies*?

20

The Blockbuster as Time Machine

In a season of history when technology has combined with political and social change to open vast new markets, we are a company equipped to reap the greatest benefits.[1]

Everything Connects

About two-thirds of the way into JURASSIC PARK, there is a scene where Hammond and Sattler talk in the Jurassic Park restaurant. The scene begins, however, with the camera exploring the adjacent gift shop. It is a slightly eerie moment, because it is as if the movie was at this point turning round and looking at us, but in the future tense. Set within a theme- and adventure park, which only exists as a fiction, the film invites us to imitate the characters in the fiction, for this fiction of a fiction will produce "real memorabilia," and in this way the film is itself an advertisement for the games, gadgets and toys that one can buy after one has seen the movie. The scene already anticipates that we will like the film so much that we will want to buy the merchandise, and to make it easy for us, it displays it in the film itself. It therefore does not come as a surprise to learn that six months before the release of the film, Spielberg's company, Amblin Films, issued a JURASSIC PARK style book, for advertisers and merchandisers, which alone cost $500,000 to produce.

Arguably this is merely another instance of the fact that in today's media-world—to (mis-) quote E.M. Forster—"everything connects." Especially a feature film, a theme park, a toy-store and a computer game have a lot in common: they feed off each other as they play off each other. When one considers that THE LION KING took $80 million at the box-office, but made $220 million as a video cassette, one can understand why some commentators argue that a film in today's media culture is merely the big advertising billboard stretched out in time, designed to showcase tomorrow's classics in the video-stores and the television re-runs. And even that is not entirely true when TERMINATOR II: THE VIDEO GAME sold three times as many copies as the video cassette! I would not be surprised if the world's toyshops had made more money with JURASSIC PARK dinosaurs than the film, the video and the *Lost World* video game together. Nonetheless, the way JURASSIC PARK makes the connections explicit is rather special, or especially symptomatic, insofar as it mimics the links within its own fiction, but in a way that plumbs the depths rather than multiplies the surfaces and their effects. "Everything connects," it would seem, does not mean that "everything goes."

And yet, since the 1980s, it was precisely as if everything did go and the sky was the limit. New Hollywood staged such an extraordinary comeback from its premature burial and put on such a permanent revolution of the eternally same, that one has to ask, who or what did the trick? Was it the charisma of the directors, who revamped the old story-telling techniques by vampirizing 1950s B-pictures and 1960s late-night television? Or was it the new generation of stars, with their talent agents and deal-makers? Was it the "synergies" with the music business, the new technologies of sound-design, of special effects and digital imaging devices? To most observers, the answer to why the contemporary Hollywood cinema climbed back to popularity all over the world was simple: money. First, at the production end, as spectacular sets, star salaries and huge promotion budgets hiked up the cost of movie making to unprecedented levels. But at the exhibition end, too, the potential and actual rewards at the box office have been staggering. If globalized capitalism, with its mergers and multi-national conglomerates, is the untranscendable horizon of the contemporary film industry, and money is the answer, it is also clear, however, that money cannot be an explanation, being the symptom rather than the cause. As one tries to understand the all-new Hollywood, it would seem that money is very nearly that which blinds one's insights, and not merely because it catches one in an economic or even technological determinism. The energies that feed the system, the aggregates of power that circulate, the creative manias, cunning strategies and ingenuity that animate the makers, as well as the fictions and fantasies that stir and attract audiences: all find in the exchange of money only their most convenient, and probably most banal materialization. For it is evident that with the conglomerates currently put together by the software firms, the music industries, the creative agencies and broadcast television companies, a power-potential is in the making that seems to be on the brink of realizing—in both senses of the word: becoming aware of, and translating into action—not only its economic clout but also its political might. DreamWorks, the name that Spielberg, David Geffen and Jerry Katzenberg gave to their studio is brilliantly and nonchalantly candid: the manufacture of fantasies that "work."

To argue this assertion, I want to look at some of the more internal or micro-links alongside the macro-level connections that hold today's media culture together, at a site where many roads cross and divergent paths intersect, namely the big picture, or blockbuster. The macro-level comprises the profit-oriented connections, while the micro-level would encompass the pleasure-oriented connections. Among the latter, with their focus on spectators and subjectivities, one could further differentiate between, say, the "film-as-text" and the "film-as-event," a distinction which in one way or another (as "narrative" versus "spectacle," or as "film semiotics" versus "cultural studies") has exercised film scholars of contemporary Hollywood. At the macro-level, too, it is possible to distinguish further, for instance, between the "horizontal" links, where everything connects in the world of entertainment and leisure (advertising, consumption, fashion, toys, as well as other aspects of popular or everyday culture), and the "vertical" ones, where everything connects at the level of business, industry, technology and finance. The former I have (elsewhere) called "Hollywood at street-level" and the latter I shall later here refer to as "Hollywood, the pinball machine." More broadly speaking, the macro-level points to the relations that exist between the film industry and other forms of modern capitalist business practice, where the big business methods of the multinationals do not differ all that much, whether they produce/sell cars or movies, silicone-chips or television programs, computer software or stars, soft drinks and junk-food or sounds and images. The micro-level, on the other hand, is at first glance more mystifying, but not altogether mysterious: why do we go to the movies, rather than watch individual films, why does one get addicted to "bad" movies, to the extent that the industry can cater for this new taste elite of the "dumber and dumber"? The micro-levels of pleasure highlight, among other things, the fact that as scholars we may have much at stake in the distinction between "film-as-text" and "film-as-event," but as audiences we evidently have resolved for ourselves in a practical manner one of the central, but rarely asked questions of film studies, which is not whether a film is "art" or "entertainment," but whether films are "products" or "services."

Product-Definition: Is a Film a Commodity or a Service?

The industry talk of money and profits, of merchandising and franchising, of tie-ins and spin-offs, of secondary markets and residual exploitation rights at once disguises and underlines what lies at the heart not only of contemporary Hollywood, but of the American film industry ever since its beginning: the struggle to define a product, to decide what it actually is that it is in the business of. The history of Hollywood from the late 1910s onwards could be written as the successive moves to install and define the *commodity* "*film*," while at the same time extending and refining the *service* "*cinema*." As to the first, it has not always been as self-evident as it now seems that a strip of celluloid, a can of film, or "two hours spent in the dark" can be a commodity. As to the second point, the cinema had to oust and/or compete with other providers of the same service, whether we call it mass entertainment or performance art, leisure activity or spectacle: the circus, the music hall, vaudeville or boulevard theater.

A commodity is something whose value to the consumer is both material and immaterial, something that both enhances the self and can be used to communicate or signify to others. A car, for instance, is a perfect commodity: its material value is as an individualized means of mass transport, but its immaterial value is that of a status symbol, and as a status symbol—say a BMW—it enhances the self-(image) of the owner and signifies something to others (such as "irresponsible, unmarried thirty-something showing off"). These self-images and the meanings attached to them by the culture at large, however, are not fixed and eternal, they can change over time and are always embedded in history and ideology. In the 1970s, for instance, BMWs in Germany were known as Baader-Meinhof Wagen (after the names of the two leading members of a German terrorist group), because they were the preferred getaway cars during the group's frequent shoot-outs and bank robberies.

A film, on the other hand, was once quite difficult to define as a commodity. Not only because what distinguishes the cinema from an automobile is the peculiar and remarkable convergence of money and culture, of commerce and art. It has also been difficult because a film essentially commodifies an experience, which by its nature is highly subjective, context dependent and comprises other variables and imponderables. The fact that the product of the film industry is thus in some sense always merely the peculiar aggregate state, both potential and actual, of this experience has led to an intense effort to establish and enforce "norms" while at the same time, keeping the parameters of those norms susceptible to the (historically, but also demographically) changing modalities of pleasure and self-enhancement. This reference to norms is what we mean by "classical cinema," while the changing modalities of self-imaging explain why the movies belong to the world of fashion and lifestyle, of consumption, leisure and tourism as well as to the world of art, literature, philosophy and psychology. It makes it necessary to define "film" as material *and* immaterial, a combination that would seem to cut across the distinction between commodity and service, unless one defines the cinema as a "service supported by commodities," where "service" means such diverse states of mind and feeling as "an evening out" alone, or with friends, the "thrill and excitement of danger and risk," a "special occasion," or even a parentally sanctioned way to arrange a date if you're a teenager. Correspondingly, ". . . supported by commodities" would mean: soft drinks and popcorn, the "book of the film," the "movie soundtrack" as CD, the Batman movie logo on a tee-shirt or a bicycle wheel, the movie characters as toys, the video of the film, the visit to a movie theme park or—to come back to my JURASSIC PARK example—the visit to the studio gift shop after the tour, where you buy a pair of dino slippers for your grandfather or Aunt Meg.

Going to the movies, in other words, involves all kinds of things other than watching a film. It presupposes the simultaneous coexistence of two systems: one—we can now say—is concerned with producing an object as experience as a commodity: in this case, a film, that is, an assemblage of moving images and sound, taking up a slice of time. The other, however, is concerned with providing a service: the cinema, the comfortable seats, the ice-cream and soft drinks, the pleasant atmosphere of simulated luxury for time out with friend or lover. Going to the movies is an event in which the film is only one of the elements, and maybe sometimes not even the most crucial or memorable one. The cinema, once one looks at it as both an industry and a culture, is really these two systems sitting on top of each other, loosely connected, or rather connected in ways intriguingly intertwined. One is the system that links a space and a site (the movie house) to bodies endowed with perception (the audience) via a certain set of expected and anticipated pleasures or gratifications. The other system is that which connects writers, directors, producers, cinematographers, actors around an activity called making a film, and resulting in roughly 90–120 minutes of continuous flow of sounds, shapes and colors. That the two systems have sometimes very little to do with each other is indicated by the fact that some filmmakers can make films that never get shown in cinemas, and some films do not get made until they are already sold—and sometimes even booked—to the cinemas. For a professional filmmaker, the ratio of projects to finished films can be as little as 5:1, which not only means that out of five projects only one becomes a film, but also that a director may spend five years working on them, without a single film in the can. When one thinks of how many films get shown at a film festival like Cannes or Rotterdam and how few of them end up getting general release, then one cannot but conclude that the system is incredibly wasteful. It just does not seem to "connect" in a meaningful, rational way to the audiences. But if this is so, why is it so?

The Slow Climb Back: Reversing the Paramount Decree

From the point of view of the cinema owners, movies are a nuisance, they are a pain in the neck! Some have been quoted as saying "if I could sell my customers popcorn and coke while locking them into a lift for two hours, I'd prefer that to showing them a film." Because the truth is, a cinema-owner does not have to be a cinephile in order to be successful. He is a businessman whose skill is "locking up" people, or more politely, "gathering an audience," and providing the amenities, the ambience and the setting that makes this audience come back, again and again. For him, the film is merely the hook by which he brings them to his house, because in truth, he often makes more money by what he sells before and after or in the breaks by way of drinks and refreshments than by the percentage he gets from the box-office receipts. Should we spare a thought for the poor owner, if his profits are not in the cinema ticket, but in the stuff you ingest? Only if the owner is Mr. So-and-so, or Mr. and Mrs. What-you-may-call-it, running a little family cinema. But as we know, those days are long gone. They are the last picture shows, belonging to the era of the slow decline and death-agony of the cinema in the 1960s and 1970s. Family cinemas all over the world have almost all closed (except for the little "art-cinema" houses, run by ex-film students or former avant-garde filmmakers) and the big cinemas are (once more) "chains," owned either by large multinational conglomerates or big entrepreneurs—which means that they are effectively controlled by American distributors: an important aspect of how the American film industry has clawed back "vertical integration," after the Paramount decree of the late 1940s and the splitting up of the industry during the 1950s, with the advent of television.

The history of Hollywood since 1945 is the history of the responses to the forced separating of production, distribution and exhibition, and the consequences of yet again having had to redefine its product, re-design its markets and re-target its audiences. In the battles that followed, the production companies or studios took many different measures to try and re-establish vertical integration. Yet for a time in the 1960s and early 1970s, it seemed that nothing connected anymore. Very quickly after the war, de-cartelization and demographic changes introduced "competition," which is to say, it introduced uncertainty at all levels: Hollywood no longer knew what products to make, what services to offer and what audiences to appeal to. Effectively, it took Hollywood thirty to forty years to reverse the implications of the Decree and the advent of television, namely to re-establish some form of vertical integration and to win back the family audience. It took a change in the nature of international capitalism—what we call "post-Fordism"—to make the system of "flexible specialization," "outsourcing" and "contract labor" also the standard practice in Hollywood. In fact, in this sense, the film and media industries sometimes "pioneered" (if this is the right word) the neo-capitalist conditions of labor not only in the new information industries.

The main aim of Hollywood, then, has been to achieve new forms of vertical integration, even if by other means and by another name. The name of the game is to create *synergies*, for instance, by consolidating, rather than diversifying business operations, but instead of consolidating manufacture, the idea is to bring together activities with which the consumer associates (music business, publishing, movie business, television channels, telephone companies), while at the level of production, the word is "outsourcing" or "sub-contracting." But synergy also has to do with "unexpected connections" or differences at one level, which turn out to be similarities at another level. In fact, it could be compared to the production of hot-dogs and ice-cream: both are similar in that they are convenience food that you eat with your hands, and they are different not only because one is savory and the other is sweet, but because the seasonal peak of consumption for each complements the other: more ice-cream in the summer and more hot-dogs in the winter. But you only get synergy when something connects the two at a deeper level. And in the case of sausages and ice-cream, the deeper level lies in the economics of recycling. Something that for obvious reasons is not terribly well known is the fact that a key waste product of sausage making is unsaturated fat. This is waste when you make sausages, but it is an ideal raw material when you make ice-cream and need something that is stiff when cold and gets creamy when warmed—for instance, by your warm tongue. If you therefore combine an ice-cream factory and a sausage factory, the result is Walls: Europe's largest producer of both sausages and ice-cream: here, too, the tail is wagging the dog—but then, what exactly is tail and what is (hot-)dog?

But in the meantime, what exactly is happening at the micro-level? What is this "experience" that best describes how everything connects for an audience, and yet does so in a highly structured manner? The structure of desire that the movies work on is a well-known one: we perceive the cinema as a window on the world, but we also apprehend the films as a mirror of the self. If this is a notoriously complex theoretical issue, it nonetheless also comes down to some simple points, of which one is the importance of repetition in popular entertainment. The same as different: genre cinema and the norms of story-construction involve us in remembered pleasure and anticipated memory, both of which bring us back to "the movies," locking us into a kind of repetition compulsion, and tying the cinema experience to anticipation and expectation. The other point has to do with the fact that these shifting structures of temporality and the moment not only constitute aspects of our subjectivity, but that this subjectivity (call it "desire" or "fantasy") can be attached to objects and products. This is what we understand by commodity-fetishism, because what defines the commodity in this context is precisely the ability of an object to attract and fix a desire or a fantasy. One way of therefore resolving the dilemma of the definition for the cinema as a commodity *and* a service would be to argue as follows. When buying a movie ticket, we are effectively taking out a contract, which in exchange for our money guarantees that we are receiving a normative, quality-controlled (material) product. Conversely, our part of the deal is to be "prepared to pay" not for the product itself and not even for the commodified experience which it represents, but simply "for the possibility of pleasure."[2]

The Blockbuster, Holding it all Together

My contention would thus be that the blockbuster in its contemporary form combines (in the most exemplary, but also the most efficient and evolved form) the two systems (film-as-production/ cinema-as-experience), the two levels (macro-level of capitalism/micro-level of desire), and the two aggregate states of the cinema experience (commodity/service). When, on a Friday night, we go to the movies, what do we want to see? Nine times out of ten it will be the big movie, the one we have been hearing about on television, reading about in the papers, of which a tantalizing trailer has been showing for months prior to its release, which has announced itself like a weather-front weeks before by its paraphernalia in the media, the novelty shops and the department stores. In short, we want to see the movie that promises to be an event, thanks to advance advertising, thanks to word of mouth, thanks to a media blitz and special websites. This movie may have many different titles, but essentially it has one generic name: it's called a blockbuster. What characterizes a blockbuster? First of all, a big subject and a big budget (world war, disaster, end of the planet, monster from the deep, holocaust, death-battle in the galaxy). Second, a young male hero, usually with a lot of fire power, or secret knowledge or an impossibly difficult mission (battle, confrontation, good versus evil, humans versus aliens). In other words, a blockbuster involves a mythic story or an epic journey (based on fairy tale, myth or religious narrative). The hero founds—or rescues—a civilization, he survives a meteorite or a deadly virus, and he saves the planet: Moses, Luke Skywalker, Aladdin, Elliott from E.T. . . .—sometimes a young woman has an action part and a life-saving role as well, such as in THE TERMINATOR, and more likely in Disney films (Esmeralda, Pocahontas), but mostly it is the young men—the Tom Cruises, the Brad Pitts, the Keanu Reeves or Leonardo di Caprios who get to do the dangerous and spectacular things. The big movie is therefore necessarily based on traditional stories, sometimes against the background of historical events, more often a combination of fantasy or sci-fi, with the well-known archetypal heroes from Western culture on parade. In one sense, this makes blockbusters the natural, that is, technologically more evolved extension of fairy tales, as told or in books. In another sense, these spectacle "experiences," these media "events" are also miracles, and not at all natural. Above all, they are miracles of engineering and industrial organization. They are put together like super-tankers, aircraft carriers or—yes, skyscrapers, office blocks, shopping malls. They resemble military campaigns, and that's one of the main reasons they cost so much to make.

It is a notorious fact that the cost of movie making has spiralled to astronomical heights. Today, the sort of movie that premiers under the conditions just described costs between $80 and $120 million to make, with some (like TITANIC) consuming $200 million. That's enough to build 4,000 homes, provide uncontaminated drinking water for 600,000 people for one year, or renew the telephone system of an entire city the size of Rome. In fact, the only other kind of product that costs as much, and on the scale of basic human necessities is as useless and frivolous as a movie is an assault helicopter, a set of intercontinental missiles in a submarine, or an atomic test on the Muraroa Atoll in the Pacific. And at this level, the Hollywood story has much in common with the arms race. What Hollywood has done is to have continually raised the stakes: by making filmmaking ever more costly and extravagant, in order for the number of competitors to become smaller and smaller. Again, it's rather like the nuclear deterrent: Ronald Reagan's Star Wars initiative, borrowed from George Lucas' and Steven Spielberg's movies, brought the Soviet Union to its knees. Of course, I am exaggerating. But the hiking of the cost of movie making is rather like the membership fees to country clubs and golf courses: it is designed to keep out the undesirables, the upstarts. In this case, it is designed to keep most of the world's countries from being able to afford a film industry, and from keeping most of the world's independent filmmakers from getting their films into the cinemas. Once upon a time, most European nations could afford a film industry. Today, with the possible exception of France, none can: not Italy, not Spain, not Britain, nor Germany. Once upon a time, second-run cinemas and art-houses would show independent productions. Now, the multiplexes keep one screen out of fifteen for the art-cinema audience, and they only show movies which have received a prize at Cannes, Venice, Berlin or Rotterdam.

For another kind of synergy is represented by the globalization of exhibition, which—to use Europe as an example—has given the American majors a virtual monopoly over distribution, and via its bargaining power as a "producer" has also had a stranglehold on the "service," down to the colors of the carpets in the multiplexes or the flavors of the popcorn. Via its dominance of the outlets, the cinemas, the American film industry has achieved the extraordinary feat of being able to open the same film in thousands of cinemas on the same Friday night, drawing attention to the question why such a feat should be desirable in the first place, namely the shifting economics of international box-office earnings. While Hollywood in the 1940s and 1950s could recover its production costs in the huge US home market alone, so that export earnings were pure profit or the financial clout behind an overseas investment policy, over the last ten to fifteen years, the foreign markets have accounted for almost 50 percent of the US film industry's total earnings, making economies of scale in the advertising and marketing of a big budget picture not only desirable but essential.

Not unconnected with the changes in exhibition is a third development by which the contemporary equivalent of vertical integration has been achieved between 1975 and 1990. Synergies not only occurred through the new management practices in the production sector (fewer, but more expensive, one-offs and prototypes) and the control of cinema exhibition via the hegemony in distribution. Synergy concerned the management of the software libraries, meaning the exploitation of film- and TV rights via cable stations, or the "dumping" practices on foreign (TV) markets, such as the re-packaging of repeats, and turning it into a whole channel, such as "TV-Gold" or the "TNT-Movie Channel." It allowed parts of the industry to live off these accumulated assets and thereby, especially in the TV production sector, to spread the risk invested in a new product. They could, for a short while, survive when there was no new product, for instance, during one of the rare strikes. The explosive growth of channels has proved the importance of owning these libraries of films or television programs: even if a studio was bankrupt like MGM, even if all its physical assets had been sold or dispersed, it was still a gold-mine because of the rights to old films. Hence the sentiment quoted by Tino Balio: "if you're a big corporation you can *never not* make money with movies."[3] You can contrast this with the conclusion drawn by James Shamus (producer and screenwriter of THE ICE STORM) in his essay "To the Rear of the Back End": if you are an independent production company, then you can *never* make money with movies, even if they are successful at the box office and with critics.[4] Why this difference?

The Pinball Machine

The answer to this question probably lies in the fact that the new consolidation/synergy model could be seen as a sort of pinball machine. The principle behind it would be something like this: you launch with great force the little steel ball, shoot it to the top, and then you watch it bounce off the different contacts, pass through the different gates, and whenever it touches a contact, your winning figures go up. The AV media entertainment business is such a pinball machine: the challenge is to "own" not only the steel ball, but also as many of the contacts as possible because the same "ball" gets you more and more "points," that is, profits. The contact points are the cinema-screens and video-stores, theme parks and toyshops, restaurant chains and video-arcades, bookstores and CD-record shops. By contrast, the independent producer only has his little steel ball, and if he is not careful, he has to stand by and watch as all the others that have the contact points make money out of his film. Hence the importance of the different attempts at independent distribution analyzed by Justin Wyatt in the case of Tom Laughlin's BILLY JACK.[5] By "road-showing" and "four-walling" the film, the producer himself booked whole districts and entire cinemas for his single film, reinventing, so to speak, the zoning and block booking of old, but as a one-off.

The impossibility of making money with a film alone is yet another form of the wagging the dog scenario: combined with television, cable, home video and DVD, the cinema has become a sort of huge advertising machine for generating not only money, but first of all, cultural "recognition value"—that is what a film has to have, before it can even begin to become a shiny steel ball, before it is sold to television and becomes a hit in video rentals and pre-recorded tapes. In the words of Siegfried Zielinski, who uses a different metaphor: the film is a *Durchlauferhitzer*, a machine that heats up cold water, brings it to the boil, and then lots of people can turn on the tap and out comes a shower (of gold). This would be the fourth meaning of "blockbuster," after standing for the bringing together of text-production and social experience, of capital and desire, of commodity and service: that it is a generator of recognition power and cultural capital. TITANIC was such an event movie that accumulated not only dollars but also recognition value, and so was THE MATRIX, which did not make mega-millions, but scored high as cultural capital.

This generation of cultural capital, when the cinema is considered not only as a money-making, but also as a meaning-making machine is a phenomenon that is beginning to be studied closer, and forms one of the justifications of a "cultural studies" approach to the Hollywood blockbuster. For from this, only slightly different perspective, the blockbuster is engineered for maximum meaning, which is to say that culturally it is a collage of very different elements, consciously chosen and deliberately put together in a particular manner. Often, these parts are "attractions," which come together in the film, but which in the process of the marketing, can be exploited separately. Thus my motto from the opening, namely that "everything connects," but not "everything goes" is already well known to industry insiders, film critics and scholars alike: it is what is meant by "high concept filmmaking," which Justin Wyatt has summed up as "the book, the look, and the hook."[6]

Catch Them when You Can, Keep them Forever—From the Disney Formula to the Spielberg Concept

"High Concept" returns us to the "internal connections" or the micro-level. For it is not the money, the corporate clout, the production values, the stars as such that makes a movie "big." It is what these entities represent, what they can "buy." If the delivery of recognition value or cultural capital is one way to put it, another would be to say: what these values, accumulated in the blockbuster, buy is time. Paradoxically, not so much the time of the viewing of the film, but time past and time future.

Foremost among the strategies with which the blockbuster multiplies these temporalities, it seems to me, are the kinds of "doubling" or repetition-effects with which I started. The souvenir-display-within-the-film, as in the example from JURASSIC PARK is only one such doubling-effect. The same goes for the internal repetitions of the "film-within-the-film," as in the opening scenes of TITANIC. Another modality would be the event-within-the-film doubling the situation of the viewer (as in the films that are released around Christmas and feature wintry celebrations, e.g. GREMLINS), or the films that feature vacations and are released for the vacations, such as HOME ALONE, a practice initiated by the prototype of all modern blockbusters, Spielberg's JAWS.

The special thing about a film like JURASSIC PARK, then, is not the doubling itself, but how tightly all this is synchronized and orchestrated, how neatly the different aspects of art and technology, of entertainment and adventure, of fantasy and merchandising fit into each other around the time-shifting axis of past, present and future. If one of the most remarkable features of the contemporary media are their mirroring functions generally, often called the *mise-en-abyme* effect, or self-reference, or self-reflexivity, with the film "doubling" the reality of what is being shown, by making us aware that we are watching a movie, then we have to conclude that in the blockbuster, instead of "breaking the illusion," this kind of effect actually deepens our fascination. It catches us in its multiple mirrors, using this doubling as a powerful tool in order to bind us into the film, as a special kind of experience that joins anticipation with repetition, and imitation with memory. I am tempted therefore to call this type of effect not *mise-en-abyme*, but to think about it in terms of a sort of "situation-synergy."

My argument would be that the reason a blockbuster usually concerns topics and themes that have to do with childhood and adolescence, with mythologies and fairytales, with major disasters and the forces of nature, with the supernatural and the boundaries between the human and the non-human is that these are all subjects that allow for a dramatization of time and temporality. They are all about connecting the past with the future. And while the most successful example of "connecting the past with the future" is still the Disney Corporation, directors like Tim Burton and Robert Zemeckis, but above all, Spielberg have become strong competitors of this aspect of the Disney-formula. The Disney corporation has been described as engineers of fantasy and they call themselves "imagineers," but the corporation is also in the business of engineering childhood, nostalgia, the need to return home (from Walt Disney and Bambi to Steven Spielberg and E.T.)—all time-based fantasies. What America has learnt from the European fairy-tale is not only insights into the world of the childhood fears and longings. It has also appreciated the fact that if you get children used to things early, they'll stick with it all their lives. What we do in our formative years will always remain a utopia, a backward utopia—we'll always want to go "home" to our childhood. The secret of going to the cinema—what I called the time structure of fantasy—is embodied to perfection in Disney, but by now not only the Disney corporation has become expert in turning this into a goldmine.

In Disney films and in Disneyland, for instance, it is always "now," and every film is an instant "classic," whether Snow White, The Lion King, Pocahontas, Hercules, The Hunchback of Notre Dame. Only George Lucas' Star Wars and Spielberg—with E.T. and since 1996, with his DreamWorks productions—seem to have tapped as deeply into the roots of the time structure of fantasy as Disney. Disney saw mass entertainment as a vital support for the family (and "family values"), giving children "worlds," "icons" and "currency" when they talk to each other, but also support to the parents. We know that the movies on television, almost as much as the cartoons in the morning and at the weekend, have become the automatic plug-in baby-sitters. But by successfully adapting the Disney formula, Spielberg has expanded it to include wars and human disasters (Schindler's List, Saving Private Ryan), the boundaries between the human and the pre-human or post-human (Jaws, Jurassic Park, Close Encounters of the Third Kind). His films have transformed the ability of the cinema to connect past and future into a mythic "now" in ways which make them the templates also for the "adult" blockbuster and future "classic."

To summarize once more the major reasons why the blockbuster is so important, both for the contemporary media scene (it is responsible for "saving" Hollywood and thus "saving" the cinema as a popular entertainment medium), and for understanding the history of the cinema in the last fifty years. In the contemporary scene the blockbuster provides a focus, an event, it divides the year and the seasons. No more than six to eight potential blockbusters compete for our attention, usually around the holiday seasons, such as Christmas and Easter, and before the summer vacation and at the start of the autumn. With its macro-structure of commodity-and-service and its micro-structure of "plumbing-the-depths," with its connections and synergies, it energizes the entire audio-visual field, as well as related sectors of the entertainment world. As a billboard, pinball machine or hot-water heater, it is the tail wagging the dog, although—as we saw—it is a moot point what here is tail and what is dog.

If the blockbuster in this respect has been instrumental in bringing about—in fact become the symbol of—a new kind of "vertical integration" in the audio-visual and entertainment industries, its ability to create an event is also an aspect of something else. One of its foremost tasks is the role it plays in our culture's time-management, both at the level of the day-to-day, the week-to-week, the seasons of the year, and at the life-cycle level of childhood and its eternal return. As an instrument of time-management, the blockbuster wants to be nothing less than our life-calendar. At one end, the event movie allows us to share and to exchange the feeling of "being there" and "having been there." At the other end, the blockbuster, being designed from the outside to the inside, and assembled out of several moving parts, so to speak, erects a kind of superstructure in time, memory and space, inviting us to "enter into" the material-immaterial "environment" and its "world." In actual fact, the *mise-en-abyme* effect with which I started here works the other way round: it takes our everyday habits, such as shopping, "by the hand" and mirrors them in so many ways that they are magnified or amplified into an adventure, an event, something never to forget.

After all the "external" forms of connection, the synergies and the deals, the concentration and the diversifications, the point about the "inner" connections is at once simple and complex. Between past and future, between childhood and parenthood, the cinema has increasingly become a kind of time machine, with the blockbuster as the "engine" that simultaneously raises expectations, stirs memories and unites us with our previous selves. Across mythical stories of disaster and renewal, trauma and survival, it also reconciles us to our mortality. That is a tall order for a movie, but in a world where money is the bottom line and the blockbuster picture the generator of sky-high profits, the movies taking on the mandate of secular redemption may not be too much to ask, not even of Hollywood. There, we are told, anything goes, but sometimes it even connects.

21

Auteurism Today: Signature Products, Concept-Authors and Access for All: AVATAR

> Lucas and Spielberg are the descendants of Griffith and, even more directly, of Chaplin, who made millions from the movies he starred in: they are artist-businessmen. The type is as old as Hollywood.
>
> (Louis Menand)[1]

The Hollywood *Auteur* in the Digital Age

There is general agreement that since the late 1980s, one of the founding narratives of the *auteur* theory no longer has either intellectual credibility or plausibility in practice.[2] The original narrative, it will be remembered, established the term *auteur* as the proper name for a film director, who under specific circumstances can be acknowledged as the author of a commercially produced film, even if hundreds of other professionals were involved in its making.[3] It gave credibility to the idea that in an industrial context, too, the director could manifest the skill, talent and "genius" of an "artist," achieving personal vision, autonomy and independence over the constraints and against the demands of a system, whose primary goal is to manage an industry on behalf of investors expecting profits. However, it seems that on both sides of this divide—the film director as *auteur*, and the system as business management—a more nuanced and differentiating picture is required, if one is to understand the situation as it has evolved over the past two to three decades in Hollywood picture making. Sometimes the sum of these changes tends to be subsumed under the word "digital," but "digital" would here function as either a metonymy, the part-for-the-whole, or as a convenient label, making a technical process stand in as a determining cause for a much more complex field of cause-and-effect, or even effects without apparent causes: "digital" in the phrase "digital cinema" not only means special effects and computer wizardry, but also the oblique and quasi-magical nexus that today ties reality to images, audiences to the cinema, film authors to studios and studios to multi-media corporations, whose workings and interactions once in a while produce spectacular economic or "real world" effects, such as the three billion dollars box-office gross of James Cameron's AVATAR, a figure so staggering that it demands, besides metaphors (of incredulity and black magic) and metonymies (of technical prowess and white magic) perhaps also an attempt at a more rational explanation.

Such an attempt might start with a very general observation, namely that in the late 20th and beginning 21st century, the traditional gap between culture and the arts on one side, and commerce and industry on the other, has narrowed significantly. As the social geographer Allen J. Scott puts it:

> One of the defining features of contemporary society, at least in the high-income countries of the world, is the conspicuous convergence that is occurring between the domain of the economic on the one hand and the domain of the cultural on the other. Vast segments of the modern economy are inscribed with significant cultural content, while culture itself is increasingly being supplied in the form of goods and services produced by private firms for a profit under conditions of market exchange. . . . An especially dramatic case of this peculiar conjunction of culture and economics is presented by the motion picture industry of Hollywood.[4]

In other words, when thinking about authorship today, it is not a matter of pitting art against commerce, critical acclaim against box-office figures, or conversely, asking rhetorically whether the arts have ever flourished without either patronage or a "market." Instead, it seems more productive to track the implications of what Scott calls a "recursive relationship": extending it from the place "Hollywood" and the industry "Hollywood" to the different forms of creativity—artistic and artisanal, but also financial and managerial—that filmmaking implies, and to assess the conditions of possibility that exist for authorship in the sense of autonomy and authority outlined above, to thrive or survive in today's conjuncture. The challenge is to examine the individual options and the practical choices certain filmmakers have made, in light of the systemic givens and the general logic of a "creative industry" that likes to call itself "the business". In the case of some of the most successful names in this "business," can the phrase "the director as author"—such would be the question—be more than a euphemistic-nostalgic or actively misleading expression, and should it, therefore, along with the *auteur* theory itself, be definitively retired?

I shall try to make the counter-case, and in what follows, I want to take the director James Cameron and his blockbuster film AVATAR as the occasion for testing Scott's conjunction of culture and economics, of place and people, of art and industry. I hope to take account of their reciprocal-recursive interdependence, as well as to clarify the stages and negotiations—internal to the film industry as well as between the industry, the audience and the author—particular to this conjunction. Cameron (born in 1954) is by no means the only director working in or for Hollywood, whose career might merit such an examination. Among his generation, one could cite Robert Zemeckis (b. 1951), the Coen Brothers (b. 1954/57), Ang Lee (b. 1954) or Katherine Bigelow (b. 1951). In the subsequent generation, Peter Jackson (b. 1961), David Fincher (b. 1962), Steven Soderbergh (b. 1963), Quentin Tarantino (b. 1963) and Christopher Nolan (b. 1970) suggest themselves as exemplars of the salient aspect in this evolving history of Hollywood authors, the career of each readable (and needing to be read) as an index that the director in question pursues an individual, reflexive-self-reflexive, as well as strategic and systemic response to a common situation.[5]

Yet in order to talk meaningfully about any of them, one has to go back at least another generation—or ten years in terms of dates of birth—and discuss the templates or prototypes of the Hollywood author in the post-studio era: Francis Ford Coppola, Martin Scorsese, George Lucas and Steven Spielberg. The most helpful entry point has been Jon Lewis' essay on George Lucas and Steven Spielberg.[6] Lewis regards these two not just as the economically most successful Hollywood directors in the history of the cinema, but as standing for what he terms the second wave of "New Hollywood" *auteurs*, to be distinguished from the first, of which Coppola and Scorsese are the outstanding representatives. Lewis starts by reminding us that in the early 1970s, these four filmmakers had more in common than separated them, with Coppola the oldest (b. 1939) and Spielberg the youngest (b. 1946), Scorsese (b. 1942) and Lucas (b. 1944) in between. Their passion for the movies as cinephile fans from an early age, their film school background, their immense knowledge of both American and European film history made them a distinct group, different from Robert Altman or William Friedkin (who came to filmmaking through television).[7] But whereas Coppola and Scorsese might be said to have emulated their Paris peers, presenting themselves as *auteurs*, and taking care to evolve a personal style and a unique *mise-en-scène*, while proclaiming their opposition to the old Hollywood system, Spielberg and Lucas were more cautious and diffident about adopting such postures. Coppola, for instance, from early on, consciously inscribed himself in a great American tradition of geniuses that failed magnificently: a line extending from D.W. Griffith and Erich von Stroheim to Orson Welles and Nicholas Ray.[8] Spielberg, on the other hand—as Lewis points out—singularly avoided working on his place in film history, preferring, in the discourse that has become increasingly important since the 1970s, namely the directorial interview, to dumb himself down to a mere popcorn entertainer:

> In virtually all of the early interviews, Spielberg espouses a child-like joy in filmmaking. And in doing so he discounts the very pretensions that supported seventies *auteurism*: personal signature, marginal and/or antagonistic relations with studio Hollywood, a priority on artistic integrity and a seeming disinterest . . . in a film's stake in the marketplace.[9]

Scorsese and Coppola, Spielberg and Lucas: Signature Style vs Signature Product

From these different stances, Lewis deduces an important distinction. After acknowledging that Hollywood readily embraced *auteurism*, "as a marketing tool," he points out that the new wave of *auteurs* are notable less for a *signature style* than for a *signature product*.[10] Lucas and Spielberg are directors, producers (and writers), as were some of the classic *auteurs* of the post-Paramount Decree era, but now they have protégés, who make films similar to those of the masters (Tobe Hooper and Robert Zemeckis in the case of Spielberg), or whom they let direct their films (in the case of Lucas, who has more or less passed on directing since the initial success of the STAR WARS series). Evidently, these different roles (producer, director, writer) no longer quite mean what they once did even in Hollywood, if they suggest that only by directing can someone be an *auteur*. Spielberg, with a producer's or co-producer's credit for more than 120 films, arguably has been more influential on the development of Hollywood in these roles than he has as director. As Lewis puts it: "[Lucas and Spielberg's] *oeuvre* presents a model of contemporary filmmaking in an industry that is no longer (just) about making movies."[11]

This latter state of affairs is often referred to as the "blockbuster mindset," and as such I have discussed it in the previous chapter. But other current terms for this new mode are: "high concept" filmmaking,[12] "franchise" filmmaking[13] and "total entertainment"[14] filmmaking. Each label puts the emphasis slightly differently, and once the perspective shifts to the makers, *signature product* seems a useful term, even if, as I shall argue in the final chapter, this does not altogether resolve the issue whether Hollywood is primarily about "products" or "services." Indeed, the signature product can be seen as a crucial element on the "service" side, which is where the accent lies when speaking of "total entertainment." Lewis, elaborating on signature product, points out that:

> Lucas and Spielberg's initial impact at the box office was unprecedented and remains unmatched. It is the ground zero of their importance, an importance that begins and according to their many critics maybe ends with money. Lucas' break-through film, *American Graffiti* (1973), was until 1999 the highest grossing low budget film in motion picture history. In what was a sign of things to come, the film, picked up reluctantly by Universal only after Francis

Coppola signed-on as executive producer in 1973, was brilliantly cross-marketed with an LP of its nostalgic pop music score. Spielberg's *Jaws*, released two years later, broke the box office record set by *The Godfather* (1972). Its success created the summer season and in doing so presented a model of filmmaking for a generation of "summer films." In 1977, Lucas' *Star Wars* broke *Jaws*' record and did so in dramatic fashion. Like *American Graffiti, Star Wars* was a model new Hollywood product. It was easily cross-promoted and it exploited markets in several parallel entertainment and consumer industries. Given the scale of its financial success, questions regarding its artistic merit seemed altogether beside the point.[15]

From Production to Post-production

The reasons why the shift from "signature style"—already a self-conscious, postmodern or "reflexive" turn on the old *auteur* principles of style and *mise-en-scène*—to "signature product" is so important are multiple and symptomatic. First of all, it reflects the fact that Hollywood, since the 1980s, has faced a distinctly different media-landscape: an increase in competitors, made up of rival media and new, so-called "disruptive" technologies, which in turn presented challenges to all aspects of Hollywood's business model as well as to the manufacture and identity of its core product, the feature film.[16]

Films have had to perform equally well on different media-platforms, at least since the 1970s: as theatrical releases, as television re-runs, as pre-recorded videotapes. Since the 1990s, however, both the market place has expanded (it has become global, rather than merely US-domestic, European, Japanese and Australian) and the platforms have diversified. Besides the ones named, they have been joined by a film's Internet site, the movie trailer, the video game and the DVD as both textual and promotional entities. And while scholars can draw up useful binary distinctions—between special effects and intricate plotting, between cinema of attraction and narrative integration, between narrative structure and game logic, between linearity and seriality, between "optical" vision and "haptic" vision, between classical and post-classical cinema, between "home entertainment" and "event movie"—Hollywood has no such luxury. As the phrase goes: in order to exist at all, the American film industry has to be "a major presence in all the world's markets," but also, one can add, have "a major presence in all the world's modes of representation." This proliferation of reception contexts and media-platforms, as well as modes of production that Hollywood has embraced (event movies, family entertainment, animation films, indie films and even niche market art films), makes relevant and indeed requires a new concept of the "author," as expressed in and through the signature product, rather than merely through a signature style.[17]

Second, while the core product of the film industry, the roughly two-hour length feature film, has remained remarkably stable over an extremely long period of time—almost a hundred years—the manner of its production has changed significantly in the last two decades, with more and more time (and money) being spent on editing, special effects (even for non-fantasy subjects), as well as on sound-design and sound effects. Most, if not all of this work is done digitally, partly for cost reasons but also because of the extended possibilities that digital technology affords in the manipulation of image and sound, the look and the feel of a picture. Together, these activities are referred to as "post-production," to distinguish them from "production." Post-production is often "outsourced" to specialized companies, involving a good deal of painstaking manual work, done by armies of trained experts—far away from, say, the locations, the sets and the actors of the film-in-progress. Here, too, the first and second wave New Hollywood *auteurs* differ from each other:

> The first wave *auteurs* [Coppola, Scorsese] focused primarily on mise-en-scene and took pride and care in directing actors, set design and lighting, all things accomplished during the

production phase. Lucas and Spielberg are almost exclusively post-production directors, experts in sound and special effects and action editing. Popular directors in Hollywood today are significantly cut from the second-wave cloth. James Cameron, the director of the ultimate nineties blockbuster, TITANIC, first made his mark doing post-production special effects.[18]

The shift to post-production thus highlights one of the key areas in Hollywood's new way of doing things, one where digitization has come to play a determining role over the past twenty years. Yet especially in this instance an aspect resurfaces which refers back to the heart of the *auteur* theory. It is sometimes assumed, for instance, that Lucas abandoned directing and retreated to post-production out of an adolescent, nerdy desire to play with cool toys, undisturbed by "reality" and insulated from the demands of human interaction, as if Industrial Light & Magic, the special effects company he founded, was some expensive train-set he could afford with the money he made with STAR WARS. But once one accepts that in a business that is most profitable when it implements some version of the "total entertainment" concept, the film shown on the big screen is only one element in a vast array of products and services accumulated around a property, a brand or franchise, then questions of independence and autonomy once more pose themselves, even if they pose themselves on a different scale: it is still a matter of how to acquire, keep and retain control over one's work. For the classical Hollywood director during the studio era, there were two major ways of ensuring this control: either by having the right to the final cut written into the contract (Orson Welles being an example of a director whose films—notably THE MAGNIFICENT AMBERSONS [1942] and TOUCH OF EVIL [1958]—suffered from the director *not* having had final cut), or to shoot a given script in such a manner that only the director can make sense of the rushes: Alfred Hitchcock called it "editing in the camera." In the digital age, the equivalent of "editing in the camera" is to give a film its decisive shape in post-production, thereby redefining the role of the producer who might be said to have (once more) acquired the powers of the *auteur*:

> Lucas and Spielberg's focus on post-production has proved to be a practical and successful industry strategy. Post-production can be painstakingly slow and lonely. But historically it has been the phase of filmmaking during which the battle to control a movie has been keenest. . . . Lucas and Spielberg understood that in such a system films are made and sometimes unmade once the talent and crew go home. In order to protect the final cut of their films, they have technically complicated the post-production process. Their films are shot in such a way that no one else could ever hope to make sense of the footage except them. Footage, after all, functions primarily to set-up complex post-production effects—effects that depend on their particular expertise. If a director or producer's claim to auteur status regards the degree to which he or she has controlled a project, Lucas and Spielberg are auteurs of the strictest and highest order. . . . Like no other directors before or since, Lucas and Spielberg have successfully challenged studio control over post-production. They have done so in order, as auteurs, to control their products completely. Lucas has gone so far as to exert control over the exhibition of his films through his THX-line of theater sound systems and videocassette, laserdisk and DVD sound reproduction.[19]

In other words, while it is true that, as Lewis also remarks, Spielberg's and Lucas' *auteur* status depended "not on a transcendence of the commercial power structure in New York and Hollywood, but rather on a deft accommodation of that power structure in the very production of their films," the matter of control remains a pressing concern and motive in their creative decisions and working methods, thus reaffirming the validity of at least one central tenet of the *auteur* theory.[20]

The Concept Author

This issue of control, however, becomes more complicated once a director has to think not only in terms of the single work or even the personal oeuvre as a whole: entities that assign value in literature and the fine arts to an author, and used to establish authorship also in the cinema during the time the *auteur* theory was in force. In the age of "total entertainment" a film is being conceived and designed in rather more ways than merely as a gripping narrative or a profound emotional and aesthetic statement—the traditional poles of "commerce" versus "art." Even where it is not a matter of devising a story that also "works" as a computer game, a big budget film nonetheless has to prove itself in several ancillary markets, in order to recoup its cost: markets where audience expectations can vary enormously.

Take, for instance, the fact that—until the rise of the HD download and streaming video—the successful DVD release had been an essential part of a film's revenue stream. From the makers' point of view, having to devise a film that works in the cinema and also "sells" as a DVD can be a dauntingly contradictory challenge.[21] On the big screen, a film has to provide a new experience (it has to be an event, a phenomenon), whose power resides in the immediate sensory affect or physical impact: effects difficult to obtain or retain on the small screen and in the DVD format. Since the DVD of a blockbuster is often purchased *because* the film is already known as an event, it must contain elements, details or materials not present or not perceived when first experienced in projection, enhancing the pleasure of the initial experience, rather than merely allowing the viewer to re-live it. Yet the DVD also makes the film into something close to a physical object, which can be treasured and possessed, quite different from the uniquely time-bound but ephemeral experience of a theatrical screening. DVDs became more like books, with chapter headings, skipping, flipping, stopping and fast-forwarding, much as one can leaf through a printed text and "bookmark" one's favorite passages. However, going beyond the book, once enriched with a "bonus package" which contains material extraneous to the projected film—the director's running commentary, out-takes and cut scenes, a "making-of" documentary, interviews with stars and other leading personalities—the DVD seriously challenges the coherence and closure of the film as a self-sufficient work.

Here, too, control and autonomy do battle with dispersal and dissemination. As a consequence, the director not only creates the work, s/he also has to craft a public persona, an image of the director as the principle of coherence that keeps creativity and motivation intact, while nonetheless being open to the culture at large, accessible to the audiences, also in the new Internet mode of "joining the conversation": authors must master the dynamics that play in popular culture and mass-entertainment, without becoming a pure product of marketing and personality cult. Quentin Tarantino's authorial persona can be understood within the tension this produces: maneuvering himself between post-studio Hollywood and the "indie" rebel director, he arguably belongs to a category that best exemplifies the author's dilemma when permeated by his public: the *auteur* has to present himself as fan and geek, barely able to manage the personality cult erupted around him, yet nurturing this cult as a valuable brand, and thus effectively identifying in his authorial discourse more with the consumer than with the creator. Weapons of choice on this new battlefront are, as already indicated, the *director's interview*, along with the optional *director's commentary* on the sound track of the DVD, and, in order to stimulate in due course another round of marketing through the re-release, the *director's cut*: a typically postmodern pastiche of and nostalgia for the old antagonism between director as *auteur* and the studio as system.

However, one should insist that these are moves on a battlefront: ever-shifting contests for control and identity in the material, physical sense (the power to program tens of thousands of screens the world over for a specific release date, or of enforcing copyright protection on DVDs or the logo and brand) as well as in an immaterial, discursive space, where even "piracy" or downloads become part of managing the fan-base. It suggests that the contemporary Hollywood *auteur*'s mode of control belongs to the flexibilization of semantic, symbolic and power structures that Gilles Deleuze—referring himself to Michel Foucault—thought typical of what he called "control societies," whose exercise of power is based on modulation, that is, keeping things moving and circulating, building up micro-circuits of assent, disssent and affirmation, in contrast to the older type of disciplinary society, based on antagonism, suppression or in the case of Hollywood, on censorship: "The disciplinary man was a discontinuous producer of energy, but the man of control is undulatory, in orbit, in a continuous network."[22] In other words, if we think of the author as possessing any kind of power to affect, connect or engage with "the public"—the fluid communities, or groups of users that once were called audiences—then this power is more impersonal and diffused across the system which makes up "total entertainment" than is ordinarily associated with the idea of authorship. Not a top-down, vertical structure of intentionality, where meaning descends, before it flows back from the audience to the author, but a horizontal, layered one, through which internal management and external engagement are linked, and meaning is kept unstable, provisional—to coalesce only at the points of reception, of which there potentially are as many as there are recipients.[23]

To give an example of the internal self-organization: in the days of the studio-system, the production process of a film relied on the film script as a kind of blueprint and account sheet: with the script in hand, budgets were calculated, sets built, shooting schedules worked out, locations booked and timetables for actors and crew coordinated. In other words, while in one sense the script was the verbal form of the visual narrative, in another sense it became something entirely different: a complex, variable, but calculable set of *instructions for actions*. In the blockbuster era, it is more likely the fully executed film, along with the script that functions as the engineering blueprint, as the map for further action, laying out a broad terrain of initiatives. Each aspect of the film—the clothes the actors wear, the props and accessories, the locations visited, the music heard, the goals pursued—can give rise to further economic activity: lines in fashion, toys, product placement, tourism, leisure pursuits, sports or hobbies have all taken off from a successful blockbuster or franchise film.

Thus, instead of the analogy of the blueprint, another comparison suggests itself: the blockbuster incorporates the classic Hollywood studio film in much the same way that in McLuhan's terms, a previous medium is embedded in a subsequent one. As he famously stated "The 'content' of any medium is always another medium . . . [while] the 'message' of any medium . . . is the change of scale or pace or pattern it introduces into human affairs."[24] Since such changes of scale or pattern also effect shifts in levels of specificity and generality, a blockbuster (considered as a new medium), would thus always also "contain" the cinema, or rather, have as its content the cinema's own history. This is indeed what characterizes not only such Spielberg-Lucas franchises as the INDIANA JONES or STAR WARS series, which have resuscitated old B-movie genres not by critically doubling or estranging them in the modernist sense, but as "remediations": their mythologies and archetypal narratives are now repurposed via special effects and extended with the technical know-how of the mechanics of suspense and multiple story-lines, while the old-fashioned ideology of heroes and villains, right and wrong, threats and dangers can now be indexed as "vintage," as another way of attaching value to obsolescence.[25]

It therefore makes sense to think of the referent "cinema" as now existing separately from any specific film, and correspondingly, to change the metaphor underlying one's mental picture of what is a major Hollywood film today. Not a "work" in the literary sense, but more like an operational manual; not a narrative, but a series of "scripted spaces," not a sequence of images and sounds synchronized with each other, but modular parts of a multi-media "installation." In each case, the first term has remained and been retained as one of the possible options or effects which the second implements or produces. By way of another comparison, blockbusters are like time and memory machines, whose architectures return us to the ancient arts of mnemotechnics, with their *loci* and *testes*, their concise layouts of place and extended spatial ensembles,[26] while adding to the uni-linear and two-dimensional action narrative a third and even a fourth dimension: a third dimension, in that its constituent parts can materialize into tangible objects and commodities, and a fourth dimension, in that it is a malleable architecture which can change and evolve over time, with its most memorable moments and images taking on a reality in their own right. If film narratives once aimed to achieve the status of a myth or archetype, their ambition is now—beyond being an unforgettable story and a moving experience—to lend body and sensuous skin to an icon or a brand. A brand is not just a name or a logo whose use and appearance can be controlled by copyright law; it is also the ability to attach an idea, an affect and a capacity for identification to a mere sign. Similarly, a narra-tivized brand in this context could be called a franchise, which is not just a way to make money out of a standardized commodity, but also requires the ability to convert a story's emotional charge and symbolic power into material form, whose meaning must be simultaneously contained and extended, spaced in intervals and across different geographical locations.[27]

The person or persons capable of planning in terms of such signs and material forms, and skilled in thinking cinema in these four dimensions simultaneously should perhaps not be thought of as *auteurs* in the classical sense. But neither should they be treated as mere salespersons or merchan-disers: it takes a special kind of creative as well as strategic intelligence to think in four dimensions, along with the institutional power to implement "on the ground" the necessary occupation of space and time. The new *auteur*, therefore, could either be thought of in military terms, as commanding officer or general, or in the way a conceptual artist shifts mental registers, categories and levels of perception and awareness, while appearing to leave the object unaltered—the aesthetic equivalent of a disruptive technology.[28] The first would bring us back to the disciplinary regime, the second is closer to the control societies. Calling the contemporary Hollywood *auteur* a "concept author" there-fore wants to draw attention both to the mode of production as "high concept," and to the resulting narrative as (in concept, if not in actuality) a brand or franchise. The objective conditions for such concept-narratives, however, may be external even to those who devise and implement them, depending on any number of historical or contingent elements present at a particular point in time. Hence Jon Lewis is right to conclude his essay with the more than rhetorical question: "Might we ask here at the end, had Lucas and Spielberg not arrived on the scene just when they did, would execu-tives in eighties' Hollywood have had to invent them?"[29]

This raises issues of agency and intentionality that are central to authorship. For instance, as far as external communication is concerned—that is, the system's exchanges with its environment—the proliferation of points of reception are indeed as crucial as they are hard to predict, indicating that the system (the locus of agency, now comprising both "author" and "Hollywood") is both master and slave, having to initiate as well as respond. If, as I argued in Chapter 12, Welles' "virtuosity" symbolized the artist's ultimate challenge (as response) to the power of the mogul and the tycoon, and thus the most perfect embodiment of the *auteur* in the classical sense, the concept-*auteur* in the Spielberg mold finds his challenge in either harnessing the external energies of the blockbuster as new medium ("changes of scale, pace and pattern," "the numbers"),[30] or he re-appropriates the priorities of the system by "personalizing" them, and in this personalized form, "responds" to the public. In either case, agency and authority (as constituent parts of the term "author") do not disappear, but become distributive, mobile or are harvested after the fact, thereby producing perhaps not a new persona, but potentially giving rise to new personal narratives. J.D. Connor cites Spielberg's "playful" retroactive claim to co-ownership of the Paramount logo (the company he was associated with from 1981 until Dreamworks split from Paramount in 2008), by weaving the studio's mountain into his own biography and name: "I just thought it would be fun to start [each of the INDIANA JONES films] with the Paramount mountain. I mean when I was a kid, my first company was called Play Mount Productions, and I had a mountain, which I painted myself. Now, Playmountain is my name in English from German. 'Spielberg' means 'playmountain.' "[31] As Connor comments:

> However inspired he might have been by Paramount "as a kid," however "fun" it would be to start with the Paramount mountain, in the end, as he says, "I had a mountain, which I painted myself." Indeed, it is not the fact of the mountain that matters here, but the fun, the play, with which it is deployed. The logo would have been there regardless. The affect behind the decision to bleed it into the film is Spielberg's patrimony. As a result of his bit of fun, Paramount may have been bound more tightly to the George Lucas-produced, Spielberg-directed film than it had any right to be, but that surplus identification of the studio with the film depended on a much larger identification of the director with the mode of production, the mode of auto-representation, as a whole.[32]

While such an overt identification of the director with his studio and thus the author with the system would seem to disqualify Spielberg from being considered an *auteur*, justifying the widely held notion that he (and Lucas) "sold out to Hollywood," while Coppola and Scorsese did not, my point (and I believe, Connor's as well) is that terms like "identification" and even "auto-representation" need to be seen within the broader concerns of Hollywood and its directors in the "digital age" (or in the era of the "control society"), namely how to reconcile creative autonomy, public persona and active engagement with the public (on the side of the director), and how to manage self-reflexivity, flexibility and self-regulation (on the part of the Hollywood studios) with regards to the State, society at large or the demands of the public.[33]

In the second part of this chapter, then, I want to examine whether in the subsequent generation, this Spielberg-Lucas legacy has been carried further, in the sense of being adopted, modified, inflected and possibly taken to another level. I could, as indicated, have chosen a number of directors, such as Robert Zemeckis or Steven Soderbergh, or jumped another ten years to David Fincher or the even younger indie-turned-blockbuster director Christopher Nolan, but clearly, in terms of high profile and economic clout, James Cameron must be considered the closest rival or successor to Spielberg and Lucas.

James Cameron and AVATAR

James Cameron is a Canadian by birth but his family moved to Southern California in 1971 when he was seventeen. According to an interview with Syd Field, after leaving school and doing odd jobs, he began reading avidly about film technology and special effects at the University of Southern California library.[34] It was Lucas' STAR WARS in 1977 that persuaded him to enter the film business, where he (like many of an earlier generation of New Hollywood directors) found his first assignments at Roger Corman's New World Pictures, making miniature models. However, unlike Coppola, Scorsese or Lucas, Cameron is largely an autodidact, never having officially enrolled in any of the New York or Los Angeles university-based film schools.[35] Working his way through the ranks of B-movies as a Corman protégé, he eventually got his break in 1984 through Orion Pictures, Warners Bros. and United Artists' boutique indie company. Orion part-financed and distributed THE TERMINATOR (1984), directed and scripted by Cameron, with Arnold Schwarzenegger in the lead role. The film proved to be a mega-hit, creating a brand, and setting new standards for action pictures, time-travel science fiction, as well as special morphing effects, shape-shifting the human body.

A look at Cameron's subsequent string of hits—Rambo First Blood II (1985), Aliens (1986), The Abyss (1989), Terminator 2: Judgment Day (1991), True Lies (1994), Titanic (1997) and Avatar (2009)—shows a Hollywood professional at work, taking on studio assignments by directing sequels, along with more "personal" projects, based on original story material, with screenplays written by himself. One can detect in these films any number of common themes, which by traditional standards qualify him as an *auteur*. His Wikipedia entry conveniently summarizes them:

> the prospects of nuclear holocaust (the Skynet takeover scenario from both Terminator films), attempts to reconcile humanity with technology (as seen in *Aliens* and *Terminator 2: Judgment Day*), humanity repeating the same mistakes, the dangers of corporate greed, strong female characters (Sarah Connor, Neytiri, and Ellen Ripley being the most famous), a strong romance subplot, the love of two worlds (*The Terminator, Titanic, Avatar*), anti-corporation (*Aliens, Avatar*), anti-military (*The Abyss, Avatar*), patchy "families" forming during the plot (*Aliens, Terminator 2: Judgment Day*), self-sacrificing—that may or may not result in actual death/termination—for a loved one or for mankind (all of his feature films as of 2011), holding breath and the danger of suffocation (*The Abyss, Terminator 2: Judgment Day, Titanic, Avatar*) and an undercurrent of feminism.[36]

One can add to this list an obsession with water, liquids, underwater diving and deep-sea exploration: topics and tropes to which I shall return.[37]

In every respect other than consistency of themes, however, Cameron is the embodiment of the post-*auteur* author, in the way I have been discussing it, following in the footsteps of Spielberg and Lucas, but with the two most economically successful films in cinema history to his name, no mere acolyte either. This (for lack of a better word) post-*auteur* authorship of the concept-author can usefully be discussed in the case of Cameron under several headings: auto-representation and personalized narrative, affective engagement with diverse publics, ambition to effect through technology a change of paradigm. The first I shall discuss as "control through access for all," the second as "control through performed self-contradiction" and the third as "control through the narrative's self-contradiction." Each requires some more detailed explanation, but all can, I hope, be exemplified through an analysis of Avatar, the much hyped 3-D science fiction fantasy which was released worldwide during the last week before Christmas, on December 16–18, 2009.

Keeping Control, Maintaining Access for All

Hollywood has always produced "texts" that are highly ambiguous, or permeable, when it comes to assigning meaning: the notorious Hays Code, introduced in 1934, was from one perspective a ludicrously prudish and hypocritical set of do's and don'ts for filmmakers and studio executives, but from another vantage-point it functioned as a devious, but also dexterous manual for producing structured ambiguity. Classical Hollywood excelled in creating movies that were ambivalent and even duplicitous, without becoming incoherent: a strategy of multiple entry-points that permitted different audiences—men and women, old and young, white and black, to have "access" to the film emotionally and intellectually, in the form of identification and (self-) recognition. There has been much debate in film theory as to what constitutes identification and recognition/miscognition of the spectatorial self with and on the screen,[38] but in the present context it corresponds to what David Bordwell has called the "excessively obvious" nature of the classical film. Bordwell and others, such as Edward Branigan, have stressed "comprehension" as the abiding priority of Hollywood storytelling, while others—with equal justification—have pointed to the lacunary, oblique and circular nature of the same classical cinema.[39] For postmodern films, the thesis of a "two-tiered system of communication" has been put forward: Hollywood films from the late 1960s onwards address them-selves to both the "naive" and the "informed" spectator simultaneously.[40] I have argued the case for this double register of knowingness elsewhere,[41] but here I want to stress that classical, postmodern as well as post-classical strategies of audience-engagement can all be accommodated under a general policy of "access for all" ("my film is a party to which everyone can bring a bottle" is how the director Robert Zemeckis once replied when asked whether FORREST GUMP had a liberal or a conservative message). However, I want this strategy to be understood also as offering the means for both director and institution to exercise control over the spectrum of reception. For to open up "access for all" in this sense should not be thought to imply "going for the lowest common denominator," or providing "something for everybody," but usually aims at a textually coherent ambiguity, the way that poetry is said to aim at maximizing the levels of meaning that specific words or works carry, thus extending interpretation while retaining control over the codes that make interpretation possible.[42]

Evidently, in the cinema, such effects of ambiguity are achieved with different means (though the screenplay is an extremely important element), but the result, when attained, represents a mastery over the "multiple entry-points," such as the ones already named: that a film must make sense to audiences of different gender, different age-groups, different national identities and different ethnic as well as educational backgrounds. But a film also quite literally must work for spectators who "enter" a film at different times during a given performance (e.g. when shown on television) or at different points in history (the permanent repeats of Hollywood classics on network and cable televi-sion being a kind of test: classics disclose themselves differently to every new generation).

When AVATAR reported box-office grosses in the region of three billion dollars within no more than six to eight weeks of its opening, critics wondered how such figures could be explained, espe-cially for a film that, by conventional standards, such as script, storyline or acting, struck them as below average in both interest and innovation even for Hollywood? An impeccably timed (and prohibitively expensive) promotional campaign and advertising offensive, first on behalf of 3-D in general and then targeting Cameron's film in particular is surely one reason: 20th Century Fox gave itself a year to make worldwide audiences aware of the launch event, raising curiosity with press reports and raising expectations with two separate trailers. But another major cause (or effect?) of the film's visibility and success were the astonishingly different, in fact contradictory and even incompatible access points for viewer identification which AVATAR managed to combine, or rather, compress into a single storyline and textual system.

One of the more surprising access points the film opened up, for example, was the enthusiasm it elicited from biologists, such as the science writer Carol Yoon:

> When watching a Hollywood movie that has robed itself in the themes and paraphernalia of science, a scientist expects to feel anything from annoyance to infuriation at facts miscon-strued or processes misrepresented. What a scientist does not expect is to enter into a state of ecstatic wonderment, to have the urge to leap up and shout: "Yes! That's exactly what it's like!" So it is time for all the biologists who have not yet done so to shut their laptops and run from their laboratories directly to the movie theaters, put on 3-D glasses and watch the film "Avatar." In fact, anyone who loves biology, or better yet, anyone who hates biology—and certainly everyone who has ever sneered at a tree-hugger—should do the same. Because the director James Cameron's otherworldly tale of romance and battle, aliens and armadas, has somehow managed to do what no other film has done. It has recreated what is the heart of biology: the naked, heart-stopping wonder of really seeing the living world.[43]

This contrasts sharply with the more "political" readings of the film. A few days earlier, in the same paper, the *New York Times* columnist David Brooks blasted AVATAR for pandering to the "White Messiah Complex":

[The White Messiah fable] rests on the stereotype that white people are rationalist and techno-cratic while colonial victims are spiritual and athletic. It rests on the assumption that nonwhites need the White Messiah to lead their crusades. It rests on the assumption that illiteracy is the path to grace. It also creates a sort of two-edged cultural imperialism. Natives can either have their history shaped by cruel imperialists or benevolent ones, but either way, they are going to be supporting actors in our journey to self-admiration.[44]

Brooks is a moderate conservative, generally quite conciliatory when it comes to Republican values of "America First." He is thus ideologically at the opposite end of the spectrum from a critic on the far left like Slavoj Žižek, who while taking a predictably stronger tone, nonetheless is in agreement with Brooks:

Beneath the idealism and political correctness of *Avatar* . . . lie brutal racist undertones. . . . The film teaches us that the only choice the aborigines have is to be saved by the human beings or to be destroyed by them. In other words, they can choose either to be the victim of imperialist reality, or to play their allotted role in the white man's fantasy.

Žižek ends on an overtly political note:

At the same time as Avatar is making money all around the world . . ., something that strangely resembles its plot is taking place. The southern hills of the Indian state of Orissa, inhabited by the Dongria Kondh people, were sold to mining companies that plan to exploit their immense reserves of bauxite (the deposits are considered to be worth at least $4trn). In reaction to this project, a Maoist (Naxalite) armed rebellion exploded.

. . . So where is Cameron's film here? Nowhere: in Orissa, there are no noble princesses waiting for white heroes to seduce them and help their people, just the Maoists organising the starving farmers. The film enables us to practise a typical ideological division: sympathising with the idealised aborigines while rejecting their actual struggle. The same people who enjoy the film and admire its aboriginal rebels would in all probability turn away in horror from the Naxalites, dismissing them as murderous terrorists. The true avatar is thus *Avatar* itself—the film substituting for reality.[45]

However, soon after Avatar became such a world success, the world heard about the Dongria Kondh, who took appropriate action: they began making their children look as beautiful and "primitive" as they possibly could, in order to present them on YouTube, explicitly suggesting analogies with the Na'vi, and appealing to Cameron to become an advocate of their plight.[46]

They were not alone in seeing Cameron's "racist" film as a useful propaganda weapon in their struggle against oppression. The Chinese government had to restrict the distribution of 2-D versions of Avatar in the countryside, since dissident bloggers quickly spotted in the land-grab of the American corporation analogies with the confiscation, appropriation and destruction of villages happening in rural China, on behalf of the land- and minerals hungry central or regional govern-ments.[47] Similarly, young Palestinians, not unlike the Chinese, saw political parallels—this time about blockades and occupation—and began to dress up as the blue creatures, in order to protest, in the village of Bilin near Ramallah, against the Israeli security fence.[48] If these might seem like carnivalesque moments of grass roots or on-line activism, using the film's ubiquity to advertise their cause, what is one to make of the response of Bolivia's president?

Evo Morales went to the cinema for the third time in his life in order to view *Avatar* which he says is "a profound sign of resistance to capitalism and the struggle for the defence of nature." ¡Viva Pandora! One of the only other films he ever travelled to the cinema for was a biopic on Pelé.[49]

Viva Pandora! might also be the slogan of a politically more sophisticated group of admirers, who would probably discount Žižek's strictures as too classically Marxist and Brooks' mock-sarcasm as too bourgeois-idealist. A Deleuzian defender of AVATAR waxes almost as ecstatically about the film, as did the biologist of the *New York Times*, recognizing in AVATAR all the forms of becoming (becoming-woman, becoming-animal), in short, the Spinozist world-picture of multiple mutualities as advocated in *Mille Plateaux*:

> The movie downloads the viewer with such ferocity and such poetic space that it bends back cinema upon itself, and introduces its content—the question of Avatarship—into the very experience, pulling out from technological increase and its inherent relatability the buried question of sensitivity, of connection and projected identification, in short, the implied organic mutuality in everything our machines have brought us. Cameron and his magicians invade our bodies and throw out our affects into the arms and sinews of operators in such a threshold defying 3D that it defies all of our repeated attempts to take a mapping of where we are. This past movie recognition, this ethnic familiarity—are the Pandorans African Maasai, elegant Native American Indians, Thai-Myanmar Pa Dong Karen, naked Amazon natives, or even cats—inundates and torques the viewer in a transport that is more than pleasured, more than reflective. It is free . . . free in only the sense that aesthetic renewal can be free. Tossed outward, amid the equally familiar ideological landscapes of ecological nightmare (however this reads for you), and you are vividly aware of its artifice. But in its practical synthetics the technological nervature examines you and opens you out, across the boundaries of even your well-honed intellectual compass.[50]

While followers of Deleuze and Guattari are thus entranced by the film and its promise of sensory plenitude, others responded more pathologically to the same deterritorializing possibilities of becoming. After spending time on Pandora, young viewers in the US contracted the inevitable "Avatar Blues," feeling so distraught that they were in need of serious professional counselling. As Žižek had predicted, "if we subtract fantasy from reality, then reality itself loses its consistency and disintegrates." For these viewers, real life turned empty and stale, to the point of sapping the will to live in the here-and-now:

> Ever since I went to see *Avatar* I have been depressed. Watching the wonderful world of Pandora and all the Na'vi made me want to be one of them. I can't stop thinking about all the things that happened in the film and all of the tears and shivers I got from it. I even contemplate suicide thinking that if I do it I will be rebirthed in a world similar to Pandora and then everything is the same as in *Avatar*.—Mike.[51]

"Access for all" in AVATAR thus functions at the level of the code, ensuring multiple readings, while not predicating or privileging any one in particular. It even effected a semantic paradigm change, when one considers that—apart from the analogy with blues as a mood—the Na'vi *blue* became the *new red* (of left-wing politics, in the case of Palestinians) *and the new green* (of environmental causes in India and China). The point, therefore, is not that the film proved controversial, and that professional critics as well as web users had many different views (which, of course, happens all the time).[52] Rather the claim is that these divergences and seeming contradictions were programmed into the film from the beginning, as part of the Cameron concept. "Access for all" in the internet era has become a complex, multi-level, multi-cultural process of mediation and appropriation, which presupposes in the fabric of the film's political and emotional texture not only a planned degree of pluralism of signs, regarding the story, its ideology and affective registers, but a new way of encoding them. Cameron has, I believe, added to the "textually coherent ambiguity" of classical Hollywood another level, which I shall provisionally call the level of "cognitive dissonance," heading towards conceptual "double-binds."

Before examining this further level, here are some of the director's more traditional (classical and post-classical) strategies for creating the kind of ambiguity that allows for the multiple access points just discussed:

First, as several of the commentators already quoted have pointed out, the story material is both extremely hybrid in its provenance and at the same time has deep mythological roots. Motifs from different religious or spiritual archetypes as well as fairy-tales and colonial fantasies are woven together and cross-pollinated. Post-classical Hollywood is well known for hybridizing its all-time classics: thus, Jurassic Park was called "Jaws with claws," and Star Wars was "High Noon in outer space." Robert Altman's The Player features a sequence satirizing the trend, and Mel Brooks famously called David Lynch "Jimmy Stewart from Mars."[53] In the case of Avatar, the Deleuzian rhapsodist, no less than David Brooks, recognized the film's cinematic ancestry:

> It's *Pocahontas* meets *Full Metal Jacket* meets *The Diving Bell and the Butterfly* meets *Alien* meets *Coming Home* meets *Dragonheart* meets *Dersu Uzala* meets *Brainstorms* meets *Total Recall* meets *The Legend of Zu* meets *Tron* meets *Dances with Wolves* meets *Final Fantasy IV* meets *Logan's Run*, all of this meeting Ecological Crisis ideology meets Indigenous nostalgia meets Disney ethnic cliché and New Age ascension, and that sum colliding with the categorical mytho-aesthetic effect of the first *Star Wars* and possibly *2001*.

Another critic, Jan Distelmeyer, only slightly less enthusiastic, sums up the story like this:

> Jesus, sitting beneath the Tree of Knowledge, is having sex with Pocahontas and converts to Buddhism, whereupon he declares the "hereafter" to be the "here-and-now" and as Tamer of the Dragon restores harmony and equilibrium to a planet, whose sole purpose is to serve as a giant data storage space. You consider this a joke? It's what happens when a James Cameron blockbuster is seeking perfect balance and happily doesn't go for the lowest common denominator.[54]

Second, Avatar in this respect is not unlike Fritz Lang's Metropolis (1927): ridiculed and derided in its time for being a synthetic myth, cobbled together from different bits of fairy-tale, folklore and politically reactionary bric-a-brac. But, as with Metropolis, whose modus operandi "the more synthetic the mythology, the better" has outlasted the critics and become an all-time classic, so perhaps with Avatar: without crippling its ability to function as a narrative, the hybridity not only allows more "things" and "signs" to attach themselves to the film, but provides the platform from which to launch a franchise, whose component parts can be separately developed and extended.[55]

Third, the ideological message of the film seems to have been precisely calibrated, for instance, regarding—in this case—the degree of anti-Americanism, the manner in which ecological motifs are touched upon, and how—within the mythological matrix of "the White Messiah" that Brooks calls "politically offensive" and Žižek calls "brutally racist"—there is enough room for these indigenous peoples to claim or reclaim through the film their "rights": whether in China or Australia, in the Middle East or Latin America. Cameron—regardless of his own politics—was well aware of the United States' deeply controversial role in the world, in the midst of two wars of aggression, but also led, for the first time, by a black president. Avatar's anti-Americanism is thus just explicit enough to flatter Hollywood's vast international market, while not too offensive for Americans of the relevant demographic to feel repelled or insulted by it. The anti-military-industrial complex message was structurally necessary: it responded to the globalization of the markets Hollywood needs to serve, full well knowing that up to 70% of total revenue for a major film might come from overseas territories.[56] Anti-Americanism is an instrument in Hollywood's arsenal for maintaining its dominance in the world market and thus another example of the paradoxical consequence of exercising power and keeping control under conditions of what Deleuze called "modulation": by giving its ideological "enemies"—who are also its customers—a "voice" and a "stake," the Cameron blockbuster does indeed restore "perfect balance" to an a-symmetrical system, though perhaps not quite in the way Distelmeyer meant it, yet very much in the sense that it is a sign of another level of (self-)reflexivity, where the film invites one to read it as an allegory of its own conditions of possibility. The reviews which accuse AVATAR of false consciousness, ideological mystification or double standards, are therefore right and yet miss the key point. They overlook the fact that Cameron systematically planned and provoked this false consciousness at all levels, making it the very principle of the film's construction, because—at the allegorical level—these are the objective conditions under which the United States maintains both its military supremacy and its cultural hegemony, the two locking together not (only) by reinforcing each other, but also by openly contradicting each other: the outlines of a double bind.

Keeping Control Through Performed Self-Presentation

Hence the importance of remembering that "access for all" is a strategy that combines *opening up* with the need of *keeping control*. Yet how does this double priority also manifest itself for the director as author in the blockbuster environment? There is the power the author has through the director's interview to shape his self-presentation through controlling the personal narrative. As we saw in the case of Coppola and Spielberg, directors have taken an active role in presenting themselves, even before the DVD bonus package along with general media interest in almost any form of celebrity allowed for more targeted interventions in the director's projected self image:

> from the moment he finished film school Coppola created a serious context for his work. In doing so, he introduced a story, a film history, in which he played the part of an artist at odds with the industry. Such a reputation is profoundly misleading of course. But it is a reputation that promises to preserve the impression that Coppola, unlike Spielberg, was once upon a time a serious filmmaker.[57]

Yet Spielberg, too, has come a long way from the days of his "popcorn" persona, realizing that he not only can but must present himself as a serious filmmaker. Besides the WWII topic in most of his films, it has been films dramatizing the fate of persecuted minorities throughout recent European and US history that have helped redefine the director's perception by the public: THE COLOR PURPLE (1985), SCHINDLER'S LIST (1993), AMISTAD (1997), SAVING PRIVATE RYAN (1998), MUNICH (2005) have elaborated an impeccable Hollywood white middle-class liberal profile, making him perhaps more the Stanley Kramer of his generation than the heir to Cecil B. DeMille or Hitchcock, but with A.I.: ARTIFICIAL INTELLIGENCE (2001), MINORITY REPORT (2002), CATCH ME IF YOU CAN (2002) and THE TERMINAL (2004) he has also made films that, thanks to their interest in complicated or dilated time schemes, their involuted narratives and post-identity protagonists, qualify for the more edgy genre of "puzzle films" or "mind-game" movies.[58]

Cameron's personal narrative, such as he presented it, for instance, at his March 2010 TED talk,[59] is notably different from that of either Coppola's film-historical or Spielberg's Jewish identity, but it also has little in common with, say, the ethnically distinct "New York-Little Italy" narrative that Scorsese so successfully traded in, or Tarantino's identity as fatherless poor white trash, brought up by the Blockbuster video store. The core of the Cameron narrative is that of "the curious boy" who, from his early years on, was as drawn to biological fieldwork and scientific experiments as he spent hours drawing pictures and doodling during maths lessons at school. Cameron establishes a clear link between science and the arts as his twin motivations: a biologist and techno-geek with an irrepressible artistic imagination, he thinks of himself as much a documentary filmmaker as he is a storyteller, even though "documentary" here clearly does not mean "realism," but more the probing, exploring mind of the scientist. It was Jacques Cousteau and his underwater expeditions that truly captivated him as a boy, much more so than the American astronauts' landing on the moon or the adventure of outer space. He even suggests that the main reason he made TITANIC was to put his hands on a budget and a topic that would justify mounting a deep sea diving expedition to the actual wreck of the *Titanic*.

Much of this personal narrative provides a perfect foil for AVATAR. Cameron can draw on excellent credentials for the pro-environmental bias of the film. His interest in biology and forests, as well as his passion for diving, snorkelling and underwater exploration sends out an eco-friendly message of someone whose pursuits and hobbies do not hurt or exploit anybody, and are respectful of nature's beauties as well as her mysteries. It echoes the enthusiasm of biologists for the film, while also making the new age mystical pantheism of Pandora and its Na'vi people seem both less naïve and less calculating.

Paradoxically, the strongest echo of Cameron's personal themes in AVATAR is the presence of water, fluids and the liquidity of metamorphosis and transformation. I am not so much thinking of the amniotic fluid in which Jake Scully's avatar is being grown and incubated, or the underwater tank that lets us witness this spectacle of rebirth. Rather, AVATAR also effects a subtle but crucial change of register in the bodily experience its images try to engage us with. One could call it the metaphoric displacement of sensations we usually associate with water and deep sea diving, into the representational space of the dense forest and outer space, which is where much of the action of AVATAR takes place. In fact, the extraordinary kinetic sensations the film conveys are based on a contradiction or impossibility: freed of gravity, bodies in space would not be able to execute—no more than in the thicket and undergrowth of the rain forest—these energetic movements of soaring flight, these leaps and swoops, which we see the Na'vi excel in, especially when they ride or tele-guide the prehistoric monsters with whom they share Pandora. Yet if we imagine, or better, if we unconsciously associate the element of water (as well as Earth's atmosphere) with these movements, then they make sense, with the force of gravity suspended and mitigated rather than abolished. Creatures at home in the depth of the oceans possess the freedom of movement in all directions, as well the agility and speed of propulsion, that Cameron deploys to such spectacular and emotionally uplifting effect in AVATAR.

"True Lies": Keeping Control via the Narrative's Self-Contradiction

However, this switch of elements from air to water (repeating his preference for Jacques Cousteau over Neil Armstrong, and bringing about a switch of sensation that puts our eyes at odds with our body), is only one of several perceptual, cognitive and narrative shifts that literally and metaphorically "animate" the film, but which are based on dissonance, discrepancy or outright contradiction. My claim would be that it is precisely through the management, rather than the elimination of these contradictions that AVATAR retains its coherence, in the face of the many different and conflicting entry-points of interpretation. The contradictions, furthermore, establish a level of reflexivity recoverable as part of the system's self-regulation through self-allegorizing, while confirming Cameron as author in the post-*auteur* mode: someone who is both "true to himself" and "keeps control" over his work.

A look at the narrative construction of AVATAR can locate there some of the contradictions or cognitive switches that give the film its "life." The Hollywood of complex narratives, but also of franchise movies has refined and perfected a mode of story-telling that can positively accommodate radical switches of story premises in its fictional worlds, when one thinks of films like THE SIXTH SENSE, THE USUAL SUSPECTS and VANILLA SKY or A BEAUTIFUL MIND, DONNY DARKO and

MEMENTO, the work of David Lynch (LOST HIGHWAY, 1997; MULHOLLAND DRIVE, 2001) and David Cronenberg (EXISTENZ, 1999; SPIDER, 2002), as well as a blockbuster like Christopher Nolan's INCEPTION (2010). In all of these cases, spectators are given to believe in one sort of reality, only to be obliged to revise their assumptions or suspend them altogether: about whether the protagonist is alive or dead, whether we see the world through a demented or distorting subjective consciousness, whether we are in a dream, or indeed in someone else's dream, whether the film begins at the beginning or we are somewhere in the middle which we mistake as the beginning. For such narratives, the geometrical term of the Moebius strip has been revived, to indicate the coexistence or continuity of one "side" of the story with its opposite, that is, the premise along with its reversal, each necessitating the other and each depending on the other.[60]

In the case of franchise movies, such cognitive dissonances or reality-switches tend to happen across several episodes, or when sequels and prequels are segued into the original story, providing causation and consequence not in a linear fashion, but through inversion—most spectacularly perhaps in Lucas' STAR WARS, where good and evil, friend and foe, protagonist and antagonist, humans and clones change sides several times across the intergalactic saga of successive generations and empires, motivated on one level by an interminably extended Oedipal family drama of fathers and sons, mothers and daughters, but presenting the spectator with the—to some intellectually onerous but to others spiritually rewarding—task of sorting out who is the representative of the Force, and when is someone or not the embodiment of evil, leading one to the conclusion that good and evil not so much change sides, as they are, across time, folded into each other, much like the recto and the verso of the Moebius strip. The complexity of the overall design, in its labyrinthine mental architecture and temporal loops is thus a source of spin-offs and proliferating add-ons that can be turned into products and commodities, but is also a way for Lucas to keep control over his sprawling "Empire" of signs and meaning, sense and non-sense.

On the face of it, none of this applies to AVATAR. As we have seen, the narrative is a more or less straightforward adaptation of so many movie stereotypes and mythological archetypes that any analogies with the mind-game or Moebius-strip films just mentioned would seem far-fetched. The plot is constructed out of relatively simple binaries: the military-industrial complex which sends Scully to Pandora is mercenary, colonialist, grossly materialist, selfish and only capable of destruction; the Na'vi are selfless, indigenous, spiritual, community-oriented and peaceful, living in harmony with nature, according to the laws of their environment and their higher Deities. Repelled by the violence, greed and cynicism of his civilization, and attracted to the lure of the exotic beautiful "other," the central character changes sides and becomes a heroic defender of these counter-values, playing both messiah and redeemer.

Unobtainium

Yet if one looks at the film's conceptual move—how we get from one world to the other, and what it is that joins them to each other—then the rhetorical figures of reversal, of mirroring and inversion are very much in evidence. The ending which seems at first the triumph of nature over technology has a built-in twist, in that the avatar is a piece of technology simulating both human and nature and thus it is in fact *the same technology* in another guise that *rescues nature from the evils of technology*. Similar in certain ways to THE MATRIX after all, but complicating the "philosophical" premise, Jake Scully here takes the red pill, not to get "deeper into the rabbit hole" but in order to enjoy the benefits and reassurance of the blue pill, as it were. Yet the principle is not that of a *choice*, or an either-or: rather the modality is closer to something that computer engineers call *bootstrapping*—namely the way a lower order of complexity produces an (imaginary) higher order and from this higher stage of organization, pulls up the lower order. It is a key technique of software production, but the term comes from the realm of fantasy: Baron Munchhausen, who pulled himself out of the swamp by his own bootstraps. Such impossibilities that nonetheless have their own persuasive plausibility we might call "true lies"—to borrow this very epitome of a self-contradiction from Cameron's own oeuvre.[61]

This, mutatis mutandis, is the principle of AVATAR, except that it depends on your beliefs and values, what you consider the "lower" or "higher" order. Jake Scully "creates" (or has the Corporation create for him) his avatar, thanks to whom he is able to transform and transport his own damaged body into a higher state of being, so that the creature here in fact re-creates the creator, in a sort of benevolent retrofitting of the Frankenstein myth. In the figure of Jake the avatar, the simulated, projected, "ideal" self rescues the "real" self, in the manner of a Kantian "transcendental subject," or according to the Hegelian dialectic of "Aufhebung" (sublation). In order to get from one realm to the other, the film posits a link, whereby the conclusion becomes its own premise, each pulling up the other by its bootstraps, so to speak, and thereby making it real, or at least making it a support of "reality."

The flip or switch operated between technology and nature or between the idealized real and the real real is not something that the film tries to hide or disguise. On the contrary, in the form of a Hitchcock MacGuffin, it is exposed and underscored: AVATAR's MacGuffin is what the Corporation's semi-military expedition force purportedly travels to Pandora for: obtaining the most precious of rare minerals, called "unobtainium." It is difficult to think of a better way of "hiding in the light," that is, of Cameron advertising his own version of "true lies"—a plausible impossibility. One's first thought is that "unobtainium" must be some kind of private joke, or Cameron thumbing his nose at the spectator by signaling that he himself does not believe the hokum he is telling in the guise of a redemptive fable about ecological catastrophe and the evils of capitalism of the military-industrial kind. But look up "unobtainium," and it turns out that its origins are in engineering, where the term designates an impossible device needed to fulfil a given purpose for a given application. "For example, a pulley made of unobtainium might be massless and frictionless. . . . Since the late 1950s, aerospace engineers have used the term "unobtainium" . . . when theoretically considering a material perfect for their needs in all respects, except that it does not exist."[62] Thus, within the philosophical construction, "unobtainium" would designate precisely the non-existing, but ideally perfect link between the two realms of the real and simulated, at once a place-holder for and the guarantee of the fully empowered agency of simulation that allows the avatar of Jake Scully to absorb the real Jake Scully, and thus, paradoxically, fulfil the initial promise the Corporation makes, namely to restore his damaged body to perfect functioning. "Unobtainium," in short, is the name for that which links and joins what cannot be brought together, and thus it is the signifier of *both* the gap *and* the cognitive switch needed to bridge the gap.

Strip-Mining or Data-Mining

Abstracting thus from "unobtainium," what is it that the expedition wants, which after all, is made up of ex-Marines, business types and lab-coat scientists? The "bad guys" from the military and the Corporation want the precious mineral (to make money for themselves and profits for the Corporation), while the "good guys," that is, the scientists—and above all the one played by Sigourney Weaver—want knowledge (of better foodstuffs, new forms of medicine, higher spirituality). Yet on reflection, both the bad and the good guys are totally committed to the logic of invasion, exploitation and appropriation. For each side acts like—and indeed, are—"miners": one strip-mines the land of the Na'vi, in order to obtain unobtainium, the other data-mines the flora, fauna, the culture, the religion and the minds of the Na'vi. In other words, a parasite-host relationship can be said to exist not just between Earth and Pandora, but also between the evil corporation and the good scientists:

what binds them together is a symbiotic relationship of antagonistic mutuality, united by an ideology of acquisition and appropriation. The action thus dramatizes conflict, competition and antagonism, while the film at the symbolic level draws parallels between the imperialism of the Sigourney Weaver character (who wants to learn and know) and that of the Corporate Yuppie (who wants to grab and seize).

Insofar as the scientists' "knowing" in the film is "knowing at a distance," through all manner of remote gathering, sampling and reading of data (rather than through "immersion") it is an entirely instrumental approach to the world. Since as spectators, in the debates aboard the space station, we are morally and emotionally aligned with the scientists, rather than with the military or the corporate stooge, this raises a further possibility for the film's narrative to become a *mise-en-abyme* of its own relation to its audience, and for such self-reflexivity to be an instrument of self-regulation. Cameron once more puts his cards on the table, comments on the multiple origins and uses of the 3-D technology that allows us to be "immersed," while the scientists probe and gather at a distance. For the instruments that identify and locate the deposits of unobtainium are shown to rely on 3-D imaging (the holographic model of the "Tree of Life" makes this evident), and thus draw attention to the fact that the exploitation of Pandora's "natural resources" (and by implication, the natural resources on earth, too) depends heavily on the technology of digital 3-D as developed for non-entertainment uses, such as land surveying, geo-tagging, weather prediction, not to mention the many military or medical uses of 3-D. These, of course, are precisely the applications which benefit from the same research and development that underlies digital 3-D in the cinema where we are watching the film, reminding us of the tight mutual interdependence between military and engineering 3-D, and movie-making and computer-gaming 3-D. Translated back into the narrative of Avatar: the technologies that are responsible for the beautiful flora and fauna of Planet Pandora—beautiful thanks to the effects that 3-D imaging creates—are the same technologies as used by Pandora's enemies, bent on destroying this beauty, by harvesting it in either material (unobtainium) or immaterial (knowledge) form.

What Avatar thus thematizes—in a form that testifies to, critiques and embodies its own contradictions—is the alliance that the high-tech Hollywood of digital special effects and 3-D graphics has entered into with the US military and defense sector, and vice versa: so much so that Tim Lenoir and Henry Lowood speak of a "military-entertainment complex" as having succeeded the famous "military-industrial complex."[63] As a consequence, what *in the film* appears explicitly as the military-industrial complex of the evil corporation is nothing other than a camouflage (or avatar) for the military-entertainment complex *that de facto sustains the film and makes it possible.*[64]

This overlay of opposites explains the touchingly obsolete and clumsy weapons the Corporation uses in order to conquer and destroy the Na'vi, when some sort of psychological warfare, preferably with such beautiful images and feel-good emotions as we ourselves are enjoying while watching, would probably have been a more effective way of getting at the Na'vi "Tree of Life" and its hidden treasures, than bulldozers, earth moving vehicles and Terminator-style techno-armor. Through yet another switch, the film owns up to Hollywood's covert collusion with the military industrial complex, which Avatar's overt ideological message would seem to contest and criticize.

From Cognitive Dissonance to Double Bind: Empowering the Audience

Where does this leave the audience, and especially the millions who watched Avatar in awe and rapt attention? Were they mere dupes, seduced by the film's glossy surface and breathtakingly beautiful pictures, misled by the ecological message, enjoying the old-fashioned man-machine fights, or secretly thrilling to the violence of the assault vehicles and massive firepower unleashed on the creatures of Pandora? Was there, after all, something for everyone in the nearly three hours of spectacle that AVATAR provides, and each viewer could pick and choose?

My thesis has been a different one: I have tried to show how the issue of control, crucial to the author's identity as *auteur*, can manifest itself in "independent" productions as much as in blockbusters through switches in the reality-status and fictional world premises of the narrative. Cameron's AVATAR does this in more muted but also more systematic ways than other films mentioned. While not every spectator may be aware of, or be troubled by them, the cumulative effect of these cognitive dissonances is to provoke the spectator into actively producing his or her own reading, in order to disambiguate the "mixed messages" or to untie the knot of the double bind, if we grant that such shifts of register are comparable to double binds, in the sense that they are as difficult to respond to as they are to resist. Double binds are classic ways of exercising control without coercion, usually effected by enlisting the "victim's" own active cooperation. If the undecidability of a film's premise motivates the spectator cognitively, it would explain these "strong readings" that AVATAR has given rise to: since the message is fundamentally self-contradictory, unraveling its meaning results in a higher "ontological commitment" on the part of the viewer to his or her particular interpretation—a commitment that works in favor of the affective bond formed with a given film. One could even say that a double bind situation gives the illusion of "empowering" the spectator, an impression confirmed by the film's reception history.

Yet there is another dimension of this empowerment of the spectator: as we have seen, one of the roles of the Na'vi is to hold in place a fantasy structure, at the same time as they function as the "conscience" of the Earth world: sensitive humans want to join the Na'vi, while no Na'vi wants to join the humans, which confirms that life on Pandora can only exist if one recognizes it as the projective/compensatory mirror for various kinds of lack on Planet Earth (peace and spirituality, pride and dignity, but also including the lack or scarcity of more material resources). The fact that the Na'vi are pure projections or idealized versions becomes even more evident when they are taken as standing for or modeled after "indigenous people" in general, whose real-life counterparts, as we know—from Native Americans, Indian Untouchables, to Australian Aborigines and Roma in Europe—tend to live in poverty and degradation, suffer from exclusion and discrimination, with their families prone to alcoholism, violence, crime and child-abuse.[65]

In this respect, the Na'vi are less "natives" than they are "navigators": not postmodern versions of "the noble savage," but cybernauts who are "digitally native," that is, savvy users and consumers of the latest communication technologies, always "plugged in" and "on-line," interacting with their game consoles or laptops the way the Na'vi plug themselves into their horses, birds or dragons. But the world of Pandora is not (merely) a metaphor for the game and fantasy environments of the geek generation. AVATAR is also an allegory: a reflexively doubled parable of the communication circuit that Hollywood seeks with its global audiences, where a studio's films are its avatars, "leading" spectators while ideologically seeming to act on their behalf. The Na'vi are the audiences, tuned in and turned on to Hollywood, so that the enthusiastic response to AVATAR as a mirror for self-recognition all over the globe was correct: spectators *are* the Na'vi, because, at the allegorical level, the Na'vi *are* spectators in their newly "empowered" role as assigned to them in the Hollywood blockbuster equation. For while audiences, thanks to the technology of digital 3-D, motion and performance capture and new ways of rendering sound and space, participate in the movie in hitherto unheard of sensory proximity, the industry is after something else. As far as Hollywood is concerned, it wants audiences *to interact* with images, while Hollywood itself *acts with the images*. Which is to say, for the industry that makes them, images are instructions for actions—they trigger further moves, purchases and events—rather than pictures to contemplate or immerse yourself in, however much "immersion" might be the stated objective. In this respect, AVATAR the film functions itself as an "avatar" in the larger system, of which it is the most successful representative. Hence my argument that when

Hollywood films allegorize their own conditions of possibility, which are by necessity contradictory, they perform cognitive switches or enact a reversibility of roles: a master-slave relationship that never stabilizes itself. The films are—in the global market they have to serve in order to survive— almost by definition agents and double agents at the same time: in the words of Cameron's own film about double agents, they are "true lies," or in terms of my argument, they are the "special effects" of the truth-trust-and-belief system which is digital Hollywood today.[66]

The Concept Author: From Shape Shifter to Paradigm Shifter

This brings me to my final point: special effects by their nature involve double binds at the perceptual level, since they encourage us to believe with our eyes what our minds know to be impossible. We know that the dinosaurs in JURASSIC PARK cannot be real, yet their density of specification in all perceptually and experientially relevant ways obliges us to accept their existence. Digital 3-D only intensifies this challenge to our mind and senses, since stereoscopic vision is both a simulation and a dissimulation technology. We see two-dimensional images in three dimensions, because the eyes, receiving mixed visual messages, pass them on to the brain, which disambiguates the optical signals by translating them into the coordinates of spatial information, using the best default values that make sense of the input. In other words, stereoscopic sight means confusing the eye and tricking the brain, and in the final instance, is a cognitive effect rather than a visual one—but it is in the hesita- tion, the oscillation and the tension between these perceptual-cognitive registers that 3-D once more becomes attractive and engaging for filmmakers and artists.

Cameron, along with Jeffrey Katzenberg, is one of Hollywood's most ardent advocates of 3-D. Yet rather than treating it merely as another special effect, made possible by digitization, 3-D for both Katzenberg and Cameron (as well as Spielberg, Zemeckis, Tim Burton and others) has become the platform or the means by which "much more pervasive" (Cameron's words) changes are being proposed and implemented. Some of these changes have to do with introducing 3-D not just on the big screen, but for television sets, laptops and mobile devices, where 3-D images can be simulated without users having to wear special glasses or otherwise adjust their viewing habits. Cameron owns patents and has stakes in a number of conversion technologies which retroactively render, that is, re-master 2-D films into 3-D, something that Cameron is in the process of doing with his own TITANIC, scheduled to be re-released in 3-D, to coincide with the centenary of the sinking of the Titanic on April 15, 2012.

However, besides the ambition to re-master our audiovisual heritage in digital 3-D, and thereby possibly revive the declining market for DVDs, I sense in Cameron's moves another motivation. This has to do with what has already been mentioned, namely his desire to marry science and technology with the visual arts and story-telling, healing the rift of the "two cultures" that has provoked the "science wars" on one side, and talk of "cyberculture" and the "post-human condition" on the other. In Cameron's case, this desire is merely a way of being true to himself and his own upbringing, and it is therefore no accident that his most explicit self-presentation to date about having been torn between the arts and sciences should have been in a lecture given before the TED community, since TED stands for *Technology, Entertainment and Design*. As we saw with reference to AVATAR, however, this can no longer be a union of equals, since both "nature" and "culture," both art and the imagination are already deeply permeated by science and technology, as well as mortgaged to their commercial applications.

If one therefore takes this performed self-presentation as "the curious boy," brought up by the twin inspirations of the natural sciences and the liberal arts, and makes a composite of it with the narrative self-presentation as the author of a film colluding with 3-D military technology in order to generate 3-D aesthetic beauty, then one faces either the tragic truth of an individual who against better knowledge continues to believe in this marriage of science and arts, or one witnesses what one might call a perfectly performed self-contradiction, under the sign of "total entertainment": Cameron, the eco-friendly environmentalist is also Cameron the beneficiary of digital software developed by and for military and industrial uses.

It also means that Cameron knows that whatever his personal convictions (the "good guy," siding with Na'vi everywhere), he is, as a Hollywood filmmaker today, also one of the "bad guys." By siding with the Na'vi, he is siding with his public, the world audiences; by siding with Hollywood, he is siding with those who "sell" this very public (the Na'vi) to commercial interests (the Corporation). That he can do both (and lets us see it in his film) means that he is totally aware of it, but also probably that he thinks of himself as the one who succeeded in "obtaining unobtainium." This might be the new definition of the Hollywood *auteur* in the digital age: managing to achieve what is impossible but necessary, being part and parcel of the military industrial complex, camouflaged as the military entertainment complex, of which the Hollywood *auteur* is now both the *avatar* and the *double agent*.

This raises the issue whether the stereoscopic or expanded 3-D technologies can still be understood within the traditional categories of either "image" or "seeing." Once one factors in the non-entertainment uses, 3-D might not actually be mainly about vision, but about the readability of vast amounts of digital data more generally, going well beyond the capacities of the human eye, because not mediated by the human eye and only processed by machine programs. At the same time, our idea of what is an image is also changing, and one might bear in mind what Lev Manovich has argued about the need to re-classify media screens, distinguishing those that are concerned with tele-presence (monitor, video-screen) from those aimed at tele-action (radar, infrared, laser, touch screens).[67] Manovich has also speculated about the differences between simulation (virtual action) and dissimulation (virtual presence) for some time,[68] and would probably argue that behind 3-D in both its entertainment and industrial-military applications lies a much more general shift in our culture towards making "seeing" a form of "action," of which, as I tried to show, AVATAR would be a striking confirmation. Children who have grown up with computers, when they see an image on a screen, rarely look without trying to click on it with a mouse or touch-pad, in the expectation of something happening, some action to take them further into the image or to another site or environment. "Image as action" would thus be the new normal, an assumption that 3-D, with its simulation of touching and grasping, at once confirms and reinforces, thus joining the vast expansion of the uses of touch screens today.

In other words, one may have to look once more at the very notion of 3-D as a "special effect," and instead see it as the most appropriate strategy for what used to be called "naturalization," and what I have elsewhere termed a switch in default-value via the logic of the supplement.[69] This would imply that 3-D is merely part of new and not so new ways of seeing, perceiving, interacting with and interpreting images (but also of recording, processing and reproducing information and data) that are becoming consumable, that is, objectified as commodities. Expressed in another vocabulary, digital 3-D, despite appearances and the hype, would therefore not be a "special effect" but the "new normal."

Extending this thought, one could take the more sceptical or critical view, and compare the implementation of 3-D technologies as norm and default value of digitally produced images, to Naomi Klein's notion of "disaster capitalism," that is, her analysis of how in liberal democracies sweeping changes are effected and unpopular or controversial policies implemented, in the wake of major natural or man-made disasters.[70] Their impact distracts attention from the new norms that are being introduced, for instance, how in the area of surveillance or privacy, civil liberties are being curtailed in the name of "security." It generalizes the old maxim that a natural catastrophe is a good place to bury bad (political) news, but also reverses it in the case of "special effects," in that it makes the extraordinary (here the exoticism of Avatar/Pandora) part of much more mundane changes and adjustments in everyday habits, such as how we look at screens of all sizes and uses. And while it follows the same logic of distraction and displacement, the relation of special effects to the new normal confirms—even without the conspiratorial overtones—the basic idea, namely that a major Hollywood film such as Avatar fulfils only one of its functions when successful as narrative and experience; even any associated merchandising and franchising does not exhaust its meaning, if one considers its potential role, as argued here, in re-setting the default values and enforcing a new normativity of assisted sight, thus helping to bring about a paradigm change in the field of vision and the image.

Cameron's efforts, if I am right, in working towards a convergence between technology, entertainment, design, the arts and education is entirely in line with mainstream liberal thinking in the US from Bill Gates to Barack Obama, from Thomas Friedman to Oprah Winfrey. His vision as a Hollywood director, too, is consistent with being the author of signature products, as defined earlier: vehicles that can attach to themselves all manner of signs and activities, as well as logos and concept-narratives, with the potential of becoming series and franchises that yield long-running lines in consumables, whether material (in the form of games, toys, make-up or fashion) or immaterial (in the form of experiences and attractions).[71]

Yet beyond this vision, there might be an ambition, secretly harbored but perhaps not altogether beyond Cameron's reach: one that, in contrast to his character the Terminator T-1000, who famously was a shape shifter, would make him a paradigm shifter. As a Hollywood concept author Cameron has made films that have been instrumental in transforming the way blockbuster movies are being conceived and received, most notably with Avatar. If it does help to establish digital 3-D as the new norm—not only of blockbuster picture making, but also of how we think about the "image" in general—Avatar would indeed illustrate the principle of the shock-doctrine in the entertainment world. It would be, as the phrase has it, a "game changer," which is to say, it would have all manner of implications for other parts of the industry and how it functions both locally and globally. But then again, it might not, and remain, despite its monster profits, a mere flash in the pan, as many are predicting about the "3-D revolution."

On the other hand, both the financial resources and the status which Titanic and Avatar have given him, might put Cameron into a different league even from Spielberg and Lucas, and bring him closer to another breed of "game changers," of which Steve Jobs—his coeval by six months—is the most famous icon. Three times in less than ten years (the time it took Cameron to produce Avatar), Jobs achieved, first with the iPod in 2001, then with the iPhone in 2007 and again with the iPad in 2010, radical change in the ways in which music players, mobile phones and laptop computers are being perceived by the public and conceived by their respective industries. And Jobs, while opening up world markets for his desirable products, has certainly understood the need, and found the means, to keep control of his operation. Cameron, as author in the flesh as well as author in the text, has exceled in combining positively perceived self-presentation with positively perceived self-contradiction: preconditions, I argued, that are necessary when functioning under the Hollywood system of "access for all," while being "true to yourself" and "keeping control over your work." What the analogy with Jobs adds to this agenda is the ability to "disrupt the market," that is, to come up with a product or service that fundamentally alters the very terms by which something is being perceived, thereby shifting the terrain on which others have to invent, innovate and do business. This, as we saw, is considered the highest achievement in the current stage of capitalism's cycles of "creative destruction," and thus would fit the world picture and aspirations of someone who, like Cameron, wants to unite technology and the arts, and bring design, education and business in line with each other. Yet it would also return us to the *auteur* theory in a somewhat unexpected way, once one remembers that defamiliarization, deviation from the norm and disruption have long been considered the modernist artist's signature traits that make him or her a true *auteur*. The romantic notion of an antagonism with the system has not disappeared; on the contrary it has shape-shifted, now reincarnating itself in the system, and as the system's most distinctive and desirable trait: Cameron would thus be the Hollywood *auteur* par excellence, not because he opposes the system, but because he embodies the system in its purest, that is, in its most contradictory but also most "disruptive" form.

V
The Persistence of Hollywood

22
Digital Hollywood: Between Truth, Belief and Trust

Beyond the Post

In an earlier chapter, I argued that film studies as a discipline first emerged in the early 1970s thanks to a double and contradictory impulse: to bury Hollywood *and* to take it into a necrophiliac embrace.[1] Both the notion of the director as *auteur* and the label "classical" partake in this gesture, because of their retrospective association and deconstructive agenda. As the 1980s progressed, however, and Hollywood began to revive economically as well as gain prominence politically in the new debates about globalization, Anglo-American film studies responded with a mixture of disbelief and suspicion—reactions that were hardly surprising, given the uncanny nature of this "return": Hollywood had once more become the vampire that no stake could impale. In the film industry and for reviewers, the *auteur* staged a comeback (having shape-shifted into the director as brand-name or superstar); in film theory the "classical" was revived, either as the undead, in its own name, or under the label "post-classical," in order to fend off the gremlins of the "postmodern"; in cultural and media studies, the ideological critiques of the 1970s around the "death of the author" and the "realism effect" were also back, now under the heading of "social constructivism" whose task it was to uncover mainstream cinema's representational regimes of race, class, gender and—more recently—nation.

At the same time, there are historical factors present that set their own pace of change, or lack of it: Hollywood's ideology, as well as its socio-economic infrastructure, has adapted to world-scale transformations, and is firmly within global capitalism: indeed, the film industry is one of its major players. Leaner and meaner production methods through outsourcing and sub-contracting, world-wide distribution and marketing strategies, blockbuster exhibition practices, merchandising, use of cutting-edge technology, aggressive anti-piracy measures and enforcement of copyright are all integral to a strategy that makes Hollywood part and parcel of the new world order of free market liberal democracy in the image of the West. In this respect, capitalism remains the "horizon" of thinking about contemporary cinema. Yet as soon as one posits a horizon, one has already envisaged the possibility of putting oneself beyond it. In what follows, I shall try to treat this horizon as the enabling condition for assuming an impossible position: to examine another horizon, which paradoxically, seems to leave everything as it is, and at the same time, changes everything: this new horizon is "digital Hollywood."

Anxieties of the Digital—Loss of the Indexical

When we use our personal computers to generate letters of the alphabet, few of us seem particularly vexed. When we listen to classical music from a CD or MP3 player, again, there is a large degree of acceptance; it is only when digitization generates images in the photographic mode that something akin to a cultural crisis occurs, with bold claims being made by some, while extravagant anxieties are being voiced by others.[2] It is as if the economy of the visible had lost its gold standard, which since the invention of photography has been the light-sensitive emulsion bearing trace and imprint of the real. To cite the former *Cahiers du cinéma* critic Jean Douchet:

> The shift towards virtual reality is a shift from one type of thinking to another, a shift in purpose, which modifies, disturbs, perhaps even perverts man's relation to what is real. All good films, we used to say in the 1960s, when the cover of *Cahiers du cinéma* was still yellow, are documentaries, . . . and filmmakers deserved to be called "great" precisely because of their near obsessive focus on capturing reality and respecting it, respectfully embarking on the way of knowledge. [Today, on the other hand], cinema has given up the purpose and the thinking behind individual shots, in favour of images—rootless, textureless images—designed to violently impress by constantly inflating their spectacular qualities.[3]

Clearly, for Douchet, the digital image is not part of cinema or film history, and the reason seems to be an absence: the lack of "roots" and "texture," which is to say, materiality and indexicality. This anxiety is the more surprising, considering that the majority of digital techniques used in films today are modeled on tricking the eye with special effects in ways that have been practiced not only by Georges Méliès, or shown off in Fritz Lang's Die Niebelungen, O'Brian's King Kong and Steven Spielberg's Jurassic Park, but also cultivated by photographers almost since Nadar and Atget. Are statements such as Douchet's part of a new round in the bout between the advocates of "realism" and the perfectors of "illusionism"? Or is something else at stake, to do with a change of cultural metaphor, a different alignment of sight and sense: away from the episteme of "representation" altogether, and touching not just on how cinema has been theorized?

The several paradigms film theory has been exploring in the past twenty years, however much they were feuding among themselves, were united by the fact that they referred themselves to the photographic image. So deeply ingrained and widely shared is the belief in script, imprint and trace as the foundation of our concepts of record and evidence, and the (peculiar kind of) "truth" preserved in them, that even where this presumed truth of the image was denounced as illusion, as ideology and cultural construction, there remained the implicit assumption that a certain type of veracity can be ascribed to the products of mechanical vision. In one sense, therefore, digitization appears to pull away the very ground that links the perceiver to the represented, while in another sense it merely marks another phase in the history of mechanical vision, so that it must in principle be possible to specify the truth conditions of the digital just as we think we know the truth conditions of the analogue.

Yet here the difficulties open up, for what exactly are the truth conditions of the photographic image? This so-called "loss of the indexical" confronts us with a paradox, or rather, with what I have called an impossible place, not so much because photographs can no longer be trusted but because the grounds on which the issue could be judged are no longer secure. For once one situates oneself on the side of digitization, André Bazin's "Ontology of the Photographic Image"[4] *as well as* its critique by Jean Louis Comolli and others becomes problematic, since both sides implicitly accept that imprint and trace, along with perspective and centered vision are what defines the cinema, from which "realism" emerges as either the cinema's "natural" or naturally "ideological" identity. Conversely, once one abandons this ontology, other, equally fundamental assumptions show themselves to be vulnerable, notably those that confer on sight and the eye the privilege of verifying or authenticating this ontology.[5]

Drawing the Line

Is this merely a question of terminology among the initiated? Attitudes held by professionals of visual culture about digital moving images vary intriguingly. For the sake of convenience, I shall identify three prevailing positions. First, there are those who posit a radical break, and situate themselves on the side of the eye of the beholder and the indexicality of the image: they feel they have to draw a line in the silicone sand. Then, there are those who also posit a radical break, but situate themselves on the other side: for them the digital is destiny, another "age-old dream" of mankind come true, with digital images freeing us of both realism and representation. Finally, there are those who take the digital in their stride: for them it is business as usual—since "as usual, it is business."

Among those generally hostile to post-photographic image making are also thinkers generally identified with postmodernism, whose opposition helps restate their commitment to the cinema, thereby effectively redefining it. Jean Douchet is in good company when one considers how Jean Baudrillard has famously distinguished the cinema from television:

> In order to have an image you need to have a scene, a certain distance without which there can be no looking, no play of glances, and it is that play that makes things appear or disappear. It is in this sense that I find television obscene, because there is no stage, no depth, no place for a possible glance and therefore no place either for a possible seduction. The image plays with the real, and play between the imaginary and the real must work. Television does not send us back to the real, it is in the hyper-real, it is the hyper-real world and does not send us to another scene. This dialectic between the real and the imaginary, necessary in order to make an image exist, and necessary to permit the *jouissance* of the image, is not, it seems to me, realized by television.[6]

Directed primarily against television, Baudrillard's argument does not consider digitization, and instead concentrates on the screen, its frame and thus on the familiar psycho-semiotic argument about absence/presence, imaginary/real and their fetishizing power binding the spectator to the image. Yet what he shares with Douchet is precisely this need to "draw a line." We can note a similar gesture in another passage, this time by Serge Daney:

> The distinction I make between the image and the visual is pragmatic. I simply found it practical to use two different words. The visual is at once reading and seeing: it's seeing what you're supposed to read. Maybe we are heading towards societies which are better and better at reading (deciphering, decoding through reflexes of reading), but less and less able to see. So I call "image" what still holds out against an experience of vision and "the visual." The visual is merely the optical verification of a procedure of power (technological power, political power, advertising power, military power). A procedure which calls for no other commentary than "reception perfect, over and out." Obviously, the visual has to do with the optical nerve, but that does not make it an image. For me, the sine qua non of the image is alterity.[7]

Here, the drawing of a line allows Daney, as it does Baudrillard, to confer upon "the cinema of the image" a powerful negativity. No doubt, as with Douchet, this negativity is in part cultural and political, but in Daney it articulates itself differently than in Douchet: the quality of alterity essential to Daney is almost the opposite of Douchet's "roots" and thus no longer needs to argue in the name of trace and imprint. And what Daney finds most reprehensible about "the visual," namely its power of interpellation and address, is precisely what—in a different vocabulary, that of seduction—most appeals to Baudrillard about the screen image as opposed to television.

Business as Usual

When turning to the arguments of those for whom the cinema of digital effects is business as usual, one encounters a different kind of pragmatism. They point out that the digital revolution around the cinema concerns an object which has not significantly changed for nearly eighty years: the narrative feature film. Special effects, digitally produced, merely confirm its aesthetics of realism and illusionism. In the second instance, if by digital cinema we mean new distribution and circulation opportunities, a novel delivery system such as digital transmission would in itself have little effect on the product, at any rate, no more than television and video transmission has had on the genres, star-system and plot structures of mainstream picture making. What have driven the rise of the blockbuster are Hollywood's new marketing and distribution practices, that is, changes that have come from business strategy, rather than technological developments or aesthetic choices.

Thus, given the central importance of the narrative, live action, star-cast feature film for the economic system, it is fair to assume that traditional ways of making films will, for the foreseeable future, continue. We know that the revolution announced by Francis Ford Coppola in the late 1970s, which he hoped to implement with his Zoetrope Studio and all-digital filmmaking, has so far not materialized, while another doyen of digital cinema, George Lucas—the inventor and owner of Industrial Light and Magic (ILM)—has voiced, at least back in 1997, a certain scepticism, and this not after failure, as in the case of Coppola's ONE FROM THE HEART, but with the tremendously successful re-launch of his digitally enhanced STAR WARS behind him, as well as a multi-billion dollar company to his name:

> Digital is like saying: "are you going to use a Panavision or an Arriflex [camera]? Are you going to write with a pen or on your little laptop? I mean, it doesn't change anything."[8]

But as Lucas also knows, digitization is a contradictory factor: there is no denying that in the film industry it has altered the relation between production and post-production, input and output. Furthermore, the blockbuster, because of the size of its budget, also acts as a starter engine, pulling along other productions, as well as often providing the funds to finance changes in the infrastructure of the industry, such as updating equipment and investment in the plant. It can also provide training-sites for new skills, talent and services, as well as occasioning other kinds of spin-offs.[9] The principle or model would be that of the "prototype," as it features in other industries, such as the car industry, which develops and tests its prototypes in-house, or in the aircraft or armament industries, where fighter planes and advanced weapon systems often function as prototypes also for civilian applications, but which are tested by the military.[10] Finally, the blockbuster as prototype helps set standards also on the service side, for the exhibition sector: for instance, it may demand the installation of better sound and projection equipment in cinemas. In each case, digitization is part of it, but it is not what regulates or disrupts the system, whose logic is, once more, commercial, entrepreneurial and capitalist-industrial.

Equally evident, this logic has not only not changed the way films are made: it has also left unaffected how viewers understand them. However, digitization is not altogether a neutral tool: to stay in Lucas' vocabulary, it could be argued that digitization has replaced the camera by the pen. Yet instead of handling like a pen, it works like a brush, but instead of using paint, the digital signal is more like electronic putty.

Back to Graphics

The last point brings me to the third position which also draws a line, but in order to outline a new continuum. It places itself on the far side of the divide, as it were, taking its stand in a future from which the present looks like a past. Faced with the increase in special effects, but also the use of digital visuals in other kinds of fields, such as advertising, medicine and warfare, it is possible to argue that this "norm" I have so far referred to, namely the Hollywood-type feature film, may in time come to be seen as what Lev Manovich has called merely the "default value" of our visions system.[11] Given that there now exist so many ways of generating moving or animated images, all of which fulfil the perceptual criteria of photographic presence (Manovich calls it "perfect photographic credibility"), their most common use today, the live action film, will be but one variant among others, a historically and culturally specific type, with no further claim to dominance, if not in the market place then conceptually.

Manovich goes even further in reversing the traditional hierarchy, arguing that we need to see the digital not as a post-photographic, but a graphic mode, one of whose many possibilities is the photographic effect, and by extension, the live action cinematic effect. Considered as a graphic mode, the digital presents itself with a long history, which not only predates the cinema and accompanies its history throughout, but which also makes crucial reference to a history that, in the modern period, has often been seen in contrast and opposition to the cinema, namely the history of painting.

This has several implications: first, the rise of photographic cinema appeared to marginalize graphic cinema, relegating animation to a minor genre, to this day confined either to avant-garde forms, such as abstract cinema and video, or more frequently associated with cartoons, which is to say, with cinema (and television) made for children. The reversal of priorities makes animation the general, higher-order category for the cinema, of which live action, photographic-effect filmmaking is a specialized sub-section within the overall possibilities of the graphic mode, especially when 3-D graphics, simulated environments and other kinds of virtual reality spaces are added.[12]

The second point is that, as a graphic mode, digital cinema joins painting also in another respect: it requires a new kind of individual input, indeed manual application of craft and skill, which is to say, it marks the return of the "artist" as source and origin of the image. In this respect, the digital image should be regarded as an expressive, rather than reproductive medium, with both the software and the "effects" it produces bearing the imprint and signature of the creator.[13] This is reminiscent of the way George Lucas describes digital filmmaking as "the process of a painter or sculptor. You work on it for a bit, then you stand back and look at it and add some more onto it, then stand back and look at it and add some more. You basically end up layering the whole thing."[14]

Lucas' and Manovich's drastic perspective corrections clear some important ground. Declaring the photographic a graphic mode, for instance, elegantly disposes of the philosophical conundrum of the "indexical," and the analogy with sculpture introduces important new aspects of "embodiment" into our speculations about the primacy of the eye.[15] At the same time, their new archaeologies of digital cinema are not unique: they echo other "alternative" histories of the cinema and the audiovisual media, propounded—once again—before digitization entered into the debate. The classical narrative film, for instance, has in recent years often been seen as an "intermediary," an "intermezzo," a "mere episode" in a historical account centered elsewhere; for instance, in the "cinema of attractions"; in "simultaneity," in "interactivity." For each case, the center chosen depended on whether the vanishing point was the post-classical cinema of "roller coaster rides,"[16] video in the form of television as both the storage medium of record as well as the mass-medium of choice,[17] or the internet as the real-time multi-directional communication and interaction mode.[18]

The general point to note is that while some of these considerations are no doubt occasioned by the digital revolution, they do not depend on digitization as the technical-electronic process of converting images into sets of numerical values. Rather, by a more or less unexpected if not erroneous route, namely the technological determinism that so readily forms around digitization, we seem to have confirmed the crisis in the validity of the ocular-specular paradigm[19] from the pragmatic end, so to speak, and quite independently from the many robust philosophical critiques it has been subjected to in recent years.[20] Media gurus, film historians, cultural analysts for very different reasons, all tend to agree: sight, eye and vision are no longer what they used to be.

A Particular Kind of Distance, However Close You Get

If there is a crisis of ocular-centrism, then it also alludes to one of the aporias of modernism, notably around the notion of distance and proximity. One of the better-known theoretical reference points for this crisis would be Walter Benjamin's notion of the loss of aura in the modern world. As we know, the aura for Benjamin was "a particular kind of distance, however close you get."[21] This distance has a temporal dimension—how "far" in historical time you are from the object you are looking at, and it is a category of place: where the object is placed and what this place says about its cultural meaning: the space you, the observer and the object share is an intermediary, a mediated category of space-time: the one in which you meet, but not the one in which either the object or you is "at home."

Consider the film experience: it organizes not only space but also temporality, since one of its central aspects concerns how a film's temporal *and* spatial frames relate to each other. Time in the cinema is externally "framed": whether a minute long or a block of one-and-a-half hours, spectators have learnt to navigate this time-frame, while internally, narrative is the frame in charge of "sculpting" duration and managing its flow. This double time-frame marks a major difference compared to television, but also distinguishes cinema from other ways of spending leisure time, almost since its beginnings. For instance, some of the most ingenious examples of using external and internal framing as a stylistic device occurs in the Lumière films, often showing processes with a predetermined end, thus drawing suspense from the fact that the time of the action on film was racing against the time of the film reel, and in DEMOLITION OF A WALL even "doubling" the invisible director and cameraman off-screen by the visible foreman and worker on-screen.[22] This double space and its alignment—the spectator space to screen space—became a key factor for the development of film style, since it implied a shift from the audience being regarded as physically present and part of a collective, to the film imagining the spectator as singular, isolated and at a constant distance from the screen (and thus virtually present on the screen, in the action). It is in this sense that the markers of distance and proximity, of scale, size and horizon, but also the temporalities of here/now or there/now—in short, characteristics of Benjamin's aura—are central to the film experience, defined in part by the relation between screen space and auditorium space, predicated on distance and separation and the ways of effacing them.

This is one of the reason why, historically, the loss of distance is an odd complaint. Benjamin thought that the cinema was responsible for it. Baudrillard, as we saw, ascribes a similar loss to the advent of television, mourning the passing of cinema. When one recalls how his theory of the simulacrum pivots around what he calls the "obscene proximity of everything" (or equally revealing, the "obscene presence of things" from which we can see that distance is indeed also a temporal category), Baudrillard emerges as a typical modernist, rather than a postmodernist. In fact, one could argue that modernist art as a whole is best understood as a renegotiation of distance, often by means other than ocular-perceptual ones, and often by deliberately transgressing or not respecting the human scale (i.e. Renaissance perspective) and the rectangular frame. Consider Duchamp with his attack on the retinal in painting, and the extreme distance which his work once more tries to establish between the object and the observer, a distance marked by the fact that Duchamp dared to cross it, when he put his piece of sanitary hardware, the urinal, in an exhibition at a museum. Or consider the spatial coordinates up/down, horizontal/vertical which abstract expressionism tried to confound. Jackson Pollock painted his canvasses on the floor, and then hung them upright again in the gallery. Then Warhol, as it were, took the piss out of Pollock with his so-called "piss paintings," where it is clear they most likely were flat on the ground for the artist to have "created" them.

As we saw in the quotations from Baudrillard and Daney, the modernist insistence on distance and separation is particularly strong in French thinking about cinema and the media. A similar anxiety about the loss of distance and alterity, for instance, can be found in Paul Virilio, who in his *Logistics of Perception* is concerned about no longer having a horizon, a state that produces in him the phobia of laying oneself open to being attacked from everywhere. Gilles Deleuze on the other hand, does not have this horror of proximity, this absence of the horizon, in fact he seems to court and welcome it. He is a thinker about the visual and the image who seems not bothered by not having distance, which may be one of the reasons he is so congenial to theorists of the so-called "new media." Compared to the play of distance and proximity around the spatial coordinates of perception which so much preoccupies modern art, one can appreciate just how conservative and retrograde the cinema has appeared to most artists. The rectangular upright space of the screen and frame, the stationary observer/spectator, the careful modulation of the represented scene around the human figure as reference for size, scale and motion within the compositions: all this furnishes a set of external and internal constraints which makes it comprehensible that today, the classical cinema—as well as its "others," such as the European art cinema and even avant-garde and documentary—can be regarded as localized, contingent instances of an audio-visuality that may well need to be resituated.

In light of this my references to Douchet, Baudrillard, Virilio, Daney outline some of the "negative" definitions of the new audiovisuality. They contrast with the positive connotations associated with the label "New Hollywood," "Post-classical" or "Post-Film Cinema," where the cinematic experience is typified quite differently, with metaphors centered on space, on embodiment, on sensation rather than visual perception, all guided by variables other than those rigid Euclidean categories of the cinematic apparatus. It would lead too far to itemize all the discourses that have accompanied these "perspective corrections," but in one of the more accessible metaphors, the movies emerge above all as an event in which to figure one's participation as member of an instant community rather than as singular spectator being seated "in front" of a picture window screen; the new image also manifests itself as a space to inhabit rather than to be scanned, scrutinized or looked at; it is experienced as a second skin or total perceptual surface by which to *dress* rather than be *addressed* as subject.[23]

Among these conceptualizations which resituate the cinema by displacing it, one of the most interesting is by Raymond Bellour, himself a leading theorist of the "classical" cinematic apparatus.[24] With his notion of the "inter-image" (*l'entr'image*) he was one of the first film scholars to argue for a broader set of spatio-temporal variables, within which the cinema and its *dispositif* can be redefined. Bellour suggests seeing both television/video and the cinema under the aspect of *installation* (the living room installation, the relative spaces it creates, how it rearranges the domestic sphere, the home; and public installations, such as the gallery, the cinema, the museum, as well as the classroom or lecture theater). In this respect *l'entr'image* is what he calls "a double helix, the crossing of two forces, that of figuration and defiguration, that of immobility and movement,"[25] which is where he situates the photographic and the cinematic, as two historically contingent manifestations. The thought behind his move seems to be the desire to valorize differently the in-between-states: from perspectival vision to the flat image, from the screen to the monitor, from projection to installation—with interactivity (understood as instability and incompleteness) forming the new "pragmatic" vanishing point. Bellour utilized the Deleuzian vocabulary of "fold" and "membrane," of perception between sense-data and hallucination, of motion and the body's various inscriptions in time and intensities or extensions in space. Thus, his installation metaphor helps to relocate the cinema by situating the spectator in a new kind of space, which could be called a "contact space" or "interface." This contact space/interface embeds, but also extends the history and practice of the cinematic apparatus, in a number of perceptual fields: besides figuration/defiguration and space/place, there is "mobility of the image/stasis of the viewer" (cinema), "mobility of the viewer/static image" (installation) and further permutations of stasis and movement, such as those applying to video or the multi-media. But in this new mobility of the apparatus, this dispersal of perception across body and space, one crucial element and critical dimension seems to be missing from Bellour's *entr'image*.

Sound: the New "Space-Station" of Ocular Truth?

This dimension is sound, for too long a structuring absence in the film theory of the ocular-specular paradigm.[26] But in the wake of the break-up of this paradigm, sound has achieved a new kind of prominence, yet it has also emerged as a peculiarly problematic "complement" or "supplement" of the image.[27] Beyond the internal logic of film studies, there are other reasons for cinema sound having come to the fore. The socio-economic environment for sound's new status, for instance, is well recognized: there is, first, the music business as organizational form and mass-market model for the restructuring of the studio system (the rock concert as prototype for the movie experience; the industrial media conglomerates driven by record companies, such as the original Time-Warner deal; the heavy merchandising of film music and sound-tracks). Second, the technological transformation of the auditorium space, where new quadraphonic sound equipment, sophisticated acoustics and Dolby noise-reduction have accustomed audiences to a different quality of sound experience. Third, the rise of the horror, thriller and sci-fi genres can be seen as symptoms of the power of sound and the instability of vision, when we think of the work of directors such as David Lynch (BLUE VELVET, THE ELEPHANT MAN, LOST HIGHWAY), Brian De Palma (BLOW-OUT), David Fincher (SE7EN) and above all, Francis Ford Coppola (THE CONVERSATION, APOCALYPSE NOW, BRAM STOKER'S DRACULA).[28]

While I cannot address all the recent theoretical elaborations of sound, music, voice and silence in contemporary cinema, I want nonetheless to point to a number of features of this theoretical context—especially the emphasis on sound creating a particular sense of space, of presence and material texture. For it seems that what is most characteristic about the new discourses on sound is their seemingly oblique, but to my mind nonetheless undeniable relation to the cultural crisis I have termed the "loss of the indexical."

Again, digitization plays an ambiguous role. It is both at the heart of the technologies of new sound and peripheral to the theoretical questions they pose. The dislocation of the spectator, the arbitrariness of the images, the simultaneous sense of empowerment and loss of control which have been noted about music videos and MTV aesthetics also apply to "New Hollywood,"[29] and these seem to me features more central to an analysis of sound than the differences between analogue and digital signal. As Edward Branigan, for instance, has pointed out, there are good physiological reasons for sound to be associated with the impression of spatial extension: "The presence or absence of sound in an environment or a film opens up our sense of space" he writes, because sound, unlike light, affects and agitates the medium through which it travels (i.e. air), thus impacting the spectator's body. "We think of sound as filling a rigid space defined by light, much like water fills a glass."[30] Film sound allows the inference that the space thus made present contains motion and volume, which are two key aspects of our sense of bodies in space. At the same time, as the space of the auditorium is put into reverberation, the reference of this spatial presence is perceived to reside in the image, or as Branigan puts it: the auditorium space "stands for the space implied by the image."[31] It has also been remarked that the darkened auditorium space at once heightens perceptual receptivity and intensifies the tactile mode of perceptual orientation and "navigation":

> [Dark space] does not spread out before me but touches me directly, envelops me, embraces me, even penetrates me, completely passes through me, so that one can almost say that while the ego is permeable by darkness it is not permeable by light. The ego does not affirm itself in relation to darkness but becomes confused with it, becomes one with it. In this way we become aware of a major difference between our manners of living light space and dark space.[32]

Michel Chion, speaking of contemporary cinema, introduces the term "superfield" to denote the highly varied soundscape of "ambient natural sounds, city noises, music, all sorts of rustling" to which multi-track recording gives body. It takes on a "quasi-autonomous existence with relation to the visual field, in that it does not depend moment by moment on what we see onscreen," which means that the "superfield provides a continuous and constant consciousness of all the space surrounding the dramatic action."[33]

But as we know from the films of David Lynch, this sense of quasi-autonomy need not be based on such a "superfield." Lynch's auditory spaces, much more than any use of special visual effects, show how sound can "inhabit" a visual space, traverse it, or provide links between different locations, while also penetrating or "violating" them, most remarkably in some of the key scenes of Lost Highway, when emanating from a single source, whether a musical instrument, the ringing of a cellular telephone or an electronic scream.

Sound, in this version, gives materiality to the objects by transferring them from the imaginary scene of the screen into the space of the auditorium and thus making them tactile, "making contact." In this respect, the massively orchestrated presence of sound in contemporary cinema could be regarded as a new sort of unmediated sonic substance, penetrating everywhere and abolishing the screen space/auditorium space separation. This in turn affects the nature of the spectacle, since spectacle (in contrast to, say, ritual or carnival) relies on the maintenance of a boundary between perceiver and perceived. Herein would lie the new sound's capacity for creating the kinds of communities which the movies have attempted to adapt from the rock concert. As Chion remarks:

> We must not forget that the definitive adoption of multi-track sound occurred in the context of musical films like Michael Wadley's WOODSTOCK and Ken Russell's TOMMY. These rock movies were made with the intent to revitalize film-going by instituting a sort of participation, a communication between the audience shown in the film and the audience in the movie theatre. The space of the film, no longer confined to the screen, in a way became the entire auditorium.[34]

This, as we can see, touches upon the argument alluded to earlier, regarding the loss of distance and the horror of proximity among the modernists in the ocular-perceptual paradigm. For Baudrillard loss of distance equals the loss of signification altogether, while in the writings of Virilio reverberates the horror that comes from the malevolent invasiveness of a world governed by sound. As a material envelope, sound suffocates and stifles, when it is contrasted to the management of distance and proximity of the eye, or when compared to the play of presence/absence in the image, considered as a signifying unit. Within traditional film semiotics, sound was regarded as not mediated, or representational, but direct, and its materiality becomes the very opposite of the symbolization by which an image signifies. Sound does not signify; rather, in its materiality, its consistency, it remains the corporeal residue that either "envelops," "bridges" and "joins," or acts as the bodily "support" of a signification which takes place in and through the image. However, given its mobility and liquidity, sound is also always poised on the brink of referentiality, its transient, fleeting and directional nature means that it will remain fickle and unpredictable in the way it "attaches" itself to, or indeed "detaches" itself from an image. This ambiguous semiotic status of sound may well be one of the reasons why it has remained undertheorized within classical semiotics, and why Branigan for one seems most suspicious of any attempt to do so, preferring the cognitive approach, in which sound is understood as apprehended not via "codes" but through schemata, processed "bottom-up," in contrast to image schemata, more often processed "top-down."[35]

However, if one retains the semiotic view, one notices that in some of the arguments about the materiality of sound this materiality is treated as if it were "indexical," which raises the possibility that in our concern with cinema sound, we are tempted to simply substitute "sound" for "image" as that part of the cinematic experience in which our culture can now invest its phantasmatic belief in and its fetish-reliance on the indexical. For instance, in the new media, it is striking how elaborate the work is that goes into the creation of sound effects, as if the digital image, even more than the moving image, needs sound in order to "anchor it," in the hope to endow it with the perceptible "truth" of the trace and the imprint.

Not only are we behaving as if we needed sound to "verify" an image. At the very limit, we need sound to see it at all. Michel Chion, for instance, has repeatedly argued that perception of objects on screen becomes only possible through sound. Whether discussing the opening of Bergman's PERSONA, a bar-room brawl in a Western or the consistency of the cartoon character Jessica's breasts in WHO FRAMED ROGER RABBIT, Chion maintains that it is the ear that makes these objects and actions visible.

But does this not risk going too far in the reversal of hierarchies and the assumption of sound as the ocular supplement or prosthetics? As a corrective, one could cite the rereading of Chion by Slavoj Žižek, who also focuses on sound's "materiality" and "supplementarity" from within the psychoanalytic paradigm, where this materiality is the very mark of the Lacanian Real in the field of representation and subjectivity. For Žižek, sound becomes a way of analyzing the process of signification and symbolization, or rather, blockages within its materiality which for Žižek indicate its status as "symptom" in relation to vision, its necessary "anamorphosis" or blind spot. Žižek agrees with Chion that sound may have little to do with "hearing" but he is keen to make a distinction between "seeing with one's ears" (Chion) and "hearing with one's eyes"—the two being related to each other, across a fundamental and constitutive a-symmetry in which "hearing with one's eyes" belongs to the mortifying terror of the Gaze rather than the animating powers of the Look.

Thus, both Chion and Žižek theorize this peculiar status of sound's materiality, between the absolutely non-symbolized substance of the Real, and a phantom indexicality of material texture, "linking" sound to vision across an indexicality of absent causes. Yet it seems that both Chion and Žižek do so from within the priority given to the ocular-specular paradigm, and thus ultimately, are still committed to the realist ontology I outlined at the start. In other words, perception in the mode of hearing, while dethroning the eye from its pre-eminence, nonetheless ends up simulating a referentiality which previously had been attributed to the indexical, implying a material link of the image to its profilmic support, whether this support is interpreted within the terms of André Bazin's realism, Christian Metz's semiology of absence/presence or Jacques Lacan's psychoanalysis of the Real.

What the new sound seems to provide is thus a kind of pseudo-indexicality: while the digital image deceives the eye, digital sound is called upon to bridge the credibility gap and step in the breach, because it appears to provide the "supplement" of a material trace, now that the specter of digitized images threatens to abolish the "truth" once guaranteed by indexicality of the photographic mode. Yet if this is so, then the reversal of hierarchies between sound and image in the New Hollywood merely replaces one kind of illusionism for another, or rather displays its ocular sense-deception, the better to hide its aural illusionism: to see with one's eyes what one knows to be impossible, but to do so from the "ontological ground" of a presence—a space and a time—simulated by sound. But just as the indexical could be said to have been one of the blind spots of the ocular-specular paradigm, so there is a danger that sound or rather its "space," its "body," its "materiality" become the blind spots of the overturning of this paradigm. Rather, to the extent that we have to re(de)fine priorities, more emphasis will have to be laid on the way moving images construct the audio-visual space also as a social space—without, however, collapsing this social space into "realist" referentiality.

From "Truth" to "Trust": Institutional Authority and its Discontents

If the indexical has become the impossible place from which to construct the truth conditions of the image, and sound cannot be the "ground" on which the image finds its place, how do we navigate the unframed time-space coordinates of the cinema beyond distance and proximity? As I have tried to argue, it cannot be from the vantage point of the digital, quite literally, our zero-degree. Instead, indexicality and our reliance on it for assuring us of the truth claim of the image has, thanks to digitization though not because of it, landed us in a theoretical fix. But supposing it had been a fixation, a fantasy even in the age of celluloid? If the status of authenticity and proof of a photograph or moving image had never resided in its indexical relation to the real at all, but had always been a function of the institutions in charge of its verification and dissemination? Such has been the argument of semio-pragmatists, for instance, as well as cognitivists.[36]

But we can test it perhaps in a more common-sense context. For instance, most of the photographs we find on the front pages of our newspapers are stills taken from video, or are photographs transmitted digitally: in either case, they have been manipulated in all kinds of ways before they reach us. But since we still accept our daily paper—tabloids perhaps excepted—as a medium of record, its digital mode of reproduction is secondary compared to the contract we expect the newspaper to honor with its readers, a contract of trust and accuracy, of good faith and public accountability, extending from the text in a newspaper to its pictures.[37]

Thus, it would seem that any threat to the "authentic," to the truth status of the moving image, too, does not come from digitization or the loss of indexicality, but might well come from, say, primarily economic and political factors such as deregulation and "market forces." If television, for instance, is no longer trusted as a public medium of record, it may be because in the commercial environment it finds itself in when competing for ratings, it no longer enjoys political or social legitimation as an institution which "polices" or self-regulates the veracity of its messages and representations. By the same token, East European countries have seen the inverse: the media were distrusted because the state controlling them lacked legitimacy, so that it was the commercial press and the newly privatized audiovisual media that—for a brief period after the fall of the Wall—were endowed with the expectation of providing reliable evidence.

Does this mean we have, after all, come back to the economic-industrial horizon with which I began, and which I wanted to bracket? Not quite. For the question of truth arising from the photographic and post-photographic would in my example neither divide along the lines of the trace and the indexical at all, nor be determined by the market. Rather, it would flow from a complex set of discursive conventions, political changes and institutional claims which safeguard (or suspend) what we might call not the "truth," but the "trust" spectators, as well as theorists, are prepared to invest in a given mode of representation, audio-visuality or imaging. Thus, perhaps more important than to reverse the sound/image hierarchies would be the task to think both sound and image's pseudo-indexicality within the cultural crisis of record, imprint, evidence and the institutional crisis of accountability and public trust, which in turn would give us an agenda for looking at contemporary

Hollywood in its wider cultural and historical significance—as one of the most acute symptoms of the loss of trust in the symbolic order, but also as a most demanding arena in which audiences can do their own "reality testing." For what lies "beyond distance and proximity," and thus also delineates a new horizon for our thinking, I would argue, are the different regimes of trust, belief and the suspension of disbelief.

Evidently, this may or may not "locate" us in space and time, or ground us in the image or sound, but it could reserve a place for us, as bodies and minds, as well as subjects and citizens. If the cinema of the event-movie and media event is still telling the same stories, is still appealing to the viewers' capacity of seeing (as well as hearing, believing, knowing), then what is New to New might be that henceforth audiences still see, hear, believe, know—but (to paraphrase Jean-Luc Godard) not necessarily precisely in that (symbolic) order.

23
The Persistence of Hollywood, Part II:
Reflexivity, Feedback and Self-Regulation

The World that is Hollywood

If one can speak of Hollywood as providing the *lingua franca* of a certain sociability, affording people from all parts of the world an instant familiarity and imaginary intimacy in the public sphere, then the case for Hollywood as a world-historical achievement along the lines sketched at the end of the first part of this essay is still far from self-evident. Despite its longevity of nearly a hundred years, and its sense of its own historical significance (annually on display during the Academy Awards Ceremony), Hollywood is too close, too much with(in) us, for one to compare it, say, to the monumental permanence of the Egyptian pyramids or the architectural and spiritual grandeur of Gothic cathedrals, or even the 19th century bourgeois novel.[1] What would be the common standard for such a comparison, forgetting for the moment that most educated people will think the very idea little short of blasphemous? Raymond Bellour has probably given the suggestion that Hollywood is more than the sum of its parts the right kind of personal inflection, hinting that the comparison might not be such hubris or folly after all:

> There are three things, and only three that I have loved in the same fashion: Greek mythology, the early writings of the Brontë sisters, the American cinema. These three worlds, at first sight so dissimilar, have one point in common, which is of immense impact: they are, precisely, worlds; that is to say, totalities complete in themselves, which respond truly, at their given point in time, to all the questions one might pose oneself about the nature, the function and the fate of the universe. This is very clear about Greek mythology. The stories of Gods and heroes leave nothing in the shadows: neither the heavens nor the earth, neither the genealogies nor the emotions; they impose the idea of an order, finite and infinite, within which a child can imagine his or her fears and desires. . . . . The American cinema found itself giving birth, at the scale of the largest modern society, to a similar phenomenon. And it expanded its reach (almost) around the entire planet. . . . To this day, the American cinema is the last attempt at a mythology of Western culture [and] since its invention, there has been an extraordinary fit between the machine that is cinema and the continent that is America. The United States immediately recognized, in this machine to reproduce reality, the instrument it needed to create its own. Its power lies in having believed in it instantly.[2]

Bellour cannily places Hollywood between the world-making mythology of the civilization whose imprint we still bear, and the personal mythology of a family of very gifted writers, thus reaffirming the foundational polarity that understands Hollywood as a complex but internally consistent secular "cosmology"—André Bazin's "genius of the system," and at the same time, as the enabling condition for a "family" of great artists—the genius of the "*auteurs*." Hollywood's strength is that it has transcended its origins in the music hall, the circus, popular theater and vaudeville of the late 19th and early 20th centuries to become a uniquely rich art form, while remaining faithful to the needs for and sources of the visual spectacle as pioneered in the magic lantern phantasmagorias and smoke-and-mirror displays of the post-Revolutionary period around 1800.

This sense of the American cinema tapping into a long tradition and a venerable, if often denigrated, pedigree has in recent years been given the name of "the cinema of attractions," emphasizing the fundamental grounding in spectacle, special effects, surprise and sensation of a cinema that is traditionally analyzed more in terms of story-lines and plotting, narrative and narration, foreshadowing and suspense—in short, highlighting linear progress, goal-directedness and the sense of closure that comes with the resolution of conflict or contradiction.[3] I want to recontextualize the other side, that of the "cinema of attractions," by linking it to what I have earlier referred to as the "event" character of movie-going in general, and the blockbuster in particular. Recall that the architectural language of movie-theaters (Egyptian, Chinese, Aztec, Gothic) often alludes to cinemas as what one might call "spaces of ritual" or of formalized behavior—temples, palaces and churches—deemed necessary for the occurrence of an event: a miracle, a sacrifice, a special effect, a transubstantiation.

What in this sense is an event? The key element I take to be that the event is in some ways unique, that it constitutes a rupture in relation to what surrounds it, and that it has an extension in time and space; an event is something taking "place" in "time." In particular, while the temporality of the event is that of "simultaneity," the media event always involves two spaces, related to each other and yet distinct from each other, a now/here space, and a now/there space, which also means, of course, that an event implies a subject, a bearer of an experience. On television, for instance, it concerns a remote location, which is being brought close; in the case of a traditional cinema experience, the key spaces designate the auditorium space and the screen space, and the time, of course, the duration of the projection, but also the time of anticipation that precedes it. Indeed, the two temporalities, as much as the two spaces have to be experienced as distinct, so that their conjuncture or melding—brought on, for instance, by the dimming of lights, sound, narration and spectacle—can actually take place.

Yet the cinema experience has the event as its organizing principle also in a different sense. One could propose a definition of cinema in the electronic age, that is, *after* television and the Internet, which, however, merely highlights a general feature of cinema since its beginnings, namely that a film requires a performance for its completion, and an event for its actualization. The event can assume various shapes, and has—over the past hundred years—taken very diverse forms. For instance, if the event character in the 1930s and 1940s was defined around the family audience, in the 1970s and 1980s it modeled itself on the leisure habits of its predominantly youthful, male audience, and since the late 1990s has—thanks to (digital) animation—increasingly found again its family audience. The constitutive elements and quality of this event, as we also know, is for exhibitors a critical factor economically, since their income from concessions and amenities can exceed that from the share of the box-office admissions.[4]

Another indication that the cinema has had an event-scenario built into its commercial exploitation almost from the very beginning is the fact that, since the 1910s, spectators have been charged according to a time advantage and a location advantage: the principle of "first run" or *première exclusivité* or now the "opening weekend" by which cinemas and admission prices are classified mean that, in effect, audiences pay a premium for seeing a film during its initial release period, when it has the attention of the press and the general public. Its commodity value resides in its temporality, here expressed as the time advantage: we are prepared to pay extra for a film while it is still an "event." The emergence of the prerecorded video-cassette and then the DVD, at a cost barely above the admission price of a cinema ticket, has further shortened the period in which the cinema film is an event, although it has, as already mentioned, given the film a substantial secondary market, in which its event character is intended to reverberate as recollection and memory.

The "event-driven" nature of cinema today also reflects the changing function of public spaces in the wake of urban renewal schemes for inner cities, where crowds no longer gather for political action or to go to work. Since the existence of television and the automobile, a whole range of other activities competes for the population's free time. But these static and mobile vehicles also mean that people who frequent the streets of city centers do so almost wholly for the purposes of shopping, leisure and entertainment: activities connected with seeing and being seen, in which "going to the movies" is part of a continuum of spectatorship, ranging from window-shopping, meeting friends at a café or eating out. But the movie-theater also marks a liminal space, at once a physical focus and social experience, defined in relation to its opposite: the home. As Edgar Reitz has put it: "cinema is a sort of consensus about going out, it gives a name and an address to the desire of leaving the house for an evening."[5]

An effect of the blockbuster as the main attraction of theatrical release and as a marketing tool for other audio-visual services and material products is that it makes "cinema" partake in the meta-genre "media-event," comparable to political events, public holidays, natural or man-made disasters. This is why we come across the cinema everywhere, but in a peculiar temporal modulation. A new film more likely than not, first hits us in the form of movie trailers, billboards, behind-the-scenes features on television and star interviews. In this respect, the blockbuster's carefully orchestrated marketing campaign involves a build-up and an intensification, followed by a media-blitz, whose nearest analogy is the weather. It is much like a hurricane gathering force (for someone living in Europe) in mid-Atlantic, as it were, showing first signs of turbulence in toy shops, on the web or on music television, before moving inland to the capital for its big release, and then finally sweeping the rest of the country's screens before gently subsiding in the videothèques and undulating through the Internet. The event-movie par excellence, the blockbuster is characterized by the fact that it takes place in a kind of countdown time and that it occupies all manner of urban, mental and media spaces. On the other hand, it can also lay waste the cinema landscape for more modest films, usually of domestic or European origin (once again, speaking from outside the US).

The new cinema space, by becoming absorbed into a different dimension (be it the theme-park atmosphere of the cineplex or the art-house ambiance modeled on museums, or the lobby areas of other high-profile high-tech public or corporate buildings), are part of an urbanism in which they figure as "cathedrals of another faith," to use a memorable phrase coined by the architect Hans Hollein for the kind of prestige buildings that today make up a metropolitan skyline.[6] John Ellis goes so far to speak of the "sacred" quality of the cinema space. For him, it is the possibility of "epiphanies" that justify the cinema's main claim to be different from television:

A cinema is a special space, one to which we are permitted a limited access. It is not our space, it is a controlled public space which we enter according to set rules—the payment of money, arrival at an appointed hour—and agree to behave according to still further established rules. These rules certainly vary according to the particular culture in which the screening is taking place, but in Europe our established convention is that we sit, we do not talk, and we attend to the spectacle. We submit—and, having submitted, we can enter into a different modality of existence, into a realm of fantasy. This process is essentially a sacred one. . . . Collective submission to rules and rituals allows the individual a degree of epiphany. . . . Television, on the other hand, occupies a different space entirely, one that has no sacred dimension to speak of. We have television of right in our society. It is a social necessity in the same way that indoor plumbing is a social necessity.[7]

Thus, compared to the old stand-alone cinemas, but especially the shoebox cinemas of the 1970s, the multiplexes since the 1990s offer not only a difference of kind and level in the amenities but a different recoding of space itself. The old cinema space is all about "drawing boundaries," marking the event is separate. By contrast, the new ones are about integration as well as differentiation, making the cinema space not merge, but be contiguous with a café, a bar or restaurant space: reflection of a different policy not only of services inside the cinema, but of how contemporary public spaces relate, communicate and connect with each other, and what experiences are being offered across these spaces. In contrast to Ellis' sacred space, which is essentially a homogeneous space, the auditorium can also be a heterogeneous space, in which the function of the screen space becomes somewhat different: not merging with the auditorium, but one where separation and distance are differently coded: one recalls the phenomenon of cult films like THE ROCKY HORROR PICTURE SHOW or THE BLUES BROTHERS, or the sing-along SOUND OF MUSIC, where the narrative action became secondary (and with it the temporality of suspense or other narrational devices). The fans' familiarity turns the film into a cue sheet for a performance. One might call such a film experience— echoing what was said earlier—a space to be entered, traversed and explored, a map to be navigated, rather than an itinerary to be followed. This sharply differentiates "going to the movies" from the home theater experience and also suggests that however much new releases are pirated or circulate on the Internet, the physical experience and the event-character will remain a key "attraction" of the Hollywood cinema.

Thus, in light of these considerations, there may be a number of factors that even for a historian invite comparison with earlier cultural achievements: blockbusters as "buildings" in time rather than space, or as media events that linger on in the memory of a generation or a community. A quite different parallel to earlier "cathedrals" might be the collective craftsmanship of Hollywood, and the often semi-anonymous authorship manifest in the multi-million spectacles (few will stay behind for the five minutes of scrolling credits). The concentration of the American film industry in one physical location over such a long period of time has meant that generations of professionals, men and women with very special skills, have invested themselves, in a uniquely American blend of imagination and engineering, competition and competence. This professionalism was passed on in the form of an impressive institutional memory: an infinitely varied body of specialized knowledge, whose talent pool has renewed itself by attracting outsiders in ways equally unique, if one compares it to similarly tightly organized areas of industry or manufacture. However, since this manufacture concerns products and services, whose historical role it was, as I shall argue further on, to partake in the "industrialization" of consciousness, of thought and of fantasy, the "power" of Hollywood is both more indirect and more insidious, but also—in the sense of world-historical achievement—more lasting in its invisible effects on minds, the senses and mental habits, than in its visible products.

In its double function as visual language of naturalization and self-evidence, coupled with a vast array of techniques of persuasion and propaganda, as well as technologies of immediacy and presence, Hollywood represents a special kind of symbolic power, not just in and through the cinema, but at the level of a more generalized code of the perceptible, the sensible and the intelligible: the news on television, the visual language of politics, the design of everyday objects, the clothes we wear, and the propagation of desirable life-styles all bear incontrovertible signs of the impact of American movies. In addition, movies have given elegance and grace to gesture and body language, pith and wit to dialogue and verbal exchange that go well beyond this particular film or that particular actor, important though these are; cinematic comportment is a recognizable measure of sophistication and "cool," it connotes physical attractiveness and what constitutes a winning personality. In this sense, with Hollywood, the sum is greater than the parts, and yet, it is also true that the parts, the films that are best remembered, the "classics," or even just a scene or a sentence, can stand for the whole. Once again, the relation of part to whole, which back in 1972, I mainly saw in terms of a "classical aesthetics" and within the canons of "organic unity" and proportionality, are more complex, more troubling, as I have tried to suggest by subsuming them under the term "continuity principle," which I turned into an oxymoron by emphasizing its inherent discontinuities, divisions, a-symmetries and reversals.

The Internal Logic of the American Film Industry

Although I have examined this in more detail in a separate chapter, it is perhaps worthwhile to just summarize how the history of Hollywood from an economic perspective has been rewritten in recent years, under the impact of three interconnected factors: the "revival" of Hollywood around the blockbuster as marketing concept; the transformation of Hollywood due to finance capitalism; and the uncertainty and opportunities arising from the introduction of digitization in production, post-production and distribution/exhibition. When recapitulating the different narratives that have evolved about the internal changes of the American film industry since 1945, one notes that a number of significant landmarks and key events keep returning in each of them. If placed on a time-line, they would oblige one to keep track of a fairly extensive list of variables, ranging from legal decisions, such as the outcome of the anti-trust case against the major studios (1948) or the change of censorship regulation and the scrapping of the Hays Code (1968), to technical innovations in lighting and sound or special effects, changes in basic technology, such as the introduction of color, wide-screen, to the opening of television studios, the mergers or takeover in the ownership of the studios, the rise of the agents and the package unit system, major flops that bankrupted studios or production companies, the rise of multiplexes, the introduction of the Dolby sound system and so on.

The broad outlines of these different histories and how they interlace are by now fairly well known, thanks to thorough scholarship along the lines of "revisionist historiography," and combining detailed monographs on specific individual topics with the ambitious multi-volume "History of American Cinema" series published by University of California Press.[8] They tend to favor the narratives of continuity over those of rupture, of break or radical renewal, and while historians differ as to the causal agents of the most recent series of transformations, the general agreement centers on a combination of changed business models (of accounting and financing) and marketing-and-distribution practices (all associated with the blockbuster, i.e. saturation release, high-concept advertising, putting exhibition chains under long-term contract).[9] Perhaps not surprisingly, these narratives have themselves analogies with Hollywood movies: for instance, the fall and rise of "Hollywood" can be personalized, in which case it is about the men who made it possible, and how they accomplished it, in a combination of ruthlessness and charm, entrepreneurial brilliance, and a gambler's instinct for risk. Yet even when personalized, the story has two (Hollywood) versions: the good guy story and the bad guy story, that is, it is about heroes and villains, although (as so often in Hollywood movies, too) the good guys and the bad guys are sometimes the same individuals: Douglas Gomery tells a "good guy" story (starring Lew Wasserman), while Jon Lewis tells the bad guy story (with a similar cast of characters).[10]

On the other hand, the story can be structural-conjunctural: symptomatic of the economic forces of "Late Capitalism" or globalization, determined by changes in technology, and affected by demographics or the shifting patterns of leisure and consumption. If these are the pressures that force CEOs, deal-makers or studio heads to decide as they do, then, their own foibles or personal vendettas are largely irrelevant, because what counts are the banks, the fund-managers or the shareholders: the famous "bottom line" on the balance sheet (this is the line taken by scholars such as Tino Balio).[11]

The net result, one can argue, is largely the same: the command-and-control structure known as "vertical integration" which had existed from the 1920s until the late 1940s (when it was broken up by the anti-trust case) has been largely re-established since the 1990s, thanks to the lax oversight of successive US administrations, as well as strong lobbying efforts by the MPAA. Integration now functions perhaps on a more horizontal axis, with "synergies" and diversification replacing the vertically integrated "production-distribution-exhibition" triad.[12] Nonetheless, from the economic-institutional perspective, Hollywood functions, in the domestic market, as a diversified yet highly coordinated cartel made up of a relatively small number of entangled entertainment conglomerates, where legal ownership rests partly in the hands of foreign multi-nationals (Canadian, Japanese, for a time also French) as well as venture capital and hedge funds.

These detailed economic histories of Hollywood are crucial to an understanding of the various challenges, and of how the many sub-systems have coordinated their crisis management, and have effected the transition from "industry" (making "products") to "business" (providing "services" that both produce surplus value, i.e. profit, and administer cultural assets, i.e. act as the nation's cultural memory). But precisely because of the latter, the cultural asset dimension, a purely economic-industrial approach also risks making Hollywood no more than a case study or illustration of a larger process in manufacturing observed in the latter half of the 20th century, namely the move from "Fordism" to "post-Fordism," initially—as the name implies—pioneered in the auto-industries, and imported into the US and Europe from Japan (Toyota, Honda).[13]

There is thus a need to also investigate other models that might explain a "business" that has typical characteristics, but also unique risks that are not shared by other forms of industrial (assembly-line) production. Three features in particular have attracted attention: the high degree of "creative" input and the importance of a specific location over a long period of time; the unique requirement for a logistics of managing time, timing and temporal flow; the "international" or global dimensions of the American film-business, and notably its relations to foreign audiences but also foreign talent and personnel. The first is associated with the work of Allen Scott and the concept of "cultural clustering," much discussed among sociologists or urbanism, but also of interest to cultural historians. Scott's *On Hollywood: The Place, the Industry* is a valuable, but so far in film studies little discussed contribution to the "persistence of Hollywood" debate.[14] The second—the logistics of time-management—can be seen as the reverse of Scott's "clustering" argument, and be related to Manuel Castells' investigations into the "network society" and especially his idea of a "space of flows."[15] But the same questions are also addressed by another ambitious study, Aida Hozic's *Hollyworld* which looks at the way the different branches of the traditional film industry have responded to both the pressures to relocate and diversify in the face of globalization (noting a shift from "producers" to "merchants"), and the need to be both present and in control of what she calls "cyberspace" (the on-line, real-time flow of information, including new marketing and distribution forms such as downloading, but also piracy and copyright protection).[16] The third topic—Hollywood's relation to its foreign markets, the import of talent and the export of labor costs—has been most thoroughly investigated in *Global Hollywood*, edited by a group of New York scholars led by Toby Miller.[17] This latter topic, on the other hand, links up with a broader theme, also often debated with Hollywood and the film industry as a prime example, namely the so-called "Cultural Imperialism" debate, begun in the late 1960s and led by US scholars critical of the dominance that US media—especially television—and US cultural exports have had notably in the developing world, to the alleged detriment of local or indigenous cultural activity and creativity.

Hollywood Hegemony, Cultural Imperialism and Creative Destruction

A typically programmatic statement of the case for seeing the economic developments which I characterized as a move from "product" to "service," and second, from "industry" to "business," and which logically implies a move from "overseas" markets to "global presence," might run something like this:

> Hollywood is a set of interconnected practices, both industrial and symbolic. . . . The theatrical exhibition of films is now merely one market among many in which the major studios are involved. Over the last three decades, the studios have become consolidated within "tightly diversified" transnational entertainment conglomerates. In this industrial context cinematically released blockbuster films are not only engineered to sell across different market segments, they have also become "launch-pads" for multi-media product lines. Successful film "brands" are exploited and disseminated internationally across a range of commodities and popular cultural experiences, from home video to theme parks, books, soundtracks, television spin-offs, toys, video games and Happy Meals. The studios also have a stake in exploiting significant niche markets, via genre production and links with the "independent" sector. In short, Hollywood is a resource for making and distributing culture worldwide.[18]

Implied in this emphasis on the symbolic, alongside the industrial prowess of Hollywood, is the point made earlier, namely that Hollywood films have evolved a peculiar kind of universality, meaning that a cultural form has been created which is very specific to a nation, an age and a century, but also universal, in the sense of being universally appreciated as well as universally understood. This is a fairly remarkable historical fact, once again ranking Hollywood alongside the powerful symbols (and symbols of power) of the great world systems (including religions), as well as—disturbingly perhaps—putting it in the company or vicinity of the great universal brands (McDonalds, Coca Cola, Nike, Sony, Mercedes, Apple—many, but by no means all of US origin).[19] Yet equally pertinent—and precisely a source of critique, once one grants Hollywood this kind of symbolic power—is Hollywood's ability, thanks to this universalism, to set the terms by which it can be discussed and analyzed, and by extension, by staking out in advance the terrain on which it can be challenged or opposed. Once one puts the question of cultural imperialism on the agenda, for instance, one has to confront the argument that Hollywood only gives to its domestic and world audiences what these audiences "want," i.e. its symbolic power is also part of a master/slave dialectic.[20]

The general definition of the cultural imperialism thesis would be something like the following, formulated by its first and foremost critic, Herbert Schiller:

> The concept of cultural imperialism today [1979] best describes the sum of the processes by which a society is brought into the modern world system and how its dominating stratum is attracted, pressured, forced, and sometimes bribed into shaping social institutions to correspond to, or even promote, the values and structures of the dominating centre of the system. The public media are the foremost example of operating enterprises that are used in the penetrative process. For penetration on a significant scale the media themselves must be captured by the dominating/penetrating power. This occurs largely through the commercialization of broadcasting.[21]

Subsequent commentators have preferred the term "dependency theory" (whereby imported communication media "vicariously establish a set of foreign norms, values, and expectations which, in varying degrees, may alter the domestic cultures and socialization processes"),[22] while yet others have stressed the continuity between cultural imperialism and 19th century imperial colonialism.[23]

The more specific formulation of Hollywood hegemony would rest on the assertion that US dominance in matters cinema have stifled, marginalized and at times even repressed many other forms of cinema. The American film industry's sheer economic power—together with the trading advantages it negotiated after the US winning the second world war in Europe, as well as its government dictating terms in economic forums like the World Trade Organization—have effectively meant that Hollywood was able to "colonize" the rest of the world, and deeply imprint on less developed countries (and minds?) its images, its fantasies, its life-styles, its dream-scenarios and the material shape of its aspirations, indeed even impose its very idea of social, but also perceptual reality.

The "Cultural Imperialism Theory" belongs in many ways to the 1960s and 1970s, when aggressive US foreign policy in South East Asia and Latin America gave additional ammunition to the "culturalist" argument. Among communication studies scholars, its central thesis has been largely abandoned since, partly because little proof could be found for it on empirical grounds, partly because—with the emergence of other media and information technologies, as well as the debate over globalization—it came to be refined and redefined, mainly in the following ways: first, cultural imperialism is best understood as the ideologically biased name for the global rise of a middle class in developing countries, whose chief characteristic it is to embrace or aspire to consumerist values and life-styles, modeled on the "West." Second, insofar as cultural imperialism is tied to media and communication, it affects rich countries more than poor countries. The latter tend to remain more "national" in their tastes of entertainment forms (music, television), not least because one has to be relatively affluent to frequent Hollywood movies in the first place, since for instance in India and other Asian countries (including China), cinemas tend to charge higher admission than for locally produced films. Third, Hollywood films and their global distribution actually make the world more culturally diverse. This is the position put forward most vigorously by Tyler Cowen, in *Creative Destruction: How Globalization is changing the World's Cultures*.[24]

Cowen systematically challenges the view that capitalism and mass consumer culture has damaged the vitality and diversity of the arts. Maintaining that a capitalist market economy is providing a largely underappreciated framework to support a wide range of artistic forms of expression, he concedes that globalization will disrupt, dislocate and transform ("Creative Destruction") many of the world's indigenous or particular cultures, but asserts that the net result will be positive for everyone concerned, not only for the culturally or economically dominant countries. Cowen is no simplistic free-marketeer; he provides detailed case studies of how markets for literature, painting, sculpture and music have arisen across the centuries, and the kind of monetary, but also immaterial incentives (similar to Bourdieu's "cultural capital") that markets create for innovation and for countering prevailing artistic traditions and institutional habits. Cowen has a separate chapter on Hollywood ("Why Hollywood rules the world and whether we should care"), whose main claim is dialectical:

> Hollywood's universality has, in part, become a central part of American national culture. Commercial forces have led America to adopt "that which can be globally sold" as part of its national culture. Americans have decided to emphasize their international triumphs and their ethnic diversity as part of their national self-image. In this regard, Hollywood's global-market position is a Faustian bargain. Achieving global dominance requires a sacrifice of a culture's initial perspective to the demands of world consumers. American culture is being exported, but for the most part it is not Amish quilts and Herman Melville. JURASSIC PARK, a movie about dinosaurs, was a huge hit abroad, but FORREST GUMP, which makes constant reference to American history and national culture, made most of its money at home.[25]

Furthermore, for Cowen, cultural dominance is not a one-way street: it forces national and local industries to become more competitive and innovative; in the case of Hollywood, it not only requires the American film industry to pay attention to its audiences overseas, but also obliges it to import personnel of diverse cultural backgrounds and local expertise, allowing for greater mobility among creative labor and talent.

Global Hollywood

This latter point—the relation of Hollywood to its foreign audiences and its importation of talent from overseas—is beginning to receive wider attention.[26] What is important, however, is to recognize that there are different historical as well as conceptual frameworks within which this transnational-global dimension can be studied. Historical fact is that from its inception, Hollywood was keen to attract the best filmmaking talent from all over the world, and especially from its most serious competitors (and most lucrative markets).[27] Better known are the periods, notably in the late 1930s and early 1940s, when Hollywood became the refuge and exile for hundreds of émigrés from Germany, France, Hungary, Austria and other countries, fleeing from anti-Semitism and other forms of persecution. Yet it would be wrong to project the refugee paradigm either back into the earlier decade or forward into the post-WWII period. In a number of articles (not included here) I have studied the complex relations which Hollywood has maintained ever since the early 1920s with, for instance, the German film industry—extending not just to the war years and the Nazi period, but resuming especially since the late 1980s, with the "import" of directors such as Wolfgang Petersen and Roland Emmerich and cinematographer Michael Ballhaus.[28] Similar case studies could be made about directors from, notably, Australia, New Zealand and Britain, but also Taiwan, Hong Kong, Mexico, Spain, France, Poland, and even The Netherlands and Finland.[29] The chapter on William Dieterle and the Warner Bros. biopic underlines many of these general points, and shows how closely economic, political and personal factors can be intertwined.

Lest, however, one should have too harmonious an impression about Hollywood's welcome of its foreign personnel, even when they are not political refugees, the study on *Global Hollywood*, already mentioned, focuses not on the high-profile directors or stars who came to Hollywood to improve their careers or win international fame as "artists," but very specifically deals with Hollywood's labor relations across different branches of the industry, and in particular, on international labor relations since the onset of globalization—thereby modifying any idealized vision one might have of the craft guilds that formally regulate the film industry's skilled labor force, or of the "anonymous authorship" I mentioned in analogy to Gothic cathedrals.

While giving up the generalized cultural imperialism thesis, *Global Hollywood* concentrates on one aspect of this thesis, namely Hollywood's hold over its foreign outlets. The authors show how much political muscle, economic clout and legal pressure the US exerts, in order to keep the world's markets open for US product, while resolutely closing off its own markets through all kinds of protectionist measures. The authors are able to make a strong case for the "proletarianization" of creative labor, via the practices of outsourcing, runaway productions and the relentless search for more cost-effective environments (locations, government subsidies, cheaper labor) for big budget film production.

The problem with the theories of *Global Hollywood* is one I mentioned above, when looking at the primarily economic accounts of Hollywood: that such studies merely demonstrate that Hollywood behaves like every other multi-national company, irrespective whether it is located in the US, in Britain, the Netherlands, Germany or China, South Korea or Japan. In this sense, we learn less about what is specific to Hollywood than the title or the project promises, especially given its polemical tone and overt hostility to academic film studies, to *auteurism* and the hermeneutics of film-interpretation. Thus, there may be a need to keep the broader perspective in view, extending it even, by pointing out not only that Hollywood has always imported talent, but that immigrants and foreigners have played a major part in making the cinema "American": Neil Gabler's book on the shaping impact Jews have had on Hollywood, for instance, or Michael Rogin's *Black Face White Noise* add to the purely economic argument a necessarily differentiating cross-cultural and ethnic dimension.[30]

This type of argument does not contradict *Global Hollywood*, but complements it, as it also complements the argument that points to the increasing dependence of American cinema on its foreign audiences, leading to a particular kind of transnationalism at the very heart of Hollywood picture making, and confirming that Hollywood has always had a multi-cultural political unconscious—within white hegemony.[31] Few reliable studies exist about Hollywood's foreign audiences, but again, specific case histories, such as a comparative study on the global reception of LORD OF THE RINGS,[32] help to get a sense of how local audiences refigure globally designed media products,[33] catching up in cinema studies with work done in the mid-1990s around the international reception of US television series such as *Dallas* and *Dynasty*.[34]

Hollywood and the Attention Economy

Earlier, I noted the many contradictions that the study of Hollywood poses to the analyst and the historian, and suggested its robustness and persistence may actually be due to these unresolved tensions, which seem to energize the system overall rather than paralyze it. Both in its internal relations—if one thinks of the permanent redefinition of what are goods and what services, or the shift in the balance of power between "merchants" and "producers"—and in its external relations (the relentless search for cheap labor, outsourcing of specialized tasks and skills, the role in the WTO in policing intellectual property, but also the firm eye on foreign audiences), Hollywood continues to repair itself by acting as a crisis-managing institution, an organism with strong survivalist instincts. By "restructuring" through bankruptcies and mergers, by being opportunist in its alliances and predatory in its marketing strategies, the American film industry behaves much in the ways analyzed by Tyler Cowen also for other industries, following the Schumpeter model of creative destruction favored by conservative economists for dealing with the crises of capitalism.

If this seems, once again, too benign an interpretation of Hollywood as multi-media conglomerate with its tentacles in all media platforms and dominant in all markets, a perspective correction is provided by the more anthropological approach mentioned earlier, where the question is "why cinema," posed now within the history of capitalism, and in particular, the Marxist problematic of how the products or objects of human labor become commodities, and commodities both reify and immaterialize themselves in (the circulation of) images. First sketched by Fredric Jameson in the context of an argument about 20th century modernism appropriating 19th century realism through the cinema as a form of commodity fetishism,[35] the argument has been elaborated and extended by Jonathan Beller, in a book called significantly, *The Cinematic Mode of Production: Attention Economy and the Society of the Spectacle*.[36] Beller is not specifically concerned with Hollywood, but tries to offer a sweeping rethink of what the cinema has contributed or destroyed during its hundred-year dominance as *the* visual medium of the 20th century. In particular, his thesis is that the most typical form that (abstract) capital has taken in the 20th century is that of "moving images," by which he understands the mobility in time and space of goods and people as allegorized by the dissemination of motion pictures; the industrialization of consciousness, as predicted by Adorno and Horkheimer; the "society of the spectacle," as analyzed by Guy Debord; the affective labor invested in sight and vision, as theorized by Michel Foucault: all of which coagulate into new potentials for exploitation and profit. If cinematic spectacles represent the different aggregate states of the abstract entity called money, they would be the latest stage of capitalism: in seizing on the senses, and converting vision and looking into reified acts of exchange, cinema readies and primes "attention" to become the most precious, but also the most profitable commodity of the 21st century. Making the case historically—from chrono-photography's time-and-motion studies, via Dziga Vertov's MAN WITH THE MOVIE CAMERA and behaviorist psychology, through psychoanalysis to the Coen Brothers' BARTON FINK—the book traces the stages by which filmic perception attains commodity status. In the central chapter, "Inspiration of Objects, Expiration of Words: Cinema, Capital of the Twentieth Century," Beller maintains that what he calls (after the Coens) "capital cinema" taps "the productive energies of consciousness and the body in order to facilitate the production of surplus value."[37] Not unlike Hardt and Negri, in their book *Empire*, Beller subscribes to the notion that human attention is a form of labor. Coded as pleasure and play, attention sustains many of the most commercial forms of circulation and exchange that depend on the flow of images, on the interaction with media and on media technologies.

The role of cinema in these processes is a historically crucial one: as the only art form which owes its existence to capitalism, "the [classical] cinema first posits and then [the post-classical cinema] presupposes 'looking' as a value-productive activity." A development of, but also an abstraction from assembly-line work, moving images have become the most prominent, because socially sanctioned, interface between the body and all the forms of abstraction that regulate the individual's relation to society: "Where factory workers first performed sequenced physical operations on moving objects in order to produce a commodity, in the cinema, spectators perform sequenced visual operations on moving montage fragments to produce an image."[38] In a further, meta-theoretical move reminiscent of Friedrich Kittler, Beller also maintains that the cinema's rapid ubiquity and universality caused the crisis in literature, language and reference, of which first psychoanalysis, then the linguistic turn in the 1960s, including post-structuralist deconstruction of the 1980s with its philosophical debates about "difference," "being" and "presence," were the unacknowledged rationalizations and reactions: cinema, as the elephant in the room, so to speak, of 20th century intellectual history, and one of the reasons why "culture" has become both the central economic force of late capitalist societies, as well as the ground for the humanities' ambivalent epistemological status. University-based film studies, in this perspective, would then become part of the symptom of what it claims to analyze.

Once one takes into account the dual implications of Beller's analysis—the (Hollywood) cinema as a (historically necessary) stage of capitalism, where critical reflection on the cinema, both direct (in the form of film studies), and indirect (in the form of philosophy and cultural studies) inevitably comes up against this "untranscendable" epistemic horizon of capitalist reification—then the paradoxes which I noted about Hollywood might very well be merely the outward projections of the contradictions within film studies itself, rather than real-existing ones. The question to ask would then be: what are the historical conditions on the side of Hollywood, that make possible the versions and inversions in the successive valorization, critique, delegitimation and re-evaluation of the American cinema from the late 1940s in France, to the present day in university courses all over the world? And in particular (with respect to the guiding idea of the present book, which tracks the tensions between the "genius of the author" and the "genius of the system"), is there a more general logic underlying the sense that it is now the "author" who *is* the "system," that is, who embodies it, represents it and promotes it—not in some obvious, salesman-like fashion (though occasionally, that too), but in the full awareness that thanks to the cinema, the traditional antinomies of art and money, creativity and industrialization, solitary artist and business entrepreneur have become redundant or are being superseded? It is this possibility—and its consequences—that I want to probe in the following sections.

Reflexivity: Self-Reference Between Literalness, Metaphor and Allegory

Trying to explain to myself the attraction the *auteur* theory held for me in the 1960s and 1970s, I wrote (in 1979):

> What seemed to make [Vincente] Minnelli exemplary. . . was that in his films the act of seeing, the constraints and power relations it gave rise to, appeared so uncannily foregrounded that the action always tended to become a metaphor of the more fundamental relation between spectator and *mise en scène*, audience and (invisible, because ubiquitous) director.

Here, the thesis expounded by Beller is mirrored back into the film itself, across the audience, before it is refocused (or reified) in the director, confirming him as *auteur*. Whereas "the act of seeing" appeared to me as a metaphor (for the manifold relations between spectator and director), "looking" for Beller is an allegory (of its commodity status within advanced capitalism). The two frames of reference are like the recto and verso of each other, with "metaphor" implying a direct relation of substitution and equivalence, whereas "allegory" suggests the indirect representation of the more abstract and extended relation between sight or vision and the capitalist reification of subject and image. Yet it is the tension between these two figures of speech that encourages me to try and bridge the gap between the symbolic-narrative practice of Hollywood (the "film as system") and the economic-industrial practice (the "film industry as system"), in short: the gap between the *history* of American cinema and the *hermeneutics* of American cinema. To do so, I propose to revise and extend the concept of "reflexivity" and examine the several of types of reflexivity present in Hollywood's institutional mode as well as Hollywood's modes of address to its audiences, where the films (as product *and* service) function not as texts, but as the "relays": dynamic and reversible circuits between Hollywood and its audiences that allow for the mirror-like doubling of metaphor as well as the more disjunctive coupling of allegory.

There are initially four such types of reflexivity that can be identified: the "modernist" self-reference just cited and associated with the director as *auteur*; the self-reference of the industry as a whole, manifest on the one hand in a persistent concern with self-regulation, and on the other, with annual rituals of self-celebration; the self-reference of the individual studios, in the form of intellectual property right protection, logo management and branding; finally, the self-reference and recursiveness established through the circuits of promotion and audience research that bind producers to consumers and regulate reception of a given film as story, event and experience (via poster, tag-line, advertising, press coverage). Despite their crucial differences, all of these forms of reflexivity can be read as manifestations of constitutive and ongoing power-struggles both *within the industry* (in the early years, between editorial control on the part of the exhibitors versus editorial control by the producers; in later years, vertical integration, its loss in 1948 and reinstatement since the 1980s) and *between the industry and its audiences* (in the early years: disruption through censorship, followed by pre-emptive self-censorship via the Hays Code, to be replaced by more covert forms of self-regulation and more aggressive marketing techniques, as well as more sophisticated tools of audience research and technology-backed feedback loops). That the site of such struggles can be the film itself is what is fascinating about studying Hollywood's modes of address, because the means of address and control—expanding on Beller's diagnostics—could well be reflexivity itself, in the form of complicity and knowingness, by which the film implicates the viewer at the story level and a meta-level. The latter enfolds the audience in cognitive double-binds, counters blasé indifference with immersive sensory overload, or acknowledges fan power through narrative complexity, while also answering (by performing within the film) the conspiratorial-paranoid readings of Hollywood that professional academics and critics are fond of.[39]

Modernist-Auteurist *Reflexivity*

As several of the chapters in the present collection—those on Minnelli, Nicholas Ray, Sam Fuller, Orson Welles, Alfred Hitchcock and Fritz Lang—are written from the implicit assumption of *auteurist* self-reference and with an explicit media-reflexivity in mind, not much more needs to be said about modernist self-reference. In the chapters on Altman, Kubrick and Coppola the media-reflexivity is often allegorizing the history of Hollywood (and its "decline-demise") more than making "the cinema" a metaphor, as in the case of Lang or Hitchcock. If my primary concern at the time was to assert this reflexivity on the side of the director, in order to claim for the work (and thus for the cinema) the status of modernist art, I would now extend, but thereby also revise this claim by saying that one of the hallmarks of much of Hollywood, both in its classical and post-classical phase, is that the work "is" what it "is about", that is, that films generally instantiate their subject matter also in their own form and mode of address. However, the exact means that manifest this level of self-reference—and the reasons for it—can differ considerably from the medium specificity or decon-structive self-interrogation of (high) modernist art; they need to be investigated in each case separately, and as a result, such self-reference can be more literal than metaphoric, while its literalism can also be quite allegorical, in the sense that it is not always self-evident what is the implied referent to which the level of reflexivity addresses itself: it could be the audience, the studio or even an individual.

Self-reference as Self-celebration and Self-regulation

Over its long history, one highly publicized aspect of the persistence of Hollywood has been the annual self-celebration of its own existence, called the Academy Awards Ceremony, or *Oscar Night*.[40] It functions not merely in order to award to insiders prizes and peer-recognition; it also is an occasion for the industry to consolidate its own history, to work on the invention of traditions, to recycle and perpetuate its tried and true mythologies. There has been relatively little scholarly work to my knowledge, which analyses and evaluates the Awards Ceremony from the vantage point of memory-creation and self-regulation. Despite the show-biz elements and thus the camouflage of hidden agendas, a meta-history of sorts is being written annually in the Kodak Theater in Los Angeles.

One remarkable feature of Hollywood's self-celebration, for instance, is that the professionals assembled at the Awards Ceremony each year take themselves deadly seriously, but they do so in the mode of comic self-denigration and self-parody. A claustrophobic world of in-jokes and self-reference, the annual ritual exhibits a peculiar combination of amnesia and memory that can be read as both a protective cover and the performative display of one of the industry's most noteworthy institutional achievements: its successful form of self-regulation—originally meant to fend off government interference, but now also to enforce collective self-discipline—paradoxically confirmed by the mixture of self-aggression, self-aggrandizement and sentimentality that characterizes Oscar Night.

If "classic Hollywood" is the coinage mainly of academics, "Hollywood classics" is what the industry itself likes to take credit for, revalorizing its film libraries by declaring them to be America's individual and collective memory, and feeding with them entire television networks.[41] "Classic" thus becomes a retronym, an expression that not so much designates a practice or an object, as it retroac-tively confers on it an identity that it cannot itself have known that it possesses. This is also true for the academic use of the term, put in circulation (for instance, by myself in 1972), at a time when the studio system seemed to have disintegrated, but the industry's own use since the rise of the VCR and cable television highlights the connotations of nostalgia and pastiche that the "classic" Hollywood cinema now invariably carries in the post-classical era. On the other hand, if "classic/al" is a retronym from the start, then the very sign of the post-classical would be that it aspires to the "classical" as its dominant effect: each term would name the other, and be dependent on the other, which might explain why historians like David Bordwell see a continuation of the "classical Hollywood cinema" without a notable break, whereas others (myself included) have argued not only for the existence of a "post-classical" Hollywood, but for the epistemic necessity of placing oneself outside the classical, in order to understand the classical. Both positions would be "correct" and "untenable" at the same time.

Self-regulation, this core feature by which Hollywood has managed to minimize outside pressure as well as maximize internal authority via the MPAA, has been studied quite closely in recent years. In particular, the Hays Code, usually ridiculed as a sign of the film community's prudishness and moral double standards, has undergone substantial re-evaluation. Chief among the historians of this re-evaluation are Richard Maltby and Ruth Vasey.[42] Maltby in particular has built much of his approach to the study of Hollywood on the centrality of self-regulation, whose external, reflexive dimension he characterizes by the "principle of deniability." It is a political term originally used by Vasey to characterize Hollywood's stance on sensitive topics, when it came to its dealings with foreign and export markets, but developed by Maltby into a more general strategy of both equivocation and ambivalence. Deniability allows Hollywood to disavow "authorial responsibility for whatever moral or political intent" a spectator might attribute to, or an institution, like the Church, might detect in a film,[43] and thus becomes a tool to defend elliptical narratives and even contradictory modes of address, that is, to manage the communication feedback loop with audiences under adverse or hostile conditions. Maltby is able to show that such a tactic of double address, said to be typical of post-modern or "New" Hollywood, and first described by Nöel Carroll,[44] actually dates back to the early days of the Hays Code. He cites the Code's first administrator, who argued that the movies needed a system of representational conventions:

> from which conclusions might be drawn by the sophisticated mind, but which would mean nothing to the unsophisticated and inexperienced.... This involved devising systems and codes of representation, where "innocence" was inscribed in the text, while "sophisticated viewers" could "read into" the movies whatever meanings they pleased to find, so long as producers could use the Hays Code to deny that they had put them there.[45]

Maltby's best-known example is the scene from Casablanca (1942), when Humphrey Bogart and Ingrid Bergman finally meet in a shabby hotel. After reminiscences and recriminations, a 3½ second fade leaves the viewer with mutually incompatible information: we never find out whether they actually made love or not during this furtive encounter.[46] Maltby's essay is in turn cited by Slavoj Žižek, to illustrate his theory that belief is always "delegated," involving either "interpassivity" or an appeal to the "Big Other."[47]

Studio Self-Reference: Intellectual Property, Logo-Management and Branding

One of the most productive areas of the so-called revisionist historiography of American cinema since the 1970s has been the study of how the industry has developed new marketing strategies, has taken advantage of new technologies in sound and vision, and has turned its genre prototypes into "franchises." Authors such as Douglas Gomery, Thomas Schatz, Justin Wyatt, Janet Wasco, Tino Balio and many others have presented valuable empirical research on how Hollywood has managed changes in the demographics and the geographic location of its audiences, implemented key technologies, such as computer-generated special effects and digital post-production methods, and exploited its intellectual property, that is, the individual studios' film holdings ("libraries"), trademarks ("logos") and universally recognized heroes, whether derived from popular literature (James Bond, Harry Potter, etc.) or comic books (Batman, Spiderman, etc.). Although less concerned with either self-reference or self-regulation, these studies confirm that the changing business models and organizational structures adopted by the film industry in the crucial years between the 1970s and

1990s, when the "event movie" or blockbuster became the new norm, brought about an industry posture that put more emphasis (and money) on marketing and promotion, and relied on the skills of different kinds of middlemen (notably agents and brokers), in order to position the films within and across the different platforms and markets necessary to generate the revenue streams that can recoup the enormous sums invested in major productions.

Yet just as promotion also means self-promotion and marketing is marketing of awareness and attention, these forms of reflexivity can also be regulatory. The blockbuster not only connotes "high concept" ("the book, the look and the hook")[48] but also "total entertainment," which in turn is a category of control, as well as access. It means that individual films are merely the local, temporary instances (the means) of practices and strategies that need to be put in place at several levels and over several years (the ends), aligning films with theme-parks and rides, converting cinemas into multi-purpose entertainment centers, and promoting them with discourses of "security and comfort zones" in the manner of shopping malls, pedestrian areas and gated communities.[49] The cinema, in its reflexive doubling as a "product" selling a "service," that is, a slice of time and a piece of place, necessarily falls in line with, or models itself after several of the prevailing surveillance paradigms, turning the service offered into a new form of "control," in the sense of Foucault or Deleuze.

At the same time, franchise films, such as Lord of the Rings, Pirates of the Caribbean, Shrek, Harry Potter, Toy Story or the various superhero series, sequels and prequels, are obvious examples of films that are both spectacles in their own right (providing thrills and sensory experiences in safe surroundings) and service platforms on which products (books, toys, t-shirts, costumes, decals, songs, DVDs) can be promoted and sold.[50] This awareness of "place" and "time" is also a form of recursiveness, often projected from the films to the spectator. Peter Krämer, for instance, has shown how films like Jaws, The Last Action Hero, Gremlins or Home Alone reference in their plots the family constellation and seasonal situation of their target audience,[51] observations I have also explored and expanded in Chapter 20, "The Blockbuster as Time Machine."[52]

The idea of "total entertainment" introduced by Maltby and Acland, as an umbrella term of some complexity, to indicate the range of activities within which a specific film is both central and only one element among others, is also taken up by Paul Grainge, in his study of the pervasiveness of branding in contemporary Hollywood.[53] He calls branding "a means of imbuing goods with symbolic or aesthetic content, and then using the laws of intellectual property to control their circulation." Focusing initially on merchandising, franchises and product placement, Grainge wants to reframe these phenomena under the heading of branding, understood as such by the film industry itself, for whom the idea of promoting an identity while staking a property claim is not especially new. The studio logo, used as a branding device, goes back to the very early days of cinema, when the company's initials or icon were often incorporated into the sets more or less inconspicuously, in order to prevent unauthorized copying. The logo functioned like a watermark on a banknote, to discourage forgers: the Biograph logo (a blended AB, for American Mutoscope and Biograph Company) was used this way, as was the Pathé rooster, but especially with Pathé in the United States, it was also brand-advertising and product placement, functioning as a subliminal self-reference: you are in a (Pathé) theater, watching a (Pathé) film.[54] Since then, Hollywood branding and advertising has featured in many studies, though perhaps nowhere more critically than in T.W. Adorno's condemnation of "The Culture Industry": "Today every monster close-up of a star is an advertisement for her name, and every hit song a plug for its tune. Advertising and the culture industry are merging technically no less than economically."[55]

What in *The Dialectic of Enlightenment* is still a critical insight, intended to disqualify mainstream cinema from serious consideration as art, has, in the meantime, become an object of study in itself: with the twist that we can now see this self-same advertising in the form of putting up front the trademark or logo as another version of the kind of reflexivity—"foregrounding the 'device'"[56] once espoused by artists to protect their work from commodification and consumption, that is, to rescue its aesthetic autonomy from the culture industry!

Grainge's study of different branding strategies—ranging from the placing of (and playing with) the shape and tactility of the Warner Bros. studio logo to the promotion of Dolby technology via its differently "themed" sound signature, from THE MATRIX as merchandising concept to the intertextual ironies of *Looney Tunes* cartoons in contemporary animation films—shows how the studios organize their production schedules and distribution platform around the need to add value to the studio logo. As with other internationally recognized brands, "the process of selling entertainment has come to rely, increasingly, on the principle of deepening audience involvement in immersive world brands."[57] At the same time that it wants to increase recognition, a brand is an invitation to interaction and exchange between a company and its customers, supported by focus groups, neuro-personality polls and the full panoply of consumer research instruments.[58] Hence the fact that Adorno's worries have, if anything, extended to democracy itself:

> The association . . . of branding at the end of the twentieth century with a neoliberal agenda to replace society with the marketplace has resulted in debates around whether brands are part of an increased commercialism that threatens democracy and citizenship or a site for contemporary struggles for meaning and identity.[59]

However, once one traces the rationale of branding beyond its directly economic objective, it becomes evident that branding itself is an inherently contradictory process: it seeks to expand the meaning and access of the brand at the semiotic level, while simultaneously enforcing the control of meaning and access at the economic level.[60] The brand tries to overcome this contradiction, by playing with the logo in the story-lines, developing what Grainge calls "forms of corporate irony that leave [the brand] knowing but 'open' in an ideological and commercial sense."[61]

In the trade-offs between material culture and discursive practice embodied in branding, one encounters a typically postmodern form of reflexivity, poised between recognition/repetition, ironic distance and sensory immersion: confounding the "modernist" categories of defamiliarization, while also blurring the lines between aesthetics and politics, even turning history into media memory and media memory into cult-classic nostalgia.[62]

Allegorical Readings

Maltby, Acland and Grainge also provide empirical evidence for another major effort to connect Hollywood, the studio system (as an industry and a business) with Hollywood, the textual system (as narrative and social symbolic). Especially noteworthy, in light of my general argument about Hollywood reflexivity between metaphor and allegory, are studies that try to read Hollywood films as allegories of their own conditions of production, as parables of their studio's self-projection, and as commentaries on how Hollywood writes and rewrites its corporate history.[63] Different from an earlier allegorical tracking of cinematic *double entendres*, which tried to establish elaborate parallels between a genre, the Western, and contemporary politics, by distinguishing, for instance, between "Democrat" (HIGH NOON) and "Republican" (RIO BRAVO) narratives, or identifying a film as a "Barry Goldwater Western" or a "Joseph McCarthy Western,"[64] contemporary allegorical readings come with a sophisticated understanding of textual and intertextual effects. They are schooled in the techniques of deconstruction, rather than practicing the "hermeneutics of suspicion" of another generation of film critics.[65] Journals such as *Representations* (Berkeley) and *Critical Inquiry* (Chicago) made a name for themselves showcasing such allegorical readings between deconstruction and the new historicism, notably with essays by Michael Rogin and Carol Clover.[66] Also focused on Hollywood are the contributions by Jerome Christensen and J.D. Connor. In several important articles, discussing films from the classic period as diverse as Mrs Miniver, The Philadelphia Story, Fountainhead and The Bandwagon, and taking on Spike Lee, the Time Warner Batman franchise and You've Got Mail, Christensen, for instance, extracts a second narrative from the primary one, in which the particular studio responsible for the film seems to be speaking to its managers and employees about the challenges they face and the objectives they need to implement.[67] Reminiscent of Claude Lévi-Strauss' dictum that myth is a form of speech by which a society communicates with its members through objects and relations, the allegories allow Christensen to reconstruct what he calls "corporate authorship," a term partly taken from Peter Drucker's management theories (according to which, well-run corporations seek to create customers through advertising)[68] and partly deployed as a critique of *auteurism* as practiced in film studies. Focusing on Time Warner (which echoes Grainge's preoccupation with Warner Bros.' reflexive and self-conscious branding strategies), Christensen sees both Tim Burton's Batman (1989) and Oliver Stone's JFK (1991) not as manifestations of these two highly idiosyncratic directors' personal vision or obsessions, but as "corporate expressions":

> Formed in 1989, . . . Time Warner, the corporate merger of fact and fiction, was deeply invested in a vision of American democracy gone sour and sore in need of rescue. That investment is most salient in two films: *Batman*, released in 1989 during the merger negotiations between Time Inc. and Warner, and *JFK*, the signature film of the new organization. I will argue that *Batman* and *JFK* are corporate expressions: the former an instrumental allegory contrived to accomplish corporate objectives, the latter a scenario that effectively expands the range of what counts as a corporate objective. *Batman* is an allegory addressed to savvy corporate insiders, some of whom are meant to get the message, while others err. *JFK* aspired to turn everyone into an insider. It inducts its viewers into a new American mythos wired for an age in which successful corporate financial performance presupposes a transculturalist politics: corporate populism. Under corporate populism the old, corporate liberal agencies for integrating a *pluribus* of individuals into a social *unum* are to be superseded by a mass entertainment complex capable of projecting a riveting logo that summons all people's attention, that offers membership in an invisible body by virtue of collective participation in a spectacular event or cathexis of a corporate person or enthrallment in a sublime virtuality, and that substitutes for credal [sic] affiliation a continuously renewable identification with logo, trademark, slogan, or brand.[69]

Such an interpretation first of all reads film texts against other texts: as Christensen freely admits, he is indebted to two book-length studies of the Time Warner merger, its key players and boardroom struggles.[70] Second, one once more senses the concern for democracy and the social contract being hollowed out by the a-social bond between the consumer and the commodity, across the fetish of the brand. But the allegorical mode is also symptomatic of the felt need to account for the frequently acknowledged reflexivity of contemporary Hollywood films, while expressing dissatisfaction with the usual attribution of such reflexivity to an all-purpose, "anything goes" postmodernism.[71]

J.D. Connor, who studied with Christensen, similarly takes the massive organizational changes that have reshaped the American film industry during the post-studio era of mergers and horizontal diversification in the 1980s and 1990s as the subtexts he expects to find allegorically represented in major Hollywood productions. He is especially interested in narratives that respond to several significant developments: the tapping of fresh talent while reducing the risk, through incorporating the "independent" sector; the practice of "outsourcing" certain specialized activities, such as computer generated imaging; the creative dependence of Hollywood on foreign personnel and the economic dependence on foreign audiences; the need to exploit the substantive holdings of old films via DVD sales and other subsidiary markets.[72] In an article on Braveheart (Mel Gibson, 1995; distributor: Paramount) Connor highlights first of all the synergies between Mel Gibson, Hollywood's Australian "bad boy" insider-as-outsider, and the genre of the "Scottish film," often used by Hollywood for "working out particularly vexing industrial problems under the guise of tackling U.S. political problems." Connor then goes on to elaborate on the economic history and theoretical models supporting such readings, explaining that:

> my thinking here, influenced by critics as different as Richard Maltby, Thomas Schatz, and Victor Navasky, is that the studio system strongly encouraged its workers to understand the films they made as corporate representations, and that it was as normal for films to allegorize the conditions and ideologies of the corporations. .. as it was for them to allegorize the medium itself.... In today's neoclassical Hollywood, then, the reflection on self-imposed conventions that marks the classical includes the convention of, the reality of, the allegory of industrial crisis, even when the instance that displays that crisis is as assured as BRAVEHEART.[73]

One key aspect of the allegory centers on Gibson's quasi-feudal relations with Warner Bros., on whose "land" Gibson has established his own production company *Icon*, granted to him because of the star's loyalty to the Warner Bros. LETHAL WEAPON franchise. Braveheart/Gibson's "rebellion," then, consists of his defection to Paramount for the rights to distribute his film. The pressure of "opening wide" and the anxieties over the first weekend's box office take are, furthermore, allegorized in the *jus prima nocte*, the feudal right of the lord to take any bride's virginity, which in the film is the ostensible cause of Wallace's rebellion against Longshanks.

When discussing Oliver Stone's ALEXANDER (2004, Warner Bros.), Connor emphasizes the anti-Bush themes one can safely attribute to the director (which makes the film the prequel to W, Stone's 2008 film about the youthful George W. Bush), but he doubles these with the corporate themes and anxieties—and the directors' self-identification with them—put in the mouth of Ptolemy, survivor of an earlier Babylonian/Iraq quagmire and guardian of Alexander's legacy:

> These days any commercial filmmaker (and particularly one with a fondness for casts of thousands and lavish period detail) needs a certain amount of imperial hubris: that is, he needs to believe that audiences will flock to his or her films around the globe. Call it cultural imperialism or a superior distribution network, filmmakers with $200 million budgets need Hollywood's power, and it is not hard to convince them to pay obeisance to it. When Alexander or Achilles yells about "everlasting glory," the hearts of studio marketing executives beat a little faster: everlasting glory equals more downstream revenue.... No wonder Anthony Hopkins, as the old general Ptolemy, narrates "Alexander" from the great library at Alexandria: Library rights are where it's at, and they're certainly why Sony bought MGM this fall.[74]

In grounding his allegorical readings in an epistemology, Connor is more explicit than Christensen. In fact, he comes close to arguing that while for classical Hollywood metaphoric doubling is the dominant mode, neoclassical (as Connor calls it) Hollywood subscribes to allegorical modes of reflexivity. For the classical mode, he cites Jean-Claude Lebensztejn's definition of the classical frame:

> First, a painting should be framed to avoid confusion between its objects and surrounding objects.... This separation is a landmark of classicism, which aims at the values of order, clarity, and distinction.... The classical frame both enables classical space and serves as an emblem of the themes that will be dealt with in that space. The order the frame makes allows the painting to address "order." The second point. ..is that the frame should be there, but not insistently there; it should not attract too much attention to itself. This balance should give the appearance of a "natural constraint."[75]

Through Lebensztejn, Connor is able to propose a definition of the classical different from the one given by Bordwell, Staiger and Thompson:

[Hollywood's] classicism lies in the balance it can strike between the conditions of its production and the demands of its literal narrative. For the authors of *The Classical Hollywood Cinema*, the system is so overwhelming that the actual instances that system produces can have no effect on its operation. There is no need to read the films of classical Hollywood for their self-understanding of that system because no such understanding is permissible.[76]

But Connor's classicism also wants to distance itself from other versions that define the classical (positively or negatively) via transparency, such as the realist one attributed to André Bazin, and critiqued in *Screen*, by among others, Jean Louis Comolli, Stephen Heath or Colin MacCabe:

What is stable or ordered about this system is. . . the division within [cinematic] space between the "insistently there" and the "naturally constrained." Since the frame must encompass both the classically constrained and the unclassically insistent, the relatively simple emblematization of the frame's ordering as the picture's order appears at one remove. Emblematization becomes the complicated allegorization of the attempt to balance the insistent against the constrained.[77]

In this reading, the classical becomes neoclassical, when this balance between narrative and meta-narrative can be staged as a mere effect. As a consequence:

what makes neoclassical Hollywood neo is this difficulty in containing its self-consciousness, not, as a Romantic account of neoclassicism might put it, the self-consciousness itself. The mismatch between the attention given to the allegorical and the attention given to the literal is what gives these films. . . their whiff of pomposity. Neoclassical Hollywood films are often overwhelmed by their allegories.[78]

The "insistently there" trumps the "naturally constrained," and allegory consumes metaphor.

Reflexivity as Feedback

Connor and Christensen still adhere to what one might call "allegories of representation," even if their referents blend "American politics" with the internally generated reflexivity of the corporation's self-representation at an abstract level, as if to suggest that contemporary Hollywood fights its own "identity politics," when protecting its intellectual property and extending its reach, in the face of competition from other forms of entertainment, but perhaps just as much, in the face of competition from the weight of its own history. I have found their discussions illuminating, even where their interpretations of specific films remained suggestive rather than persuasive, and perhaps too narrowly framed to lend themselves to generalization. Their great merit is that, without minimizing the difficulties of doing so, they insist that a historically informed analysis of Hollywood as a high-tech California industry and a global business, must have something to say about the films as highly skilled, multi-layered narratives and multi-purpose vehicles, which must function equally well on different platforms, in different media formats, for different audiences. By positing allegory as the hermeneutics of choice, they intertwine the economic and the textual as a kind of *a priori* requirement, recognizing and respecting the fact that anyone working in Hollywood lives corporate strategy day to day, and is only too aware of the conflicts between financial creativity, marketing creativity and personal creativity. The choice of films across the classical/post-classical chronological divide indicate that forms of allegorizing have always existed, even if the internal upheavals of the industry over the past three decades have given these allegories a new self-correcting and self-regulating urgency. The Disney-Pixar "partnership," for instance, has produced a string of animation franchise films, such as Toy Story and Shrek, which are prime candidates for tracking the recto and verso of individual directors performing an internalized corporate authorship and the studios asserting authorship through these individuals' self-presentation as *auteurs*, while representing the changed power relationships and and reassigning the roles between the different "players."

But Christensen and Connor also convinced me that one of my previous definitions of the post-classical as a special kind of "knowingness" about the classical might require further clarification. After what has been said, the more general principle at issue would be that the classical and post-classical cinema are neither diachronically successive, nor the same in a different guise or context, but rather that they are reflexive in relation to each other, in that each determines the other and is in turn determined by it. This is indeed the technical definition of "reflexivity," especially in the social sciences, where the term refers to circular or bi-directional relationships between cause and effect, each changing or defining the other in such a way that both function as causes and as effects. If reflexivity, however, names situations of self-reference, where an action refers back to, and thereby alters or affects the instance or agent instigating the action, then it might be more correct to speak of "feedback," both positive and negative.

Might this change of spatial metaphor from reflexivity as frame, mirror and reversible relations of inside and outside, to the dynamic metaphors of positive and negative feedback, input and output, and reversible relations of cause and effect help render moot or "sublate" some of the contradictions discussed earlier, such as the one between the self-contained, closed nature of Hollywood storytelling (where a film comes with its own instruction manual and proceeds in a highly predictable, formulaic way) and the open way that a Hollywood film allows for entry and comprehension at almost any point in time along its narrative arc? Can feedback reconcile the category of *product* (the self-sufficiency of a film as a rounded story, complete and replete for all time) with that of *service* (the time-bound and place-specific unique experience of the event), by suggesting for both a new aggregate state, not just of "performance" but also highlighting the instant availability, the fluidity and iterative nature of a film that now exists and reaches its audience as download or streaming video?

If the classical represents in some sense the dominance of negative feedback (of self-regulation and deniability) then the post-classical would signal the presence and appreciation of the positive feedback loops that the new technologies and social networks have added to the managerial to-do list of running a film company or studio in the post-classical period. Balancing the more traditional negative feedback loops against these more recent positive feedback loops, as they have emerged around Amazon, Facebook, Twitter and YouTube, is perhaps the major challenge that Hollywood has faced in the past ten years, and it is directly and indirectly the subject of Henry Jenkins' *Convergence Culture*.[79] Jenkins' frame of reference, however, is different from the one here proposed, insofar as it is more in line with the emancipatory discourse of self-empowerment around popular culture, which he had already championed in his previous bestseller, *Textual Poachers*.[80] Focusing instead on feedback loops, one can distinguish between negative feedback (the controlling instances of the system, providing an internal frame of reference as stabilizing element), and positive feedback (the fan community that cannot be anticipated, but that has become essential, perhaps not for its "user-generated content" per se, but for its participatory involvement in the institution Hollywood, even at the limits of incoherence and cacophony).[81] Intensifying the focus on branding and the logo in the sense discussed above, would then be more like a principle of homeostasis, a way of not only renegotiating the relationship between product and consumers, but—under conditions of positive, that is, self-reinforcing feedback, as generated by social networks—a chief strategy for capturing and managing these volatile masses and markets.

Conclusion

As I go over the texts presented here, almost everything I have written about the American cinema, in one form or another, relates to aspects of feedback: its loops and repetitions, its interferences and amplifications, and the subsequent attempts at regulation, auto-correction and the homeostasis of credibly or persuasively attributing meaning. Indeed, I began to realize that Hollywood has always been for me a case of positive feedback, in the full ambiguity of the term: it has always been post-classical, even as I tried to define it as classical.

To recapitulate once more some of the semantic aspects that this ambiguity entails:

- Positive feedback in everyday language refers to all kinds of "therapeutic" interpersonal encouragement, for the purpose of self-regulation, but in a more technical sense it connotes its opposite: the aggravating interferences and conflict escalation that result from intersubjective or transferential over-identification.
- Positive feedback is also a term familiar from performed music, and in particular it occurs when a body, a voice or an electric guitar gets audio feedback from the microphone, which then amplifies the disturbance, also called "oscillation." Performers like Jimi Hendrix, or The Who would exploit such audio feedback for the creative (or even political) potential it afforded as "interference" that could be shaped, modulated and passed along, in a kind of dialogue between artist, instrument and audience.
- Positive feedback is a major factor in financial markets, at least according to George Soros. Contrary to equilibrium theory, which stipulates that markets move towards equilibrium and that non-equilibrium fluctuations are merely random noise, so that share prices in the long run at equilibrium reflect the underlying fundamentals, Soros argues that prices do in fact influence the fundamentals and that this newly influenced set of fundamentals then proceeds to change expectations, thus influencing prices; the process continues in a self-reinforcing pattern. Because the pattern is self-reinforcing, markets tend towards disequilibrium. Sooner or later they reach a point where the sentiment is reversed and negative expectations become self-reinforcing in the downward direction, thereby explaining the familiar pattern of boom and bust cycles.
- Positive feedback in cybernetics describes the situation when the output of a system is fed back as input, amplifying the possibility of divergence, and thus enabling change and branching, and thus new states of equilibrium and self-regulation. But positive feedback may also lead to collapse, implosion and the self-destruction of the system, for instance when a suspension bridge breaks up, because a storm amplifies the vibration of the cables.
- Finally, certain forms of self-reference or recursiveness in the arts, literature, philosophy and computer science might be said to be instances of positive feedback, such as the rhetorical trope and heraldic emblem of *mise-en-abyme*, the logical paradoxes associated with Zeno ("Achilles and the tortoise") or the process of a simple system activating a more complex system, also known as "bootstrapping."

A theory of the cinema centered on feedback would highlight the following features: at the micro-level of the textual system, for instance, of classical Hollywood cinema, feedback in general would characterize the uneven circulation of information. Its regulation via sequential narrative of cause-and-effect, and its distribution among characters, and between characters and spectator, via narration and focalization would be instances of "negative feedback," while the sheer amount of data produced by mechanical reproduction of sound and image, much of it neither contained nor constrained by style, technique and narrative, would fall under "positive feedback." *Identification*, as opposed to comprehension, *cinephilia* and cult cinema, as opposed to film appreciation or criticism, would thus respond to this excess or contingent flow of information, and therefore also be effects of positive feedback. Melodrama—in the way I have written about it—would be the example par excellence of positive feedback, as the genre that not only exceeds the norm, but whose affective data (as manifest, for instance, in what we usually refer to as the *mise-en-scène*) comprises all those elements *not* governed by controlling instances: be they linear narrative, the conventions of genre, the social symbolic of patriarchy, or the super-ego of the Law.

At the macro-level, positive feedback would be relevant as the category that accounts for the peculiarity of Hollywood cinema in the public sphere, for instance, the apparent fickleness of popular taste, the unpredictability of box-office success, as well as the nature of the ancillary industries that sustain the multi-media "event movie" we call the blockbuster, and are sustained by it: Hollywood will always need positive feedback for innovation and change, and negative feedback as self-regulation or self-censorship in self-celebration. Rather than concentrating on the classical *auteurs* within the system (Ford, Hawks), this collection puts more emphasis on the feedback loops that underlie the antagonistic-cooperative relations between *auteur* and system, Hollywood and Europe, *maudit* and mainstream, or the parasite-host relationships that developed around émigré directors in the 1940s and the New Hollywood directors in relation to New Economy Hollywood in the 1970s. What regulates talent transfers, characterizes the film festival circuit, or can explain the "pilot fish" function of the independent sector for global Hollywood all takes place in the force field of negative *and* positive feedback.

Throughout the 20th century, the cinema would have been fulfilling a special role in society at large: as the mainstay of mankind's audio-visual heritage, it has an extraordinarily central "memory function," increasingly taking over the role previously assigned to the fine arts, to literature and the study of languages. But the American cinema also partakes in society's "oscillation function" (to use a distinction made by Niklaus Luhmann),[82] which is more generally associated with technological change, with cutting edge design, new life-style opportunities or activism: the "creative destruction" discussed earlier. According to Luhmann, culture is the name we give to the memory of social systems, but not in the form of spatial repositories that one can enter or leave, open or close. Rather, the memory function of a society would be that continuous process of recursive erasure and recall of significant symbols or images, through which the constitutive contingency of the moment becomes "reflexive" and therefore active. Extending this thought further, I want to conclude by suggesting that the cinema in general and Hollywood in particular is engaged in precisely such processes of permanent erasure and recall, and thus constitutes the most technologically developed form of this "recursive memory" of social systems, which could indeed be called "culture," but which I have been specifying as "the persistence of Hollywood."

Endnotes

General Introduction

1 The May '68 events started for me with the demonstrations against the sacking of Henri Langlois by the then Minister of Culture, André Malraux in February 1968. For a semi-documentary fictionalized version of this episode, see the opening of Bernardo Bertolucci's THE DREAMERS (2003).

2 By defending Hollywood movies as in many ways exemplary, we are not claiming that they are inherently a superior form of filmmaking, nor that the Hollywood aesthetic is the only possible one. What we are insisting on is that the cinema, in spite of its comparative youth and novelty does have a tradition and that this tradition is to a large part constituted by the American cinema. And like every art, however public and commercial, the cinema derives its complexity and richness not only from its relation to felt and experienced life, but also from its internal relation to the development and history of the medium.

Editorial Statement, *Monogram* 1 (April 1971), 1.

3 The complaint runs through virtually all of Jonathan Rosenbaum's writings since the mid-1990s. For a concise summary, see Nick James, "Who Needs Critics?," *Sight & Sound* 10 (October 2008): 16–29.

4 Siegfried Kracauer, *From Caligari to Hitler* (Princeton, NJ, Princeton University Press, 1947) and Lotte Eisner, *The Haunted Screen* (London: Secker & Warburg, 1963).

5 This point was first made by Paul Willemen, "Through the Glass Darkly: Cinephilia Reconsidered," in *Looks and Frictions: Essays in Cultural Studies and Film Theory* (London: BFI Publishing, 1993), 236–37.

6 Originally published as "Two Decades in Another Country: Hollywood and the Cinephiles," in *Superculture*, ed. Chris Bigsby (London: Elek, 1975), 199–216. Reprinted in Thomas Elsaesser, *European Cinema: Face to Face with Hollywood* (Amsterdam: Amsterdam University Press, 2005), 233–50.

7 "John Ford's *Young Mr. Lincoln*: A Collective Text by the Editors of *Cahiers du Cinéma*," in *Movies and Methods*, ed. Bill Nichols (Berkeley: University of California Press, 1976), 493–529; Jean-Louis Comolli and Jean Narboni, "Cinema/Ideology/Criticism," in *Movies and Methods*, 22–30; Comolli, "Technique and Ideology: Camera, Perspective, Depth of Field," in *Movies and Methods*, Vol. 2, ed. Bill Nichols (Berkeley: University of California Press, 1985), 40–57.

8 See Colin MacCabe, "Class of '68: Elements of an Intellectual Autobiography, 1967–81," in *Theoretical Essays: Film, Linguistics, Literature* (Manchester: Manchester University Press, 1985), 1–32; Mark Nash, "The Moment of *Screen*," in *Screen Theory Culture* (Basingstoke: Palgrave Macmillan, 2008), 1–27. During the early 1970s, *Screen* translated many key essays from the French: Comolli and Narboni (cited in note 5), Gérard Leblanc, Jean-Paul Fargier and Marcelin Pleynet. These translations can be found in *Screen Reader 1: Cinema/Ideology/Politics*, ed. John Ellis (London: Society for Education in Film and Television, 1977).

9 For a backlash against these theories in American universities, see David Weddle's "Lights, Camera, Action. Marxism, Semiotics, Narratology," *Los Angeles Times Magazine*, July 13 (2003).

10 Important was Ray Durgnat's "Paint It Black: The Family Tree of Film Noir," published in *Monogram*'s rival *Cinema* 6/7 (August 1970): 49–56.

11 Peter Wollen, "The Auteur Theory," in *Signs and Meaning in the Cinema* (London: Secker & Warburg, 1969), 74–115.

12 David Bordwell has on occasion referenced the *Monogram* articles in this respect as a precursor (e.g., in *Classical Hollywood Cinema: Film Style and Mode of Production to 1960*), but I have also been quoted by some of Bordwell's critics, Richard Maltby (e.g. in *Hollywood Cinema: An Introduction*) and by Vivian Sobchack, for instance.

13 Thomas Elsaesser, "Film Studies in Search of the Object," *Film Criticism* 17, 2–3 (Winter/Spring 1993): 40–47.

14 Colin MacCabe, "Realism and the Cinema: Notes on Some Brechtian Theses," *Screen* 15, 2 (Summer 1974): 7–27.

15 Stephen Heath, "Film and System: Terms of Analysis," *Screen* 16, 1 (Spring 1975): 7–77, and *Screen*, 16, 2 (Summer 1975): 91–113; "Narrative Space," *Screen*, 17, 3 (Autumn 1976): 19–75.

16 Laura Mulvey, "Visual Pleasure and Narrative Cinema," *Screen* 16, 3 (Autumn 1975): 6–18.

17 Richard Dyer, "Entertainment and Utopia," *Movie* 24 (Spring 1977): 2–13.

18 Robin Wood, "An Introduction to the American Horror Film," in *The American Nightmare: Essays on the Horror Film*, ed. Robin Wood and Richard Lippe (Toronto: Festival of Festivals, 1979), 7–28.

19 Originally published in German; reasons of space prevent me from including the English version in this volume: "Raoul Walsh und The Roaring Twenties" (w. Winfried Fluck), in *Amerikastudien – Theorie, Geschichte, interpretatorische Praxis*, ed. Martin Christadler and Günter Lenz (Stuttgart: Metzler, 1977), 161–78.

20 "History will remember each person only for their beautiful moments on film—the rest is off the record." Andy Warhol, *The Philosophy of Andy Warhol (From A to Be and Back Again)* (New York: Harcourt Brace Jovanovich, 1975), 68.

21 See Jean-Luc Godard, Youssef Ishaghpour, *Cinema: The Archeology of Film and the Memory of a Century* (Oxford & New York: Berg, 2005).

22 See Peter Wollen, "Godard and Counter Cinema: Vent d'Est," *Afterimage* 4 (Autumn 1972): 6–17.

23 I also published essays on François Truffaut and Jacques Demy, Anthony Mann, King Vidor and Otto Preminger, Luchino Visconti and Jean Renoir, Luis Bunuel and Jean-Luc Godard—an orthodox mix of European auteurs and marginal, forgotten or *maudit* filmmakers within the Hollywood system.

24 Pauline Kael, *The Citizen Kane Book* (New York: Little, Brown, 1971),

25 Thomas Elsaesser and Warren Buckland, *Studying Contemporary American Film* (London: Arnold, 2002).

26 Thomas Elsaesser, "Fantasy Island: Dream Logic as Production Logic," in *Cinema Futures: Cain, Abel or Cable? The Screen Arts in the Digital Age*, ed. T. Elsaesser and K. Hoffmann (Amsterdam: Amsterdam University Press, 1998), 143–58.

1 Film Studies in Britain: Cinephilia, Screen Theory and Cultural Studies

1 I began a similar task once more in Amsterdam in 1991, setting up a department of Film & Television Studies, which (besides television and digital media studies) developed Film Studies at BA, MA, and PhD level.

2 A detailed account of these transformations is expected in Geoffrey Nowell-Smith's long-awaited study of the BFI. A brief overview can be found in G. Nowell-Smith, "The British Film Institute," *Cinema Journal*, 47, 4 (Summer 2008): 126–32.

3 For the militant critics from *Movie* magazine the choice was easy: they could very persuasively argue that Hollywood not only meant more to more people all over the world than any other movies, and therefore deserved critical attention, but that the *mise-en-scène*, the editing rhythm, the camera movements supporting, fleshing out and giving substance to often very ordinary stories, made its films superior examples of cinematic art than, say, the "big subjects" in the work of British directors like Lewis Gilbert, Peter Glenville or Jack Clayton.

4 Lawrence Alloway, "Iconography of the Movies," *Movie*, 7 (1963): 4–6. See also Lawrence Alloway, *Violent America: The Movies 1946–1964* (New York: MOMA, 1971).

5 www.belkin-gallery.ubc.ca/lastcall/current/page1.html

6 In *Screen Education: From Film Appreciation to Media Studies* (Bristol: Intellect, 2009), Terry Bolas presents a satellite map of this small topographical "square" in Central London, as well as photographs of the individual buildings. See the block of photographs between pages 196 and 197.

7 A good account of *Screen* theory can be found in the introductions and texts assembled in *Narrative, Apparatus, Ideology: A Film Theory Reader*, ed. Phil Rosen (New York: Columbia University Press, 1986).

8 As I pointed out in the general introduction to this volume, this ambivalence is demonstrated by the translation of *Cahiers du cinéma*'s Lacanian deconstruction of John Ford's YOUNG MR LINCOLN, Stephen Heath's massive two-part essay on Orson Welles' TOUCH OF EVIL, Laura Mulvey's feminist critique of voyeurism in Hitchcock and Sternberg, as well as by Geoffrey Nowell-Smith's debate on Ford's THE SEARCHERS ("Six Authors in Pursuit of *The Searchers*," *Screen*, 17, 1 [Spring 1976]: 26–33) and Colin MacCabe's article on AMERICAN GRAFFITI ("Theory and Film: Principles of Realism and Pleasure," *Screen*, 17, 3 [Autumn 1976]: 7–28; reprinted in his *Theoretical Essays*, 58–81). All of which make Hollywood at once the target of relentless deconstruction and yet the obsessively chosen object of study.

9 Stephen Heath, "Narrative Space," *Screen*, 17, 3 (Autumn 1976): 19–75; and Laura Mulvey, "Visual Pleasure and Narrative Cinema," *Screen*, 16, 3 (Autumn 1975): 6–18.

10 See, for instance, James Donald (ed.), *Formations of Pleasure* (London: Routledge and Kegan Paul, 1983).

11 See Peter Wollen, "Godard and Counter Cinema: Vent d'est," *Afterimage*, 4 (Autumn 1972): 6–17.

12 On Peter Gidal, see Deke Dusinberre, "Consistent Oxymoron: Peter Gidal's Theoretical Strategy," *Screen* (Summer 1977): 79–88 and on the London Coop generally, see Peter Gidal (ed.), *Structural Film Anthology* (London: BFI, 1974).

13 This said, there are now highly successful film studies departments within London University, at Birkbeck College, King's College London, Queen Mary College, University College, Goldsmith's College and Royal Holloway College.

14 "John Ford's *Young Mr. Lincoln*: A Collective Text by the Editors of *Cahiers du Cinéma*," in *Movies and Methods*, ed. Bill Nichols (Berkeley: University of California Press, 1976), 496.

15 The academic and non-academic career of Colin MacCabe can stand as exemplary for these contradictions, twists and turns. See "Class of '68: Elements of an Intellectual Autobiography 1967–81," in C. MacCabe, *Tracking the Signifier: Theoretical Essays on Film, Linguistics, Literature* (Minneapolis: University of Minnesota Press, 1985), 6–24.

16 Susan Sontag, "The Decay of Cinema," *New York Times*, February 25, 1996; Godfrey Cheshire, "The Death of Film/The Decay of Cinema," *New York Press*, 12, 34 (August 26, 1999); Michael Witt, "The Death(s) of Cinema According to Godard," *Screen*, 40, 3 (Autumn 1999): 333–45; Paolo Cherchi Usai, *The Death of Cinema: History, Cultural Memory and the Digital Dark Age* (London: BFI, 2001); Stefan Jovanovic, "The Ending(s) of Cinema: Notes on the Recurrent Demise of the Seventh Art, Part 1 & 2," online at: www.horschamp.qc.ca/new_offscreen/death_cinema.html

17 The extensive critical and historical work on film festivals reflects some of these shifts. For bibliographies and ongoing research, see the Film Festival Research Network (www.filmfestivalresearch.org/index.php/tag/necs/).

18 For Brecht's theories of the active spectator, see *Brecht on Film and Radio*, ed. and trans. Marc Silberman (London: Methuen, 2000), on which were built H.M. Enzensberger's famous "Constituents of a Theory of the Media," *New Left Review*, 1, 64 (November–December 1970): 13–36.
19 Mikhail M. Bakhtin, *The Dialogic Imagination: Four Essays*, ed. Michael Holquist, trans. Caryl Emerson and Michael Holquist (Austin: University of Texas Press, 1981).
20 See the work of Henry Jenkins, for instance: *Textual Poachers: Television Fans & Participatory Culture: Studies in Culture and Communication* (New York: Routledge, 1992) and *Convergence Culture: Where Old and New Media Collide* (New York: New York University Press, 2006).

2 The Name for a Pleasure that has No Substitute: Vincente Minnelli

1 "Vincente Minnelli," *Brighton Film Review*, 15 (December 1969): 11–13, and 18 (February 1970): 20–22.
2 I am thinking of Jim Kitses, *Horizons West. Anthony Mann, Budd Boetticher, Sam Peckinpah. Studies of Authorship within the Western* (London: Thames and Hudson/BFI, 1969) and Colin McArthur, *Underworld USA* (London: BFI, 1972).
3 Paul Mayersberg, "The Testament of V. Minnelli," in *Movie* (London, October 1962): 10–13. On testament films more generally, see Joe McElhaney, *The Death of Classical Cinema* (Albany: State University of New York Press, 2006) and A.O. Scott, "Directors in their Magic Hour," *New York Times*, April 15, 2009.
4 For a more recent appreciation of Minnelli's career, see Joe McElhaney, "Great Directors: Vincente Minnelli," *Senses of Cinema*, 31 (2004), www.sensesofcinema.com/2004/great-directors/minnelli/ (last accessed March 9, 2011). as well as the collection edited by McElhaney, *Vincente Minnelli: The Art of Entertainment* (Detroit: Wayne State University Press, 2009).

3 All the Lonely Places: The Heroes of Nicholas Ray

1 The essay was originally published as "Nicholas Ray I and II," *The Brighton Film Review*, 20 (1970): 12–16, and 21 (1970): 15–17 (text corrected and slightly revised in 2008).
2 At the time I was writing about Ray, I knew next to nothing about his life, so was hardly in a position to specify what I meant by "autobiographical." For instance, I was unaware of his bisexuality, a theme now often dwelt on. John Houseman, the producer of THEY LIVE BY NIGHT, said of Ray:

> Reared in Wisconsin in a household dominated by women, he was a potential homosexual with a deep, passionate and constant need for female love in his life. This made him attractive to women, for whom the chance to save him from his own self-destructive habits proved an irresistible attraction of which Nick took full advantage and for which he rarely forgave them. He left a trail of damaged lives behind him—not as a seducer, but as a husband, lover and father.

Others have read this sexuality back into the films: "Bisexual for much of his life, Ray was arguably a director who invested both kinds of pairings with similar erotic as well as romantic dynamics." Jonathan Rosenbaum, *Essential Cinema: On the Necessity of Film Canons* (Baltimore: Johns Hopkins University Press, 2004), 334.
3 "There are no Ray films that do not have a scene at the close of day; he is the poet of nightfall, and of course everything is permitted in Hollywood except poetry." Francois Truffaut; "There was theatre (Griffith), poetry (Murnau), painting (Rossellini), dance (Eisenstein), music (Renoir). Henceforth there is cinema. And the cinema is Nicholas Ray." Jean-Luc Godard; "A taste for paroxysm, which imparts something of the feverish and impermanent to the most tranquil of moments." Jacques Rivette.
4 The most thorough biography of Nicholas Ray to date is Bernard Eisenschitz, *Nicholas Ray—An American Journey* (London: Faber & Faber, 1993). Also well worth reading is Geoff Andrew, *Nicholas Ray: The Poet of Nightfall* (London: British Film Institute, 2000). When I first wrote about Ray, there was little available on him in English. A famous polemical article, comparing Nicholas unfavorably to Satyajit Ray, was Penelope Huston's "Ray or Ray," *Sight & Sound*, April 1969.

5 > Ray has always displayed an exciting visual style. For example, if one compares *They Live by Night* with Huston's *The Asphalt Jungle*—and these two films are strikingly similar in mood, theme and plot—one will notice that where Ray tends to cut between physical movements, Huston tends to cut between static compositions. *Ray's style tends to be more kinetic, Huston's more plastic, the difference between dance and sculpture. Johnny Guitar* was his most bizarre film, and probably his most personal. . . . *Johnny Guitar* has invented its own genre. Philip Yordan set out to attack McCarthyism, but Ray was too delirious to pay any heed as Freudian feminism prevailed over Marxist masochism, and Pirandello transcended polemics.
>
> Andrew Sarris, *The American Cinema* (New York: Dutton, 1968), 107–8.

6 "In the late 1950s and early 1960s, as everything began to go wrong for Ray, he became not just a cult but a living fictional character, the American who wanted to make pictures and who had been forced out of his own country. His tattered life became the movie he could not quite make." David Thompson, the *Guardian*, December 27, 2003.
7 All direct quotations are from Nicholas Ray's NFT-lecture, given on January 19, 1969 at the National Film Theatre, South Bank, London.
8 Also a regular at the Ray retrosepctive in 1969 was Victor Perkins, writing for *Movie*:

> The director's control is proved not so much by the perfection of individual performances as by the consistency with which Ray's actors embody his vision. This consistency is the result—it's an ancient paradox—of the

director's search for the particular truth of each particular situation. Johnny Guitar's isolation is depicted in such specific terms that we appreciate, without directorial emphasis, the wider significance of his remark "I've a great respect for a gun, and, besides, I'm a stranger here myself." In THEY LIVE BY NIGHT Cathy O'Donnell is unable to put her watch right because "there's no clock here to set it by."

> V.F. Perkins, "The Cinema of Nicholas Ray," in *Movies and Methods*, ed.
> Bill Nichols (Berkeley: University of California Press, 1976), 351–52.

9 Charles Barr, "CinemaScope: Before and After," *Film Quarterly*, 16, 4 (Summer 1963): 4–24.
10 Celebrated review essays on PARTY GIRL are Fereydoun Hoveyda, "Nicholas Ray's Reply: *Party Girl*," and "Sunspots," in *Cahiers du Cinéma, 1960–1968: New Wave, New Cinema, Reevaluating Hollywood*, ed. Jim Hillier (London: Routledge, 1986), 122–31 and 135–45. Originally published as: "La Réponse de Nicholas Ray: *Party Girl*," *Cahiers du cinéma*, 107 (May 1960): 13–23, and "Taches de soleil" *Cahiers du cinéma*, 110 (August 1960): 41–46.
11 See also Charles Barr's description of a comparable scene in THE TRUE STORY OF JESSE JAMES, in "CinemaScope: Before and After," *Film Quarterly* 16, 4 (Summer 1963): 9.

4 Sam Fuller's Productive Pathologies: The Hero as (His Own Best) Enemy

1 The essay on SHOCK CORRIDOR was originally published in *Sam Fuller*, edited by Peter Wollen and David Will (Edinburgh International Film Festival, 1969). Reprinted in *Movies and Methods Vol. I*, ed. Bill Nichols (Berkeley: University of California Press, 1976), 290–97. The review of THE CRIMSON KIMONO has now been added. Both texts have been revised and are slightly expanded to include plot summaries. All the footnotes have been added.
2 Thomas Elsaesser, THE CRIMSON KIMONO, *The Brighton Film Review* 8 (1969): 11–12.
3 Phil Hardy, *Samuel Fuller* (London: Studio Vista, 1970).
4 Peter Wollen also discovered Sam Fuller in Paris:

> I was living in Paris in 1959, the year of both Jean-Luc Godard's *Breathless* and Budd Boetticher's *The Rise and Fall of Legs Diamond*, and I went to see both of these films the week they were released. . . . Samuel Fuller's extraordinary *Crimson Kimono* also came out in 1959 and, sure enough, Sam Fuller shows up in Godard's films six years later, in *Pierrot le Fou*.
> > Peter Wollen, "When the beam of light has gone," *London Review of Books*, 20, 18
> > (September 17, 1998), 19.

Gilbert Adair and Bernardo Bertolucci pay tribute to Fuller and SHOCK CORRIDOR in their film THE DREAMERS (2003). From a discussion with David Thomson, at the National Film Theatre, London, on November 10, 2003:

> **GA:** At the beginning of *The Dreamers*, for example, when Matthew goes to the Cinémathèque and sees *Shock Corridor* . . . and it's got those French subtitles—to me that's a little Proustian thing. Watching old American movies at the Cinémathèque was a French experience, not really American—it was American culture filtered through a French sensibility.
> **DT:** Why did you choose SHOCK CORRIDOR?
> **BB:** I think we chose it together, no?
> **GA:** I think we felt that there were a lot of corridors in the movie. The characters are constantly walking along corridors, no?
> **BB:** I don't think so. [laughter]
> **GA:** Maybe I thought so and didn't say so.
> **BB:** No, because the title was already in the screenplay before we built the set. We made some changes in an old flat in a Haussmann kind of building in Paris and I think maybe the opposite was true: that we built so many corridors in the film *because* of SHOCK CORRIDOR.
> **DT:** This was also a film that was much beloved by the *Cahiers* critics, the *Positif* critics and so forth . . .
> **GA:** Fuller wasn't taken seriously in the States, but in France he was considered one of the most important American directors.
> > www.bfi.org.uk/features/interviews/bertolucci.html (last accessed February 20, 2011).

5 Bill Nichols, *Movies and Methods* (Berkeley: University of California Press, 1976), 289–90.
6 Jean-Luc Godard, one of Sam Fuller's early admirers in France, has Jean Paul Belmondo, his hero in PIERROT LE FOU (1965) accost the director at a party, who, when asked to define "what is cinema," replies: "Film is like a battleground. Love. Hate. Action. Violence. Death. In one word . . . Emotion."
7 Perhaps the most notorious line from any Fuller film is: "if you die, I'll kill you" (Zack [Gene Evans], in THE STEEL HELMET, 1951). It is now the subtitle of a full-length book, Lisa Dombrowski, *A Fuller View: The Films of Samuel Fuller: If You Die, I'll Kill You!* (Middletown, CT: Wesleyan University Press, 2008).
8 Herbert Marcuse, *One Dimensional Man: Studies in the Ideology of Advanced Industrial Society* (Boston: Beacon Books, 1964), 55.

9 In a famous shot in CRIMSON KIMONO, a police detective (Glenn Corbett) aims a karate kick right in the viewer's face. Extreme close-ups (the "two big eyes" shot, years before Sergio Leone made it his own) contrast no less violently with distant, telephoto views of violence in the street.
> Dave Kehr, "Tabloid Auteur: Muscular Vision of Samuel Fuller," *New York Times*, November 6, 2009:
> www.nytimes.com/2009/11/08/movies/homevideo/08kehr.html (last accessed February 20, 2011).

10 Sam Fuller, *A Third Face: My Tale of Writing, Fighting and Filmmaking* (New York: Applause Books, 2004), 376.

11 THE CRIMSON KIMONO was almost operatic in its tone. I was trying to make an unconventionally triangular love story, laced with reverse racism, a kind of narrow-mindedness that's just as deplorable as outright bigotry. I wanted to show that whites aren't the only ones susceptible to racist thoughts. Joe is a racist because he transfers his fears to his friend.

Fuller, *A Third Face*, 376.

12 I wanted to get the kendo scene right because that sword fight sends an emotional message about Joe that's essential to my yarn. When Joe blows his stack and tries to beat up Charlie during the exhibition, he transgresses the protocol of a discipline whose basic rules have been developed over the last two thousand years of Japanese culture. He strikes out at his best friend and at the basic mores of his people. A person that far overboard is in terrible pain. Joe goes off the deep end and may never regain his balance.

Fuller, *A Third Face*, 380.

13 In this respect, Joe is not only an inverted racist, but also emotionally inverted, displaying behavior that is "aggressive-defensive." As Fuller says: "I wanted to show that the violence [in the kendo fight] was directed as much at himself as at his buddy" (*A Third Face*, 380).

5 Cinephilia: Or the Uses of Disenchantment

1 Paul Willemen's essay on "Cinephilia" accurately echoes this severity of tone and hints at disapproval. See "Through the Glass Darkly: Cinephilia Reconsidered," in his *Looks and Frictions. Essays in Cultural Studies and Film Theory* (Bloomington: Indiana University Press, 1994), 223–57.
2 The Andrew Sarris/Pauline Kael controversy can be studied in Andrew Sarris, "Notes on the *Auteur* Theory in 1962," *Film Culture* 27 (1962–63): 1–8; Pauline Kael, "Circles and Squares," *Film Quarterly* 16, 3 (Spring 1963): 12–26. For biographical background to Sarris' position, see www.dga.org/news/v25_6/feat_sarris_schickel.php3 (last accessed October 1, 2010).
3 ANNIE HALL (USA, 1977):

We saw the Fellini film last Tuesday. It was not one of his best. It lacks a cohesive structure. You know, you get the feeling that he's not absolutely sure what it is he wants to say. Course, I've always felt he was essentially a—a *technical* film maker. Granted, LA STRADA was a great film. Great in its use of negative imagery more than anything else. But that simple, cohesive core … Like all that JULIET OF THE SPIRITS or SATYRICON, I found it incredibly *indulgent*. You know, he really is. He's one of the most *indulgent* filmmakers. He really is. …

4 Susan Sontag, "The Decay of Cinema," *New York Times*, February 25, 1996.
5 Jean Paul Sartre returned to Paris from his visit to New York in 1947, full of admiration for the movies and the cities, and especially about Orson Welles' CITIZEN KANE (USA: 1941). See *Situations IV: Portraits* (Paris: Gallimard, 1964), 34–56.
6 Antoine de Baecque, *La cinéphilie. Invention d'un regard, histoire d'une culture, 1944–1968* (Paris: Fayard, 2003).
7 Jonathan Rosenbaum, *Moving Places. A Life at the Movies* (New York: Harper & Row, 1980), 19–35.
8 Adrian Martin, "No Flowers for the Cinephile: The Fates of Cultural Populism 1960–88," in *Island in the Stream: Myths of Place in Australian Cinema*, ed. Paul Foss (Sydney: Pluto Press, 1988), 128.
9 For Latin American cinephilia, apart from Manuel Puig's novel *Kiss of the Spider Woman* (1979), see Gilberto Perez, *The Material Ghost: Films and Their Medium* (Baltimore: The Johns Hopkins University Press, 2000).

10 Charlton Heston is an axiom. By himself alone he constitutes a tragedy, and his presence in any film whatsoever suffices to create beauty. The contained violence expressed by the somber phosphorescence of his eyes, his eagle's profile, the haughty arch of his eyebrows, his prominent cheekbones, the bitter and hard curve of his mouth, the fabulous power of his torso; this is what he possesses and what not even the worst director can degrade.

Michel Mourlet, quoted in Richard Roud, "The French Line," *Sight & Sound*, 29, 4 (Autumn 1960): 167–71, 168.

On Lang see Luc Moullet, *Fritz Lang* (Paris: Seghers, 1963); Alfred Eibel (ed.), *Fritz Lang* (Paris: Présence du Cinéma, 1964). On Hitchcock see Eric Rohmer and Claude Chabrol, *Hitchcock* (Paris: Éditions universitaires, 1957); François Truffaut, *Le cinéma selon Hitchcock* (Paris: Robert Laffont, 1966); Jean Douchet, *Alfred Hitchcock* (Paris: Éditions de l'Herne, 1967).
11 Raymond Bellour, "Nostalgies," *Autrement: Europe-Hollywood et Retour*, 79 (1986): 231–32.
12 *Movie Mutations. The Changing Face of World Cinephilia*, ed. Adrian Martin and Jonathan Rosenbaum (London: British Film Institute, 2003).
13 The terms "pull" and "push" come from marketing and constitute two ways of making contact between a consumer and a product or service. In a push medium, the producer persuades the customer actively of the advantages of the product (via adverting, marketing campaigns or mailing). In a pull medium, the consumer "finds" the product or service by appearing to freely exercise his/her choice, curiosity or by following an information trail, such as word-of-mouth. The search engines of the internet make the world wide web the typical "pull" medium, obliging traditional "push" media to redefine their communication strategies.
14 Dominic Pettman, remark at the Cinephilia II Conference, Amsterdam 2003.

15 Books, special issues of magazines, dossiers and debates on cinephilia have proliferated in recent years to an unprecedented extent. See for instance, Christian Keathley, *Cinephilia and History, or The Wind in the Trees* (Bloomington: Indiana University Press, 2005); Malte Hagener and Marijke de Valck (eds.), *Cinephilia, Movies, Love and Memory* (Amsterdam: Amsterdam University Press, 2005); "Dossier on Cinephilia," *Framework*, 50 (Fall 2009); "Dossier on Cinephilia," *Cinema Journal*, 49, 2 (Winter 2010); and Jonathan Rosenbaum, *Goodbye Cinema Hello Cinephilia* (Chicago: Chicago University Press, 2010).

6 The Persistence of Hollywood, Part I: The Continuity Principle

1 Susan Sontag, "The Decay of Cinema," *New York Times*, February 25, 1996.

2 David Thomson: "Who Killed the Movies?," *Esquire* (December 1996), 56–63; William Goldman: *The Big Picture: Who Killed Hollywood?* (New York: Applause 2000); and Peter Bart, *Who Killed Hollywood . . . and Put the Tarnish on Tinseltown?* (Los Angeles: Renaissance Books, 1999).

3 Louis Menand has pointedly satirized the obsession with the "death of cinema":

> The cinema, like the novel, is always dying. The movies were killed by sequels; they were killed by conglomerates; they were killed by special effects. "HEAVEN'S GATE" was the end; "STAR WARS" was the end; "JAWS" did it. It was the ratings system, profit participation, television, the blacklist, the collapse of the studio system, the Production Code. The movies should never have gone to colour; they should never have gone to sound. The movies have been declared dead so many times that it is almost surprising that they were born, and, as every history of the cinema makes a point of noting, the first announcement of their demise practically coincided with the announcement of their birth. "The cinema is an invention without any commercial future," said Louis Lumière [sic], the man who opened the world's first movie theatre, in Paris, in 1895. He thought that motion pictures were a novelty item, and, in 1900, after successfully exhibiting his company's films around the world, he got out of the business. It seemed the prudent move.
>
> Louis Menand, "Gross Points: Is the blockbuster the end of cinema?,"
> *New Yorker*, February 7, 2005.

4 Italy's neo-realism after 1945, France's nouvelle vague in the 1950s and 1960s, the New Polish Cinema after the "thaw" in the 1960s, Brazil's Cinema Novo around 1968 and the anti-imperialist struggles, the New German Cinema in the 1970s, and various avant-garde counter-cinema and materialist film co-operatives in London, Vienna and New York.

5 The history of Hollywood is a:

> comic routine of bad guesses, unintended outcomes and pure luck. . . . in life there never is just one secret, and there never is just one cause. In the case of a collaborative, semi-regulated, high-cap, worldwide, mass-market entertainment like a Hollywood movie, identifying causes is like predicting next year's weather. A butterfly flutters its wings in Culver City, and a decade later you get *The Terminator*.
>
> Menand, "Gross Points."

6 I review other theorists' version of classical cinema Chapter 9, "Film as System, or How to Step Through an Open Door."

7 Neil Postman, *Amusing Ourselves to Death: Public Discourse in the Age of Show Business* (New York: Penguin, 1986); Michael Medved, *Hollywood vs. America: Popular Culture and the War on Traditional Values* (New York: Harper, 1993).

8 Toby Miller, Nitin Govall, John McMurria, Ting Wang and Richard Maxwell, *Global Hollywood*, 2nd edition (London: BFI Publishing, 2008); Aida Hozic, *Hollyworld: Space, Power, and Fantasy in the American Economy* (Ithaca: Cornell University Press, 2001).

9 Tim Lenoir, "All but War is Simulation: The Military Entertainment Complex," *Configurations* 8, 3 (2000): 289–335; Norman Klein, *The Vatican to Vegas: The History of Special Effects* (New York: The New Press, 2003).

10 Peter Kramer, "Post-Classical Hollywood," in *American Cinema: Critical Approaches*, ed. John Hill and Pamela C. Gibson (Oxford: Oxford University Press, 2000), 289–309; Richard Maltby, "Nobody Knows Everything," in *Contemporary Hollywood Cinema*, ed. Murray Smith and Steve Neale (London: Routledge, 1998), 21–44; David Bordwell, *The Way Hollywood Tells It* (Berkeley: California University Press, 2006).

11 Olivier Zunz, in *Why the American Century?* (Chicago: University of Chicago Press, 2000) identifies four chief factors: a. Government, universities and corporations worked closely with one another in search for economically useful knowledge and its practical applications; b. The creation of a society based on mass consumption; c. the political effort to promote a concept of citizenship that balanced ethnic and religious diversity with one-nation patriotism; d. the projection of military power together with the values of soft power, delivered though mass media and commodity culture. Hollywood had an active share in several of these factors, notably by a close alliance with US foreign policy about the projection of soft power; second, by fitting humans to the machine it tended to resolve the question "what is a human being?" in engineering terms, not on the basis of religious or philosophical arguments; third, it practiced, from early on, the cooperation and collusion of cinema with industry and the military: from Edweard Muybridge and Howard Hughes to George Lucas and James Cameron.

12 Chalmers Johnson, *Blowback: The Costs and Consequences of American Empire* (New York: Holt, 2000); Robert Kagan, *Of Paradise and Power: America and Europe in the New World Order* (New York: Knopf, 2003); Niall Ferguson, *Colossus: The Rise and Fall of the American Empire* (New York: Penguin, 2005); Michael Hardt, Antonio Negri, *Empire* (Cambridge, MA: Harvard University Press, 2001).

13 Benjamin R. Barber, *Jihad Versus McWorld* (New York: Times Books, 1995); Richard Pells, *Not Like Us: How Europeans Have Loved, Hated, and Transformed American Culture Since World War II* (New York: Basic Books, 1997).

14 Allen J. Scott, *On Hollywood The Place, The Industry* (Princeton: Princeton University Press, 2005).

15 In an underappreciated essay, Fredric Jameson has tried to apply a Hegelian periodization scheme to the question "why cinema?" See "The Existence of Italy," in *Signatures of the Visible* (New York: Routledge, 1992), 155–229.

16 Miriam Bratu Hansen, "The Mass Production of the Senses: Classical Cinema as Vernacular Modernism," *Modernism/Modernity* 6, 2 (1999): 59–77; Thomas Elsaesser and Malte Hagener, *Film Theory: An Introduction Through the Senses* (New York: Routledge, 2010).

17 Thomas Elsaesser, "The Mindgame Film," in *Puzzle Films*, ed. Warren Buckland (Oxford: Blackwell 2009), 13–41 and "Casting Around: Hitchcock's Absence," in *Looking for Alfred: The Hitchcock Castings*, Johan Grimonprez (Ostfieldern: Hatje Cantz, 2007), 139–61.

18 Craigie Horsfield pointed out recently that film is essentially a socializing medium. We constantly ask each other, "What film have you seen? Did you like the new so-and-so?" Everybody wants to share their experiences of seeing a narrative film. Film creates a kind of connective tissue, socially and culturally, much more than anything else—novels or TV, for instance.
   Chrissie Iles, "The Projected Image in Contemporary Art," *October*, 104 (Spring 2003), 73.

19 Tyler Cowen, "Some Countries Remain Resistant to American Cultural Exports," *New York Times*, February 22, 2007: www.nytimes.com/2007/02/22/business/22scene.html (last accessed April 13, 2009).

20 The Italian director Gianni Amelio once bitterly complained:

   Young people today want a product that is not to be consumed individually, but rather collectively. They go to the cinema in groups of 20 to 25 and need it as an accomplice to their behaviour, a cinema with regular gags, for example, that allow you to slap the person beside you on the shoulder. This sort of movie-going functions much like being in a bar or discotheque: you go to the cinema, not primarily in order to see a film, but to enjoy yourself and each other, preferably at the expense of the film.
   Jörg Hermann, " 'Wir gehen auf den Tod des Kinos zu': Ein Gespräch mit Gianni Amelio," in *Neue Medien contra Filmkultur?*, ed. Arbeitsgemeinschaft der Filmjournalisten/Hamburger Filmbüro (Berlin: Spiess, 1987), 28–37.

21 Perhaps European filmmakers are too individualistic and their works lack mythological resonance? Are non-Hollywood films too much the self-expression of an individual and therefore—an often heard argument—too difficult, too self-indulgent or too demanding for a wider audience? Or have the Americans simply taken the best from European and Asian cinema artistically, while adding their own culturally conditioned, feel-good optimism and can-do pragmatism?

22 Digital technologies of storage such as the DVD have become crucial not only for Hollywood; they are vital to art films as well as documentaries and avant-garde films, creating new film cultures and invigorating old ones. The result has been a resurgence of discussions on "cinephilia": see, for instance, M. Hagener and M. de Valck (eds.), *Cinephilia—Movies, Love and Memory* (Amsterdam: Amsterdam University Press, 2005); Christian Keathley, *Cinephilia and History, or The Wind in the Trees* (Bloomington: Indiana University Press, 2005).

23 The American cinema is a classical art, but why not then admire in it what is most admirable, i.e. not only the talent of this or that film-maker, but the genius of the system, the richness of its ever-vigorous tradition, and its fertility when it comes into contact with new elements?
   André Bazin, "De la politique des auteurs," *Cahiers du Cinéma* 70 (April 1957): 10.

7 Why Hollywood?

1 Cited in the German journal *Filmkritik* (October 1970), 516.

2 The text is based on a lecture given at the National Film Theatre in 1970, as one of a series, where the editors of different film journals had been invited to present their basic editorial positions. Hence the polemical tone of these opening passages. It was first published in *Monogram* 1 (April 1971), 4–10.

3 William Faulkner memorably said about Hawks, after co-writing the script of LAND OF THE PHARAOHS: "it's the same movie Howard has been making for 35 years. . . . But the thing about Howard is he knows it's the same movie, and he knows he made it." Quoted in Peter Hogue, "Hawks and Faulkner: *Today We Live*," *Literature/Film Quarterly*, 9, 1 (1981), 51.

4 Parker Tyler, *Sex, Psyche, Etcetera in the Film* (Harmondsworth: Penguin, 1966), 222.

5 Georg Lukács, "Narrate or Describe (1936)," in *Writer and Critic and Other Essays*, ed. and trans. Arthur D. Kahn (New York, 1970), 172.

6 Erwin Panofsky, "Style and Medium in the Motion Picture," originally published as "On Movies" in the *Bulletin of the Department of Art and Archaeology*, Princeton University (June 1936): 5–15. The 1947 revised edition appears in Gerald Mast and Marshall Cohen (eds.), *Film Theory and Criticism* (New York: Oxford University Press, 1985), 215–33.

7 For succinct accounts of genre theory, see Steve Neale, *Genre* (London: British Film Institute, 1980); Rick Altman, "An Introduction to the Theory of Genre Analysis," *The American Film Musical* (New York: Knopf, 1992); and Francesco Casetti, "Les Genres cinématographiques," *Ça Cinéma*, 18 (1980): 37–43.

8 This intervention was, I shall try to show in another chapter, driven by an ideological agenda, as in the case of German émigré directors and *film noir*, or the gender-politics of melodrama. On *film noir*, see the special issue of *iris* (Paris/Iowa), 21 (Spring 1996), (European precursors of *film noir*).

9 Psycho-semiotics has also given us models of how to understand the working of generic codes, as in Steve Neale's brief monograph, where apparatus theory, interpellation and enunciation are deployed in order to distinguish mainstream Hollywood genres according to their different subject-effects and modes of address, notably the different regimes of illusion and belief, or the different axes of verisimilitude and credibility by which the spectator's visual pleasure is engaged and his sense of mastery is solicited. See Steve Neale, *Genre* (London: British Film Institute, 1980).

8 Narrative Cinema and Audience Aesthetics: The *Mise-en-Scène* of the Spectator

1 Originally delivered as a paper to a seminar organized by the Educational Advisory Service of the British Film Institute, March 29, 1974. Edited, shortened and slightly revised, 2001.

2 When I presented this paper at a British Film Institute evening seminar, I received quite a drubbing at the hands of Sam Rohdie and Ben Brewster, the editor and his second-lieutenant at *Screen*. It was a useful experience, because it led me to immerse myself more seriously in the French theorists *Screen* was promoting. Not only, it has to be said, out of fear of political isolation and intellectual ostracism. For some of the very problems that preoccupied me, Jean Louis Baudry's cinematic apparatus, Christian Metz's "primary identification," and Lacanian psychosemiotics were indeed more theoretically elegant, politically radical and academically hip syntheses than my own theoretical bricolage, cobbled together from Sigmund Freud's *Interpretation of Dreams* and *Psychopathology of Everyday Life*, Roman Jakobson's "poetics" from his famous *Closing Statement*, E.H. Gombrich's pragmatics of realism from *Art and Illusion* and *Meditations on a Hobby Horse*, Anton Ehrenzweig's *The Hidden Order of Art*, Herbert Marcuse's "repressive desublimation" from *One-Dimensional Man*, and a book I come across in my comparative literature studies, Norman Holland's *The Dynamics of Literary Response*.

3 I have returned to the problems of deictics, shifters and markers of the "here, me and now" in several of my essays on Early Cinema and new media, such as "The New Film History as Media Archaeology," *Cinémas* 14, 2–3 (Spring 2004): 75–117.

4 Christian Metz, *L'enonciation impersonnelle ou le site du film* (Paris: Méridiens Klincksieck, 1991).

5 This idea is elaborated in my essay "The Blockbuster: Everything Connects, but Not Everything Goes," in *The End of Cinema as We Know It: American Film in the Nineties*, ed. Jon Lewis (New York: NYU Press, 2001), 11–22.

6 As to the question of signification, or meaning-making, which is not taken up further in these essays, one might invoke Eisenstein. He, too, was interested in how films direct the spectatorial attention, bypassing the thematics of illusionist identification. Richard Allen, in an e-mail from 2006 has suggested that Eisenstein offers a different version of cognitivism, a sort of "cognitivist unconscious."

7 This was a reference to the essays on Brecht and Benjamin, which were discussed in previous sessions of the seminar and which became the famous "Brecht issue" of *Screen*, 15, 2 (Summer, 1974), with essays by Stephen Heath, Ben Brewster and Colin MacCabe among others.

8 According to the linguist Roman Jakobson, the "phatic" dimension refers to those elements of the communication process whose aim is simply to establish contact and ensure that channels are open. Its most obvious form is in expressions like "Good morning," "How are you," where the aim is not to solicit or provide information, but simply to establish linguistic contact. A phatic expression is thus one whose function is to perform a social task, as opposed to conveying information. The term was originally coined by Bronislaw Malinowski, "The Problem of Meaning in Primitive Languages," in *The Meaning of Meaning*, Charles K. Ogden and Ian A. Richards (London: Routledge and Kegan Paul, 1923), 146–52.

9 Cathexis is a term first used by Freud in 1922 (German: "Besetzung" occupation), defined as the process of investment of libidinal (or more generally, affective) energy in a person, object or idea. It is here used to highlight the affective investment of the spectator in both the cinema experience and in the film experience.

10 Quoted in Siegfried Kracauer, *From Caligari to Hitler* (Princeton, NJ: Princeton University Press, 1947), 187.

11 "Interview with Ruy Guerra," *Monogram* 5 (1975): 27–33.

9 Film as System: Or How to Step Through an Open Door

1 This essay is an adaptation of the first three introductory lectures of my MA course on Film Theory, begun in 1992 at the University of Amsterdam. As indicated in the introduction, once I had assumed my role of introducing "film studies" into the university curriculum, some of my polemical and cinephile preoccupations as a working critic took second place to the need to establish an academically viable method of close textual analysis. For reasons also touched upon in the previous chapters, I made the "system" the master text, rather than the "author," the individual film or the genre. This explains why I opted for an "anthropological" version of French structuralism, while retaining my interest in Freud, in order to extend my analysis of the spectator's work in making meaning. The chapter, along with the subsequent one (which does focus on an individual film: "Gangsters and Grapefruits") summarizes some of the implications of structuralist analysis but also tests the limits of their applications.

2 See Ari Hiltunen, *Aristotle in Hollywood: Visual Stories That Work* (Bristol: Intellect, 2001) and Michael Tierno, *Aristotle's Poetics for Screenwriters: Storytelling Secrets from the Greatest Mind in Western Civilisation* (New York: Hyperion, 2002).

3 See Christian Metz, "Story/Discourse (A Note on Two Kinds of Voyeurism)," in his *Psychoanalysis and Cinema: The Imaginary Signifier* (London: MacMillan, 1982), 91–98.

4 For an extensive discussion, see Thomas Elsaesser and Emile Poppe, "Film and Language," in *Encyclopedia of Language and Linguistics*, ed. R.E. Asher and J.M.Y Simpson (Oxford: Pergamon Press, 1993), 1225–41.

5 Christian Metz, "The Cinema: Language or Language System?," in his *Film Language: A Semiotics of the Cinema* (New York: Oxford University Press, 1974), 31–91.

6   For a critique of semiotics, see Noël Carroll, *Mystifying Movies: Fads and Fallacies in Contemporary Film Theory* (New York: Columbia University Press, 1988).

7   See Warren Buckland (ed.), *The Film Spectator: From Sign to Mind* (Amsterdam: Amsterdam University Press, 1995) and *The Cognitive Semiotics of Film* (Cambridge: Cambridge University Press, 2000).

8   To cite three English-language texts: David Bordwell, *Narration in the Fiction Film* (Madison: University of Wisconsin Press, 1985); Edward Branigan, *Narrative Comprehension and Film* (New York: Routledge, 1992); Seymour Chatman, *Coming to Terms: The Rhetoric of Narrative in Fiction and Film* (Ithaca: Cornell University Press, 1990).

9   Among a host of books, one can name Richard Allen, *Projecting Illusion* (Cambridge: Cambridge University Press, 1995) and Murray Smith, *Engaging Characters* (Oxford: Clarendon Press, 1995).

10 For a representative sample of feminist film theory essays, see *Feminism and Film*, ed. E. Ann Kaplan (Oxford: Oxford University Press, 2000).

11 Raymond Bellour, "The Obvious and the Code," in his *The Analysis of Film* (Bloomington: Indiana University Press, 2001), 69–76.

12 Kristin Thompson, *Storytelling in the New Hollywood* (Cambridge, MA: Harvard University Press, 1999); David Bordwell, "Since 1960: The Persistence of a Mode of Film Practice," chapter 30 of D. Bordwell, J. Staiger, and K. Thompson, *The Classical Hollywood Cinema: Film Style and Mode of Production to 1960* (London: Routledge, 1985), 367–77; Bordwell, *The Way Hollywood Tells It: Story and Style in Modern Movies* (Berkeley: University of California Press, 2006).

13 See Peter Wollen, "*North by Northwest*: A Morphological Analysis," in his *Readings and Writings: Semiotic Counter-Strategies* (London: Verso, 1982), 18–33; David Bordwell, "ApProppriations and ImProprieties: Problems in the Morphology of Film Narrative," *Cinema Journal* 27, 3 (Spring 1988): 5–20.

14 Bellour, *The Analysis of Film*; Wollen, "The Auteur Theory" and "Conclusion," in *Signs and Meaning in the Cinema*, 2nd edition (London: BFI, 1972).

15 Michael Hauge, *Writing Screenplays That Sell* (London: Elm Tree Books, 1988), 83.

16 A further reduction of Propp's function is exemplified by Greimas's semiotic square, as explained in A.J. Greimas, *Structural Semantics: An Attempt at a Method*, trans. Daniele McDowell, Ronald Schleifer and Alan Velie (Lincoln: University of Nebraska Press, 1983). For a brief exposition, see Thomas Elsaesser and Warren Buckland, *Studying Contemporary American Film: A Guide to Movie Analysis* (London: Hodder, 2002), 32–35.

17 George Lakoff, *Women, Fire, and Dangerous Things: What Categories Reveal About the Mind* (Chicago: University of Chicago Press, 1987).

18 Michel Foucault, in the Preface to *The Order of Things: An Archaeology of the Human Sciences* (London: Tavistock, 1970).

19 See Lévi-Strauss, *Structural Anthropology*, trans. Claire Jacobson and Brooke Grundfest Schoepf (New York: Basic Books 1963), 224.

20 See *The Analysis of Film*, Chapters 2, 5, 8 respectively.

21 *The Analysis of Film*, Chapter 4.

22 Hauge, *Writing Screenplays that Sell*, 83.

23 Bellour, in Janet Bergstrom, "Alternation, Segmentation, Hypnosis: Interview with Raymond Bellour," *Camera Obscura*, 3/4 (1979): 88.

24 Thierry Kuntzel, "The Film Work 2," *Camera Obscura*, 5 (1980): 8–9, 10.

25 Kuntzel, "The Film Work," *Enclitic*, 2, 1 (Spring 1978): 60.

26 David Thomson, "At the Acme Book Shop," *Sight & Sound* (Spring 1981): 122–25, 124.

27 This overt sexualization operating at the micro-level of the opening of THE BIG SLEEP also has significance on the film's macro-level, for it helps to disguise and compensate the fundamental but wholly covert fairy-tale subtext, already hinted at in the dynastic dilemma. For what is the typical Proppian structure? The king sends out the hero to slay the dragon, and, if successful, he gets the daughter as prize: but in order to become the hero, the contender has to pass three "tests," which is precisely what happens in THE BIG SLEEP. Bogart, as Marlowe, so sure of himself, is tested verbally and physically by the General and the butler, as well as by both the sisters: this sets up the nature of the hero: not a superman, but a man always able to turn a situation to his advantage whatever the initial handicap. All the verbal play not only establishes the layout of the dramatic terrain, the geography of the narrative, so to speak, but also gives us confidence in our hero because we know how many different kinds of weapons he has at his disposal for the mission: verbal wit, attractiveness to women, physical courage, masculinity, worldliness, ingenuity—all his character traits are tested in the opening scene. From the moment he pushes the doorbell button, the action takes over like a machine, almost of its own accord, but that is because we have a hero who makes the effort seem easy, to whom the "next, please" comes very naturally. But the suave sophistication of the smooth surface is, as so often in Hollywood films, firmly anchored in the deep-structure of our myths and fairy tales.

28 Given the subtlety of the narrative construction, the verbal wit and visual glamor of ANGEL, it is surprising that the film does not enjoy more of a reputation. I could find no serious discussion of the film, but more than one snide or disparaging remark: "Dietrich is glamour in double dress. This time she is wearing eyelashes you could hang your hat on and every now and then the star flicks 'em as though a dust storm was getting in her way" (*Variety*). Even more critical: "This was a disappointing venture for the Dietrich-Lubitsch team, as this slight story provided no sparks for the magic expected. This empty film helped name Dietrich as 'Box Office Poison' in 1937." http://homepages.sover.net/~ozus/angel.htm (last accessed March 5, 2011).

10 Gangsters and Grapefruits: Masculinity and Marginality in *The Public Enemy*

1   Internet Movie Database, Trivia on THE PUBLIC ENEMY: www.imdb.com/title/tt0022286/trivia (last accessed December 15, 2010).

2 Billy Wilder's SOME LIKE IT HOT (1959) paid tribute to all three films:

> The crime lord "Little Bonaparte" stems from LITTLE CAESAR, while Spats Columbo threatens to smash a grape-fruit in the face of one of his henchmen (James Cagney's famous scene from THE PUBLIC ENEMY). He then grabs a coin from the air as it is being flipped by another gangster, a cliché that originated with Raft's character in Howard Hawks' SCARFACE—thus making Raft's line "Where did you pick up that cheap trick?" a bit of meta-humor.
> Book Rags: www.bookrags.com/wiki/Some_Like_It_Hot (last accessed December 15, 2010).

3 Tom Keough, quoted on "dvd today": www.dvd-today.com/actor/James-Cagney/dvd.html (last accessed December 15, 2010).

4 David Thompson, *The New Biographical Dictionary of Film*, 4th revised edition (New York: Little, Brown & Company, 2003), 126–27.

5 Richard Dyer, *Stars*, new edition (London: BFI, 1998).

6 See Patrick McGilligan, "Just a Dancer Gone Wrong," in his *Cagney: The Actor as Auteur* (New York: A.S. Barnes and Co., 1975), 29–96; and Robert Sklar, *City Boys: Cagney, Bogart, Garfield* (Princeton: Princeton University Press, 1992).

7 For a consideration of genre in post-classical Hollywood, see Peter Kramer, "Post-classical Hollywood," in *The Oxford Guide to Film Studies*, ed. John Hill and Pamela Church Gibson (Oxford: Oxford University Press, 1998), 289–309; and Barry Langford, *Film Genre: Hollywood and Beyond* (Edinburgh: Edinburgh University Press, 2005).

8 One of the most acute analyses of film as a combat zone of cultural memory is J. Hoberman, *The Magic Hour: Film at fin de siècle* (Philadelphia: Temple University Press, 2003).

9 Historically informed and wide-ranging examples of this approach are Michael Rogin, *Blackface, White Noise: Jewish Immigrants in the Hollywood Melting Pot* (Berkeley: University of California Press, 1998); and Linda Williams, *"Playing the Race Card:" Melodramas of Black and White from Uncle Tom to O.J. Simpson* (Princeton: Princeton University Press, 2001).

10 Peter Wollen, "The Auteur Theory," in his *Signs and Meaning in the Cinema* (London: Secker & Warburg, 1969), 74–115; Jim Kitses, *Horizons West. Anthony Mann, Budd Boetticher, Sam Peckinpah. Studies of Authorship within the Western* (London: Thames and Hudson/BFI, 1969); Colin McArthur, *Underworld USA* (London: BFI, 1972); Geoffrey Nowell-Smith, *Visconti* (London: Secker and Warburg/BFI, 1969).

11 Claude Lévi-Strauss, "The Structural Study of Myth," in *Structural Anthropology*, trans. Claire Jacobson and Brooke Grundfest Schoepf (New York: Basic Books, 1963); Vladimir Propp, *Morphology of the Folktale* (Austin: University of Texas Press, 1968); Brian Henderson, "Critique of Cine-Structuralism," *Film Quarterly* 27, 1 (Fall 1973): 25–34; Charles Eckert, "The English Cine-Structuralists," *Film Comment* 9, 3 (May–June 1973): 46–51.

12 "John Ford's *Young Mr. Lincoln*: A Collective Text by the Editors of *Cahiers du Cinéma*," in *Movies and Methods*, ed. Bill Nichols (Berkeley: University of California Press, 1976), 493–529.

13 Brian Henderson, "*The Searchers*: An American Dilemma," *Film Quarterly* 34, 2 (Winter 1980–81), 9–23; Charles W. Eckert, "The Anatomy of a Proletarian Film: Warner's *Marked Woman*," *Film Quarterly* 27, 2 (Winter, 1973–74), 10–24.

14 Published in Robert Warshow, *The Immediate Experience: Movies, Comics, Theatre & Other Aspects of Popular Culture* (New York: Doubleday, 1962).

15 I take the phrase from Fredric Jameson's famous book on literary interpretation, *The Political Unconscious: Narrative as a Socially Symbolic Act* (Ithaca, NY: Cornell University Press, 1981).

16 George Chabot, *Public Enemy*: www.epinions.com/mvie-review-5A90-BA0673A-39E4AB34-prod1 (last accessed December 15, 2010).

17 Richard Maltby, "Public Enemy," *Senses of Cinema*: www.sensesofcinema.com/2003/cteq/public_enemy/ (last accessed December 15, 2010). *Senses of Cinema*, 29 (November–December 2003). Copyright 1999–2011 Senses of Cinema Inc and the contributor. Reproduced by permission.

18 Maltby, "Public Enemy."

19 Maltby, "Public Enemy."

20 Maltby, "Public Enemy."

21 Eckert, "The Anatomy of a Proletarian Film," 21.

22 Eckert, "The Anatomy of a Proletarian Film," 20.

23 Eckert, "The Anatomy of a Proletarian Film," 17–18.

24 Noël Burch and Jorge Dana, "Propositions," *Afterimage* 5 (Spring 1974), 40–66 (56).

25 Martin Luther King, in response to comparisons between black underachievers and other immigrant groups' success stories, used to point out that while European immigrants came voluntarily, blacks came in chains, and thus, they cannot be compared. It is debatable that the Irish during the potato famine came voluntarily, any more than the Jews who fled Hitler, but clearly patriotism can be relative to the conditions under which you had to join the host nation.

26 The mother-fixation is a theme of the Cagney persona developed in later films, notably WHITE HEAT, and, apparently, present in his real life. See Lucy Fisher, "Mama's Boy: Filial Hysteria in WHITE HEAT," in *Screening the Male: Exploring Masculinities in Hollywood Cinema*, ed. Steven Cohan and Ina Rae Hark (New York: Routledge, 1992), 70–84.

27 According to the Wikipedia entry, this scene was cut for the 1941 post-Hayes Code re-release, as was the seduction scene with Paddy Ryan's wife Jane: http://en.wikipedia.org/wiki/The_Public_Enemy (last accessed December 15, 2010).

28 Cagney's Tom Power cultivates a number of distinct mannerisms of ambivalence and excess, such as the sudden lunge with the fist, either lethal or playful, or both: the fist through the speakeasy door, the fist on his mother's chin and so on; or the little dance on the pavement, just after he meets Gwen (Jean Harlow), whom he impresses with his manliness and gravitas.

29 What Lucy Fisher, in "Mama's Boy," calls "filial hysteria," in respect to WHITE HEAT, also applies to THE PUBLIC ENEMY.

30 See in this context Janet Bergstrom, "Alternation, Segmentation, Hypnosis: Interview with Raymond Bellour," *Camera Obscura* 3/4 (1979): 87.

31 One additional dimension of its astonishing afterlife are the many explanations given for why it was inserted or kept in the film, whose sheer number renders them either implausible or inadequate. Wikipedia cites William Wellman (the director), Ben Mankiewicz (grandson of the screenwriter Herman J. Mankiewicz), Mae Clark, James Cagney and even Mae Clark's ex-husband with (sometimes contradictory) accounts of the why and how of the scene: http://en.wikipedia.org/wiki/The_Public_Enemy (last accessed December 15, 2010).

11 Transatlantic Triangulations: William Dieterle and the Warner Bros. Biopics

1 The most analytical study of the biopic as genre is Henry M. Taylor's (as yet untranslated) *Rolle des Lebens. Die Filmbiographie als narratives System* (Marburg: Schüren, 2002). Evaluations of Dieterle and Warner Bros. biopics can be found in Richard Maltby's chapters "History as Production Value" and "The Lessons from History" in his *Hollywood Cinema* (Oxford: Blackwells, 2003), 436–48. For the most comprehensive general history of biopics, see George Frederick Custen, *Bio/pics: How Hollywood Constructed Public History* (Brunswick, NJ: Rutgers University Press, 1992). An analysis of Dieterle's biopic of scientists can be found in T. Hugh Crawford, "Screening Science: Pedagogy and Practice in William Dieterle's Film Biographies of Scientists," *Common Knowledge* G.2 (Fall 1997), 52–68. For the role of the left-wing émigré community and the biopic's internationalism, see Saverio Giovacchini, *Hollywood Modernism: Film and Politics in the Age of the New Deal* (Philadelphia: Temple University Press, 2001).

2 This chapter is based on a lecture given at the "Eminent Europeans" conference, King's College London May 17–18, 2007. It incorporates material originally published as "Film History as Social History: The Dieterle/Warner Brothers Bio-Pic," *WideAngle* 8, 2 (1986): 15–31.

3 David Quinlan, quoted on the website "They Shoot Pictures, Don't They?": www.theyshootpictures.com/dieterlewilliam.htm (last accessed October 23, 2010).

4 Hortense Powdermaker, *Hollywood, the Dream Factory* (Boston: Little, Brown and Company, 1950).

5 The key text on Hollywood as a "cluster" phenomenon is Allen J. Scott, *On Hollywood: The Place The Industry* (Princeton, NJ: Princeton University Press, 2005).

6 David Bordwell, Janet Staiger and Kristin Thompson, *The Classical Hollywood Cinema: Film Style and Mode of Production to 1960* (London: Routledge, 1985).

7 The foremost scholars studying the organizational and cultural implications are Richard Maltby and Ruth Vasey. See Richard Maltby, "The Production Code and the Hays Office," in Tino Balio (ed.), *Grand Design: Hollywood as a Modern Business Enterprise, 1930–1939* (New York: Scribner's, 1993), 37–72; Ruth Vasey, *The World According to Hollywood, 1918–1939* (Madison: University of Wisconsin Press, 1997); and also Richard Maltby, *Hollywood Cinema*, 2nd edition (Oxford: (Oxford: Basil Blackwell, 2003), 59–73.

8 Robert Warshow, "The Gangster as Tragic Hero," originally *Partisan Review* (New Brunswick, NJ, 1948), reprinted in his *The Immediate Experience* (New York: Doubleday, 1970, 127–34.

9 Lea Jacobs, *The Wages of Sin: Censorship and the Fallen Woman Film, 1928–1942* (Madison: University of Wisconsin Press, 1991). Jacobs' study covers films from a number of studios, including Paramount's BLONDE VENUS, MGM's ANNA KARENINA, Goldwyn/UA's STELLA DALLAS and RKO's KITTY FOYLE, as well as Warner Bros. If self-regulation is vital to the stability of the system then it cannot be limited to a single studio, but requires cartel-like agreements among all the studios.

10 See Robert C. Allen, "William Fox presents SUNRISE," *Quarterly Review of Film Studies* 2, 3 (August 1977): 327–38.

11 For a more extensive discussion of self-fashioning in the émigré community, see Thomas Elsaesser, "Ethnicity, Authenticity, and Exile: A Counterfeit Trade?—German filmmakers and Hollywood," in *Home, Exile, Homeland: Film, Media and the Politics of Place*, ed. Hamid Naficy (London: Routledge, 1999): 97–123.

12 Dieterle, quoted in Tom Flinn, "William Dieterle: The Plutarch of Hollywood," *The Velvet Light Trap* 15 (Fall 1975), 25.

13 Dieterle, quoted in Flinn, "William Dieterle," 25.

14 See *The Classical Hollywood Cinema*, 326.

15 In an essay focusing on the biopic and the American Left, Chris Robé has corroborated this suggestion, citing a contemporary review by Peter Ellis in *The New Masses*. Chris Robé, "Taking Hollywood Back: The Historical Costume Drama, the Biopic, and Popular Front U.S. Film Criticism," *Cinema Journal* 48, 2 (Winter 2009), 79.

16 Bertolt Brecht, "Wilhelm Dieterles Galerie grosser bürgerlicher Figuren," in *Von Deutschland nach Hollywood: William Dieterle 1893–1972* (Berlin: Internationale Filmfestspiele, 1973), 5–7.

17 For a fuller argument on this point, see the section "Allegorical Readings" in Chapter 23, "The Persistence of Hollywood Part II: Reflexivity and Self-Reference."

18 Dieterle, quoted in Flinn, "William Dieterle," 26.

19 Blanke, quoted in Ezra Goodman, *The Fifty Year Decline and Fall of Hollywood* (New York: Simon and Schuster, 1962), 179–80.

20 Wolfgang Gersch, *Film bei Brecht: Bertolt Brechts praktische und theoretische Auseinandersetzung mit dem Film* (Munich: Hanser, 1975).

21 Plot summary of JUAREZ, on imdb: www.imdb.com/title/tt0031516/plotsummary (last accessed October 23, 2010).

22 Other evaluations of Dieterle's status and talent include the following: "Dieterle proved a prolific workhorse, serving Paramount, Warners, and David Selznick.... By the mid-1940s Dieterle was under Selznick's wing and his sense of almost supernatural atmosphere was not unsuited to the producer's dreamy-mystical conception of Jennifer Jones in

PORTRAIT OF JENNIE—indication of how often the women's picture encourages moderate talent into abandoning caution" (David Thomson, *The New Biographical Dictionary of Film*, 2002). "Bosley Crowther referred to Dieterle as the 'Plutarch of the screen,' in reference to the filmmaker's brilliant series of cinema biographies throughout the 1930s. Dieterle was influenced by expressionism, and his work is usually slow moving, occasionally top-heavy, but more often penetrating" (William R. Meyer (*The Film Buff's Catalog*, 1978): www.theyshootpictures.com/dieterlewilliam.htm (last accessed August 2, 2011).

23 See Eric Barnouw, *The Golden Web: A History of Broadcasting in the United States 1933–1953* (New York: Oxford University Press, 1968).

24 The best example is Nick Browne, "System of Production/System of Representation: Industry Context and Ideological Form in Capra's MEET JOHN DOE," in *Meet John Doe*, ed. Charles Wolfe (New Brunswick, NJ: Rutgers University Press, 1989), 269–88.

12 Welles and Virtuosity: *Citizen Kane* as Character-Mask

1 This essay began life as a two-part introductory lecture on authorship at the University of East Anglia in the mid-1980s, at around the time of Welles' death. Meta-theoretical in intent, it presupposed a substantial amount of prior acquaintance and preparatory reading. It has been revised, and complemented by additional footnotes. It neither provides a survey of the literature on CITIZEN KANE nor has it been updated to include the more recent writings on Welles, authorship and CITIZEN KANE. Merely noted, for instance is the existence of Laura Mulvey's BFI Classic volume on CITIZEN KANE (London: BFI 2008) and Youssef Ishagpour's almost 400 page book on CITIZEN KANE, part of his three-volume set *Orson Welles Cinéaste*. Not mentioned is Robert Carringer's *The Making of Citizen Kane* (revised edition, 1996) nor the books edited by Ron Gottesman *Focus on CK* and *Perspectives on CK*.

2 To name just a few: Dudley Andrew, "The Unauthorized Auteur Today," in *Film Theory Goes to the Movies*, ed. Jim Collins, Hilary Radner and Ava Preacher Collins (New York: Routledge, 1993), 77–85; Timothy Corrigan, "Auteurs and the New Hollywood," in *The New American Cinema*, ed. Jon Lewis (London: Duke University Press, 1998), 38–63; James Naremore, "Authorship," in *A Companion to Film Theory*, ed. Toby Miller and Robert Stam (Oxford: Blackwells, 1999), 9–24; David A. Gerstner and Janet Staiger (eds.), *Authorship and Film* (New York: Routledge, 2003); Dana Polan, "Auteur Desire," *Screening the Past* (March 2001): www.latrobe.edu.au/screeningthepast/firstrelease/fr0301/dpfr12a.htm (last accessed March 9, 2011).

3 The phrase is often cited, but seldom precisely sourced. See for instance, the *New York Times* Obituary, "Orson Welles is Dead at 70; Innovator of Film and Stage," October 11, 1985 or Roger Ebert on his blog in 2009: http://blogs.suntimes.com/ebert/2009/03/the_best_train_set_a_boy_could.html (last accessed July 25, 2011).

4 See the obituaries published in 1985, which made the fact very plain.

5 Quoted in Joseph McBride, *Orson Welles* (London: Secker & Warburg, 1972), 38–39.

6 Few film directors have had as many biographies written about them as Welles. Among the most noteworthy are books by André Bazin, Charles Higham, Barbara Leaming, Peter Bogdanovich, Joseph McBride, David Thomson, Jonathan Rosenbaum, Simon Callow and Peter Conrad. In France, the philosopher-filmmaker-critic Youssef Ishaghpour has said that his creative (and much of his personal) life had been nothing but a forty-year preparation for writing the definitive study of Orson Welles. The books, totalling some 1500 pages, finally appeared in 2005: *Orson Welles Cinéaste* in three volumes: *Mais notre dépendance à l'image est énorme . . .; Les films de la période américaine; Les films de la période nomade: Une Caméra Visible* (Paris: Edition de la Différance, 2005).

7 Paramount Studio memo, dated November 30, 1938, sent from Russell Holman to A.M. Botsford, and passed on to the directors Albert Lewin, Wesley Ruggles, William Wellman, Fritz Lang, as well as producer Arthur Hornblow and several others:

> I have had a long talk with Orson Welles yesterday. Let me say that I believe it might be a good and profitable thing if Welles could be associated with Paramount production. He is a good and striking character actor but he has even more important talents as a director and producer. . . . His *War of the Worlds* broadcast was just another example of how this man's mind works showmanwise. Following this broadcast, Welles received several Hollywood offers, including one from us for *Air Raid*. . . . Welles is a husky fellow of 23, a little on the pudgy side but with quite good height. His best feature is his eyes, which are deep-set and quite striking. His worst features are his mouth and chin. His mouth is bowed like that of a child's and has a somewhat effeminate appearance, although I understand he is thoroughly masculine, in fact, has a deep, resounding voice. His chin is too round and undeveloped although not receding.
>
> Private collection, given to the author by Fritz Lang's widow, Lily Latté, September 1982.

8 Schaefer signed Welles to a two-year, two-picture contract as producer-director-writer-actor in July 1939. Shown around the RKO studio lot, Welles is supposed to have uttered the "train-set" remark cited above.

9 Welles had made a number of home movies when he was seventeen. See Truffaut, "Foreword" to André Bazin, *Orson Welles: A Critical View* (Venice, CA: Acrobat Books, 1991), 9.

10 Charles Higham, *Orson Welles: The Rise and Fall of an American Genius* (London: New English Library, 1986), 167.

11 Higham, *Orson Welles*, 209–10.

12 Looking at his filmography, it seems that the ratio of unfinished projects to completed films is about six-to-one.

13 François Truffaut, *The Films in My Life* (New York: Simon & Schuster, 1978), 286.

14 Richard Corliss, quoted in Frank Mankiewicz, "John Houseman, With Honors; Producer, Actor Joyous Spirit: A Friend's Fond Look Back," *Washington Post*, November 6, 1988.

15   Gregg Toland was the "hottest" photographer in Hollywood at the time he called Welles and asked to work with him; in March he had won the Academy Award for WUTHERING HEIGHTS, and his other recent credits included THE GRAPES OF WRATH and the film in which he had experimented with deep focus, THE LONG VOYAGE HOME.

Pauline Kael, "Raising Kane," in *The Citizen Kane Book* (New York: Bantam Books, 1974), 113.

16   Pauline Kael, "Circles and Squares," *Film Quarterly* 16, 3 (1963): 12–26; Andrew Sarris, "The Auteur Theory and the Perils of Pauline," *Film Quarterly* 16, 4 (1963): 26–33; Sarris responded to Kael's "Raising Kane" in "Films in Focus," *Village Voice*, April 15, 1971.

17   Rick Altman, "Deep-Focus Sound: *Citizen Kane* and the Radio Aesthetic," *Quarterly Review of Film and Video* 15, 3 (December 1994): 25.

18   From radio, and in particular from Welles's peculiar narrational form of radio, *Kane* borrows one convention after another:

- establishment of three separate volume ranges (loud for discursive passages, medium for foreground speech, low for background sound), rather than film's two traditional ranges (medium for foreground, low for background);
- overdetermined use of volume and distance effects for discursive as well as narrative purposes;
- use of spatial effects as transitions between discursive and narrative sections;
- use of sound continuities to link separate scenes ("lightning mixes", cross fades, sound bridges, etc.);
- division of the film into a large number of short, clearly delineated units, each one beginning and ending with a high- (or unusually low-) volume sound event.

"Deep-Focus Sound," 24.

Altman goes on to argue that "much more than separate techniques, however, radio contributes an overall structure to *Citizen Kane*" ("Deep-Focus Sound," 24).

19   Martin Scorsese, quoted in Barbara Leaming, *Orson Welles: A Biography* (New York: Viking Press, 1985), 200.

20   See Chapter 19, "The Love that Never Dies: Francis Ford Coppola and BRAM STOKER'S DRACULA."

21   "When I saw CITIZEN KANE as an adolescent film buff, I was overcome with admiration for the film's main character. I thought he was marvellous, splendid. . . . When I saw it again, after I'd become a critic . . . I discovered its true critical point of view: satire." Truffaut, *The Films in My Life*, 284.

22   See Chapter 11, "Transatlantic Triangulations: William Dieterle and the Warner Bros. Biopics."

23   Truffaut also called it a "cheap Freudian gimmick," "Foreword," 8. See also Chapter 10 for more "in-your-face" Freudian-isms and overpowering mothers.

24   For sound-effects (radio, lightning mixes and sound bridges; cuing of the story) see Altman, "Deep-Focus Sound" and Truffaut, "Foreword," 10.

25   Noël Burch and Jorge Dana list eight of the film's technical innovations: long take/*mise en scène* in depth; exaggerated perspective effect; low angle shots; emphatic back lighting; "arrested" dissolves; overlapping and multi-dimensional dialogue; exaggerated echo effects; rhetorical montage. "Propositions," *Afterimage* 5 (1974), 55. Peter Wollen lists six: "the lightning mixes, the stills which come to life, the complex montages, the elasticity of perspective, the protracted dissolves, the low-angle camera movements." "Introduction to *Citizen Kane*," *Readings and Writings: Semiotic Counter-Strategies* (London: Verso, 1982), 60. David Bordwell lists five: "the diagonal perspectives (with ceilings), the splitting of action into two or more distinct planes, the use of an enlarged foreground plane (close-up or even extreme close-up), the low key lighting, and the persistent frontality." *The Classical Hollywood Cinema: Film Style and Mode of Production to 1960* (London: Routledge, 1985), 347.

26   The London-based magazine *The Cine-Technician* ran a special section in its November 1941–January 1942 issue "Technicians Discuss Citizen Kane" (134–38), with contributions from Anthony Asquith, Roy Boulting, Bernard Knowles, Mutz Greenbaum, Thorold Dickinson, Frank Sainsbury, Jack Cardiff. The contributions reflect just how controversial the film was among professionals.

27   "You have to hate the camera and regard it as a detestable machine, because it should be doing better than what it can do . . . you have to whip it through the movie and not approach it on your knees." Welles, quoted in Leaming, *Orson Welles*, 196.

28   See Bordwell, *The Classical Hollywood Cinema*, 347–49, for an account of the film's innovations in cinematography.

29   The French critic Roger Tailleur, for instance, called LAST YEAR IN MARIENBAD "Citizen Kane in the fourth dimension." *Les Lettres Nouvelles* 16 (July–September 1961): 167.

30   Kerry Brougher uses both Welles' CITIZEN KANE and his LADY FROM SHANGHAI as emblematic for a thesis about the decline of Hollywood producing a new kind of self-reflexivity, which he calls a "Hall of Mirrors," in *Art and Film after 1945: Hall of Mirrors*, ed. Kerry Brougher (Los Angeles: Monacelli, 1996).

31   Apart from Jean Paul Sartre, one of the most quoted celebrity critics of CITIZEN KANE was Jorge Luis Borges, who called it:

a kind of metaphysical detective story. . . . Forms of multiplicity and incongruity abound in the film: the first scenes record the treasures amassed by Kane; in one of the last, a poor woman, luxuriant and suffering, plays with an enormous jigsaw puzzle on the floor of a palace that is also a museum. At the end we realize that the fragments are not governed by any secret unity: the detested Charles Foster Kane is a simulacrum, a chaos of appearances.

Jorge Luis Borges, "Citizen Kane," in *Perspectives on Citizen Kane*, ed. Ronald Gottsman (New York: G.K. Hall, 1966), 54–55.

32   André Bazin, *What is Cinema?* (Berkeley: University of California Press, 1967), 33.

33   Bazin, *What is Cinema?*, 37.

34 Bordwell "Citizen Kane," in *Movies and Methods*, ed. Bill Nichols (Berkeley: University of California Press, 1976), 285.
35 Burch and Dana, "Propositions," 54–55.
36 Burch and Dana, "Propositions," 57.
37 Burch and Dana, "Propositions," 56–57.
38 Wollen "Introduction to *Citizen Kane*," 61.
39 Already in Scott Fitzgerald's *The Great Gatsby* there was the self-realization, the materialism and the American Dream on one side, and on the other the sophisticated social comedy, with the light touch that takes materialism for granted, celebrating its energy rather than worrying about the human cost.
40 This is also noted by Peter Wollen in "Introduction to *Citizen Kane*," 61.

13 The Dandy in Hitchcock

1   This essay was initially given as a lecture in late April 1980, at a conference in Rome, organized by Eduardo Bruno ("Aprile Hitchcock"). Hitchcock was to be the guest of honor; instead, it turned into a wake (he died on April 29). Present were, apart from critics like Peter Wollen, Raymond Bellour, also Tippi Hedren, Ernest Lehman, Farley Granger and Fernando Rey. My paper was published in Italian, in *Per Alfredo Hitchcock*, ed. E. Bruno (Montepulciano: Editore del Grifo, 1981), 93–105; first appearance in English in *The MacGuffin* 14 (November 1994), 15–21.
2   It is this paradox that has made biographical enterprises such as John Russell Taylor's *Hitch: Life and Work of Alfred Hitchcock* (London: Faber and Faber, 1978) and Donald Spoto's *The Dark Side of Genius: The Life of Alfred Hitchcock* (New York: Little, Brown & Company, 1983) at once tempting and troubling explorations of the man "behind" the mask.
3   Robin Wood, *Hitchcock's Films* (London: Studio Vista, 1965), 26.
4   Lindsay Anderson, "Alfred Hitchcock," in *Focus on Hitchcock*, ed. A. LaValley (Englewood Cliffs, NJ: Prentice Hall, 1972), 58.
5   Peter Wollen, "Hitchcock's Vision," in *Cinema* (UK) 3 (June 1969): 2.
6   Wollen, "Hitchcock's Vision," 4.
7   Raymond Durgnat, *The Strange Case of Alfred Hitchcock* (London: Faber and Faber, 1974), 38.
8   Ellen Moers, *The Dandy*, quoted in Martin Green, *Children of the Sun* (New York: Basic Books, 1976), 9.
9   Taylor, *Hitch*, 159.
10 Taylor, *Hitch*, 159.
11 Oscar Wilde, "The Decay of Lying," in *Intentions* (London: James R. Osgood, McIlvaine & Co., 1891), 1.
12 Quoted in François Truffaut, *Hitchcock* (London: Secker & Warburg, 1967), 81.
13 Alfred Hitchcock, "I Wish I Didn't Have to Shoot the Picture," in LaValley, *Focus on Hitchcock*, 24.
14 Quoted in Chris Hodenfield, "Murder by the Babbling Brook," in *Rolling Stone*, July 29, 1976: 26.
15 See, for instance, Peter Noble (ed.), "Index to the Work of Alfred Hitchcock," *Sight and Sound*, 3 (1949):

> I aim to give the public good healthy mental shake-ups. Civilisation has become so screening and sheltering that we cannot experience sufficient thrills at first hand. Therefore, to prevent our becoming sluggish and jellified we have to experience them artificially, and the screen is the best medium for this.

16 Truffaut, *Hitchcock*, 112.
17 Quoted in André Bazin, "Hitchcock vs Hitchcock," in LaValley, *Focus on Hitchcock*, 64.
18 Truffaut, *Hitchcock*, 164.
19 See Robert Mundy, "Another Look at Hitchcock," *Cinema* (UK) 6/7: 11:

> The view of Hitchcock as a Catholic moralist is untenable when I Confess [1952] is compared to Downhill [1927]: public school morality is assigned the same significance as Catholic dogma. The situation where guilt is transferred is what appeals to Hitchcock, and this situation is not necessarily charged with any religious significance. Religion is almost a MacGuffin.

20 Raymond Bellour, "Symbolic Blockage," in *The Analysis of Film* (Bloomington: Indiana University Press, 2001), Chapter 4.
21 "His idea of character is rather primitive." Raymond Chandler, quoted in LaValley, *Focus on Hitchcock*, 102.
22 Quoted in Chris Hodenfield, "Murder by the Babbling Brook," 24.
23 One might add Joseph Cotten as Uncle Charlie in Shadow of a Doubt (1943) and the Right Honourable Charles Adare in Under Capricorn (1949).
24 The suggestion of listing among Hitchcock's dandies one of his female heroines would have to contend, as Ken Mogg, editor of *The MacGuffin* has remarked, with a statement flatly contradicting it: " 'Woman', wrote Baudelaire, 'is the opposite of the dandy. Therefore she must inspire horror.... Woman is *natural*, that is to say, abominable'." *The MacGuffin* 14 (November 1994), 1.
25 Martin Green, *Children of the Sun*, 13.

14 Too Big and Too Close: Alfred Hitchcock and Fritz Lang

1   For an excellent discussion of Hitchcock and German Expressionism, see Sidney Gottlieb, "Early Hitchcock: The German Influence," *Hitchcock Annual*, vol. 8 (1999–2000): 100–130.
2   Cf. the camera descending the elevator in the opening scene of The Last Laugh.

3 Particularly famous is the tracking in and out of the apartment in FRENZY before and after the murder.

4 According to Patrick McGilligan, Hitchcock also admired the sets of DIE NIEBELUNGEN when Lang was away and tore down part of the set to film THE BLACKGUARD. See *Alfred Hitchcock: A Life in Darkness and Light* (New York: HarperCollins, 2003), 63.

5 The prospect of dirty old men frightening young girls is perhaps another Edwardian element in Hitchcock, and also a possible connection to Lang. This motif is archetypally embodied in the mesmerizing, manipulative and sinister lust of Dr. Caligari, in the way this charlatan lecher lures the heroine Jane into his fairground tent, and then has her abducted by his medium Cesare. A tantalizing case for Hitchcock having been influenced by THE CABINET OF DR. CALIGARI is made by Bettina Rosenblatt in "Doubles and Doubts in Hitchcock: The German Connection," in *Hitchcock: Past and Future*, ed. Richard Allen and Sam Ishii-Gonzalès (New York: Routledge, 2004), 37–63. Given Lang's purported role in setting up and almost directing CALIGARI, there would thus be another connection between the two men, however tenuous.

6 François Truffaut, *Hitchcock*, with the collaboration of Helen G. Scott, revised edition (New York: Simon and Schuster, 1984), 131.

7 See Peter Wollen, "*North by Northwest*: A Morphological Analysis" and "Hybrid Plots in *Psycho*," in *Readings and Writings: Semiotic Counter-Strategies* (London: Verso, 1982), 18–33 and 34–39.

8 Hitchcock's pervasive use of the archetypal/mythical structure of the romance genre is fully argued in Lesley Brill, *The Hitchcock Romance* (Princeton: Princeton University Press, 1988).

9 For an elaboration on this point, see my introduction, "The Griffith Legacy in Europe," in *Early Cinema Space Frame Narrative*, ed. Thomas Elsaesser (London: BFI, 1989), 306–13.

10 See Tom Gunning, "Continuity, Non-continuity, Discontinuity: A Theory of Genres of Early Cinema," in Elsaesser, *Early Cinema*, 86–94.

11 A screening at the Gradisca Spring School 2003 suggests that a detailed analysis and comparison of MURDER! and MARY, which differ significantly, would add greatly to our knowledge of Hitchcock and sound, and highlight the different audience expectations inscribed in two versions.

12 Hitchcock was courted by Myron Selznick as early as 1931. See Patrick McGilligan, "Hitchcock Dreams of America," *Hitchcock Annual*, vol. 11 (2002–3): 1–31.

13 It is possible that Hitchcock met Lang at the dinner that Cukor arranged when hosting Luis Buñuel. We know that Lang left the dinner early, so that is why he is not in the photograph of the event. Did Hitchcock arrive late? Why did Lang leave early? If they did meet, this was surely the place. For a brief discussion of this dinner, see McGilligan, *Alfred Hitchcock*, 714–15.

14 Patrick McGilligan, *Fritz Lang: The Nature of the Beast* (London: Faber, 1997), 353.

15 McGilligan, *Fritz Lang*, 357.

16 Sid Gottlieb has noted that Hitchcock considered the property BEYOND A REASONABLE DOUBT before it went to Lang. See "Unknown Hitchcock: The Unrealized Projects," in Allen and Ishii-Gonzalès, *Hitchcock: Past and Future*, 90. Hitchcock was also interested in MINISTRY OF FEAR, but Graham Greene was not; he favored Lang over Hitchcock as we know, but then detested Lang's film for the same reason he disliked Hitchcock.

17 For a detailed analysis of KÄMPFENDE HERZEN, see my "Time, Space and Causality: Joe May, Fritz Lang and the Modernism of the German Detective Film," *Modernist Cultures* 5, 1 (May 2010): 79–105.

18 Quoted in McGilligan, *Fritz Lang*, 281.

19 A possible link between Hitchcock and Lang, according to Richard Allen, could be John Buchan, in whose writings a Mabuse-type villain is very significant. The man with the missing finger in THE 39 STEPS can be seen as a Mabuse figure, but whereas Hitchcock's narrative is always freighted towards the ordinary hero in extraordinary circumstances, Lang's narrative is centered on the Mabuse figure himself. Jean-Luc Godard, in Histoire(s) du Cinéma, at one point links Hitchcock's "mastery of the universe" to a shot from THE TESTAMENT OF DR MABUSE.

20 McGilligan, *Fritz Lang*, 306.

21 Quoted in McGilligan, *Fritz Lang*, 353. More recently, Tom Gunning has discussed the REBECCA/SECRET BEYOND THE DOOR relationship in the context of a broader claim that by this stage, Lang was indeed copying, or shadowing Hitchcock on a regular basis. See *The Films of Fritz Lang: Allegories of Vision and Modernity* (London: BFI, 2000), 343–48.

22 Walter Metz, "While Lang Criticism Sleeps: Authorship, Canonicity, and Historicizing Film Studies," *Revisiting Fritz Lang* panel, SCS conference, San Diego, 1998.

23 See the Fritz Lang catalog, published by the Kinemathek Berlin, on occasion of the Berlin Film Festival 2001 Lang Retrospective.

24 Patrick McGilligan has begun to unearth material that sheds light on Hitchcock's politics, at least during the 1930s while he was still in England. See *Alfred Hitchcock: A Life in Darkness and Light* (New York: HarperCollins, 2003), 158.

25 Pascal Bonitzer, "Partial Vision: Film and the Labyrinth," trans. Fabrice Ziolkowski, *Wide Angle* 4, 4 (1981): 56–63.

26 These examples were first suggested and elaborated by Walter Metz "While Lang Criticism Sleeps."

27 Hitchcock, too, had a tendency, as evidenced in the interviews with Truffaut, to explain the occasional box-office failure of his films with a complaint about unsuitable or wooden actors.

28 Robin Wood, *Hitchcock's Films* (London: Zwemmer, 1965).

29 On the history of Hitchcock's reputation, especially in England and the USA, one can usefully consult Robert Kapsis, *Hitchcock: The Making of a Reputation* (Chicago: University of Chicago Press, 1992).

30 For Hitchcock this was initiated by Claude Chabrol and Eric Rohmer, and then consolidated by Truffaut. For Lang, the key articles were those written by Michel Mourlet, and again, Rohmer.

31 For a recent evaluation of Hitchcock's reputation in France, see James Vest, *Hitchcock in France: The Forging of an Auteur* (Westport: Praeger, 2003).

32 Lotte Eisner, "Notes sur le style de Fritz Lang," *La Revue de cinéma* 5 (February 1947): 22–24.

33 Eric Rohmer:

> Mise en scene was for us a critical concept, not a battle cry. We rejected the word "realisateur" because we were convinced that the work of cinematic mise-en-scene was not a question of realizing a scenario or directing players, but a matter of conception. Mise-en-scene is an unsuitable term insofar as it is derived from the theatre, but correct if we understand by it an organization of space and time. Fritz Lang's films embody the precise example and the most demanding conception of the mise-en-scene.
>
> Quoted in Stephen Jenkins (ed.), *Fritz Lang: The Image and the Look* (London: BFI, 1981), 2.

34 Michel Mourlet wrote in 1959:

> [In Lang] Expressionism was cast into a Euclidian mould which transformed its meaning . . . . So a liturgy was created, based on a purely formal hieratism. Already the principal feature of Lang's later attitude to actors is prefigured in this liturgy, where they are its servants: in other words, turning them into a completely neutralized vehicle for *mise-en-scène* considered as pure movement, whereas the reverse is generally true of other filmmakers, for whom *mise-en-scène* is a means to glorify the actors. Hence Lang's predilection for actors who are more negative than positive, and whose reticence, diffidence or passivity more readily suffers the annihilation imposed on them.
>
> "Fritz Lang's Trajectory," in Jenkins, *Fritz Lang*, 13.

35 Raymond Bellour, "On Fritz Lang," in Jenkins, *The Image and the Look*, 26–37; Noël Burch, "Notes on Fritz Lang's First Mabuse," *Cine-tracts* 13 (Spring 1981): 1–13; Thierry Kuntzel, "The Film Work," *Enclitic* 2, 1 (Spring 1978): 39–64.

36 Noël Burch, "Fritz Lang: German Period," in *Cinema: A Critical Dictionary*, vol. 2, ed. Richard Roud (New York: Viking Press, 1980), 583–99.

37 Bellour, "On Fritz Lang," 29.

38 Laura Mulvey, "Visual Pleasure and Narrative Cinema," *Screen* 16, 3 (1975): 6–18; Stephen Heath, "Narrative Space," *Screen* 17, 3 (Autumn 1976): 68–112; Raymond Bellour "Hitchcock, the Enunciator," *Camera Obscura* 2 (Fall 1977): 66–91, and "Psychosis, Neurosis, Perversion," *Camera Obscura* 3–4 (1979): 104–34; Mary Ann Doane, *The Desire to Desire* (Bloomington: Indiana University Press, 1987); Tania Modleski, *The Women Who Knew Too Much: Hitchcock and Feminist Theory* (New York: Methuen, 1988).

39 Ann E. Kaplan (ed.) *Women in Film Noir* (London: BFI, 1978) and *Fritz Lang: A Guide to Resources* (Englewood Cliffs: G.K. Hall, 1981).

40 Jenkins, *The Image and The Look*; Reynold Humphries, *Fritz Lang, Cinéaste américain* (Paris: Albatros, 1982), trans. by Humphries as *Fritz Lang: Genre and Representation in His American Films* (Baltimore: Johns Hopkins University Press, 1989).

41 For a more extended assessment, see my review essay of McGilligan's book, under the title "Fritz Lang: Traps for the Mind and Eye," *Sight & Sound* (July–August 1997): 28–30.

42 Initiated in part by the Fritz Lang retrospective in 2000, organized through the British Film Institute, which commissioned Tom Gunning's monograph on Lang, and also published two BFI Classics on M (Anton Kaes) and METROPOLIS (Thomas Elsaesser), there has been a revival of interest in Lang. For reasons argued in the present essay, it remains to be seen, however, whether this will give the broader agendas of film studies a new direction, in the way Hitchcock did and still does.

43 See Raymond Bellour, "Pourquoi Lang pourrait devenir préférable à Hitchcock," *Trafic* 41 (2002): 163–72.

44 Patrick McGilligan, *Fritz Lang, the Nature of the Beast* and *Hitchcock: A Life in Darkness and Light*.

45 Slavoj Žižek (ed.), *Everything you Wanted to Know about Lacan but were Afraid to Ask Hitchcock* (London: Verso, 1992).

46 Jure Mikuz and Zdenko Vrdlovec, *Fritz Lang* (Ljubljana: Kinoteka Slovenska, 1990).

47 For illustrations of these figures, see Heide Schönemann, *Fritz Lang Filmbilder Vorbilder* (Berlin: Hentrich 1992).

48

> Hitchcock as the theoretical phenomenon that we have witnessed in recent decades—the endless flow of books, articles, university courses, conference panels—is a postmodern phenomenon par excellence. It relies on the extraordinary transference his work sets in motion: [his] elevation into a God-like demiurge . . . is simply the transferential relationship where Hitchcock functions as the "subject supposed to know".
>
> Žižek, "Introduction: Alfred Hitchcock, or, the Form and Its Historical Mediation," in *Everything You Wanted to Know About Lacan*, 10.

49 The issue of Hitchcock and deconstruction has in the meantime received its own book-length study: Christopher Morris, *The Hanging Figure: On Suspense and the Films of Alfred Hitchcock* (Westport, CT: Greenwood Press, 2002).

50 I have tried to look at the German Lang within such a triple perspective in my chapter on Lang in *Weimar Cinema and After: Germany's Historical Imaginary* (London: Routledge, 2000), 145–94.

51 The *Revue belge du cinéma* devoted an entire issue to the close up (10, Winter 1984/85), as did *Iris*, with a special number on "The Kuleshov Effect" (*Iris* 12, 1991).

52 Pascal Bonitzer "Le gros plan obscene," in Philippe Dubois (ed.), "Gros plan," *Revue belge du cinéma*, 10 (Winter 1984/85): 19–44.

53 For an illuminating essay on Hitchcock in this respect, see Joe McElhaney, "The Object and the Face: *Notorious*, Bergman and the Close-Up," in Allen and Ishii-Gonzalès, *Hitchcock: Past and Future*, 64–84.

54 One recalls the Hitchcock punch line in his explanation of the MacGuffin: ". . . but there are no lions in the Scottish highlands"—"then this is no MacGuffin." More recently, there have been attempts to show that Hitchcock's films, too, can be read as MacGuffins at the macro- as well as the micro-level (see Morris, *The Hanging Figure*). This would support my point in extending Žižek's analysis of Hitchcock to Lang: that the similarities/differences between the two directors

are also the result of the directors' function as mirrors of contemporary concerns, currently at the interface of film and philosophy.

55 Jacques Rivette, "La Main," *Cahiers du cinéma*, 76 (November 1957), 48–51. Sabrina Barton has written on "Hitchcock and Hands," *Hitchcock Annual*, vol. 9 (2000–1): 47–72, briefly mentioning Lang.

56 Thomas Pynchon, *Gravity's Rainbow* (New York: Bantam Books, 1972), 674.

57 Pynchon, *Gravity's Rainbow*, 674.

58 Brigitte Peucker discusses the close-up and the cut in terms of violence in "The Cut of Representation: Painting and Sculpture in Hitchcock," in *Alfred Hitchcock: Centenary Essays*, ed. Richard Allen and Sam Ishii-Gonzalès (New York: BFI, 1999), 141–58.

59 Lang's care for the specificity of his social world in Dr Mabuse is matched by his attention to detail, the carefully chosen decor in each of the settings. Close-ups highlight the planting/discovering/misplacing of clues: letters, notes, handkerchiefs, attaché cases, keys wrapped in balls of wool: a world of objects full of hidden significance, with close ups making them not better identifiable but more mysterious.

60 Hitchcock is here quoting himself, since an even more striking example of this effect occurs in Murder! What is remarkable about Frenzy is that such a trick, typical of the early sound period, should be invoked nostalgically almost forty years later, proving how attached Hitchcock was to the cinema of the early period.

61 "In His Bold Gaze My Ruin is Writ Large," in *Everything You Wanted to Know about Lacan*, 224. It is his gloss on Freud's concept of *Nachträglichkeit*, or "deferred action."

62 Sid Gottlieb has coined the term "perspectival chain" to describe Hitchcock's recurrent presentation of "a series of observers watching observers finally watching someone who cannot return this compounded gaze." See "Kissing and Telling in Hitchcock's Easy Virtue," *Hitchcock Annual*, vol. 1 (1992), 25.

63 Richard Allen has pointed out (in a letter to the author) that this is indeed a difference between Lang and Hitchcock, one that makes Stanley Kubrick's much-noted coldness (because he also gives the viewer the sense of having been had) similar to that of Lang:

> I don't think "being had" is characteristic of Hitchcock (he regretted "having had" the spectator in Sabotage). The difference is that Hitchcock characteristically lets the spectator in on the superiority he has over the character (the play of subjective and objective). For a while we know but Marion doesn't that she is being watched by the cop in *Psycho*. Hitchcock doesn't laud it over the audience because he also in some sense thinks of himself as an audience member.

See also Susan Smith's analysis of Sabotage in *Hitchcock: Suspense, Humour and Tone* (London: BFI, 2000), 1–15.

64 For a similar point, see "In His Bold Gaze My Ruin is Writ Large," 218, 242.

65 The most notable complement of the extreme close-up in Lang is the dissolve, which also often makes his image illegible as well as impossible to place in its temporal sequence.

66 Truffaut, *Hitchcock*, 203.

67 See in this regard Gilles Deleuze on Hitchcock, in *The Movement Image* (Minneapolis: University of Minnesota Press, 1986), 200–5.

68 If this suggests that vision is not necessarily what is at stake in such forms of allegorizing self-reference, one needs to remember that vision is also not *not* what is at issue: the aggression towards vision in two of Lang's early admirers, Buñuel and Hitchcock, is well known. Their own poke in the eye, so to speak, might have originated in Lang's Die Niebelungen (Siegfried's sword gouging the Dragon's eye). The motif is elaborately staged in Un Chien Andalou, which is itself parodied by the fried-egg of To Catch a Thief, before descending into the metaphysical horror of Janet Leigh's eye metaphorically draining into the bathtub plug-hole of Psycho.

69 "In His Bold Gaze My Ruin is Writ Large," 257.

15 Robert Altman's *Nashville*: Putting on the Show

1 Paul Gardner, "Altman Surveys Nashville and Sees Instant America," *New York Times*, June 13, 1976, II, 26.

2 "Has there ever been another director who failed at the box office so often, and so regularly? Most Hollywood directors don't survive one flop, let alone twenty-five. But Altman the gambler, the schemer, kept finding ways to make films." Nathaniel Rich, "The Gambler," *New York Review of Books* 57, 4 (March 11, 2010): www.nybooks.com/articles/archives/2010/mar/11/the-gambler-3/ (last accessed October 25, 2010).

3 For a symptomatic reading of these two films, as the recto and verso of the US Zeitgeist and its ideology at this point in time, see J. Hoberman, "*Nashville* Contra *Jaws* or 'The Imagination of Disaster' Revisited," in *The Last Great American Picture Show: New Hollywood Cinema in the 1970s*, ed. Thomas Elsaesser, Alexander Horwath, and Noel King (Amsterdam: Amsterdam University Press, 2004), 195–222.

4 Rich, "The Gambler."

5 See Virginia Wright Wexman and Gretchen Bisplinghoff, *Robert Altman: A Guide to References and Resources* (Boston: G.K. Hall, 1984), and the listing of articles (only up to 1999) at www.filmreference.com/Films-My-No/Nashville.html. The 25th anniversary in 2000 produced another slew of books and articles, including a survey by Ray Sawhill, "A Movie called 'Nashville,'" *Salon*, June 27, 2000.

6 We used an 8-track system and it's really unmixing rather than mixing sound. We'd just put microphones on all the principals . . . [and] they all go down on different tracks, pretty much the way music is done today. And in our musical sequences we had an additional 16 tracks.
    Altman quoted in Connie Byrne and William O. Lopez, "*Nashville*," *Film Quarterly* 29, 2 (Winter 1975–76), 15.

7 "Nashville is one of the great examples of why 'dated' is sometimes impotent criticism to level at a movie. This one was made to be dated, and as such it is a brilliant satire of America immediately prior to the Bicentennial. It is a movie about the moment, but the moment lives on." Matthew Kennedy, "The Nashville Chronicles: The Making of Robert Altman's Masterpiece", *Bright Lights Film Journal* 32 (April 2001): www.brightlightsfilm.com/32/nashville.php (last accessed October 25, 2010).

8 Altman has been credited with having predicted—and accused of having inspired—the assassination of John Lennon five years later. See the director's response in an interview included in the 2000 DVD release, also cited verbatim on the film's Wikipedia page: http://en.wikipedia.org/wiki/Nashville_%28film%29 (last accessed August 10, 2010).

9 Virginia Wright Wexman "The Rhetoric of Cinematic Improvisation," *Cinema Journal* 20, 1 (Autumn 1980): 29–41.

10 "Altman's storytelling is so clear in his own mind, his mastery of this complex wealth of material is so complete, that we're never for a moment confused or even curious. We feel secure in his hands, and apart from anything else, 'Nashville' is a virtuoso display of narrative mastery." Roger Ebert, "Nashville" (1975): http://rogerebert.suntimes.com/apps/pbcs.dll/article?AID=/19750101/REVIEWS/501010346/1023

11 Almost as famous as the film is Pauline Kael's gushingly enthusiastic, but perceptive pre-release review in the *New Yorker*, which apparently irritated many industry professionals on the West Coast, unless it merely made them envious. Pauline Kael, "The Current Cinema," *New Yorker*, March 3, 1975. For more on the Broadway-to-Hollywood generation, see Chapter 12 on Orson Welles and Citizen Kane.

12 See my "Pathos of Failure: Notes on the Unmotivated Hero," *Monogram* 6 (October 1975): 13–19 (reprinted in this volume, see Chapter 17).

13 Thomas Elsaesser, "Ou finit le spectacle?" *Positif* (Paris) 197 (September 1977): 23–27.

14 The term had made its entry a few years earlier, with Guy Debord's manifesto *La Société du spectacle*, first published in 1967 and translated into English in 1970 and 1977 (Detroit: Black & Red, 1977).

15 It is a musical. . . . It is a docudrama about the Nashville scene. It is a political parable, written and directed in the immediate aftermath of Watergate. . . . It tells interlocking stories of love and sex, of hearts broken and mended. And it is a wicked satire of American smarminess.

Roger Ebert, review of *Nashville* DVD (Paramount), *Chicago Sun Times*, August 6, 2000: http://rogerebert.suntimes.com/apps/pbcs.dll/article?AID=/20000806/REVIEWS08/8060301/1023 (last accessed August 10, 2010).

16 "Country music, like much of our popular culture, feeds on contradictions—extremes of long-suffering and self-indulgence, mildness and brutality, piety and hedonism, discipline and misrule." Roy P. Clark, "Unbuckling the Bible Belt," *New York Times*, July 6, 1976, E: 12. Cited also by Roger B. Rolin, "Robert Altman's *Nashville*: Popular Film and the American Character," *South Atlantic Bulletin* 42, 4 (November 1977): 50.

17 [Nashville] is, in one significant respect, a popular film *about* popular film and about popular culture in general, though, paradoxically, it implies that popular film is less popular, less central to popular culture, than such media as television, radio, and records. However, as a film, Nashville also bridges the gap between popular and "elite" culture by being at once an entertainment and a formidably artistic metaphor for nothing less than the United States of America in the latter quarter of the twentieth century.

Rolin, "Robert Altman's *Nashville*," 41.

18 Michel Ciment, "Jouer avec Altman: Rencontres avec Ronee Blakley et Keith Carradine," *Positif* 176 (December 1975): 45–49.

19 For family melodramas in the tragic mode during the 1970s, the central reference is Francis Coppola's Godfather II (1974), which, in the genre of the gangster film, details the corrosive effects of capitalism—as well as show business—on the family and on gender roles.

20 John Marks, "Molecular Biology in the Work of Deleuze and Guattari," *Paragraph* 29, 2 (July 2006), 81.

21 At the airport arrival scene, Altman prominently features the presence of the local TV news, to which his own camera provides the counterpoint. While the TV camera pans left to anticipate some action, Altman's camera leisurely sweeps to the right, in a movement that commands attention as it takes control, putting the rival in the junior place.

22 Jonathan Rosenbaum, "Improvisations and Interactions in Altmanville," *Sight & Sound* 44, 2 (Spring 1975), 91.

23 For a detailed discussion of Altman, Nashville and improvisation, see Wexman, "The Rhetoric of Cinematic Improvisation."

24 Geraldine Chaplin, who plays Opal, remembers the first day on the set: "Altman said, 'Have you brought your scripts?' We said yes. He said, 'Well, throw them away. You don't need them.'" Cited by Rich, "The Gambler," from Mitchell Zuckoff, *Robert Altman: The Oral Biography* (New York: Knopf, 2010).

25 Michael Henry, "La Palette de l'action painter," *Positif* 166 (February 1975): 3–7.

26 Altman, in Byrne and Lopez, "*Nashville*," 15.

27 As Buck Henry observed: "An Altman set was different because everyone felt they were collaborating—of course they weren't." Quoting this line, Nathaniel Rich (in "The Gambler") concludes: "The deepest contradiction with Altman lies in this disparity between the spontaneous, anarchic feel of his films and the rigorous planning that produced them."

28 Robert Benayoun has compared Altman with Kurt Vonnegut, Jr., in an important article, "Altman, USA," *Positif* 176 (December 1975): 32. Vonnegut in turn has called Nashville "a spiritual inventory of America, frank and honest." "Nashville," *Vogue* 165 (June 1975), 103.

29 See Michel Ciment's interview in *Positif* 166 (February 1975), with Carradine and Blakley, from which the remarks here attributed to them are taken.

30   Commercially the biggest problem with the film is that it doesn't have a shark. So nobody really knows except by word of mouth. . . . And you say What's it about? And, well, you can't answer that. So that's the problem every time you do a film that doesn't have an absolute, one focal point.

Altman, in Byrne and Lopez, "*Nashville*," 13.

31   To a considerable extent, Altman resists [the] temptation [of satire], electing to strive for something that is far more difficult, more ambitious, and in the end more humane—a depiction of our national character that is as comprehensive as one movie will allow, employing a variety of points of view ranging from the satiric to the sympathetic.

Rolin, "Robert Altman's *Nashville*," 42.

32   *The Nashville Banner* ran a big front-page headline saying "Altman's *Nashville* Down on Nashville".—[W]e had a screening before we opened in New York for the people in Nashville who contributed to the film. They had a lot of press down there, but it didn't amount to very much. The musicians like it. Some people thought it was too long. Some people thought that the music was not authentic, and some thought it was. It was kind of a bore.

Altman, in Byrne and Lopez, "*Nashville*," 16.

For more on NASHVILLE in Nashville, see Jan Stuart, *The Nashville Chronicles: The Making of Robert Altman's Masterpiece* (New York: Simon & Schuster, 2000).

33   There is still some uncertainty as to whether NASHVILLE was considered by the industry a success or not. Altman claims that it was the first of his films since M*A*S*H to make him any money, but Hollywood producers seem to have thought otherwise: "Originally I came out here with a script with a lot of scenes in it and a lot of characters. A former head of Columbia, who was the producer I was talking to at the time, said, 'Oh, that's very Nashvilleian'. And I said, 'Oh, great!' I took it as a positive, not knowing he meant it as a negative." Scott MacDonald, "Hollywood Insider-Outsider: An Interview with Chuck Workman," *Film Quarterly* 57, 1 (Autumn 2003), 7.

34   Michael Henry, "Altmanscope (sur le plateau de 'Nashville')," *Positif* 166: 19.

35   The reference here is to Herbert Marcuse's then widely read *One-Dimensional Man: Studies in the Ideology of Advanced Industrial Society* (Boston: Beacon Press, 1964), which argued that the supposed freedoms of liberal democracy disguised the coercion to consume and entailed the unfreedom of neurotic needs. The final song in NASHVILLE, with its refrain "some might say that I ain't free, but it don't worry me" could be taken as an ironic response to Marcuse.

36   "I don't think we've found a format for movies yet. I don't believe the film should be limited to photographing people talking or walking from a car into a building, that kind of stuff we do. It can be more abstract, impressionistic, less linear." Altman, quoted by Chris Holdenfield, "Zoom Lens Voyeur," *Rolling Stone* (July 17, 1975): 31.

37   Altman, in Byrne and Lopez, "*Nashville*," 25.

16 Stanley Kubrick's Prototypes: The Author as World-Maker

1   David Denby, cited in John Baxter, *Stanley Kubrick: A Biography* (New York: Harper Collins, 1997), 233.

2   See the John Alcott and Garret Brown interviews in Mario Falsetto, *Perspectives on Stanley Kubrick* (New York: G.K. Hall, 1996), 214; 273. Note also www.wendycarlos.com/kubrick.html and Frederic Raphael's book about his experience with Kubrick, *Eyes Wide Open* (New York: Ballantine, 1999). Raphael commented in the *Observer*, Sunday, July 11, 1999: "The thing about Kubrick is he was a serious recluse. Whether that was a form of drawing attention by not drawing attention, I don't know. [But] I think he wasn't interested in himself."

3   His official address was Childwickbury Manor, Harpenden, Hertfordshire. Some visitors thought it was grand while others, like Sara Maitland, were surprised rather than impressed: "He lived, rather unromantically between Luton and St Albans, in the house originally built for the founder of Maples furniture store: an Edwardian pomposity set in large grounds." (Sara Maitland, "My Year with Stanley," the *Independent*, March 12, 1999).

4   "His name has become an adjective for over-control. It is said that Kubrick sent his scripts—or pages thereof—around in plastic bags, to be read by the intended recipient and then returned via hovering messengers." David Edelstein, "Stanley Kubrick: Take 1, Take 2," *Slate*, March 8, 1999: www.slate.com/id/1000948/ (last accessed May 20, 2010).

5   "One morning in 1995 the telephone rang. I answered and a gruff voice said, 'This is Stanley Kubrick. Would you like to write a film script for me?' Assuming this was a joking friend, I replied, 'And this is Marilyn Monroe and I've been dead 30 years.' He laughed. It really was Stanley Kubrick." Maitland, "My Year with Stanley." Malcolm McDowell: "Uh, well, Kubrick rang me up one day two years ago; we'd never met. 'Can you come and see me?' he said." Candia McWilliam was another such contributor. She also noted "I could not bear the idea of contact with other people to the degree that Stanley, in his professional life, had it." Candia McWilliam, "Remembering Kubrick," *Guardian*, March 13, 1999.

6   According to Steven Spielberg, Kubrick was a "great communicator. . . . When we spoke on the phone, our conversations lasted for hours. He was constantly in contact with hundreds of people all over the world."

7   These were some of the comments by New York critics about 2001: A SPACE ODYSSEY: "It's a monumentally un-imaginative movie" (Pauline Kael, *Harper's* magazine); "A major disappointment" (Stanley Kaufman, *New Republic*); "Incredibly boring" (Renata Adler, *New York Times*); "A disaster" (Andrew Sarris, *Village Voice*). *Variety* wrote, prior to its release:

2001 is not a cinematic landmark. It compares with but does not best, previous efforts at film science-fiction; lacking the humanity of FORBIDDEN PLANET, the imagination of THINGS TO COME and the simplicity of OF STARS AND MEN. It actually belongs to the technically slick group previously dominated by George Pal and the Japanese.

Quoted in Michel Ciment, *Kubrick, The Definitive Edition* (London: Faber and Faber, 2003), 43.

8   Edelstein, "Stanley Kubrick: Take 1, Take 2."
9   Other extremes and contradictions:

While his movies are thought of as huge (they are certainly hugely expensive), Kubrick's crews were legendarily tiny—in many cases no more than 15 people—and the director himself would go around arranging the lights in the manner not of a deity but of an electrician or plumber. Where most people think of Kubrick's films as having been storyboarded to death—pre-digested—others report that he often wandered his sets with a camera lens, groping for shots on the spot. He spoke in an engaging nebbishy Bronx-Jewish accent that was always a shock to hear—like the voice of the unmasked Wizard of Oz, it didn't belong. On his sets he wore the same outfits; it is said that, like Einstein, he had five or more each lined up on hangers. The act of making choices was clearly excruciating to him; that's why the choices he made are so memorable.

Edelstein, "Stanley Kubrick: Take 1, Take 2."

10   The context is relevant to Kubrick, however short-lived this renaissance should prove to be, and however little he finally participated in it—in contrast to that other expatriate US self-exiled director in Britain, Joseph Losey, if one thinks of his collaboration with Harold Pinter.
11   See Joseph Gelmis, "Interview with Kubrick," in *Perspectives on Stanley Kubrick*, ed. Mario Falsetto (New York: G.K. Hall, 1996), 29–32, and a chapter in John Baxter's biography.
12   See David A. Cook, *Lost Illusions. American Cinema in the Shadow of Watergate and Vietnam, 1970–1979* (Berkeley: California University Press, 2002).
13   "I received hundreds and hundreds of phone calls and thousands of faxes [during our 30-year collaboration]. I guess you could say he was unrelenting." Terry Semel, at the Warner Brothers Kubrick memorial service.
14   See Alexander Walker, *Hollywood UK: The British Film Industry in the Sixties* (New York: Stein and Day, 1974).
15   Roland Barthes, "The Death of the Author" (1968), in *Image, Music, Text*, ed. and trans. Stephen Heath (New York: Hill & Wang, 1977) and Peter Wollen, "The Auteur Theory," in *Signs and Meaning in the Cinema* (London: Secker & Warburg, 1969), 74–115.
16   Dennis Bingham highlights this aspect in "The Displaced Auteur—A Reception History of THE SHINING," in Falsetto, *Perspectives on Stanley Kubrick*, 284–306.
17   "Ten feature motion pictures, each one totally different from the others in both content and style. He has never twice made the same film." John Alcott, in Falsetto, *Perspectives on Stanley Kubrick*, 124.
18   Fredric Jameson, "Historicism in *The Shining*" (1981), in *Signatures of the Visible* (New York: Routledge, 1990), 82–83.

19   Is it ungrateful to long from time to time for something both more ugly and less proficient or expert, more home-made and awkward, than those breathtaking expanses of sunlit leaf-tracery, those big screen flower-bowls of an unimaginably intense delicacy of hue, that would have caused the Impressionists to shut up their paint boxes in frustration?

Jameson, "Historicism in *The Shining*," 83.

20   Jameson, "Historicism in *The Shining*," 82, 83.

21   After an initial bout of work on AI with Aldiss in the early 70s, it was shelved, partly in response to *Star Wars*. So The Aryan Papers was the frontrunner after Kubrick finished *Full Metal Jacket* in 1987. "Kubrick always wanted to do a film on the Holocaust, but he never got a good script," says Harlan. He had tried to commission an original screenplay from the novelist Isaac Bashevis Singer (who turned it down on the grounds that he knew nothing about the Holocaust), before settling on an adaptation of the novel *Wartime Lies*, by Lewis Begley. "We were very committed to do this film," Harlan recalls. "We had done enormous amounts of research and preparation, but there came a point when he and Warner boss Terry Semel decided it would be better to do AI first. It had to do with SCHINDLER'S LIST," he said. "It was such a good film and so successful, and Stanley's film would have come out about a year later. He'd already had this experience with FULL METAL JACKET, which came out the year after PLATOON, and that hurt us, there's no question about it." So in 1995, The Aryan Papers was abandoned and Kubrick returned to *AI*.

Steve Rose, "Kubrick, Spielberg and the AI project," *Guardian*, May 5, 2000.

22   Candia McWilliam, *Guardian*, March 13, 1999.
23   James Joyce, *A Portrait of the Artist as a Young Man* (New York: Huebsch, 1916), Chapter 5.
24   Kubrick Interview, *Observer*, December 4, 1960.
25   See Robert Hughes, "The Décor of Tomorrow's Hell," *Time Magazine*, December 27, 1971.
26   "An obituary in the *New York Times* used the word *cold* three times, and for good measure added *chilly, icy, bleak*, and *grim*. Kubrick the Cold is a cliché that cropped up in the columns of Pauline Kael and now serves as a comfy sofa for those who don't want to deal with Kubrick's ambition." Alex Ross, "A Tribute to Stanley Kubrick," *Slate* March 8, 1999: www.slate.com/id/1000948/ (last accessed May 20, 2010).
27   Frederic Raphael noted in *Eyes Wide Open*: "Stanley was so determined to be aloof and unfeeling that my heart went out to him. Somewhere along the line he was still the kid in the playground who had been no one's first choice to play with." The latter may or may not have been the case, but the "cold persona" evidently only begins (and ends) as an aesthetic construct, if this "kid" becomes an artist.

28 See Helmut Lethen, *Cool Conduct* (Berkeley: University of California Press, 2002), whose book identifies this "cold persona" as a "survival strategy" among some prominent writers, philosophers and artists of the post-war (WWI) generation in Germany.

29 To briefly recall the story: a gang of violent suburban thugs, led by the charismatic, but wholly a-moral Alex, spend their evenings routinely raping, beating up and murdering whoever happens to cross their path. Betrayed by one of his Droogs, Alex is put in prison, where he is selected as a guinea-pig in a new type of behaviorist aversion therapy, the so-called Ludovico Treatment. He is released from prison, but every time he now hears Beethoven's Ninth Symphony or is confronted with an act of aggression, he cannot retaliate but gets physically sick. This makes him incapable of dealing with the day-to-day reality of post-urban life, with its routine violence and aggression. Eventually, after the intervention of the prison chaplain, the aversion therapy is reversed, and Alex is once more free to give unbridled reign to his ultra-violence.

30 Slavoj Žižek devotes part three of *The Ticklish Subject* ("Whither Oedipus"), to "The Demise of Symbolic Efficiency." There, he details instances of the falling apart of the double paternal function, from False Memory Syndrome to the Moral Majority Promise Keepers, from the obsession with code-crackers and hackers, to the reason why there is no sex between the protagonists in the *X-files*. Žižek also points to the return of what he calls "ferocious Superego figures," with their command to enjoy!, or their own display of obscene enjoyment, either by inhibiting male identity formation under the sign of consumerist self-indulgence, or unleashing infantile rage or "tightening the Master-Slave matrix of passionate attachments," as in films that try to re-inscribe the non-phallic father, such as LA VITA E BELLA. Slavoj Žižek, *The Ticklish Subject* (London: Verso, 2000), 374.

31 Gilles Deleuze, "Postscript on the Societies of Control," *October* 59 (1992), 4.

32 Deleuze, "Postscript," 4.

33 Perhaps only Kubrick himself was fully aware of the double-edged praise in a sentence like "Stanley Kubrick does not simply create films—he creates entire *worlds*." "Photographing Stanley Kubrick's BARRY LYNDON," *American Cinematographer* (March 1976), 268.

17 The Pathos of Failure: Notes on the Unmotivated Hero

1 First published in *Monogram* 6 (October 1975): 13–19. The essay was originally intended as the second part of "Why Hollywood?" (*Monogram* 1 [April 1971]: 4–10). Appearing with a four-year delay, the context of the argument had slightly changed, and it was now, together with an essay by my co-editor Mark LeFanu, the thematic centerpiece of an issue devoted to "Spectacle, Gesture, Violence." LeFanu's article dealt mostly with the turn to history in (recent) European cinema, but towards the end picked up also on changes in the American cinema, which I had taken as my subject. In the following, I cite from LeFanu in the text and the footnotes, in memory of our conversations when preparing the issue, which was to be our last.

2   The "discovery" over the last ten years of Sirk and Fuller and other directors like them has been largely the discovery of [a] secret discourse which although not exactly subversive is nevertheless the clue on the level of form to these movies' ambiguous message. They are disquieting where they should be conformist, intransigent where they seem to offer the easy option.

Mark LeFanu, "Pageants of Violence," *Monogram* 6 (October 1975), 12.

3 "The function of narrative in American pictures is exactly to translate the inner pulsion of these men into formal and graspable signs by giving it a goal. Thus it provides the framework in which the asceticism of *gesture* can be substituted for that abundance of *speech*." LeFanu, "Pageants of Violence," 12.

4 Paul Schrader, himself a director of the New Hollywood, asked why he felt attracted to European films, replied: "in Hollywood movies the hero has a problem, in the European cinema, he faces a dilemma." TV broadcast, "Pictures of Europe," *Channel Four*, April 25, 1990.

5 LeFanu, "Pageants of Violence," 12.

6 LeFanu, "Pageants of Violence," 12.

7 "The loss of confidence in the way things are going at present politically, is a signal to re-examine the roots of the disaster in the past; or, if not to examine them, to forget them in the revisionist history which forgives everything by seeing it through the eyes of a child." LeFanu, "Pageants of Violence," 12.

18 *Auteur* Cinema and the New Economy Hollywood

1 David Thomson, "Who Killed the Movies," *Esquire* (December 1996), 56–63; William Goldman, *The Big Picture: Who Killed Hollywood* (New York: Applause 2000); and Peter Bart, *Who Killed Hollywood . . . and Put the Tarnish on Tinseltown?* (Los Angeles: Renaissance Books, 1999). See also Noel King's "'The Last Good Time We Had': Remembering the New Hollywood Cinema," in *The Last Great American Picture Show*, ed. Thomas Elsaesser, Alexander Horwath and Noel King (Amsterdam: Amsterdam University Press, 2004), 19–36.

2 See Jonathan Rosenbaum, "New Hollywood and the Sixties Melting Pot," in *The Last Great American Picture Show*, 131–54. For J. Hoberman, see "How the Western Was Lost," in his *The Magic Hour* (Philadelphia: Temple University Press, 2003), 128. Roy Grundmann has researched a similar encounter in "Subtext, Context, Intertext: Andy Warhol's Midnight Movie Hustlers and Hollywood's MIDNIGHT COWBOY" (unpublished manuscript, 2003).

3 Tom Schatz, "The New Hollywood," in *Film Theory Goes to the Movies*, ed. J. Collins, H. Radner, A. Preacher Collins (New York: Routledge, 1993), 10.

4   For a journalist's account, based on interviews conduced twenty years later, see Peter Biskind, *Easy Riders Raging Bulls—How the Sex "n" Drugs "n" Rock "n" Roll Generation Saved Hollywood* (New York: Simon & Schuster, 1998).

5   Beverly Walker, "Go West Young Man," *Sight & Sound* 41, 4 (Winter 1971/72): 22–25.

6   André Bazin, "On the *politique des auteurs*," in *Cahiers du cinéma: The 1950s*, ed. Jim Hillier (London: RKP, 1985), 257–58.

7   See the introduction by Steve Neale and Murray Smith in their *Contemporary Hollywood Cinema* (London: Routledge, 1998), xiv–xxii, and my chapter "Classical/Post-classical Narrative (DIE HARD)" in *Studying Contemporary American Film*, Thomas Elsaesser and Warren Buckland (London: Arnold, 2002), 26–79.

8   Peter Bogdanovich, *Who the Devil Made It* (New York: Alfred A. Knopf, 1997), 8.

9   See Jonathan Rosenbaum, *Moving Places: A Life at the Movies* (New York: Harper & Row, 1980); and *Midnight Movies* (with J. Hoberman) (New York: Harper & Row, 1983).

10 Rosenbaum, "New Hollywood and the Sixties Melting Pot," in *The Last Great American Picture Show*, 129–49.

11 See Dennis Giles, "The Outdoor Economy: A Study of the Contemporary Drive-In," *Journal of the University Film and Video Association* 35, 2 (Spring 1983): 66–76.

12 Douglas Gomery, *Shared Pleasures: A History of Movie Presentation in the United States* (London: BFI, 1992); and Tino Balio, "'A major presence in all of the world's important markets': The globalization of Hollywood in the 1990s," in *Contemporary Hollywood Cinema*, ed. Steve Neale and Murray Smith, 58–73.

13 Justin Wyatt, *High Concept: Movies and Marketing in Hollywood* (Austin: University of Texas Press, 1994).

14 Peter Bogdanovich talks about the change of generations as a baton relay race (*Who the Devil Made It*, 13). He is candid about the mother and father substitutes, that is, the generation paradigm, especially when filling in his own background in theater and acting, in order to counter the myth that he was just a writer switching to directing, like the French critics-turned-directors of the *nouvelle vague* (12–16).

15 Maitland McDonagh, "The Exploitation Genre, or: How Marginal Movies Came in from the Cold," in *The Last Great American Picture Show*, 107–30.

16 Jon Lewis, *Whom God Wishes to Destroy: Francis Coppola and the New Hollywood* (Durham, NC: Duke University Press, 1995).

17 See the sections devoted to the individual directors in David Cook's *Lost Illusions. American Cinema in the Shadow of Watergate and Vietnam 1970–1979* (New York: Charles Scribner's Sons, 2000).

18 Murray Smith, "Theses on the Philosophy of Hollywood History," in Neale and Smith, *Contemporary Hollywood Cinema*, 14–15.

19 See Corman's ghosted, boastfully titled autobiography: Roger Corman (with Jim Jerome), *How I Made a Hundred Movies in Hollywood and Never Lost a Dime* (New York: Delta Books, 1990).

20 Michael Storper, "Flexible Specialisation in Hollywood: A Response to Aksoy and Robins," *Cambridge Journal of Economics* 17 (1993): 479–84: also quoted in Smith, in *Contemporary Hollywood Cinema*, 9.

21 Smith, quoting Nicholas Garnham, in *Contemporary Hollywood Cinema*, 9.

22 Howard Hampton, "Everyone Knows This is Nowhere: The Uneasy Ride of Hollywood and Rock," in *The Last Great American Picture Show*, 249–66.

23 "Three American LPs," in Wim Wenders, *Emotion Pictures* (London: Faber and Faber, 1992).

24 David Cook, *Lost Illusions: American Cinema in the Shadow of Watergate and Vietnam, 1970–1979* (New York: Charles Scribner's Sons, 2000), xv–xvi.

25 Robin Wood, *Hollywood from Vietnam to Reagan* (New York: Columbia University Press, 1986; revised expanded edition, 2003); Andrew Britton, "Blissing Out: The Politics of Reaganite Entertainment," *Movie* 31/32 (Winter 1986): 1–42. For reflections on 1980s movies by notable cultural critics, see Fredric Jameson, "Nostalgia for the Present," *South Atlantic Quarterly* 88, 2 (Spring 1989), 517–37; and Fred Pfeil, "Plot and Patriarchy in the Age of Reagan," *Another Tale to Tell* (New York: Verso, 1990), 227–42.

26 Alexander Horwath, "A Walking Contradiction (Partly Truth and Partly Fiction)," in *The Last Great American Picture Show*, 83–106. Robin Wood, "An Introduction to the American Horror Film," in *Movies and Methods II*, ed. Bill Nichols (Berkeley: University of California Press, 1985), 196–220.

27 Jim Hoberman, "NASHVILLE contra Jaws, or 'The Imagination of Disaster'," in *The Last Great American Picture Show*, 195–222.

28 Fredric Jameson, "Totality as Conspiracy," in *The Geopolitical Aesthetic* (Bloomington: Indiana University Press, 1995), 9–86.

29 See James Bernardoni, *The New Hollywood: What the Movies did with the New Freedoms of the Seventies* (Jefferson, NC: McFarland Press, 1991).

30 See Peter Biskind, *Easy Riders Raging Bulls* for a very full account of the sexual mores of the 1970s auteur-film community.

31 Adrian Martin, "Grim Fascination: FINGERS, James Toback and 1970s American Cinema," and Drehli Robnik "Allegories of Post-Fordism in 1970s New Hollywood: Countercultural Combat Films and Conspiracy Thrillers as Genre Recycling," in *The Last Great American Picture Show*, 309–32 and 333–58.

32 Christian Keathley, "Trapped in the Affection Image: Hollywood's Post-Traumatic Cycle," in *The Last Great American Picture Show*, 293–308.

33 See, for instance, Julia Phillips, *You'll Never Eat Lunch In This Town Again* (New York: Signet, 1991).

19 The Love that Never Dies: Francis Ford Coppola and *Bram Stoker's Dracula*

1   Jon Lewis, *Whom God Wishes to Destroy* (Durham, NC: Duke University Press, 1995), 160.

2 The subtitle of *Whom God Wishes to Destroy* is "Francis Coppola and the New Hollywood." See also James Monaco, *American Film Now* (New York: Oxford University Press, 1979).

3 Tom Schatz, "The New Hollywood," in *Film Theory Goes to the Movies*, ed. J. Collins, H. Radner and A. Preacher Collins (London: Routledge, 1993), 8–36.

4 Michael Pye and Lynda Myles, *The Movie Brats* (London: Studio Vista, 1985).

5 Schatz, "The New Hollywood," 26–28.

6 Tino Balio (ed.), *Hollywood in the Age of Television* (Cambridge, MA: Unwyn Hyman, 1990).

7 Justin Wyatt, *High Concept: Movies and Marketing in Hollywood* (Austin: University of Texas Press, 1994).

8 Tim Corrigan, *A Cinema Without Walls: Movies and Culture after Vietnam* (New York: Routledge, 1991).

9 Robin Wood, *Hollywood from Vietnam to Reagan* (New York: Columbia University Press, 1986).

10 Since the mid-seventies, the international film industry has been defined by more economic and productive contention and alteration than coherence. . . . This . . . follows clearly from the uncertainty and instability about the reception of a product that has too many audiences or too vague an audience: an audience that can only be designated, in the jargon of Hollywood producers today, as "fly-overs", a mass of undifferentiated desires that lives below planes moving between Los Angeles and New York City.

Corrigan, *A Cinema Without Walls*, 22–23.

11 See Ien Ang, *Desperately Seeking the Audience* (London: Routledge, 1995).

12 Andrew Higson, "National Cinema: The Competition with Hollywood," *Skrien* 186 (October–November 1992): 50–53.

13 Thomas Elsaesser, "German Postwar Cinema and Hollywood," in *Hollywood and Europe*, ed. D. Ellwood and R. Kroes (Amsterdam: Vrije Universiteit, 1994), 283–302.

14 The boom of allusionism is a legacy of American auteurism, a term that . . . denotes the frenzy for film that seized this country in the 60s and early 70s. Armed with lists from Andrew Sarris and compatible aesthetic theories from Eisenstein, Bazin, Godard and McLuhan, a significant part of the generation raised in the 50s went movie mad and attacked film history. They passionately sought out films they had missed, returned obsessively to old favourites, and tried to classify them all. Among those engaged in this discovery of film history—particularly American film history—were some people who would become filmmakers.

Noël Carroll, "The Future of an Allusion," *October* 21 (1982), 54.

15 Robert Ray, *A Certain Tendency of the Hollywood Cinema* (Princeton: Princeton University Press, 1985), 244.

16 Fredric Jameson, *The Political Unconscious* (London: Methuen, 1981), 207.

17 Chris Hugo, "The Economic Background (of New Hollywood), pt I and II," *Movie* 27/28 (1984): 43–49 and 31/32 (1986): 84–87.

18 Another round of acquisitions began in the early 1990s: the media mergers continue to make headlines, involving Time-Warner, Disney, Turner Broadcasting, Viacom, and in 1995 the foundation of a new studio was announced, SKG DreamWorks, headed by Jerry Katzenberg, Steven Spielberg and David Geffen.

19 Corrigan, *A Cinema Without Walls*; Schatz, "The New Hollywood"; Wyatt, *High Concept*; Lewis, *Whom God Wishes to Destroy*.

20 "I would give anything to have a life like Orson Welles." Quoted in Peter Cowie, *Coppola* (London: Faber, 1990), 222.

21 Cowie, *Coppola*, 43–58.

22 Beverle Houston, "Power and Dis-Integration in the Films of Orson Welles," *Film Quarterly* (Summer 1982): 2.

23 Wood, *Hollywood from Vietnam to Reagan*, 49–50.

24 Michel Chion, *Audiovision: Sound on Screen* (New York: Columbia University Press, 1994).

25 In APOCALYPSE NOW, both times the patrol boat is attacked by Vietcong guerillas, their presence is first indicated by the sound of their guns and arrows, and when they finally are visually located in the image (and noticed by the American soldiers), it is too late to escape: both times a soldier loses his life.

26 Thomas Elsaesser and Michael Wedel, "The Hollow Heart of Hollywood: Sound Space in APOCALYPSE NOW," in *Conrad on Film*, ed. Gene M. Moore (Oxford: Oxford University Press, 1997), 151–75. Some of the material used here is taken from this essay and I gratefully acknowledge Michael Wedel's contribution.

27 Post-classical cinema is associated with East Coast directors like Scorsese, de Palma, Schrader, David Lynch and West Coast directors like Spielberg, Lucas, Coppola (from USC and UCLA film schools). But post-classical films are also directed by Adrian Lyne and Alan Parker, Ridley Scott and Paul Verhoeven, and more recently by Wolfgang Petersen, with Michael Ballhaus, the cameraman on BRAM STOKER'S DRACULA a conspicuous presence: there is thus not only an input from advertising (in which the British excel), but also from continental European cinema talent.

28 See Richard Dyer, "Dracula and Desire," *Sight & Sound* 3, 1 (January 1993): 8–11.

29 Pierre Sorlin, "Ist es möglich, eine Geschichte des Kinos zu schreiben?," *montage a/v* 5, 1 (1996): 27.

30 See Steve Biodrowski, "Coppola's Dracula," *Cinefantastique* 23, 4 (December 1992): 24.

31 Omar Calabrese, "I Replicanti," paper given at the Semiotics Conference 1986 in Urbino.

32 For more on the relation between the female characters and technologies of recording and transmission, see my, "Six degrees of Nosferatu," *Sight & Sound* 11, 2 (February 2001): 12–15.

33 See special issue of *Sight & Sound*, January 1993, especially the review essays by Ian Sinclair and Richard Dyer.

34 The terms used by Raymond Bellour, to describe the functioning of the classical cinema's visual-narrative economy. See Bellour, "The Obvious and the Code," in *Narrative, Apparatus, Ideology*, ed. Philip Rosen (New York: Columbia University Press, 1986), 93–101.

35 In order to have an image you need to have a scene, a certain distance without which there can be no looking, no play of glances, and it is that play that makes things appear or disappear. It is in this sense that I find television

obscene, because there is no stage, no depth, no place for a possible glance and therefore no place either for a possible seduction.

Jean Baudrillard, Baudrillard Live (London: Verso, 1989), 69.

36　This ironic-indulgent stance vis-à-vis film history itself seems to me one difference between Coppola and other practitioners of the multi-media mode in cinema. In Peter Greenaway's experiments with video (e.g. Prospero's Books) or his cinema films, such as The Pillow Book, for instance, one senses the director's conviction that the whole tradition of classical Hollywood is for him an irrelevance, and that the real business of cinema is to finally develop into an art form.

20　The Blockbuster as Time Machine

1　Time Warner Inc., 1989 Annual Report (New York: Time Warner Inc., 1990), 1.
2　The phrase is taken from John Ellis, Visible Fictions: Cinema, Television, Video 2nd edition (New York: Routledge, 1992), 26.
3　Tino Balio, "A major presence in all of the world's important markets," in Contemporary Hollywood Cinema, ed. Murray Smith and Stephen Neale (London: Routledge, 1998), 62.
4　James Schamus, "To the Rear of the Back End: The Economics of Independent Cinema," in Smith and Neale, Contemporary Hollywood Cinema, 91–105.
5　Justin Wyatt, High Concept: Movies and Marketing in Hollywood (Austin: University of Texas Press, 1994), 110–111.
6　Wyatt, High Concept, 22.

21　Auteurism Today: Signature Products, Concept-Authors and Access for All: Avatar

1　Louis Menand, "Gross Points: Is the blockbuster the end of cinema?," New Yorker, February 7, 2005, 85.
2　See Tim Corrigan, A Cinema Without Walls: Movies and Culture After Vietnam (New Brunswick, NJ: Rutgers, 1991); James Naremore, "Authorship and the Cultural Politics of Film Criticism," Film Quarterly 44, 1 (Autumn 1990): 14–23; Dudley Andrew, "The Unauthorized Auteur Today," in Film Theory Goes to the Movies, ed. Jim Collins, Hilary Radner, Ava Preacher Collins (New York: Routledge, 1993), 77–85; Toby Miller and Noel King, "Auteurism in the 1990s," in The Cinema Book, 2nd edition, ed. Pam Cook and Mieke Bernink (London: BFI Publishing, 1999), 311–14.
3　The canonical versions of (and debates around) the auteur theory can be found in John Caughie (ed.), Theories of Authorship (London: Routledge & Kegan Paul, 1981). Many of the original French articles, in translation, are in Jim Hillier (ed.), Cahiers du Cinéma (Cambridge, MA: Harvard University Press, 1985). A more recent attempt to recast the classical versions and extend them to minority filmmakers is David A. Gerstner and Janet Staiger, Authorship and Film (New York: Routledge, 2002).
4　Scott goes on:

> In purely geographic terms, Hollywood proper is a relatively small district lying just to the northwest of downtown Los Angeles. . . . This geographic area is the stage over which the main features of Hollywood as a productive milieu are laid out. At the same time, greater Hollywood, the place, is not simply a passive receptacle of economic and cultural activity, but is a critical source of successful system performance. This recursive relationship between place and industrial performance is a recurrent feature throughout the space-economy of modern capitalism.
> Allen J. Scott, Hollywood: The Place, the Industry (Princeton, NJ: Princeton University Press, 2005), 1.

5　I should explain that I am not including in this list directors such as Gus van Sant, Jim Jarmush, Hal Hartley, Richard Linklater, Terrence Malick, John Waters, Wes Anderson or Todd Haynes: to these and other authors of independent American cinema most of the traditional criteria and definitions of the auteur apply, as they continue to be used in Europe and other parts of the world for art cinema directors or international festival directors. Soderbergh and Spike Lee qualify as special cases, insofar as they tend to alternate between making one film "for the industry" and one film "for themselves": a well-established if oversimplifying distinction that, however, hides as much as it clarifies. See Jerome Christensen, "Spike Lee, Corporate Populist," Critical Inquiry 17, 3 (Spring 1991): 582–95.
6　Jon Lewis, "The Perfect Money Machine(s): George Lucas, Steven Spielberg and Auteurism in the New Hollywood," in Looking Past the Screen: Case Studies in American Film History and Method, ed. Eric Smoodin and Jon Lewis (Durham, NC: Duke University Press, 2007), 61–86 (an earlier version appeared in Film International 1. 1 (January 2003): 12–26).
7　Other directors of this generation, with a consistent (if uneven) body of work would be Brian de Palma (b. 1940), Oliver Stone (b. 1946) and Paul Schrader (b. 1946).
8　See Chapter 19 on Coppola, as well as Jon Lewis, Whom God Wishes to Destroy: Francis Coppola and the New Hollywood (Durham, NC: Duke University Press, 1996).
9　Lewis, "The Perfect Money Machine(s)," 73. He goes on (73–74):

> By embracing high concept filmmaking, Spielberg expressed (according to his critics at least) undue interest in what works and doesn't work with audiences. By seeming to prioritize public relations over personal artistic principles, he effectively snubbed the very filmmaking practice that reviewers, critics and historians idealize. Reviewers and critics and film teachers routinely maintain that certain American filmmakers, ones deserving of the term auteur, transcend the system and make great art.

10　Lewis, "The Perfect Money Machine(s)," 68.

11 Lewis, "The Perfect Money Machine(s)," 68.

12 The term "high concept" was deployed most fully in Justin Wyatt, *High Concept: Movies and Marketing in Hollywood* (Austin; University of Texas Press, 1994). As an example, Wyatt quotes Spielberg: "If a person can tell me the idea in 25 words or less," Spielberg boasted to J. Hoberman in 1985, "it's going to make a good movie. I like ideas, especially movie ideas you can hold in your hand," Wyatt, *High Concept*, 13.

13 See Kristin Thompson, *The Frodo Franchise: The Lord of the Rings and Modern Hollywood* (Berkeley: University of California Press, 2007).

14 For "total entertainment," see Richard Maltby, *Hollywood Cinema*, 2nd edition (Oxford: Basil Blackwell, 2003), 73; Charles R. Acland, *Screen Traffic: Movies, Multiplexes, and Global Culture* (Durham, NC: Duke University Press, 2003), 106; and Paul Grainge, *Brand Hollywood: Selling Entertainment in a Global Media Age* (New York: Routledge, 2008), 175.

15 Lewis, "The Perfect Money Machine(s)," 67–68. He continues (68): "As Fox executive Mark Pepvers reflected in a 1983 *Business Week* article, 'George Lucas created Star Wars with the toy byproducts in mind. He was making much more than a movie.' Indeed, he was. Within its first year *Star Wars*' merchandise accounted for $300 million in revenue."

16 The term "disruptive technology" (in a positive sense) was first introduced by Clayton M. Christensen in 1995, to describe an innovation that changes the nature or impact of a product or service, in ways that force competitors to adapt or reconfigure their business model. See http://en.wikipedia.org/wiki/Disruptive_technology (last accessed March 24, 2011).

17 Lewis quotes Coppola ruefully remarking about Lucas: "If I'm like America, then George was my Japan—he saw what I did wrong and perfected what I did right." Lewis, "The Perfect Money Machine(s)," 82.

18 Lewis, "The Perfect Money Machine(s)," 70.

19 Lewis, "The Perfect Money Machine(s)," 71.

20 By naming Lucas and Spielberg in one breath, one should not overlook the very complex relationship that ties these two directors-producers together and also puts them in competition with each other. On the "sibling rivalry" between Spielberg and Lucas, and how this in turn has shaped important decisions, see Tom Shone, "Lucas vs. Spielberg: The Worst Best Friends in Hollywood," *Slate*, June 14, 2005: www.slate.com/id/2120697/ (last accessed March 25, 2011).

21   As the entertainment market expanded, these corporations began to insist that films be efficiently distributed in a variety of forms and formats to better exploit the vertically and horizontally integrated marketplace. Lucas and Spielberg were the first and best at the very sort of filmmaking designed to succeed under such an economic policy.

Lewis, "The Perfect Money Machine(s)," 86.

22 Gilles Deleuze, "Postscript on the Societies of Control," *October* 59 (Winter 1992), 4.

23 One might quote in this context the well-known medical dictum "ablata causa, tolluntur effectus" (if the cause is taken away, its effect will disappear), but here meaning, "take away the first cause, and the effects can proliferate."

24 Marshall McLuhan, *Understanding Media: The Extensions of Man* (New York: Doubleday, 1964), 23–24.

25 "Remediation" is the term now generally favored for describing McLuhan's "the media is the message." See Jay David Bolter and Richard Grusin, *Remediation: Understanding New Media* (Cambridge, MA: The MIT Press, 2000).

26 The best-known studies of mnemotechnics are Frances A. Yates, *The Art of Memory* (Chicago: University of Chicago Press, 1966) and Mary Carruthers, *The Craft of Thought* (Cambridge: Cambridge University Press, 1998).

27 There is some debate about the correct use of the word franchise in connection with long-running film series, since franchises are usually businesses operated on behalf of another business, which owns the name, recipe and/or branded product or service. But the term movie franchise has entered the language and now refers to an intellectual property whose characters, settings and story-elements give rise to sequels and/or prequels. What distinguishes the franchise from the series is that in the case of the former all manner of ancillary activities are associated with it, such as video game spin-offs, merchandising deals or endorsements, which are licensed for separate exploitation in the way of franchises. Among the most profitable film franchises are LORD OF THE RINGS, HARRY POTTER, STAR WARS, BATMAN, James Bond, INDIANA JONES and PIRATES OF THE CARIBBEAN, with James Bond the longest running.

28 "In conceptual art the idea or concept is the most important aspect of the work. When an artist uses a conceptual form of art, it means that all of the planning and decisions are made beforehand and the execution is a perfunctory affair. The idea becomes a machine that makes the art." Sol LeWitt, "Paragraphs on Conceptual Art," *Artforum* 5, 10 (June 1967): 79–83. Evidently, in Hollywood, the execution is not a "perfunctory affair," but the idea becomes a machine, while the blockbuster is both a continuation of the classical Hollywood movie and an engine to implement decisive shifts of register.

29 Lewis, "The Perfect Money Machine(s)," 86.

30 "The numbers" are the weekly—now often daily—charts of box office receipts, which play such an inordinate role in the self-perception of Hollywood, as well as the media coverage of films even in the general press. See www.the-numbers.com/ (last accessed August 2, 2011).

31 A very similar strategy can be observed in the "making of" film accompanying the 2004 DVD re-edition of SAVING PRIVATE RYAN, where Spielberg elaborates on how his father's home movies from the Korean War inspired him to feature aspects of WWII in virtually every picture he has made.

32 J.D. Connor, "Logorrhea, or, how should we watch a neoclassical Hollywood film?" in Connor, *The Studios after the Studios: Hollywood in the Neoclassical Era, 1970–2005* (forthcoming). Connor also points out that "throughout Spielberg's career, every solicitation of studio concern has been tempered, subverted, even completely undone by his assertion of a particularly broad claim of authorship."

33 The self-reflexivity and self-regulation of Hollywood in the post-Studio era will be dealt with more fully in the concluding, second part of "The Persistence of Hollywood" (Chapter 23).

34 Cameron interview with Syd Field, quoted in "James Cameron—Terminator 2: Judgement Day (Part I)": www.sydfield.com/featured_jamescameron.htm (last accessed August 2, 2011).

35   Cameron went to Fullerton College, where he studied Physics, then English, before dropping out in 1974. It should be said that being a "drop out" is, of course, both *de rigueur* and a badge of honor for some of the USC, UCLA and NYU alumni, not to mention for the "nerds" that founded Microsoft, Apple, Google or Facebook.

36   "James Cameron," Wikipedia: http://en.wikipedia.org/wiki/James_Cameron (last accessed March 29, 2011).

37   In the time between making Titanic and his return to feature films with Avatar, Cameron spent several years creating many documentary films (specifically underwater documentaries), and also co-developed the digital 3-D Fusion Camera System. Described by a biographer as part-scientist and part-artist, Cameron has also contributed to underwater filming and remote vehicle technologies.

                                                                                           "James Cameron," Wikipedia.

38   An overview of identification from a cognitivist perspective can be found at: www.latrobe.edu.au/screeningthepast/20/entranced.html; from a sociological one at: www.aber.ac.uk/media/Students/pjv9801.html; and from an anthropological-narratological one at: www.latrobe.edu.au/screeningthepast/classics/cl0499/jdcl1.html (all last accessed August 2, 2011). See also Thomas Elsaesser and Malte Hagener, *Film Theory: An Introduction Through the Senses* (New York: Routledge, 2010), especially chapters 2 ("Cinema as door: screen and threshold"), 3 ("Cinema as mirror and face") and 4 ("Cinema as eye: look and gaze").

39   See Chapter 9, "Film as System: Or how to Learn to Step through an Open Door," for a more extensive examination of the classical system.

40   Nöel Carroll, "The Future of Allusionism," *October* 20 (Spring 1982): 51–81. Carroll credits (or blames) Roger Corman for this two tier-strategy: "Increasingly Corman's cinema came to be built with the notion of two audiences in mind—special grace notes for insiders, appoggiatura for the cognoscenti, and a soaring, action-charged melody for the rest. In this, he pioneered the two-tiered system," 77.

41   Thomas Elsaesser and Warren Buckland, *Studying Contemporary American Film* (London: Arnold, 2002), 26–79.

42   See for instance, William Empson, *Seven Types of Ambiguity* (London: Chatto & Windus, 1949 [first published in 1930]), one of the most influential books on close textual analysis in literature.

43   Carol Kaesuk Yoon, "Luminous 3D Jungle Is a Biologist's Dream," *New York Times*, January 18, 2010.

44   David Brooks, "The Messiah Complex," *New York Times*, January 7, 2010.

45   Slavoj Žižek, "Return of the natives," *New Statesman*, March 4, 2010.

46   "Dongria Kondh—The Real Avatar: Mine—Story of a Sacred Mountain": www.youtube.com/watch?v=R4tuTFZ3wXQ. The video now has a banner, reading: UPDATE: Victory! The Dongria Kondh have stopped Vedanta from mining their sacred mountain (last accessed March 28, 2011).

47   Non-3D versions of Avatar to be pulled next week, in order to protect the nation's home grown films. The country's censors ruled that the epic had become too dominant and also worried about its effect on audiences, according to reports. . . . Some Chinese bloggers had already said parallels between the plight of the film's Na'vi creatures—who are forced to flee their homes—and Chinese people who have faced the threat of eviction would have raised concerns. One wrote: "For audiences in other countries, such brutal eviction is something outside their imagining. It could only take place on another planet or in China."

                                                                    Izzy Broughton, *Sky News Online*, January 20, 2010.

48   "Bilin Reenacts Avatar Film 12-02-2010": www.youtube.com/watch?v = Chw32qG-M7E (last accessed August 2, 2011).

49   Morales is quoted at http://notas.guanabee.com/2010/01/evo-morales-avatar/ (last accessed January 27, 2010). In the "conversation" following this item one blogger denounces Morales: "Morales is an idiot who spouts platitudes, he is the 'brown guy' front for Álvaro Garcia Linera. Alvaro is using Evo to trap the indigenous populations"; while anther replies: "this movie Avatar has a lot of meanings for different people. Green peace activists would draw their own meanings, Iraqis who feel they were invaded for their vast oil resources, would have their own. What Evo Morales drew out of this movie, is relevant to most of us on this planet earth. Capitalism will eat us away, if we don't do something in time."

50   Frames/sing, "Avatar the Density of Being": http://kvond.wordpress.com/2009/12/18/avatar-the-density-of-being/ (last accessed March 30, 2011).

51   "Post Avatar Depression Hits Thousands of Fans": http://mashable.com/2010/01/12/post-avatar-depression-hits-thousands-of-fans-video/ (last accessed March 29, 2011).

52   The Wikipedia entry on Avatar lists more than dozen different voices, pairing the ones that flatly contradict the other: http://en.wikipedia.org/wiki/Avatar_%282009_film%29 (last accessed August 2, 2011).

53   It was The Elephant Man's executive producer Smart Cornfeld (and not Mel Brooks, to whom it was attributed) who so adroitly represented this paradox with the phrase "Jimmy Stewart from Mars." This works both as a humorous binary description and as deceptively simple shorthand for a more complex picture.

                                                        David Lynch, Chris Rodley, *Lynch on Lynch* (London: Faber & Faber, 2004), xii.

54   Jan Distelmeyer, "*Avatar—Aufbruch nach Pandora*," *epd Film* (January 2010), 34.

55   The IMDb entry on Cameron lists Avatar 2 and Avatar 3 as in the works for respectively 2014 and 2015. However, it should not be forgotten that unlike other franchise movies, Avatar presented, by Hollywood standards, original story-content:

          "The movie might be derivative of many movies in its story and themes," [Brandon Gray] said, "but it had no direct antecedent like the other top-grossing films: Titanic (historical events), the Star Wars movies (an established film franchise), or The Lord of the Rings (literature). It was a tougher sell."

                                                        Sarah Ball, "Why Avatar could out-earn Titanic," *Newsweek*, January 9, 2010:
                                        http://en.wikipedia.org/wiki/Avatar_%282009_film%29—cite_note-www.newsweek.com-206
                                                                                        (last accessed March 29, 2011).

56 According to Box Office Mojo, by early 2011, AVATAR had grossed $760 million in the USA and Canada, but $2.022 billion in other territories, bringing the worldwide total to over $2.780 billion, meaning that nearly 75 percent of income was foreign earned.

57 Lewis, "The Perfect Money Machine(s)," 73.

58 Thomas Elsaesser, "The Mindgame Film," in *Puzzle Films: Complex Storytelling in Contemporary Cinema*, ed. Warren Buckland (Oxford: Wiley Blackwell, 2009), 13–41.

59 www.ted.com/talks/james_cameron_before_avatar_a_curious_boy.html (last accessed March 30, 2011).

60 The Moebius Strip subverts the normal, i.e. Euclidean way of spatial (and, ultimately: temporal) representation, seemingly having two sides, but in fact having only one. At one point the two sides can be clearly distinguished, but when you traverse the strip as a whole, the two sides are experienced as being continuous. This figure is one of the topological figures studied and put to use by Lacan. On the one hand, Lacan employs the Moebius Strip as a model to conceptualize the "return of the repressed," . . . On the other hand, it can illustrate the way psychoanalysis conceptualizes certain binary oppositions, such as inside/outside, before/after, signifier/signified etc . . . These oppositions are normally seen as completely distinct; the Moebius Strip, however, enables us to see them as continuous with each other: the one, as it is, is the "truth" of the other, and vice versa.
    Slavoj Žižek, "How to make a Moebius Strip": http://the-zizek-site.blogspot.com/2007/01/digression-2-how-to-make-mobius-strip.html (last accessed March 12, 2011).

61 TRUE LIES is the title of Cameron's 1994 action comedy, whose husband-and wife protagonists not only lead double lives, but their different kinds of duplicity have to be doubled by another layer of undercover disguise, in order for the couple to find "true love." Although two lies do not make a truth even in this film, the principle is broadly that of a double negative becoming an affirmative.

62 The quotations are taken from the Wikipedia entry: http://en.wikipedia.org/wiki/Unobtainium (last accessed March 31, 2011).

63 Tim Lenoir and Henry Lowood, "Theaters of War: The Military-Entertainment complex": www.stanford.edu/class/sts145/Library/Lenoir-Lowood_TheatersOfWar.pdf (last accessed August 2, 2011) and Tim Lenoir, "All but War Is Simulation: The Military-Entertainment Complex," *Configurations* 8, 3 (Fall 2000): 289–335. See also Nick Turse, "The New Military Entertainment Complex": www.commondreams.org/views03/1017–09.htm (last accessed August 2, 2011). An early definition and use of the term can be found in an essay in the *New York Times*:

> Call it the military-entertainment complex. The aerospace and entertainment industries, which in the past inhabited parallel universes even as they sat side by side in southern California, are starting to cross-pollinate, bringing a new level of technology to entertainment and perhaps returning dividends to the Pentagon as well.
> Andrew Pollack, "Building the military-entertainment complex,"
> *New York Times*, October 10, 1997.

64 This is evidently even more the case with computer-games, where the US army is an important client and partner of the film industry in developing the digital tools and technical capacities for recruiting, training and combat use of 3-D simulation. A succinct overview is given by Stephen Stockwell and Adam Muir, "FCJ-004 The Military Entertainment Complex: A New Facet of Information Warfare," *The Fibreculture Journal* 1 (November 2003): http://one.fibreculturejournal.org/fcj-004-the-military-entertainment-complex-a-new-facet-of-information-warfare/print/ (last accessed August 2, 2011).

65 It is a point also made by Slavoj Žižek in "Return of the Natives," cited above, accusing AVATAR of racism.

66 For an examination of the truth-belief-trust system, see Chapter 22, "Digital Hollywood: BetweenTruth, Belief, and Trust."

67 Lev Manovich, "Archeology of a Computer Screen," *NewMediaLogia* (Moscow: Soros Center for the Contemporary Art, 1996): www.manovich.net/TEXT/digital_nature.html (last accessed March 28, 2011).

68 Lev Manovich, "To Lie and to Act: Cinema and Telepresence," in *Cinema Futures: Cain, Abel or Cable? The Screen Arts in the Digital Age*, ed. Thomas Elsaesser, Kay Hoffmann (Amsterdam: Amsterdam University Press, 1996), 189–200.

69 Thomas Elsaesser, "Tiefe des Raums, Angriff der Dinge," *epd Film* 27, 1 (2010): 22–27.

70 Naomi Klein, *The Shock Doctrine: The Rise of Disaster Capitalism* (New York: Metropolitan Books, 2007).

71 Avatar spawned legions of YouTube videos, giving tips and instructions how and what make-up to use in order to turn yourself into a Na'vi, for example: www.youtube.com/watch?v = QgtSvXd0ssg; www.youtube.com/watch?v = lYk_eUQ1h48; www.youtube.com/watch?v = 0BcAxgcuTRY (last accessed August 2, 2011).

22 Digital Hollywood: Between Truth, Belief and Trust

1 See Chapter 1, "Film Studies in Britain."

2 This fear is well conveyed, for instance, in Kevin Robbins, "The Virtual Unconscious in Postphotography," in *Electronic Culture*, ed. Tim Druckrey (New York: Aperture 1996), 154–63.

3 *Le Cinéma: Vers son deuxième siècle*, conference held at the Odéon, Paris, March 20, 1995. Press handout of Jean Douchet's lecture, in English, 1.

4 André Bazin, *What is Cinema?* (Berkeley: University of California Press, 1967), 9–16.

5 See the vigorously conducted debate about "visuality" by writers such as Jonathan Crary, *Techniques of the Observer* (Cambridge, MA: MIT Press, 1991) and Martin Jay, *Downcast Eyes* (Berkeley: University of California Press, 1993), as well as contributions in *Vision and Visuality*, ed. Hal Foster (Seattle: Bay Press, 1991).

6   Jean Baudrillard, "The television screen seems to be the place where images disappear," in *Baudrillard Live* (London: Verso, 1989), 69.

7   Serge Daney, "Before and After the Image," reprinted in *Documenta X, The Book*, ed. Jean-Francois Chevrier (Cantz Editions, 1997), 610, originally in *Revue des études palestiniennes* 40 (Summer 1991).

8   Kevin Kelly and Paula Parisi, "Beyond *Star Wars* what's next for George Lucas?" *Wired*, February 1997: 164.

9   Companies like Disney, Pixar or Industrial Light & Magic fund extensive in-house research-and-development units, staffed with graduates recruited from leading academic centers like Stanford University, Harvard, the MIT media lab of the University of Utah Graphics progam. See Tim Lenoir, "All but War is Simulation: The Military Entertainment Complex," *Configurations* 8, 3 (2000): 289–335.

10   "The cinema of the future will be a simulated roller coaster ride. Go see *Star Tours* at Disneyland. That is the prototype. The cinema auditorium of the future will be a modified flight simulator. You will literally fasten your seat belt for the ultimate flight of fancy. That's why you're seeing alliances forming between the motion picture and aircraft industries." Conrad Schoeffter, "Scanning the Horizon," in *Cinema Futures: Cain, Abel or Cable? The Screen Arts in the Digital Age*, ed. Thomas Elsaesser and Kay Hoffmann (Amsterdam: Amsterdam University Press, 1998), 115.

11   [Real-live action films with actors] may become merely the default values of the system cinema, in the future, all kinds of other options are possible, so that both narrative and live action may seem to be options rather than constitutive features of cinema.
   Lev Manovich, "Digital Cinema": www.jupiter/ucsd.edu/~manovich (last accessed August 2, 2011).

12   "Born from animation, cinema pushed animation to its boundary, only to become one particular case of animation in the end. . . . The same applies for the relationship between production and post-production." Lev Manovich, "Digital Cinema."

13   For an interesting account of this "expressive" mode in contemporary television, see John T. Caldwell, *Televisuality: Style, Crisis and Authority in American Television* (New Brunswick, NJ: Rutgers University Press, 1995).

14   Kevin Kelly and Paula Parisi, "Beyond *Star Wars*," 163.

15   "As a media technology, cinema's role was to capture and to store visible reality. The difficulty of modifying images once they were recorded was exactly what gave cinema its value as a document, assuring its authenticity." Lev Manovich, "Digital Cinema."

16   The literal interpretation of cinema as a roller coaster ride is brought to the fore whenever a new technology comes along. A new technology comes along whenever television becomes too big. There was a roller coaster ride in THIS IS CINERAMA. One of the first films in Sensurround was called ROLLER COASTER. One of the first IMAX films featured roller coaster and similar rides.
   Conrad Schoeffter, "Scanning the Horizon," 115.

17   But see Siegfried Zielinski, *Audiovisions: Cinema and Television as Entr'actes in History* (Amsterdam: Amsterdam University Press, 1999) arguing that we have already entered the "fin de siècle" of television.

18   See, among many possible sources, William J. Mitchell, *City of Bits* (Cambridge, MA: MIT Press, 1995).

19   By ocular-specular paradigm I mean that geometry of looks as the architecture of cinematic representation which prevailed in film studies. *Narrative, Apparatus, Ideology* ed. Philip Rosen (New York: Columbia University Press, 1986) and Stephen Heath, *Questions of Cinema* (London: Macmillan, 1981).

20   See the critique of Stephen Heath and Christian Metz in Noël Carroll, *Mystifying Movies: Fads and Fallacies in Contemporary Film Theory* (New York: Columbia University Press, 1988) and Richard Allen, *Projecting Illusion: Film Spectatorship and the Impression of Reality* (Cambridge: Cambridge University Press, 1995).

21   Walter Benjamin, "The Work of Art in the Age of Mechanical Reproduction," in *Illuminations*, ed. Hannah Arendt (New York: Schocken, 1969), 217–52.

22   Thomas Elsaesser, "Louis Lumière—the Cinema's First Virtualist?" in *Cinema Futures*, 46.

23   Stripped of its negative connotations, and replacing "television" by "new images," one could almost quote Baudrillard in support of the latter, with a passage immediately preceding the one already quoted:

   The television screen seems to me a place where images disappear, in the sense that each one of the images is undifferentiated and to the extent that the succession of images becomes total. Contents, emotions, things of great intensity, all take place on a screen that has no depth, a pure surface, while the cinema is also a screen, of course, but has depth, be it fantastic, imaginary or something else. Television is there, it's immanent, and it turns you into a screen. You have a quick, tactile perception of it, little definition. Basically there is no strong image; what it requires of you is a sort of immediate, instantaneous participation, in order to read it, make it exist but not make it signify.
   Jean Baudrillard, *Baudrillard Live*, 69.

24   Raymond Bellour, *The Analysis of Film* (Bloomington: Indiana University Press, 2000).

25   Raymond Bellour, "The Double Helix," in *Electronic Culture*, 173–99.

26   The first serious considerations given to sound in the post-semiotic period of film theory were Rick Altman (ed.), *Sound Theory Sound Practice* (New York: Routledge, 1992); John Belton and Elisabath Weis (eds.), *Film Sound* (New York: Columbia University Press, 1985); and Kaja Silverman, *The Acoustic Mirror* (Bloomington: Indiana University Press, 1988).

27   See the books by Rick Altman, Claudia Gorbman (e.g., *Unheard Melodies* [Bloomington: Indiana University Press, 1987]) and, above all, Michel Chion, *Audiovsion: Sound on Screen* (New York: Columbia University Press, 1994).

28   Thomas Elsaesser and Michael Wedel, "The Hollow Heart of Hollywood: *Apocalypse Now* and the New Sound Space," in *Conrad on Film*, ed. Gene M. Moore (Cambridge: Cambridge University Press, 1997), 151–75.

29 To quote from an article I wrote in the early 1980s:

> The New Hollywood cinema at once amplifies and multiplies the sensory input, leading an audience into the echo chambers of its own palpitating heartbeat. The spectator enters the films as if sucked into a space unbounded and unlocalizable, and yet strangely familiar and interior. Not unlike the operation of the probes, scanners and spectroscopes used in medicine or by the military, the cinema today colonizes both the visible and the sense of vision itself. Deprived of gravity or scale, the suspended and immersed spectator no longer trusts the eye, and in free fall, he suddenly relies on sound. This sound, however, has an ominous force, or rather, it is an acoustic Moebius strip on which the spectator takes his roller-coaster ride. The auditorium becomes the outerspace-as-innerspace-as-outerspace: an externalized, publicly shared solid wall of sound, produced directly in one's head. The cinema becomes a magnified walkman stereo, itself a listening experience in the active mode, and once described as similar to Nicolas de Cusa's definition of God, namely as one of being fully present both at the world's centre and at every point of its circumference.
>
> Thomas Elsaesser, "American Graffiti," in *Postmoderne— Zeichen eines kulturellen Wandels*, ed. Klaus Scherpe and Andreas Huyssen (Reinbek: Rowohlt, 1986), 313.

30 Edward Branigan, "Sound and Epistemology in Film," *Journal of Aesthetics and Art Criticism* 47, 4 (Autumn 1989): 312 and 314.

31 Branigan "Sound and Epistemology in Film," 312, where this point is footnoted to Tom Levin "The Acoustic Dimension," in *Screen* 25, 3 (May–June 1984).

32 Eugene Minkovski, quoted in Sue L. Cataldi, *Emotion, Depth and Flesh: A Study of Sensitive Space—Reflections on Merleau-Ponty's Philosophy of Embodiment* (New York: State University of New York Press, 1993), 50. I want to thank Warren Buckland for drawing my attention to this passage. See also Chapter 8, "Narrative Cinema and Audience Aesthetics: The *Mise-en-Scène* of the Spectator."

33 Chion, *Audiovision*, 151.

34 Chion, *Audiovision*, 151.

35 Branigan discusses Comolli's view of sound as an indexical sign, and seems to dismiss it—though without altogether explaining why: rather, he moves in a different terminology, calling sound "adjectival"—maybe because his purpose is to redefine how we can describe sound, that is, a problem of description/ontology. But he then goes on to argue that we do not need to think of sound either adjectivally or indexically, but rather in terms of two types of perception, top-down and bottom-up processing. This distinction for him makes obsolete the difference between "perception" and "cognition" as two separate kinds of mental activities (Branigan, "Sound and Epistemology in Film," 320).

36 See Roger Odin, "For a Semio-Pragmatics of Film" and "A Semio-Pragmatic Approach to the Documentary Film," in *The Film Spectator: From Sign to Mind*, ed. Warren Buckland (Amsterdam: Amsterdam University Press, 1995) 213–26 and 227–35.

37 In its edition of October 7, 2010 the *New York Times* felt obliged to append the following Editor's Note to a review essay:

> A photograph with an art review on Oct. 1 about the show "Abstract Expressionist New York: The Big Picture" at the Museum of Modern Art, and several other pictures in an online slide show, appeared to show museum visitors viewing the exhibit. In fact, the people shown were museum staff members, who were asked by museum officials to be present in the galleries to provide scale and context for the photographs. The photographer acknowledged using the same procedure in other cases when an exhibition was not yet opened to the public. Such staging of news pictures violates *The Times*'s standards and the photographs should not have been published.
>
> www.nytimes.com/2010/10/01/arts/design/01abex.html (last accessed March 10, 2011).

23 The Persistence of Hollywood, Part II: Reflexivity, Feedback and Self-Regulation

1 In a famous scene in Victor Hugo's novel *Notre Dame de Paris*, the archdeacon Frollo says, pointing first to a book and then to the Cathedral, "ceci tuera cela"—this (the printed book) will kill that (the built Cathedral). If similar (and equally unfounded) worries have accompanied the 20th century, when the cinema was said to have killed literature (and painting), the scene does illustrate the possibility of a transfer of iconic achievements across the succession of media. In a self-referential turn "ceci" might well have stood in Hugo's mind for his own novel, so that *Notre Dame de Paris* "killed" Notre Dame de Paris, just as Charles Laughton/William Dieterle's Notre Dame de Paris would—a hundred years later—"kill" Hugo's *Notre Dame de Paris*.

2 Raymond Bellour, "Nostalgies," *Autrement 79* (April 1986), special issue "Europe-Hollywood et retour," 231–32.

3 Tom Gunning, "The Cinema of Attractions: Early Film, its Spectator and the Avant-Garde," in *Early Cinema: Space Frame Narrative*, ed. Thomas Elsaesser (London: British Film Institute, 1990), 58–59.

4 For blockbusters, exhibitors might retain as little as 10 percent of the ticket price (the so-called "house nut," i.e. the running costs of the theater), and are therefore obliged to maximize income generated though the sale of soft drinks and popcorn. See: www.skillset.org/film/knowledge/article{_}5084{_}1.asp (last accessed March 4, 2011).

5 Edgar Reitz, "Das Kino der Zukunft," *Telepolis* 2 (June 1997), 71.

6 Hans Hollein, "Alles ist Architektur," *Bau: Schrift für Architektur und Städtebau*, 23, 1/2 (Vienna 1968).

7 John Ellis, "Cinema and Television: Laios and Oedipus," in *Cinema Futures: Cain, Abel or Cable? The Screen Arts in the Digital Age*, ed. Thomas Elsaesser and Kay Hoffmann (Amsterdam: Amsterdam University Press, 1998), 127.

8 The narratives—by Douglas Gomery (*The Hollywood Studio System*, London: British Film Institute, 2008); by Tom Schatz ("The New Hollywood," in *Film Theory Goes to the Movies: Cultural Analyses of Contemporary Film*, ed. James Collins,

Hilary Radner, and Ava Collins, New York: Routledge, 1993, 8–37); and Jon Lewis ("Money Matters: Hollywood in the Corporate Era", in *The New American Cinema*, ed. Jon Lewis, Durham: Duke University Press, 1998, 87–121)—have each a different emphasis, but they broadly outline or flesh out the same story.

9 See Charles R. Acland, *Screen Traffic: Movies, Multiplexes, and Global Culture* (Durham, NC: Duke University Press, 2003), especially Chapter Six, "Zones and Speeds of International Cinematic Life."

10 Douglas Gomery, "Hollywood Corporate Business Practice and Periodizing Contemporary Film History," in *Contemporary Hollywood Cinema*, ed. Steve Neale and Murray Smith (London: Routledge, 1998), 47–57; and Jon Lewis, "Money Matters: Hollywood in the Corporate Era," in *The New American Cinema*, ed. Jon Lewis (Durham, NC: Duke University Press, 1998), 87–121.

11 Tino Balio, *The American Film Industry* (Madison: University of Wisconsin Press, 1985).

12 The new business model tries to consolidate services, bringing together under one corporate roof activities which the consumers (rather than the producer) associate as belonging together, that is, based on a common pattern of service and use, as opposed to a common technology. For instance, the common denominator between the music business, publishing, movie business, television channels and telephone companies is access to typical domestic entertainment forms. This convergence of services is often called "synergy" and is part of how vertical integration was re-established along horizontal lines, after the Supreme Court lifted the ban on distributors owning exhibition platforms in 1986.

13 One of the key essays on Hollywood as an example of post-Fordism is Michael Storper, "The Transition to Flexible Specialisation in the U.S. Film Industry: External Economies, the Division of Labour, and the Crossing of Industrial Divides," *Cambridge Journal of Economics* 13, 2 (June 1989): 273–305.

14 Allen J. Scott, *On Hollywood: The Place, the Industry* (Princeton: Princeton University Press, 2005).

15 Manuel Castells, *The Network Society* (Oxford: Blackwell, 1999).

16 Aida Hozic, *Hollyworld: Space, Power, and Fantasy in the American Economy* (Ithaca, NY: Cornell University Press, 2001).

17 Toby Miller, Nitin Govall, John McMurria, Ting Wang and Richard Maxwell, *Global Hollywood*, 2nd edition (London: BFI Publishing, 2008).

18 Thomas Austin, "Hollywood Industry and Imaginary," Course description, University of Sussex, Autumn 2000: www.docstoc.com/docs/17839854/HOLLYWOOD-INDUSTRY-AND-IMAGINARY (last accessed June 12, 2009).

19 The James Bond franchise has become a classic case of product placement. For instance, Tomorrow Never Dies (Roger Spottiswoode, 1997) had tie-ins with Visa, Avis, BMW, Smirnoff vodka, Heineken, Omega watches, Ericsson cell phones and L'Oréal cosmetics. For a history of product placement, see Kerry Segrave, *Product Placement in Hollywood Films* (Jefferson, NC: McFarland, 2004) and Jean-Marc Lehu, *Branded Entertainment: Product Placement & Brand Strategy in the Entertainment Business* (London: Kogan Page, 2007).

20 This is the argument put forward by the art historian Boris Groys, "Versklavte Götter. Filmstudio und Realität oder Hollywoods metaphysische Wende," *Lettre International* 52 (Winter 2001): 268–84.

21 Herbert I. Schiller, *Communication and Cultural Domination*. (White Plains, NY: International Arts & Science Press, 1979), 9–10.

22 Thomas L. McPhail, *Electronic Colonialism: The Future of International Broadcasting and Communication* (London: Sage Publications, 1987), 18.

23 Imperialism is the conquest and control of one country by a more powerful one. Cultural imperialism signifies the dimensions of the process that go beyond economic exploitation or military force. In the history of colonialism, (i.e., the form of imperialism in which the government of the colony is run directly by foreigners), the educational and media systems of many Third World countries have been set up as replicas of those in Britain, France, or the United States and carry their values. Western advertising has made further inroads, as have architectural and fashion styles. Subtly but powerfully, the message has often been insinuated that Western cultures are superior to the cultures of the Third World.
J. Downing, A. Mohammadi and A. Sreberny-Mohammadi, *Questioning the Media* (London: Sage, 1995), 482.

24 Tyler Cowen, *Creative Destruction: How Globalization is changing the World's Cultures* (Princeton: Princeton University Pres, 2002).

25 Cowen, *Creative Destruction*, 89–90.

26 See Lauren A. Shuker, "Plot Change: Foreign Forces Transform Hollywood Films," *Wall Street Journal*, August 2, 2010: http://online.wsj.com/article/0,SB10001424052748704913304575371394036766312,00.html (last accessed March 3, 2011).

27 In the 1910s and 1920s, foreign filmmakers would come to Hollywood from France (Léonce Perret, Maurice Tourneur, Jacques Feyder), Germany (Ernst Lubitsch and F.W. Murnau) and Scandinavia (Victor Sjostrom and Mauritz Stiller). See Andrew Higson and Richard Maltby (eds.), *"Film Europe" and "Film America": Cinema, Commerce and Cultural Exchange 1920–1939* (Exeter: University of Exeter Press, 1999).

28 Thomas Elsaesser, "Ethnicity, Authenticity and Exile: A Counterfeit Trade?," in *Exile, Home and Homeland*, ed. Hamid Naficy (New York: Routledge, 1998), 97–124; "Walter Reisch: Vienna-Berlin-London-Hollywood," in *Pix3*, ed. Ilona Halberstadt (London: BFI Publishing, 2001), 43–67; "German Cinema Face to Face with Hollywood: Looking into a Two-Way Mirror," in *Americanization and Anti-Americanism: The German Encounter with American Culture after 1945*, ed. Alexander Stephan (New York: Berghahn Books, 2005), 166–87.

29 See Melis Behlil, *Home Away From Home: Global Directors in New Hollywood*. PhD Thesis, University of Amsterdam, 2007.

30 Neal Gabler, *An Empire of their Own: How the Jews Invented Hollywood* (New York: Anchor Books, 1989); Michael Rogin, *Black Face White Noise: Jewish Immigrants in the Hollywood Melting Pot* (Berkeley: University of California Press, 1998).

31 Ever since Richard Dyer's seminal studies in *White: Essays on Race and Culture* (London: Routledge, 1997) there have been several book-length studies on Hollywood's "equal-opportunity racism," among them Linda Williams, *Playing the Race Card: Melodramas of Black and White from Uncle Tom to O.J. Simpson* (Princeton: Princeton University Press, 2001); Daniel J. Bernardi (ed.), *Classic Hollywood, Classic Whiteness* (Minneapolis: University of Minnesota Press, 2000); Vera Hernan and Andrew Gordon, *Screen Saviors: Hollywood Fictions of Whiteness* (Lanham, MD: Rowman & Littlefield, 2003).

32 Martin Barker and Ernest Mathijs (eds.), *Watching the Lord of the Rings: Tolkien's World Audiences* (New York: Peter Lang, 2007); see also Kristin Thompson, *The Frodo Franchise* (Berkeley: University of California Press, 2007).

33 The controversies and eventual success of Slumdog Millionaire (Danny Boyle, 2008) in India have focused on the issue of local reception, as well as on Hollywood—and Bollywood—aiming for each other's global audiences. See Nandini Lakshman, "Hollywood Meets Bollywood as India's Movies Go Global," *Bloomberg News*, February 20, 2009: www.businessweek.com/globalbiz/content/feb2009/gb20090220{_}330804.htm (last accessed March 3, 2011).

34 Tamar Liebes and Elihu Katz, *The Export of Meaning: Cross-Cultural Readings of Dallas* (London: Polity, 1994) and Jostein Gripsrud, *The Dynasty Years: Hollywood Television and Critical Media Studies* (London: Routledge, 1995).

35 Fredric Jameson, "The Existence of Italy," in *Signatures of the Visible* (New York: Routledge, 1992), 155–229.

36 Jonathan Beller, *The Cinematic Mode of Production: Attention Economy and the Society of the Spectacle* (Lebanon, NH: University Presses of New England, 2006).

37 See also Jeff Bell's review of Beller's "Cinema, capital of the 20th century," *Postmodern Culture* 5, 1 (September 1994): http://pmc.iath.virginia.edu/text-only/issue.994/bell.994 (last accessed March 3, 2011).

38 Beller, *The Cinematic Mode of Production*, 5.

39 These options are examined in more detail in Thomas Elsaesser, "The Mindgame Film," in *Puzzle Films*, ed. Warren Buckland (Oxford: Blackwell 2009), 13–41.

40 The first Academy Awards ceremony was held on May 16, 1929. It gave the Oscar for best picture to Wings and Sunrise: A Song of Two Humans; best actor: Emil Jannings (The Last Command; The Way of All Flesh); best actress: Janet Gaynor (Seventh Heaven; Street Angel; Sunrise); best director: Frank Borzage (Seventh Heaven)/Lewis Milestone (Two Arabian Knights); best adapted screenplay: Benjamin Glazer (Seventh Heaven); best original story: Ben Hecht (Underworld); best cinematography: Charles Rosher and Karl Struss (Sunrise). See also Emmanuel Levy, *All About Oscar: The History and Politics of the Academy Awards* (New York: Continuum, 2003).

41 For an astute analysis of Hollywood's memory management and the "invention of tradition," see Vinzenz Hediger, "The Original Is Always Lost: Film History, Copyright Industries and the Problem of Reconstruction," in *Cinephilia: Movies, Love and Memory*, ed. Marijke de Valck and Malte Hagener (Amsterdam: Amsterdam University Press, 2005), 135–49 and Vinzenz Hediger, "Politique des archives: European Cinema and the Invention of Tradition in the Digital Age": http://www.rouge.com.au/12/hediger.html (last accessed March 4, 2011).

42 Richard Maltby, "The Production Code and the Hays Office," in *Grand Design: Hollywood as a Modern Business Enterprise, 1930–1939*, ed. Tino Balio (New York: Scribner's, 1993), 37–72; Ruth Vasey, *The World According to Hollywood, 1918–1939* (Madison: University of Wisconsin Press, 1997). See also Richard Maltby, *Hollywood Cinema*, Second Edition (Oxford: Basil Blackwell, 2003), 59–73.

43 Maltby, *Hollywood Cinema*, 61.

44 Nöel Carroll, "The Future of Allusion: Hollywood in the Seventies and Beyond," *October* 34 (Summer 1981): 51–80.

45 Maltby, *Hollywood Cinema*, 63.

46 Richard Maltby, "A Brief Romantic Interlude: Dick and Jane go to 3½ seconds of the Classical Hollywood Cinema," in *Post-Theory—Reconstructing Film Studies*, ed. David Bordwell and Noel Carroll (Madison: University of Wisconsin Press, 1996), 434–59.

47 Recapitulating the argument of the sophisticated and the innocent viewer ("Dick and Jane"), Žižek adds: "our only correction to Maltby would be that we do not need two spectators sitting next to each other: one and the same spectator, split in itself, is sufficient." Slavoj Žižek, "Shostakovich in Casablanca," *Lacanian Ink*, 2007: www.lacan.com/zizcasablanca.htm (last accessed March 4, 2011).

48 The terms are taken from Justin Wyatt, *High Concept: Movies and Marketing in Hollywood* (Austin: University of Texas Press, 1994).

49 The 1986 Supreme Court Paramount ruling allowed major US distributors (which is what the studios had become by then) to enter the exhibition sector, making vertical integration once more an economic reality. The consequence was the concept of the multiplex/megaplex, a new type of cinema, whose purpose was to create "spaces of total entertainment," defined by "upscaling, comfort, courteousness, cleanliness, total entertainment, and prestige." Acland, *Screen Traffic*, 106.

50 For an account of how media images become "things" and vice versa, and how communication (once more) takes place through (totemic) objects, see Scott Lash and Celia Lury, *Global Culture Industry: The Mediation of Things* (London: Polity, 2007).

51 Peter Krämer, "Would You Take Your Child To See This Film? The Cultural and Social Work of the Family-Adventure Movie," in Neale and Smith, *Contemporary Hollywood Cinema*, 294–311.

52 Originally published as Thomas Elsaesser, "The Blockbuster: Everything Connects, but Not Everything Goes," in *The End of Cinema as We Know It: American Film in the Nineties*, ed. Jon Lewis (London: Pluto Press, 2002), 11–22.

53 "Total entertainment refers to industrial structures of corporate ownership as well as to particular textual and consumption practices that have developed at a junction where entertainment content is inclined, and designed, to travel in mobile ways across media platforms and ancillary/territorial markets." Paul Grainge, *Brand Hollywood: Selling Entertainment in a Global Media Age* (New York: Routledge, 2008), 175.

54 On Pathé's (and other companies') promotional strategies, see Richard Abel, *The Red Rooster Scare: Making Cinema American, 1900–1910* (Berkeley: University of California Press, 1999), 14–19.

55 Theodor W. Adorno, with Max Horkheimer, "Culture industry: Enlightenment as Mass-Deception," *The Dialectic of Enlightenment*, trans. Edmund Jephcott (Stanford: Stanford University Press, 2002), 133. The passage is also quoted in J.D. Connor, "Logorrhea, or, how should we watch a neoclassical Hollywood film?," in Connor, *The Studios after the Studios: Hollywood in the Neoclassical Era, 1970–2005* (forthcoming). I am grateful to the author for letting me see a draft of this essay while I was completing this chapter.

56 The "foregrounding of the device" is a key concept of the Russian Formalist School, based on the insight that poetic effects are achieved by defamiliarizing language, often by means of repetition or a change of context. Jan Mukarovsky developed the notion into a literary concept, but it was given a politically progressive meaning mainly via Bert Brecht's estrangement or alienation effect.

57 Grainge, *Brand Hollywood*, 175.

58 [*Brand Hollywood*'s] chapter on the Lord of the Rings trilogy and the Harry Potter franchise shows that the need to nurture brands over a longer period, to be "credible" with fans and stay true to the brands' "core values" forced Warner Bros to enter into "careful forms of negotiation" with fan communities about content, even while their marketing and promotional materials could be tailored more strategically to target new (non-fan) markets and age groups.

> Liz Moor, "Global Brands," *Global Media and Communication* 5, 1 (2009): 101–2.

59 Catherine Johnson, review of *Brand Hollywood* in *Screen* 50, 2 (2009), 254.

60 The economic value of brands is reflected in the increasing protection given to them through changes to copyright and trademark law, as well as the valuation given of brands on the stock market and other financial markets. The semiotic value of a brand is the degree of recognition and the field of associations attached to it.

61 Grainge, *Brand Hollywood*, 128.

62 It is the aesthetic/affective combination of studio memory and blockbuster hype that can be applied more widely to the symbolic economy of post-classical logos. By tailoring the form and appearance of logos for specific presentational ends, and by occasionally insinuating themselves into a film's (promotional) diegesis, logos have helped code the event status of the modern blockbuster while visibly asserting the industrial history and position of their corporate progenitors.

> Paul Grainge, "Branding Hollywood: Studio Logos and the Aesthetics of Memory and Hype,"
> *Screen* 45, 4 (2004), 360.

63 For an example from the 1930s of a studio writing and rewriting its history through a genre, see Chapter 11, "Transatlantic Triangulations: William Dieterle and the Warner Bros. Biopics."

64 See for instance, Philip French, *Westerns, Aspects of a Movie Genre* (New York: The Viking Press, 1973).

> French categorized Westerns by the American political figures he thought they most resembled. Thus High Noon and Johnny Guitar are McCarthy Westerns because both show individuals persecuted or abandoned by hostile political environments. The Magnificent Seven was judged Kennedy-esque by virtue of its Peace Corps-style American professional supermen taking their superior skills and firepower out to right wrongs beyond U.S. borders. Goldwater Westerns, on the other hand, tended to take the patronizing Republican/conservative tack of upholding the past and "old ways" as the ideal to be aspired to; there was nothing wrong with men, women or conflicts that good old-fashioned brawling, spanking, or mayhem couldn't solve.... French further inflected his thesis by subcategorizing films having Kennedy content treated in Goldwater style (the LBJ Western), and Goldwater content with a Kennedy style (the William Buckley Western).
>
> Glenn Erickson, "Foreign Intervention and the American Western" (1999):
> www.dvdtalk.com/dvdsavant/s80west.html (last accessed March 5, 2011).

65 An example would be J. Hoberman's *An Army of Phantoms: American Movies and the Making of the Cold War* (New York: The New Press, 2011), as well as his "'Nashville' Contra 'Jaws' or 'The Imagination of Disaster' Revisited," in *The Last Great American Picture Show: New Hollywood Cinema in the 1970s*, ed. T. Elsaesser, A. Horwath and N. King (Amsterdam: Amsterdam University Press, 2004), 195–222.

66 Michael Rogin, "The Two Declarations of American Independence," *Representations*, 55 (Summer 1996): 13–30; Carol Clover, "Dancin' in the Rain," *Critical Inquiry* 21, 4 (Summer 1995): 722–47.

67 Jerome Christensen, "Delirious Warner Bros: Studio Authorship and The Fountainhead," *Velvet Light Trap* (Spring 2005): 17–31; "Taking it to the Next Level: You've Got Mail," *Critical Inquiry* 30 (Autumn 2003): 198–215; "The Time Warner Conspiracy: JFK, Batman, and the Manager Theory of Hollywood Film," *Critical Inquiry* (Spring 2002): 591–616; "Studio Identity, Studio Art: MGM, Mrs. Miniver, and Planning the Postwar Era," *ELH* 67, 1 (Winter 1999): 257–92; "Spike Lee: Corporate Populist," *Critical Inquiry* 17 (Spring 1991): 582–95.

68 Peter Drucker, *The Practice of Management* (New York: Harper Collins, 1954).

69 Christensen, "The Time Warner Conspiracy," 591.

70 The two chief accounts are Richard M. Clurman, *To the End of Time: The Seduction and Conquest of a Media Empire* (New York, 1992) ... and Connie Bruck, *Master of the Game: Steve Ross and the Creation of Time Warner* (New York, 1994).... My version of the negotiations is completely indebted to Clurman and Bruck, unless otherwise indicated.

> Christensen, "The Time Warner Conspiracy," footnote 4.

71 Christensen has in turn had to endure quite harsh criticism of arbitrariness and tautology by Peter Havholm and Philip Sandifer, in "Corporate Authorship: A Response to Jerome Christensen," *Critical Inquiry* 30, 1 (Autumn 2003): 187–97,

to which Christensen replied with "Taking it to the Next Level: You've Got Mail," *Critical Inquiry* 30, 1 (Autumn 2003): 198–215.

72 On the economics of studio libraries, see Jan-Christopher Horak, "The Hollywood History Business," in Lewis, *The End of Cinema as we Know it*, 33–42.

73 J.D. Connor, " 'The Projections': Allegories of Industrial Crisis in Neoclassical Hollywood," *Representations*, 71 (Summer, 2000), 50.

74 J.D. Connor, "The anxious epic," *The Boston Globe*, November 28, 2004.

75 Jean-Claude Lebensztejn, "Framing Classical Space," *Art Journal* (Spring 1988): 37–38.

76 Connor, "The Projections," 60. Connor is referring to David Bordwell, Janet Staiger and Kristin Thompson, *The Classical Hollywood Cinema: Film Style and Mode of Production to 1960* (New York: Routledge & Kegan Paul, 1986).

77 Connor, "The Projections," 60.

78 Connor, "The Projections," 61.

79 Henry Jenkins, *Convergence Culture: Where Old and New Media Collide* (New York: NYU Press, 2006).

80 Henry Jenkins, *Textual Poachers: Television Fans and Participatory Culture* (New York: Routledge, 1992).

81 Involving the fans in the scripting of a film has turned out to be a mixed blessing. SNAKES ON A PLANE (2006, David R. Ellis, New Line Cinema) was not the success that its initiators had hoped for: "In response to the Internet fan base, New Line Cinema incorporated feedback from online users into its production, and added five days of reshooting. . . . Despite the immense Internet buzz, the film's gross revenue did not live up to expectations, earning US$15.25 million in its opening weekend" (Wikipedia entry, accessed March 7, 2011).

82 Niklaus Luhmann, "Globalization or World Society? How to Conceive of Modern Society," *International Review of Sociology* 7, 1 (March 1997): 67–69: *www.generation-online.org/p/fpluhmann2.htm* (last accessed March 7, 2011).

Index